T0212495

Lecture Notes in Computer Science   9763

Commenced Publication in 1973
Founding and Former Series Editors:
Gerhard Goos, Juris Hartmanis, and Jan van Leeuwen

More information about this series at http://www.springer.com/series/7407

Rocco De Nicola · Eva Kühn (Eds.)

Software Engineering and Formal Methods

14th International Conference, SEFM 2016
Held as Part of STAF 2016
Vienna, Austria, July 4–8, 2016
Proceedings

 Springer

Editors
Rocco De Nicola
IMT - School for Advanced Studies
Lucca
Italy

Eva Kühn
Institute of Computer Languages
TU Wien
Wien
Austria

ISSN 0302-9743   ISSN 1611-3349 (electronic)
Lecture Notes in Computer Science
ISBN 978-3-319-41590-1   ISBN 978-3-319-41591-8 (eBook)
DOI 10.1007/978-3-319-41591-8

Library of Congress Control Number: 2016943040

LNCS Sublibrary: SL1 – Theoretical Computer Science and General Issues

Printed on acid-free paper

This Springer imprint is published by Springer Nature
The registered company is Springer International Publishing AG Switzerland

Foreword

Software Technologies: Applications and Foundations (STAF) is a federation of leading conferences on software technologies. It provides a loose umbrella organization with a Steering Committee that ensures continuity. The STAF federated event takes place annually. The participating conferences may vary from year to year, but all focus on foundational and practical advances in software technology. The conferences address all aspects of software technology, from object-oriented design, testing, mathematical approaches to modeling and verification, transformation, model-driven engineering, aspect-oriented techniques, and tools.

STAF 2016 took place at TU Wien, Austria, during July 4–8, 2016, and hosted the five conferences ECMFA 2016, ICGT 2016, ICMT 2016, SEFM 2016, and TAP 2016, the transformation tool contest TTC 2016, eight workshops, a doctoral symposium, and a projects showcase event. STAF 2016 featured eight internationally renowned keynote speakers, and welcomed participants from around the world.

The STAF 2016 Organizing Committee thanks (a) all participants for submitting to and attending the event, (b) the program chairs and Steering Committee members of the individual conferences and satellite events for their hard work, (c) the keynote speakers for their thoughtful, insightful, and inspiring talks, and (d) TU Wien, the city of Vienna, and all sponsors for their support. A special thank you goes to the members of the Business Informatics Group, coping with all the foreseen and unforeseen work (as usual ☺)!

July 2016   Gerti Kappel

Preface

The 14th edition of the International Conference on Software Engineering and Formal Methods (SEFM) presented new advances and research results in the fields of software engineering and formal methods. The conference brought together leading researchers and practitioners from academia and industry, to advance the state of the art in formal methods, to facilitate their uptake in the software industry, and to encourage their integration within practical software engineering methods and tools.

Authors were invited to submit full research papers describing original research results, case studies, and tools; and short new ideas/work-in-progress papers describing new approaches, techniques, and/or tools not fully validated yet. The topics of interest for submission included the following aspects of software engineering and formal methods:

- New frontiers in software architecture: self-adaptive, service-oriented, and cloud computing systems; component, object, and multi-agent systems; real-time, hybrid, and embedded systems; reconfigurable systems
- Software verification and testing: model checking, theorem proving, and decision procedures; verification and validation; probabilistic verification and synthesis; testing, re-engineering, and reuse
- Software development methods: requirement analysis, modeling, specification, and design; light-weight and scalable formal methods; software evolution, maintenance, and reuse
- Application and technology transfer: case studies, best practices, and experience reports; tool integration, education, HCI, interactive systems, and human error analysis
- Security and safety: security and mobility; safety-critical, fault-tolerant, and secure systems; software certification
- Design principles: programming languages, domain-specific languages, type theory, abstraction, and refinement.

SEFM 2016 received 114 submissions of abstracts that materialized as 88 papers. All submitted papers underwent a rigorous review process, and each paper received at least three reviews. After a careful discussion phase, the international Program Committee decided to select 20 research papers and five new ideas/work-in-progress short papers. These papers cover a wide variety of topics from areas where formal methods can be applied to software engineering. They also address a broad range of application domains.

The conference featured two keynote talks, by Erika Ábrahám (RWTH Aachen University, Germany) and Gul Agha (University of Illinois at Urbana-Champaign, USA); their presentations were accompanied by the invited papers that can be found at the beginning of this volume.

We would first like to thank the STAF general chair, Gerti Kappel, for her support with planning and running the conference, the local Organization Committee for taking care of the local arrangements, the SEFM Steering Committee for their assistance, and the SEFM local support team for the local and technical support. We are grateful to EasyChair for the support with the paper submission and reviewing process, and with the preparation of this volume. We were able to put together an exciting technical program that would not have been possible without the excellent work of the Program Committee members and their external reviewers.

Finally, we would like to thank the authors of all submitted papers, our invited speakers, and all the participants of the conference in Vienna, all of whom contributed to the success of the 2016 edition of SEFM.

July 2016   Rocco De Nicola
                                                                      Eva Kühn

Organization

Program Committee

Wolfgang Ahrendt	Chalmers University of Technology, Sweden
Dalal Alrajeh	Imperial College London, UK
Farhad Arbab	CWI and Leiden University, The Netherlands
Luis Barbosa	Universidade do Minho, Portugal
Jiri Barnat	Masaryk University, Czech Republic
Antonia Bertolino	ISTI-CNR, Italy
Jonathan P. Bowen	London South Bank University, UK
Mario Bravetti	University of Bologna, Italy
Ana Cavalcanti	University of York, UK
Zhenbang Chen	National Laboratory for Parallel and Distributed Processing, Changsha, China
Alessandro Cimatti	Fondazione Bruno Kessler, Trento, Italy
Hung Dang Van	UET, Vietnam National University, Hanoi, Vietnam
Jim Davies	University of Oxford, UK
Rocco De Nicola	IMT Lucca, Italy
John Derrick	University of Sheffield, UK
George Eleftherakis	The University of Sheffield International Faculty, Thessaloniki, Greece
José Luiz Fiadeiro	Royal Holloway, University of London, UK
Wan Fokkink	Vrije Universiteit Amsterdam, The Netherlands
Hubert Garavel	Inria Rhone-Alpes/VASY, France
Dimitra Giannakopoulou	NASA Ames Research Center, USA
Stefania Gnesi	ISTI-CNR, Italy
Klaus Havelund	Jet Propulsion Laboratory, California Institute of Technology, USA
Rob Hierons	Brunel University, UK
Michaela Huhn	TU Clausthal, Germany
Einar Broch Johnsen	University of Oslo, Norway
Gabriel Juhas	Slovak University of Technology Bratislava, Slovakia
Jens Knoop	TU Vienna, Austria
Paddy Krishnan	Oracle Labs, Brisbane, Australia
Eva Kühn	Vienna University of Technology, Austria
Kung-Kiu Lau	The University of Manchester, UK
Zhiming Liu	Birmingham City University, UK
Antónia Lopes	University of Lisbon, Portugal
Mercedes Merayo	Universidad Complutense de Madrid, Spain
Viet Yen Nguyen	RotoStadt, Ottawa, Canada

Fernando Orejas	Universitat Politècnica de Catalunya, Barcelona, Spain
Corina Pasareanu	CMU/NASA Ames Research Center, USA
Marinella Petrocchi	IIT-CNR, Italy
Anna Philippou	University of Cyprus, Nicosia, Cyprus
Sanjiva Prasad	Indian Institute of Technology Delhi, India
Geguang Pu	East China Normal University, China
Leila Ribeiro	Universidade Federal do Rio Grande do Sul, Brazil
Bernhard Rumpe	RWTH Aachen University, Germany
Gwen Salaün	Grenoble INP, Inria, LIG, France
Augusto Sampaio	Federal University of Pernambuco, Brazil
Bernhard Schätz	TU München, Germany
Vesna Sesum-Cavic	TU Vienna, Austria
Marjan Sirjani	Reykjavik University, Iceland
Graeme Smith	University of Queensland, Australia
Markus Stumptner	University of South Australia
Francesco Tiezzi	Università di Camerino, Italy
Cláudia Werner	Universidade Federal do Rio de Janeiro, Brazil
Danny Weyns	Linnaeus University, Sweden

Additional Reviewers

Aravantinos, Vincent
Arellanes, Damian
Arshad, Rehman
Bagheri, Maryam
Basile, Davide
Baxter, James
Bendík, Jaroslav
Bouajjani, Ahmed
Bruintjes, Harold
Bubel, Richard
Cerna, Ivana
Chen, Xiaohong
Cheng Hum Yuen, Steven
Crass, Stefan
de Frutos Escrig, David
Di Cola, Simone
Din, Crystal Chang
Doherty, Simon
Edmunds, Andrew
Eikermann, Robert
Evrard, Hugues
Fantechi, Alessandro
Fazzolari, Michela

Filali Amine, Mamoun
Fornari, Fabrizio
Grossmann, Georg
Guedemann, Matthias
Gupta, Pragya Kirti
Hamid, Brahim
Jebali, Fatma
Johansson, Moa
K.R., Raghavendra
Khamespanah, Ehsan
Li, Qin
Lima, Lucas
Machado, Rodrigo
Margheri, Andrea
Markey, Nicolas
Mateescu, Radu
Mayer, Wolfgang
Mazzanti, Franco
Miyazawa, Alvaro
Mrázek, Jan
Muske, Tukaram
Muzi, Chiara
Nogueira, Sidney

Nuñez, Manuel
Plotnikov, Dimitri
Preguiça, Nuno
Qian, Chen
Raco, Deni
Re, Barbara
Robillard, Simon
Roth, Alexander
Ročkai, Petr
Sabouri, Hamideh
Santos, André
Sasse, Ralf
Schots, Marcelo
Schulze, Christoph
Selway, Matt
Serwe, Wendelin
Sinha, Rohit
Sokolova, Ana
Stumpf, Johanna Beate
Štill, Vladimír
Su, Ting
Taylor, Ramsay
Tiezzi, Francesco

Tran, Cuong
Truong, Hoang
van Breugel, Franck
Vandin, Andrea
Vanzetto, Hernán

Varshosaz, Mahsa
von Rhein, Alexander
Wang, Shuling
Winter, Joost
Winter, Kirsten

Young, Bill
Yu, Hengbiao
Zhao, Liang

Contents

Model Checking

Verification

Interaction and Adaptation

Development Methods

Invited Papers

Abstractions, Semantic Models and Analysis Tools for Concurrent Systems: Progress and Open Problems
(Extended Abstract)

Gul Agha[(✉)]

University of Illinois at Urbana-Champaign, Champaign, USA
agha@illinois.edu
http://osl.cs.illinois.edu

Abstract. The growth of mobile and cloud computing, cyberphysical systems and the internet of things has arguably made scalable concurrency the central to computing. Actor languages and frameworks have been widely adopted to address scalability. Moreover, new tools that combine static and dyamic analysis are making software safer. This presentation describes the actor programming model and reasoning tools for scalable concurrency. As we scale up cyberphysical applications and build the internet of things, a key limitation of current languages and tools becomes apparent: the difficulty of representing quantitative and probabilistic properties and reasoning about them. The paper concludes by discussing some techniques to address reasoning about the behavior of complex scalable concurrent applications.

1 Introduction

The increasing use of web services, web applications, cloud computing, multi-core computers, and sensor networks have made concurrency central to software development. The software industry is adapting to these changes by adopting concurrent programming as a key to achieving the performance goals of software product lines. Because many applications require scalable computing, the Actor model of concurrent computation [12] has naturally found increased applicability. A number of actor languages and frameworks are being used by software developers in industry today. Erlang [4], originally developed by Ericsson, has been used to implement Ericsson's backbone system, the Facebook Chat system [5], and the Vendetta game engine. Google released DART [2], an actor language for the *in-browser application* market. Actors in Scala are used by Twitter to program its backbone system [6]. Microsoft's Orleans actor framework [13] has hundreds of industrial users. Other applications written using one of these actor frameworks include WhatsApp [3], LinkedIn, the Halo 4 game engine [1], and the British National Health Service backbone [7]. We first describe the actor model and then discuss how we can test actor programs. We then discuss some techniques to scale up reasoning in order to increase confidence in large systems.

© Springer International Publishing Switzerland 2016
R. De Nicola and E. Kühn (Eds.): SEFM 2016, LNCS 9763, pp. 3–8, 2016.
DOI: 10.1007/978-3-319-41591-8_1

The Actor Model. An *actor* is an autonomous, interacting unit of computation with its own memory. An actor could be a computer node, a virtual process, or a thread with only private memory. If we were trying to model a shared memory computation using actors, we would have to represent each variable as a (simple) actor. But scalable systems require greater abstraction and the Actor model is more useful for modeling such systems. Each actor operates asynchronously rather than on a global clock. This models distributed systems where precise synchronization between actions of subcomponents is not feasible.

Actors communicate by sending each other messages. Because there is no action at a distance, these messages are by default asynchronous. Abstractions for synchronous messaging must be defined using asynchronous messages (e.g., [9]). Finally, an actor may create new actors. In software, this models creation of new concurrent objects and in operating system it can model process creation. In the case of hardware, it may model adding modules to an existing system. The concept of actors is closely related to that of autonomous agents [16].

Variants of the Actor Model. In real-time systems, sometimes a global clock is used [20]. In modeling networks, probability is added to transition [8,11]. However, as I noted in 2003, there is a need for more complex models of time than the current extremes of asynchronous or synchronous computation and communication. In physics, the notion of distance and the speed of light bounds the synchrony of events at different objects. Similarly, a richer model of concurrent systems should have a notion of "virtual" distance with which the degree of synchronization varies. However, this degree of synchronization need not be exact: the model needs to incorporate probability so that we can reason about the stochastic nature of message delivery, or about failures, or other hard to control variables.

2   Concolic Testing

The behavior of a computing system can be represented as a *binary tree* (a higher arity tree can be reduced to a binary tree), where the internal nodes of a computation tree represent decision points (resulting from *conditional statements* or from *nondeterminism*), and the branches represent (one or more) sequential steps. Note that the nondeterminism may be a way of modeling the results of different mechanisms: probabilistic transitions, scheduling of actors, or communication delays. For simplicity, we will call these nondeterministic choices *scheduling choices*. System verification is a process of examining a tree of potential executions to see if some property holds at each step.

The most common form of correctness reasoning is *testing*. Testing involves executing a system, which in turn requires picking some data values for the inputs and fixing an order for the scheduling choices. In order to make testing feasible, only a finite approximation of the potentially infinite behavior is considered. Such approximation is done in two ways: first, by restricting the domain of inputs. Second, by bounding the depth of the loops. The bound on the depth is typically arbitrary.

Of course, termination is undecidable, but more pragmatically, even though for many computations termination may be decidable, it may not be feasible to automatically determine what bound to use for a loop. Finally, only a small number of potential scheduling choices are considered.

Even with these restrictions, the space of possible behaviors is generally too large to examine fully. To overcome the problem, *symbolic testing* was proposed. The idea of symbolic testing is quite simple. Instead of using concrete values for data inputs, a symbolic value (variable) can be associated with each value. Then at each branch point, a constraint is generated on the variable. If there are values for which the constraint holds, the branch in which the constraint is true is explored, carrying the constrained forward. At the next branch point, the constraint on that branch is added to the constraint which has been carried forward, and again solved to see if there are values satisfying it. Similarly, if there are values satisfying the negation of the constraint, the other branch is explored. During the exploration, the symbolic state is checked to see if the constraints implied by the specification could be violated.

The problem with using symbolic testing is that the constraints involved are often unsolvable or computationally intractable. For example, if these constraints involve some complex functions or use of dynamic memory. In this case, it is unclear if a branch might be taken. When a constraint at a branch point cannot be solved, tools based on symbolic checking assume that both branches might be taken, leading to a large number of erroneous bug reports and causing tool users to ignore the tool.

To overcome this difficulty, *concolic testing* was proposed [15][1]. The idea is to simultaneously do concrete testing and symbolic testing on the same system. When a constraint cannot be solved, use randomization to simplify the constraint and find a partial solution. This increases coverage, but of course, does not provide completeness. We extended this concept to systems with dynamic memory, and to systems with concurrency, both the actor and the Java multi-threaded variety.

In case of concurrent systems, there are a large number of possible executions which are result in the same causal structure. This is because independent events (e.g. those on two different actors that have no causal relation) are simply interleaved. However, considering different orders may not affect the outcome. It is important to reduce or eliminate the number of such redundant executions as there are an exponential number of choices. Such reductions are called *partial order reduction*. A number of techniques, such as a macro-step semantics for actors have been developed to facilitate partial order reduction. We have also used concolic testing to dynamically detect interleavings that are redundant.

Concolic testing has been implemented in two tools which enable automatic unit (as opposed to system) testing of software written in C [24], JAVA [23], and actor programs [22]. Although the idea behind concolic testing is rather simple, concolic testing has proved very effective in efficiently finding previously undetected bugs in real-world software, in some cases, in software with a large

---

[1] Although the term first appears in [24].

user base which had gone through testing before being deployed. It has since been adopted in a number of commercial tools, including PEX from Microsoft[2].

Partial Order Reductions for Testing. In case of concurrent systems, there are a large number of possible executions which are result in the same causal structure [21]. This is because independent events (e.g. those on two different actors that have no causal relation) are simply interleaved. However, considering different orders may not affect the outcome. It is important to reduce or eliminate the number of such redundant executions as there are an exponential number of choices. Such reductions are called *partial order reduction*. A number of techniques, such as a macro-step semantics for actors have been developed to facilitate partial order reduction [10].

We have also used concolic testing to dynamically detect interleavings that are redundant. The macro-step semantics of actors is independent of the particularly library or language used: because the processing of a message by an actor is atomic, it can be done to an arbitrary depth before another actor takes a transition. Such properties have been used to provide a path exploration interface which can be common to all actor frameworks in Java [19].

Concolic Walk. When concolic testing encounters a constraint that a constraint solver cannot handle, it needs to do a heuristic search in the space defined by the subset of constraints that it can solve. Many heuristics have been proposed to address this problem. In fact, we have shown that it is often possible to essentially use a combination of linear constraint solving and heuristic search to address this problem [14].

3   Reasoning About Large-Scale Concurrent Systems

In large-scale concurrent systems, we are often interested in probabilistic guarantees on the behavior of the system, and in quantitative properties (energy consumption, throughput, etc.) of such systems.

Statistical Model Checking. One possibility is sampling the behavior of a system: in the real world, engineers often use Monte Carlo simulations to analyze systems. This process can be made more rigorous by expressing the desired properties of a system in a formal logic such as *continuous stochastic logic* (CSL). We have proposed using an approach we call *Statistical Method Checking* to verify properties expressed in a sublogic of CSL [25]. This work was extended to verify properties involving *unbounded untils* in [26]. The methods are implemented in a tool called VESTA [26] which has been used in a number of applications.

---

[2] http://research.microsoft.com/en-us/projects/pex/.

Verifying Quantitative Properties in Large State Spaces. The notion of global state also needs to be richer. In statistical physics, one often looks at the probability distribution over states to reason about aggregate properties such as temperature. Similarly, we can effectively measure certain quality of service parameters by representing the global state of systems not as a nondeterministic interleaving of the local states of components, but as a superposition of the individual states. We have developed a notion of state based on this concept. The notion of state as a probability mass function allows us to use a variant of linear temporal logic to express properties and to solve the model checking problem by using linear algebra for systems that are Markovian [17]. The technique is particularly useful for systems such as sensor networks [18].

Acknowledgements. The work on this paper has been supported in part by Air Force Research Laboratory and the Air Force Office of Scientific Research under agreement number FA8750-11-2-0084, and by National Science Foundation under grant number CCF-1438982.

References

1. Building Halo 4, a video game, using the actor model. http://www.infoq.com/news/2015/03/halo4-actor-model
2. Dart. http://www.dartlang.org
3. Erlang-powered Whatsapp. https://www.erlang-solutions.com/about/news/erlang-powered-whatsapp-exceeds-200-million-monthly-users
4. Erlang programming language
5. Facebook chat. https://www.facebook.com/note.php?note_id=14218138919
6. How and why Twitter uses Scala. https://www.redfin.com/devblog/2010/05/how_and_why_twitter_uses_scala.html
7. NHS to deploy Riak for new IT backbone. http://basho.com/posts/press/nhs-to-deploy-riak-for-new-it-backbone-with-quality-of-care-improvements-in-sight/
8. Agha, G., Gunter, C., Greenwald, M., Khanna, S., Meseguer, J., Sen, K., Thati, P.: Formal modeling and analysis of DOS using probabilistic rewrite theories. In: Workshop on Foundations of Computer Security (FCS 2005), vol. 20, pp. 1–15 (2005)
9. Agha, G., Houck, C.R., Panwar, R.: Distributed execution of actor programs. In: Banerjee, U., Gelernter, D., Nicolau, A., Padua, D.A. (eds.) Languages and Compilers for Parallel Computing. LNCS, vol. 589, pp. 1–17. Springer, Heidelberg (1992)
10. Agha, G., Mason, I.A., Smith, S.F., Talcott, C.L.: A foundation for actor computation. J. Funct. Program. **7**(1), 1–72 (1997)
11. Agha, G., Meseguer, J., Sen, K.: PMaude: rewrite-based specification language for probabilistic object systems. Electron. Notes Theoret. Comput. Sci. **153**(2), 213–239 (2006)
12. Agha, G.A.: ACTORS - A Model of Concurrent Computation in Distributed Systems. MIT Press Series in Artificial Intelligence. MIT Press, Cambridge (1990)
13. Bernstein, P.A., Bykov, S., Geller, A., Kliot, G., Thelin, J.: Orleans: distributed virtual actors for programmability and scalability. Technical report MSR-TR-2014-41, Microsoft Research (2014)

14. Dinges, P., Agha, G.: Solving complex path conditions through heuristic search on induced polytopes. In: Proceedings of the 22nd ACM SIGSOFT International Symposium on Foundations of Software Engineering, FSE 2014, pp. 425–436. ACM (2014)

15. Godefroid, P., Klarlund, N., Sen, K.: Dart: directed automated random testing. In: Sarkar, V., Hall, M.W. (eds.) PLDI, pp. 213–223. ACM (2005)

16. Jamali, N., Thati, P., Agha, G.A.: An actor-based architecture for customizing and controlling agent ensembles. IEEE Intell. Syst. **2**, 38–44 (1999)

17. Kwon, Y., Agha, G.: Verifying the evolution of probability distributions governed by a DTMC. IEEE Trans. Softw. Eng. **37**(1), 126–141 (2011)

18. Kwon, Y., Agha, G.: Performance evaluation of sensor networks by statistical modeling and Euclidean model checking. ACM Trans. Sensor Netw. **9**(4), 39:1–39:38 (2013)

19. Lauterburg, S., Karmani, R.K., Marinov, D., Agha, G.: Basset: a tool for systematic testing of actor programs. In: Roman, G.-C., Sullivan, K.J. (eds.) 2010 Proceedings of the 18th ACM SIGSOFT International Symposium on Foundations of Software Engineering, 7–11 November 2010, Santa Fe, NM, USA, pp. 363–364. ACM (2010)

20. Ren, S., Agha, G.: RTsynchronizer: language support for real-time specifications in distributed systems. In: Gerber, R., Marlowe, T.J. (eds.) Proceedings of the ACM SIGPLAN 1995 Workshop on Languages, Compilers, & Tools for Real-Time Systems (LCT-RTS 1995), 21–22 June 1995, La Jolla, California, pp. 50–59. ACM (1995)

21. Sen, K., Agha, G.: CUTE and jCUTE: concolic unit testing and explicit path model-checking tools. In: Ball, T., Jones, R.B. (eds.) CAV 2006. LNCS, vol. 4144, pp. 419–423. Springer, Heidelberg (2006)

22. Sen, K., Agha, G.: Automated systematic testing of open distributed programs. In: Baresi, L., Heckel, R. (eds.) FASE 2006. LNCS, vol. 3922, pp. 339–356. Springer, Heidelberg (2006)

23. Sen, K., Agha, G.: A race-detection and flipping algorithm for automated testing of multi-threaded programs. In: Bin, E., Ziv, A., Ur, S. (eds.) HVC 2006. LNCS, vol. 4383, pp. 166–182. Springer, Heidelberg (2007)

24. Sen, K., Marinov, D., Agha, G.: Cute: a concolic unit testing engine for C. In: Wermelinger, M., Gall, H. (eds.) Proceedings of the 10th European Software Engineering Conference held jointly with 13th ACM SIGSOFT International Symposium on Foundations of Software Engineering, 5–9 September 2005, Lisbon, Portugal, pp. 263–272. ACM (2005)

25. Sen, K., Viswanathan, M., Agha, G.: Statistical model checking of black-box probabilistic systems. In: Alur, R., Peled, D.A. (eds.) CAV 2004. LNCS, vol. 3114, pp. 202–215. Springer, Heidelberg (2004)

26. Sen, K., Viswanathan, M., Agha, G.: Vesta: a statistical model-checker and analyzer for probabilistic systems. In: Second International Conference on the Quantitative Evaluaiton of Systems (QEST 2005), 19–22 September 2005, Torino, Italy, pp. 251–252. IEEE Computer Society (2005)

Satisfiability Checking: Theory and Applications

Erika Ábrahám$^{(\boxtimes)}$ and Gereon Kremer

RWTH Aachen University, Aachen, Germany
`abraham@cs.rwth-aachen.de`

Abstract. Satisfiability checking aims to develop algorithms and tools for checking the satisfiability of existentially quantified logical formulas. Besides powerful SAT solvers for solving propositional logic formulas, sophisticated SAT-modulo-theories (SMT) solvers are available for a wide range of theories, and are applied as black-box engines for many techniques in different areas. In this paper we give a short introduction to the theoretical foundations of satisfiability checking, mention some of the most popular tools, and discuss the successful embedding of SMT solvers in different technologies.

1 Introduction

First-order-logic is a powerful modelling formalism frequently used to specify problems in different areas like verification, termination analysis, test case generation, controller synthesis, equivalence checking, combinatorial tasks, scheduling, planning, and product design automation and optimisation, just to mention a few well-known examples. Once the problem is formalised, algorithms and their implementations are needed to check the validity or satisfiability of the formulas, and in case they are satisfiable, to identify satisfying solutions. Algorithms to solve this problem are called *decision procedures*.

In mathematical logic, in the early 20th century some novel decision procedures were developed for arithmetic theories. With the advent of computer systems, big efforts were made to provide automated solutions in form of practically feasible implementations of decision procedures. In the area of symbolic computation, this development led to computer algebra systems supporting all kinds of scientific computations. Another line of research, *satisfiability checking* [10], started to focus on the more specific aim of checking the *satisfiability* of *existentially* quantified logical formulas.

For Boolean propositional logic, which is known to be NP-complete, in the late '90s impressive progress was made in the area of satisfiability checking, resulting in powerful *SAT solvers*. The first idea used *resolution* for quantifier elimination [30], but it had serious problems with the explosion of the memory requirements with increasing problem size. A combination of *enumeration* and *Boolean constraint propagation* [29] brought important enhancements. Another major improvement was achieved by a novel combination of enumeration, Boolean constraint propagation and resolution, leading to *conflict-driven*

© Springer International Publishing Switzerland 2016
R. De Nicola and E. Kühn (Eds.): SEFM 2016, LNCS 9763, pp. 9–23, 2016.
DOI: 10.1007/978-3-319-41591-8_2

clause-learning and *non-chronological backtracking* [50]. Later on, this impressive progress was continued by novel efficient implementation techniques (*e.g.*, sophisticated decision heuristics, two-watched-literal scheme, restarts, cache performance, etc.). Also different extensions are available, for example QBF solvers for quantified Boolean formulas, Max-SAT solvers to find solutions which satisfy a maximal number of clauses, or #SAT solvers to find all satisfying solutions of a propositional logic formula. State-of-the-art SAT solvers are able to solve such impressively large propositional logic problems that they became not only applicable in industry, but one of the most important engines in, *e.g.*, hardware verification.

Driven by this success, the satisfiability checking community started to enrich propositional SAT solvers with solver modules for different theories. Nowadays, sophisticated *SAT-modulo-theories* (*SMT*) solvers are available for a wide range of theories like equalities and uninterpreted functions, bit-vector arithmetic, floating-point arithmetic, array theory, difference logic, (quantifier-free) linear real/integer/mixed arithmetic, and (quantifier-free) non-linear real/integer/mixed arithmetic. Latest research led also to functional extensions, going beyond satisfiability checking for existentially quantified formulas towards providing an unsatisfiable core for unsatisfiable input problems, proof of unsatisfiability, solving quantified formulas, and solving optimisation problems. Some solvers also exploit parallelisation to make use of multi-core hardware architectures.

The strength of SMT solvers is that they offer fully automated push-button solutions. Thanks to efficient data structures and elaborate search heuristics, their increasing efficiency is coupled with increasing popularity and success in applications. An important enabling factor to applications was the introduction of a standard input language SMT-LIB [8] with a first release in 2004, which allows users to specify their problems in the standard language and to feed it to different solvers to find the optimal tool for a given purpose.

The standard also enabled the collection of reference benchmark sets and the start of annual competitions [7]. The first competition took place in 2005 with 12 participating solvers in 7 divisions (theories, theory combinations, or fragments thereof) on 1360 benchmarks, which increased in 2015 to 21 solvers competing in 40 divisions on 154238 benchmarks in the main track. All these activities contributed to the consolidation of an SMT solving community and to the visibility of the SMT-solving technologies. Nowadays, SMT solvers are widely used and are key components of many techniques in different academic and industrial areas.

In the following we give a short introduction to the theoretical foundations of satisfiability checking in Sect. 2, give a nutshell-overview about state-of-the-art SMT solvers including our own SMT solver SMT-RAT in Sect. 3, and discuss the efficient embedding of SMT solvers in different technologies in Sect. 4. We conclude the paper in Sect. 5. For further reading on SMT solving we refer to, *e.g.*, [9,46].

Quantifier-free theory	SMT-LIB name	Example theory constraints
equality and uninterpreted functions	QF_UF	$a = f(b, g(a, c))$
theory of (fixed-size) bit-vectors	QF_BV	$(a|b) \leq (a\&b)$
theory of arrays with extensionality	QF_AX	$select(store(a, i, v), i) = v$
floating point arithmetic	QF_FP	$x_2 = x_1 + 5(x_1 - y_1)$
real difference logic	QF_RDL	$x - y > 0$
integer difference logic	QF_IDL	
linear real arithmetic	QF_LRA	$3x + 7y - 8 \leq 0$
linear integer arithmetic	QF_LIA	
non-linear real arithmetic	QF_NRA	$x^{42} - 2yz^2 + 5 = 0$
non-linear integer arithmetic	QF_NIA	
theory of bit-vectors and bit-vector arrays extended with uninterpreted functions	QF_AUFBV	$select(a, bv[32]) < bv[32]$
linear real arithmetic with uninterpreted functions	QF_UFLRA	$3x + 7f(y) - 8 \geq 0$

Fig. 1. Example theory constraints from some logics that are included in the SMT-LIB standard language. The involved operators are: f, g, h are uninterpreted functions; | and & are bit-wise *or* and *and*, respectively; finally, for arrays $write(a, i, v)$ is the array a after setting its ith field to v, whereas $read(a, j)$ stays for the jth field of a. For readability, the examples are not in SMT-LIB syntax, *e.g.*, they use infix notation.

2   Satisfiability Checking

Satisfiability checking aims at automated solutions for determining the satisfiability of existentially quantified first-order-logic formulas. Such formulas are Boolean combinations of *theory constraints*, where the form of the theory constraints depends on with which theory we instantiate first-order logic. For example, existentially quantified non-linear real arithmetic formulas can be built from polynomial equalities and inequalities, and their Boolean combinations. Some example theory constraints from different theories that are included in the SMT-LIB standard input language are depicted in Fig. 1. Exemplarily, we mention also two *combined* theories in the last two rows.

2.1   SAT Solving

Before we discuss SAT-modulo-theories solving for checking the satisfiability of quantifier-free first-order-logic formulas, we first make a short excursion to *SAT solving*. SAT solvers implement decision procedures to check the satisfiability of *propositional logic* formulas, being the Boolean combinations of atomic (Boolean) propositions.

Here we only explain the DPLL-style SAT solving algorithm, which is implemented in most state-of-the-art SAT solver technologies. The input formula

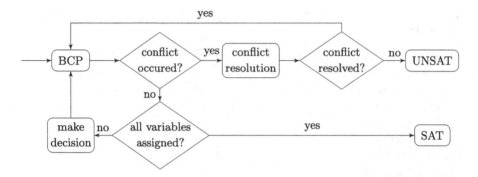

Fig. 2. The DPLL framework

is expected to be in conjunctive normal form (CNF), *i.e.*, the conjunction of *clauses*, each clause being the disjunction of *literals*, and each literal being a proposition or its negation. Each formula can be transformed into CNF in linear time and space at the cost of linearly many fresh propositions using Tseitin's transformation [67].

The DPLL algorithm has three main ingredients:

1. To explore the state space, the algorithm iteratively makes *decisions*, *i.e.*, it iteratively assigns truth values to some heuristically chosen propositions.
2. After each such decision, the algorithm applies *Boolean constraint propagation* (*BCP*) to determine further variable assignments that are implied by the last decision.
3. If BCP leads to a *conflict*, *i.e.*, if the value of a proposition is implied to be true as well as false at the same time, *conflict-driven clause-learning* and *non-chronological backtracking* [50] are applied: The algorithm follows back the chain of implications and applies *resolution* [30] to derive a reason for the conflict in form of a *conflict clause*, which is added to the solver's clause set. Backtracking removes previous decisions and their implications until the conflict clause can be satisfied.

If the input has clauses consisting of a single literal, these literals will be directly assigned. Therefore, the algorithm starts with BCP, as show in Fig. 2, to detect implications. If BCP leads to a conflict, the algorithm tries to resolve the conflict. If the conflict cannot be resolved, the input formula is unsatisfiable. Otherwise, if the conflict was successfully resolved, the algorithm backtracks and continues with BCP. If BCP could be completed without any conflicts, a new decision will be made if there are any unassigned propositions. Otherwise, a satisfying solution is found.

Example 1. Assume as input the CNF $(a) \wedge (\neg a \vee b) \wedge (c \vee d) \wedge (\neg b \vee c \vee \neg d)$. First a is set to true. BCP implies by the second clause that b must be true in order to complete the current partial assignment to a full satisfying solution. As no conflict appeared and there are still unassigned variables, a new decision will be made. Assume that this decision assigns `false` to c. BCP will assign `true` to d based on the third clause, however, now the fourth clause is conflicting. Resolution applied to the last two clauses will result in the conflict clause $(\neg b \vee c)$, which is added to the clause set. Backtracking removes the last decision, and BCP implies that c must be `true`. As all variables are assigned, a complete solution if found and the algorithm returns SAT.

The above algorithm is complete for propositional logic. It should be noted that many further optimisations were proposed, which led to major improvements, but cannot be discussed here.

2.2   SMT Solving

To check the satisfiability of quantifier-free first-order-logic formulas with an underlying theory (or combined theories [54]), *SAT-modulo-theories* (*SMT*) solvers can be applied. *Eager* SMT solving approaches translate the input formula to a satisfiability-equivalent propositional logic formula, whose satisfiability can be decided using a SAT solver. In the following we focus on *lazy* SMT-solving approaches.

Lazy SMT solvers combine a SAT solver with one or more *theory solvers*. Thereby the SAT solver handles the input formula's logical structure and is responsible for finding solutions for the *Boolean skeleton* of the input formula, which is gained by substituting fresh propositions for the theory atoms. To be able to check the consistency of theory atoms, the SAT solver communicates with the theory solvers, which implement decision procedures for the underlying theory.

Figure 3 illustrates the lazy SMT solving framework. The SAT solver iteratively searches for a satisfying solutions for the Boolean skeleton. During its search, it consults the theory solver(s) to check whether the current Boolean assignment is consistent in the theory. To do so, it collects all theory constraints whose abstraction proposition is `true` and appears non-negated in the formula, and those whose abstraction proposition

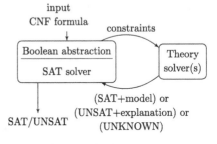

Fig. 3. The SMT solving framework

is `false` and appears negated in the formula. The resulting theory constraint set is sent to the theory solver(s), which checks whether it is consistent. In the *full* lazy approach, this communication takes place only for full Boolean solutions, whereas in the *less* lazy approach usually after each conflict-free BCP execution.

If the constraints are consistent in the theory and the SAT solver's assignment is already complete then a satisfying solution is found for the input formula. If the constraints are consistent but the Boolean assignment is not yet complete, the SAT solver continues its search. Otherwise, if the theory constraints are conflicting, the invoked theory solver returns an *explanation* for the conflict.

The explanation is often an *infeasible subset* $\{c_1, \ldots, c_n\}$ of the theory solver's input constraints, which leads to a tautology $(\neg c_1 \vee \ldots \neg c_n)$, whose abstraction can be added to the SAT solver's clause set. As the newly added clause is conflicting, conflict resolution is applied and the SAT solver continues its search in other parts of the search space.

Example 2. Assume as input the linear real-arithmetic formula

$$(x - y > 10) \wedge (x + y = 4 \vee x = 2y \vee x < y)$$

with Boolean abstraction

$$(a) \wedge (b \vee c \vee d) \ .$$

Assume that the SAT solver's current assignment is $a = \texttt{true}$, $b = \texttt{false}$, $c = \texttt{true}$ and $d = \texttt{true}$. The constraint set $\{x - y > 10, x = 2y, x < y\}$ is sent to a theory solver, which reports back inconsistency. A possible explanation is $\{x - y > 10, x < y\}$, whose abstraction $(\neg a \vee \neg d)$ assures that in the further search either a or d will be set to $\texttt{false}$.

The above-described approach clearly separates the Boolean search and theory solving. There are also other approaches in which Boolean and theory solving are more closely integrated.

First SMT solvers addressed more light-weight theories like equality logic and uninterpreted functions. Aiming at program verification, theories for arrays, bit-vectors and floating-point arithmetic followed. Nowadays there are also highly tuned SMT solvers for linear arithmetic theories. Latest developments also allow solving non-linear arithmetic problems [26,41], quantified formulas, optimisation problems [13], and exploit parallelisation [70].

3   SMT Solvers

The aforementioned SMT competitions [7] compare the abilities of participating SMT solvers on SMT-LIB benchmark sets. The latest results from 2015 [64] give a good overview of state-of-the-art solvers and their range of applicability. Table 1 shows a rough survey of these solvers for existentially quantified logics. There is a large number of further SMT solvers, which did not participate in last year's competition. Other SMT solvers under active development, which we are aware of, are Alt-Ergo [25] and iSAT3 [34,62]. Further examples for SMT solvers are Ario, Barcelogic, Beaver, clasp, DPT, Fx7, haRVey, ICS, LPSAT, MiniSmt, Mistral, OpenCog, RDL, SatEEn, Simplics, Simplify, SMCHR, SONOLAR, Spear, STeP, SVC, SWORD, and UCLID.

SMT-solver technologies cover a wide range of theories and their combinations. The embedding of theory decision procedures into the SMT solving context requires not only a deep understanding of the individual decision procedures, but also a careful software design. We illustrate how an SMT solver can be designed to support a broad range of logics, and how a user of such a solver can exploit the

Table 1. An overview of the SMT solvers for solving quantifier-free logical formulas that participated in SMT-COMP 2015 (for the naming of the logics see Fig. 1 and the SMT-LIB page [8]).

Solver	Website	Supported SMT-LIB logics QF_XXX
AProVE [37]	aprove.informatik.rwth-aachen.de	NIA
Boolector [55]	fmv.jku.at/boolector	ABV, AUFBV, BV, UFBV
CVC4 [6]	cvc4.cs.nyu.edu	All not involving FP
MathSAT5 [22]	mathsat.fbk.eu	All not involving integers
OpenSMT2 [18]	verify.inf.usi.ch/opensmt2	UF
raSAT [43]	github.com/tungvx/raSAT	NIA, NRA
SMTInterpol [21]	github.com/ultimate-pa/smtinterpol	All not involving BV, FP, NRA and NIA
SMT-RAT [26]	github.com/smtrat/smtrat/wiki	BV, LIA, LIRA, LRA, NIA, NIRA, NRA, UF
STP [35]	stp.github.io	BV
veriT [16]	www.verit-solver.org	All not involving BV, FP, NRA and NIA
Yices2 [32]	yices.csl.sri.com	All not involving FP and NIA
Z3 [51]	z3.codeplex.com	All

versatility, on the example of our SMT-RAT [26] solver. SMT-RAT's focus is on non-linear arithmetic. It adapts algebraic decision procedures to the needs of SMT solving and exploits powerful combinations of these procedures. Currently, it offers SMT-compliant implementations of the Fourier-Motzkin variable elimination, the simplex method [28], interval constraint propagation [36,39], methods based on Gröbner bases [68], the virtual substitution method [69], the cylindrical algebraic decomposition method [24], and a generalised branch-and-bound method. Additionally it provides a DPLL-style SAT solver as well as several preprocessing modules.

In SMT-RAT, all these procedures – including the SAT solver and preprocessing modules – are implemented in encapsulated modules, which share a common module interface. This modularisation allows for a strategic combination [52] of these solver modules: whenever a module is unable to solve a specific problem, it can forward the problem – or sub-problems – to other modules that might be better suited for the given task.

The strategic combination of solver modules is governed by a user-defined SMT-RAT *strategy*. Basically, a strategy is a directed tree, whose nodes are solver module instances, and whose edges are labelled with conditions. These conditions are evaluated in the context of a formula; an example for such a condition could

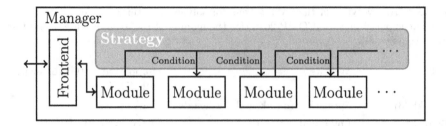

Fig. 4. Basic structure of an SMT-RAT strategy

be that the formula is linear, or that the maximal degree of polynomials in the formula is at most 2.

Figure 4 illustrates how such a strategy drives the solving procedure. A dedicated initial module (the root of the tree) receives the input formula and starts processing. If an executing module wants to pass on (sub-)problems to other modules, the conditions on the edges to its children are tested whether they hold for the given (sub-)problem. For each edge, if its condition holds, the child module will be invoked to solve the (sub-)problem. If a call to a child-module terminates, the calling module uses the returned result to continue its solving process. Note that this way also parallel execution can be implemented. Note furthermore that also the child modules can invoke further modules on their (sub-)problems.

In this framework, we can easily generate and test novel combinations of solving techniques, extend the range of supported logics, or employ parallel execution without the need to modify the previous implementation. Given a module that implements a certain decision procedure, it can be directly embedded within a strategy and thus participate in the overall solving process. Still, it does not save us the burden of handling the combination of two or more different theories. Theory combination schemes like Nelson-Oppen [54] are not yet implemented in SMT-RAT which is why it only supports a relatively small number of individual logics.

4   Applications

After the previous introduction to satisfiability checking and SMT solvers, let us turn to applications. In the following we mention some applications from the most popular areas. SMT solvers are employed in such a wide context that we cannot claim completeness, not only regarding single applications, but even regarding the application domains.

Program Verification. The perhaps most prominent SMT application example is program verification. In this area, the success of explicit model checking is complemented with symbolic and deductive approaches.

Bounded model checking [11] can be used to unroll the transition relation and to generate, for increasing path lengths, formulas that state the existence of a property-violating path. SMT solvers can be used to check the involved formulas for satisfiability, *i.e.*, to determine whether counterexamples exist. Whereas the basic approach cannot prove correctness but is rather suited to find counterexamples, it can be extended with, *e.g.*, k-induction to be able to prove the correctness of programs.

Deductive verification approaches generate verification conditions; if these conditions hold, the program is provably correct. In this context, SMT solvers can be used to check whether the verification conditions hold. Further methods related to, *e.g.*, invariant generation, interpolation and predicate abstraction can be invoked to increase the verification success.

Examples for tools in this area, which embed SMT-solving technologies, are CBMC [47] (bounded model checker for C and C++ programs), IC3 [17,48] (induction-based verification approach), PKIND [42] (a parallel k-induction-based model checker), the Microsoft software model checkers Boogie [15] (intermediate-language verification) and SLAM [5] (device driver verification), the Rodin platform [31] for formal development in Event-B, and the SRI tool SAL [60] (infinite bounded model checker).

Symbolic Execution. Besides static analysis, SMT solvers are also used for *symbolic execution*. For example, the Avalanche tool [3] was developed to identify input data that reproduces critical bugs and vulnerabilities in programs. The tool is based on the Valgrind dynamic instrumentation framework. It analyses the target program by tracing and produces modified input data sets (corresponding to different execution paths) from the collected data. Finally, every possible execution path in the target program is traversed and checked for critical runtime defects. This way, buggy traces can be identified from a single test case.

Test-Case Generation. Due to the growing size of software, verification is not always applicable. Though the importance of thorough testing is undisputed among software engineers, crafting meaningful *test cases* remains a complex task. An ideal set of test cases should cover every possible code path and be reasonably concise and readable.

SMT-solving can be of help also in this area. The basic idea is similar to that of bounded model checking: we can encode paths with certain properties, *e.g.*, assuming that certain branches are followed or that certain loops are executed a given number of times, and use SMT solvers to find paths satisfying the given requirements. The work [19] reports on a successful application to generate test cases that cover most of the source code of the GNU Coreutils which "arguably are the single most heavily tested set of open-source programs in existence". The resulting code coverage was improved significantly and ten individual new bugs were found, therefrom three existing since at least 1992. Another approach for automated test case generation with SMT solving and abstract interpretation is proposed in [56].

Superoptimiser Compiler Backends. In the area of compiler construction, *superoptimisation* techniques assist to find optimal instruction sequences that are semantically equivalent to the original code fragment. The tool Souper [65] uses an SMT solver to automatically find *optimisations* missed by LLVM (low-level virtual machine) bit-code optimisers. Another work from this area is [57], where a simulator is used to evaluate the correctness of a candidate program on concrete test cases. If a candidate passes all test cases, the search technique verifies the *equivalence* of the candidate program and the reference program on all possible inputs using an SMT solver.

Termination Analysis. An important question in formal verification is whether a given program *terminates.* Though this question is undecidable in general, an active field of research has emerged on finding provable upper bounds on the runtime of a program. Usually, finding such complexity bounds requires solving non-linear integer problems. SAT and SMT techniques are routinely used by all leading termination analysis tools, for example AProVE [37], T_TT_2 [45] or NaTT[71].

Program Synthesis. The paper [66] presents an SMT-based approach for component-based *program synthesis.* In this work, the synthesis problem is reduced to a satisfiability checking problem and an SMT solver is employed to synthesise bit-vector manipulation programs, padding-based encryption schemes, and block cipher modes of operations.

Planning. *Planning as satisfiability* was introduced in the area of artificial intelligence by Kautz and Selman in 1990 for domain-independent planning. This approach was limited to asynchronous discrete systems expressible in propositional logic, therefore SAT solvers could be applied. Later the approach was extended with numeric state variables and continuous time. Both of these extensions include integer- and real-valued state variables, which cannot be effectively handled by SAT solvers. As described in [59], SMT solvers can successfully solve such problems, but one needs to pay attention that the problem encoding is done carefully. To mention some further examples, SMT solvers in the area of planning were also applied for sequential numeric planning [61]. Another example is the work [38] which combines planning as satisfiability and SMT to perform efficient reasoning about actions that occupy realistic time. SMT solving for integrated task and motion planning is discussed in [53].

Scheduling. Many practical problems involve the *scheduling* of some tasks or processes. Oftentimes, their nature is not only combinatorial but also involves arithmetic constraints. For example, we might need to consider running times or certain resource demands in order to satisfy deadlines or to assure that enough memory is available for execution. SMT solvers, being designed to handle both combinatorial as well as arithmetic aspects, have been applied for numerous scheduling problems. The work [14] uses SMT solvers to solve resource-constrained project scheduling problems, where minimum as well as maximum delays between tasks are considered. Other examples are, *e.g.*, [2,27,58,72].

Cloud Applications. With the rise of cloud platforms, web applications have become much more flexible regarding scalability. However, *designing* a cloud application that consists of multiple components – for example database backends, webservers and a load balancer – poses the question, how many individual components are needed and how they shall be distributed among virtual machines. This problem has been solved in the Zephyrus tool [20] by the employment of constraint solving techniques. Based on an ongoing work of the authors with the tool developers we can state that SMT solvers equipped with linear optimisation are a valuable addition for such applications and can outperform previously used solutions. Implementing optimisation techniques for SMT solvers has seen a lot of progress in the last few years, for example in [13,49,63], thus we expect further interesting applications in domains that are so far dominated by constraint programming techniques.

Another work [12] is devoted the the analysis of *cloud contracts*, which capture architectural requirements in datacenters. The contracts are checked using the SecGuru tool, which is based on SMT solving and models network configurations in bit-vector arithmetic. SecGuru was also used to automatically validate network connectivity policies [40].

Hybrid Systems Reachability Analysis. *Hybrid systems* are systems with mixed discrete-continuous behaviour, typical examples being physical plants whose behaviour is controlled by a discrete controller. While the controller senses the plant state and executes control actions in a discrete manner, the dynamic state of the plant evolves continuously. For such systems, *reachability analysis* can be applied to assure that the plant never reaches any critical states.

One way to employ SMT solving technologies for reachability analysis is, similarly to programs, bounded model checking. However, as the dynamic behaviour is usually modelled using differential equations, the invoked SMT solvers need to be able to deal with the theory of differential equations. Suitable solvers for this task are dReach [23,44] and iSAT-ODE [33]. Beyond reachability analysis, the recent work [4] shows how various verification problems for complex synchronous hybrid PALS (physically asynchronous, logically synchronous) models can be reduced to SMT solving.

5   Conclusion

In this paper we gave a short introduction to SAT and SMT solving, discussed software design issues, and gave a number of SMT-solving applications.

The research area of satisfiability checking is highly active. New results and novel software engineering solutions constantly improve the power and the practical applicability of solver technologies. This holds not only for the efficiency, but also for the functionality of SMT solvers: Latest developments show that SMT solvers can also be successfully extended to handle, *e.g.*, quantified formulas or optimisation problems.

We expect this trend to be continued, on the one hand because there are still unused potentials (for example through building closer interactions with the symbolic computation community to improve on non-linear arithmetic theories [1]), and on the other hand because there is still a wide variety of problems, whose solutions could be improved by using SMT solving.

References

1. Ábrahám, E.: Building bridges between symbolic computation and satisfiability checking. In: Proceedings of ISSAC 2015, pp. 1–6. ACM (2015)
2. Ansótegui, C., Bofill, M., Palahı, M., Suy, J., Villaret, M.: Satisfiability modulo theories: An efficient approach for the resource-constrained project scheduling problem. In: Proceedings of SARA 2011, pp. 2–9. AAAI (2011)
3. Avalanche.: Dynamic program analysis tool. http://www.ispras.ru/en/technologies/avalanche_dynamic_program_analysis_tool/
4. Bae, K., Ölveczky, P.C., Kong, S., Gao, S., Clarke, E.M.: SMT-based analysis of virtually synchronous distributed hybrid systems. In: Proceedings of HSCC 2016 (2016). (to appear)
5. Ball, T., Bounimova, E., Levin, V., De Moura, L.: Efficient evaluation of pointer predicates with Z3 SMT solver in SLAM2. Technical report, Microsoft Research (2010)
6. Barrett, C., Conway, C.L., Deters, M., Hadarean, L., Jovanović, D., King, T., Reynolds, A., Tinelli, C.: CVC4. In: Gopalakrishnan, G., Qadeer, S. (eds.) CAV 2011. LNCS, vol. 6806, pp. 171–177. Springer, Heidelberg (2011)
7. Barrett, C.W., de Moura, L., Stump, A.: SMT-COMP: satisfiability modulo theories competition. In: Etessami, K., Rajamani, S.K. (eds.) CAV 2005. LNCS, vol. 3576, pp. 20–23. Springer, Heidelberg (2005)
8. Barrett, C., Fontaine, P., Tinelli, C.: The Satisfiability Modulo Theories Library (SMT-LIB) (2016). www.SMT-LIB.org
9. Barrett, C., Sebastiani, R., Seshia, S.A., Tinelli, C.: Satisfiability modulo theories. In: Biere, A., Heule, M.J.H., van Maaren, H., Walsh, T. (eds.) Handbook of Satisfiability, Chap. 26. Frontiers in Artificial Intelligence and Applications, vol. 185, pp. 825–885. IOS Press, Amsterdam (2009)
10. Biere, A., Biere, A., Heule, M., van Maaren, H., Walsh, T.: Handbook of Satisfiability. Frontiers in Artificial Intelligence and Applications, vol. 185. IOS Press, Amsterdam (2009)
11. Biere, A., Cimatti, A., Clarke, E., Zhu, Y.: Symbolic model checking without BDDs. In: Cleaveland, W.R. (ed.) TACAS 1999. LNCS, vol. 1579, pp. 193–207. Springer, Heidelberg (1999)
12. Bjørner, N., Jayaraman, K.: Checking cloud contracts in microsoft azure. In: Natarajan, R., Barua, G., Patra, M.R. (eds.) ICDCIT 2015. LNCS, vol. 8956, pp. 21–32. Springer, Heidelberg (2015)
13. Bjørner, N., Phan, A.-D., Fleckenstein, L.: νZ - an optimizing SMT solver. In: Baier, C., Tinelli, C. (eds.) TACAS 2015. LNCS, vol. 9035, pp. 194–199. Springer, Heidelberg (2015)
14. Bofill, M., Coll, J., Suy, J., Villaret, M.: A system for generation and visualization of resource-constrained projects. In: Proceedings of CCIA 2014. Frontiers in Artificial Intelligence and Applications, vol. 269, pp. 237–246. IOS Press (2014)
15. Boogie.: An intermediate verification language. http://research.microsoft.com/en-us/projects/boogie/
16. Bouton, Thomas, de Oliveira, D.C.B., Déharbe, D., Fontaine, P.: veriT: an open, trustable and efficient SMT-solver. In: Schmidt, Renate A. (ed.) CADE-22. LNCS, vol. 5663, pp. 151–156. Springer, Heidelberg (2009)
17. Bradley, A.R.: SAT-based model checking without unrolling. In: Schmidt, D., Jhala, R. (eds.) VMCAI 2011. LNCS, vol. 6538, pp. 70–87. Springer, Heidelberg (2011)

18. Bruttomesso, R., Pek, E., Sharygina, N., Tsitovich, A.: The OpenSMT solver. In: Esparza, J., Majumdar, R. (eds.) TACAS 2010. LNCS, vol. 6015, pp. 150–153. Springer, Heidelberg (2010)

19. Cadar, C., Dunbar, D., Engler, D.: KLEE: Unassisted and automatic generation of high-coverage tests for complex systems programs. In: Proceedings of OSDI 2008, pp. 209–224. USENIX Association (2008)

20. Catan, M., et al.: Aeolus: mastering the complexity of cloud application deployment. In: Lau, K.-K., Lamersdorf, W., Pimentel, E. (eds.) ESOCC 2013. LNCS, vol. 8135, pp. 1–3. Springer, Heidelberg (2013)

21. Christ, J., Hoenicke, J., Nutz, A.: SMTInterpol: an interpolating SMT solver. In: Donaldson, A., Parker, D. (eds.) SPIN 2012. LNCS, vol. 7385, pp. 248–254. Springer, Heidelberg (2012)

22. Cimatti, A., Griggio, A., Schaafsma, B.J., Sebastiani, R.: The MathSAT5 SMT solver. In: Piterman, N., Smolka, S.A. (eds.) TACAS 2013 (ETAPS 2013). LNCS, vol. 7795, pp. 93–107. Springer, Heidelberg (2013)

23. Cimatti, A., Mover, S., Tonetta, S.: A quantifier-free SMT encoding of non-linear hybrid automata. In: Proceedings of FMCAD 2012, pp. 187–195. IEEE (2012)

24. Collins, G.E.: Quantifier elimination for real closed fields by cylindrical algebraic decomposition. In: Brakhage, H. (ed.) Automata Theory and Formal Languages. LNCS, vol. 33, pp. 134–183. Springer, Heidelberg (1975)

25. Conchon, S., Iguernelala, M., Mebsout, A.: A collaborative framework for nonlinear integer arithmetic reasoning in Alt-Ergo. In: Proceedings of SYNASC 2013, pp. 161–168. IEEE (2013)

26. Corzilius, F., Kremer, G., Junges, S., Schupp, S., Ábrahám, E.: SMT-RAT: an open source C++ toolbox for strategic and parallel SMT solving. In: Heule, M., et al. (eds.) SAT 2015. LNCS, vol. 9340, pp. 360–368. Springer, Heidelberg (2015). doi:10.1007/978-3-319-24318-4_26

27. Craciunas, S.S., Oliver, R.S.: SMT-based task- and network-level static schedule generation for time-triggered networked systems. In: Proceedings of RTNS 2014, p. 45. ACM (2014)

28. Dantzig, G.B.: Linear Programming and Extensions. Princeton University Press, Princeton (1963)

29. Davis, M., Logemann, G., Loveland, D.: A machine program for theorem-proving. Commun. ACM **5**(7), 394–397 (1962)

30. Davis, M., Putnam, H.: A computing procedure for quantification theory. J. ACM **7**(3), 201–215 (1960)

31. Déharbe, D., Fontaine, P., Guyot, Y., Voisin, L.: Integrating SMT solvers in Rodin. Sci. Comput. Program. **94**(P2), 130–143 (2014)

32. Dutertre, B.: Yices 2.2. In: Biere, A., Bloem, R. (eds.) CAV 2014. LNCS, vol. 8559, pp. 737–744. Springer, Heidelberg (2014)

33. Eggers, A., Ramdani, N., Nedialkov, N.S., Fränzle, M.: Improving the SAT modulo ODE approach to hybrid systems analysis by combining different enclosure methods. Softw. Syst. Model. **14**(1), 121–148 (2012)

34. Fränzle, M., Herde, C., Teige, T., Ratschan, S., Schubert, T.: Efficient solving of large non-linear arithmetic constraint systems with complex Boolean structure. J. Satisf. Boolean Model. Comput. **1**(3–4), 209–236 (2007)

35. Ganesh, V., Dill, D.L.: A decision procedure for bit-vectors and arrays. In: Damm, W., Hermanns, H. (eds.) CAV 2007. LNCS, vol. 4590, pp. 519–531. Springer, Heidelberg (2007)

36. Gao, S., Ganai, M., Ivančić, F., Gupta, A., Sankaranarayanan, S., Clarke, E.M.: Integrating ICP and LRA solvers for deciding nonlinear real arithmetic problems. In: Proceedings of FMCAD 2010, pp. 81–90. IEEE (2010)
37. Giesl, J., et al.: Proving termination of programs automatically with AProVE. In: Demri, S., Kapur, D., Weidenbach, C. (eds.) IJCAR 2014. LNCS, vol. 8562, pp. 184–191. Springer, Heidelberg (2014)
38. Hallin, M.: SMT-Based Reasoning and Planning in TAL. Master's thesis, Linköping University (2010)
39. Herbort, S., Ratz, D.: Improving the efficiency of a nonlinear-system-solver using a componentwise Newton method. Technical report 2/1997, Inst. für Angewandte Mathematik, University of Karlsruhe (1997)
40. Jayaraman, K., Bjrner, N., Outhred, G., Kaufman, C.: Automated analysis and debugging of network connectivity policies. Technical report MSR-TR-2014-102, Microsoft Research (2014). http://research.microsoft.com/apps/pubs/default.aspx?id=225826
41. Jovanović, D., de Moura, L.: Solving non-linear arithmetic. In: Gramlich, B., Miller, D., Sattler, U. (eds.) IJCAR 2012. LNCS, vol. 7364, pp. 339–354. Springer, Heidelberg (2012)
42. Kahsai, T., Tinelli, C.: PKIND: A parallel k-induction based model checker. arXiv preprint (2011). arXiv:1111.0372
43. Khanh, T.V., Vu, X., Ogawa, M.: raSAT: SMT for polynomial inequality. In: Proceedings of SMT 2014, p. 67 (2014)
44. Kong, S., Gao, S., Chen, W., Clarke, E.: dReach :δ-reachability analysis for hybrid systems. In: Baier, C., Tinelli, C. (eds.) TACAS 2015. LNCS, vol. 9035, pp. 200–205. Springer, Heidelberg (2015)
45. Korp, M., Sternagel, C., Zankl, H., Middeldorp, A.: Tyrolean termination tool 2. In: Treinen, R. (ed.) RTA 2009. LNCS, vol. 5595, pp. 295–304. Springer, Heidelberg (2009)
46. Kroening, D., Strichman, O.: Decision Procedures: An Algorithmic Point of View. Springer, New York (2008)
47. Kroening, D., Tautschnig, M.: CBMC – C bounded model checker. In: Ábrahám, E., Havelund, K. (eds.) TACAS 2014 (ETAPS). LNCS, vol. 8413, pp. 389–391. Springer, Heidelberg (2014)
48. Lange, T., Neuhäußer, M.R., Noll, T.: IC3 software model checking on control flow automata. In: Proceedings of FMCAD 2015, pp. 97–104. IEEE (2015)
49. Li, Y., Albarghouthi, A., Kincaid, Z., Gurfinkel, A., Chechik, M.: Symbolic optimization with SMT solvers. In: Proceedings of POPL 2014, pp. 607–618. ACM (2014)
50. Marques-silva, J.P., Sakallah, K.A.: Grasp: a search algorithm for propositional satisfiability. IEEE Trans. Comput. **48**, 506–521 (1999)
51. de Moura, L., Bjørner, N.S.: Z3: an efficient SMT solver. In: Ramakrishnan, C.R., Rehof, J. (eds.) TACAS 2008. LNCS, vol. 4963, pp. 337–340. Springer, Heidelberg (2008)
52. de Moura, L., Passmore, G.O.: The strategy challenge in SMT solving. In: Bonacina, M.P., Stickel, M.E. (eds.) Automated Reasoning and Mathematics. LNCS, vol. 7788, pp. 15–44. Springer, Heidelberg (2013)
53. Nedunuri, S., Prabhu, S., Moll, M., Chaudhuri, S., Kavraki, L.E.: SMT-based synthesis of integrated task and motion plans from plan outlines. In: Proceedings of ICRA 2014, pp. 655–662. IEEE (2014)
54. Nelson, G., Oppen, D.C.: Simplification by cooperating decision procedures. ACM Trans. Program. Lang. Syst. **1**(2), 245–257 (1979)

55. Niemetz, A., Preiner, M., Biere, A.: Boolector 2.0. J. Satisf. Boolean Model. Comput. **9**, 53–58 (2015)
56. Peleska, J., Vorobev, E., Lapschies, F.: Automated test case generation with SMT-solving and abstract interpretation. In: Bobaru, M., Havelund, K., Holzmann, G.J., Joshi, R. (eds.) NFM 2011. LNCS, vol. 6617, pp. 298–312. Springer, Heidelberg (2011)
57. Phothilimthana, P.M., Thakur, A., Bodik, R., Dhurjati, D.: GreenThumb: Superoptimizer construction framework. In: Proceedings of CCC 2016, pp. 261–262. ACM (2016)
58. Pike, L.: Modeling time-triggered protocols and verifying their real-time schedules. In: Proceedings of FMCAD 2007, pp. 231–238. IEEE (2007)
59. Rintanen, J.: Discretization of temporal models with application to planning with SMT. In: Proceedings of AAAI 2015, pp. 3349–3355. AAAI (2015)
60. Symbolic analysis laboratory. http://sal.csl.sri.com/introduction.shtml
61. Scala, E., Ramirez, M., Haslum, P., Thiebaux, S.: Numeric planning with disjunctive global constraints via SMT. In: Proceedings of ICASP 2016 (2016, to appear)
62. Scheibler, K., Kupferschmid, S., Becker, B.: Recent improvements in the SMT solver iSAT. In: Proceedings of MBMV 2013, pp. 231–241. Institut für Angewandte Mikroelektronik und Datentechnik, Fakultät für Informatik und Elektrotechnik, Universität Rostock (2013)
63. Sebastiani, R., Trentin, P.: OptiMathSAT: a tool for optimization modulo theories. In: Kroening, D., Păsăreanu, C.S. (eds.) CAV 2015. LNCS, vol. 9206, pp. 447–454. Springer, Heidelberg (2015)
64. SMT-COMP 2015 result summary (2015). http://smtcomp.sourceforge.net/2015/results-summary.shtml
65. Souper. http://github.com/google/souper
66. Tiwari, A., Gascón, A., Dutertre, B.: Program synthesis using dual interpretation. In: Felty, A., Middeldorp, A. (eds.) CADE-25. Lecture Notes in Computer Science, vol. 9195, pp. 482–497. Springer, Heidelberg (2015)
67. Tseitin, G.S.: On the complexity of derivation in propositional calculus. In: Siekmann, J.H., Wrightson, G. (eds.) Automation of Reasoning, pp. 466–483. Springer, New York (1983)
68. Weispfenning, V.: A new approach to quantifier elimination for real algebra. In: Caviness, B.F., Johnson, J.R. (eds.) Quantifier Elimination and Cylindrical Algebraic Decomposition. Texts and Monographs in Symbolic Computation, pp. 376–392. Springer, NEw York (1998)
69. Weispfenning, V.: Quantifier elimination for real algebra - the quadratic case and beyond. Appl. Algebra Eng. Commun. Comput. **8**(2), 85–101 (1997)
70. Wintersteiger, C.M., Hamadi, Y., de Moura, L.: A concurrent portfolio approach to SMT solving. In: Bouajjani, A., Maler, O. (eds.) CAV 2009. LNCS, vol. 5643, pp. 715–720. Springer, Heidelberg (2009)
71. Yamada, A., Kusakari, K., Sakabe, T.: Nagoya termination tool. In: Dowek, G. (ed.) RTA-TLCA 2014. LNCS, vol. 8560, pp. 466–475. Springer, Heidelberg (2014)
72. Yuan, M., He, X., Gu, Z.: Hardware/software partitioning and static task scheduling on runtime reconfigurable FPGAs using an SMT solver. In: Proceedings of RTAS 2008, pp. 295–304. IEEE (2008)

Concurrency and Non-interference

Automatic Derivation of Platform Noninterference Properties

Oliver Schwarz[1,2(✉)] and Mads Dam[2]

[1] SICS Swedish ICT, Kista, Sweden
oschwarz@kth.se
[2] KTH Royal Institute of Technology, Stockholm, Sweden
mfd@kth.se

Abstract. For the verification of system software, information flow properties of the instruction set architecture (ISA) are essential. They show how information propagates through the processor, including sometimes opaque control registers. Thus, they can be used to guarantee that user processes cannot infer the state of privileged system components, such as secure partitions. Formal ISA models - for example for the HOL4 theorem prover - have been available for a number of years. However, little work has been published on the formal analysis of these models. In this paper, we present a general framework for proving information flow properties of a number of ISAs automatically, for example for ARM. The analysis is represented in HOL4 using a direct semantical embedding of noninterference, and does not use an explicit type system, in order to (i) minimize the trusted computing base, and to (ii) support a large degree of context-sensitivity, which is needed for the analysis. The framework determines automatically which system components are accessible at a given privilege level, guaranteeing both soundness and accuracy.

Keywords: Instruction set architectures · ARM · MIPS · Noninterference · Information flow · Theorem proving · HOL4

1 Introduction

From a security perspective, isolation of processes on lower privilege levels is one of the main tasks of system software. More and more vulnerabilities discovered in operating systems and hypervisors demonstrate that assurance of this isolation is far from given. That is why an increasing effort has been made to formally verify system software, with noticeable progress in recent years [1,6,10,14,16]. However, system software depends on hardware support to guarantee isolation. Usually, this involves at least the ability to execute code on different privilege levels and with basic memory protection. Kernels need to control access to their own code and data and to critical software, both in memory and as content of registers or other components. Moreover, they need to control the management of the access control itself. For the correct configuration of hardware, it is essential to understand how and under which circumstances information flows through

© Springer International Publishing Switzerland 2016
R. De Nicola and E. Kühn (Eds.): SEFM 2016, LNCS 9763, pp. 27–44, 2016.
DOI: 10.1007/978-3-319-41591-8_3

the system. Hardware must comply to a contract that kernels can rely on. In practice, however, information flows can be indirect and hidden. For example, some processors automatically set control flags on context switches that can later be used by unprivileged code to see if neighbouring processes have been running or to establish a covert channel [19]. Such attacks can be addressed by the kernel, but to that end, kernel developers need machinery to identify the exact components available to unprivileged code, and specifications often fail to provide this information in a concise form. When analysing information flow, it is insufficient to focus on direct register and memory access. Confidentiality, in particular, can be broken in more subtle ways. Even if direct reads from a control flag are prevented by hardware, the flag can be set as an unintended side effect of an action by one process and later influence the behaviour of another process, allowing the latter to learn something about the control flow of the former.

In this paper we present a framework to automate information flow analysis of instruction set architectures (ISAs) and their operational semantics inside the interactive theorem prover HOL4 [11]. We employ the framework on ISA models developed by Fox et al. [7] and verify *noninterference*, that is, that secret (*high*) components can not influence public (*low*) components. Besides an ISA model, the input consists of desired conditions (such as a specific privilege mode) and a candidate labelling, specifying which system components are already to be considered as low (such as the program counter) and, implicitly, which components might possibly be high. The approach then iteratively refines the candidate labelling by downgrading new components from high to low until a proper noninterference labelling is obtained, reminiscent of [12]. The iteration may fail for decidability reasons. However, on successful termination, both soundness and accuracy are guaranteed unless a warning is given indicating that only an approximate, sound, but not necessarily accurate solution has been found.

What makes accurate ISA information flow analysis challenging is not only the size and complexity of modern instruction sets, but also particularities in semantics and representation of their models. For example, arithmetic operations (e.g., with bitmasks) can cancel out some information flows and data structures can contain a mix of high and low information. Modification of the models to suit the analysis is error prone and requires manual effort. Automatic, and provably correct, preprocessing of the specifications could overcome some, but not all, of those difficulties, but then the added value of standard approaches such as type systems over a direct implementation becomes questionable. By directly embedding noninterference into HOL4, we can make use of machinery to address the discussed difficulties and at the same time we are able to minimize the trusted computing base (TCB), since the models, the preprocessing and the actual reasoning are all implemented/represented in HOL4. Previous work on HOL4 noninterference proofs for ISA models [13] had to rely on some manual proofs, since its compositional approach suffered from the lack of sufficient context in some cases (e.g., the secrecy level of a register access in one step can depend on location lookups in earlier steps). In contrast, the approach suggested in the present paper analyses ISAs one instruction at a time, allowing for accuracy and automation at the same time. However, since many instructions involve a number of subroutines, this instruction-wide context introduces complexity challenges. We address those by unfolding definitions of transitions in such a way that their effects can be extracted in an efficient manner.

Our analysis is divided into three steps: (i) *rewriting* to unfold and simplify instruction definitions, (ii) the *actual proof attempt*, and (iii) automated counterexample-guided *refinement of the labelling* in cases where the proof fails. The framework can with minor adaptations be applied to arbitrary HOL4 ISA models. We present benchmarks for ARMv7 and MIPS. With a suitable labelling identified, the median verification time for one ARMv7 instruction is about 40 seconds. For MIPS, the complete analysis took slightly more than one hour and made configuration dependencies explicit that we had not been aware of before. We report on the following contributions: (i) a backward proof tactic to automatically verify noninterference of HOL4 state transition functions, as used in operational ISA semantics; (ii) the automated identification of sound and accurate labellings; (iii) benchmarks for the ISAs of ARMv7-A and MIPS, based on an SML-implementation of the approach.

2   Processor Models

2.1   ISA Models

In the recent years, Fox et al. have created ISA models for x86-64, MIPS, several versions of ARM and other architectures [7,8]. The instruction sets are modelled based on official documentations and on the abstraction level of the programmer's view, thus being agnostic to internals like pipelines. The newest models are produced in the domain-specific language L3 [7] and can be exported to the interactive theorem prover HOL4. Our analysis targets those purely-functional HOL4 models for single-core systems. An ISA is formalized as a state transition system, with the machine state represented as record structure (on memory, registers, operational modes, control flags, etc.) and the operational semantics as functions (or *transitions*) on such states. The top-level transition NEXT processes the CPU by one instruction. While L3 also supports export to HOL4 definitions in monadic style, we focus our work on the standard functional representation based on let-expressions. States resulting from an *unpredictable* (i.e., underspecified) operation are tagged with an exception marker (see Sect. 7 for a discussion).

2.2   Notation

A *state* $s = \{C_1 := c_1, C_2 := c_2, \ldots\}$ is a record, where the fields $C_1, C_2, \ldots$ depend on the concrete ISA. As a naming convention, we use R_i for fields that are records themselves (such as control registers) and F_i for fields of a function/mapping type (such as general purpose register sets). The *components* of a state are all its fields and subfields (in arbitrary depth), as well as the single entries of the state's mappings. The value of field C in s is derived by $s.C$. An update of field C in s with value c is represented as $s[C := c]$. Similarly, function updates of F in location l by value v are written as $F[l := v]$. Conditionals and other case distinctions are written as $\mathbb{C}(b, a_1, a_2, \ldots, a_k)$, with b being the selector and $a_1, a_2, \ldots, a_k$ the alternatives. A transition Φ transforms a pre-state s into a return-value v and a post-state s', formally $\Phi s = (v, s')$. Usually, a transition contains subtransitions $\Phi_1, \Phi_2, \ldots, \Phi_n$, composed of some structure ϕ of abstractions, function applications, case distinctions, sequential compositions and other semantic operators, so that $\Phi s = \phi(\Phi_1, \Phi_2, \ldots, \Phi_n)s$. Transition definitions can be recursively unfolded: $\phi(\Phi_1, \ldots, \Phi_n)s = \phi(\phi_1(\Phi_{1,1}, \ldots, \Phi_{1,m}), \ldots, \Phi_n)s = \ldots = \vec{\phi}s$, where $\vec{\phi}$ is the completely unfolded transition, called the *evaluated form*. For the transitions of the considered instruction sets, unfolding always terminates. Note that '$=$' is used here for the equivalence of states, transitions or values, not for the syntactical equivalence of terms. Below we give the definition of the ARMv7-NOOP-instruction and its evaluated (and simplified) form:

```
dfn′NoOperation s
= BranchTo(s.REG RName_PC + C(FST (ThisInstrLength () s) = 16, 2, 4)) s
= ((), s[REG := s.REG[RName_PC := s.REG RName_PC + C(s.Encoding = Thumb, 2, 4)]])
```

NOOP branches to the current program counter (s.REG RName_PC) plus some offset. The offset depends on the current instruction length, which in turn depends on the current encoding. Here, FST selects the actual return value of the ThisInstrLength transition, ignoring its unchanged post-state.

2.3 Memory Management

For simplicity, our analysis focuses on core-internal flows (e.g., between registers) and abstracts away from the concrete behaviour of the memory subsystem (including address translation, memory protection, caching, peripherals, buses, etc.). Throughout the course of the - otherwise core internal - analysis, a contract on the memory subsystem is assumed that then allows the reasoning on global properties. The core can communicate with the memory subsystem through an interface, but never directly accesses its internal state. The interface expects inputs like the type of access (read, fetch, write, ...), the virtual address, the privilege state of the processor, and other parameters. It updates the state of the memory subsystem and returns a success or error message along with possibly read data. While being agnostic about the concrete behaviour of the memory subsystems, we assume that there is a secure memory configuration $\mathcal{P}_m$, restricting unprivileged accesses, e.g., through page table settings. Furthermore, we assume the existence of a low-equivalence relation $\mathcal{R}_m$ on pairs of memory subsystems. Typically, two memories in $\mathcal{R}_m$ would agree on memory content accessible in an unprivileged processor mode. When in unprivileged processor mode and starting from secure memory configurations, transitions on memory subsystems are assumed to maintain both the memory relation and secure configurations. Consider an update of state s assigning the sum of the values of register y and the memory at location a to register x, slightly simplified: $s[x := s.y + \texttt{read}(a, s.\text{mem})]$. Since read - as a function of the memory interface - satisfies the constraints above, for two pre-states s_1 and s_2 satisfying

$\mathcal{P}_m s_1.\text{mem} \wedge \mathcal{P}_m s_2.\text{mem} \wedge \mathcal{R}_m(s_1.\text{mem}, s_2.\text{mem})$, we can infer that read will return the same value or error. Overall, with preconditions met, two states that agree on x, y, and the low parts of the memory before the computation, will also agree after the computation. That is, as long as read fulfils the contract, the analysis of the core (and in the end the global analysis) does not need to be concerned with details of the memory subsystem.

3   ISA Information Flow Analysis

3.1   Objectives

Consider an ISA model with an initial specification determining some preconditions (e.g., on the privilege mode) and some system components, typically only the program counter, that are to be regarded as observable (or *low*) by some given actor. If there is information flow from some other component (say, a control register) to some of these initially-low components, this other component must be regarded as observable too for noninterference to hold. The objective of the analysis is to identify all these other components that are observable due to their direct or indirect influence on the given low components.

A *labelling* $\mathcal{L}$ assigns to each atomic component (component without subcomponents) a label, high or low.[1] It is *sound* if it does not mark any component as high that can influence, and hence pass information to, a component marked as low. In the refinement order the labelling $\mathcal{L}'$ refines $\mathcal{L}$ ($\mathcal{L} \sqsubseteq \mathcal{L}'$), if low components in $\mathcal{L}$ are low also in $\mathcal{L}'$. The labelling $\mathcal{L}$ is *accurate*, if $\mathcal{L}$ is minimal in the refinement order such that $\mathcal{L}$ is sound and refines the initial labelling.

Determining whether a labelling is accurate is generally undecidable. Suppose $\mathbb{C}(P(x), s.C, 0)$ is assigned to a low component. Deciding whether C needs to be deemed low requires deciding whether there is some valid instantiation of x, such that $P(x)$ holds, which might not be decidable. However, it appears that in many cases, including those considered here, accurate labellings are feasible. In our approach we check the necessity of a label refinement by identifying an actual flow from the witness component to some low component. We cannot guarantee that this check always succeeds, for undecidability reasons. If it does not, the tool still tries to refine the low equivalence and a warning that the final relation may no longer be accurate is generated. For the considered case studies the tool always finds an accurate labelling, which is then by construction unique.

Labellings correspond to low-equivalence relations on pairs of states, relations that agree on all low components including the memory relation $\mathcal{R}_m$ and leave all other components unrestricted. *Noninterference* holds if the only components affecting the state or any return value are themselves low. Formally, assume the two pre-states s_1 and s_2 agree on the low-labelled components, expressed by a low-equivalence relation $\mathcal{R}$ on those states. Then, for a given transition Φ and preconditions $\mathcal{P}$, noninterference $\mathcal{N}(\mathcal{R}, \mathcal{P}, \Phi)$ holds if after Φ the post-states are again in $\mathcal{R}$ and the resulting return values are equal:

---

[1] We have not found a use for ISA security lattices of finer granularity.

$$\mathcal{N}(\mathcal{R}, \mathcal{P}, \Phi) := \forall s_1, s_2, v_1, v_2, t_1, t_2 :$$
$$((v_1, t_1) = \Phi s_1) \wedge ((v_2, t_2) = \Phi s_2) \wedge \mathcal{R}(s_1, s_2) \wedge \mathcal{P} s_1 \wedge \mathcal{P} s_2$$
$$\Rightarrow \mathcal{R}(t_1, t_2) \wedge (v_1 = v_2)$$

Preconditions on the starting states can include architecture properties (version number, present extensions, etc.), a secure memory configuration and a specification of the privilege level. In our framework the user defines relevant preconditions and an initial low-equivalence relation $\mathcal{R}_0$ for an input ISA. The goal of the analysis is to statically and automatically find an accurate refinement of $\mathcal{R}_0$ so that noninterference holds for $\Phi = \texttt{NEXT}$. The analysis yields the final low-equivalence relation, the corresponding HOL4 noninterference theorem demonstrating the soundness of the relation, and a notification of whether the analysis succeeded to establish a guarantee on the relation's accuracy. The proof search is not guaranteed to terminate successfully, but we have found it robust enough to reliably produce accurate output on ISA models of considerable complexity (see Sect. 5). We do not treat timing and probabilistic channels and leave safety-properties about unmodified components for future work.

3.2 Challenges

Our goal is to perform the analysis from an initial, user-supplied labelling on a standard ISA with minimal user interaction. In particular, we wish to avoid user supplied label annotations and error-prone manual rewrites of the ISA specification, that a type-based approach might depend on to eliminate some of the complications specific to ISA models. Instead, we address those challenges with symbolic evaluation and the application of simplification theorems. Since both are available in HOL4, and so are the models, we verify noninterference in HOL4 directly. This also frees us from external preprocessing and soundness proofs, thus minimizing the TCB. Below, we give examples for common challenges.

Representation. The functional models that we use represent register sets as mappings. Static type systems for (purely) functional languages [9,17] need to assign secrecy levels uniformly to all image values, even if a mapping has both public and secret entries. Adaptations of representation and type system might allow to type more accurately for lookups on constant locations. But common lookup patterns on locations represented by variables or complex terms would require a preprocessing that propagates constraints throughout large expressions.

Semantics. Unprivileged ARMv7 processes can access the current state of the control register CPSR. The ISA specifies to (i) map all subcomponents of the control register to a 32-bit word and (ii) apply the resulting word to a bitmask. As a result, the returned value does actually not depend on all subcomponents of the CPSR, even though all of them were referred to in the first step. For accuracy, an actual understanding of the arithmetics is required.

Context-Sensitivity. Earlier work on ISA information flow [13] deals with ARM's complex operational semantics in a stepwise analysis, focusing on one subprocedure at a time. This allows for a systematic solution, but comes with the risk of insufficient context. For example, when reading from a register, usually two steps are involved: first, the concrete register identifier with respect to the current processor mode is looked up; second, the actual reading is performed. Analysing the reading operation in isolation is not accurate, since the lack of constraints on the register identifier would require to deem all registers low. In order to include restrictions from the context, [13] required a number of manual proofs. To avoid this, we analyse entire instructions at a time, using HOL4's machinery to propagate constraints.

4   Approach

We are not the first to study (semi-)automated hardware verification using theorem proving. As [5] points out for hardware refinement proofs, a large share of the proof obligations can be discharged by repeated unfolding (rewriting) of definitions, case splits and basic simplification. While easy to automate, these steps lead easily to an increase in complexity. The challenge, thus, is to find efficient and effective ways of rewriting and to minimize case splits throughout the proof. Our framework traverses the instruction set instruction by instruction, managing a task queue. For each instruction, three steps are performed: (i) rewriting/unfolding to obtain evaluated forms, (ii) attempting to prove noninterference for the instruction, (iii) on failure, using the identified counterexample to refine the low-equivalence relation. This section details those steps. After each refinement, the instructions verified so far are re-enqueued. The steps are repeated until the queue is empty and each instruction has successfully been verified with the most recent low-equivalence relation. Finally, noninterference is shown for NEXT, employing all instruction lemmas, as well as rewrite theorems for the fetch and decode transitions. Soundness is inherited from HOL4's machinery. Accuracy is tracked by the counterexample verification in step (iii).

4.1   Rewriting Towards an Evaluated Form

The evaluated form of instructions is obtained through symbolic evaluation. Starting from the definition of a given transition, (i) let-expressions are eliminated, (ii) parameters of subtransitions are evaluated (in a call-by-value manner), (iii) the subtransitions are recursively unfolded by replacing them with their respective evaluated forms, (iv) the result is normalized, and (v) in a few cases substituted with an abstraction. Normalization and abstraction are described below. For the first three steps we reuse evaluation machinery from [7] and extend it, mainly to add support for automated subtransition identification and recursion. Preconditions, for example on the privilege level, allow to reduce rewriting time and the size of the result. Since they can become invalid during instruction execution, they have to be re-evaluated for each recursive invocation.

Throughout the whole rewriting process, various simplifications are applied, for example on nested conditional expressions, case distinctions, words, and pairs, as well as conditional lifting, which we motivate below. For soundness, all steps produce equivalence theorems.

Step Library. The ISA models are provided together with so-called *step libraries*, specific to every architecture [7]. They include a database of pre-computed rewrite theorems, connecting transitions to their evaluated forms. Those theorems are computed in an automated manner, but are guided manually. Our tool is able to employ them as hints, as long as their preconditions are not too restrictive for the general security analysis. Otherwise, we compute the evaluated forms autonomously. Besides instruction specific theorems, we use some datatype specific theorems and general machinery from [7].

Conditional Lifting. Throughout the rewriting process, the evaluated forms of two sequential subtransitions might be composed by passing the result of the first transition into the formal parameters of the second. This often leads to terms like $\gamma(s) := \mathbb{C}(b, s[C_1 := c_1], s[C_2 := c_2]).C_3$. However, in order to derive equality properties in the noninterference proof (e.g., $[s_1.C_3 = s_2.C_3] \vdash \gamma(s_1) = \gamma(s_2)$) or to check validity of premises (e.g., $\gamma(s) = 0$), conditional lifting is applied:

$$
\begin{aligned}
\gamma(s) &= \mathbb{C}(b, s[C_1 := c_1], s[C_2 := c_2]).C_3 && \text{lifting} \\
&= \mathbb{C}(b, (s[C_1 := c_1]).C_3, (s[C_2 := c_2]).C_3) && \text{simplifying} \\
&= \mathbb{C}(b, s.C_3, s.C_3) && \text{merging} \\
&= s.C_3
\end{aligned}
$$

To mitigate exponential blow-up, conditional lifting should only be applied where needed. For record field accesses we do this in a top-down manner, ignoring fields outside the current focus. For example, in $\gamma(s)$ there is no need to process c_1 at all, even in cases where c_1 itself is a conditional expression.

Normalization. With record field accesses being so critical for performance, both rewriting and proof benefit from (intermediate) evaluated forms being normalized. A state term is *normalized* if it only consists of record field updates to a state variable s, that is, it has the form

$$
s[C_1 := c_1, \ldots, C_n := c_n, R_1 := s.R_1[C_{1,1} := c_{1,1}, \ldots, C_{1,k} := c_{1,k}], \ldots].
$$

For a state term τ updating state variable s in the fields $C_1, \ldots, C_n$ with the values $c_1, \ldots, c_n$, we verify the normalized form in a forward construction (omitting subcomponents here and below for readability; they are treated analogously):

$$
\begin{aligned}
\tau &= \tau[C_1 := \tau.C_1, \ldots, C_n := \tau.C_n] && (1) \\
&= s[C_1 := \tau.C_1, \ldots, C_n := \tau.C_n] && (2) \\
&= s[C_1 := c_1, \ldots, C_n := c_n] && (3)
\end{aligned}
$$

We significantly improve proof performance with the abstraction of complex expressions by showing (1) independently of the concrete τ and (2) independently of the values of the updates, both those inside τ and those applied to τ. We obtain $c_1, \ldots, c_n$ by similar means to those shown in the lifting example of γ above.

In [7], both conditional lifting and normalization are based on the precomputation of datatype specific lifting and unlifting lemmas for updates. Our procedures are largely independent of record types and update patterns. However, because of the performance benefits of [7], we plan to generalize/automate their normalization machinery or combine both approaches in future work.

Abstracted Transitions. Even with normalization, the specification of a transition grows quickly when unfolding complex subtransitions, especially for loops. We therefore choose to abstract selected subtransitions. To this end, we substitute their evaluated forms with terms that make potential flows explicit, but abstract away from concrete specifications. Let the normalized form of transition Φ be $\vec{\phi}s = (\beta(s), s[C_1 := \gamma_1(s), \ldots, C_n := \gamma_n(s)])$. The values of all primitive state updates $\gamma_1(s), \ldots, \gamma_n(s)$ on s and the return value $\beta(s)$ of Φ are substituted with new function constants $f_0, f_1, \ldots, f_n$ applied to relevant state components actually accessed instead of to the entire state:

$$\Phi s = \vec{\phi}s = (f_0(s.C_{0,1}, \ldots, s.C_{0,k_0}),$$
$$s[C_1 := f_1(s.C_{1,1}, \ldots, s.C_{1,k_1}), \ldots, C_n := f_n(s.C_{n,1}, \ldots, s.C_{n,k_n})])$$

Except for situations that suggest the need for a refinement of the low-equivalence relation, $f_0, \ldots, f_n$ do not need to be unfolded in the further processing of Φ. Low-equivalence of the post-states can be inferred trivially:

$$[(s_1.C_{1,1} = s_2.C_{1,1}) \wedge \ldots] \vdash f_1(s_1.C_{1,1}, s_1.C_{1,2}, \ldots) = f_1(s_2.C_{1,1}, s_2.C_{1,2}, \ldots))$$

To avoid accuracy losses in cases where $\vec{\phi}$ mentions components that neither return value nor low components actually depend on, we unfold abstractions as last resort before declaring a noninterference proof as failed.

4.2   Backward Proof Strategy

Having computed the evaluated form for an instruction Φ, we proceed with the verification attempt of $\mathcal{N}(\mathcal{R}, \mathcal{P}, \Phi)$ through a backward proof, for the user-provided preconditions $\mathcal{P}$ and the current low-equivalence relation $\mathcal{R}$. The sound backward proof employs a combination of the following steps:

- **Conditional Lifting:** Especially in order to resolve record field accesses on complex state expressions, we apply conditional lifting in various scopes (record accesses, operators, operands) and degrees of aggressiveness.
- **Equality of Subexpressions:** Let F be a functional component and n and m be two variables ranging over $\{0, 1, 2\}$. The equality

$$\mathbb{C}(n = 2, 0, s_1.F(\mathbb{C}(n, a, b, c))) + s_1.F(\mathbb{C}(m, a, b, a))$$
$$= \mathbb{C}(n = 2, 0, s_2.F(\mathbb{C}(n, a, b, c))) + s_2.F(\mathbb{C}(m, a, b, a))$$

can be established from the premises $s_1.F(a) = s_2.F(a)$ and $s_1.F(b) = s_2.F(b)$ by lifting the distinctions on n and m outwards or - alternatively - by case splitting on n and m. Either way, equality should be established for each summand separately, in order to limit the number of considered cases to $3 + 3$ instead of 3×3. Doing so in explicit subgoals also helps in discarding unreachable cases, such as the one where c would be chosen. We identify relevant expressions via pre-defined and user-defined patterns.

- **Memory Reasoning:** Axioms and derived theorems on noninterference properties of the memory subsystem and maintained invariants are applied.
- **Simplifications:** Throughout the whole proof process, various simplifications take effect, for example on record field updates.
- **Case Splitting:** Usually the mentioned steps are sufficient. For a few harder instructions or if the low-equivalence relation requires refinement, we apply case splits, following the branching structure closely.
- **Evaluation:** After the case splitting, a number of more aggressive simplifications, evaluations, and automatic proof tactics are used to unfold remaining constants and to reason about words, bit operations, unusual forms of record accesses, and other corner cases.

4.3   Relation Refinement

Throughout the analysis, refinement of the low-equivalence relation is required whenever noninterference does not hold for the instruction currently considered. Counterexamples to noninterference enable the identification of new components to be downgraded to low. When managed carefully, failed backward proofs of noninterference allow to extract such counterexamples. However, backward proofs are not complete. Unsatisfiable subgoals might be introduced despite the goal being verifiable. For accuracy, we thus verify the necessity of downgrading a component C before the actual refinement of the relation. To that end, it is sufficient to identify two witness states that fulfil the preconditions $\mathcal{P}$, agree on all components except C, and lead to a violation of noninterference in respect to the analysed instruction Φ and the current (yet to be refined) relation $\mathcal{R}$. We refer to the existence of such witnesses as $\overline{\mathcal{N}}$:

$$\overline{\mathcal{N}}(\mathcal{R}, \mathcal{P}, \Phi, C) := \exists s, x_1, x_2, v_1, v_2, t_1, t_2 :$$
$$((v_1, t_1) = \Phi(s[C := x_1])) \wedge ((v_2, t_2) = \Phi(s[C := x_2]))$$
$$\wedge \mathcal{P}(s[C := x_1]) \wedge \mathcal{P}(s[C := x_2]) \wedge (\neg \mathcal{R}(t_1, t_2) \vee (v_1 \neq v_2))$$

If such witnesses exist, any sound relation $\mathcal{R}'$ refining $\mathcal{R}$ will have to contain some restriction on C. With the chosen granularity, that translates to $\forall s_1, s_2 : \mathcal{R}'(s_1, s_2) \Rightarrow (\mathcal{R}(s_1, s_2) \wedge s_1.C = s_2.C)$. We proceed with the weakest such relation, i.e., $\mathcal{R}'(s_1, s_2) := (\mathcal{R}(s_1, s_2) \wedge s_1.C = s_2.C)$. As discussed in Sect. 3.1, it can be undecidable whether the current relation needs refinement. However, for the models that we analyzed, our framework was always able to verify the existence of suitable witnesses. The identification and verification of new low components consists of three steps:

1. **Identification of a new low component.** We transform subgoal G on top of the goal stack into a subgoal `false` with premises extended by $\neg G$. In this updated list of premises for the pre-states s_1 and s_2, we identify a premise on s_1 which would solve the transformed subgoal by contradiction when assumed for s_2 as well. Intuitively, we suspect that noninterference is prevented by the disagreement on components in the identified premise. We arbitrarily pick one such component as candidate for downgrading.
2. **Existential verification of the scenario.** To ensure that the extended premises alone are not already in contradiction, we prove the existence of a scenario in which all of them hold. We furthermore introduce the additional premise that the two pre-states disagree on the chosen candidate, but agree on all other components. An instantiation satisfying this existential statement is a promising suspect for the set of witnesses for $\overline{\mathcal{N}}$. The existential proof in HOL4 refines existentially quantified variables with patterns, e.g., symbolic states for state variables, bit vectors for words, and mappings with abstract updates for function variables (allowing to reduce $\exists f : P(f(n))$ to $\exists x : P(x)$). If possible, existential goals are split. Further simplifications include HOL4 tactics particular to existential reasoning, the application of type-specific existential inequality theorems, and simplifications on word and bit operations. If after those steps and automatic reasoning existential subgoals remain, the tool attempts to finish the proof with different combinations of standard values for the remaining existentially quantified variables.
3. **Witness verification.** We use the anonymous witnesses of the existential statement in the previous step as witnesses for $\overline{\mathcal{N}}$. After initialisation, the core parts of the proof strategy from the failed noninterference proof are repeated until the violation of noninterference has been demonstrated.

In order to keep the analysis focused, it is important to handle case splits before entering the refinement stage. At the same time, persistent case splits can be expensive on a non-provable goal. Therefore, we implemented a depth first proof tactical, which introduces hardly any performance overhead on successful proofs, but fails early in cases where the proof strategy does not succeed. Furthermore, whenever case splits become necessary in the proof attempt, the framework strives to diverge early, prioritizing case splits on state components.

5   Evaluation

We applied our framework to analyse information flows on ARMv7-A and MIPS-III (64-bit RS4000). For ARM, we focus on user mode execution without security or virtualization extension. Since unprivileged ARM code is able to switch between several instructions sets (ARM, Thumb, Thumb2, ThumbEE), the information flow analysis has to be performed for all of them. For MIPS, we consider all three privilege modes (user, kernel, and supervisor). The single-core model does not include floating point operations or memory management instructions.

Table 1 shows the initial and accurate final low-equivalence relations for the two ISAs with different configurations. All relations refine the memory relation. The *final relation* column only lists components not already restricted by

Table 1. Identified flows (model components might deviate from physical systems)

ISA	Mode	Initial relation	Final relation
ARMv7-A	user mode	program counter	user registers; control register CPSR (all flags); floating point registers of FP.REG and FP.FSPCR; TEEHBR register (coprocessor 14); Encoding ghost component; system control register SCTLR (coprocessor 15, flags: EE, TE, V, A, U, DZ)
MIPS-III	user *or* kernel *or* supervisor mode	program counter; BranchTo; BranchDelay; CP0.Count; exception marker; CP0.Status.KSU; CP0.Status.EXL; CP0.Status.ERL	all modelled system components
MIPS-III	*restricted* user mode		general purpose register set; LLbit; lo; hi; CP0.Config.BE; CP0.Status.RE; CP0.Status.BEV; exceptionSignalled

the corresponding initial relations. For simplicity, the initial relation for MIPS restricts three components accessed on the highest level of NEXT. The corresponding table cell also lists components already restricted by the preconditions. Initially unaware of the privilege management in MIPS, we were surprised that our tool first yielded the same results for all MIPS processor modes and that even user processes can read the entire state of system coprocessor CP0, which is responsible for privileged operations such as the management of interrupts, exceptions, or contexts. To restrict user privileges, the CU0 status flag must be cleared (see last line of the table). While ARMv7-processes in user mode can not read from banked registers of privileged modes, they can infer the state of various control registers. Alignment control register flags (CP15.SCTLR.A/U in ARMv7) are a good example for implicit flows in CPUs. Depending on their values, an unaligned address will either be accessed as is, forcibly aligned, or cause an alignment fault. Table 2 shows the time that rewriting, instruction proofs (including relation refinement), and the composing proof for NEXT took on a single Xeon® X3470 core. The first benchmark for MIPS refers to unrestricted user mode (with similar times as for kernel and supervisor mode), the second one to restricted user mode. Even though we borrowed a few data type theorems and some basic machinery from the step library, we did not use instruction specific

Table 2. Proof performance (in seconds)

ISA	Rewrite	Instr	NEXT	Total	
ARMv7	29,829	46,146	2,171	78,146	(21 h, 42 min)
MIPS (1)	537	1,790	1,594	3,921	(1 h, 5 min)
MIPS (2)	537	1,216	562	2,315	(38 min)

Table 3. Performance ARMv7 proof

Step	Min	Median	Mean	Max
rewrite	1	25	167	2,384
instr. (success)	1	15	96	3,605
instr. (fail)	3	26	72	1,544
refinement	7	50	89	1,326

theorems for the MIPS verification. Both ISAs have around 130 modelled instructions, but with 9238 lines of L3 compared to 2080 lines [7], the specifications of the ARMv7 instructions are both larger and more complex. Consequently, we observed a remarkable difference in performance. However, as Table 3 shows, minimum, median, and mean processing times (given in seconds) for the ARM instructions are actually moderate throughout all steps (rewriting, successful and failed noninterference proofs, and relation refinement). Merely a few complex outliers are responsible for the high verification time of the ARM ISA. While we believe that optimizations and parallelization could significantly improve performance, those outliers still demonstrate the limits of analyzing entire instructions as a whole. Combining our approach with compositional solutions such as [13] could overcome this remaining challenge. We leave this for future work.

6 Related Work

While most work on processor verification focuses on functional correctness [4,5, 21] and ignores information flow, we survey hardware noninterference, both for special separation hardware and for general purpose hardware.

Noninterference Verification for Separation Hardware. Wilding et al. [24] verify noninterference for the partitioning system of the AAMP7G microprocessor. The processor can be seen as a separation kernel in hardware, but lacks for example user-visible registers. Security is first shown for an abstract model, which is later refined to a more concrete model of the system, comprising about 3000 lines of ACL2. The proof appears to be performed semi-automatically.

SAFE is a computer system with hardware operating on tagged data [2]. Noninterference is first proven for a more abstract machine model and then transferred to the concrete machine by refinement. The proof in Coq does not seem to involve much automation.

Sinha et al. [20] verify confidentiality of x86 programs that use Intel's Software Guard Extensions (SGX) in order to execute critical code inside an SGX enclave, a hardware-isolated execution environment. They formalize the extended ISA axiomatically and model execution as interleaving between enclave and environment actions. A type system then checks that the enclave does not contain insecure code that leaks sensitive data to non-enclave memory. At the same time, accompanying theorems guarantee some protection from the environment, in particular that an adversary can not influence the enclave by any instruction other than a write to input memory. However, [20] assumes that SGX management data structures are not shared and that there are no register contents that survive an enclave exit and are readable by the environment. Once L3/HOL4 models of x86 with SGX are available, our machinery would allow to validate those assumptions in an automated manner, even for a realistic x86 ISA model. Such a verification would demonstrate that instructions executed by the environment do not leak enclave data from shared resources (like non-mediated registers) to components observable by the adversary.

Noninterference Verification for General Purpose Hardware. Information flow analysis below ISA level is discussed in [15,18]. Procter et al. [18] present a functional hardware description language suitable for formal verification, while the language in [15] can be typed with information flow labels to allow for static verification of noninterference. Described hardware can be compiled into VHDL and Verilog, respectively. Both papers demonstrate how their approaches can be used to verify information flow properties of hardware executing both trusted and untrusted code. We are not aware of the application of either approach to information flow analysis of complex commodity processors such as ARM.

Tiwari et al. [23] augment gate level designs with information flow labels, allowing simulators to statically verify information flow policies. Signals from outside the TCB are modelled as *unknown*. Logical gates are automatically replaced with label propagating gates that operate on both known and unknown values. The authors employ the machinery to verify the security of a combination of a processor, I/O, and a microkernel with a small TCB. It is unclear to us how the approach would scale to commodity processors with a more complex TCB. From our own experience on ISA-level, the bottleneck is mainly constituted by the preprocessing to obtain the model's evaluated form and by the identification of a suitable labelling. The actual verification is comparatively fast.

In earlier work [13] we described a HOL4 proof for the noninterference (and other isolation properties) of a monadic ARMv7-model. A compositional approach based on proof rules was used to support a semi-automatic analysis. However, due to insufficient context, a number of transitions had to be verified manually or with the support of context-enhancing proof rules. In the present work, we overcome this issue by analysing entire instructions. Furthermore, our new analysis exhibits the low-equivalence relation automatically, while [13] provides it as fixed input. Finally, the framework described in the present paper is less dependent of the analysed architecture.

Verification of Binaries. Fox's ARM model is also used to automatically verify security properties of binary code. Balliu et al. [3] does this for noninterference, Tan et al. [22] for safety-properties. Despite the seeming similarities, ISA analysis and binary code analysis differ in many respects. While binary verification considers concrete assembly instructions for (partly) known parameters, ISA analysis has to consider all possible assembly instructions for all possible parameters. On the other hand, it is sufficient for an ISA analysis to do this for each instruction in isolation, while binary verification usually reasons on a sequence (or a tree of) instructions. In effect, that makes the verification of a binary program an analysis on imperative code. In contrast, ISA analysis (in our setting) is really concerned with functional code, namely the operational semantics that describe the different steps of single instructions. In either case, to enable full automation, both analyses have to include a broader context when the local context is not sufficient to verify the desired property for a single step in isolation. As discussed above, we choose an instruction-wide context from the beginning. Both [3,22] employ a more local reasoning. In [22] a Hoare-style logic is used and context is provided by selective synchronisation of pre- and postconditions between neighbouring code blocks. In [3] a forward symbolic analysis carries the context in a path condition when advancing from instruction to instruction. SMT solvers then allow to discard symbolic states with non-satisfiable paths.

7   Discussion on Unpredictable Behaviour

ISA specifications usually target actors responsible for code production, like programmers or compiler developers. Consequently, they are often based on the assumption that executed code will be composed from a set of well-defined instructions and sound conditions, so that no one relies on combinations of instructions, parameters and configurations not fully covered by the specification. This allows to keep instructions partly underspecified and leave room for optimizations on the manufacturer's side. However, this practice comes at the cost of actors who have to trust the execution of unknown and potentially malicious third-party code. For example, an OS has an interest in maintaining confidentiality between processes. To that end, it has different means such as clearing visible registers on context switches. But if the specification is incomplete on which registers actually are visible to an instruction with uncommon parameters, then there is no guarantee that malicious code can not use underspecified instructions (i.e., instructions resulting in unpredictable states) to learn about otherwise secret components. ARM attempts to address this by specifying that "*unpredictable* behaviour must not perform any function that cannot be performed at the current or lower level of privilege using instructions that are not *unpredictable*".[2] While this might indeed remedy integrity concerns, it is still problematic for noninterference. An underspecified instruction can be implemented by two different "safe" behaviours, with the choice of the behaviour depending on an otherwise secret component. The models by Fox et al. mark the post-states of underspecified operations as unpredictable by assigning an exception marker to those states. In addition, newer versions still model a reasonable behaviour for such cases, but there is no guarantee that the manufacturer chooses the same behaviour. A physical implementation might include

---

[2] ARMv7-A architecture reference manual, issue C: http://infocenter.arm.com/help/index.jsp?topic=/com.arm.doc.ddi0406c.

flows from more components than the model does, or vice versa. A more conservative analysis like ours takes state changes after model exceptions into account, but can still miss flows simply not specified. To the rescue might come statements from processor designers like ARM that *"unpredictable* behaviour must not represent security holes".[3] In one interpretation, flows not occurring elsewhere can be excluded in underspecified instructions. The need to rely on this interpretation can be reduced (but not entirely removed) when the exception marker itself is considered low in the initial labelling. As an example, consider an instruction that is well-defined when system component C_1 is 0, but underspecified when it is 1. The manufacturer might choose different behaviours for both cases, thus possibly introducing a flow from C_1 to low components. At the same time, the creator of the formal model might implement both cases in the same way, so that the analysis could miss the flow. But with a low exception marker, C_1 would also be labelled low, since it influences the marker. However, an additional undocumented dependency on another component C_2 that only exists when C_1 is 1 can still be missed.

8   Conclusions and Future Work

We presented a sound and accurate approach to automatically and statically verify noninterference on instruction set architectures, including the automatic identification of a least restrictive low-equivalence relation. Besides applying our framework to more models such as the one of ARMv8, we intend to improve robustness and performance, and to cover integrity properties as well.

Integrity Properties. We plan to enhance the framework by safety-properties such as nonexfiltration [10,13] and mode switch properties [13]. Nonexfiltration asserts that certain components do not change throughout (unprivileged) execution. Mode switch properties make guarantees on how components change when transiting to higher privilege levels, for example that the program counter will point to a well-defined entry point of the kernel code. We believe that both properties can be derived relatively easily from the normalized forms of the instructions.

Performance Optimization. While our benchmarks have demonstrated that ISA information flow analysis on an instruction by instruction basis allows for a large degree of automation, they also have shown that this approach introduces severe performance penalties for more complex instructions. To increase scalability and at the same time maintain automation, we plan to investigate how to combine the compositional approach of [13] with the more global reasoning demonstrated here. Furthermore, there is potential for improvements in the performance of individual steps. E.g., our normalization could be combined with the one of [7].

---

[3] ARMv7-A architecture reference manual, issue B.

Acknowledgments. Work supported by the Swedish Foundation for Strategic Research, by VINNOVA's HASPOC-project, and by the Swedish Civil Contingencies Agency project CERCES. Thanks to Anthony C. J. Fox, Roberto Guanciale, Nicolae Paladi, and the anonymous reviewers for their helpful comments.

References

1. Alkassar, E., Hillebrand, M.A., Paul, W., Petrova, E.: Automated verification of a small hypervisor. In: Leavens, G.T., O'Hearn, P., Rajamani, S.K. (eds.) VSTTE 2010. LNCS, vol. 6217, pp. 40–54. Springer, Heidelberg (2010)
2. Azevedo de Amorim, A., Collins, N., DeHon, A., Demange, D., Hriţcu, C., Pichardie, D., Pierce, B.C., Pollack, R., Tolmach, A.: A verified information-flow architecture. In: Principles of Programming Languages, POPL, pp. 165–178 (2014)
3. Balliu, M., Dam, M., Guanciale, R.: Automating information flow analysis of low level code. In: Proceedings of the 2014 ACM SIGSAC Conference on Computer and Communications Security, CCS, pp. 1080–1091 (2014)
4. Beyer, S., Jacobi, C., Kröning, D., Leinenbach, D., Paul, W.J.: Putting it all together - formal verification of the VAMP. Int. J. Softw. Tools Technol. Transf. **8**(4), 411–430 (2006)
5. Cyrluk, D., Rajan, S., Shankar, N., Srivas, M.K.: Effective theorem proving for hardware verification. In: Kumar, R., Kropf, T. (eds.) TPCD 1994. LNCS, vol. 901, pp. 203–222. Springer, Heidelberg (1995)
6. Dam, M., Guanciale, R., Khakpour, N., Nemati, H., Schwarz, O.: Formal verification of information flow security for a simple ARM-based separation kernel. In: Computer and Communications Security, CCS, pp. 223–234 (2013)
7. Fox, A.C.J.: Improved tool support for machine-code decompilation in HOL4. In: Urban, C., Zhang, X. (eds.) ITP 2015. LNCS, pp. 187–202. Springer, Heidelberg (2015)
8. Fox, A., Myreen, M.O.: A trustworthy monadic formalization of the ARMv7 instruction set architecture. In: Kaufmann, M., Paulson, L.C. (eds.) ITP 2010. LNCS, vol. 6172, pp. 243–258. Springer, Heidelberg (2010)
9. Heintze, N., Riecke, J.G.: The SLam calculus: programming with secrecy and integrity. In: Principles of Programming Languages, POPL, pp. 365–377 (1998)
10. Heitmeyer, C., Archer, M., Leonard, E., McLean, J.: Applying formal methods to a certifiably secure software system. IEEE Trans. Softw. Eng. **34**(1), 82–98 (2008)
11. HOL4 project. http://hol.sourceforge.net/
12. Hunt, S., Sands, D.: On flow-sensitive security types. In: Principles of Programming Languages, POPL, pp. 79–90 (2006)
13. Khakpour, N., Schwarz, O., Dam, M.: Machine assisted proof of ARMv7 instruction level isolation properties. In: Gonthier, G., Norrish, M. (eds.) CPP 2013. LNCS, vol. 8307, pp. 276–291. Springer, Heidelberg (2013)
14. Klein, G., Elphinstone, K., Heiser, G., Andronick, J., Cock, D., Derrin, P., Elkaduwe, D., Engelhardt, K., Kolanski, R., Norrish, M., Sewell, T., Tuch, H., Winwood, S.: seL4: formal verification of an OS kernel. In: SOSP, pp. 207–220 (2009)
15. Li, X., Tiwari, M., Oberg, J.K., Kashyap, V., Chong, F.T., Sherwood, T., Hardekopf, B.: Caisson: A hardware description language for secure information flow. In: Programming Language Design and Implementation, PLDI, pp. 109–120 (2011)

16. Murray, T.C., Matichuk, D., Brassil, M., Gammie, P., Bourke, T., Seefried, S., Lewis, C., Gao, X., Klein, G.: seL4: From general purpose to a proof of information flow enforcement. In: Security and Privacy, pp. 415–429 (2013)

17. Pottier, F., Simonet, V.: Information flow inference for ML. In: Principles of Programming Languages, POPL, pp. 319–330 (2002)

18. A. Procter, W. L. Harrison, I. Graves, M. Becchi, and G. Allwein.: Semantics driven hardware design, implementation, and verification with ReWire. In: Languages, Compilers and Tools for Embedded Systems, LCTES, pp. 13:1–13:10 (2015)

19. Sibert, O., Porras, P.A., Lindell, R.: The Intel 80x86 processor architecture: Pitfalls for secure systems. In: Security and Privacy, SP, pp. 211–222 (1995)

20. Sinha, R., Rajamani, S., Seshia, S., Vaswani, K.: Moat: verifying confidentiality of enclave programs. In: Computer and Communication Security, pp. 1169–1184 (2015)

21. Srivas, M., Bickford, M.: Formal verification of a pipelined microprocessor. IEEE Softw. **7**(5), 52–64 (1990)

22. Tan, J., Tay, H.J., Gandhi, R., Narasimhan, P.: AUSPICE: automatic safety property verification for unmodified executables. In: Gurfinkel, A., et al. (eds.) VSTTE 2015. LNCS, vol. 9593, pp. 202–222. Springer, Heidelberg (2016). doi:10.1007/978-3-319-29613-5_12

23. Tiwari, M., Oberg, J.K., Li, X., Valamehr, J., Levin, T., Hardekopf, B., Kastner, R., Chong, F.T., Sherwood, T.: Crafting a usable microkernel, processor, and I/O system with strict and provable information flow security. In: International Symposium on Computer Architecture, ISCA, pp. 189–200 (2011)

24. Wilding, M.M., Greve, D.A., Richards, R.J., Hardin, D.S.: Formal verification of partition management for the AAMP7G microprocessor. In: Hardin, D.S. (ed.) Design and Verification of Microprocessor Systems for High-Assurance Applications, pp. 175–191. Springer, New York (2010)

Linearizability and Causality

Simon Doherty$^{(\boxtimes)}$ and John Derrick

Department of Computing, University of Sheffield, Sheffield, UK
s.doherty@sheffield.ac.uk

Abstract. Most work on the verification of concurrent objects for shared memory assumes sequential consistency, but most multicore processors support only *weak memory models* that do not provide sequential consistency. Furthermore, most verification efforts focus on the *linearizability* of concurrent objects, but there are existing implementations optimized to run on weak memory models that are not linearizable.

In this paper, we address these problems by introducing *causal linearizability*, a correctness condition for concurrent objects running on weak memory models. Like linearizability itself, causal linearizability enables concurrent objects to be composed, under weak constraints on the client's behaviour. We specify these constraints by introducing a notion of *operation-race freedom*, where programs that satisfy this property are guaranteed to behave as if their shared objects were in fact linearizable.

We apply these ideas to objects from the Linux kernel, optimized to run on TSO, the memory model of the x86 processor family.

1 Introduction

The past decade has seen a great deal of interest in the verification of highly optimized, shared-memory concurrent objects. This interest is partly motivated by the increasing importance of multicore systems. Much of this verification work has assumed that these concurrent implementations run on the sequentially consistent memory model. However, contemporary multicore architectures do not implement this strong model. Rather, they implement *weak memory models*, which allow reorderings of memory operations, relative to what would be legal under sequential consistency. Examples of such models include TSO (implemented on the x86) [10], POWER and ARM [2]. These models create significant challenges for verifying that an implementation satisfies a particular correctness condition [5].

Furthermore it is not always clear *what* correctness conditions are appropriate for an implementation running on a weak memory model. Specifically, the standard correctness condition for concurrent objects is *linearizabilty* [8]. However, as described in Sect. 1.1, there are implementations of concurrent objects optimized to run on weak memory models that are not linearizable. Nevertheless, these implementations are used in important contexts, including the Linux kernel. This is possible because when these objects are used in a stereotypical fashion, their nonlinearizable behaviours are not observable to their clients.

© Springer International Publishing Switzerland 2016
R. De Nicola and E. Kühn (Eds.): SEFM 2016, LNCS 9763, pp. 45–60, 2016.
DOI: 10.1007/978-3-319-41591-8_4

Our goal in this paper is to define a correctness condition appropriate for these nonlinearizable objects. We introduce a correctness condition called *causal linearizablilty*. Roughly speaking, an object is causally linearizable if all its executions can be transformed into linearizable executions, in a way that is not observable to any thread. As we shall see, causal linearizability is stronger than sequential consistency, and therefore programmers can reason about causally linearizable systems using established intuitions and verification techniques. Furthermore, unlike some competing proposals, causal linearizability places no constraints on the algorithmic techniques used in the implementation of concurrent objects.

Causal linearizability enables concurrent objects to be composed, under certain constraints on the client's behaviour. We specify these constraints by introducing a notion of *operation-race freedom*, where programs that satisfy this property are guaranteed to behave as if their shared objects were linearizable.

In the remainder of the introduction we motivate our work by describing a nonlinearizable data structure designed for a particular weak memory model (in this case, TSO). The structure of the rest of the paper is as follows. Section 2 outlines our contribution, and compares it to related work. Section 3 defines the formal framework and notation, and Sect. 4 defines independence and causal ordering, which are key concepts in our definition of causal linearizability. Section 5 defines causal linearizability itself. Section 6 then defines operation-race freedom and outlines a proof method for proving causal linearizability. Section 7 applies our ideas to the TSO memory model. Section 8 concludes.

1.1   Motivation - Nonlinearizable Objects on TSO

The Total Store Order (TSO) memory model optimizes write operations by first *buffering* a write to a local *write buffer*, and later *flushing* the write to shared memory. The effect of the write is immediately visible to the core that issues it, but is only visible to other cores after the write has been flushed. The x86 instruction set provides primitives for ensuring that the effect of a write is visible to other threads on other cores. The *barrier* operation flushes all writes of the executing core that have not previously been flushed. In addition, memory operations that both read and modify shared memory may be *locked*. A locked operation appears to execute atomically, and the locking mechanism causes the executing core's write buffer to be emptied both before and after the execution of the locked operation. We formalize this memory model in Sect. 7.

Locked operations and barriers are typically costly, relative to simple reads and writes. For this reason, optimized datastructures often avoid such synchronization primitives where possible. Here we describe a simple example of such an algorithm: a *spinlock* algorithm for x86 processors that is adapted from an implementation in the Linux kernel. Figure 1 presents pseudocode for the algorithm, which uses a simple boolean flag (F below) to record whether the lock is currently held by some thread. A thread acquires the lock using the `try_acquire` procedure, which fails if the lock is currently held (an unconditional `acquire` procedure can be implemented by repeatedly invoking `try_acquire` until successful).

```
bool F := false;


void release() {
R1  F := false;
}
```

```
bool try_acquire() {
T1  locked {
T2    held := F;
T3    F := true;
T4  }
T5  return !held;
}
```

Fig. 1. Nonlinearizable spinlock implementation

The `try_acquire` procedure uses a locked operation to atomically determine whether the lock is held and to set the flag to true. (This operation is called an atomic *test-and-set*). Note that this operation has no effect if the flag is already true. Thus, if the lock is not held, then `try_acquire` successfully acquires the lock and returns `true`. Otherwise, the acquisition attempt fails, and `try_acquire` returns `false`. The optimised `release` operation simply sets the flag to `false`, without using any locked or barrier operations.

The spinlock implementation is *not* linearizable. Intuitively, linearizability requires that each operation on the lock appears to take effect at some point between its invocation and response. To see how this fails, consider the execution in Fig. 2. In this example, two threads, t_1 and t_2 attempt to acquire the lock L, using the `try_acquire` operation. The first acquisition attempt (of t_1) succeeds, because the lock is free; t_1 then releases the lock (presumably after accessing some shared state protected by the lock), but the write that changes the lock's state is not yet flushed to shared memory. Now t_2's lock acquisition fails, despite being invoked after the end of t_1's `release` operation. This is because, in the example, the releasing write is not flushed until after the completion of t_2's `try_acquire`. Thus, t_2's `try_acquire` appears to take effect between t_1's acquisition and release operations. Linearizability requires that the `try_acquire` appear to take effect *after* t_1's release.

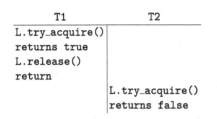

Fig. 2. Nonlinearizable spinlock history.

Despite the fact that it is not linearizable, there are important circumstances in which this spinlock implementation can be correctly used. Indeed, a spinlock essentially identical to this has been used extensively in the Linux kernel. Fundamentally, the goal of this paper is to investigate and formalize conditions under which objects like this spinlock may be used safely on weak memory models.

2 Our Contribution

In this paper, we describe a weakening of linearizability which we call *causal linearizability*. Note that in the execution of Fig. 2, no thread can observe that the invocation of thread t_2's `try_acquire` occurred after the response of t_1's release, and therefore no thread can observe the failure of linearizability. Causal linearizability allows operations to be linearized *out of order*, in cases where no thread can observe this reordering.

However, the lock L is the only object in execution in Fig. 2. In general, clients of the lock may have other means of communicating, apart from operations on L. Therefore, under some circumstances, clients may observe that the execution is not linearizable. Our second contribution is to define a condition called *operation-race freedom* (ORF) on the *clients* of nonlinearizable objects like the TSO spinlock, such that clients satisfying ORF cannot observe a failure of linearizability. ORF is inspired by *data-race freedom* (DRF) approaches, which we discuss below. However, unlike DRF, ORF is defined in terms of high-level invocations and responses, rather than low-level reads and writes.

Finally, we provide a proof method for verifying causal linearizability. We define a correctness condition called *response-synchronized linearizability* (RS-linearizability). In the context of TSO, proving that a data structure satisfies RS-linearizability amounts to proving that the structure is linearizable in all executions where every write executed during an operation are flushed by the time any operation completes. Because of this, we can prove RS-linearizability using essentially standard techniques used for proving linearizability. In Sect. 6, we show that any set of RS-linearizable objects is causally linearizable, when the objects' clients satisfy ORF.

Related Work. One way to address the issues raised by weak memory models is based on the observation that locks and other synchronization primitives are typically used in certain stereotypical ways. For example, a lock is never released unless it has been first acquired; and the shared state that a lock protects is not normally accessed without holding the lock. As shown in [9], these circumstances mean that the spinlock's nonlinearizable behaviour can never be observed by any participating thread.

The analysis given in [9] belongs to a class of approaches that define conditions under which a program running on a weak memory model will behave as if it were running on a sequentially-consistent memory. These conditions are often phrased in terms *data-races*: a data-race is a pair of operations executed by different threads, one of which is a write, such that the two operations can be adjacent in some execution of the (multithreaded) program. Data-race free (DRF) programs are those whose executions never contain data races, and the executions of DRF programs are always sequentially consistent.

Data-race free algorithms that are linearizable on the sequentially-consistent model will appear to be linearizable on the appropriate weak memory model. Thus the problem of verifying a DRF algorithm on weak-memory is reduced to that of verifying it under the standard assumption of sequential consistency. However, DRF-based approaches have the drawback that algorithms that are not DRF cannot be verified. Our approach does not suffer from this limitation: implementations are free to use any algorithmic techniques, regardless of DRF.

Furthermore, the ORF property only constrains the ordering of high-level invocations and responses, rather than low level reads and writes.

[3,7] define correctness conditions for TSO by weakening linearizability. [3]
introduces abstract specifications that manipulate TSO-style write-buffers such
that the abstract effect of an operation can be delayed until after the operation's
response. [7] proposes adding nondeterminism to concurrent objects' specifications to account for possible delay in the effect of an operation becoming visible. Neither work systematically addresses how to reason about the behaviour
of clients that use these weakened abstract objects. In our work, the abstract
specifications underlying linearizability are unchanged, and programs satsifying
the ORF constraint are guaranteed to behave as if their shared objects were
linearizable.

RS-linearizability is a generalisation of *TSO-linearizability*, described in [5].
That work shows that TSO-linearizability can be verified using more-or-less
standard techniques for proving linearizability. However, [5] does not address
how to reason about the behaviour of clients that use TSO-linearizable objects,
as we do with the ORF constraint.

3   Modelling Threads, Histories and Objects

As is standard, we assume a set of invocations I and responses R, which are
used to represent operations on a set X of *objects*. The invocations and responses
of an object define its interactons with the external environment so we define
$Ext = I \cup R$ to be the set of *external actions*. We denote by $obj(a)$ the object
associated with $a \in Ext$. We also assume a set of *memory actions Mem*, which
typically includes reads, writes and other standard actions on shared-memory.
Operational definitions of weak memory models typically involve *hidden actions*
that are used to model the memory system's propagation of information between
threads, so we assume a set $Hidden \subseteq Mem$ (for example, in TSO the hidden
actions are the flushes). Let $Act = Ext \cup Mem$ be the set of *actions*.

In our model, each action is executed either on behalf of a thread (e.g.,
invocations, or read operations), or on behalf of some memory system (these are
the hidden actions). To represent this, we assume a set of threads T, a function
$thr : Act \rightarrow T \cup \{\perp\} = T_\perp$, such that $thr(a) = \perp$ iff $a \in Hidden$.

Executions are modelled as *histories*, which are sequences of actions. We
denote by gh the concatenation of two histories g and h. When h is a history
and A a set of actions, we denote by $h \downharpoonright A$ the sequence of actions $a \in A$
occurring in h. For a history h, the *thread history of* $t \in T$, denoted $h \downharpoonright t$, is
$h \downharpoonright \{a : thr(a) = t\}$. Two histories h and h' are *thread equivalent* if $h \downharpoonright t = h' \downharpoonright t$,
for all threads $t \in T$. (Note that two histories may be thread equivalent while
having different hidden actions.)

For example, the behaviour shown in Fig. 2 is represented by the history:

$$L.try\_acq_{t_1}, locked_{t_1}(TAS, F, false), resp_{t_1}(L, true), L.release_{t_1}, write_{t_1}(F, false),$$

$$resp_{t_1}(L), L.try\_acq_{t_2}, locked_{t_2}(TAS, F, true), resp_{t_2}(L, false), flush(F, false) \quad (1)$$

Let $a = L.try\_acq_{t_1}$. Then a is an invocation of the `try_acquire` operation, $thr(a) = t_1$ and $obj(a) = L$. The action $resp_{t_1}(L, true)$ is a response from object L, of the thread t_1, returning the value $true$. $locked_{t_1}(TAS, F, false)$ is a locked invocation of the test-and-set operation on the location F, again by thread t_1 that returns the value $false$. $flush(F, false)$ is a flush action of the memory subsystem, that sets the value of F to false in the shared store. This history is thread equivalent to the following:

$$L.try\_acq_{t_1}, locked_{t_1}(TAS, F, false), resp_{t_1}(L, true),$$
$$L.try\_acq_{t_2}, locked_{t_2}(TAS, F, true), resp_{t_2}(L, false),$$
$$L.release_{t_1}, write_{t_1}(F, false), flush(F, false), resp_{t_1}(L) \,(2)$$

A history is well-formed if for all $t \in T$, $h \restriction t \restriction Ext$ is an alternating sequence of invocations and responses, beginning with an invocation. Note that well-formedness only constrains invocations and responses. Memory operations may be freely interleaved with the external actions. From now on, we assume that all histories are well-formed. A history is *complete* if every thread history is empty or ends in a response.

An *object system* is a prefix-closed set of well-formed histories. A *sequential object system* is an object system where every invocation is followed immediately by a response, in every history. If O is an object system then $acts(O)$ is the set of actions appearing in any history of O.

We wish to reason about orders on the actions appearing in histories. In general, each action may appear several times in a history. Strictly speaking, to define appropriate orders on the actions, we would need to tag actions with some identifying information, to obtain an *event* which is guaranteed to be unique in the history. However, for the sake of simplicity, we assume that each action only appears at most once in each history. For example, each thread may only execute at most one write for each location-value pair. This restriction can be lifted straightforwardly, at the cost of some notational complexity.[1]

Given a history h, the *real-time order* of h, denoted $\rightarrow_h$ is the strict total order on actions such that $a \rightarrow_h b$ if a occurs before b in h. The *program order*, denoted $\xrightarrow{p}_h$, is the strict partial order on the actions of h such that $a \xrightarrow{p}_h b$ if $thr(a) = thr(b)$ and $a \rightarrow_h b$. For example, in History 1 above, $L.release_{t_1} \xrightarrow{p}_h write_{t_1}(F, false)$ and $write_{t_1}(F, false) \rightarrow_h flush(F, false)$.

4   Independence and Causal Ordering

In this section, we develop a notion of causal ordering. Roughly speaking, an action a is causally prior to an action b in a history h if $a \rightarrow_h b$ and some thread can observe that a and b occurred in that order. Therefore, we can safely reorder events that are not causally ordered. Causal order itself is expressed in

---

[1] The full version of the paper, which can be found at arXiv.org/abs/1604.06734, presents a model of histories in which events are unique.

terms of an independence relation between actions, which we now define. The notion of independence, and the idea of using independence to construct a causal order has a long history. See [6] for a discussion in a related context.

Given an object system S, two actions a and b are S-independent if $thr(a) \neq thr(b)$ and for all histories g and h,

$$g\langle a, b\rangle h \in S \Leftrightarrow g\langle b, a\rangle h \in S \tag{3}$$

(Here, $\langle a, b\rangle$ denotes the sequence of length two containing a and then b.) According to this definition, TSO flushes are independent iff they are to distinct locations. Again in TSO, read and write actions in different threads are always independent, but two actions of the same thread never are. (Inter-thread communication only occurs during flush or locked actions.)

We define the causal order over a history in terms of this independence relation. We say that h is S-causally equivalent to h' if h' is obtained from h by zero or more transpositions of adjacent, S-independent actions. Note that causal equivalence is an equivalence relation. Actions a and b are S-causally ordered in h, denoted $a \hookrightarrow_h^S b$ if for all causally equivalent histories h', $a \to_{h'} b$. This is a transitive and acyclic relation, and therefore $\hookrightarrow_h^S$ is a strict partial order.

For example, because the release operation does not contain any locked actions, Histories 1 and 2 on page 6 are causally equivalent. On the other hand, the actions $locked_{t_2}(TAS, F, true)$ and $flush(F, false)$ are not independent, and therefore $locked_{t_2}(TAS, F, true) \hookrightarrow_h flush(F, false)$.

Note that independence, causal equivalence, and causal order are all defined relative to a specific object system. However, we often elide the object system parameter when it is obvious from context.

One key idea of this work is that a history is "correct" if it can be transformed into a linearizable history in a way that is not observable to any thread. The following lemma is our main tool for effecting this transformation. It says that a history can be reordered to be consistent with any partial order that contains the history's causal ordering. The thrust of our compositionality condition, presented in Sect. 6, is to provide sufficient conditions for the existence of a strict partial order satisfying the hypotheses of this lemma.[2]

Lemma 1. *Let S be an object system, let $h \in S$ be a history, and let $<$ be a strict partial order on the events of h such that $\hookrightarrow_h^S \subseteq <$. Then there exists an h' causally equivalent to h such that for all events a, b in h (equivalently in h') $a < b$ implies $a \to_{h'} b$.* □

We are now in a position to formally define causal linearizability. Essentially, an object system is causally linearizable if all its histories have causally equivalent linearizable histories. The key idea behind linearizablity is that each operation should appear to take effect atomically, at some point between the operation's invocation an response. See [8] or [4] for a formal definition.

---

[2] For reasons of space, this paper does not contain proofs of Lemma 1 or the other results presented in this paper. The full version of the paper contains the proofs, and can be found at arXiv.org/abs/1604.06734.

Definition 1 (Causal Linearizability). *An object system S is causally linearizable to a sequential object system T if for all $h \in S$, h is S-causally equivalent to some history h' such that $h' \downarrow acts(T) \cap Ext$ is linearizable to T.*

Note that causal linearizability is defined in terms of histories that contain both external and internal actions. Typically linearizability and related correctness conditions are defined purely in terms of external actions. Here, we preserve the internal actions of the object, because those internal actions carry the causal order.

5   Observational Refinement and Causal Linearizability

In this section, we introduce a notion of *client* and a notion of composition of a client with an object system (Definition 5). We then define a notion of *observational refinement* for object systems. One object system S observationally refines another object system T for a client C if the external behaviour of C composed with S is included in the external behaviour of C composed with T. These notions have a twofold purpose. First, they provide a framework in which to show that causal linearizability is a reasonable correctness condition: the composition of a client with a causally linearizable object system has only the behaviours of the client composed with a corresponding linearizable object system (Theorem 1). Second, these notions allow us to specify a constraint on the behaviour of a client, such that the client can safely use a composition of nonlinearizable objects.

A *client* is a prefix-closed set of histories, where each history contains only one thread, and all actions are thread actions (so that the client contains no hidden actions). Each client history represents a possible interaction of a client thread with an object system. While each client history contains only one thread, the client itself may contain histories of several threads. For example, consider the histories that might be generated by a thread t_1 repeatedly executing spinlock's `try_acquire` operation (Fig. 1) until the lock is successfully acquired. The set of histories generated in this way for every thread is a client. One such history is $L.try\_acq_{t_1}$, $locked_{t_1}(TAS, F, false)$, $resp_{t_1}(L, true)$, where t_1 successfully acquires the lock on the first attempt. A history where the thread acquires the lock after two attempts is

$$L.try\_acq_{t_1}, locked_{t_1}(TAS, F, true), resp_{t_1}(L, false),$$
$$L.try\_acq_{t_1}, locked_{t_1}(TAS, F, false), resp_{t_1}(L, true) \quad (4)$$

Thus, the client histories contain the memory operations determined by the implementations of the shared objects.

The composition of an object system O and client program C, denoted $C[O]$ is the object system defined as follows:

$$C[O] = \{h : h \downarrow acts(O) \in O \wedge \forall t \in T.\ h \downarrow t \in C\} \quad (5)$$

So for all $h \in C[O]$, h is an interleaving of actions of the threads in C, and every thread history of h is allowed by both the object system and the client program.

We need a notion of observational refinement relative to a given client.

Definition 2 (Observational Refinement). *An object system S observationaly refines an object system T for a client C if for every $h \in C[S]$, there exists some $h' \in C[T]$ where $h \restriction Ext$ and $h' \restriction Ext$ are thread equivalent.*

The following theorem shows that causal linearizability is sound with respect to observational refinement. Because of this, a causally linearizable object can be used instead of a linearizable object, while preserving correctness of the client's behaviour.

Theorem 1 (Causal Linearizability Implies Observational Refinement). *Let T be a sequential object system, and let T' be its set of linearizable histories. Let S be an object system such that $acts(T) \cap Ext = acts(S) \cap Ext$. If $C[S]$ is causally linearizable to T, then S observationally refines T' for C.*

6   Flush-Based Memory and Operation-Race Freedom

Causal linearizability is a general correctness condition, potentially applicable in a range of contexts. Our goal is to apply it to objects running on weak memory models. To this end, we formally define a notion of *flush-based memory*. Flush-based memory is a generalisation of TSO and some other memory models, including *partial store order* [1]. This section develops a proof technique for causal linearizability of an object system running on flush-based memory, and hence for observational refinement.

Our proof technique can be encapsulated in the following formula: Operation-race freedom + Response-synchronized linearizabilty $\Rightarrow$ *Causal linearizability*. Response-synchronized linearizability, a weakening of linearizability, is a correctness property specialised for flush-based memory, and is adapted from *TSO linearizability* studied in [5]. That work presents techniques for verifying TSO linearizability and proofs that spinlock and seqlock are TSO linearizable. Theorem 2 below shows that a multi-object system composed of response-synchronized linearizable objects is causally linearizable, under a constraint on the multi-object system's clients. This constraint is called *operation-race freedom*, given in Definition 6.

A *flush-based memory* is an object system whose histories do not contain invocations or responses (so its only actions are memory actions), together with a *thread-action* function $thr\_act_h : Hidden \rightarrow Act$, for each history h in the memory model. Hidden actions model the propagation of writes and other operations that modify shared memory. We use the thr_act function to record the operation that each hidden action propagates. Therefore, for each $f \in Hidden$, we require that $thr\_act_h(f) \notin Hidden$. ($f$ is short for *flush*.) For example, in TSO, the hidden actions are the flushes, and thr_act_h associates with each flush the write that created the buffer entry which is being flushed.

Flush based memories must satisfy a technical constraint. We require that the effect of a flush be invisible to the thread on whose behalf the flush is being performed. This captures the idea that flushes are responsible for propagating the effect of operations from one thread to another, rather than affecting the behaviour of the invoking thread.

Definition 3 (Local Flush Invisible). *A memory model M is* local flush invisible *if for all histories $h \in M$, actions a, b, f in h such that $a = thr\_act(f)$ and $a \xrightarrow{p}_h b \rightarrow_h f$, b and f are M-independent.*

For the rest of this section, fix a memory model M with thread action function thr_act. Furthermore, fix an object system S, such that for all $h \in S$, $h \mid Mem \in M$. Thus, S is an object system that may contain both external and internal actions.

Definition 4 (Response Synchronization). *Given a history h, the response-synchronization relation of h is*

$$\xrightarrow{RS}_h = \hookrightarrow^S_h \cup \{(f, resp_h(thr\_act_h(f))) : f \in Hidden\} \tag{6}$$

A *response-synchronized history* is one where each flush appears before its associated response. That is, $h \in S$ is response-synchronized if $\xrightarrow{RS}_h \subseteq \rightarrow_h$. An object system is *response-synchronized linearizable* (or RS-linearizable) if all its response synchronized histories are linearizable.

It is relatively easy to verify RS-linearizability. The idea is to construct a model of the system such that response actions are not enabled until the operation's writes have been flushed, and then to prove that the implementation is linearizable on this stronger model. See [5] for a careful development of the technique.

Operation-race freedom requires that clients provide sufficent synchronization to prevent any thread from observing that a flush has taken place after its corresponding response action. Definition 5 formalizes which actions count as synchronizing actions, for the purposes of operation-race freedom. Operation-race freedom has one key property not shared by standard notions of data-race freedom: invocations and responses can count as synchronizing actions. This has two advantages. First, we can reason about the absence of races based on the presence of synchronizing invocations and responses, rather than being based on low-level memory operations that have synchronization properties. Second, implementations of concurrent objects are free to employ racey techniques within each operation.

Definition 5 (Synchronization Point). *An action b is a synchronization point in $h \in S$, if for all actions a such that $a \xrightarrow{p}_h b$ or $a = b$, all actions c such that $thr(c) \neq thr(a)$ and $b \hookrightarrow^S_h c$, and all hidden actions f such that $thr\_act(f) = a$, not $c \hookrightarrow^S_h f$.*

For example, in TSO, barrier operations are synchronization points. This is because such operations ensure that the issuing thread's write buffer is empty before the barrier is executed. Therefore, any write before the barrier in program order is flushed before the barrier executes, and so the write's flush cannot be after the barrier in causal order. For the same reason, locked operations are also synchronization points in TSO.

Under this definition, invocations and responses may also be synchronization points. An invocation is a synchronization point if its first memory action is a synchronization point, and a response is a synchronization point if its last memory action is a synchronization point. This is because any external action is independent of any hidden action.

Definition 6 (Operation Race). *An* operation race *(or o-race) in a history* h *is a triple* r_0, i, r_1, *where* r_0, r_1 *are responses,* i *is an invocation such that* $r_0 \xrightarrow{p}_h i$, $i \hookrightarrow^S_h r_1$, $thr(r_0) \neq thr(r_1)$, $obj(r_0) = obj(r_1)$, *there is some hidden action* f *such that* $r_0 = resp_h(thr\_act_h(f))$, *and there is no synchronization point between* r_0 *and* i *(inclusive) in program order.*

We say that an object system is *o-race free* (ORF) if no history has an o-race.

Below we provide an example of an execution containing an o-race. This example and the next use a datastructure called a *seqlock*, another concurrent object optimised for use on TSO, and adapted from an implementation in the Linux kernel [9]. Seqlock is an object providing *read* and *write* operations with the usual semantics, except that several values can be read or written in one operation. Seqlock has the restriction that there may only be one active write operation at a time, but there may be any number of concurrent read operations and reads may execute concurrently with a write. Seqlock does not use any locking mechanism internally, instead relying on a counter to ensure that read operations observe a consistent set of values. Seqlock does not use any locked or barrier operations, and the read operation never writes to any location in memory. Other details of the algorithm do not matter for our purposes. See [3] for a complete description.

Consider the behaviour presented in Fig. 3, adapted from [9]. Here, three threads interact using an instance L of the spinlock object, and an instance S of seqlock. In this example execution, the flush correponding to the write of t_2's release operation is delayed until the end of the execution, but the flushes associated with the writes of t_1's seqlock write operation occur immediately (note that because the seqlock does not use any barrier or locked operations, this flush could have occurred at any point after the write to memory). This history is not sequentially consistent. If it were sequentially consistent, thread t_2's release would need to take effect before thread t_1's write, which in turn would take effect before thread t_3's read. However, this is inconsistent with the fact that t_3's try-acquire appears to take effect before thread t_2's release. Because it is not sequentially consistent, this execution would be impossible if the spinlock and seqlock were both linearizable objects. Therefore, the composition of spinlock and seqlock do not observationally refine a composition of linearizable objects,

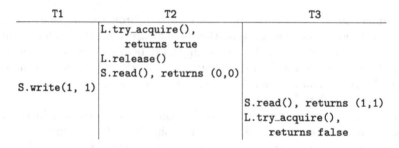

T1	T2	T3
	L.try_acquire(),	
	returns true	
	L.release()	
	S.read(), returns (0,0)	
S.write(1, 1)		
		S.read(), returns (1,1)
		L.try_acquire(),
		returns false

Fig. 3. A racey execution of a spinlock L and a seqlock S. Operation-race freedom prohibits the race between t_2's release and read, and t_3's try-acquire.

for any client capable of producing this behaviour. There is a race between the response of t_2's release operation, the invocation of t_2's subsequent read, and the release of t_3's try-acquire.

Theorem 2 below shows that an ORF multi-object system composed of response-synchronized linearizable objects is causally linearizable, under one technical assumption. We require that the objects themselves must not *interfere*. That is, each action of each object must be independent of all potentially adjacent actions of other objects. This constraint is implicit in the standard composition result for linearizability, and is satisfied by any multi-object system where each object uses regions of shared-memory disjoint from all the other objects. If a multi-object system does not satisify this property, then one object can affect the behaviour of another object by modifying its representation. Therefore, a composition of individually linearizable objects may not be linearizable itself.

Definition 7 (Noninterfering Object System). *An object system S is noninterfering if for all histories $h \in S$, and actions a, b adjacent in h, if $thr(a) \neq thr(b)$ and $obj(a) \neq obj(b)$ then a and b are independent.*

The following lemma shows that the response-synchronization relation is acyclic for an operation-race free object system. This allows us to prove Theorem 2 by applying Lemma 1.

Lemma 2 (Acyclicity of the Response-synchronization Relation). *If M is a memory model and C[M] is a noninterfering, ORF object system, then for all $h \in C[M]$, the response-synchronisation relation is acyclic.*

We can now state our compositionality result. This result says that any client composed with a set of RS-linearizable objects observationally refines the client when composed with linearizable objects, so long as the client is ORF when composed with the RS-linearizable objects. In this case, RS-linearizable objects can be used instead of linearizable objects, while preserving correctness of the client.

Theorem 2 (Composition). *Let X be a set of objects and for each $x \in X$, let T_x be a sequential object system. If M is a flush-based memory and C[M] is* an *ORF noninterfering multi-object system such that for each $x \in X$, $C[M] \downharpoonright x$ is response-synchronized linearizable to T_x, then $C[M]$ is causally linearizable to $T = h : \forall\, x \in X.\ h \downharpoonright acts(T_x) \in T_x$, and thus $C[M]$ observationally refines $C[T]$.*

7   Operation-Race Freedom on TSO

We apply our technique to the well-known *total store order* (TSO) memory model, a version of which is implemented by the ubiqitous x86 processor family. Indeed, we closely follow the formalization of TSO for x86 given in [10]. We then argue that TSO has the properties required of a flush-based memory, including the local flush invisibility property. Finally, we demonstrate how to determine whether a client is operation-race free.

We model TSO as a labelled transition system (LTS) $T = \langle S_T, A_T, I_T, R_T \rangle$. Each state $s \in S_T$ has the form $\langle M, B \rangle$ where

- M is the contents of shared memory, $M : Loc \to \mathbb{Z}$, where Loc is the set of *locations.*
- B records for each thread the contents of its buffer, which is a sequence of location/value pairs. Thus, $B : T \to (Loc \times \mathbb{Z})^*$.

The initial state predicate I_T says only that every buffer is empty (formally, $\forall\, t \in T.\ B(s) = \langle\rangle$). The transition relation R_T is given in Fig. 4. The labels (or *actions*) in the set A_T are as follows. For each thread $t \in T$, location $x \in Loc$ and value $v, r \in \mathbb{Z}$, there is a write action $write_t(x, v)$, a read action $read_t(x, r)$, a flush action $flush(t, x, v)$ and a barrier action $barrier_t$. Further, there is a locked action $lock_t(f, x, v, r)$, for each $f : \mathbb{Z} \times \mathbb{Z} \to \mathbb{Z}$ taken from an appropriate list of *read-modify-write* (RMW) operations. Locked actions model the atomic application of an RMW operation to shared memory. For example, $lock_t(+, x, 1, r)$ models the atomic increment of the value at x, and r is the value in location x immediately before the increment. The x86 instruction set supports a range of other RMW operations, such as *add* and *test-and-set*.

The set of traces of this TSO LTS is prefix-closed and thus forms an object system, which we denote by *TSO*. The system actions of *TSO* are just the flush actions, so the *TSO thr* function returns $\bot$ for flush actions, and the thread index of all other actions. The thr_act_h function associates with each flush f the write that is being flushed. *TSO* has the flush invisibility property, of Definition 3, because a flush is independent of any action of the issuing thread, except for the write that is being flushed (as proved in the full version of the paper).

We now explain by example how to check that a client is ORF. Our example is the double-checked locking implementation presented in Fig. 5. Double-checked locking is a pattern for lazily initializing a shared object at most once in any execution. The `ensure_init` procedure implements this pattern. Here, the shared object is represented using a seqlock X. The `ensure_init` procedure first reads the values in X, and completes immediately if X has already been initialised. Otherwise, `ensure_init` acquires a spinlock L and then checks again whether

$$\frac{(last\_write(B(t), x) = \bot \wedge M(x) = r) \vee last\_write(B(t), x) = r}{(M, B) \xrightarrow{read_t(x,r)} (M, B)} \quad Read$$

$$\frac{b' = B(t)\langle(l, v)\rangle}{(M, B) \xrightarrow{write_t(x,v)} (M, B \oplus \{t \mapsto b'\})} \quad Write$$

$$\frac{B(t) = \langle(l, v)\rangle b'}{(M, B) \xrightarrow{flush(t,x,v)} (M \oplus \{l \mapsto v\}, B \oplus \{t \mapsto b'\})} \quad Flush$$

$$\frac{B(t) = \langle\rangle}{(M, B) \xrightarrow{barrier_t} (M, B)} \quad Barrier$$

$$\frac{B(t) = \langle\rangle \quad r = M(x)}{(M, B) \xrightarrow{lock_t(f,x,v,r)} (M \oplus \{x \mapsto f(c, v)\}, B)} \quad Locked\text{-}RMW$$

Fig. 4. Transition relation of the TSO memory model. If b is a write buffer, $latest\_write(b, x)$ returns the value of the last write to x in b, if it exists, or $\bot$ otherwise.

```
val ensure_init() {
1.    (v0, v1) = X.read();
2.    if (v0 == null) {
3.       L.acquire();
4.       (v0, v1) = X.read();
5.       if (v0 == null) {
6.          (v0, v1) = initial_value;
7.          X.write(v0, v1);
8.          Barrier();
9.       }
10.      L.release();
11.   }
12. return (v0, v1);
}
```

Fig. 5. Pseudocode for a client executing a double checked locking protocol.

X has already been initialised (by some concurrent thread), again completing if the initialisation has already occurred. Otherwise, ensure_init initialises the object, executes a barrier, releases the lock and returns.

To show that this code is ORF, we must employ knowledge about which invocations and responses of our objects are synchronization points, and which operations do not execute write actions. As we described in the discussion after Definition 5, in TSO all barriers and locked operations are synchronization points.

Furthermore, because the try-acquire's only memory operation is a locked operation, both the invocation and response of try-acquire are synchronization points. Finally, the read operation of seqlock can never execute a write action.

To show that `ensure_init` has no o-races, we must consider the relationship between each operation, and the next operation in program order. For each case, we must show that no o-race is possible.

- The read on Line 1 never executes a write, so its response cannot form an o-race with the subsequent invocation.
- The response of the acquire on Line 3 is a synchronization point, so it cannot form an o-race with the subsequent read.
- As with the read on Line 1, the read on Line 4 never executes a write operation, and so its response cannot form an o-race.
- The write on Line 7 is followed by the barrier on Line 8, so this cannot form an o-race.

Note that during this argument, we only need to consider whether or not the invocation or response of each operation is a synchronization point, or whether the operation never executes write actions. We do not require any further information about the operation's implementation. Again, this means that operations may themselves be racey.

8   Concluding Remarks

Although the details of the paper are fairly technical the essence of the contribution is simple: how can we use non-linearizable algorithms safely. The context that we work in here is that of weak memory models, where TSO provides an important example. This work should also be applicable to other flush-based memory models. Such an extension is work for the future.

To enable our multi-object systems to be composed safely we introduced a notion of operation-race freedom. However, what about non-operation-race free programs? Our formulation provides no composability guaranteess for a family of objects where even *one* of those objects is not response-synchronized. As indicated in Sect. 6, this is a less severe restriction than other proposals based on some notion of data race freedom (because of its modularity). However, it seems reasonable to expect that some compositionality result would hold for the subset of response-synchronized objects. Again this is left as future work.

References

1. Adve, S.V., Gharachorloo, K.: Shared memory consistency models: a tutorial. Computer **29**(12), 66–76 (1996)
2. Alglave, J., Fox, A., Ishtiaq, S., Myreen, M.O., Sarkar, S., Sewell, P., Nardelli, F.Z.: The semantics of power and ARM multiprocessor machine code. In: Petersen, L., Chakravarty, M.M.T. (eds.) DAMP 2009, pp. 13–24. ACM (2008)

3. Burckhardt, S., Gotsman, A., Musuvathi, M., Yang, H.: Concurrent library correctness on the TSO memory model. In: Seidl, H. (ed.) Programming Languages and Systems. LNCS, vol. 7211, pp. 87–107. Springer, Heidelberg (2012)
4. Derrick, J., Schellhorn, G., Wehrheim, H.: Mechanically verified proof obligations for linearizability. ACM Trans. Program. Lang. Syst. **33**(1), 4:1–4:43 (2011)
5. Derrick, J., Smith, G., Dongol, B.: Verifying linearizability on TSO architectures. In: Albert, E., Sekerinski, E. (eds.) IFM 2014. LNCS, vol. 8739, pp. 341–356. Springer, Heidelberg (2014)
6. Filipović, I., O'Hearn, P., Rinetzky, N., Yang, H.: Abstraction for concurrent objects. Theor. Comput. Sci. **411**(51–52), 4379–4398 (2010)
7. Gotsman, A., Musuvathi, M., Yang, H.: Show no weakness: sequentially consistent specifications of TSO libraries. In: Aguilera, M.K. (ed.) DISC 2012. LNCS, vol. 7611, pp. 31–45. Springer, Heidelberg (2012)
8. Herlihy, M.P., Wing, J.M.: Linearizability: A correctness condition for concurrent objects. ACM Trans. Program. Lang. Syst. **12**(3), 463–492 (1990)
9. Owens, S.: Reasoning about the implementation of concurrency abstractions on x86-TSO. In: D'Hondt, T. (ed.) ECOOP 2010. LNCS, vol. 6183, pp. 478–503. Springer, Heidelberg (2010)
10. Owens, S., Sarkar, S., Sewell, P.: A better x86 memory model: x86-TSO. In: Berghofer, S., Nipkow, T., Urban, C., Wenzel, M. (eds.) TPHOLs 2009. LNCS, vol. 5674, pp. 391–407. Springer, Heidelberg (2009)

Refinement-Based Verification
of Communicating Unstructured Code

Nils Jähnig[1]([⊠]), Thomas Göthel[2], and Sabine Glesner[1]

[1] Technische Universität Berlin, Berlin, Germany
nils.jaehnig@tu-berlin.de
[2] Universität Potsdam, Potsdam, Germany

Abstract. Formal model refinement aims at preserving safety and live-ness properties of models. However, there is usually a verification gap between model and executed code, especially if concurrent processes are involved. The reason for this is that a manual implementation and further code optimizations can introduce implementation errors. In this paper, we present a framework that allows for formally proving a failures refinement between a CSP specification and its low-level implementation. The implementation is given in a generic unstructured language with `gotos` and an abstract communication instruction. We provide a failures-based denotational semantics of it with an appropriate Hoare calculus. Since failures-based refinement is compositional w.r.t. parallel composition of concurrent components and preserves safety and liveness properties, this contributes to reducing the verification gap between high-level specifications and their low-level implementations.

Keywords: gotos · Unstructured code · Formal semantics · Hoare calculus · CSP · Failures refinement

1 Introduction

Verification is usually performed on abstract models, as usually proofs are more manageable than corresponding proofs on an implementation model. However, when the model is transformed to executable (low-level) code, bugs can be introduced. This is especially the case for manual transformations, which are often necessary as an abstract model is strictly more abstract than the implementation model, and as such is missing implementation details. Furthermore, if done automatically, optimizations and their implementations are usually not verified as this is hard to do at a general level.

Still, the verified properties of the abstract model need to be carried over to the implementation. To preserve *safety and liveness* properties when refining the model, the notion of *stable failures refinement* of *Communicating Sequential Processes* (CSP) is suitable. Additionally, CSP is specifically designed for verification of *communicating* and *non-terminating systems*. It allows a refinement from abstract models to concrete models, but only within CSP, not to relate CSP with other executable code.

© Springer International Publishing Switzerland 2016
R. De Nicola and E. Kühn (Eds.): SEFM 2016, LNCS 9763, pp. 61–75, 2016.
DOI: 10.1007/978-3-319-41591-8_5

To overcome the problem described above, we present a framework that allows for formally proving stable failures refinement between CSP specifications and *Communicating Unstructured Code* (CUC) implementations, which preserves *safety and liveness* properties. CUC is a generic low-level language with gotos and an abstract communication instruction. Our contribution includes a stable failure semantics for CUC and a corresponding Hoare calculus. The stable failures refinement implies that all *liveness and safety* properties of the specification also hold for the implementation.

The rest of this paper is structured as follows. We provide necessary background information about CSP in the next section. In Sect. 3, we present our framework for relating CSP specifications with CUC implementations. In Sect. 4, we define the stable failures semantics for CUC and in Sect. 5 the corresponding Hoare calculus. We illustrate the applicability of our framework in Sect. 6. In Sect. 7, we discuss related work. We give a conclusion and pointers to future work in Sect. 8.

2   Communicating Sequential Processes (Background)

Communicating Sequential Processes (CSP) is a process algebra, originally introduced in [Hoa78]. It is designed specifically to model concurrent processes that communicate via events. Communication is synchronous and can thus be used to synchronize processes or exchange data.

Processes can be constructed from the basic processes STOP and SKIP and using operators such as event prefixing, external and internal choice, interrupts, and sequential and parallel composition. In CSP, the *channels* are introduced as syntactic sugar on events. The event $c.v$ is said to communicate the value v over channel c. To describe an input in CSP, $c?x : T$ is used, which denotes an external choice over all events of the form $c.x$ with $x \in T$. An output is denoted as $c!v$ and means simply $c.v$. Note, that there is no actual native concept of sending and receiving in CSP, only synchronization. Therefore CUC needs only a single communication instruction.

There are two important semantic models for CSP with raising complexity and expressiveness: *(1)* The trace semantics $\mathcal{T}$, which describes the communication histories of processes and preserves *safety* properties. *(2)* The stable failures semantics $\mathcal{SF}$, which additionally captures the events a process can refuse after a trace, and thereby preserves safety and *liveness* properties. In this paper, we focus on the stable failures semantics.

A *failure* is a pair of a trace and a refusal set (tr, X). A process is *stable*, if no internal progress can be made. Thus the process is either waiting to communicate or has stopped (i.e., behaves like $STOP$). We call the former *communication* failures and the latter *terminal* failures. A *stable* failure (tr, X) is a failure where, after engaging in the events in tr, the process is stable and refuses to engage in events from X. When sequentially combining processes P and Q, terminal stable failures of P can become unstable as the combined process might not longer stop after those traces.

The semantic models of CSP allow for modeling various layers of abstraction as described in [Sch99]: Specification, design and implementation, where specification is most abstract, and implementation is closer to an actual implementation. CSP processes can be put into relation across all abstraction levels via *refinements*. Informally, stable failures refinement ($P \sqsubseteq_{\mathcal{SF}} Q$) describes the reduction of (internal) non-determinism.

An important property of all the semantical models of CSP is their compositionality. From the refinements $P \sqsubseteq P'$ and $Q \sqsubseteq Q'$ it follows that in any arbitrary composition $\otimes$ also $P \otimes Q \sqsubseteq P' \otimes Q'$ holds, i.e., refinement can be shown component-wise. This enables modular verification in CSP.

The automatic refinement checker FDR3 [GABR14] supports refinement checks for both mentioned semantics.

3 Framework for Formally Relating CSP Specifications and CUC Implementations

In this section, we give an overview of our framework for establishing the relation between a CSP specification and a low-level implementation. We assume that a CSP specification *Spec* is given, as well as an implementation *Impl* thereof in CUC. To preserve liveness and safety properties from *Spec* to *Impl*, we aim at showing that $Spec \sqsubseteq_{\mathcal{SF}} Impl$ holds in the stable failures model. Our proposed workflow is depicted in Fig. 1a and consists of three steps:

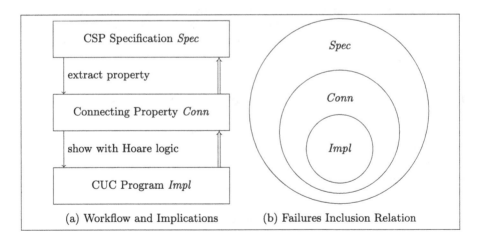

(a) Workflow and Implications   (b) Failures Inclusion Relation

Fig. 1. Overview of the workflow

(1) Manually constructing a *connecting property Conn* from *Spec*,
(2) showing that *Conn* is sufficient for *Spec*, and
(3) showing that *Conn* holds for *Impl*.

The property *Conn* that is constructed from *Spec* in step *(1)* is a predicate on CSP failures and needs to be *stronger* than *Spec*. Thus, a connecting property *Conn* has to be sufficiently strong in the sense that it contains the semantics of a concrete CUC program *Impl* while being contained in the semantics of the original CSP specification *Spec*. The inclusion relation is visualized in Fig. 1b. It also shows that the weaker *Conn* is, the more implementations can be shown to be a refinement. The ideal property *Conn* is describing exactly the possible failures of *Spec*. This is similar to finding an invariant, and as such, there is no automatic way of finding it in general. For our framework, we just require a proof showing that the failures captured by *Conn* are failures of *Spec*.

It is hard to establish a refinement between *Spec* and *Impl* directly, as they are structurally very different: CSP is structured and unstructured languages (such as CUC) are not. In structured languages the control flow is visible in the structure. This is not the case for languages with unrestricted jumps.

In step *(3)*, it needs to be shown that the property *Conn* holds for the CUC program *Impl* with the Hoare logic presented in Sect. 5. In such a proof it has to be shown that starting with a precondition *Pre*, describing the initial states, the program fulfills the postcondition *Post*, which doubles as an invariant for traces due to the way the semantics is defined (this will be explained in Sects. 4.2 and 5). In Sect. 6, we will conduct such a proof for an example consisting of a parallel combination of two simple buffers. This is formally captured by $(tr, s, X) \in [\![Impl]\!] \implies Conn(tr, X)$, i.e., ignoring the state, the failures of *Impl* fulfill *Conn*. Here, (tr, s, X) is a tuple of trace, state, and refusal set, and $[\![Impl]\!]$ denotes the stable failures semantics of *Impl*.

After completing all three steps, we get by transitivity that $(tr, s, X) \in [\![Impl]\!] \implies (tr, X) \in \mathcal{SF}(Spec)$ holds, which is equivalent to our goal $Spec \sqsubseteq_{\mathcal{SF}} Impl$. In the next section we introduce CUC and its stable failure semantics, which we need for step *(3)*.

4   Communicating Unstructured Code and Its Semantics

We published the language CUC and its operational semantics in [JGG15]. In this section, we give a brief overview of CUC and then proceed to one of the contributions of this paper, the *stable failures semantics*. We discuss its properties and finally define the parallel composition.

4.1   Communicating Unstructured Code

We start with a rationale and continue with some type definitions and a description of the instructions.

We aim at being as close to low-level code as possible to reduce the gap between executed code and verified code. CUC focuses on abstract communication and not its detailed implementation. The detailed implementation of the communication can be verified separately, which is not the focus of this paper. Therefore, we decided to study a generic, unstructured language with a higher level construct for communication. CUC is generic and simple, which allows for manageable semantics design and proofs without compromising expressiveness.

A *state* s consists of a *program counter* s_{pc} and a *register store* $s_{rs} \in RS$. CUC uses events to model communication. As in CSP, let Σ denote the set of all *events ev*. In the stable failures semantics, we consider *traces tr* that are sequences of events, and *refusal sets* $X \subseteq \Sigma$.

Being a low-level language, instructions are labeled. We choose set of labels to be $\mathbb{N}$. A simple form of a program is a set of labeled instructions. To facilitate compositional reasoning about programs, we use a tree structure [SU05, JGG15] in the denotational semantics instead. In either case it is important, that labels are *unique*. The program counter points to the label of the current instruction.

$$instruction := \texttt{do } f \mid \texttt{cbr } b\ m\ n \mid \texttt{comm } ef\ f$$
$$code := (label :: instruction) \mid code \oplus code$$

Fig. 2. Syntax of CUC programs

The tree structure of CUC and its instructions are depicted in Fig. 2. The three basic instructions are explained below. We consider as (part of) a program a tree of labeled instructions. $\oplus$ connects two program parts. All potential jumps between them are considered. When using a Hoare calculus a suitable tree structure can be used to reason compositionally. For more details, we refer to [SU05].

do f – The command **do** is a generalized assignment. f is a function $f \colon RS \to \mathcal{P}(RS)$ and is applied to the current state. The register store of the resulting state is one element of the set returned by **f**. The instruction can thus be thought of as a nondeterministic multiple assignment, i.e., multiple variables can be manipulated in one step. The program counter is increased by one.

cbr $b\ m\ n$ – The instruction **cbr** is a usual conditional branch. If the function $b \colon RS \to \{\text{TRUE}, \text{FALSE}\}$ evaluates to TRUE then the program counter is set to m else to n.

comm $ef\ f$ – The command **comm** is the communication primitive. It communicates an event from the result of $ef \colon RS \to \mathcal{P}(\Sigma)$ and then changes the state according to $f \colon RS \times \Sigma \to RS$. Observe that here f is deterministic to ease reasoning. The **comm** instruction needs to modify the register store to record input data. We reserve nondeterminism of the successor state to the instruction **do** f. The program counter is increased by one.

4.2 Stable Failures Semantics

In [JGG15] we presented a *trace* semantics for CUC. We enhance this semantics to carry refusal information, i.e., the information on which communications are not possible after performing a particular trace. As a result, we get a stable failures semantics for CUC that is designed to capture stable failures similarly to CSP.

In CSP, there are two kinds of stable processes (i.e., where no internal transitions are possible): Processes ready to communicate and *STOP*. Let us call failures resulting from the former *communication* failures and from the latter *terminal* failures. When a process is combined with another, a terminal failure might no longer be terminal and thus become unstable. The unstable failures are removed in the sequential composition (see Sect. 2).

To be able to differentiate between terminal failures and communication failures in CUC, we introduce two kinds of states: *normal states* and *communication states*. In the former, the next instruction can be executed. In the latter, the execution is in the middle of a comm instruction and ready to communicate. Formally, we define a sum type over the state defined in Sect. 4.1:

$$NCstate := normal\ state \mid communication\ state$$

We introduce a predicate $N(\cdot)$ to test if a state is *normal*, and a function $\cdot^C$ which converts a normal state to a communication state. We define a *failure* in CUC to be a triple (tr, s, X), where tr is a trace, s a normal-/communication-state, and X a refusal set. Let $\mathcal{SF}$ be the type of all failures. It will be clear from the context, whether we talk about CSP or CUC failures. We can now express terminal failures in CUC: A failure with normal state whose program counter is not among the labels of the considered program part is a terminal failure. As we remove (former) terminal failures with specific program counters frequently, we introduce an operator, which removes all failures with a normal state and a program counter from a given set.

$$S\backslash_{pcs} := S\backslash\big\{(tr, s, X) \mid s_{pc} \in pcs \wedge N(s)\big\}$$

Lastly, let $labels(code)$ be the set of all labels in $code$ and let $pc \in_\ell code$ denote whether pc points to a label within $code$, i.e., $pc \in labels(code)$.

Our failures semantics is given in Fig. 3. We first explain the general structure of the semantics and then the rules individually. The failures semantics is a denotational semantics, which assigns every code tree a function (also called denotation) $[\![code]\!]\colon \mathcal{P}(\mathcal{SF}) \to \mathcal{P}(\mathcal{SF})$. Allowing sets of failures as input eases the sequential composition. We also allow bogus traces as input, thus the semantics is only meaningful if used with sensible initial failures, which usually means triples of: an empty trace, a normal state, and the maximal refusal set or a subset. All failures from the initial input set that are still stable after the execution of the code are carried over to the semantics of the code. This has two reasons. *(1)* To be compatible with CSP, the semantics needs to be prefix closed w.r.t. traces. *(2)* States that do not point into the code are not processed and remain as they are.

We illustrate this with the first rule D-DO: Consider the initial input set $\{(\langle\rangle, t, X), (\langle\rangle, s, Y)\}$, where $\langle\rangle$ is the empty trace, X, Y are arbitrary refusal sets, $t_{pc} = 5$, $s_{pc} = 1$, both normal, and the instruction (1:: do $\lambda\sigma.\ \{\sigma\}$), which does nothing but increment the program counter. As the pc of t is not pointing

---

D-DO
$$[\![\ell :: \mathbf{do} \ f]\!](S) := S\setminus_\ell \cup \Big\{ (tr, t, X) \ \Big| \ (tr, s, \_) \in S \wedge s_{pc} = \ell \wedge N(s) \ \wedge X \subseteq \Sigma \ \wedge$$
$$t_{pc} = \ell + 1 \wedge t_{rs} \in f(s_{rs}) \Big\}$$

D-CBR
$$[\![\ell :: \mathbf{cbr} \ b \ m \ n]\!](S) := S\setminus_\ell \cup \Big\{ (tr, t, X) \ \Big| \ (tr, s, \_) \in S \wedge s_{pc} = \ell \wedge N(s) \ \wedge X \subseteq \Sigma \ \wedge$$
$$\Big(b(s_{rs}) \wedge t_{pc} = m \ \vee \neg b(s_{rs}) \wedge t_{pc} = n \Big) \Big\}$$

D-COMM
$$[\![\ell :: \mathbf{comm} \ ef \ f]\!](S) := S\setminus_\ell \cup \Big\{ \big(tr, s^C, X\big) \ \Big| \ (tr, s, \_) \in S \wedge s_{pc} = \ell \wedge N(s) \ \wedge$$
$$X \subseteq \Sigma \setminus ef(s_{rs}) \Big\}$$
$$\cup \Big\{ (tr^\frown ev, t, X) \ \Big| \ (tr, s, \_) \in S \wedge s_{pc} = \ell \wedge N(s) \ \wedge$$
$$X \subseteq \Sigma \ \wedge$$
$$ev \in ef(s_{rs}) \wedge t = f(s_{rs}, ev) \Big\}$$

D-SEQ
$$[\![code_1 \oplus code_2]\!](S) := \Big(\big(\mu d. \ extend(code_1, code_2) \ (d)\big)(S) \Big)\setminus_{labels(code_1 \oplus code_2)}$$

D-EXT
$$extend(code_1, code_2) \ (d) := \lambda S. \ S \cup d\big([\![code_1]\!](S)\big) \cup d\big([\![code_2]\!](S)\big)$$

Fig. 3. Stable failures semantics for CUC

to this instruction, the failure is still terminal. There is no successor failure of $(\langle\rangle, t, X)$. Within the state s, the program counter s_{pc} points to the instruction, so there is "a" successor failure $\{(\langle\rangle, s', Z) \mid s' = s[pc \leftarrow 2] \wedge Z \subseteq \Sigma\}$. The initial failure $(\langle\rangle, s, X)$ is not terminal anymore, thus no longer stable and needs to be removed. Thus the resulting failures are

$$[\![1::\mathbf{do} \ \lambda\sigma. \ \{\sigma\}]\!](\{(\langle\rangle, t, X), (\langle\rangle, s, Y)\}) = \{(\langle\rangle, t, \_)\} \ \cup$$
$$\{(\langle\rangle, s', Z) \mid s' = s[pc \leftarrow 2] \wedge Z \subseteq \Sigma\}$$

The rule D-CBR works in similar way, but alters the subsequent program counter instead of the register store. The rule D-COMM adds two kinds of failures: The terminal failures after the execution of the instruction, in the same way as the two previous rules. Furthermore, it adds the communication failures, when it is ready to communicate.

The rule D-SEQ is the most complex, and it is based on D-EXT. The latter takes a denotation d and extends it with the execution of $code_1$ and $code_2$, separately.

More specifically, the input set S is first evaluated with the denotations for $code_1$ and $code_2$ and then passed to d, which corresponds to executing $code_1$ or $code_2$ first, and then executing d. In D-SEQ, we "loop" this construct now indefinitely, and obtain as a result all possible interleavings of $code_1$ and $code_2$. To this end, we use the *least fixpoint* over the *complete partial order* of functions $\mathcal{P}(\mathcal{SF}) \to \mathcal{P}(\mathcal{SF})$, with the pointwise subset inclusion a ordering $\left(f \leq g := \forall S. \ f(S) \subseteq g(S)\right)$.[1] As in the other rules, we need to remove all former terminal failures.

We illustrate the rule D-SEQ with an example. Consider the initial failure $(\langle\rangle, s, X)$ with $s_{pc} = 1$, X arbitrary, and the program

$$(1\text{:: comm } \lambda\sigma. \ \{a\} \ \lambda\sigma \ event. \ \{\sigma\}) \oplus (2\text{:: cbr } \lambda\sigma. \ True \ 1 \ 1)$$

It is a non-terminating program communicating a repeatedly with its environment. According to D-SEQ, both instructions are evaluated separately, where initially comm modifies the set accordingly (e.g., append a to the trace) and cbr does nothing, as s_{pc} does not point to it. In the next iteration of the fixpoint iteration, both instructions are again executed. This time comm does nothing (new) but cbr will now generate failures whose program counter points to comm, so in the next iteration the loop will be executed from the beginning. As a global fixpoint we get the failure set

$$[\![(1\text{::comm } ...) \oplus (2\text{::cbr } ...)]\!](\{(\langle\rangle, s, X)\}) = \{(\langle a\rangle^*, s^C, Y) \mid Y \subseteq \Sigma\backslash\{a\}\}$$

As this program does not terminate, there are no normal states in its semantics.

4.3   Compatibility to CSP

In this section, we show that our CUC semantics enjoys basic properties of the CSP semantics. This allows us to show that CUC is compatible with CSP, which finally allows us to prove failures refinement between a CUC implementation and its CSP specification. As the refinement relation is basically just a subset relation, its use is clear for safety properties, but for liveness properties the considered failure sets need to fulfill some properties (simply speaking they may not be too small). We introduce and explain adapted versions of the properties of the CSP failures semantics (see e.g., in [Sch99]) and briefly discuss why they hold. We omit the program and the initial failures set for brevity. For each of the following properties, we require that it holds for the initial set of failures. Let $\mathcal{SF}$ be the stable failures of the omitted program, and $\mathcal{T}$ the traces according to the trace semantics given in [JGG15].

SF1: $(tr, s, X) \in \mathcal{SF} \implies (tr, s) \in \mathcal{T}$ – All trace-state pairs are included in the trace semantics. This property ensures that we still have all benefits of the traces semantics (safety properties). The trace semantics for CUC and its properties are published in [JGG15]. It holds as we extended the trace semantics in a safe way.

---

[1] For an introduction to denotational semantics and fixpoints see, e.g., [Rey98].

SF2: $(tr, s, X) \in \mathcal{SF} \wedge X' \subseteq X \implies (tr, s, X') \in \mathcal{SF}$ – Refusal sets are subset closed. This holds by construction.

SF3: $(tr, s, X) \in \mathcal{SF} \wedge \forall a \in X', t. (tr^\frown \langle a \rangle, t) \notin \mathcal{T} \implies (tr, s, X \cup X') \in \mathcal{SF}$ – The refusal set can be augmented with events not possible. This is the important property ensuring that there are "enough" refusals to show liveness properties. This also holds by construction.

SF4: $(tr, s) \in \mathcal{T} \wedge s_{pc} \notin_\ell code \implies (tr, s, X) \in \mathcal{SF}$ – Terminal failures are stable. This also holds by construction.

Properties SF3 and SF4 ensure that all stable failures are included, and thus guarantee that the stable failures refinement relation allows to carry over (safety and) liveness properties.

4.4 Concurrent Semantics

Having defined the sequential semantics in Sect. 4.2, we now define the concurrent semantics. It is defined as close a possible to the concurrent CSP semantics. The purpose is to inherit the compositionality of the parallel composition of CSP and thus the compositionality of its refinement relation. This enables us to refine each component separately. It is important to notice that we only define *top-level* parallel composition, so components can be composed in parallel, but may themselves not contain parallel components.

To define the concurrent semantics of CUC, we first define the notion of a concurrent state. As components communicate via events, the states of components do not share variables. We define a concurrent state to be a normal-/communication-state or pair of concurrent states:

$$concurrent\ state := NCstate \mid concurrent\ state \parallel concurrent\ state$$

The nesting structure of a concurrent state should match the nesting structure of a parallel program. We choose *alphabetized parallel* as the most general parallel combination in CSP that can be used to represent the other two, namely interface parallel and interleaving. We closely follow the CSP definition of alphabetized parallel and adjust it to CUC. As in CSP, the concurrent composition of two components considers all interleavings of the traces of the components, synchronizing on the given alphabets. As we only allow top-level composition, we assume initial failures to have an empty trace and a normal state.

$$
\begin{aligned}
[\![code_1 \,_\alpha\|_\beta\, code_2]\!](S) = \{ &(tr, t_1 \parallel t_2, X) \mid \exists X_1, X_2. \\
&(\langle\rangle, s_1 \parallel s_2, Y) \in S \wedge N(s_1) \wedge N(s_2) \wedge \\
&X \cap (\alpha \cup \beta) = (X_1 \cap \alpha) \cup (X_2 \cap \beta) \wedge \\
&(tr \upharpoonright \alpha, t_1, X_1) \in [\![code_1]\!](\{(\langle\rangle, s_1, Y)\}) \wedge \\
&(tr \upharpoonright \beta, t_2, X_2) \in [\![code_2]\!](\{(\langle\rangle, s_2, Y)\}) \wedge \\
&set(tr) \subseteq (\alpha \cup \beta)\}
\end{aligned}
$$

We have created a semantics which fulfills our needs, and in particular, preserves the properties from the previous section. We are now able to combine CUC programs in parallel. As we have defined parallel composition within CUC like in CSP, we enjoy its compositionality. We thus need only to refine single components and can combine the results, thanks to the compositionality of the stable failures refinement w.r.t. parallel composition. This is the reason, why we do not need a rule for parallel composition in our Hoare calculus, which we introduce in the following section.

5   Hoare Calculus

Our assertions are predicates on single $NCstates$. We define a Hoare triple as usual with one catch:

$$\{P\} \, code \, \{Q\} := \forall \, s. \left(P(s) \longrightarrow \forall \, t \in [\![code]\!](\{s\}). \, Q(t) \right)$$

Observe that our semantics yields a set that includes *all intermediate* stable failures. Postconditions in our Hoare calculus are thus also *invariants for communication failures*. We still can construct usual postconditions, e.g., by setting $Q(t) := t_{pc} \notin code \longrightarrow Q'(t)$.

We present our Hoare calculus for stable failures of CUC in Fig. 4. In H-DO, H-CBR and H-COMM, it is described how pre- and postconditions can be connected for the basic instructions. As all sequential compositions potentially introduce loops in CUC, H-SEQ is based on an invariant I, which is tailored to its placement in the rule: For $code_i$, only the relevant parts of the invariant have to hold as its precondition. In the postcondition of the combination, all parts of the invariant that deal with now former terminal failures are ignored by the conjunction with the requirement that all normal states do not point into the code. H-CONS is the usual rule of consequence.

All rules of the calculus are correct w.r.t. the definition at the start of this section. This can be shown by structural induction over the structure of an arbitrary CUC program. This corresponds to a partial correctness for normal states where the program terminates (we do not show termination). However, for communication failures the postcondition holds universally thus can be used as invariant about trace-refusal pairs (CSP failures). This is important, as this enables us to show properties for reactive systems, i.e., communicating, non-terminating systems. Our Hoare calculus is not complete.

In this paper, we assume that sequential system components are refined only separately. Due to the compositionality of failures refinement w.r.t. parallel composition, we do not need an additional rule for concurrent components. In summary, our overall framework allows for proving properties about sequential components and their parallel combination in a compositional way. We demonstrate its applicability with an example in the next section.

H-DO
$$P(tr, s, X) \equiv \neg(N(s) \land s_{pc} = \ell) \longrightarrow Q(tr, s, X) \land$$
$$N(s) \land s_{pc} = \ell \longrightarrow (\forall t. \ N(t) \land t_{pc} = \ell + 1 \land t_{rs} \in f(s_{rs})$$
$$\longrightarrow \forall Y \subseteq \Sigma. \ Q(tr, t, Y))$$
$$\overline{\{P\} \ \ell :: \textbf{do} \ f \ \{Q\}}$$

H-CBR
$$P(tr, s, X) \equiv \neg(N(s) \land s_{pc} = \ell) \longrightarrow Q(tr, s, X) \land$$
$$N(s) \land s_{pc} = \ell \longrightarrow (\forall t. \ (b(s_{rs}) \land t_{pc} = m \lor \neg b(s_{rs}) \land t_{pc} = n) \land$$
$$N(t) \land s_{rs} = t_{rs} \longrightarrow \forall Y \subseteq \Sigma. \ Q(tr, t, Y))$$
$$\overline{\{P\} \ \ell :: \textbf{cbr} \ b \ m \ n \ \{Q\}}$$

H-COMM
$$P(tr, s, X) \equiv \neg(N(s) \land s_{pc} = \ell) \longrightarrow Q(tr, s, X) \land$$
$$N(s) \land s_{pc} = \ell \longrightarrow (\forall t. \ N(t) \land e \in ef(s_{rs}) \land t_{pc} = \ell + 1 \land t_{rs} = f(s_{rs}, e)$$
$$\longrightarrow (\forall Y \subseteq \Sigma \setminus ef(s_{rs}). \ Q(tr, s^{C}, Y)) \land (\forall Y \subseteq \Sigma. \ Q(tr^\frown e, t, Y)))$$
$$\overline{\{P\} \ \ell :: \textbf{comm} \ ef \ f \ \{Q\}}$$

H-SEQ
$$\{\lambda(tr, s, X). \ I(tr, s, X) \land s_{pc} \in_\ell code_1 \land N(s)\} \ code_1 \ \{I\}$$
$$\{\lambda(tr, s, X). \ I(tr, s, X) \land s_{pc} \in_\ell code_2 \land N(s)\} \ code_2 \ \{I\}$$
$$\overline{\{I\} \ code_1 \oplus code_2 \ \{\lambda(tr, s, X). \ I(tr, s, X) \land (N(s) \longrightarrow s_{pc} \notin_\ell code_1 \oplus code_2)\}}$$

H-CONS
$$\frac{P \Longrightarrow P' \qquad \{P'\} \ code \ \{Q'\} \qquad Q' \Longrightarrow Q}{\{P\} \ code \ \{Q\}}$$

Fig. 4. Hoare calculus for CUC

$Spec = in?x : T \rightarrow out!x \rightarrow Spec$

$Impl :=$
        1 :: **do** $(\lambda\sigma. \ \{\sigma[free \leftarrow \text{TRUE}]\})$
$\oplus$ 2 :: **comm** $ef \ f$ **where**
              $ef = (\lambda\sigma. \ \{in.x \ | \ \sigma(free) = \text{TRUE} \land x \in T\}$
                    $\cup \{out.x \ | \ \sigma(free) = \text{FALSE} \land x = \sigma(buffer)\})$
              $f \ = (\lambda\sigma \ event. \ \textbf{case} \ event \ \textbf{of}$
                    $| \ in.x \ \Rightarrow \sigma[buffer \leftarrow x, free \leftarrow \text{FALSE}]$
                    $| \ out.x \Rightarrow \sigma[free \leftarrow \text{TRUE}])$
$\oplus$ 3 :: **cbr** $(\lambda\sigma. \ \text{TRUE}) \ 2 \ 2$

Fig. 5. CSP specification and CUC implementation of a one place buffer

6   Example

We demonstrate the applicability of our formal framework as presented above and show that a given CSP specification *Spec* for a one place buffer is refined by a given CUC implementation *Impl* of a buffer. Both are shown in Fig. 5. The elements that can be stored in the buffer are of type T. *Spec* waits for an input on channel *in*, i.e., synchronizes on any event $\{in.x \mid x \in T\}$, outputs the received value x on channel *out*, and then starts over. We define $\oplus$ to be right associative. Next, we explain *Impl* line by line:

(1::do) – This is the initialization. The boolean *free* indicates that the *buffer* is ready to store data.

(2::comm) – The comm-instruction both offers the events and changes the state after the communication happened. The events offered by *ef* are all values of type T on channel *in* if the buffer is free, else the output event with the value stored in the buffer is offered. According to the event communicated, it either stores the input value and sets the buffer to not free, or it just sets the buffer to free.

(3::cbr) – The conditional branch is used in this case to model an unconditional branch and always jumps back to the comm-instruction at label 2.

Step 1: Manual Extraction of *Conn* from *Spec*

First, we need to extract a connecting property *Conn* which is only true for the failures of *Spec*. Let *trace** mean *trace* zero or more times concatenated, where the variable $x \in T$ is fresh in every occurrence of *trace*. We define

$$Conn(F) := F \in \mathbb{F}_{even} \vee F \in \mathbb{F}_{odd} \qquad \text{where}$$

$$\mathbb{F}_{even} := \left\{ \left((in.x^\frown out.x)^*, X\right) \,\middle|\, X \subseteq \Sigma \backslash \{in.y \mid y \in T\} \right\}$$

$$\mathbb{F}_{odd} := \left\{ \left((in.x^\frown out.x)^* {}^\frown in.y, X\right) \,\middle|\, y \in T \wedge X \subseteq \Sigma \backslash \{out.y\} \right\}$$

This means, we choose pairs of matching inputs and outputs and at most one "free" input at the end. Initially and after an output only inputs are possible. After an input only the matching output is possible.

Step 2: Relation Between *Conn* and *Spec*

We need to prove that this holds *only* for stable failures of *Spec*, i.e., $Conn(F) \implies F \in \mathcal{SF}(Spec)$, but in this simple case it is easy to see, as *Conn* describes exactly the failures of *Spec*.

Lemma 1. $Conn(F) \implies F \in \mathcal{SF}(Spec)$.

Step 3: Relation Between *Conn* and *Impl*

In the next step, we need to show that *Conn* holds for all failures of the program *Impl*, or more exactly for all elements of the projection of the failures of

Impl onto the traces-refusal pairs. To this end, we need an invariant *Inv*, which implies *Conn* but is effectively stronger, as we need state information such as the current program counter. We also need to specify the initial failures with a precondition *Pre*. We omit *Pre* in the formulation of several lemmas for brevity. In the following, we show {*Pre*} *Impl* {*Inv*}. First, we define *Pre* and *Inv*:

$$Pre(tr, s, X) := s_{pc} = 1 \land tr = \langle\rangle$$

$$Inv := Pre \lor I_{2,3}$$

$$I_{2,3}(tr, s, X) := t_{pc} \in \{2, 3\} \land$$
$$((tr, X) \in \mathbb{F}_{even} \land s_{rs}(free) = \text{TRUE} \lor$$
$$(tr, X) \in \mathbb{F}_{odd} \land s_{rs}(free) = \text{FALSE}$$
$$\land \exists x.\, t_{rs}(buffer) = x \land last(tr) = in.x)$$

Lemma 2. $(tr, s, X) \in [\![Impl]\!] \implies Conn(tr, X)$.

Proof. We show $(tr, s, X) \in [\![Impl]\!](\{(tr, t, Y) \mid Pre(tr, t, Y)\}) \implies Inv(tr, s, X)$ with our Hoare calculus, i.e., {*Pre*} *Impl* {*Inv*} holds. For brevity we denote the instruction by their label and instruction name, e.g., 1:: do. The idea of the Hoare calculus proof is that starting in *Pre*, 1:: do leads to the loop (2:: comm ⊕ 3:: cbr) and $I_{2,3}$ holds. During execution of the loop, the invariant $I_{2,3}$ is preserved, thus overall the invariant $Inv \equiv Pre \lor I_{2,3}$ holds. As $Inv(tr, s, X) \implies Conn(tr, X)$ holds too, we conclude

$$(tr, s, X) \in [\![Impl]\!](\{(tr, t, Y) \mid Pre(tr, t, Y)\}) \implies Conn(tr, X)$$

□

From Lemmas 1 and 2 we conclude Theorem 1 that all trace-refusal pairs of *Impl* are failures of *Spec*, i.e., *Spec* $\sqsubseteq_{\mathcal{SF}}$ *Impl* holds. $\sqsubseteq_{\mathcal{SF}}$ being CSP (stable) failures refinement, *Impl* thus enjoys all liveness and safety properties of *Spec*.

Theorem 1. *Spec* $\sqsubseteq_{\mathcal{SF}}$ *Impl*.

6.1   Concurrency

Thanks to the compositionality of refinement and parallel composition of CSP, we are able to model a two place buffer by letting two buffers communicate. Still, all safety and liveness properties are preserved. Consider the following CSP processes:

$$Spec_1 = in?x : T \to mid!x \to Spec_1$$
$$Spec_2 = mid?x : T \to out!x \to Spec_2$$
$$Spec_\| = Spec_1 \,_{\{mid\}}\|_{\{mid\}} Spec_2$$

We can show that two programs $Impl_1$ and $Impl_2$ (similar to the code in Fig. 5) refine $Spec_1$ and $Spec_2$ respectively (see Theorem 1). Let

$$Impl_\| = Impl_1 \,_{\{mid\}}\|_{\{mid\}} Impl_2$$

Due to the compositionality of CSP and the equal nature of the parallel compositions of CSP and CUC, we can immediately follow that $Spec_{\|} \sqsubseteq_{\mathcal{SF}} Impl_{\|}$, which demonstrates the compositionality of our approach. Please observe that it scales well with the number of components: a system with N components requires only N separate refinement proofs. For homogeneous systems (as the in the buffer example) we even can reuse the refinement proof.

7 Related Work

To the best of our knowledge there exists no other approach to define a stable failures semantics for low-level code.

A denotational semantics and a proof calculus for a high-level language with communication are defined by Zwiers [Zwi89]. The semantics deals with traces and *ready sets*, which are similar in intention to refusals. As low-level code is not considered, the semantics is not directly applicable.

There are some attempts to give unstructured code a semantics for later verification. Tews [Tew04] developed a compositional semantics for a C-like language with goto, which is used to verify Duff's device. However, this approach does not model communication, and is thus not appropriate to describe non-terminating systems. Saabas and Uustalu [SU05] present a compositional bigstep semantics of an unstructured language. To this end, a generic structuring mechanism for the code is presented, which makes the semantics compositional and also allows for a compositional proof calculus. Although they formally relate a high-level and a low-level language, they do not relate a process specification with the low-level language. Communication is not considered. CUC uses their structuring mechanism [JGG15].

CUC, presented in [JGG15], is based on our previous work [BJ14] enhanced with communication capabilities. The approach in [BJ14] focuses on a small-step and a bigstep operational semantics based on which a compositional proof calculus is built. We used similar semantics in [BG11] to show correspondence between unstructured code and (Timed) CSP processes. We used events as observation points, but did not consider actual communication. Furthermore, the use of a bisimulation to relate unstructured code and CSP processes allows only for equivalence, which is inappropriate for an implementation process.

8 Conclusion

In this paper, we have defined a stable failures semantics and a Hoare calculus for CUC. Both are used in our framework, which allows for formally proving stable failures refinement between specifications in CSP and implementations in CUC. Our framework thus contributes to reducing the verification gap between behavioral abstract specification and executed low-level code. This relation preserves all safety and liveness properties of the specification. Our approach is compositional w.r.t. parallel system components, i.e., we only need to show refinements for the sequential components of the system, as the properties are preserved for the entire system due to compositionality of stable failures refinement.

In future work, we aim at extending our existing Isabelle/HOL [NPW02] formalization of the trace semantics for CUC and the corresponding Hoare calculus for stable failures. To enable a further refinement of the CUC implementation, we plan to model the detailed implementation of the comm instruction in a low level language with primitives to implement a channel, such as shared variables and locks. We aim at investigating the applicability of our approach with more complex systems. We are especially interested in the utility of the intra-component compositionality of CUC. Finally, our framework could be combined with other frameworks, e.g., the CSP++ framework [GGC15], where a C++ communication backbone is generated from a CSP specification.

References

[BG11] Bartels, B., Glesner, S.: Verification of distributed embedded real-time systems and their low-level implementation using timed CSP. In: APSEC 2011, pp. 195–202. IEEE Computer Society (2011)

[BJ14] Bartels, B., Jähnig, N.: Mechanized, compositional verification of low-level code. In: Badger, J.M., Rozier, K.Y. (eds.) NFM 2014. LNCS, vol. 8430, pp. 98–112. Springer, Heidelberg (2014)

[GABR14] Gibson-Robinson, T., Armstrong, P., Boulgakov, A., Roscoe, A.W.: FDR3 — a modern refinement checker for CSP. In: Ábrahám, E., Havelund, K. (eds.) TACAS 2014 (ETAPS). LNCS, vol. 8413, pp. 187–201. Springer, Heidelberg (2014)

[GGC15] Gardner, W.B., Gumtie, A., Carter, J.D.: Supporting selective formalism in CSP++ with process-specific storage. In: ICESS 2015, pp. 1057–1065 (2015)

[Hoa78] Hoare, C.A.R.: Communicating sequential processes. Commun. ACM **21**(8), 666–677 (1978)

[JGG15] Jähnig, N., Göthel, T., Glesner, S.: A denotational semantics for communicating unstructured code. In: FESCA 2015. EPTCS, vol. 178, pp. 9–21 (2015)

[NPW02] Nipkow, T., Paulson, L.C., Wenzel, M.: The basics. In: Nipkow, T., Paulson, L.C., Wenzel, M. (eds.) Isabelle/HOL. LNCS, vol. 2283, p. 3. Springer, Heidelberg (2002)

[Rey98] Reynolds, J.C.: Theories of Programming Languages. Cambridge University Press, Cambridge (1998)

[Sch99] Schneider, S.: Concurrent and Real Time Systems: The CSP Approach. Wiley, New York (1999)

[SU05] Saabas, A., Uustalu, T.: A compositional natural semantics and hoare logic for low-level languages. SOS **156**(1), 151–168 (2005). Elsevier

[Tew04] Tews, H.: Verifying Duff's device: a simple compositional denotational semantics for goto and computed jumps. Technical report, Technische Universität Dresden (2004)

[Zwi89] Zwiers, J.: Compositionality, Concurrency, and Partial Correctness. LNCS, vol. 321. Springer, Heidelberg (1989)

Guided Dynamic Symbolic Execution Using Subgraph Control-Flow Information

Josselin Feist[✉], Laurent Mounier, and Marie-Laure Potet

Univ. Grenoble Alpes, 38000 Grenoble, France
josselin.feist@imag.fr

Abstract. Dynamic symbolic execution (DSE) is an efficient SMT-based path enumeration technique used in software testing. In this work in progress, we consider here the case of guided DSE, where the paths to enumerate should be part of a given program slice. We propose a new path selection criterion, which aims to minimize the number of queries to the SMT solvers. This criterion is based on the probability of a path to exit the program slice. Experiments show that this information can be computed in a reasonable time for DSE purpose.

1 Guided Dynamic Symbolic Execution

Dynamic symbolic execution (DSE) is a technique used in software testing and vulnerability analysis. This subject has received a large interest these past years [5]. DSE mixes a concrete execution trace and a symbolic reasoning on it. From a given symbolic execution path, a logical formula called *path predicate* is built, from which conditional instructions can be inverted using an SMT solver. This operation leads to the generation of a new *input*, which can be used to obtain a new path, and so on. Exploring all bounded paths in a software is not realistic, due to the large number of paths. This limitation is well known as the *path explosion* problem [2]. A key feature of DSE is thus the strategy used to select which part of the program should be explored first, either to maximize path coverage or to reach specific locations. Our work falls in the latter category: exploration is led towards a goal and focuses on a specific part of the program. This approach is called Guided Dynamic Symbolic Execution. For example, [8] uses DSE to reach a given instruction, while [1,6] use it to confirm results coming from static analysis. In order to reach a goal, two kinds of strategies are used: *Control Flow Guided* and *Data Flow Guided*. For example, [8] belongs to the first family: distance between the source and the destination is used to select which part of the program will be explored first. Meanwhile, [6] belongs the second one: taint analysis is used to guide the exploration.

We focus on *Control Flow Guided* strategies. We observed that most of the strategies in this family are not well adapted in a context of program slice exploration. We propose a new metric based on subgraph information, that we combine with random walks to guide the exploration. The paper is organized as follows. In Sect. 1.1, we give a motivating example and explain limitations of

© Springer International Publishing Switzerland 2016
R. De Nicola and E. Kühn (Eds.): SEFM 2016, LNCS 9763, pp. 76–81, 2016.
DOI: 10.1007/978-3-319-41591-8_6

state of the art techniques on it. Then we present our subgraph representation in Sect. 2.1 and define our new metric in Sect. 2.2. We give a criterion on subgraph extraction for which our approach is well adapted in Sect. 2.3. Afterwards, we present related work on guided strategies in Sect. 3. Finally, in Sect. 4 we discuss possible improvements.

1.1 Motivating Example

Figure 1 is used to illustrate our proposition. The right side of the Figure is the control-flow graph representation of the source code, where node numbers fit with source code lines. We assume that the objective of the DSE is to reach the call to function **goal** (line 11), and that **long_computation** (line 9) is a very large subgraph, with all internal paths leading to node 11. The explored slice is represented by nodes in the subgraph: $\{3, 4, 9, 11\}$ (nodes in the dotted square). Starting from node 3, there are three path categories: *(i)* paths that do not reach destination node 11 and so are outside the subgraph (called $Path_{out}$) *(ii)* paths that reach destination node 11 through node 4 (called $Path_{sp}$, those in shortest paths), and *(iii)* paths that reach destination node 11 through node 9 (called $Path_{lp}$, those in longest paths). Paths in $Path_{lp}$ are assumed to be significantly longer[1] than paths in $Path_{sp}$ and $Path_{out}$. Paths containing the node 4 can either be in $Path_{out}$ or $Path_{sp}$. So, going through node 4 can potentially lead to not reach the destination. Conversely, paths containing node 9 can only be in $Path_{lp}$ and choosing such paths will ensure to reach the destination.

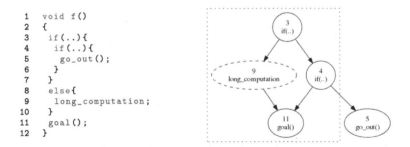

```
1   void f()
2   {
3     if(..){
4       if(..){
5         go_out();
6       }
7     }
8     else{
9       long_computation;
10    }
11    goal();
12  }
```

Fig. 1. Motivating example

1.2 Proposition

We observe that most *Control Flow Guided* strategies are based on shortest path, without taking into account the context of program slice exploration (see Sect. 3). In Fig. 1, state of the art strategies will first select node 4 rather than node 9 in order to reach node 11 from node 3. However, this choice is clearly not the most appropriate. A path going through node 9 requires no further inversion,

---

[1] In number of nodes and comparisons.

while passing through node 4 there is a 50 % chance to need an inversion (that requires one more solver query). We notice that classical exploration of program slice does not take into account branches that do not reach the destination. For example, by removing node 5 and its incoming edge, the information needed to choose node 9 over 4 is lost. Our metric is based on this particular information.

We propose a new path selection heuristic, based on the number of instruction inversions necessary to reach the goal, rather than on the length of a path. More specifically, we compute the probability of a path starting from a node to reach the destination, while taking into account that it can go out of the subgraph.

2   Using Subgraph Control-Flow Information

2.1   Subgraph Transformation

We define $G = (V, E)$, where G is the control-flow graph representation of the analyzed program, V a set of nodes n_i and E a set of directed edges. $e_{i,j}$ denotes the edge between nodes n_i and n_j. A program slice is given as a pair (n_{dst}, φ) where $n_{dst} \in V$ and φ is a property on paths. $G_{dst} = (V', E')$ is the subgraph of G with n_{dst} as destination node. V' is the set of nodes satisfying φ. All nodes that do not satisfy φ are merged into one single node: n_{out}. In a context of line reachability, φ states if a node can reach the destination or not. In more complex contexts, as in static analysis validation, φ can describe more specific properties [4]. n_{out} and n_{dst} are both absorbing nodes, meaning that we replace their out-edges by self-loops. Figure 2 explains the subgraph extraction algorithm.

$$V' = \{v \in V \mid \varphi(v, n_{dst})\} \cup \{n_{out}\}$$
$$E' = \{e_{i,j} \in E \mid n_i \in V' \wedge n_j \in V' \wedge n_i \neq n_{dst}\} \cup$$
$$\{e_{i,out} \mid \exists e_{i,j} \in E \wedge n_i \in V' \wedge n_j \notin V'\} \cup$$
$$\{e_{dst,dst}\} \cup \{e_{out,out}\}$$

Fig. 2. Subgraph transformation

2.2   Using Random Walk to Guide the Exploration

The main idea is now to compute the probability to reach rather n_{dst} than n_{out}. From a node, this probability can be seen as the number of elementary[2] paths reaching n_{dst} rather than n_{out}. Unfortunately, elementary paths computation is exponential. In order to be scalable, we propose a more realistic heuristic. A way to approximate program paths is to use random walks. Computing the probability for a random walk to reach n_{dst} starting from a node yields the desired probability. This can be computed using the *transition matrix* of the graph [7]. A *transition matrix* T is a $|N| * |N|$ matrix where $|N|$ is the number of nodes and $T(n_i, n_j)$ represents the probability for a random walk to move

---

[2] A elementary path is a path where no node appears more than once.

from n_i to n_j in one step. If there is no edge between n_i and n_j, this probability is 0, otherwise it is equal to 1 divided by the number of out-edges of n_i in a unweighted graph:

$$T(n_i, n_j) = \begin{cases} 0 & \text{if } e_{i,j} \notin E, \\ \frac{1}{deg_{out}(n_i)} & \text{otherwise.} \end{cases}$$

An absorbing node a is a special node, where $T(a, a) = 1$ and $T(a, j) = 0, \forall j \neq a$. Absorbing nodes are used to stop the random walk. From our subgraph transformation (Sect. 2.1), n_{dst} and n_{out} are both absorbing nodes. Then $T^l(i, j)$ represents the probability of a random walk to be in j starting from i after l steps [7]. An interesting point is that we focus only on two specific destinations: n_{dst} and n_{out}. Since they are absorbing nodes, paths represented by $T^l(n_i, n_{dst})$ (resp. $T^l(n_i, n_{out})$) contain the one represented by $T^{l-1}(n_i, n_{dst})$ (resp. $T^{l-1}(n_i, n_{out})$). For our example in Fig. 1 we have[3]:

$$T = \begin{array}{c} \\ n_3 \\ n_4 \\ n_{out} \\ n_9 \\ n_{11} \end{array} \overset{\displaystyle n_3\ n_4\ n_{out}\ n_9\ n_{11}}{\begin{pmatrix} 0 & \frac{1}{2} & 0 & \frac{1}{2} & 0 \\ 0 & 0 & \frac{1}{2} & 0 & \frac{1}{2} \\ 0 & 0 & 1 & 0 & 0 \\ 0 & 0 & 0 & 0 & 1 \\ 0 & 0 & 0 & 0 & 1 \end{pmatrix}}$$

$$T^2 = \begin{array}{c} \\ n_3 \\ n_4 \\ n_{out} \\ n_9 \\ n_{11} \end{array} \overset{\displaystyle n_3\ n_4\ n_{out}\ n_9\ n_{11}}{\begin{pmatrix} 0 & 0 & \frac{1}{4} & 0 & \frac{3}{4} \\ 0 & 0 & \frac{1}{2} & 0 & \frac{1}{2} \\ 0 & 0 & 1 & 0 & 0 \\ 0 & 0 & 0 & 0 & 1 \\ 0 & 0 & 0 & 0 & 1 \end{pmatrix}}$$

We define $P^l(n_i, e_{i,j})$ as the probability to reach the destination n_{dst} in at most l steps starting from n_i and going through $e_{i,j}$, as follows:

$$P^l(n_i, e_{i,j}) = T^l(n_j, n_{dst})$$

P^l is computed before the DSE exploration and it is used as score during the exploration to prioritize over the choice of edges. In case of equality, a classical shortest path, or $T^l(n_i, n_{out})$[4], can be used to settle the choice. In our example, $P^2(n_3, e_{3,4}) = T^2(n_4, n_{11}) = \frac{1}{2}$ and $P^2(n_3, e_{3,9}) = T^2(n_9, n_{11}) = 1$, so $e_{3,9}$ is chosen.

2.3   Subgraph Pattern

Our proposed strategy makes sense only if nodes in shortest paths could lead out of the subgraph. Yet this corresponds to concrete programming patterns as shown in Fig. 3. The first one is close to the example given in Fig. 1. Here, the true branch of a comparison leads to a short function, but with paths inside this function that do not satisfy the property φ (see Sect. 2.1). On the contrary, the false branch leads to a longer function, with all paths satisfying φ. The second pattern appears every time there is a list of comparisons and only the first one contains another comparison leading paths to not satisfy φ. More generally, our

---

[3] There are at most 2 steps in this example, so we choose $l = 2$.

[4] $T^l(n_i, n_{dst}) + T^l(n_i, n_{out}) \leq 1$ since a random walk ends not necessary in an absorbing node after l steps.

approach differs from shortest path algorithms whenever subgraph respects the following criterion:

Criterion 1. *In the subgraph, nodes in the shortest paths to n_{dst} also appear in numerous paths leading out of the subgraph.*

```
if(cond)
  small_calc() // small_calc
      contains paths that do
      not satisfy the desired
      property
else
  long_calc() // in long_calc
      all paths satisfy the
      desired property
```

```
if(cond){
  if(cond){
    ...    // the desired
           property is not
           satisfy
  }
  return ;
}
else if(cond){
  return ;
}
return;
```

Fig. 3. Pattern examples

2.4 Overhead

Our approach is not yet implemented in a DSE. However we compute P^l on a slice coming from *Jasper-JPEG-2000*[5]. The slice contains 2000 nodes and 2600 edges. For random walks with a length of 200000 steps ($l = 200000$), the computation takes 8 s. Since we only need to compute P one time (as preprocessing), it is clearly negligible compared to the computation time needed by a guided DSE to explore this slice.

3   Related Work

As discussed in previous sections, state of the art strategies are mostly based on different variants of shortest path and on data-flow analysis. For example, [8] mixes a shortest path analysis with a backward analysis to reach a specific line of code. [11] uses a *proximity heuristics* that computes the shortest path on basic blocks. [9] combines shortest paths on conditional instructions with a data-flow analysis to remove unreachable paths. In [1], data-flow analysis is combined with shortest path in the *Visible Pushdown Automaton* (VPA) representation of the program. [12] proposes to join a data-flow analysis with *Finite State Machine* (FSM) to select a path that satisfies a property as soon as possible. There are many other strategies and it is not in the scope of this paper to list them all. Yet, to the best of our knowledge, there are no *Control Flow Guided* strategies that are not based on shortest paths.

---

[5] https://www.ece.uvic.ca/~frodo/jasper/#overview.

4 Conclusion and Perspectives

We present in this paper the use of a new heuristic, using control-flow information and random walks to guide a DSE towards a goal in a program slice. It still has a large possibility of improvement. First of all, our metric needs to be integrated in a DSE and compared with state of the art strategies. It would be also relevant to test our metric on results of static analysis [4,10], to determine if some analyses create subgraphs that fit well with Criterion 1. We plan to integrate our work inside the BINSEC/SE framework [3] and use it in a security oriented purpose. More specifically, this work is driven by the need to confirm results coming from an *use-after-free* static analyzer [4]. Another perspective is also to correlate our approach with data-flow analysis, by weighing the random walk from its results, or directly during subgraph transformation. We also believe that strategies in DSE exploration currently lack of an adapted use of graph theory metrics. One of future directions is to better integrate these notions in DSE usage.

References

1. Babic, D., Martignoni, L., McCamant, S., Song, D.: Statically-directed dynamic automated test generation. In: ISSTA (2011)
2. Cadar, C., Sen, K.: Symbolic execution for software testing: three decades later. ACM Commun. **56**(2), 82–90 (2013)
3. David, R., Bardin, S., Ta, T.D., Feist, J., et al.: BINSEC/SE: a dynamic symbolic execution toolkit for binary-level analysis. In: SANER (2016)
4. Feist, J., Mounier, L., Potet, M.L.: Statically detecting use-after-free on binary code. JCVHT **10**(3), 211–217 (2014)
5. Godefroid, P.: 500 machine-years of software model checking and SMT solving (invited speaker). In: SEFM (2014)
6. Haller, I., Slowinska, A., Neugschwandtner, M., Bos, H.: Dowsing for overflows: a guided fuzzer to find buffer boundary violations. In: USENIX SEC (2013)
7. Lovász, L.: Random walks on graphs: a survey. In: Erdős, P., Miklós,D., Sós, V.T., Szőnyi, T., Bolyai János Matematikai Társulat (eds.) Combinatorics, Paul Erdös is Eighty. Bolyai Society Mathematical Studies, vol. 2, pp. 1–46. János Bolyai Mathematical Society (1996)
8. Ma, K.-K., Yit Phang, K., Foster, J.S., Hicks, M.: Directed symbolic execution. In: Yahav, E. (ed.) Static Analysis. LNCS, vol. 6887, pp. 95–111. Springer, Heidelberg (2011)
9. Marinescu, P.D., Cadar, C.: Katch: high-coverage testing of software patches. In: ESEC/SIGSOFT FSE (2013)
10. Rawat, S., Mounier, L.: Finding buffer overflow inducing loops in binary executables. In: SERE (2012)
11. Zamfir, C., Candea, G.: Execution synthesis: a technique for automated software debugging. In: EuroSys (2010)
12. Zhang, Y., Chen, Z., Wang, J., Dong, W., Liu, Z.: Regular property guided dynamic symbolic execution. In: ICSE (2015)

Program Analysis

Correlating Structured Inputs and Outputs in Functional Specifications

Oana Fabiana Andreescu[1,2]([✉]), Thomas Jensen[1,2], and Stéphane Lescuyer[1]

[1] Prove & Run, 75017 Paris, France
{oana.andreescu,thomas.jensen,stephane.lescuyer}@provenrun.com
[2] INRIA Rennes – Bretagne Atlantique, Rennes, France

Abstract. We present a static correlation analysis that computes a safe approximation of what part of an input state of a function is copied to the output state. This information is to be used by an interactive theorem prover to automate the discharging of proof obligations concerning unmodified parts of the state. The analysis is defined for a strongly-typed, functional language that handles structures, variants and arrays. It uses partial equivalence relations as approximations of fine-grained correlations between inputs and outputs. The analysis is interprocedural and summarizes not only what is modified but also how and to what extent. We have applied it to a functional specification of a micro-kernel, and obtained results that demonstrate both its precision and its scalability.

1 Introduction

Any complete formal software verification endeavour focuses on two fundamental, mutually dependent questions: what are the effects of program operations on their environment, i.e. what do program operations do, and what do they leave unmodified, i.e. what are they *not* doing. The latter concern inevitably leads to some manifestation of the *frame problem* [8], imposing superfluous manual verification effort and having notoriously tedious consequences. These are particularly visible in the context of complex transitions systems, which consist of complex states and transitions between them, i.e. state changes. States are defined using associative arrays and algebraic data types (structures and variants). Transitions map an input state to an output state. In reality, the transitions' effects are often restricted to a small subset of the state, thus impacting only a limited number of invariants simultaneously. However, a considerable amount of time is spent on proof obligations concerning unmodified parts. Though intuitively easy, these are in practice a lengthy and repetitive task. Specifying and proving the preservation of logical properties for the unmodified part thus becomes a natural target for automation [9]. We propose to tackle the inference of preserved invariants for the unmodified parts by answering the following two questions, by means of *static analysis*:

© Springer International Publishing Switzerland 2016
R. De Nicola and E. Kühn (Eds.): SEFM 2016, LNCS 9763, pp. 85–103, 2016.
DOI: 10.1007/978-3-319-41591-8_7

(1) What is the input subset on which a logical property depends?
(2) How does the output relate to the input of an operation?

In [1], we have presented a static dependency analysis that addresses the first question and automatically determines the input subsets on which a property depends. This paper deals with the second question. More specifically, given an operation that manipulates a structured input, we strive to determine the subset that remains unchanged and is propagated into the output. Our goal is thus to summarize the behaviour of an operation by computing relations between parts of the input and parts of the output. To this end, we present a *correlation analysis*, meant to be used in an interactive verification context, that tracks the origin of subparts of the output and relates it to subparts of the input. The analysis produces expressive results without sacrificing scalability. By unifying these correlation and dependency results and thus by knowing the effects of an operation, after having detected that a property only depends on unmodified parts, the preservation of some invariants can be inferred.

1.1 Motivating Example

The motivation and ideas behind the correlation analysis presented in this paper stemmed from the formal verification of *ProvenCore* [7], a full-featured industrial isolation micro-kernel. To exemplify the addressed problem and the fine-grained correlation results that we are targeting, we consider an abstract process manager and the data structures for its fundamental components: process and thread, shown in Fig. 1-a. A process is an executing instance of an application that can consist of multiple threads that share the same address space. A thread is a path of execution within a process and it is modeled as a structure having fields such as the thread's identifier and the memory region for its stack. The current state of a thread is defined as a variant having three alternatives: READY, BLOCKED, RUNNING. Similarly, a process is a structure including an identifier for the currently running thread and an array of possibly inactive threads associated with it. Whether a thread in the thread array is active or has terminated is indicated by a variant of type option_thread = | Some(thread t) | None.

```
type proc = {                      type thread = {
  threads : array<option_thread>;    identifier : int;
  pid : int;                         current_state : state;
  current_thread : int;              stack : mem_region; }
  address_space : address_space;  }
}
```
a) Data Structures

```
predicate stop(proc in, int i) -> [true: proc o | inval]
```
b) Signature for the Example Function

Fig. 1. Example – data structures and functions of an abstract process manager

The signature of a function stop, written in a modeling language that we present in Sect. 2, is shown in Fig. 1-b. It has two possible execution scenarios: true, when the given index i corresponds to an active thread, and inval otherwise. In the former case, stop copies the i-th element of the threads array to a local variable th, sets its state to BLOCKED and leaves everything else unmodified. The new state o of the process is then returned, with its i-th element set to th and everything else copied from in. The body of stop is detailed in Fig. 2.

Our analysis should infer that between the input process in and the output o, the values of the fields pid, current_thread and address_space are equal. Furthermore, it should detect that all elements of the array threads are equal, except the value of the i-th element, for which only the current_state differs.

By tracking only equalities between pairs of variables of the same type, we can detect the equality of the values of the pid, current_thread and address_space fields between the input and the output. However, if we ignore the flow of an input's subelement value to a variable (or conversely, the flow of a variable's value to an output's subelement) valuable information is lost. We are not only losing information between inputs and outputs of different types, but by accumulating imprecisions, we also lose information concerning inputs and outputs of the same type. This is exactly what can happen in our example. The equality between the values extracted from the input in and copied into th as well as the relation between the value of th and o.threads[i] are ignored because th is not of the same type as in and o. As a consequence, we lose the information concerning the relation between in's and o's threads value altogether. It is therefore imperative to track (cor)relations between variables of different types as well.

The contributions of this paper include an interprocedural domain and a static analysis that allow us to compute expressive correlations between parts of the inputs and parts of the outputs in a flexible manner. An in-depth presentation of these is given in Sect. 3. Results obtained on a functional specification of an operating system are discussed in Sect. 4.

2   Language

We briefly present the unified programming and specification language targeted by our analysis. This is an idealized version of a language developed at *Prove & Run*[1], designed with a focus on subsequent proof facilitation. It is a first-order, purely functional and strongly-typed language with algebraic data types and arrays. The basic building blocks of programs written in our language are *predicates*, the equivalent of functions in common programming languages.

2.1   Types and Statements

We let $\mathbb{T}$ be the universe of type identifiers and $T_0 \subset \mathbb{T}$ the set of base type identifiers. The sets of structure field identifiers and variant constructors are denoted by $\mathscr{F}$ and $\mathscr{C}$, respectively.

---

[1] http://www.provenrun.com/.

A *structure* represents the *Cartesian product* of the different types of its elements, called *fields*. A *variant* is the *disjoint union* of different types. It represents data that may take on multiple forms, where each form is marked by a specific tag called the *constructor*. *Arrays* group elements of data of the same type (given in angle brackets) into a single entity; elements are selected by an index whose type is included (as denoted by the superscript) in the array's definition.

$$
\begin{aligned}
\tau \in \mathbb{T}, \tau := \ & | \ \tau_0 \in T_0 & \text{base types} \\
& | \ \textbf{struct}\{f_1 : \tau, \ldots, f_n : \tau\} & f_i \in \mathscr{F}, 0 \leq n \ \text{structures} \\
& | \ \textbf{variant}[C_1 : \tau \ | \ \ldots \ | \ C_m : \tau] \ C_i \in \mathscr{C}, 1 \leq m \ \text{variants} \\
& | \ \textbf{arr}^\tau \langle \tau \rangle & \text{arrays}
\end{aligned}
$$

Variants and structures can be used together to model traditional algebraic variants with zero or several parameters. For instance, the `option_thread` type given in Sect. 1.1 is actually modeled as:

$$
\textit{variant}[\texttt{Some} : \textbf{struct}\{\texttt{t} : \texttt{thread}\} \ | \ \texttt{None} : \textbf{struct}\{\}].
$$

A program in our language is a collection of predicates. A predicate has input and output parameters and a body of statements of the form shown in Table 1. The first statement represents a generic predicate call and is described later. All other statements can be seen as special cases of it, representing calls to built-in predicates. They all have a functional nature and handle immutable data. Thus, setting the value of a structure's field, shown in (4), returns a *new* structure where all fields have the same value as in r, except f_i which is set to e. Similarly, updating the i-th cell of an array, shown in (8), returns a *new* array where all cells have the same value as in a, except the i-th cell which is set to e.

2.2   Exit Labels

In addition to input and output parameters, the declaration of a predicate also includes a non-empty set of *exit labels*, which behave like *exit codes*. When called, a predicate exits with one of the specified exit labels, thus summarizing and returning to its callers further information regarding its execution.

Table 1. Subset of supported statements

statement :=		
$\| \ p(e_1, \ldots, e_n) \ [\lambda_1 : \bar{o}_1 \ | \ldots | \ \lambda_m : \bar{o}_m]$	(1)	predicate call
$\| \ o := e$	(2)	assignment
$\| \ o := r.f_i$	(3)	access field f_i
$\| \ r' := \{r \ \textbf{with} \ f_i = e\}$	(4)	update field f_i
$\| \ v := C_p[e]$	(5)	create v with constructor C_p
$\| \ \textbf{switch}(v) \ \textbf{as} \ [o_1| \ldots |o_n]$	(6)	variant matching
$\| \ o := a[i]$	(7)	array access at index i
$\| \ a' := [a \ \textbf{with} \ i = e]$	(8)	array update at index i

Table 2. Statements and their exit labels

Statement	Exit Labels		Statement	Exit Labels
$p(e_1, \ldots, e_n)$ $[\lambda_1 : \bar{o}_1 \mid \ldots \mid \lambda_m : \bar{o}_m]$	$\begin{bmatrix} \lambda_1 \mapsto \bar{o}_1 \\ \vdots \quad \ddots \quad \vdots \\ \lambda_m \mapsto \bar{o}_m \end{bmatrix}$ (1)		$v := C_p[e]$	$\begin{bmatrix} \text{true} \mapsto v \end{bmatrix}$ (5)
$o := e$	$\begin{bmatrix} \text{true} \mapsto o \end{bmatrix}$ (2)		$switch(v)$ as $[o_1 \mid \ldots \mid o_n]$	$[\ldots \lambda_{C_i} \mapsto o_i \ldots]$ where $C_1, \ldots, C_n$ are the constructors of the type of variant v (6)
$o := r.f_i$	$\begin{bmatrix} \text{true} \mapsto o \end{bmatrix}$ (3)		$o := a[i]$	$\begin{bmatrix} \text{true} \mapsto o, \text{false} \mapsto \emptyset \end{bmatrix}$ (7)
$r' := \{r \; with \; f_i = e\}$	$\begin{bmatrix} \text{true} \mapsto r' \end{bmatrix}$ (4)		$a' := [a \; with \; i = e]$	$\begin{bmatrix} \text{true} \mapsto a', \text{false} \mapsto \emptyset \end{bmatrix}$ (8)

Exit labels play an important role for control flow management, which is expressed and directed by catching and transforming labels. Furthermore, they condition the existence of output parameters, as these are associated to the exit labels of a predicate. Whenever a predicate exits with an exit label λ, all the outputs associated to it are effectively produced, whereas all other outputs are discarded. If no output is associated to an exit label, it means that no output is generated when the predicate exits with this particular label. We can now explain the generic predicate call statement (1) from Table 1: the predicate p is called with inputs $e_1, \ldots, e_n$ and yields one of the declared exit labels $\lambda_1, \ldots, \lambda_m$, each having its own set of associated output variables $\bar{o}_1, \ldots, \bar{o}_m$, respectively.

As shown in Table 2, statement (6) has a label corresponding to each constructor of the input variant. Statements (7) and (8) are bilabeled, using false as an "out of bounds" exception and generating an output only for the label true.

Figure 2 details the body of our example predicate from Sect. 1.1, where arrows show the control-flow between the various statements of the predicate.

```
1: ta := in.threads
2: th := ta[i]                          false
3: switch(th) as [Some:ti | None]
4: s  := BLOCKED                         None
5: ti := {ti with current_state=s}
6: th := Some(ti)
7: ta := [ta with i=th]                  false
8: o  := {in with threads=ta}
9: true
                                    10: inval
```

Fig. 2. Body of the stop predicate

3 Correlation Analysis

We present a flow-sensitive, conservative static analysis inferring what is modified by an operation and to *what* extent. It approximates the flow of input values into output values, by uncovering *equalities* and computing *correlations* as pairs between input parts and the output parts into which these are injected.

Outputs are often complex compounds of different subparts of different input variables: a subset of the input is modified, while the rest is injected as is. We track the origin of subparts of the output and relate it to subparts of the input. As previously explained in Sect. 1.1, we prevent avoidable over-approximations by considering pairs of different types and granularities. As a consequence, in order to avoid dealing with data in a monolithic manner, we are forced to introduce an extra level of granularity below variables. At the intraprocedural level, illustrated in Fig. 3(a), we define the *correlation* domain as mappings between pairs of inputs and outputs to which we associate mappings between pairs of valid inner *paths* and the relations binding them. Correlations for arrays and variants are shown in Fig. 3(b, c).

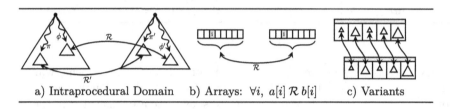

a) Intraprocedural Domain   b) Arrays: $\forall i,\ a[i]\ \mathcal{R}\ b[i]$ c) Variants

Fig. 3. Intraprocedural domain - general representation and examples

3.1 Partial Equivalence Relations

The first step towards automatically reasoning about the propagation of input subelements into output subelements is the definition of an abstract *partial equivalence type* $\mathscr{R}$ that mimics the structure of algebraic data types and arrays. A partial equivalence $\mathcal{R} \in \mathscr{R}$ is defined inductively from the two atomic elements, Equal and Any, and mirrors the structure of the concrete types:

$$
\begin{aligned}
\mathcal{R} := &\mid \mathsf{Equal} \mid \mathsf{Any} && \text{atomic cases} \\
&\mid \{f_1 \mapsto \mathcal{R}_1; \ldots; f_n \mapsto \mathcal{R}_n\} && f_1, \ldots, f_n \text{ fields} && \text{(i)} \\
&\mid [C_1 \mapsto \mathcal{R}_1; \ldots; C_n \mapsto \mathcal{R}_n] && C_1, \ldots, C_n \text{ constructors} && \text{(ii)} \\
&\mid \langle \mathcal{R}_{def} \rangle && \text{array} && \text{(iii)} \\
&\mid \langle \mathcal{R}_{def} \rhd i\ :\ \mathcal{R}_{exc} \rangle && i \text{ array index} && \text{(iv)}
\end{aligned}
$$

Such relations represent fine-grained partial equivalences between pairs of values of the same type. Equal and Any represent respectively equal and unrelated values. Partial equivalence relations for structures (given by (i)) and for variants (given by (ii)), are expressed in terms of the partial equivalences of their subparts, by mapping each field or constructor to the corresponding relations. For arrays, we distinguish between two cases, namely arrays with a general relation applying to all of the cells (as given by (iii)) or to all but one exceptional cell (as given by (iv)), for which a specific relation is known.

Even if the syntactic partial equivalences are untyped, their interpretation is made in the context of a type $\tau \in \mathbb{T}$. The semantics of a partial equivalence $\mathcal{R}$ for a type τ is a partial equivalence relation over values of type τ. Cases other than Equal and Any only have non-empty interpretations for types τ which are compatible with their shape. For instance, the structured relation $\{f \mapsto \mathcal{R}\}$ only really makes sense for structured types with a single field f, whose type itself is compatible with $\mathcal{R}$, and shall not be used in connection with variant or array types for example.

To describe the semantics of elements in $\mathcal{R}$, we define for each type τ the set $\mathbb{D}_\tau$ of semantic values of that type. For each primitive type $t \in T_0$, we suppose a given $\mathbb{D}_t$. Other semantic values are defined inductively as follows:

$$
\begin{aligned}
\mathbb{D}_{struct\{f_1:\tau_1,\ldots,f_n:\tau_n\}} &= \{\{f_1 = v_1, \ldots f_n = v_n\} \mid \forall i, v_i \in \mathbb{D}_{\tau_i}\} \\
\mathbb{D}_{variant[C_1:\tau_1 \mid \ldots \mid C_n:\tau_n]} &= \biguplus_{1 \leq i \leq n}\{C_i[v_i] \mid v_i \in \mathbb{D}_{\tau_i}\} \\
\mathbb{D}_{arr^{\tau_i}\langle \tau \rangle} &= \{(\mathcal{P}, (v_k)_{k \in \mathcal{P}}) \mid \mathcal{P} \subseteq \mathbb{D}_{\tau_i}, \forall k, v_k \in \mathbb{D}_\tau\}.
\end{aligned}
$$

Given a *valuation* E from variables to semantic values, the interpretation of a relation $\mathcal{R} \in \mathcal{R}$ with respect to some type τ is a binary relation over $\mathbb{D}_\tau$ defined as shown in Table 3.

Table 3. Partial equivalence relations – semantics

$$
[\![\mathsf{Equal}]\!]^\tau = \{(x,x) \mid x \in \mathbb{D}_\tau\} \qquad [\![\mathsf{Any}]\!]^\tau = \mathbb{D}_\tau \times \mathbb{D}_\tau
$$

$$
\begin{aligned}
&[\![\{f_1 \mapsto \mathcal{R}_1; \ldots; f_n \mapsto \mathcal{R}_n\}]\!]^{struct\{f_1:\tau_1,\ldots,f_n:\tau_n\}} = \\
&\quad \{(\{f_1 = v_1; \ldots; f_n = v_n\}, \{f_1 = w_1; \ldots; f_n = w_n\}) \mid \forall i, 1 \leq i \leq n, (v_i, w_i) \in [\![\mathcal{R}_i]\!]^{\tau_i}\}
\end{aligned}
$$

$$
\begin{aligned}
&[\![[C_1 \mapsto \mathcal{R}_1; \ldots; C_n \mapsto \mathcal{R}_n]]\!]^{variant[C_1:\tau_1 \mid \ldots \mid C_n:\tau_n]} = \\
&\quad \{(C_i[v_i], C_i[w_i]) \mid \forall i, 1 \leq i \leq n, (v_i, w_i) \in [\![\mathcal{R}_i]\!]^{\tau_i}\}
\end{aligned}
$$

$$
[\![\langle \mathcal{R}_{def} \rangle]\!]^{arr^{\tau_i}\langle \tau \rangle} = \{((\mathcal{P}, (v)_k), (\mathcal{P}, (w)_k)) \mid \forall k, (v_k, w_k) \in [\![\mathcal{R}_{def}]\!]^\tau\}
$$

$$
\begin{aligned}
&[\![\langle \mathcal{R}_{def} \triangleright i : \mathcal{R}_{exc} \rangle]\!]^{arr^{\tau_i}\langle \tau \rangle} = \{((\mathcal{P}, (v)_k), (\mathcal{P}, (w)_k)) \mid \\
&\quad E(i) \in \mathcal{P} \implies (v_{E(i)}, w_{E(i)}) \in [\![\mathcal{R}_{exn}]\!]^\tau, \forall k \neq E(i), (v_k, w_k) \in [\![\mathcal{R}_{def}]\!]^\tau\}
\end{aligned}
$$

The preorder relation of the partial equivalence lattice is denoted by $\sqsubseteq_\mathcal{R}$. It is defined in Table 4.

$$
\sqsubseteq_\mathcal{R} \subseteq \mathcal{R} \times \mathcal{R} \qquad \vee_\mathcal{R}: \mathcal{R} \times \mathcal{R} \to \mathcal{R} \qquad \wedge_\mathcal{R}: \mathcal{R} \times \mathcal{R} \to \mathcal{R}.
$$

The defined *join* and *meet* operations, denoted by $\vee_\mathcal{R}$ and $\wedge_\mathcal{R}$, are *commutative* operations, applied pointwise on each subelement. *Join* has Equal as its identity element and Any as its absorbing element. *Meet* has Equal as its absorbing element and Any as its identity element.

Additionally, the following extraction functions are defined:

$$
\begin{aligned}
extr_f &: \mathcal{R} \rightharpoonup \mathcal{R} \text{ extraction of a field's relation} \\
extr_C &: \mathcal{R} \rightharpoonup \mathcal{R} \text{ extraction of a constructor's relation} \\
extr_{\langle i \rangle} &: \mathcal{R} \rightharpoonup \mathcal{R} \text{ extraction of a cell's relation.}
\end{aligned}
$$

These are partial functions and can only be applied on relations of the corresponding types. For example, the field extraction $extr_f$ only makes sense for

Table 4. $\sqsubseteq_{\mathcal{R}}$ – Comparison of two domains

$$\frac{}{\mathcal{R} \sqsubseteq_{\mathcal{R}} \text{Any}} \text{ TOP} \qquad \frac{}{\text{Equal} \sqsubseteq_{\mathcal{R}} \mathcal{R}} \text{ BOT}$$

$$\frac{\mathcal{R}_1 \sqsubseteq_{\mathcal{R}} \mathcal{R}'_1 \quad \cdots \quad \mathcal{R}_n \sqsubseteq_{\mathcal{R}} \mathcal{R}'_n}{\{f_1 \mapsto \mathcal{R}_1; \ldots; f_n \mapsto \mathcal{R}_n\} \sqsubseteq_{\mathcal{R}} \{f_1 \mapsto \mathcal{R}'_1; \ldots; f_n \mapsto \mathcal{R}'_n\}} \text{ STR}$$

$$\frac{\mathcal{R}_1 \sqsubseteq_{\mathcal{R}} \mathcal{R}'_1 \quad \cdots \quad \mathcal{R}_n \sqsubseteq_{\mathcal{R}} \mathcal{R}'_n}{[C_1 \mapsto \mathcal{R}_1; \ldots; C_n \mapsto \mathcal{R}_n] \sqsubseteq_{\mathcal{R}} [C_1 \mapsto \mathcal{R}'_1; \ldots; C_n \mapsto \mathcal{R}'_n]} \text{ VAR}$$

$$\frac{\mathcal{R} \sqsubseteq_{\mathcal{R}} \mathcal{R}'}{\langle \mathcal{R} \rangle \sqsubseteq_{\mathcal{R}} \langle \mathcal{R}' \rangle} \text{ ADEF} \qquad \frac{\mathcal{R}_{def} \sqsubseteq_{\mathcal{R}} \mathcal{R}'_{def} \quad \mathcal{R}_{exc} \sqsubseteq_{\mathcal{R}} \mathcal{R}'_{exc}}{\langle \mathcal{R}_{def} \triangleright i : \mathcal{R}_{exc} \rangle \sqsubseteq_{\mathcal{R}} \langle \mathcal{R}'_{def} \triangleright i : \mathcal{R}'_{exc} \rangle} \text{ AI}$$

$$\frac{\mathcal{R}_{def} \sqsubseteq_{\mathcal{R}} \mathcal{R}' \quad \mathcal{R}_{exc} \sqsubseteq_{\mathcal{R}} \mathcal{R}'}{\langle \mathcal{R}_{def} \triangleright i : \mathcal{R}_{exc} \rangle \sqsubseteq_{\mathcal{R}} \langle \mathcal{R}' \rangle} \text{ AIA} \qquad \frac{\mathcal{R} \sqsubseteq_{\mathcal{R}} \mathcal{R}'_{def} \quad \mathcal{R} \sqsubseteq_{\mathcal{R}} \mathcal{R}'_{exc}}{\langle \mathcal{R} \rangle \sqsubseteq_{\mathcal{R}} \langle \mathcal{R}'_{def} \triangleright i : \mathcal{R}'_{exc} \rangle} \text{ AAI}$$

$$\frac{i \neq j \quad \mathcal{R}_{def} \sqsubseteq_{\mathcal{R}} \mathcal{R}'_{def} \quad \mathcal{R}_{def} \sqsubseteq_{\mathcal{R}} \mathcal{R}'_{exc} \quad \mathcal{R}_{exc} \sqsubseteq_{\mathcal{R}} \mathcal{R}'_{def} \quad \mathcal{R}_{exc} \sqsubseteq_{\mathcal{R}} \mathcal{R}'_{exc}}{\langle \mathcal{R}_{def} \triangleright i : \mathcal{R}_{exc} \rangle \sqsubseteq_{\mathcal{R}} \langle \mathcal{R}'_{def} \triangleright j : \mathcal{R}'_{exc} \rangle} \text{ AIJ}$$

atomic or structured relations having a field named f, which should be the case if the relation connects two values of a structured type with a field f. For any of the two atomic relations $\mathcal{R}_a$, applying any of these extractions yields $\mathcal{R}_a$.

3.2 Paths and Correlations

Partial equivalence relations are enough to represent fine-grained information for values of the same structured type. For the example introduced in Sect. 1.1 and detailed in Fig. 2 these would suffice to express the equality of the `pid`, `current_thread` and `address_space` fields between the input process `in` and the output process `o`, by simply mapping this pair to {`threads` $\mapsto$ Any; `pid` $\mapsto$ Equal; `current_thread` $\mapsto$ Equal; `address_space` $\mapsto$ Equal}. However, the partial equivalence relations cannot, for example, be used to convey the equality at line 1 in Fig. 2 between the value of the `threads` field of `in` and the local `ta` variable. In order to express this information, we first need to be able to refer to the substructure `in.threads` and relate its value to the one of `ta`.

Rather than handling only partial equivalences between pairs of variables of the same type and approximating the rest to Any – the element that conveys no information – we introduce an intermediate level, allowing us to store relations between subparts of values. To this end, we begin by introducing *paths*.

A *path* is rooted at one of the program's variables and represents a unique sequence of internal accesses inside some value's structure, i.e. it is a traversal from one value to one of its subparts. Each path is a unique chain of accesses leading to a nested element. We define a recursive type Π encompassing this:

$$\pi \in \Pi,\ \pi := \mid \varepsilon \qquad \text{empty} - \text{root}$$
$$\mid .f\pi \quad f \in \mathcal{F}$$
$$\mid @C\pi \ C \in \mathcal{C}$$
$$\mid \langle i \rangle \pi \ i \text{ index, program variable.}$$

The *empty* path, denoted by ε, is the special case denoting an access to an entire element, i.e. the root. The action of appending a *non-empty* path π' to another path π is denoted by $\pi :: \pi'$.

Meaningful information is conveyed by associating paths and partial equivalence relations. For example, the equality between in.threads and ta at line 1 in Fig. 2 can be expressed by associating Equal to the pair of subelements identified by the .threads path in in and by ε in ta. Thus, we introduce *correlation maps* $\hat{c} \in \hat{\mathcal{C}}$, which are finite mappings from pairs of paths to relations $\mathcal{R} \in \mathscr{R}$:

$$\hat{\mathcal{C}} : \Pi \times \Pi \rightarrow \mathscr{R}$$

Generally, for two given variables e and o, a correlation $(\pi, \rho) \mapsto \mathcal{R}$ specifies that e and o have nested subelements, respectively identified by the inner paths π and ρ, whose values are related by the relation $\mathcal{R}$.

There is no clear canonical form for correlations. For instance, it is equivalent to write $(\varepsilon, \varepsilon) \mapsto \{f \mapsto \mathcal{R}\}$ and $(.f, .f) \mapsto \mathcal{R}$. Operations can create and manipulate them in different manners, that are hard to predict. New correlations can also be introduced while considering *def-use* chains in the transfer function presented later in Sect. 3.3. This trait renders the definition of a partial order between correlation maps difficult. In order to compare two correlation maps $\hat{c}_1$ and $\hat{c}_2$, we cannot simply verify if the path pairs are identical and compare their associated relations. A correlation of the second map could be *linked*, in different manners, to multiple mappings of the first. For example, between a process p of the type defined in Sect. 1.1 and an array ta of the same type as the field threads of the process, we might have the following correlation maps:

$$\hat{c}_1 : \begin{array}{l} (.\texttt{threads}, \varepsilon) \mapsto \langle \textsf{Equal} \vartriangleright \texttt{i} : \textsf{Any} \rangle \\[6pt] (.\texttt{threads}\langle \texttt{i} \rangle @\texttt{Some.t}, \langle \texttt{i} \rangle @\texttt{Some.t}) \mapsto \left\{ \begin{array}{r} \texttt{identifier} \mapsto \textsf{Equal} \\ \texttt{current\_state} \mapsto \textsf{Any} \\ \texttt{stack} \mapsto \textsf{Equal} \end{array} \right\} \end{array}$$

$$\hat{c}_2 : (.\texttt{threads}, \varepsilon) \mapsto \left\langle \left[\begin{array}{l} \textsf{None} \mapsto \textsf{Any} \\[4pt] \textsf{Some} \mapsto \left\{ \texttt{t} \mapsto \left\{ \begin{array}{r} \texttt{identifier} \mapsto \textsf{Equal} \\ \texttt{current\_state} \mapsto \textsf{Any} \\ \texttt{stack} \mapsto \textsf{Equal} \end{array} \right\} \right\} \end{array} \right] \right\rangle .$$

To compare two correlation maps $\hat{c}_1$ and $\hat{c}_2$, we need to collect for each pair (π, ρ) mapped to $\mathcal{R}$ in $\hat{c}_2$ all the information contained by $\hat{c}_1$ that refers to the elements identified by (π, ρ) and verify if this covers at least the same information as the relation $\mathcal{R}$. This information could be scattered across multiple mappings of the correlation map $\hat{c}_1$. For example, in the given map $\hat{c}_1$, in addition to the relation associated to $(.\texttt{threads}, \varepsilon)$, the relation associated to $(.\mathtt{threads}\langle i\rangle@\mathtt{Some.t}, \langle i\rangle@\mathtt{Some.t})$ expresses information about the values of the process' $\mathtt{threads}$ field and $\mathtt{ta}$ as well. These are nested in the i-th element of each, as identified by $\langle i\rangle@\mathtt{Some.t}$. To compare these two correlation maps, we have to first determine the relationships between the pair of paths $(.\mathtt{threads}, \varepsilon)$ from $\hat{c}_2$ and each pair of paths of $\hat{c}_1$. The first pair of paths in $\hat{c}_1$ is identical, whereas the second pair refers to elements that are further away from the root. Based on these relationships, we have to extract all the information relevant to $(.\mathtt{threads}, \varepsilon)$ from $\hat{c}_1$. This amounts to:

$$(.\mathtt{threads}, \varepsilon) \mapsto \left\langle \mathsf{Equal} \triangleright i : \begin{bmatrix} \mathtt{None} \mapsto \mathsf{Any} \\ \mathtt{Some} \mapsto \left\{ \mathtt{t} \mapsto \left\{ \begin{matrix} \mathtt{identifier} \mapsto \mathsf{Equal} \\ \mathtt{current\_state} \mapsto \mathsf{Any} \\ \mathtt{stack} \mapsto \mathsf{Equal} \end{matrix} \right\} \right\} \end{bmatrix} \right\rangle .$$

which is more precise than the relation associated to $(.\mathtt{threads}, \varepsilon)$ in $\hat{c}_2$. We call this process *alignment*. It is necessary in the absence of a canonical form, a trait of our approach that is both a weakness and a strength: it leads to complex computations but gives considerable flexibility.

For aligning, we first determine the relationships between paths by determining the relationship between the sequences of internal accesses that they represent. These can be identical, representing the same traversal to the same subelement of a value or they can be completely unrelated, such as $.f$ and $.g$ for example, representing accesses to two different fields of a structure. They can also represent sequences of accesses of different depths, one being the prefix of the other, i.e. being closer to the root. For example, the path $.f$ is a prefix of the path $.f\langle i\rangle$; the first represents the access to the field f, whereas the second one represents an access to the i-th element of the array nested in the field f.

To distinguish between these cases, we have defined a *link* type, $\mu \in \mathcal{M}$:

$$\mu := \mid \mathsf{Identical} \mid \mathsf{Left}\ \pi \mid \mathsf{Right}\ \pi \mid \mathsf{Incompatible}$$

and a *matching* operator $\curlywedge$:

$$\curlywedge : \Pi \times \Pi \to \mathcal{M} \qquad \curlywedge(\pi, \rho) = \begin{cases} \mathsf{Identical}, & \pi = \rho \\ \mathsf{Left}\ \pi', & \pi :: \pi' = \rho \\ \mathsf{Right}\ \rho', & \rho :: \rho' = \pi \\ \mathsf{Incompatible}, & \text{otherwise} \end{cases}$$

that retrieves the link between two paths. *Aligning* a correlation $(\pi, \rho) \mapsto \mathcal{R}$ to another pair of paths (π', ρ'), is denoted by $\|$.

$$\| : \hat{\mathcal{C}} \times (\Pi \times \Pi) \to \mathcal{R} \qquad [(\pi, \rho) \mapsto \mathcal{R}] \| (\pi', \rho') = \mathcal{R}^{(\pi, \rho)}_{\|(\pi', \rho')}.$$

From $\mathcal{R}$ we obtain the information referring to the elements identified by (π', ρ') and denote it by $\mathcal{R}^{(\pi, \rho)}_{\|(\pi', \rho')}$. This is done by *matching* on π and π' on the one hand and on ρ and ρ' on the other and by distinguishing between the different cases. When the paths are identical, we can simply return the relation $\mathcal{R}$.

When the links between the paths differ or when the paths are incompatible, we have to approximate to the least precise relation, thus returning Any. When π and ρ are more shallow paths, i.e. closer to the root, we need to make a *projection*, denoted by $\leadsto$. For example, aligning $(.f, \varepsilon) \mapsto \{a \mapsto \mathcal{R}_a; b \mapsto \mathcal{R}_b; c \mapsto \mathcal{R}_c\}$ to $(.f.b, .b)$ consists in projecting $.b$ on the relation $\{a \mapsto \mathcal{R}_a; b \mapsto \mathcal{R}_b; c \mapsto \mathcal{R}_c\}$ and thus obtaining $\mathcal{R}_b$. On the contrary, if π' and ρ' are closer to the root, we need to perform an *injection*, denoted by $\curvearrowright$. For example, aligning $(.f.b, .b) \mapsto \mathcal{R}_b$ to $(.f, \varepsilon)$ consists in creating a relation $\{a \mapsto \mathsf{Any}; b \mapsto \mathcal{R}_b; c \mapsto \mathsf{Any}\}$.

$$
\mathcal{R}_{\|(\pi', \rho')}^{(\pi, \rho)} = \begin{cases} \mathcal{R} & \text{when } \lambda\,(\pi, \pi') = \lambda(\rho, \rho') = \mathsf{Identical} \\ \leadsto(\sigma, \mathcal{R}) & \text{when } \lambda\,(\pi, \pi') = \lambda(\rho, \rho') = \mathsf{Left}\ \sigma \\ \curvearrowright(\mathcal{R}, \sigma) & \text{when } \lambda\,(\pi, \pi') = \lambda(\rho, \rho') = \mathsf{Right}\ \sigma \\ \mathsf{Any} & \text{otherwise} \end{cases}
$$

$$
\text{where} : \leadsto\, :\, \Pi \times \mathscr{R} \twoheadrightarrow \mathscr{R} \quad \curvearrowright\, :\, \mathscr{R} \times \Pi \twoheadrightarrow \mathscr{R}
$$

$$
\leadsto(\pi, \mathcal{R}) = \begin{cases} \mathcal{R} & \text{when } \pi = \varepsilon \\ \leadsto(\pi', \mathit{extr}_f(\mathcal{R})), & \text{when } \pi = .f\pi' \\ \leadsto(\pi', \mathit{extr}_C(\mathcal{R})), & \text{when } \pi = @C\pi' \\ \leadsto(\pi', \mathit{extr}_{\langle i \rangle}(\mathcal{R})), & \text{when } \pi = \langle i \rangle\pi' \end{cases}
$$

$$
\curvearrowright(\mathcal{R}, \pi) = \begin{cases} \mathcal{R} & \text{when } \pi = \varepsilon \\ \{f_1 \mapsto \mathsf{Any}; \dots; f_i \mapsto \curvearrowright(\mathcal{R}, \pi'); \dots; f_n \mapsto \mathsf{Any}\}, & \text{when } \pi = .f\pi', f = f_i \\ [C_1 \mapsto \mathsf{Any}; \dots; C_i \mapsto \curvearrowright(\mathcal{R}, \pi'); \dots; C_n \mapsto \mathsf{Any}], & \text{when } \pi = @C\pi', C = C_i \\ \langle \mathsf{Any} \rhd i : \curvearrowright(\mathcal{R}, \pi') \rangle, & \text{when } \pi = \langle i \rangle\pi' \end{cases}
$$

Aligning a correlation map $\hat{c} \in \hat{\mathcal{C}}$ to (π', ρ'), amounts to performing this operation for each element $(\pi, \rho) \mapsto \mathcal{R}$ of $\hat{c}$ and intersecting the results with the $\wedge_\mathscr{R}$ operator:

$$
\hat{c} \parallel (\pi', \rho') = \bigwedge_{\mathscr{R}}_{(\pi, \rho) \mapsto \mathcal{R} \in \hat{c}} \mathcal{R}_{\|(\pi', \rho')}^{(\pi, \rho)}.
$$

Finally, we can define the preorder for correlation maps:

$$
\hat{c}_1 \sqsubseteq \hat{c}_2 \iff \forall\, [(\pi, \rho) \mapsto \mathcal{R}] \in \hat{c}_2,\ \hat{c}_1 \parallel (\pi, \rho) \sqsubseteq_\mathscr{R} \mathcal{R}.
$$

Any correlation map $\hat{c} \in \hat{\mathcal{C}}$ is smaller than $\emptyset$, the empty correlation map. The defined join operation between two correlation maps is denoted by $\hat{\bigvee}$:

$$
\hat{c}_1 \hat{\bigvee} \hat{c}_2 = \hat{c}_3 \iff \forall\, [(\pi, \rho) \mapsto \mathcal{R}] \in \hat{c}_1, \hat{c}_3(\pi, \rho) = \mathcal{R} \vee_\mathscr{R} (\hat{c}_2 \parallel (\pi, \rho)).
$$

The *meet* operation between two correlation maps is denoted by $\hat{\bigwedge}$:

$$
\hat{c}_1 \hat{\bigwedge} \hat{c}_2 = \hat{c}_3 \iff \hat{c}_3(\pi, \rho) = \hat{c}_1(\pi, \rho) \wedge_\mathscr{R} \hat{c}_2(\pi, \rho),\ \forall(\pi, \rho).
$$

3.3   Intraprocedural Analysis and Correlation Summaries

We work with a control flow graph (CFG) representation of the predicates' bodies. Nodes represent program states and edges are defined by statements with a particular exit label λ. In our case, all the outgoing edges of a node n

bear the different cases of the same statement s found at the program point n. For each statement s there is an edge labeled s, λ_k for each of its possible exit labels λ_k. However, the analysis does not depend on this specificity.

Correlation information has to be kept at each point of the CFG, for each input and output pair of the node. An *intraprocedural* correlation summary:

$$\Delta \in \mathcal{D}, \quad \Delta : \mathcal{V} \times \mathcal{V} \to \hat{\mathcal{C}}.$$

is thus a mapping from pairs of variables $v \in \mathcal{V}$ to correlation maps.

For each node of a given control flow graph, $\Delta(e, o)$ retrieves the correlation map between the local variable e and the output variable o. If a mapping for e and o does not currently exist, $\Delta(e, o)$ retrieves the correlation $(\varepsilon, \varepsilon) \mapsto$ Equal when $e = o$ or the empty correlation map $\emptyset$, otherwise. Establishing the partial order $\sqsubseteq$ and the join operation $\bigvee : \mathcal{D} \times \mathcal{D} \to \mathcal{D}$ is straightforward: $\hat{\sqsubseteq}$ and $\hat{\bigvee}$ are extended pointwise to an intraprocedural summary, for each ordered input-output pair and its associated correlation map.

$$\sqsubseteq \subseteq \mathcal{D} \times \mathcal{D} \quad \Delta_1 \sqsubseteq \Delta_2 \iff \forall e, o \in \mathcal{V}, \; \Delta_1(e, o) \hat{\sqsubseteq} \Delta_2(e, o)$$

$$\Delta_1 \bigvee \Delta_2 = \Delta_3 \iff \forall(e, o), \; \Delta_3(e, o) = \Delta_1(e, o) \hat{\bigvee} \Delta_2(e, o)$$

Our correlation analysis is a *backward* data-flow analysis, computing an intraprocedural summary at each point of the control flow graph. This represents the correlations at the node's *entry point*. For each exit label, it traverses the control flow graph starting with its corresponding exit node. The intraprocedural summary for the currently analyzed label is initialized with pairs between the local value of each associated output variable of the label and the final value of the same output variable, mapped to $(\varepsilon, \varepsilon) \mapsto$ Equal. The analysis traverses the control flow graph and gradually refines the correlations, using Kildall's worklist algorithm [5], until a fixed point is reached. Table 5 summarizes the representation and general equation of the statements. For each statement, the presented data-flow equation operates on the intraprocedural summaries of the statement's *successor* nodes. The intraprocedural summary at the *entry point* of the node is obtained by *joining* the contributions of each *outgoing* edge. The contribution of an edge (n, n_i) labeled with s and λ_i is given by $\mathbb{C}^s_{\lambda_i}(\Delta_{n_i}) \in \mathbb{C}$ where $\mathbb{C}^s_{\lambda_i}(.)$ is the *transfer function* of the edge labeled s, λ_i.

The transfer function $\mathbb{C}^s_{\lambda}(.)$ formalizes the correlations created by the statement s on the label λ between its local input variables and its local output variables, denoted by δ^s_{λ}, as well as the set $kill_{\lambda}$ of variables whose values have been redefined by the statement s on the label λ. These are shown in Table 5. There is one crucial difference between transfer functions $\mathbb{C}^s_{\lambda}(.)$ and intraprocedural summaries Δ. An intraprocedural summary Δ implicitly maps any pair (v, v) for $v \in \mathcal{V}$ to $(\varepsilon, \varepsilon) \mapsto$ Equal. On the contrary, in δ^s_{λ}, when the variable v is used as both input and output by the statement s, the pair (v, v) is mapped to the correlation known between the input's v old value and the output's v fresh value. Otherwise, when v is an output, i.e. $v \in kill_{\lambda}$, but not an input of s, (v, v) is mapped to $\emptyset$.

Table 5. Statements – representations and data-flow equations

Representation	Equation

$$\Delta_n = \bigvee_{n \xrightarrow{s,\lambda_i} n_i} \mathbb{C}^s_{\lambda_i}(\Delta_{n_i})$$

Statement		$\mathbb{C}^s_\lambda(.)\colon \delta^s_\lambda$	$kill_\lambda$
Assignment	$o := e$	$\{(e,o) \mapsto [(\varepsilon,\varepsilon) \mapsto \mathsf{Equal}]\}$	$\{o\}_{true}$
Get Field	$o := r.f_i$	$\{(r,o) \mapsto [(.f_i,\varepsilon) \mapsto \mathsf{Equal}]\}$	$\{o\}_{true}$
Set Field	$r' := \{r \ \textbf{with} \ f_i = e\}$	$\{(r,r') \mapsto [(\varepsilon,\varepsilon) \mapsto$	$\{r'\}_{true}$
		$\{f_1 \mapsto \mathsf{Equal}; \dots; f_i \mapsto \mathsf{Any}; \dots; f_n \mapsto \mathsf{Equal}\}]$	
		$(e,r') \mapsto [(\varepsilon,.f_i) \mapsto \mathsf{Equal}]\}$	
Create Var.	$v := C_p[e]$	$\{(e,v) \mapsto [(\varepsilon,@C_p.e) \mapsto \mathsf{Equal}]\}$	$\{v\}_{true}$
Var. Switch	$\textbf{switch}(v) \ \textbf{as} \ [o_1|\dots|o_n]$	$\{(v,o_i) \mapsto [(@C_i.e,\varepsilon) \mapsto \mathsf{Equal}]\}$	$\{o_i\}_{\lambda_{C_i}}$
Array Get	$o := a[i]$	$\{(a,o) \mapsto [(\langle i \rangle,\varepsilon) \mapsto \mathsf{Equal}]\}$	$\{o\}_{true}$
Array Set	$a' := [a \ \textbf{with} \ i = e]$	$\{(a,a') \mapsto [(\varepsilon,\varepsilon) \mapsto \langle \mathsf{Equal} \rhd i \ : \ \mathsf{Any} \rangle]$	$\{a'\}_{true}$
		$(e,a') \mapsto [(\varepsilon,\langle i \rangle) \mapsto \mathsf{Equal}]\}$	

In order to obtain the contribution $\mathbb{C}^s_{\lambda_i}(\Delta_{n_i})$ of an edge labeled with s and λ_i, we need to connect the information given by the $\delta^s_{\lambda_i}$ to the information contained in the intraprocedural summary Δ_{n_i}. For example, at the entry of node 3 in Fig. 2, when considering the scenario in which the predicate exits with true, the intraprocedural summary contains the mapping:

$$(\mathtt{th},\mathtt{o}) \mapsto \left[(@\mathsf{Some}.\mathtt{t}, .\mathtt{threads}\langle \mathtt{i} \rangle @\mathsf{Some}.\mathtt{t}) \mapsto \left\{ \begin{array}{r} \mathtt{identifier} \mapsto \mathsf{Equal} \\ \mathtt{current\_state} \mapsto \mathsf{Any} \\ \mathtt{stack} \mapsto \mathsf{Equal} \end{array} \right\} \right].$$

On the true edge statement 2 creates the mapping: $(\mathtt{ta},\mathtt{th}) \mapsto [(\langle \mathtt{i} \rangle, \varepsilon) \mapsto \mathsf{Equal}]$. Intuitively, since we are traversing the graph backwards and mapping ordered (local) input-output pairs, $(\mathtt{ta}, \mathtt{th})$ and $(\mathtt{th}, \mathtt{o})$ can be seen as a *def-use* pair: the correlation associated to $(\mathtt{ta}, \mathtt{th})$ expresses the relation between the *defined* value of $\mathtt{th}$ and the input $\mathtt{ta}$ used for creating it, while the correlation associated to $(\mathtt{th}, \mathtt{o})$ shows a subsequent *use* of that value of $\mathtt{th}$ for creating $\mathtt{o}$. The contribution of statement 2 on the true edge should capture this flow of $\mathtt{ta}$'s value to $\mathtt{o}$'s value, through the variable $\mathtt{th}$. Thus, it should contain a mapping for the pair $(\mathtt{ta}, \mathtt{o})$. In the general case we need to detect any variable r such that $[(p,r) \mapsto \hat{c}] \in \delta^s_{\lambda_i}$, $[(r,q) \mapsto \hat{c}'] \in \Delta_{n_i}$ and compute the mapping for (p,q) in $\mathbb{C}^s_{\lambda_i}(\Delta_{n_i})$.

In order to compute the correlation map associated to $(\mathtt{ta}, \mathtt{o})$, we take into account the fact that both the right path ε of $\delta^s_\lambda(\mathtt{ta},\mathtt{th})$ and the left path $@\mathsf{Some}.\mathtt{t}$ of $\Delta_{n_3}(\mathtt{th}, \mathtt{o})$ refer to the $\mathtt{th}$ variable. However, they do not represent traversals of the same depth: ε refers to the entire value of $\mathtt{th}$, while $@\mathsf{Some}.\mathtt{t}$ refers to the value below the constructor Some. Between $\mathtt{ta}$ and $\mathtt{o}$ we can conclude that the values nested under the Some constructor of the $\mathtt{i}$-th elements are related:

$$(\texttt{ta},\texttt{o}) \mapsto \left[\langle\texttt{i}\rangle\texttt{@Some.t}, .\texttt{threads}\langle\texttt{i}\rangle\texttt{@Some.t}\rangle \mapsto \left\{ \begin{array}{r} \texttt{identifier} \mapsto \mathsf{Equal} \\ \texttt{current\_state} \mapsto \mathsf{Any} \\ \texttt{stack} \mapsto \mathsf{Equal} \end{array} \right\} \right].$$

We call the process of obtaining the correlation map associated to $(\texttt{ta},\texttt{o})$ from the correlations associated to $(\texttt{ta},\texttt{th})$ and $(\texttt{th},\texttt{o})$ *composition* and denote it by $\odot$. In the general case, we obtain the link between ρ and π' by *matching* with $\curlywedge$. In the context of the example given above, ρ and π' are the paths referring to the $\texttt{th}$ variable, i.e. ε and $\texttt{@Some.t}$, respectively. If these paths are compatible, we compose the correlation elements $(\pi,\rho) \mapsto \mathcal{R}$ and $(\pi',\rho') \mapsto \mathcal{R}'$, obtaining a new correlation element, $(\pi_\bullet,\rho_\bullet) \mapsto \mathcal{R}_{\bowtie}$, computed as follows:

$$(\pi_\bullet,\rho_\bullet) = (\pi,\rho) \bullet (\pi',\rho') \overset{def}{=} \begin{cases} (\pi,\rho') & \text{when } \curlywedge(\rho,\pi') = \mathsf{Identical} \\ (\pi::\sigma,\rho') & \text{when } \curlywedge(\rho,\pi') = \mathsf{Left}\ \sigma \\ (\pi,\rho'::\sigma) & \text{when } \curlywedge(\rho,\pi') = \mathsf{Right}\ \sigma \end{cases}$$

$$\mathcal{R}_{\bowtie} = \mathcal{R} \bowtie \mathcal{R}' \overset{def}{=} \begin{cases} \mathcal{R} \vee_{\mathscr{R}} \mathcal{R}' & \text{when } \curlywedge(\rho,\pi') = \mathsf{Identical} \\ \rightsquigarrow(\sigma,\mathcal{R}) \vee_{\mathscr{R}} \mathcal{R}' & \text{when } \curlywedge(\rho,\pi') = \mathsf{Left}\ \sigma \\ \mathcal{R} \vee_{\mathscr{R}} \rightsquigarrow(\sigma,\mathcal{R}') & \text{when } \curlywedge(\rho,\pi') = \mathsf{Right}\ \sigma \end{cases}$$

Note that given the special form of partial relations $\mathcal{R} \in \mathscr{R}$, the compose operation at this level is equivalent to $\vee_{\mathscr{R}}$. However, this would not be the case anymore for a more complex partial relation type.

The composition of correlation maps is denoted by $\bigcirc$. Computing $\hat{c}_1 \bigcirc \hat{c}_2$ amounts to intersecting the composition of all correlation elements from $\hat{c}_1$ and $\hat{c}_2$:

$$(\hat{c}_1 \bigcirc \hat{c}_2)(\pi_\bullet,\rho_\bullet) = \bigwedge_{\substack{\mathcal{R} \\ (\pi,\rho)\mapsto\mathcal{R}\in\hat{c}_1 \\ (\pi',\rho')\mapsto\mathcal{R}'\in\hat{c}_2 \\ (\pi_\bullet,\rho_\bullet)=(\pi,\rho)\bullet(\pi',\rho')}} \mathcal{R} \bowtie \mathcal{R}'.$$

Finally, the contribution $\mathbb{C}^s_{\lambda_i}(\Delta_{n_i})$ is obtained by:

$$\odot : \mathbb{C} \times \mathscr{D} \to \mathscr{D} \quad \delta^s_\lambda \odot \Delta = \Delta' \quad \text{where } \Delta'(p,q) = \bigwedge_r (\delta^s_\lambda(p,r) \bigcirc \Delta(r,q)).$$

Interprocedural Level. Our analysis is performed label by label and interprocedural correlation domains associate an intraprocedural summary to each exit label of the analyzed predicate. Therefore, interprocedural domains encapsulate an intraprocedural summary for each possible execution scenario of a predicate.

An interprocedural domain of a predicate p is thus defined as follows:

$$\Xi_p : \Lambda_p \to \Delta \quad \text{where } \Lambda_p \text{ is the set of output labels of predicate } p.$$

The intraprocedural summary associated to each label is *filtered* so as to contain only ordered pairs of variables where the left member is an input of the analyzed predicate and the right member is an output associated to the analyzed label. The correlation maps associated to such pairs are built so as to contain correlations where only input variables may appear in array cell paths. Similarly, the exception index in partial equivalence relations of arrays must be an input variable. Registering exceptions in array correlations only for input variables is not a consequence of a language restriction on array operations, but simply a consequence of the fact that at the interprocedural level, only correlation information between inputs and outputs makes sense.

The interprocedural domain of a predicate is used for deducing the transfer functions for a predicate call statement.

In the following we detail the equation corresponding to a call to a predicate:

$$p(e_1, \ldots, e_n)[\lambda_1 : \bar{o}_1 \mid \ldots \mid \lambda_m : \bar{o}_m]$$

having the following signature:

$$p(\epsilon_1, \ldots, \epsilon_n)[\lambda_1 : \bar{\omega}_1 \mid \ldots \mid \lambda_m : \bar{\omega}_m].$$

The general equation form applies:

$$\Delta_n = \bigvee_{n \xrightarrow{s, \lambda_i} n_i} \mathbb{C}_{\lambda_i}^{p(e_1, \ldots, e_n) [\lambda_1 : \bar{o}_1 \mid \ldots \mid \lambda_m : \bar{o}_m]}(\Delta_{n_i}).$$

The transfer functions for the predicate call statement are deduced from the predicate's interprocedural domain in the following fashion:

$$\mathbb{C}_{\lambda_i}^s(\Delta_{n_i}) = \delta_{\lambda_i}^s \odot \Delta_{n_i}, \quad kill_{\lambda_i} = \{\bar{o}_i\}$$
$$\delta_{\lambda_i}^s(e_j, o_i^k) = \hat{c}_i^{j,k}, \forall j \in \{1, \ldots, n\}, \forall k \in \{1, \ldots, h\}$$

where

$$\hat{c}_i^{j,k} = \Xi_p(\lambda_i)(\epsilon_j, \omega_i^k) \blacktriangleleft (\bar{\epsilon} \mapsto \bar{e})$$
$$s = p(e_1, \ldots, e_n) \, [\lambda_1 : \bar{o}_1 \mid \ldots \mid \lambda_m : \bar{o}_m]; \quad \bar{o}_i = \{o_i^1, \ldots, o_i^h\}.$$

Namely, the contribution of a predicate call to each (e_j, o_i^k) input-output pair stems from the contribution of the interprocedural domain for label λ_i and formal input-output pair (ϵ_j, ω_i^k). In these, all the formal input parameters $\bar{\epsilon}$ in array partial equivalences and in array cell paths are substituted by the corresponding effective input parameters from $\bar{e}$ or approximated away.

The substitution operation is denoted by $\blacktriangleleft (\sigma)$ where σ is a substitution from formal to effective parameters.

4   Preliminary Results and Experiments

Our analysis has currently been applied to a functional specification of *Proven-Core* [7], a general-purpose microkernel inspired by Minix 3.1 that ensures *isolation*. Its proof is based on multiple refinements between successive models, from the most abstract, on which the *isolation* property is defined and proved, to the most concrete, i.e. the actual model used for code generation.

Some of the abstract layers of *ProvenCore* are the *Refined Security Model* (RSM), the *Functional Specification* (FSP) and the *Target of Evaluation Design* (TDS). RSM is an abstract layer located just below the top-most layer of the refinement chain; the FSP is a model closely resembling the most concrete layer – TDS – but using data structures and algorithms that facilitate reasoning. Each layer is characterized by a global state with numerous fields, and different transitions, i.e. supported commands such as *fork, exec, exit*. Each of these receives as an input the global state before executing the command and returns the state of the system after execution. Most supported commands affect only a limited subset of the input state. For example, in FSP there are 25 possible transitions. Its state contains 15 fields; it is characterized by 70 invariants. In the TDS these figures are doubled. Each invariant is concerned with a different subset of the global's state fields. Some of these invariants concern all the processes held in the process store. Processes are complex structures in their own right, having more than 20 fields themselves. However, most transitions affect only a few of these fields.

We have applied our analysis on the RSM, FSP and TDS layers. These are medium-sized experiments. An overview of their characteristics and the time needed to obtain the correlation results are given in Table 6. The first column shows the total number of predicates of the analysed layers. In parentheses, we indicate the number of predicates that only read information, i.e. logical properties, as well as the number of opaque predicates for which a pessimistic assumption is made. The second column shows the total number of lines of code (LoC) for each. The next two columns indicate the number of LoC corresponding to type definitions and comments, respectively. The average time needed to compute the correlation and dependency results are shown in the last two columns. Unlike the correlation analysis that only computes information for predicates that actually modify data structures, the dependency analysis computes information for code as well as specifications, i.e. logical properties, in a unified manner. This explains the time difference between the two analyses.

Table 6. Abstract layers - evaluation data and analysis timing

	Predicates	Total LoC	Types	Comments	Correlation	Dependency
RSM/FSP	633 (235/65)	9853	596	855	0.90 s	1.84 s
TDS	418 (58/105)	6804	460	623	0.62 s	1.09 s

One of the analyzed predicates is do_auth. It is a system call clearing or granting an authorization to some process to read from or write to some memory range of the current process. It receives a global state in and an index i as inputs and produces, on the true label, the new global state out, after modifying the permission for the i-th process in the process store. The code of do_auth performs various system-wide checks before registering the permission change, and is therefore not trivial, although its effect is quite limited. Indeed, the correlation results computed by our analysis for the **true** label of this predicate are shown below. The analysis detects that out of the 15 fields of **out**, only the **i**-th element of the **procs** field is changed. Furthermore, it detects that if this element is an active process, only the **mem_auth** field is modified out of the total of 26 fields. Everything else is copied from the input state **in**.

$$\text{true} : (\text{in}, \text{out}) \mapsto \big[$$

$$(\varepsilon, \varepsilon) \mapsto \{ \ \ldots \quad\quad \mapsto \text{Equal}\} \ 14 \text{ fields}$$
$$\text{procs} \ \mapsto \text{Any} \ \}$$
$$(\text{.procs}, \text{.procs}) \mapsto \langle \ \text{Equal} \triangleright \text{i} : \ [\text{None} \ \mapsto \text{Equal}$$
$$\text{Some} \mapsto \{\text{v} \mapsto \{ \ \ldots \quad\quad \mapsto \text{Equal} \ \} \ 25 \text{ fields}$$
$$\text{mem\_auth} \mapsto \text{Any}\}\}]\rangle\big]$$

Combined with dependency results for logical properties, these results would allow us to infer the preservation of all invariants that are not concerned with the memory permissions. All but one out of the 70 properties fall into this category. This is the *relevant memory permissions* property, which states that a process has permissions covering a valid range of memory addresses and referring only to existing processes. It has to hold for every process in the process store. After executing **do_auth**, this property is threatened and needs to be verified only for the **i**-th process of the store. It is preserved for all others.

Space constraints prevent us from discussing more examples here. However, various other examples are provided and explained on the web page[2] dedicated to our analysis. Users can devise and test their own examples as well.

5   Related Work

In [3], Chang and Leino present the congruence-closure abstract domain, designed for an object-oriented context and implemented in the Spec# program verifier. They infer and express relations between fields of variables, a goal similar to ours. The congruence-closure domain maintains equivalence graphs mapping field accesses to symbolic locations. On its own, this domain allows the inference and expression of relations for accessed fields. In order to take into account updates as well, this needs to use the heap succession domain as a base. Unlike us, they can express preorders between fields, depending on the base domains used. However, our domain handles both accesses and updates to structures, arrays and variants in a uniform manner, independent of additional information.

Rakamarić and Hu report in [12] a method to infer frame axioms of procedures and loops based on static analysis. As a starting point, they use the DSA shape analysis, presented by Lattner et al. [6]. DSA provides a summary of points-to relations as a graph, that is used to compute a set of memory locations that are modified by a procedure or its callers. By a pass through the graph,

---

[2] http://ajl-demo.fr/2016.

for each node reachable from the globals or procedure parameters, they generate expressions representing a path to that node. The generated frame axioms are used internally by an extended static checker of C programs, i.e. in a purely automatic setting. In contrast, our analysis is designed for an interactive verification context. Our technique focusing on a purely functional language is not concerned by aliasing and does not depend on an external points-to framework.

In [15], Taghdiri et al. present a technique for extracting procedure summaries for object-oriented procedures, used to prove verification conditions. Procedures are executed symbolically and the environment of the post-state is computed so as to express every variable and field in terms of the values of the variables and fields of the pre-state. Their goal is broader than ours. However, unlike their summaries, our correlation results encompass only information that is visible from the outside (to the callers).

The literature on shape analysis [2,4,11,13] and side effects analyses [10,14] is vast. The former is aimed at deep-heap mutations, while we are focusing on deep-state modifications, in the context of complex transition systems. The latter determine memory locations that may be modified by an operation. Reasoning about heap locations is beyond our scope. We treat mappings between variables and their values, analyze their evolution in a side-effect free environment and detect not only what is modified, but also how and to what extent.

6   Conclusion and Future Work

Identifying precise information concerning the effects of program operations is possible by means of static analysis without sacrificing scalability. We have presented a flow-sensitive, interprocedural correlation analysis that has been applied to a functional specification of an operating system. The analysis tracks the origin of subparts of the output and relates it to subparts of the inputs thus detecting not only what is modified, but also how and to what extent. It is designed as a companion tool to be used during interactive program verification.

We have plans for future work along two main directions. The first is to go beyond the detection of equivalences and to handle *preorders*. This would allow us to detect the evolution of constructors for variants. Tracking this would allow the inference of properties that are not affected by a transition from a stronger state to a weaker state. Also, experiments show that the simultaneous use of dependency and correlation information can lead to a substantial reduction of proof obligations. Our priority is to employ the two, to develop a proof tactic for the inference of preserved invariants and to integrate it in our prover.

Acknowledgments. We would like to thank the anonymous referees for helpful comments and suggestions. For their excellent comments and sharp observations, we are particularly grateful to Olivier Delande and Georges Dupéron. Our article also benefited from the remarks of B. Montagu and H. Chataing.

References

1. Andreescu, O.F., Jensen, T., Lescuyer, S.: Dependency analysis of functional specifications with algebraic data structures. In: Formal Methods and Software Engineering - 17th International Conference on Formal Engineering Methods, ICFEM 2015, Proceedings, pp. 116–133 (2015). doi:10.1007/978-3-319-25423-4_8
2. Calcagno, C., Distefano, D., O'Hearn, P.W., Yang, H.: Compositional shape analysis by means of Bi-abduction. In: Proceedings of the 36th ACM SIGPLAN-SIGACT Symposium on Principles of Programming Languages, POPL 2009, pp. 289–300 (2009). http://doi.acm.org/10.1145/1480881.1480917
3. Chang, B.E., Leino, K.R.M.: Abstract interpretation with alien expressions and heap structures. In: Verification, Model Checking, and Abstract Interpretation, 6th International Conference, VMCAI 2005, Proceedings, pp. 147–163 (2005). http://dx.doi.org/10.1007/978-3-540-30579-8_11
4. Jones, N.D., Muchnick, S.S.: Flow analysis and optimization of lisp-like structures. In: Conference Record of the Sixth Annual ACM Symposium on Principles of Programming Languages, 1979, pp. 244–256 (1979). http://doi.acm.org/10.1145/567752.567776
5. Kildall, G.A.: A unified approach to global program optimization. In: Conference Record of the ACM Symposium on Principles of Programming Languages, 1973, pp. 194–206 (1973). http://doi.acm.org/10.1145/512927.512945
6. Lattner, C., Lenharth, A., Adve, V.S.: Making context-sensitive points-to analysis with heap cloning practical for the real world. In: Proceedings of the ACM SIGPLAN 2007 Conference on Programming Language Design and Implementation, 2007, pp. 278–289 (2007). http://doi.acm.org/10.1145/1250734.1250766
7. Lescuyer, S.: ProvenCore: towards a verified isolation micro-kernel (2015). http://milsworkshop2015.euromils.eu/downloads/hipeac_literature/04-mils15_submission_6.pdf
8. Mccarthy, J., Hayes, P.J.: Some philosophical problems from the standpoint of artificial intelligence. In: Machine Intelligence. Edinburgh University Press (1969)
9. Meyer, B.: Framing the frame problem. In: Dependable Software Systems Engineering, pp. 193–203 (2015). http://dx.doi.org/10.3233/978-1-61499-495-4-193
10. Milanova, A., Rountev, A., Ryder, B.G.: Parameterized object sensitivity for points-to analysis for Java. ACM Trans. Softw. Eng. Methodol. **14**(1), 1–41. http://doi.acm.org/10.1145/1044834.1044835 (2005)
11. Montenegro, M., Peña, R., Segura, C.: Shape analysis in a functional language by using regular languages. Sci. Comput. Program. **111**, 51–78 (2015). http://dx.doi.org/10.1016/j.scico.2014.12.006
12. Rakamaric, Z., Hu, A.J.: Automatic inference of frame axioms using static analysis. In: 23rd IEEE/ACM International Conference on Automated Software Engineering (ASE 2008), pp. 89–98 (2008). http://dx.doi.org/10.1109/ASE.2008.19
13. Sagiv, S., Reps, T.W., Wilhelm, R.: Parametric shape analysis via 3-valued logic. In: POPL 1999, Proceedings of the 26th ACM SIGPLAN-SIGACT Symposium on Principles of Programming Languages, 1999, pp. 105–118 (1999). http://doi.acm.org/10.1145/292540.292552
14. Sălcianu, A., Rinard, M.: Purity and side effect analysis for Java programs. In: Cousot, R. (ed.) VMCAI 2005. LNCS, vol. 3385, pp. 199–215. Springer, Heidelberg (2005)
15. Taghdiri, M., Seater, R., Jackson, D.: Lightweight extraction of syntactic specifications. In: Proceedings of the 14th ACM SIGSOFT International Symposium on Foundations of Software Engineering, FSE 2006, pp. 276–286 (2006). http://doi.acm.org/10.1145/1181775.1181809

Combining Predicate Abstraction
with Fixpoint Approximations

Tuba Yavuz$^{(\boxtimes)}$

University of Florida, Gainesville, USA
tuba@ece.ufl.edu

Abstract. In this paper we consider combining two techniques that have
been effective in analyzing infinite-state systems: predicate abstraction
and fixpoint approximations. Using a carefully crafted model of Airport
Ground Network Control, we show that when predicate abstraction in a
CEGAR loop fails to verify temporal logic properties of an infinite-state
transition system, a combination of predicate abstraction with fixpoint
approximations may provide improved performance for both safety and
liveness property verification.

Keywords: Predicate abstraction · Widening · Model checking

1 Introduction

State-explosion is an inherent problem in model checking. Every model checking
tool - no matter how optimized - will report or demonstrate one of the following
for systems that push its limits: out of memory error, non-convergence, or inconclusive result. As the target systems of interest (hardware, software, or biological
systems) grow in terms of complexity, and consequently in size, a great deal of
manual effort is spent on verification engineering to produce usable results. We
admit that this effort will always be needed. However, we also think that hybrid
approaches should be employed to push the limits for automated verification.

Abstract interpretation framework [6] provides a theoretical basis for sound
verification of finite as well as infinite-state systems. Two major elements of this
framework are abstraction and approximation. Abstraction defines a mapping
between a concrete domain and an abstract domain (less precise) in a conservative way so that when a property is satisfied for an abstract state the property
also holds for the concrete states that map to the abstract state. Approximation,
on the other hand, works on values in the same domain and provides a lower or
an upper bound. Abstraction is a way to deal with the state-explosion problem
whereas approximation is a way to achieve convergence and hence potentially
a conclusive result. When an infinite-state system is considered there are three
basic approaches that can be employed: pure abstraction, pure approximation[1],
and a combination of abstraction and approximation.

---

[1] Assuming the logic that describes the system is decidable.

© Springer International Publishing Switzerland 2016
R. De Nicola and E. Kühn (Eds.): SEFM 2016, LNCS 9763, pp. 104–120, 2016.
DOI: 10.1007/978-3-319-41591-8_8

The most popular abstraction technique is predicate abstraction [9], in which the abstract domain consists of a combination of valuations of Boolean variables that represent truth values of a fixed set of predicates on the variables from the concrete system. Since it is difficult to come up with the right set of predicates that would yield a precise analysis, predicate abstraction has been combined with the counter-example guided abstraction refinement (CEGAR) framework. Predicate abstraction requires computing a quantifier-free version of the transformed system and, hence, potentially involves an exponential number of queries to the underlying SMT solver.

A widely used approximation technique is *widening*. The widening operator takes two states belonging to the same domain and computes an overapproximation of the two. A key point of the widening operator is the guarantee for stabilizing an increasing chain after a finite number of steps. So one can apply the widening operator to the iterates of a non-converging fixpoint computation and achieve convergence, where the last iterate is an over-approximation of the actual fixpoint. In this paper we use an implementation of the widening operator for convex polyhedra [8] that is used in the infinite-state model checker Action Language Verifier (ALV) [18]. ALV uses fixpoint approximations to check whether a CTL property is satisfied by an infinite-state system [2].

In [7] it is demonstrated that both model checking and automated testing can benefit from a combination of carefully designed abstractions and approximations that improve precision of the analysis. In this paper, we take a modest step by combining predicate abstraction with widening for infinite-state systems described in terms of Presburger arithmetic. Our approach requires the user to provide the set of predicates to be considered. *In our approach only the variables that are involved in the predicates are abstracted and all other variables are preserved in their concrete domains.* We implemented the combined approach by extending the Action Language Verifier (ALV) [18] with automated predicate abstraction capability. We show the need for such a combined approach through a specially crafted infinite-state model that requires fixpoint approximation. Our experimental results show that combining the two techniques can provide improved performance for safety as well as liveness property specification.

The rest of the paper is organized as follows. We first present the basic definitions and key results of the two approaches, approximate fixpoint computations and predicate abstraction in the context of CTL model checking, in Sect. 2. Section 3 presents the hybrid approach and demonstrates soundness of combining the two techniques. Section 4 presents the experimental results. Section 5 discusses related work and Sect. 6 concludes with directions for future work.

2   Preliminaries

In this paper, we consider transition systems that are described in terms of boolean and unbounded integer variables.

Definition 1. *An infinite-state transition system is described by a Kripke structure $T = (S, I, R, V)$, where S, I, R, and V denote the state space, set of initial states, the transition relation, and the set of state variables, respectively. $V = V_{bool} \cup V_{int}$ such that $S \subseteq \mathcal{B}^{|V_{bool}|} \times \mathcal{Z}^{|V_{int}|}$, $I \subseteq S$, and $R \subseteq S \times S$.*

Definition 2. *Given a Kripke structure, $T = (S, I, R, V)$ and a set of states $A \subseteq S$, the post-image operator, $post[R](A)$, computes the set of states that can be reached from the states in A in one step:*

$$post[R](A) = \{b \mid a \in A \ \wedge \ (a, b) \in R\}.$$

Similarly, the pre-image operator, $pre[R](A)$, computes the set of states that can reach the states in A in one step:

$$pre[R](A) = \{b \mid a \in A \ \wedge \ (b, a) \in R\}.$$

Model Checking via Fixpoint Approximations. Symbolic Computation-Tree Logic (CTL) model checking algorithms decide whether a given Kripke structure, $T = (S, I, R, V)$, satisfies a given CTL correctness property, f, by checking whether $I \subseteq [\![f]\!]_T$, where $[\![f]\!]_T$ denotes the set of states that satisfy f in T. Most CTL operators have either least fixpoint (EU, AU) or greatest fixpoint (EG, AG) characterizations in terms of the pre-image operator.

Variables	s, t, a_1, a_2, z: integer
	$pc1$, $pc2$: think, try, cs
Initial State:	$s = t \wedge pc_1 = think \wedge pc_2 = think$
Transitions:	
r_i^{try}	$\equiv pc_i = think \wedge a_i' = t \wedge t' = t + 1 \wedge pc_i' = try$
r_i^{cs}	$\equiv pc_i = try \wedge s \geq a_i \wedge z' = z + 1 \wedge pc_i' = cs$
r_i^{think}	$\equiv pc_i = cs \wedge s' = s + 1 \wedge z' = z - 1 \wedge pc_i' = think$
Transition Relation:	$\bigvee_{i=1,2} r_i^{try} \vee r_i^{cs} \vee r_i^{think}$

Fig. 1. The ticket mutual exclusion algorithm for two processes. Variable z is an addition to demonstrate the merits of the proposed approach.

Symbolic CTL model checking for infinite-state systems may not converge. Consider the so-called ticket mutual exclusion model for two processes [1] given in Fig. 1. Each process gets a ticket number before attempting to enter the critical section. There are two global integer variables, t and s, that show the next ticket value that will be available to obtain and the upper bound for tickets that are eligible to enter the critical section, respectively. Local variable a_i represents the ticket value held by process i. We added variable z to model an update in the critical region. It turns out that checking $AG(z \leq 1)$ for this model does not terminate.

One way is to compute an over or an under approximation to the fixpoint computations as proposed in [2] and check $I \subseteq \llbracket f \rrbracket_T^-$, i.e., check whether all initial states in T satisfy an under-approximation (denoted by superscript $-$) of the correctness property or check $I \cap \llbracket \neg f \rrbracket_T^+ \neq \emptyset$, i.e., check whether no initial state satisfies an over-approximation of the negated correctness property. If so, the model checker certifies that the property is satisfied. Otherwise, no conclusions can be made without further analysis.

The key in approximating a fixpoint computation is the availability of over-approximating and under-approximating operators. So we give the basic definitions and a brief explanation here and refer the reader to [2,8] for technical details on the implementation of these operators for Presburger arithmetic.

Definition 3. *Given a complete lattice* $(L, \sqsubseteq, \sqcap, \sqcup, \bot, \top)$, $\triangle : L \times L \rightarrow L$, *is a widening operator iff*

- $\forall x, y \in L.\ x \sqcup y \sqsubseteq x \triangle y$,
- *For all increasing chains* $x_0 \sqsubseteq x_1 \sqsubseteq ...x_n$ *in* L, *the increasing chain* $y_0 = x_0, ..., y_{n+1} = y_n \triangle x_{n+1}, ...$ *is not strictly increasing, i.e., stabilizes after a number of terms.*

Definition 4. *Given a complete lattice* $(L, \sqsubseteq, \sqcap, \sqcup, \bot, \top)$, $\nabla : L \times L \rightarrow L$, *is a dual of the widening operator iff*

- $\forall x, y \in L.x \nabla y \sqsubseteq x \sqcap y$,
- *For all decreasing chains* $x_0 \sqsupseteq x_1 \sqsupseteq ...x_n$ *in* L, *the decreasing chain* $y_0 = x_0, ..., y_{n+1} = y_n \nabla x_{n+1}, ...$ *is not strictly decreasing, i.e., stabilizes after a number of terms.*

The approximation of individual temporal operators in a CTL formula is decided recursively based on the type of approximation to be achieved and whether the operator is preceded by a negation. The over-approximation can be computed using the widening operator for least fixpoint characterizations and terminating the fixpoint iteration after a finite number of steps for greatest fixpoint characterizations. The under-approximation can be computed using the dual of the widening operator for the greatest fixpoint characterizations and terminating the fixpoint iteration after a finite number of steps for the least fixpoint characterizations. Another heuristic that is used in approximate symbolic model checking is to compute an over-approximation (denoted by superscript $+$) of the set of reachable states $((\mu Z.I \vee post[R](Z))^+)$, a least fixpoint characterization, and to restrict all the fixpoint computations within this set.

Lemma 1. *Given an infinite-state transition system* $T = (S, I, R, V)$ *and* $T^+ = ((\mu Z.I \vee post[R](Z))^+, I, R, V)$, *and a temporal property* f, *the conclusive results obtained using fixpoint approximations for the temporal operators and the approximate set of reachable states are sound, i.e.,* $(I \subseteq \llbracket f \rrbracket_{T^+}^- \vee I \cap \llbracket \neg f \rrbracket_{T^+}^+ = \emptyset) \rightarrow T \models f$ *(see [2] for the proof).*

So for the example model in Fig. 1, an over-approximation to $EF(z > 1)$, the negation of the correctness property, is computed using the widening operator. Based on the implementation of the widening operator in [18], it turns out that the initial states do not intersect with $[\![EF(z > 1)]\!]^{+}_{ticket2}$ and hence the model satisfies $AG(z \le 1)$.

Abstract Model Checking and Predicate Abstraction.

Definition 5. *Let φ denote a set of predicates over integer variables. Let φ_i denote a predicate in φ and b_i denote the boolean variable that corresponds to φ_i. $\bar{\varphi}$ represents an ordered sequence (from index 1 to $|\varphi|$) of predicates in φ. The set of variables that appear in φ is denoted by $V(\varphi)$. Let φ' denote the set of next state predicates obtained from φ by replacing variables in each predicate φ_i with their primed versions. Let b denote the set of b_i that corresponds to each φ_i. Let $V_\natural = V_\natural \cup b \setminus V(\varphi)$, where $V_\natural$ denotes the set of variables in the concrete model.*

Abstracting states. A concrete state $s^\natural$ is predicate abstracted using a mapping function α via a set of predicates φ by introducing a predicate boolean variable b_i that represents predicate φ_i and existentially quantifying the concrete variables $V(\varphi)$ that appear in the predicates:

$$\alpha(s^\natural) = \exists V(\varphi).(s^\natural \wedge \bigwedge_{i=1}^{|\varphi|} \varphi_i \iff b_i). \tag{1}$$

Concretization of abstract states. An abstract state $s^\sharp$ is mapped back to all the concrete states it represents by replacing each predicate boolean variable b_i with the corresponding predicate φ_i:

$$\gamma(s^\sharp) = s^\sharp[\bar{\varphi}/\bar{b}] \tag{2}$$

Abstraction function α provides a safe approximation for states:

Lemma 2. *(α, γ), as defined in Eqs. 1 and 2, defines a Galois connection, i.e., α and γ are monotonic functions and $s^\natural \subseteq \gamma(\alpha(s^\natural))$ and $\alpha(\gamma(s^\sharp)) = s^\sharp$ (see the Appendix for the proof).*

A concrete transition system can be conservatively approximated by an abstract transition system through a simulation relation or a surjective mapping function involving the respective state spaces:

Definition 6. *(Existential Abstraction) Given transition systems $T_1 = (S_1, I_1, R_1, V_1)$ and $T_2 = (S_2, I_2, R_2, V_2)$, T_2 approximates T_1 (denoted $T_1 \sqsubseteq_h T_2$) iff*

- *$\exists s_1.(h(s_1) = s_2 \wedge s_1 \in I_1)$ implies $s_2 \in I_2$,*
- *$\exists s_1, s'_1.(h(s_1) = s_2 \wedge h(s'_1) = s'_2 \wedge (s_1, s'_1) \in R_1)$ implies $(s_2, s'_2) \in R_2$,*

where h is a surjective function from S_1 to S_2.

It is a known [13] fact that one can use a Galois connection (α, γ) to construct an approximate transition system. Basically, α is used as the mapping function and γ is used to map properties of the approximate or abstracted system to the concrete system:

Definition 7. *Given transition systems $T_1 = (S_1, I_1, R_1, V_1)$ and $T_2 = (S_2, I_2, R_2, V_2)$, assume that $T_1 \sqsubseteq_\alpha T_2$, the ACTL formula ϕ describes properties of T_2, and (α, γ) forms a Galois connection. $C(\phi)$ represents a transformation on ϕ that descends on the subformulas recursively and transforms every atomic atomic formula a with $\gamma(a)$ (see [4] for details).*

For example, let ϕ be $AG(b_1 \vee b_2)$, where b_1 and b_2 represent $z = 1$ and $z < 1$, respectively, when the model in Fig. 1 is predicate abstracted wrt to the set of predicates $\varphi = \{z = 1, z < 1\}$ and the Galois connection (α, γ) defined as in Eqs. 1 and 2. Then, $C(\phi) = AG(z \leq 1)$.

The preservation of ACTL properties when going from the approximate system to the concrete system is proved for existential abstraction in [4]. Here, we adapt it to an instantiation of existential abstraction using predicate abstraction as in [5]:

Lemma 3. *Assume $T_1 \sqsubseteq_\alpha T_2$, ϕ denotes an ACTL formula that describes a property of T_2, $C(\phi)$ denotes the transformation of the correctness property as in Definition 7, and (α, γ) forms a Galois connection and defines predicate abstraction and concretization as given in Eqs. 1 and 2, respectively. Then, $T_2 \models \phi$ implies $T_1 \models C(\phi)$.*

Proof. Preservation of atomic properties: *If a state s_2 in T_2 satisfies an atomic abstract property ϕ, due to the correctness preserving property of a Galois connection, s_2 also satisfies $\gamma(\phi)$ [14]. Due to soundness of the mapping between the states in T_1 to states in T_2 and monotonic property of α and γ, any state s_1 in T_1 that gets mapped to s_2, that is every state in $\gamma(s_2)$ also satisfies $\gamma(\phi)$.*
Preservation of ACTL Properties: *Follows from Corollary 1 in [4] and using α as the mapping function h in [4].*

3   A Hybrid Approach

In Sect. 3.1, we introduce a symbolic abstraction operator for transitions and an over-approximating abstract post operator derived from it. The abstract post operator enables partial predicate abstraction of an infinite-state system. Section 3.2 elaborates on the proposed hybrid approach that combines predicate abstraction and fixpoint approximations to perform CTL model checking of infinite-state systems. It also demonstrates soundness of the hybrid approach, which follows from the soundness results of the individual approaches and the over-approximating nature of the proposed abstract post operator.

3.1   Computing a Partially Predicate Abstracted Transition System

We compute an abstraction of a given transition system via a set of predicates such that only the variables that appear in the predicates disappear, i.e., existentially quantified, and all the other variables are preserved in their concrete domains and in the exact semantics from the original system. As an example, using the set of predicates $\{z = 1, z < 1\}$, we can partially abstract the model in Fig. 1 in a way that z is removed from the model, two new boolean variables b_1 (for $z = 1$) and b_2 (for $z < 1$) are introduced, and s, t, a_1, a_2, pc_1, and pc_2 remain the same as in the original model.

Abstracting transitions. A concrete transition $r^\natural$ is predicate abstracted using a mapping function α^τ via a set of current state predicates φ and a set of next state predicates φ' by introducing a predicate boolean variable b_i that represents predicate φ_i in the current state and a predicate boolean variable b'_i that represents predicate φ_i in the next state and existentially quantifying the current and next state concrete variables $V(\varphi) \cup V(\varphi')$ that appear in the current state and next state predicates:

$$\alpha^\tau(r^\natural) = \exists V(\varphi).\exists V(\varphi').(r^\natural \wedge CS \wedge \bigwedge_{i=1}^{|\varphi|} \varphi_i \Longleftrightarrow b_i \wedge \bigwedge_{i=1}^{|\varphi|} \varphi'_i \Longleftrightarrow b'_i), \quad (3)$$

where CS represents a consistency constraint that if all the abstracted variables that appear in a predicate remains the same in the next state then the corresponding boolean variable is kept the same in the next state:

$$CS = \bigwedge_{\varphi_i \in \varphi} ((\bigwedge_{v \in V(\varphi_i)} v' = v) \implies b'_i \Longleftrightarrow b_i).$$

Concretization of abstract transitions. An abstract transition $r^\sharp$ is mapped back to all the concrete transitions it represents by replacing each current state boolean variable b_i with the corresponding current state predicate φ_i and each next state boolean variable b'_i with the corresponding next state predicate φ'_i:

$$\gamma^\tau(r^\sharp) = r^\sharp[\bar{\varphi}, \bar{\varphi}'/\bar{b}, \bar{b}']$$

For instance, for the model in Fig. 1 and predicate set $\phi = \{z = 1, z < 1\}$, partial predicate abstraction of r_i^{cs}, $\alpha^\tau(r_i^{cs})$, is computed as

$$pc_i = try \wedge s \geq a_i \wedge ((b_1 \wedge \neg b_2 \wedge \neg b'_1 \wedge \neg b'_2) \vee (\neg b_1 \wedge b_2 \wedge (b'_1 \vee b'_2))$$
$$\vee (\neg b_1 \wedge \neg b_2 \wedge \neg b'_1 \wedge \neg b'_2)) \wedge pc'_i = cs. \quad (4)$$

It is important to note that the concrete semantics pertaining to the integer variables s and a_i and the enumerated variable pc_i are preserved in the partially abstract system.

Abstraction function α^τ represents a safe approximation for transitions:

Lemma 4. $(\alpha^\tau, \gamma^\tau)$ *defines a Galois connection (see the Appendix for the proof).*

One can compute an over-approximation to the set of reachable states via an over-approximating abstract post operator that computes the abstract successor states:

Lemma 5. α^τ *provides an over-approximate post operator:*

$$post[r^\natural](\gamma(s^\sharp)) \subseteq \gamma(post[\alpha^\tau(r^\natural)](s^\sharp))$$

Proof.

$$post[\tau^\natural](\gamma(s^\sharp)) \subseteq post[\gamma^\tau(\alpha^\tau(\tau^\natural))](\gamma(s^\sharp))(due \ to \ Lemma \ 4) \qquad (5)$$

We need to show the following:

$$post[\gamma^\tau(\alpha^\tau(\tau^\natural))](\gamma(s^\sharp)) \subseteq \gamma(post[\alpha^\tau(\tau^\natural)](s^\sharp))$$
$$post[\gamma^\tau(\tau^\natural)](\gamma(s^\sharp)) \subseteq \gamma(post[\tau^\sharp](s^\sharp))$$
$$(\exists V_\natural. \ \tau^\sharp[\bar\varphi, \bar\varphi'/\bar b, \bar b'] \ \wedge \ s^\sharp[\bar\varphi/\bar b])[V_\natural/V_\natural'] \subseteq (\exists V_\sharp. \ \tau^\sharp \ \wedge \ s^\sharp)[V_\sharp/V_\sharp'][\bar\varphi/\bar b] \qquad (6)$$
$$(\exists V_\natural. \ \tau^\sharp[\bar\varphi, \bar\varphi'/\bar b, \bar b'] \ \wedge \ s^\sharp[\bar\varphi/\bar b])[V_\natural/V_\natural'] \subseteq (\exists V_\sharp. \ \tau^\sharp \ \wedge \ s^\sharp)[\bar\varphi'/\bar b'][V_\natural/V_\natural']$$
$$(\exists V_\natural.(\ \tau^\sharp \ \wedge \ s^\sharp)[\bar\varphi, \bar\varphi'/\bar b, \bar b'])[V_\natural/V_\natural'] \subseteq (\exists V_\sharp. \ \tau^\sharp \ \wedge \ s^\sharp)[\bar\varphi'/\bar b'][V_\natural/V_\natural']$$

$$post[\tau^\natural](\gamma(s^\sharp)) \subseteq \gamma(post[\alpha^\tau(\tau^\natural)](s^\sharp))(due \ to \ Eqs. \ 5 \ \& \ 6) \qquad (7)$$

3.2 Combining Predicate Abstraction with Fixpoint Approximations

At the heart of the hybrid approach is a partially predicate abstracted transition system and we are ready to provide a formal definition:

Definition 8. *Given a concrete infinite-state transition system* $T^\natural = (S^\natural, I^\natural, R^\natural, V^\natural)$ *and a set of predicates* φ, *where* $V(\varphi) \subseteq V_{int}^\natural$, *the partially predicate abstracted transition system* $T^\sharp = (S^\sharp, I^\sharp, R^\sharp, V^\sharp)$ *is defined as follows:*

- $S^\sharp \subseteq \mathcal{B}^{|V_{bool}^\natural| + |\varphi|} \times \mathcal{Z}^{|V_{int}^\natural \setminus V(\varphi)|}$
- $S^\sharp = \bigcup_{s^\natural \in S^\natural} \alpha(s^\natural)$.
- $I^\sharp = \bigcup_{is^\natural \in I^\natural} \alpha(is^\natural)$.
- $R^\sharp = \bigcup_{r^\natural \in R^\natural} \alpha^\tau(r^\natural)$.

A partially predicate abstracted transition system $T^\sharp$ defined via α and α^τ functions is a conservative approximation of the concrete transition system.

Lemma 6. *Let the abstract transition system* $T^\sharp = (S^\sharp, I^\sharp, R^\sharp, V^\sharp)$ *be defined as in Definition 8 with respect to the concrete transition system* $T^\natural = (S^\natural, I^\natural, R^\natural, V^\natural)$ *and the set of predicates* φ. $T^\sharp$ *approximates* $T^\natural$: $T^\natural \sqsubseteq_\alpha T^\sharp$.

Proof. It is straightforward to see, i.e., by construction, that $\exists s_1.(\alpha(s_1) = s_2 \wedge s_1 \in I^\natural)$ implies $s_2 \in I^\sharp$. To show $\exists s_1, s_1'.(\alpha(s_1) = s_2 \wedge \alpha(s_1') = s_2' \wedge (s_1, s_1') \in R^\natural)$ implies $(s_2, s_2') \in R^\sharp$, we need to show that $\exists s_1, s_1'.(\alpha(s_1) = s_2 \wedge \alpha(s_1') = s_2' \wedge s_1' \in post[R^\natural](s_1))$ implies $s_2' \in post[\alpha^\tau(R^\natural)](s_2)$, which follows from Lemma 5: $s_1' \in \gamma(post[\alpha^\tau(R^\natural)](s_2))$ and $\alpha(s_1') \in \alpha(\gamma(post[\alpha^\tau(R^\natural)](s_2)))$, and hence $s_2' \in post[\alpha^\tau(R^\natural)](s_2)$.

Therefore, ACTL properties verified on $T^\sharp$ also holds for $T^\natural$:

Lemma 7. *Let the abstract transition system $T^\sharp = (S^\sharp, I^\sharp, R^\sharp, V^\sharp)$ be defined as in Definition 8 with respect to the concrete transition system $T^\natural = (S^\natural, I^\natural, R^\natural, V^\natural)$ and the set of predicates φ. Given an ACTL property $f^\sharp$, $T^\sharp \models f^\sharp \rightarrow T^\natural \models \gamma(f^\sharp)$.*

Proof. Follows from Lemmas 3 and 6.

Using fixpoint approximation techniques on an infinite-state partially predicate abstracted transition system in symbolic model checking of CTL properties [2] preserves the verified ACTL properties due to Lemmas 1 and 7.

Restricting the state space of an abstract transition system $T^\sharp = (S^\sharp, I^\sharp, R^\sharp)$ with an over-approximation of the set of reachable states $T_{RS}^\sharp = (\mu Z.post[R^\sharp](Z) \vee I^\sharp)^+, I^\sharp, R^\sharp)$ also preserves the verified ACTL properties:

Lemma 8. *Let the abstract transition system $T^\sharp = (S^\sharp, I^\sharp, R^\sharp, V^\sharp)$ be defined as in Definition 8 with respect to the concrete transition system $T^\natural = (S^\natural, I^\natural, R^\natural, V^\natural)$. Let $T_{RS}^\sharp = ((\mu Z.I^\sharp \vee post[R^\sharp](Z))^+, I^\sharp, R^\sharp, V^\sharp)$. Given an ACTL property $f^\sharp$, $I^\sharp \subseteq [\![f^\sharp]\!]_{T_{RS}^\sharp}^- \rightarrow T^\natural \models \gamma(f^\sharp)$.*

Proof. Follows from Lemma 1 that approximate symbolic model checking is sound, i.e., $I^\sharp \subseteq [\![f^\sharp]\!]_{T_{RS}^\sharp}^-$ implies $T^\sharp \models f^\sharp$, and from Lemma 7 that ACTL properties verified on the partially predicate abstracted transition system holds for the concrete transition system, i.e., $T^\sharp \models f^\sharp$ implies $T^\natural \models \gamma(f^\sharp)$.

As an example, using the proposed hybrid approach one can show that the concrete model, $T_{ticket2}^\natural$ given in Fig. 1 satisfies the correctness property $AG(z \leq 1)$ by first generating a partially predicate abstracted model, $T_{ticket2}^\sharp$, wrt the predicate set $\{z = 1, z < 1\}$ and performing approximate fixpoint computations to prove $AG(b_1 \vee b_2)$. Due to Lemma 8, if $T_{ticket2,RS}^\sharp$ satisfies $AG(b_1 \vee b_2)$, it can be concluded that $T_{ticket2}^\natural$ satisfies $AG(z \leq 1)$.

The main merit of the proposed approach is to combat the state explosion problem in the verification of problem instances for which predicate abstraction does not provide the necessary precision (even in the case of being embedded in a CEGAR loop) to achieve a conclusive result. In such cases approximate fixpoint computations may turn out to be more precise. The hybrid approach may provide both the necessary precision to achieve a conclusive result and an improved performance by predicate abstracting the variables that do not require fixpoint approximations. In Sect. 4, we present a crafted model that embeds bigger instances of the ticket mutual exclusion model and provide empirical evidence on the merits of the hybrid approach.

4   Experiments

The hypothesis we would like to test in this paper is that *the hybrid approach would be more effective than the individual techniques alone if the analysis does not converge without computing an approximation to the fixpoint and the number of integer variables pushes the limits of of the underlying symbolic, e.g., polyhedral, representation for the integer domain.* The ticket mutual exclusion model shown in Fig. 1 is too small to be a useful case study for the hypothesis that we set to test. So we combined a model for Airport Ground Network Traffic Control (AGNTC) [18] with the mutual exclusion algorithm shown in Fig. 1. AGNTC is a resource sharing model for multiple processes, where the resources are taxiways and runways of an airport ground network and the processes are the arriving and departing airplanes. We changed the AGNTC model given in [18] by (1) using the mutual exclusion algorithm for synchronization on one of the taxiways and (2) making parked arriving airplanes fly and come back to faithfully include the mutual exclusion model, i.e., processes go back to *think* state after they are done with the critical section to attempt to enter the critical section again. The mutual exclusive use of the taxiway and the progress of an airplane attempting to use the taxiway could not be verified for the final model we obtained without using approximate fixpoint computations.

Although we will be using the AGNTC model to present our results, we would like to start by presenting verification results for the ticket mutual exclusion algorithm using ALV [18] and NuXmv [3]. ALV is a symbolic model checker that can represent the state space of an infinite-state system through a composition of symbolic representations so that each state variable can be encoded with the most suitable symbolic representation. It uses BDD representation for the boolean domain and supports two alternative representations for the integer domain: polyhedra based representation[2] (using the Omega library [12]) and automata based representation. ALV leverages the widening operator defined by the underlying integer representations to compute over-approximations for the fixpoint computations of EU, AU, EF, AF operators (-A flag) and the set of reachable states (-F flag). The reason we chose NuXmv is that it is a symbolic model checker that supports full CTL and implements an efficient CEGAR loop in connection with k-induction [16]. So we tried to verify safety property of the ticket model with both tools and the results are given in Fig. 1. The experiments have been executed on a 64-bit Intel Xeon(R) CPU with 8 GB RAM running Ubuntu 14.04 LTS.

We varied the size of the model by varying the number of processes that try to have mutual exclusive access to the critical section. ALV using fixpoint approximations only could verify all 4 cases; the biggest model taking around 20 min, which is a perfect example of state-explosion as one smaller instance was verified in less than 4 s. NuXmv's explicit predicate abstraction did not finish. So we tried implicit predicate abstraction. In that mode NuXmv could successfully

---

[2] Experimental results are based on the widening operator implemented for the polyhedral representation.

Table 1. Comparison of ALV's fixpoint approximation based approach with NuXmv's CEGAR loop using predicate abstraction and k-induction.

Model	ALV (Appr.)		NuXmv (CEGAR, k-induction)	
	Memory	Time	Memory	Time
ticket2	1.73 M	0.06	79.43 M	2.01 (bound=24, verified)
ticket3	3.71 M	0.88	-	>2700 (bound >115, unable to prove)
ticket4	6.64 M	3.49	-	>2700 (bound >58, unable to prove)
ticket5	280.77 M	1170.36	-	>2700 (bound >24, unable to prove)

verify the smallest instance in 2 secs by inferring the necessary predicates. However, for all the remaining instances it could neither prove nor falsify the models in 45 mins. So this experiment shows that the ticket mutual exclusion algorithm is a benchmark for which widening based fixpoint approximation is more effective than predicate abstraction in a CEGAR loop (Table 1).

To find out whether combining predicate abstraction with fixpoint approximations has any benefit, we extended ALV with predicate abstraction and conducted some experiments. In our implementation, we did not instantiate predicate abstraction in the context of a CEGAR loop. So we used predicates that can be easily inferred from the model. Therefore, for all the configurations we made sure that the set of predicates produce a conclusive result.

Table 2 shows sizes of the Airport Ground Network Control models for 2, 3, 4, and 5 arriving airplanes and one departing airplane. There are 2 taxiways and 2 runways. The number of integer variables, Int, and the number of boolean variables, $Bool$, are due to the state variables in the model for the fixpoint approximation only case. For the predicate abstraction, we used different sets of predicates for safety and liveness. In the case of safety, we abstracted the 6 integer variables that modeled the taxiways and runways and used 6 predicates whereas in the case of liveness, we abstracted two integer variables that represent the runways and used 2 predicates. The difference in the number of predicates are reflected in the memory consumption during transition system construction for safety verification and liveness verification cases. We used predicates in the form of $rc < 1$ and $rc = 1$ for verification of safety and liveness properties, respectively. Here, rc denotes the number of airplanes on ground network resource r.

Tables 3 and 4 show various statistics for safety and liveness verification of the Airport Ground Network Control model, respectively. *Size* column presents data about the last fixpoint iterate. Time includes the transition relation construction time and the verification time in seconds. *In the case of safety property verification, the combined approach provides significant improvements for the total time as the model gets bigger. The memory overhead could be tolerated as long as the memory is not exhausted. In the case of liveness property verification, the combined approach shows improvement both in terms of time and memory. This is due to the greatest fixpoint computation (EG) for the negated property and the conjunction*

Table 2. Comparison of the transition system size in terms of memory (M) in MBs and the sizes of the symbolic representations (I for integer constraints, $|B|$ for BDDS size) and the number of integer (Int) and boolean variables ($Bool$) for fixpoint approximation only mode versus the mixed mode of predicate abstraction and fixpoint approximation.

	Fix. Apr.		Pred. Abs + Fix. Apr.			
	Safety & Liveness		Safety		Liveness	
	$M, \#I, |BDD|$	$Int, Bool$	$M, \#I, |BDD|$	$Int, Bool$	$M, \#I, |BDD|$	$Int, Bool$
2A	4.53, 354, 726	10, 10	214.66, 26, 566	4, 16	29.26, 102, 553	8, 12
3A	7.31, 547, 1590	11, 14	281.27, 43, 883	5, 20	45.79, 133, 922	9, 16
4A	10.32, 760, 2794	12, 18	348.08, 64, 1248	6, 24	64.33, 168, 1339	10, 20
5A	13.64, 993, 4338	13, 28	417.10, 89, 1661	7, 26	85.20, 207, 1804	11, 24

Table 3. Comparison of using fixpoint approximation only versus a combination of predicate abstraction and fixpoint approximation for **safety property** verification of the Airport Ground Network Control model *using the approximate set of reachable states* (-F flags).

Model	Fix. Apr.		Pred. Abs + Fix. Apr.	
	Size	Time	Size	Time
	$M, \#Int, |BDD|$		$M, \#Int, |BDD|$	
2A	10.02, 558, 791	1.76	414.67, 21, 1019	16.30
3A	32.46, 2176, 4466	59.29	511.78, 73, 3872	52.67
4A	95.76, 6072, 17586	1216.47	676.19 , 185, 10175	271.48
5A	245.92, 12272, 50162	11199.00	912.34, 381, 22850	639.33

Table 4. Comparison of using fixpoint approximation only versus a combination of predicate abstraction and fixpoint approximation for **liveness property** verification of the Airport Ground Network Control case study *using the approximate set of reachable states* (-F flag).

Model	Fix. Apr.		Pred. Abs. + Fix. Apr.	
	Size	Time	Size	Time
	$M, \#Int, |BDD|$		$M, \#Int, |BDD|$	
2A	47.84, 474, 680	5.71	43.76, 138, 412	3.85
3A	194.70, 1856, 3908	174.62	106.41, 538, 2101	96.81
4A	451.76, 5216, 15596	3142.21	273.78, 1625, 8006	1850.27
5A	>1772.30, 12272, 50139	> 11431.70	>288.60, 3980, 40434	>7867.00

causing an exponential blow-up in the symbolic representation as the number of fixpoint iterations increase. For both safety and liveness verification, we used ALV's approximate reachable state computation.

Table 5. Percentage of reductions achieved using ALV's simplification heuristic. The reductions are shown for the number of integer constraints ($\#Int$) and the sizes of the BDDs ($|BDD|$). The time taken by the simplification stage is given in secs.

# of Preds.	2A			3A			4A		
	Reduction		Time	Reduction		Time	Reduction		Time
	$\#Int$	$|BDD|$		$\#Int$	$|BDD|$		$\#Int$	$|BDD|$	
1	%71.62	%59.68	0.29	%77.56	%66.56	0.53	%80.66	%71.14	0.93
2	%85.47	%78.59	0.54	%88.35	%81.81	1.03	%89.87	%84.62	1.75
3	%93.27	%89.84	0.96	%94.64	%91.73	1.96	%95.35	%92.90	3.46
4	%97.34	%95.34	1.81	%97.78	%96.16	3.90	%98.01	%96.67	7.23
5	%98.82	%97.80	4.45	%98.99	%98.17	9.75	%99.11	%98.41	18.08
6	%99.56	%98.98	11.83	%99.60	%99.16	25.83	%99.62	%99.27	45.86

Unlike traditional implementation of predicate abstraction, our approach to generation of the abstract transition system does not involve weakest precondition computation with respect to the predicates. Also, our approach does not use an SMT solver, in the traditional sense, to compute the abstraction. This is because we literally perform the existential quantification in Eqs. 1 and 3 using ALV's polyhedral symbolic representation that uses the Omega Library [12]. However, in our approach the price is paid by having a blow-up in the abstract transition system that is exponential in the number of predicates. We deal with this blow-up by using the simplification heuristic of ALV [17] after the existential quantification is computed as part of the abstraction process (Eq. 3). The existential quantification yields an exponentially large (in the number of predicates) transition system. Table 5 shows the reductions we obtained in the sizes of the transition relations and the time the simplification stages took. As the table shows the range of reductions is approximately [%60, %99.56] and the reductions increase with the increasing number of predicates as well as the model size.

Predicate Abstraction Only With ALV, generating a finite-state abstraction of the model using predicate abstraction only, i.e., abstracting all integer variables, has not been effective as it ended up in an out of memory error while building the abstract transition system. Since the predicate abstraction in ALV is not optimized, we wanted to use another tool that has an optimized implementation to see if using predicate abstraction alone would be more effective than the combined approach. As we did for the ticket example, we chose to use NuXmv. In the context of this model checking tool, explicit predicate abstraction did not scale as building the model for 2A instance did not finish in 40 min. NuXmv's implicit predicate abstraction, which can verify invariant properties of infinite-state systems using a combination of predicate abstraction inside a CEGAR loop and Bounded Model Checking, could neither verify nor refute the same model in 40 min. So even for the smallest instance of the case study, predicate abstraction alone has not been effective in verifying the safety property. Since NuXmv cannot handle liveness properties when it uses implicit predicate abstraction, we were not able to compare its performance for that case.

5 Related Work

In [10] a new abstract domain that combines predicate abstraction with numerical abstraction is presented. The idea is to improve precision of the analysis when the predicates involve numeric variables that are represented by an abstract numeric domain, e.g., a predicate on an array cell, where the domain of the index variables are represented using polyhedral domain. In our approach the predicates and the numeric variables do not have any interference. Although [10] has evaluated the combined approach in the context of software model checking, our evaluation in the context of CTL model checking shows similar improvement in performance over complete numeric representation.

In [11] Jhala et al. point out the inadequacy of generating predicates for integer domain based on weakest preconditions over counter-examples. They propose a complete technique for finding effective predicates when the system satisfies the property and involves a bounded number of iterations. The technique limits the range of constants to be considered at each refinement stage and avoids generation of diverging predicates in the interpolation stage by discovering new constraints that relate program variables. Unlike the examples considered in [11], the presented mutual exclusion algorithm does not have a bound and, therefore, it is not obvious whether that technique would be successful on ticket-like models.

Transition predicate abstraction [15] is a technique that overcomes the inherent imprecision of state-based predicate abstraction with respect to proving liveness properties. Although we also consider primed versions of variables in the predicate as part of the transition, our approach cannot handle predicates that directly relate primed and unprimed variables. In [15] such predicates can be handled as it uses the abstract transitions to label nodes of the abstract program. However, our approach is able to handle liveness properties that relate abstracted and concrete variables.

6 Conclusion

We have implemented a hybrid approach that combines predicate abstraction with fixpoint approximations so that when approximate fixpoint computation is more effective than predicate abstraction in terms of providing the necessary precision, the state explosion can be dealt with the help of predicate abstraction. We have implemented the proposed approach in the context of Action Language Verifier, an infinite-state symbolic model checker that performs approximate CTL model checking. Experimental results show cases of improved performance for both safety and liveness verification when the hybrid approach is used. For future work, we would like to incorporate a CEGAR loop that would be capable of inferring a suitable partitioning of the state space between predicate abstraction and fixpoint approximations.

A Appendix

Let $\bar{A}$ denote an ordered list of terms from set A. Let $cube^{\bar{A}} = \bigwedge_{k=1}^{|A|} a_k$, where $a_k \in A$ or $\neg a_k \in A$ and k denotes the index of a_k in $\bar{A}$. Let $cube_i^{\bar{A}}$ denote the cube that evaluates to i when regarded as a $|A|$ bit number when the terms' encoding are interpreted as 0 for those that are negated and as 1 for the non-negated. For instance $cube_0^{\bar{A}}$ denotes $\bigwedge_{k=1}^{|A|} \neg a_k$, where $a_k \in A$. Also, let $|\varphi| = n$.

Lemma 2.

Proof.

$$s \wedge cube_i^{\varphi} \rightarrow \exists V_{\varphi}.s \wedge cube_i^{\varphi} \text{ (due to Existential Introduction)}$$

$$s \wedge cube_i^{\varphi} \wedge cube_i^{\varphi} \rightarrow (\exists V_{\varphi}.s \wedge cube_i^{\varphi}) \wedge cube_i^{\varphi}$$

$$s \wedge cube_i^{\varphi} \rightarrow (\exists V_{\varphi}.s \wedge cube_i^{\varphi}) \wedge cube_i^{\varphi}$$

$$\bigvee_{i=0}^{2^n-1} s \wedge cube_i^{\varphi} \rightarrow \bigvee_{i=0}^{2^n-1} (\exists V_{\varphi}.s \wedge cube_i^{\varphi}) \wedge cube_i^{\varphi}$$

$$s \wedge \bigvee_{i=0}^{2^n-1} cube_i^{\varphi} \rightarrow \bigvee_{i=0}^{2^n-1} (\exists V_{\varphi}.s \wedge cube_i^{\varphi}) \wedge cube_i^{\varphi}$$

$$s \wedge true \rightarrow \bigvee_{i=0}^{2^n-1} (\exists V_{\varphi}.s \wedge cube_i^{\varphi}) \wedge cube_i^{\varphi}$$

$$s \rightarrow \bigvee_{i=0}^{2^n-1} (\exists V_{\varphi}.s \wedge cube_i^{\varphi}) \wedge cube_i^{\varphi}$$

$$s \rightarrow (\bigvee_{i=0}^{2^n-1} \exists V_{\varphi}.(s \wedge cube_i^{\varphi}) \wedge cube_i^{b}))[\bar{\varphi}/\bar{b}]$$

$$s \rightarrow (\bigvee_{i=0}^{2^n-1} \exists V_{\varphi}.(s \wedge cube_i^{\varphi} \wedge cube_i^{b}))[\bar{\varphi}/\bar{b}] \text{ (due to } V_{\varphi} \cap V_b = \emptyset)$$

$$s \rightarrow (\exists V_{\varphi}.(\bigvee_{i=0}^{2^n-1} s \wedge cube_i^{\varphi} \wedge cube_i^{b}))[\bar{\varphi}/\bar{b}]$$

$$s \rightarrow (\exists V_{\varphi}.(s \wedge \bigvee_{i=0}^{2^n-1} cube_i^{\varphi} \wedge cube_i^{b}))[\bar{\varphi}/\bar{b}]$$

$$s \rightarrow \gamma(\exists V_{\varphi}.(s \wedge \bigvee_{i=0}^{2^n-1} cube_i^{\varphi} \wedge cube_i^{b}))$$

$$s \rightarrow \gamma(\exists V_{\varphi}.(s \wedge \bigwedge_{j=1}^{|\varphi|} \varphi_j \iff b_j))$$

$$s \rightarrow \gamma(\alpha(s))$$

$$(8)$$

Lemma 4.

Proof. **Showing** $r^{\natural} \rightarrow \gamma^{\tau}(\alpha^{\tau}(r^{\natural}))$: Also, let $\overline{\varphi''}$ and $\overline{b''}$ denote the ordered list of terms from the set $\varphi \cup \varphi'$ and the ordered list of terms from the set $b \cup b'$, respectively. Let $n = |\varphi| = |\varphi'|$ and $CS' = \bigwedge_{\varphi_i \in \varphi}((\bigwedge_{v \in V(\varphi_i)} v' = v) \implies \varphi_i' \iff \varphi_i)$.

$$r^\natural \wedge CS' \wedge \overline{cube_i^{\varphi''}} \to \exists V_{\varphi \cup \varphi'}.r^\natural \wedge CS' \wedge \overline{cube_i^{\varphi''}}$$

$$r^\natural \wedge CS' \wedge \overline{cube_i^{\varphi''}} \wedge \overline{cube_i^{\varphi''}} \to (\exists V_{\varphi \cup \varphi'}.r^\natural \wedge CS' \wedge \overline{cube_i^{\varphi''}}) \wedge \overline{cube_i^{\varphi''}}$$

$$r^\natural \wedge CS' \wedge \overline{cube_i^{\varphi''}} \to (\exists V_{\varphi \cup \varphi'}.r^\natural \wedge CS' \wedge \overline{cube_i^{\varphi''}}) \wedge \overline{cube_i^{\varphi''}}$$

$$\bigvee_{i=0}^{2^{2n}-1} r^\natural \wedge CS' \wedge \overline{cube_i^{\varphi''}} \to \bigvee_{i=0}^{2^{2n}-1} (\exists V_{\varphi \cup \varphi'}.r^\natural \wedge CS' \wedge \overline{cube_i^{\varphi''}}) \wedge \overline{cube_i^{\varphi''}}$$

$$r^\natural \wedge CS' \wedge \bigvee_{i=0}^{2^{2n}-1} \overline{cube_i^{\varphi''}} \to \bigvee_{i=0}^{2^{2n}-1} (\exists V_{\varphi \cup \varphi'}.r^\natural \wedge CS' \wedge \overline{cube_i^{\varphi''}}) \wedge \overline{cube_i^{\varphi''}}$$

$$r^\natural \wedge true \to \bigvee_{i=0}^{2^{2n}-1} (\exists V_{\varphi \cup \varphi'}.r^\natural \wedge CS' \wedge \overline{cube_i^{\varphi''}}) \wedge \overline{cube_i^{\varphi''}}$$

$$r^\natural \to \bigvee_{i=0}^{2^{2n}-1} (\exists V_{\varphi \cup \varphi'}.r^\natural \wedge CS' \wedge \overline{cube_i^{\varphi''}}) \wedge \overline{cube_i^{\varphi''}}$$

$$r^\natural \to (\bigvee_{i=0}^{2^{2n}-1} \exists V_{\varphi \cup \varphi'}.(r^\natural \wedge CS \wedge \overline{cube_i^{\varphi''}}) \wedge \overline{cube_i^{b''}}))[\overline{\varphi''}/\overline{b''}]$$

$$r^\natural \to (\bigvee_{i=0}^{2^{2n}-1} \exists V_{\varphi \cup \varphi'}.(r^\natural \wedge CS \wedge \overline{cube_i^{\varphi''}} \wedge \overline{cube_i^{b''}}))[\overline{\varphi''}/\overline{b''}]$$

$$(\text{due to } V_{\varphi \cup \varphi'} \cap V_b = \emptyset)$$

$$r^\natural \to (\exists V_{\varphi \cup \varphi'}.(\bigvee_{i=0}^{2^{2n}-1} r^\natural \wedge CS \wedge \overline{cube_i^{\varphi''}} \wedge \overline{cube_i^{b''}}))[\overline{\varphi''}/\overline{b''}]$$

$$r^\natural \to (\exists V_{\varphi \cup \varphi'}.(r^\natural \wedge CS \wedge \bigvee_{i=0}^{2^{2n}-1} \overline{cube_i^{\varphi''}} \wedge \overline{cube_i^{b''}}))[\overline{\varphi''}/\overline{b''}]$$

$$r^\natural \to \gamma^\tau(\exists V_{\varphi \cup \varphi'}.(r^\natural \wedge CS \wedge \bigvee_{i=0}^{2^{2n}-1} \overline{cube_i^{\varphi''}} \wedge \overline{cube_i^{b''}}))$$

$$r^\natural \to \gamma^\tau(\exists V_{\varphi \cup \varphi'}.(r^\natural \wedge CS \wedge \bigwedge_{j=1}^{|\varphi|} \varphi_j \iff b_j \wedge \bigwedge_{j=1}^{|\varphi'|} \varphi_j' \iff b_j'))$$

$$r^\natural \to \gamma^\tau(\alpha^\tau(r^\natural))$$

Showing $r^\sharp = \alpha(\gamma(r^\sharp))$:

$$\equiv \alpha(\gamma(r^\sharp))$$

$$\equiv \exists V(\varphi).\exists V(\varphi').(r^\sharp[\overline{\varphi}, \overline{\varphi'}/\overline{b}, \overline{b'}] \wedge CS \wedge \bigwedge_{i=1}^{|\varphi|} \varphi_i \iff b_i \wedge \bigwedge_{i=1}^{|\varphi|} \varphi_i' \iff b_i')$$

$$\equiv \exists V(\varphi).\exists V(\varphi').(r^\sharp[\overline{\varphi}, \overline{\varphi'}/\overline{b}, \overline{b'}] \wedge \bigwedge_{i=1}^{|\varphi|} \varphi_i \iff b_i \wedge \bigwedge_{i=1}^{|\varphi|} \varphi_i' \iff b_i')$$

$$\equiv r^\sharp$$

(9)

References

1. Andrews, G.R.: Concurrent Programming: Principles and Practice. Benjamin-Cummings Publishing Co., Inc., Redwood City (1991)
2. Bultan, T., Gerber, R., Pugh, W.: Symbolic model checking of infinite state systems using Presburger arithmetic. In: Grumberg, O. (ed.) CAV 1997. LNCS, vol. 1254, pp. 400–411. Springer, Heidelberg (1997)
3. Cavada, R., et al.: The NUXMV symbolic model checker. In: Biere, A., Bloem, R. (eds.) CAV 2014. LNCS, vol. 8559, pp. 334–342. Springer, Heidelberg (2014)
4. Clarke, E.M., Grumberg, O., Long, D.E.: Model checking and abstraction. ACM Trans. Program. Lang. Syst. **16**(5), 1512–1542 (1994)
5. Clarke, E., Grumberg, O., Talupur, M., Wang, D.: Making predicate abstraction effcient: how to eliminate redundant predicates. In: Hunt Jr., W.A., Somenzi, F. (eds.) CAV 2003. LNCS, vol. 2725, pp. 126–140. Springer, Heidelberg (2003)
6. Cousot, P., Cousot, R.: Abstract interpretation: a unified lattice model for static analysisof programs by construction or approximation of fixpoints. In: Conference Record of the Fourth Annual ACM SIGPLAN-SIGACTSymposium on Principles of Programming Languages, Los Angeles, California, pp. 238–252. ACM Press, New York (1977)
7. Cousot, P., Cousot, R.: On abstraction in software verification. In: Brinksma, E., Larsen, K.G. (eds.) CAV 2002. LNCS, vol. 2404, pp. 37–56. Springer, Heidelberg (2002)
8. Cousot, P., Halbwachs, N.: Automatic discovery of linear restraints among variables of a program. In: Conference Record of the Fifth Annual ACM Symposium on Principles of Programming Languages, Tucson, Arizona, USA, pp. 84–96, January 1978
9. Graf, S., Saïdi, H.: Construction of abstract state graphs with PVS. In: Grumberg, O. (ed.) CAV 1997. LNCS, vol. 1254, pp. 72–83. Springer, Heidelberg (1997)
10. Gurfinkel, A., Chaki, S.: Combining predicate and numeric abstraction for software model checking. STTT **12**(6), 409–427 (2010)
11. Jhala, R., McMillan, K.L.: A practical and complete approach to predicate refinement. In: Hermanns, H., Palsberg, J. (eds.) TACAS 2006. LNCS, vol. 3920, pp. 459–473. Springer, Heidelberg (2006)
12. Kelly, W., Maslov, V., Pugh, W., Rosser, E., Shpeisman, T., Wonnacott, D.: The omega library interface guide. Technical report, University of Maryland at College Park, College Park, MD, USA (1995)
13. Loiseaux, C., Graf, S., Sifakis, J., Bouajjani, A., Bensalem, S.: Property preserving abstractions for the verification of concurrent systems. Form. Methods Syst. Des. **6**(1), 11–44 (1995)
14. Nielson, F., Nielson, H.R., Hankin, C.: Principles of Program Analysis. Springer-Verlag New York Inc., Secaucus (1999)
15. A. Podelski and A. Rybalchenko. Transition predicate abstraction and fair termination. ACM Trans. Program. Lang. Syst. **29**(3), May 2007
16. Tonetta, S.: Abstract model checking without computing the abstraction. In: Cavalcanti, A., Dams, D.R. (eds.) FM 2009. LNCS, vol. 5850, pp. 89–105. Springer, Heidelberg (2009)
17. Yavuz-Kahveci, T., Bultan, T.: Heuristics for efficient manipulation of composite constraints. In: Armando, A. (ed.) FroCos 2002. LNCS (LNAI), vol. 2309, pp. 57–71. Springer, Heidelberg (2002)
18. Yavuz-Kahveci, T., Bultan, T.: Action language verifier: an infinite-state model checker for reactive software specifications. Formal Methods Syst. Des. **35**(3), 325–367 (2009)

Finding Boundary Elements in Ordered Sets with Application to Safety and Requirements Analysis

Jaroslav Bendík$^{(\boxtimes)}$, Nikola Beneš, Jiří Barnat, and Ivana Černá

Faculty of Informatics, Masaryk University, Brno, Czech Republic
{xbendik,xbenes3,barnat,cerna}@fi.muni.cz

Abstract. The motivation for this study comes from various sources such as parametric formal verification, requirements engineering, and safety analysis. In these areas, there are often situations in which we are given a set of configurations and a property of interest with the goal of computing all the configurations for which the property is valid. Checking the validity of each single configuration may be a costly process. We are thus interested in reducing the number of such validity queries. In this work, we assume that the configuration space is equipped with a partial ordering that is preserved by the property to be checked. In such a case, the set of all valid configurations can be effectively represented by the set of all maximum valid (or minimum invalid) configurations w.r.t. the ordering. We show an algorithm to compute such boundary elements. We explain how this general setting applies to consistency and redundancy checking of requirements and to finding minimum cut-sets for safety analysis. We further discuss various heuristics and evaluate their efficiency, measured primarily by the number of validity queries, on a preliminary set of experiments.

Keywords: Requirements analysis · Formal verification · Safety analysis

1 Introduction

The motivation of this work comes from various source areas, such as parametric formal verification, requirements engineering, safety analysis, or software product lines. In these areas, the following situation often arises: We are given, as an input, a set of configurations and a property of interest. The goal is to compute the set of all the configurations that satisfy the given property. We call such configurations valid. As a short example, one may imagine a system with tunable parameters that is to be verified for correctness. The set of configurations, in that case, is a set of all possible parameter values and the goal is to find all such values that ensure the correctness of the given system. If we are given a method to ascertain the validity of a single configuration, we could try running the method repeatedly for each configuration to obtain the desired result. In the

© Springer International Publishing Switzerland 2016
R. De Nicola and E. Kühn (Eds.): SEFM 2016, LNCS 9763, pp. 121–136, 2016.
DOI: 10.1007/978-3-319-41591-8_9

case of an infinite set of configurations, this approach does not terminate, and we get at most a partial answer. However, even if the configuration space is finite, checking configurations one by one may be too costly. We are thus interested in reducing the number of validity checks in the finite case.

Although such reduction might be impossible in general, we focus on problems whose configuration space is equipped with a certain structure that is preserved by the property of interest. This may then be exploited in order to check a smaller number of configurations and still obtain the full answer. The desired structure is a set of dependencies of the form: "If configuration A violates the property then configuration B does too." Mathematically, we can either view such structure as a directed acyclic graph of those dependencies, or as a partial ordering on the set of all configurations induced by this graph. Viewed as an ordered set, the set of all the valid configurations can be effectively represented by the set of all the maximal valid (alternatively, minimal invalid) configurations.

We are interested in finding this boundary between valid and invalid configurations while minimising the number of validity queries, i.e. the potentially costly checks whether a given configuration satisfies the property.

We are not aware of any previous work which deals with exactly the same problem as we do. The most related problems can be found among the Constraint Satisfaction Problems (CSPs) where a satisfiability of a set of constraints is examined. When a set of constraints C is infeasible the most common analysis is the maximum satisfiability problem (MaxSAT, MaxCSP), which asks for a satisfiable subset of C with the greatest possible cardinality. Our problem is different from MaxSAT and more related to the maximum satisfiable subset problem (MSS) that considers maximality in the ordering sense instead of maximum cardinality. The goal of MSS is to find a subset of C that is satisfiable, and that becomes unsatisfiable if any other constraint is added to this subset. Similarly, one can define the minimum unsatisfiable subset problem (MUS).

Both MSSes and MUSes describe the boundary between the satisfiable and unsatisfiable subsets of C and both these problems were recently addressed in works [1,3,6,15,16]. To solve the problem, the papers use different approaches like the duality that exists between MUSes and MSSes [1,16] or parallel enumeration from bottom and top [3]. In [15] authors unify and expand upon the earlier work, presenting a detailed explanation of the algorithm's operation in a framework that also enables clear comparisons. Paper [6] describes an MUS extractor tool MUSer2 which implements a number of MUS extraction algorithms.

Subsets of a set of requirements are naturally ordered by the subset relation, thus our approach can be also used to solve these problems. We deal with a more general problem as we consider arbitrary graphs instead of the hypercube graphs representing subsets of requirements. Our approach has thus a wider area of potential usage. Furthermore, as is explained in Sect. 4, in the case of hypercubes our approach can be competitive with the state-of-the-art tool Marco [15].

Safety Analysis. The safety analysis techniques are widely used during the design phase of safety-critical systems. Their aim is to assure that the systems provide prescribed levels of safety via exploring the dependencies between a system-level failure and the failures of individual components. Traditionally, the various safety analyses are done manually and are based on an informal model of the systems. This leads to the process being very time-consuming and the results being highly subjective. The desire to alleviate such issues somewhat and to make the process more automated led to the development of Model-Based Safety Analysis (MBSA) approach [13]. This approach assumes the existence of a system model that is extended by an error model describing the way faults may happen and propagate throughout the system. One of the problems solved in MBSA is the computation of the so-called minimal cut-sets for a given failure, i.e. the minimal sets of low-level faults that cause the high-level failure to manifest in the system.

One can map the minimal cut-sets problem to our setting easily. The configurations are the possible sets of faults that may be enabled in the extended system model, their ordering is given by set inclusion. Note that there might be dependencies between some of the faults, which means that not all sets of faults are considered to be possible. The property of interest is the non-existence of failure and the valid configurations are exactly those sets of faults that do not cause the failure to happen. Clearly, in this case, the minimal cut-sets correspond exactly to the minimal invalid configurations. This means that the problem can be solved using our approach.

To illustrate the application on a simple example, we consider an avionics triplex sensor voter, described in [9]. The voter gains measurement data from three sensors as well as information whether the sensors are operational. It computes the differences between the sensor data and detects persistent miscompare, i.e. situations where two sensors differ above a certain threshold for a certain amount of time. If all three sensors are operational and two pairs of sensors have persistent miscompare, the common sensor is marked as invalid and data is no longer received from that sensor. If just two sensors are operational, a persistent miscompare between the two means that the output data is considered invalid.

For simplicity, let us assume that there are two kinds of faults per sensor and let us call these fault A and fault B. Fault A causes the sensor to transmit wrong data while fault B causes the sensor to stop working completely. Note that we may assume that both faults cannot occur on the same sensor, as once fault B happens, the occurrence of fault A is irrelevant. In general, we thus have six possible faults and 27 sets of faults to be checked, including the empty set of faults. However, as the situation of sensors is symmetrical, we may get rid of this symmetry and simply count the number of fault-A sensors and fault-B sensors instead. This situation is illustrated in Fig. 1. The nodes in the graph represent the various fault configurations: ∅ represents that no faults occur, AB represents that fault A occurred on one sensor and fault B occurred on another sensor, etc. The graph is created from the inclusion ordering on the fault situations.

Let us now consider the failure to deliver data to the output. As explained above, the voter fails to deliver output if either all sensors stopped working or have been eliminated, or if there are just two sensors working with persistent miscompare. We assume that the persistent miscompare situation is detected

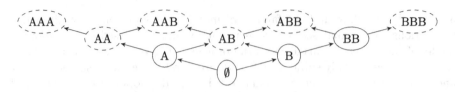

Fig. 1. Illustration of the safety analysis example

once at least one of a pair of sensors starts transmitting wrong data, i.e. fault A occurred on that sensor. For this reason, the minimum invalid configurations (i.e. the minimal cut-set) are AA, AB, and BBB, while the maximum valid configurations are A and BB.

Requirements Analysis. Establishing the requirements is an important stage in all development. Although traditionally, software requirements were given informally, recently there has been a growing interest in formalising these requirements [12]. Formal description in a kind of mathematical logic enables various model-based techniques, such as formal verification. Moreover, we also get the opportunity to check the requirements earlier, even before any system model is built. This so-called requirements sanity checking [3] aims to assure that a given set of requirements is consistent and that there are no redundancies. If inconsistencies or redundancies are found, it is usually desirable to present them to the user in a minimal fashion, exposing the core problems in the requirements. As redundancy checking can be usually reduced to inconsistency checking [2], the goal is thus to find all minimal inconsistent subsets of requirements. Such a problem may be clearly seen as an instance of our setting, where the configurations are sets of requirements and the ordering is given by the subset relation.

We illustrate the inconsistency checking on an example. Assume that we are given a set of four requirements. These requirements consider one particular component in a system and constrain the way the component is used. We formalise the requirements using the branching temporal logic CTL [8]. In the formulae we use the atomic propositions q denoting that a *query* has arrived, r denoting that the component is *running*, and m denoting that the system is taken down for *maintenance*. Our first requirement states that whenever a query arrives, the component has to become active eventually, formally $\varphi_1 := \mathbf{AG}(q \rightarrow \mathbf{AF}\, r)$. The second requirement states that once the component is started, it may never be stopped. This may be a reasonable requirement e.g. if the component's initialisation is expensive, formally $\varphi_2 := \mathbf{AG}(r \rightarrow \mathbf{AG}\, r)$. The third requirement states that the system has to be taken down for maintenance once in a while. This also means that the component has to become inactive at that time. This is formalised as $\varphi_3 := \mathbf{AG}\,\mathbf{AF}\,(m \wedge \neg r)$. Our last requirement states that after the maintenance, the system (including the component we are interested in) has to be restarted, formally $\varphi_4 := \mathbf{AG}(m \rightarrow \mathbf{AF}\,(\neg m \wedge r))$. The situation is illustrated in Fig. 2. We discover that there is one minimum inconsistent subset of the four requirements, namely $\{\varphi_2, \varphi_3, \varphi_4\}$, and that there are three maximum

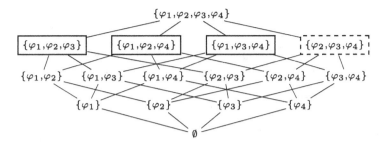

Fig. 2. Illustration of the requirements analysis example. The subset with dashed outline is the maximum inconsistent one, the subsets with solid outline are the maximum consistent ones.

consistent subsets of the requirements, namely $\{\varphi_1, \varphi_2, \varphi_3\}$, $\{\varphi_1, \varphi_2, \varphi_4\}$, $\{\varphi_1, \varphi_3, \varphi_4\}$. The consistency of the first set $\{\varphi_1, \varphi_2, \varphi_3\}$ might be surprising, as one would suspect the pair of requirements φ_2 and φ_3 to be the source of inconsistency. However, the first three requirements can hold at the same time – in systems where no queries arrive at all. In these situations we say that the requirements hold *vacuously*. There are ways of dealing with vacuity, such as employing the so-called vacuity witnesses [5].

Note that although in this example, the space of all sets of requirements had the particular shape of a hypercube, this might not always be the case. We might sometimes be interested in certain subsets of requirements instead of all of them. Such a situation may arise e.g. if there are some known implications between the requirements. Consider the example above with the added requirement that once the component is started, it may only stop after 1 h. This requirement is clearly implied by φ_2 and we would therefore omit all subsets that contain both φ_2 and this new requirement. Another way of obtaining a non-hypercube requirements graph is when considering requirements for several components at once in a component-based or software product line setting. In such cases, some of the components or product features may be incompatible and it thus only makes sense to consider subsets of requirements that reason about compatible components.

Outline of the Paper. The rest of this paper is organised as follows. In Sect. 2 we present the basic definitions and preliminaries and state our problem formally. In Sect. 3 we present our new algorithm to solve the problem and discuss several variants and heuristics of it, as well as we analyse its complexity. The algorithm is then evaluated on a set of experiments in Sect. 4 and the paper is concluded in Sect. 5.

2   Preliminaries and Problem Statement

In this section, we recall some basic notions that we use later in the paper. We also introduce the formalism of annotated directed acyclic graphs that forms the basic setting for our problem.

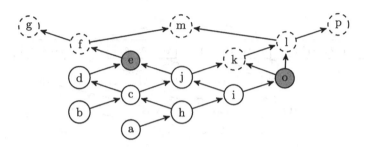

Fig. 3. An example of an ADAG, the dashed vertices are the invalid ones, the grey vertices are the maximum valid ones.

Definition 1 *(Directed Acyclic Graph). A directed graph G is a pair (V, E), where V is a finite set of vertices and $E \subseteq V \times V$ is a set of edges. An edge (u, v) is an* outgoing *edge of the vertex u and an* incoming *edge of the vertex v. The* indegree *(outdegree) of a vertex v is the number of incoming (outgoing) edges of v. A* path *from a vertex u to a vertex v in G is a sequence $\langle v_0, v_1, \cdots v_k \rangle$ of vertices such that $v_0 = u$, $v_k = v$, $k > 0$ and $(v_i, v_{i+1}) \in E$ for $i = 0, 1, \cdots, k-1$. We say that v is reachable from u if there is a path in G from u to v.*

A directed graph $G = (V, E)$ is called a directed acyclic graph (DAG) *if there is no path $\langle v_0, v_1, \cdots v_k \rangle$ in the graph such that $v_0 = v_k$. A DAG induces a strict partial order relation $\sqsubset_G$ on its vertices as follows: $u \sqsubset_G v$ if v is reachable from u. A vertex v is said to be a* minimum vertex *in G if there is no u such that $u \sqsubset_G v$. Dually, a vertex u is a* maximum vertex *in G if there is no v such that $u \sqsubset_G v$.*

Definition 2 *(Chain Cover). A* chain *in a DAG G with its induced relation $\sqsubset_G$ is a sequence of one or more vertices $\langle v_0, v_1, \ldots, v_k \rangle$ such that $v_0 \sqsubset_G v_1 \sqsubset_G \cdots \sqsubset_G v_k$. A* chain cover *of a DAG is a set of chains $C = \{c_1, \cdots, c_l\}$ such that each vertex is included in exactly one chain from C. A* minimum chain cover *is a chain cover containing the fewest possible number of chains. Note that the minimum chain cover is not given uniquely.*

Definition 3 *(Annotated DAG). An* annotated directed acyclic graph (ADAG) *is a pair $(G, valid)$, where $G = (V, E)$ is a directed acyclic graph and $valid :$ $V \to Bool$ is a validation function. The validation function is* monotone *on V, which means that for every pair $u, v \in V$ if $u \sqsubset_G v$ and $valid(u) = false$ then $valid(v) = false$.*

The problem we are interested in can be stated as finding either a set of maximum valid vertices or a set of minimum invalid vertices. We present an algorithm to obtain the former. However, the algorithm can be also used to obtain the latter, as the two formulations are dual.

Definition 4 *(Maximum Valid Vertex and Cut). Let $\mathcal{G} = ((V, E), valid)$ be an ADAG. A vertex $u \in V$ is a* maximum valid vertex *of G iff $valid(u) = true$ and $\forall v \in V$ such that $u \sqsubset_G v$ is $valid(v) = false$.*

The maximum valid cut *of $\mathcal{G}$ is a set of all its maximum valid vertices.*

Problem Formulation. Given an ADAG $\mathcal{G} = ((V, E), valid)$, find the *maximum valid cut* of $\mathcal{G}$.

As mentioned in the introduction, evaluating the function *valid* on a single configuration (a single vertex of the ADAG) might be an expensive operation. Therefore, our aim is to propose an algorithm minimising the number of evaluations of the *valid* function even for the price of the increased complexity of the algorithm with respect to the number of operations over the graph.

The problem formulation assumes that the graph is acyclic and that the validation function is monotone. We might, however, be also interested in cases where one of these preconditions is violated. We postpone the discussion of these possibilities to Sect. 3.5.

3   Algorithm

A naive solution of the maximum valid cut problem for a given ADAG G would be to evaluate the *valid* function on each vertex, compute the $\sqsubset_G$ relation for valid vertices, and choose the maximum ones. In this naive approach, the *valid* function is called once per each vertex.

3.1   Chain-Based Algorithm

Instead of dealing with each vertex of G separately we build our solution on a decomposition of G into a set of chains and we use the fact that the validation function is monotone. The algorithm takes as an input an ADAG G and one of its chain covers C. Then it iteratively handles chains and removes those vertices which cannot be the maximum valid ones.

From the definition, each vertex of the maximum valid cut of G belongs to exactly one chain from C. Moreover, every chain contains at most one maximum valid vertex of the graph and this vertex is at the same time the maximum valid vertex of the chain. Let us note that the opposite implication does not hold generally, the maximum valid vertex of a chain may not be a maximum valid vertex of the whole graph. Therefore, the set of maximum valid vertices of individual chains contains the maximum valid cut as its subset.

Let $c = \langle v_0, v_1, \cdots, v_l \rangle$ be an arbitrary chain of C. To find the maximum valid vertex v_h of this chain we use binary search. We take the *middle* vertex c_{mid} of c, $c_{mid} = v_{\lceil \frac{l}{2} \rceil}$ and evaluate the *valid* function on c_{mid}. If c_{mid} is valid, then we know for sure that none of the lower vertices from c can be the maximum valid vertex of this chain. In the other case, we claim that none of the higher vertices from c can be maximum valid vertex. This allows us to reduce c into half and recursively repeat the procedure. We finish with a chain consisting of only one vertex v_i. If v_i is a valid vertex then it is the maximum valid vertex of c, otherwise c does not have any valid vertex at all.

Once we have applied the binary search on each chain from C, we have the set H of maximum vertices of these chains. To obtain the maximum valid cut of G from H we just compute the $\sqsubset_G$ relation for each pair from H and remove from H all those vertices that are not maximum w.r.t. $\sqsubset_G$.

For an illustration of the chain based algorithm, assume that we are given the graph from Fig. 3 and as a chain cover we take these chains: $\langle b, c, d, e, f, g \rangle$, $\langle a, h, j, k, m \rangle$, $\langle i, o, l, p \rangle$. The vertices e, j, o are found to be the maximum valid vertices of these chains and the $\sqsubset_G$ relation is computed for these three vertices. Vertex j is found to be lower than e and vertices o, e are mutually unreachable, hence $\{e, o\}$ is the resulting maximum valid cut.

The number of calls to *valid* in this algorithm depends on the number of chains in C and the number of calls used in the binary searches. The number of calls is logarithmic in the length of the chain in every binary search. Therefore, the total number of calls is $\mathcal{O}(|C| \log L)$ where $|C|$ is the number of chains in C and L is the length of the longest chain in C.

Note that there are algorithms such as [7,11] that compute the minimum chain cover of a given graph. We may thus make use of these algorithms to reduce the number of chains that need to be processed by this algorithm.

3.2   Cutoff-Based Algorithm

We now improve the efficiency of our algorithm by decreasing the chain lengths and possibly eliminating some of the chains completely. The main idea makes use of the fact that a vertex v_i is recognised as the maximum valid vertex of a chain $c = \langle v_0, v_1, \cdots, v_i, \cdots, v_l \rangle$ (if c has any). From this we can deduce that not only vertices from c lower than v_i cannot belong to the maximum valid cut, but neither do any vertices from G lower than v_i. Symmetrically, none of the vertices from G higher than v_{i+1} can belong to the maximum valid cut. Therefore, we can remove all vertices lower than v_i and higher than v_{i+1}, including v_{i+1}, from all chains and thus reduce their size and possibly the number of *valid* calls in the future.

Definition 5 *(Cutoff Transformation). Let G be an ADAG and C its chain cover. Let $c = \langle v_0, v_1, \cdots, v_i, \cdots, v_l \rangle$ be a chain from C and let v_i be its maximum valid vertex. Then the* cutoff *of G is a pair $\overline{G}$ and $\overline{C}$ generated from G and C, respectively, by removing:*

- *vertices which are lower than v_i,*
- *vertices which are higher than v_{i+1}, and*
- *the vertex v_{i+1}.*

In case that c does not have a maximum valid vertex we define the cutoff *of G to be a tuple $\overline{G}$ and $\overline{C}$ created from G and C, respectively, by removing:*

- *vertices which are higher than v_0, and*
- *the vertex v_0.*

As this vertex removal may make some chains empty, we also remove the empty chains from $\overline{C}$.

Theorem 1 *(Cutoff Property). Let G be an ADAG, C its chain cover, and $\overline{G}, \overline{C}$ be their cutoff. Then graphs G and $\overline{G}$ have the same maximum valid cuts, $\overline{C}$ is a chain cover of $\overline{G}$, and $|C| \geq |\overline{C}|$.*

MAXVALID($c = \langle v_0, v_1, \ldots, v_l \rangle, IsValid()$)

```
1   if c is empty
2       then return nil
3   middle ← ⌈l/2⌉
4   if ISVALID(v_middle)
5       then x ← MAXVALID(⟨v_middle+1, ..., v_l⟩, IsValid())
6           if x = nil
7               then return middle
8               else return x
9       else
10          return MAXVALID(⟨v_0, ..., v_middle-1⟩, IsValid())
```

CUTOFF($G = (V, E), c = \langle v_0, v_1, ..., v_l \rangle, i$)

```
1   if i ≠ nil
2       then set v.cand = false for each v ∈ V lower than v_i
3            set v.cand = false for each v ∈ V higher than v_{i+1}
4            set v_{i+1}.cand = false
5       else set v.cand = false for each v ∈ V higher than v_0
6            set v_0.cand = false
```

MAXVALIDCUT($G = (V, E), IsValid()$)

```
1   set v.cand = true for each v ∈ V
2   compute the relation ⊏_G
3   ChainCover ← MINIMUMCHAINCOVER(G)
4   for each chain ∈ ChainCover
5       do PROCESSCHAIN(G, IsValid(), chain)
6   return V
```

PROCESSCHAIN($G, IsValid(), c$)

```
1   remove from c all vertices v with v.cand = false
2   index ← MAXVALID(c, IsValid())
3   CUTOFF(G, c, index)
```

Algorithm 1. Maximum Valid Cut Algorithm

Theorem 2 *(Maximal Cut Property). Let G be an ADAG and C its chain cover. Let us apply step by step the cutoff transformation on all chains from C and let $\overline{G}$ and $\overline{C}$ be the resulting graph and its chain cover respectively. Then every chain in $\overline{C}$ is just a single vertex and $\overline{C}$ is exactly the maximum valid cut of G.*

The algorithm based on the cutoff transformation is shown as Algorithm 1. The algorithm assumes that the reachability relation $\sqsubset_G$ is pre-computed. The relation is used both for computing the minimum chain cover and when detecting lower and higher vertices, however, bread-first-search can be also used for this detection. Instead of removing vertices from the graph we just mark them with a binary flag *cand* (for candidate) initially set to *true*. Once we have discovered that a vertex cannot be a maximum valid one, the flag is set to *false*.

Contrary to the previous algorithm based on chains, once the algorithm based on cutoffs processes the last chain from the chain cover of the original graph G,

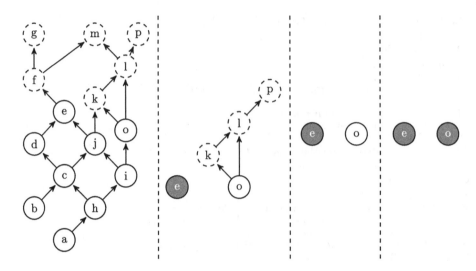

Fig. 4. Illustration of the cutoff based algorithm. The graph is covered with three chains $\langle b, c, d, e, f, g \rangle$, $\langle a, h, j, k, m \rangle$, $\langle i, o, l, p \rangle$ and they are processed in this order. At first, the vertex e is found to be the maximum valid vertex of the first chain and the consequently made cutoff reduces the set of chains to $\langle e \rangle$, $\langle k \rangle$, $\langle o, l, p \rangle$. In the next step, the chain $\langle k \rangle$ is processed and no valid vertex on this chain is found, but the cutoff is made and the set of chains is reduced to $\langle e \rangle$, $\langle o \rangle$. In the last step, the chain $\langle o \rangle$ is processed and o is found to be valid. The result of the third cutoff is the maximal valid cut $\{e, o\}$. The grey nodes are nodes which have already been determined to be valid ones.

the set C contains exactly the maximum valid cut of G and no other computation is needed.

Figure 4 illustrates the cutoff based algorithm on the graph from Fig. 3. The cutoffs significantly reduce the space of vertices that can be maximum valid ones. After processing of the first two chains only two vertices are left as the possible maximum valid ones.

3.3   Complexity

The time complexity analysis of the cutoff algorithm is given w.r.t. the size of the graph $G = (V, E)$ and we separately evaluate the number of *valid* calls and the number of all other operations.

The number of calls to the *valid* function depends on the number of chains in C and the number of calls used in the binary searches. The total number of calls is in the worst case the same as with the algorithm based on chains, i.e. $\mathcal{O}(|C| \log L)$ where $|C|$ is the number of chains in C and L is the length of the longest chain in C. Note that the size of the *minimum* chain cover can be bounded due to Dilworth's theorem.

Theorem 3 *(Dilworth's Theorem [10]). The size of the minimum chain cover of graph G equals to the size of a maximum number of pairwise unrelated elements, where u is unrelated to v if neither $u \sqsubseteq_G v$ not $v \sqsubseteq_G u$.*

To evaluate the overall complexity of the algorithm we denote by T_{valid} the time needed for one evaluation of *valid*.

The reachability relation $\sqsubseteq_G$ is in fact equal to the transitive closure of the graph and can be computed in $\mathcal{O}(|V| \cdot |E|)$ with the help of, e.g., depth-first search starting from each node of the graph.

The procedure PROCESSCHAIN first removes from the chain all vertices that have been recognised as not maximum valid in some of the previous cutoff transformations. When starting the MAXVALIDCUT algorithm, each vertex is included in exactly one chain of the chain cover. Each vertex is removed at most once, hence the overall number of removals is bounded by the size of V and the complexity of the removals only is $\mathcal{O}(|V|)$.

The procedure MAXVALID is an analogy of the binary search. It calls the validation function on the middle vertex of the given chain c, splits the chain into two halves, and recursively continues on one of these halves. The complexity of MAXVALID is $\mathcal{O}(T_{valid} \cdot \log |c|)$ where $|c|$ is the length of c. The procedure is called once for each chain of the chain cover C of G resulting in the overall complexity of $\mathcal{O}(T_{valid} \cdot |C| \cdot \log L)$ where L is the length of the longest chain from C.

The procedure CUTOFF marks those vertices which cannot be maximum valid ones. Either bread-first-search or the $\sqsubseteq_G$ relation can be used to detect the vertices, which should be marked, and each vertex is marked as *false* at most once. Therefore all the markings (including the initialisation) take time $\mathcal{O}(|V|)$.

The most time consuming part of the algorithm (excluding the *valid* calls) is the computation of the minimum chain cover taking time $\mathcal{O}(|C| \cdot |V|^2)$. For details and complexity analysis please refer to [7,11]. The total time complexity of the cutoff algorithm is thus $\mathcal{O}(|V|^3 + T_{valid} \cdot |C| \cdot \log L)$.

3.4   Heuristics

The cutoff algorithm works with the minimum chain cover, however, the algorithm does not prescribe the order in which individual chains are processed. Each cutoff transformation affects the chains that have not been processed yet. Therefore the order in which the chains are processed affects the total number of calls to the validation function.

Cutting Power Based Heuristics. The order which minimises the number of calls to the validation function cannot be determined without the information which vertices are valid and which are not. Instead, for each chain c we can identify the minimum and the maximum number of vertices that can be cut off as a result of its processing. Let us define for each vertex v_i from the chain $\langle v_0, v_1, \ldots, v_l \rangle$ its *cutting power* as the number of vertices of G lower than v_i plus the number of vertices higher than v_{i+1} plus 1 (for vertex v_{i+1}). Then the *maximum cutting power of chain c* is the maximum of cutting powers of its vertices.

Average and median cutting power of a chain can be defined in a similar way. Cutting powers of vertices can be used to propose several heuristics decreasing the number of calls to the validation function.

The first heuristic sorts the chains in descending order according to their maximum cutting powers. This heuristic can lead to a large reduction of the graph while processing the first few chains. However, this happens only if the vertices with maximum cutting power are the maximum valid vertices of these chains.

As the second heuristic we propose to compute for each chain c its average cutting power which equals to the arithmetic mean of the cutting powers of its vertices. The heuristic sorts the chains in descending order according to their average cutting power. A similar heuristic is to order the chains according to the median of the cutting powers of its vertices. These two heuristics can speed up the average performance of the algorithm.

Note that to compute the cutting power of a vertex we need to know the reachability relation of the graph. The reachability relation is pre-computed when the minimum chain cover is constructed. The only additional computation required by the heuristics is thus the sorting which takes $\mathcal{O}(|C| \cdot \log |C|)$ time and does not increase the asymptotic complexity of the cutoff algorithm.

All heuristics can be improved if we recompute the cutting powers of vertices and sort the chains after each cutoff transformation. However, this requires recomputation of the reachability relation which is rather expensive and increases the complexity of the algorithm. As explained in the introduction, our goal is to minimise the number of calls to the validation function as it is assumed to be a very expensive operation. When choosing the appropriate heuristic we have to trade off between the number of validation function calls and the complexity of the heuristic.

Cutting Power Approximation. Yet another possibility is to approximate the cutting power of vertices by some easily computable characteristic. For instance, we can take the outdegree of a vertex as a high outdegree can indicate high cutting power. The same holds for the indegree of a vertex. Again, we can sort chains according to out/indegrees, average degree or median. On the one hand, this approach could be less effective than the approaches based on cutting powers. On the other hand, it is relatively cheap and affords to recompute the ordering after each cutoff transformation.

Online Computed Chains. As the precomputation of the minimum chain cover is rather expensive, our last heuristic drops this precomputation. The chains are instead computed on the fly. To construct a chain we take an arbitrary unprocessed vertex (i.e. a vertex whose validity is not known yet) and by following its unprocessed predecessors and successors we extend it to a chain. This chain is then processed as described in the cutoff algorithm and we repeat this process as long as there are some unprocessed vertices. We call this heuristic the *online heuristic*. Obviously, the disadvantage of this approach is that the number of the on-the-fly constructed chains can be much higher than the size of the minimal chain cover. However, if we precompute the minimal chain

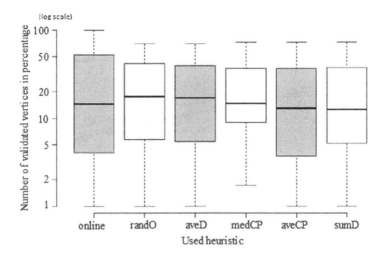

Fig. 5. Efficiency of our algorithm with online computed chain cover (online), minimum chain cover (randO), and heuristics determining the order in which individual chains are processed. The graph is in log scale.

cover, its minimality is guaranteed only before the first cutoff transformation is made as this transformation can shorten some chains of the cover and there can emerge some chains that can be joined together. The online heuristic always processes a chain that cannot be extended any more. It can thus possibly process even less chains than the original algorithm with the minimum chain cover pre-computed. Moreover, the computation of the minimal chain cover is the most expensive operation of our algorithm besides the validation calls. The online heuristic does not need this precomputation and hence the $\sqsubset_G$ relation does not need to be computed. The time complexity of the algorithm is reduced to $\mathcal{O}(|V| + |E| + T_{valid} \cdot |C| \cdot \log L)$. We compare the online heuristic with the others in the next section.

3.5   Relaxing the Preconditions

The two main preconditions of our approach are that the graph is assumed to be acyclic and that the validation function is monotone on this graph. A natural question might arise whether we could relax one of these preconditions. Consider first an arbitrary annotated graph, i.e. a directed graph with a monotone valida-tion function. The monotonicity implies that all vertices lying on one cycle are either all valid or all invalid. This means that we can preprocess the graph using any standard algorithm for decomposition into strongly connected components and work on the resulting (acyclic!) graph of strongly connected components.

Consider now a second possibility, where we retain the acyclic property of the graph yet relax the monotonicity precondition. If we run our algorithm on such a graph, we might not get the maximal valid cut of the graph. Nevertheless, the

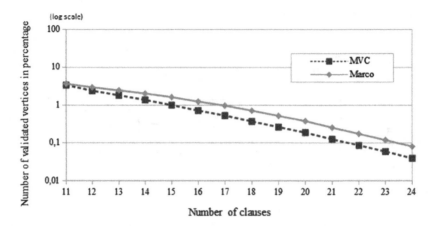

Fig. 6. A log scale graph that compares our algorithm with the Marco algorithm. The graph shows the percentage of subsets that were validated by the algorithms. Our algorithm is denoted by MVC (Maximum Valid Cut).

algorithm terminates and we obtain a set of vertices with the property that they are valid and their immediate successors in the graph are all invalid. We thus obtain at least partial evidence of the boundary between valid and invalid vertices. This can help us identify the source of errors in application areas such as software-product lines or in version control branches, which may not necessarily be monotone.

4   Experimental Evaluation

We implemented the cutoff algorithm and experimentally evaluated its behaviour on different types of graphs. While evaluating the algorithm we focused on the number of calls of the validation function as our aim is to minimise this number.

The first set of experiments was run on three different sets of randomly generated ADAGs of size up to 5000 vertices. The efficiency of the algorithm strongly depends on many factors like the relative number of pairwise unreachable vertices, the number and lengths of chains, density of the graph, etc. We tested the variant of our algorithm with online computed chain cover (online) and with precomputed minimum chain cover (randO). The results are shown in boxplot in Fig. 5, the boxplot shows the percentage of vertices which were validated. The online variant has higher third quartile but lower median.

Moreover, we tried the five heuristics described earlier. The heuristics sort chains from the minimum chain cover according to average cutting powers of individual chains (aveCP), medians of cutting powers of chains (medCP), average degrees of vertices of chains (aveD), and sum of the degrees of vertices of chains. The best performance was achieved using the sumD heuristic which has a median of 13 %.

Note that there are ADAGs for which almost all vertices have to be validated, namely graphs where almost all vertices are pairwise unreachable. These types of graphs were not included in our data sets for the experimental evaluation.

Requirements Checking. We now evaluate the performance of the algorithm on the graphs with the specific shape of a hypercube that represent all subsets of a set of requirements. For n requirements the hypercube consists of 2^n vertices and $n2^{n-1}$ edges. We used requirements specified in propositional logic and employed the SAT instances generator from [14] to generate experimental data. Experiments were run on requirements sets containing up to 24 requirements and hundred instances for each size. For these experiments we ran the online algorithm as it has shown to be the best one for hypercubes. The minimum-chain based approach performs worse on hypercubes as the minimal chain cover of a hypercube contains a large number of short chains. However, the binary search approach performs better on longer chains.

To provide a better insight into the qualitative parameters of our algorithm we compare its behaviour with two other tools solving the problem of finding the minimal unsatisfiable subsets of a set of requirements, namely [3,15]. Authors of [3] use the linear temporal logic (LTL) to specify requirements and report efficiency of around 10 % (i.e. 10 % of all vertices of the hypercube were validated). We were not able to repeat their experiments exactly as the authors do not provide their experimental data. Moreover, LTL is hard-coded in their tool. However, in our experiments with SAT instances the ratio of validated vertices decreases to 0.05 %. The MARCO tool, presented in [15], is proposed to solve any constraint sets. We compared the efficiency of our algorithm against MARCO on the same sets of SAT instances. As can be seen in Fig. 6, our tool makes less queries to the SAT-solver.

5   Conclusion

In this paper, we have focused on finding boundary elements in partially ordered sets, seen as a kind of graphs. We have discussed the mapping of this problem to various activities in software engineering; we have shown applications in safety and requirements analysis. We have presented a new general algorithm to solve this problem, including several variants and heuristics. We have found that the efficiency of the heuristics depends on the structure of the input graph. For graphs with the hypercube structure, the online variant of our algorithm performed the best.

As a future work, we consider several improvements of our basic algorithm. One possible direction of research is to aim at parallel processing of the configuration space in order to further improve the performance of our approach. Another is to focus more on the specific cases of hypercube graphs and exploit their structure more on the fly. We also want to consider more applications of our approach, such as software product line engineering and discovering incompatibilities in component-based designs. We also believe that our method can be applied to various other domains, such as the parameter synthesis for biological systems [4]. We intend to explore these applications in more detail.

Acknowledgement. The research leading to these results has received funding from the European Unions Seventh Framework Program (FP7/2007-2013) for CRYSTAL Critical System Engineering Acceleration Joint Undertaking under grant agreement No. 332830 and from specific national programs and/or funding authorities.

References

1. Bailey, J., Stuckey, P.J.: Discovery of minimal unsatisfiable subsets of constraints using hitting set dualization. In: Hermenegildo, M.V., Cabeza, D. (eds.) PADL 2004. LNCS, vol. 3350, pp. 174–186. Springer, Heidelberg (2005)
2. Barnat, J., Bauch, P., Beneš, N., Brim, L., Beran, J., Kratochvíla, T.: Analysing sanity of requirements for avionics systems. Form. Aspects Comput. **28**(1), 45–63 (2016). doi:10.1007/s00165-015-0348-9
3. Barnat, J., Bauch, P., Brim, L.: Checking sanity of software requirements. In: Eleftherakis, G., Hinchey, M., Holcombe, M. (eds.) SEFM 2012. LNCS, vol. 7504, pp. 48–62. Springer, Heidelberg (2012)
4. Barnat, J., Brim, L., Krejci, A., Streck, A., Safranek, D., Vejnar, M., Vejpustek, T.: On parameter synthesis by parallel model checking. IEEE/ACM Trans. Comput. Biol. Bioinform. **9**(3), 693–705 (2012)
5. Beer, I., Ben-David, S., Eisner, C., Rodeh, Y.: Efficient detection of vacuity in temporal model checking. Form. Methods Syst. Des. **18**(2), 141–163 (2001)
6. Belov, A., Marques-Silva, J.: MUSer2: an efficient MUS extractor. J. Satisfiability Boolean Model. Comput. **8**, 123–128 (2012)
7. Chen, Y., Chen, Y.: On the decomposition of posets. In: 2012 International Conference on Computer Science Service System (CSSS), pp. 134–138 (2012)
8. Clarke, E., Grumberg, O., Peled, D.: Model Checking. MIT Press, Cambridge (1999)
9. Dajani-Brown, S., Cofer, D., Hartmann, A.C., Pratt, T.W.: Formal modeling and analysis of an avionics triplex sensor voter. In: Ball, T., Rajamani, S.K. (eds.) SPIN 2003. LNCS, vol. 2648, pp. 34–48. Springer, Heidelberg (2003)
10. Dilworth, R.P.: A decomposition theorem for partially ordered sets. Ann. Math. **51**(1), 161–166 (1950)
11. Fulkerson, D.R.: Note on Dilworth's decomposition theorem for partially ordered sets. Proc. Am. Math. Soc. **7**(4), 701–702 (1956)
12. Hinchey, M., Jackson, M., Cousot, P., Cook, B., Bowen, J.P., Margaria, T.: Software engineering and formal methods. Commun. ACM **51**, 54–59 (2008)
13. Joshi, A., Miller, S.P., Whalen, M., Heimdahl, M.P.: A proposal for model-based safety analysis. In: The 24th Digital Avionics Systems Conference, 2005. DASC 2005, vol. 2. IEEE (2005)
14. Lauria, M.: CNFgen formula generator. http://massimolauria.github.io/cnfgen/. Accessed 11 Jan 2016
15. Liffiton, M.H., Previti, A., Malik, A., Marques-Silva, J.: Fast, flexible MUS enumeration. Constraints **21**(2), 223–250 (2016). http://link.springer.com/article/10.1007%2Fs10601-015-9183-0
16. Liffiton, M.H., Sakallah, K.A.: Algorithms for computing minimal unsatisfiable subsets of constraints. J. Autom. Reason. **40**(1), 1–33 (2008)

Combining Abstract Interpretation with Symbolic Execution for a Static Value Range Analysis of Block Diagrams

Christian Dernehl$^{(\boxtimes)}$, Norman Hansen, and Stefan Kowalewski

RWTH Aachen University, Lehrstuhl Informatik 11 - Embedded Software, Aachen, Germany
{dernehl,hansen,kowalewski}@embedded.rwth-aachen.de

Abstract. This paper presents a fully automatic verification technique for Simulink block diagrams, by combining a static value range analysis with symbolic execution. Our concept avoids a translation to other languages and, instead, extracts all necessary attributes from Simulink and interprets the model directly. With this technique, we show how user defined specifications can be validated using sound abstractions for primitives, including IEEE-754 floats, and custom data types. Moreover, we propose optimizations by exploiting the benefits of intervals and symbolic representations to apply our technique to larger models. We evaluate our solution against an industrial tool.

1 Introduction

With the growing use of software controlled embedded systems, the safety of programs plays an increasing role. As projects and teams become larger and more interdisciplinary, model-based design tends to improve the development process [4]. Model-based design uses graphical programming, which is easily understood by developers from different domains. Another reason for model-based design is the attempt to limit the designer to rules and, eventually, avoid certain classes of software failures. This technique has been acknowledged in safety standards for embedded software systems [9,15].

The landscape of tools supporting model-based design differs between industrial sectors. For instance, Matlab/Simulink has become a widely applied tool in the automotive domain, while some aerospace businesses prefer SCADE [3]. Both tools provide the user with a visual modeling interface for *block diagrams*, in which elements are connected via lines and the flow among the blocks defines the behavior. This paper presents solutions for block diagrams in Simulink, however, the concepts can be adapted to similar modeling tools.

In practice, code is generated from existing models and integrated, automatically at best, into custom software. As a side effect, this process enhances rapid prototyping by allowing the user to simulate and test models on desktop computers, independent of the target platform. Admitting that errors caused by invalid memory access and wrong pointer arithmetic occur rather seldom in

© Springer International Publishing Switzerland 2016
R. De Nicola and E. Kühn (Eds.): SEFM 2016, LNCS 9763, pp. 137–152, 2016.
DOI: 10.1007/978-3-319-41591-8_10

generated code, many design issues remain. Among these are unintended data type over-/underflows, irrelevant or unused model parts, invalid divisions and operations, unintended variable resets and out-of-bound access.

Since the resulting code might lead to a failure, formal methods and extensive testing is applied for validation. Nevertheless, these techniques are often used after code generation, requiring a linkage between code and model, necessitating a regeneration of the code. Instead, our aim is to provide the user during the design stage with important notifications and warnings about potential modeling flaws, so that these can be resolved immediately.

Contribution. In this paper, we present a detailed, sound and fully automatic verification for Simulink block diagrams using *sat modulo theory* (SMT) techniques, which are introduced in Sect. 2. Our contribution in Sect. 4 extends already existing proposals by combining a previously designed interval analysis [8] with SMT checking. We use the Microsoft Z3 SMT solver [7], which is able to represent IEEE-754 floats with bit vectors as used by Matlab/Simulink. In detail, our algorithm identifies potential design errors, including divisions by zero, under- and overflows, infinite and NaN values, out-of-bound access and boolean signals, which are constant. We classify our work with others in the field, presented in Sect. 3, and evaluate our work against an industrial tool in Sect. 5.

2 Background

Before presenting our method, we elaborate briefly the concept of SMT solving and block diagrams, which has already been explained in previous work [14].

2.1 SMT Solver

Boolean expressions combine variables with logical operators, such as and ($\wedge$), not ($\neg$) and or ($\vee$). Each variable is either true or false and thus, the boolean expression evaluates either to true or false, depending on the variables. Solving such a boolean expression is the computation of an assignment for the variables so that the expression evaluates to true. Boolean expressions can be extended, for instance, by allowing arithmetic terms which provide a broader application range. With the combination of more underlying theories such as arithmetics, bit vectors, lists or floats, the decidability, i.e. searching for a satisfying variable assignment, of the expression cannot be guaranteed [13]. SMT solvers are tools trying to find satisfying variable assignments with regard to additional theories. Because of the potential undecidability, results of the solving procedure may be either satisfiable, unsatisfiable or unknown.

For our application, we have chosen the latest Microsoft Z3 SMT solver [7] and the support of multiple theories including IEEE-754 floating point arithmetic. The interface of the solver allows users to specify either variables or constants of a given *sort*, which can be boolean, integer, real, float, bit vector or others. For real and integer expressions, a finite rational number approximation

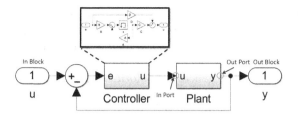

Fig. 1. Simulink block diagram example

is used, while floats are modeled as bit vectors, where each part, sign, fraction and exponent can be accessed individually. Since rational numbers behave differently than IEEE-754 floats, arithmetic operations are implemented individually, yielding the suited operation for a given sort.

One application of SMT is to interpret program variables as SMT variables and use the solver to prove properties of the code. For instance, it might be proven that a variable value is always different from 0 or does not exceed a certain range.

2.2 Block Diagram

A block diagram consists of ports P, blocks B and lines L, such that P and L form a graph. Each port is assigned to a block, whereas, subsystems, which are blocks themselves, allow a hierarchical modeling. Since subsystems can be reused, complex systems can be constructed in a bottom up approach. Figure 1 illustrates a Simulink block diagram, with subsystems *Controller* and *Plant*, root input u and root output y, respectively. The interface of a subsystem is specified with special *In-* and *Out*-blocks. Within the Controller subsystem, the block labeled u references the in port of the Controller subsystem, whereas, y references the out port.

While designing systems, a user may choose from a given palette of blocks or a set of his own. For instance, the blocks shown in Fig. 1 are all part of the Simulink standard block set. Masks are user interfaces, tied to a specific block, which allows further parametrization and configuration of the block, such as setting the value for *Constant*-blocks or changing the sign within a *Sum*-block. Finally, parameters may be set in the *model workspace*, which is a container of variables, with concrete values.

A *simulation* of a block diagram consists of a certain, possibly infinite, amount of time steps, such that each step has a certain, potentially varying duration, for example 0.01 s. Additionally, an individual sample time is assigned to each block, either automatically or specifically by the user, to model systems which run at different frequencies. Blocks are active, i.e. performing a computation, if a multiple of their sample time matches the currently considered time step. If a block is inactive, due to the sample time, a zero order hold operation is performed by default[1]. Another way to make a block inactive is by creating an enabled subsystem in which the block resides. These special systems contain an enable port with a corresponding block, making all blocks in that subsystem active or inactive.

Since loops may be constructed in block diagrams, models with circular dependencies between blocks, called algebraic loops, can be created. For example, feeding the output of a *Sum*-block back to its input yields a time synchronization problem, because the output of the block in the current time step has to be computed based on the current input, which has not yet been calculated. To avoid the occurrence of algebraic loops, a block performing a time shift or storage operation should be added within the loop. These blocks, such as delays or integrators, have therefore a *state*. On the contrary, blocks without internal states feed their input through by computing a memoryless operation.

If not otherwise specified, all states of active blocks are updated with each time step, even those, which are not needed to calculate the root outputs. Thus, the control flow of a block diagram is linear, so that at a given decision, both paths of a *Switch*-block are evaluated by default. Unnecessary computations can be avoided by using enabled subsystems.

Signals. In each time step, signals flow along lines from port to port through the entire model. Each block represents a function, taking the signal values of its input ports as parameters and writing the computed result to its output ports.

Whereas blocks, ports and lines specify the syntax of the block diagram, the semantics are described by signals between ports. A signal has a name and a certain value for each time step. *Concrete* signals are represented by a tensor with a data type, which is equal for all elements in the tensor, ranging over multiple dimensions. Consider a signal of type int8 containing a 2×2 matrix, then each element in the matrix has type int8. Except for special cases, such as matrix multiplication, operations on signals are defined element-wise.

Signals with different data types can be combined into one signal using *buses*. A bus can be constructed in a hierarchical fashion, so that a bus may contain concrete signals or further bus signals. Before arithmetic and other element wise operations are performed on buses, all elements of the bus are casted to a single concrete signal of the most expressive data type. However, signal routing or *Memory*-blocks, which do not change the content of a signal, do not perform type cast operations or the conversion of bus signals to concrete signals.

Execution Order. Finally, after the structure of block diagrams and signals has been explained, the execution order schedules the simulation of the model. Suppose a system, consisting of a *Sum*-block with feed back through a *Memory*-block, which acts like a counter, depending on the input. In the first step, the *Memory*-block, with initial output value zero, must be computed before the *Sum*-block can calculate the sum over its inputs. Therefore, a sequence, guaranteeing all inputs being available when a block is executed, is necessary. Consequently,

---

[1] See http://de.mathworks.com/help/simulink/slref/ratetransition.html.

source blocks, such as *Constant-* or *Inport*-blocks, must be executed before their connected blocks can be executed based on the source blocks output. This order is given by *execution contexts*, which form an ordered tree structure, in which the leafs are non-subsystem blocks. At each level of the tree, the order set of children represents a valid schedule yielding an order in a top-down structure.

3 Related Work

Analyzing and verifying Simulink diagrams is a task which has been addressed before. Reicherdt and Glesner [14] present a similar approach and translate Matlab/Simulink models into the intermediate verification Boogie language. The subsequent verification relies on the Microsoft Z3 SMT solver. Our algorithm abstracts feed through and bounded blocks, such as sin, cos, arctan in a similar fashion. Their algorithm supports up to 44 blocks, however, their solution has some limitations regarding buses and the soundness, since corner cases for IEEE-754 floating point types and corresponding rounding methods are not considered. Although their solution incorporates intervals specified by the user, our algorithm utilizes the fully automatically calculated intervals from a static value range analysis. Eventually, Reicherdt and Glesner prove their solution to perform in certain aspects better than the Simulink Design Verifier[2], which is a tool to verify Matlab/Simulink models, by computing reachable values and detecting design flaws. The Design Verifier uses rational numbers, as indicated by the tool, and lacks a correct abstraction of IEEE-754 floats, too. Furthermore, there are many unsupported blocks by the Design Verifier, causing large over approximations and a variety of false positive results and even undetected flaws in the model. Other techniques, such as abstract simulation by Chapoutot et al. focus on numerical errors caused by continuous models [5]. Hence, we present a static value range analysis based on abstract interpretation [6] with symbolic execution to refine derived value ranges with regard to IEEE-754 floating point arithmetic.

Apart from the verification on model level, block diagrams can be translated to intermediate representations which can subsequently be analyzed. Tripakis et al. propose in their work [16] the translation of discrete Matlab/Simulink models to Lustre. Based on the resulting Lustre representation, verification techniques can be applied. Agrawal et al. [1] convert Matlab/Simulink block diagrams to hybrid automata, which are analyzed using domain specific methods. However, the approaches based on translation of block diagrams into different representations are in general only applicable for a subset of the available Matlab/Simulink model elements and functionalities.

4 Concept

In this section, we give a basic introduction into our approach for abstract interpretation of Matlab/Simulink models. Consequently, the construction of SMT expressions and use of symbolic execution is presented before the combination of both approaches, is described.

---

[2] See http://de.mathworks.com/products/sldesignverifier/.

Overview. Before discussing the concrete analysis, we highlight the construction of our intermediate representation. First, a simulation of the model is launched and paused to retrieve the compiled data types of ports, model parameters and the execution order, using the Matlab API. For block parameters, which are expressions such as $3 * x + 5$, a resolution is used which first looks up the mask parameters of parent blocks in the model for matching variables and replaces variable occurrences in the expressions recursively. Second, the model workspace, where the user may set parameters, is investigated. Finally, the expression is evaluated with the Matlab API, yielding a concrete value.

The block diagram itself is represented as a graph with ports and lines, with a linking between ports and blocks. For simplicity, we enrich the graph and connect *In*- and *Out*-blocks with the matching in- and out-ports along potentially multiple hierarchical levels in the diagram. With these lines, plain subsystems without further configuration can be omitted in the analysis. For enabled, triggered or other subsystems, each affected block references its enable blocks. Signals are abstracted and are either concrete, buses or variable size signals[3]. A signal flow analysis, based on a depth-first-search, computes the hierarchical structure of each bus in the model, providing each port with a primitive or bus type.

The blocks of the model are interpreted during analysis based on previously defined abstractions and corresponding model parametrizations. As abstract domain for the interpretation, interval sets are used.

Limitations. Although our technique can be applied to a variety of systems, we pose some limitations on the models. First, models must be updatable and compilable, i.e. a simulation must be carried out. Note, that our method does not rely on simulation results, but rather fetches the resolved data types and signal dimensions from the model. Systems may not contain algebraic loops, since those cannot be generally resolved and no code can be generated. Furthermore, our algorithm works for discrete models with a fixed time step solver. Currently, we have implemented abstractions for over 50 blocks supporting most possible configurations and parametrizations, including basic support for custom masked blocks. Blocks without correspondent abstractions are over approximated by default.

4.1   Abstract Interpretation with Interval Sets

Intervals provide means to define a set of values by two boundaries, making it an efficient representation. Arithmetics and all other operations, which can be expressed by Matlab/Simulink, can be adapted to intervals [2,12]. For instance, $[1,2] + [3,4]$ yields $[4,6]$, which is the set of all possible sums between values x, y with $x \in [1,2], y \in [3,4]$. We have shown in previous work [8] how interval sets can be used for abstract interpretation of Simulink models. In our implementation, which is reused in this work, the interval analysis is a sound abstraction of IEEE-754 floats, including rounding modes after each operation and

---

[3] Our algorithm currently does not support all variable size operations, which are allowed by Simulink.

symbols such as $\pm\infty$ and NaN. Thus, our implemented abstract interpretation yields an interval set for each port and internal state of a block for the entire model. Although interval sets provide an efficient method for analyzing large models, interval sets lack, the capability to represent relations among multiple variables [8].

4.2   Symbolic Execution with SMT

After having referenced how abstract interpretation using interval set domains is carried out, we explain how SMT expressions, describing relations among signals of a model, are constructed from block diagrams.

Types and Casting. For the Z3 SMT expressions, there are three different sorts, *boolean*, *integer* and *float*, which we use in our algorithm. The boolean($\mathbb{B}$) and floating point ($\mathbb{F}_{32}, \mathbb{F}_{64}$) data types from Simulink can be directly mapped to the corresponding SMT sorts, while the wrapping effects or configurable saturation of integers ($\mathbb{I}_n, n = 8, 16, 32$) must be treated by adding modulo operations or respectively constraining the value. For instance, $u_0 + u_1$ becomes $(u_0 + u_1)$ mod 2^{16} if the types are uint16. The additional mod operation, which has to be added to ensure correct type behavior after every operation, increases complexity of the SMT expressions across the model and can be omitted if the intervals prove, that no under- and overflow occurs.

For floating point operations, a rounding mode according to IEEE-754 must be specified, such as towards zero or $\pm\infty$. By introducing a new variable z, the plus operation between float expressions x and y can be precisely specified by adding a global statement

$$\bigvee_{r \in R} z = \text{plus}(x, y, r) \tag{1}$$

where R is the set of rounding modes. However, this approach leads to large SMT expressions and increases the number of variables and computation effort significantly. Therefore, we allow the user to specify a concrete rounding mode, which is used for all floating point operations. This approach seems reasonable, when assuming that neither Simulink nor external code changes the rounding mode of the floating point unit.

Type casts are handled in different fashions, depending on the input and the output type. Table 1 shows an overview of type casts, where φ is the expression, which shall be casted. If both types are the same, the casting operation is ignored, yielding the input. Boolean casts are represented by the *if-then-else* (ite) operator, yielding one or zero depending on the boolean value. The ite is a ternary operator, so that the first argument is a boolean statement and the latter ones are the results, depending on the first argument. Casting integers or floats to boolean is modeled by setting the expression unequal to zero $\neg(\varphi = 0)$. Suppose both are integer types and the source type is larger than the destination type, then the implicitly added mod operator takes care of the overflow effect.

Table 1. Type casts as SMT expressions

From	To	SMT expression	From	To	SMT expression
$\mathbb{B}$	$\mathbb{I}$	$ite(\varphi, 1, 0)$	$\mathbb{I}$	$\mathbb{B}$	$\neg(\varphi = 0)$
$\mathbb{B}$	$\mathbb{F}$	$ite(\varphi, 1.0, +0.0)$	$\mathbb{I}_a$	$\mathbb{I}_b$	$\varphi \bmod b$ if $b > a$, no op otherwise
$\mathbb{F}$	$\mathbb{B}$	$\neg(\varphi = 0)$	$\mathbb{I}_{32}$	$\mathbb{F}_{32}$	bit vector to fraction if $|\varphi| \leq 2^{23}$
$\mathbb{F}$	$\mathbb{I}$	via rational and modulo	$\mathbb{I}_{<32}$	$\mathbb{F}_{32}$	via bit vector to fraction
$\mathbb{F}_{64}$	$\mathbb{F}_{32}$	fresh variable	$\mathbb{I}$	$\mathbb{F}_{64}$	via bit vector to fraction
$\mathbb{F}_{32}$	$\mathbb{F}_{64}$	copy bit vector parts			

Assume the Matlab/Simulink setting *saturate on integer overflow* is active, then the modulo operation is substituted by two ite operations

$$ite(\varphi > \max, \max, ite(\varphi < \min, \min, \varphi)) \qquad (2)$$

which restrict φ to the range $[\min, \max]$.

For the special case, in which a 32-bit integer is casted to a 32-bit float, several steps are taken. First, if the calculated interval proves the maximum absolute value below 2^{23}, then the expression fits into the fraction of a 32-bit float, since the other eleven bits are used for the exponent. In this case, we can copy the bit vector representation of the integer into the fraction and set the exponent to the bias value, i.e. such that the value of the exponent is zeroed, yielding only the fraction. If the 32-bit integer exceeds $\pm 2^{23}$, then we create a fresh variable, since we cannot make any assumptions on the typecast. For 64-bit floats, no check needs to be done, since the largest integer in Simulink with 32 bits fits into the fraction of 52 bits.

In addition to potential overflows, casts from floating point to integers need special treatment for NaN and $\pm\infty$ symbols. We wrap the expression

$$ite(isNaN(\varphi), 0, ite(isInf(\varphi), ite(sgn > 0, \max, \min), \mathbb{I}(\mathbb{Q}(\varphi)))) \mod 2^n \qquad (3)$$

around, where isNaN is translated to a bit vector operator by the SMT solver. The integer cast $(\mathbb{I}(\mathbb{Q}(\varphi)))$ is executed by a detour to rational number abstraction $(\mathbb{Q})$, which is then translated to an integer using the modulo operation. Similarly to the NaN check, we map the $\pm\infty$ symbols to either the minimum or maximum value of the integer, if the saturation option is activated. Thus, if ∞ is casted to an 8-bit integer, the result is 127. In case the saturation option of the block performing the type cast is deactivated, the first part of the isInf check is set to zero, so that a cast from $\pm\infty$ results in zero, as it does in Simulink. Consequently, the fraction and exponent are represented by rational number, which is then rounded to an integer with the configured mode. Nevertheless, a major drawback is that the bit vector constraints, which are attached to the float expression, must be propagated, causing a large overhead. Therefore, we deactivate the propagation for better efficiency, with the cost of an additional over approximation.

Finally, if both types are different floats, and the input is $\mathbb{F}_{32}$, a few checks are made. First, a fresh $\mathbb{F}_{64}$ variable is constructed and optionally constraints with respect to NaN, $\pm\infty$ are added, if the input variable cannot reach these values. This is an approximation, since no $\mathbb{F}_{32}$ except ∞ yields a $\mathbb{F}_{64}$ ∞, which holds for $-\infty$ and NaN, too. Furthermore the bit vectors from the $\mathbb{F}_{32}$ are taken into consideration, when the $\mathbb{F}_{64}$ variable is created. This procedure cannot be used the other way around, except for NaN, since certain non ∞ $\mathbb{F}_{64}$ values yield an ∞ $\mathbb{F}_{32}$ value. Furthermore, since the type and bit vectors are larger, this data cannot be copied without loss of information. Thus, a new variable with the optional NaN constraint, is created.

$$\text{ite}(\text{isNaN}(\varphi), \text{NaN}, \text{ite}(\text{isInf}(\varphi), \text{sgn}(\varphi)\infty, \varphi) \tag{4}$$

Block Functions. Block operations, as long as they are supported, are mapped to the according SMT operation. In addition, Simulink adds implicit type casts, when necessary. For example, if two float signals are connected to a logical operator block, an implicit cast to boolean is executed. All supported blocks perform the implicit casting operation.

Arithmetic operators are mapped to the corresponding integer or floating point, i.e. bit vector implementation. For integers, the absolute value function is mapped to the $\text{ite}(\varphi < 0, -\varphi, \varphi)$ expression, while for floating point types the sign bit is adjusted. Both, power and modulo can be expressed with integer expressions, while for floats a fresh variable is created, over approximating those functions. Finally, the square root on integers is expressed by a fresh variable z and adding $\exists z \, . zz = \varphi$ to the global constraints.

Functions, which are not supported by the SMT solver, such as transcendentals, are mapped to anonymous functions, allowing the solver to choose any value of the associated sort. For example, such an over approximation is applied for trigonometric or exponential functions. In addition, constraints for bounded functions, such as sine, are added to a list of global constraints, which is included, when the solver is invoked. Concretely,

$$\bigwedge_{\substack{z \in \{\pm\infty, \\ \text{NaN}\}}} \sin(z) = \text{NaN} \wedge \forall x \, \neg(x = \pm\infty \vee x = \text{NaN}) \rightarrow \sin(x) \leq 1 \wedge \sin(x) \geq 1 \tag{5}$$

expresses the limitation of the sine function except for $\pm\infty$ and NaN as arguments. Analogous expressions can be constructed for cos and arctan. For unsupported blocks, fresh variables, which can take any value, are created. However, since a data type is assigned to each port, further global constraints for the fresh variable are added, in case of an integer type. For instance, if the output is an uint8 data type, global constraints $y_0 \geq 0 \wedge y_0 \leq 2^8 - 1$ can be added for the fresh variable y_0.

Unlike intervals, which loose information about the control flow and relations between values, SMT expressions abstract switches by the ite operation, keeping the condition and relation between variables available for further analysis. This memory of the formula is expressed by an abstract syntax tree (AST), which is

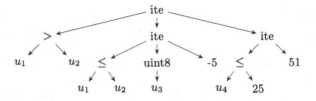

Fig. 2. Abstract syntax tree example

constructed internally by the Z3 solver. An illustration of an AST is given in Fig. 2, where each node represents an operator and the children the operands. There is the ite ternary operator, binary relational operators($>$, $\leq$) and an unary cast operation. Suppose the ite is created from a switch block, then during the evaluation of the root, no decision between the nodes uint8(u_3) and -5 has been made. Consider further, the expression

$$\text{ite}(u_1, \text{ite}(\neg u_1, u_2, u_3), u_4) \tag{6}$$

where the result is never u_2, since u_1 cannot be true and false at the same time. This is because, if u_1 would be true, then the result would be u_3, if u_1 is false, then the result is u_4. A similar problem exists in the more complex tree in Fig. 2, between the root and the second child, because the cast to u_3 is never the result.

Sometimes SMT formulas can be theoretically constructed for blocks, but in practice this is not feasible. Consider a large lookup table, which can be expressed by a nested combination of ite operators. For each point in the lookup table, a new ite expression is constructed, yielding a large overhead. In this case, our implementation omits the computation of the SMT expression and yields a fresh variable with additional constraints. These constraints are taken from the interval analysis to limit the created variable.

Finally, the selector block allows the user to select a subset from an input vector or matrix, such as the first two entries of a vector of length 20. Additionally, the selection can be specified by a signal, which potentially changes with each time step. Furthermore, if the selection signal is above 20, an unintended data access occurs. Our verification solution adds constraints to verify, that the selection signal stays within bounds.

Model Sources. Inputs to the entire system are expressed by *In*-blocks at root level, which receive a special handling, since other *In*-blocks are virtually connected to the corresponding *Out*-blocks during the enrichment of the model. For each scalar in each root *In*-block, a new variable is created $u_0, \ldots u_n$, such that the SMT sort is chosen based on the data type. Constants with an associated data type, such as block parameters, are expressed by the corresponding SMT constants. Since the inputs may change over time, new variables for the model sources have to be created for each time step.

Path Encoding. With the generation of symbolic expressions for single blocks given, this technique can be adapted to entire block diagrams. The execution order from Simulink is used as a schedule for the symbolic execution, such that for each block a symbolic output expression can be computed based on the symbolic input expression. For blocks with internal states, such as integrators, delays or others, symbolic representation is computed, too.

4.3   Combining Abstract Interpretation with Symbolic Execution

Our technique, based on abstract interpretation, terminates if a fix point for the model is found, i.e. any further considered time step does not change the computed reachable values for any signal [6,8]. Assuming an infinite run time, approximations need to be made for blocks with states and models with loops to enforce the existence of a fix point, since our analysis would potentially not terminate otherwise. After a specified time horizon, states, for which no fix point was reached yet, are widened to the biggest interval for the states type. Since each loop contains at least a block with a state, a fix point for every loop is eventually reached.

By comparison, widening for SMT formulas is hard, if no fresh variable without any constraints is used [11]. To avoid the construction of symbolic expressions over multiple considered model time steps, we introduce new variables where constructed expressions would depend on expressions of a previous time step, which is the case for blocks with states. However, our technique exploits the computed intervals and uses the interval constraints for the further analysis. For example, if an interval is only positive ($[0, \infty)$), the constraint $v_0 \geq 0$ is added for the newly created variable v_0.

Nevertheless, the calculation and evaluation of SMT operations takes the largest share of the computational time. Therefore, we add further optimizations, so that information among the two domains is shared. First, before a boolean signal is evaluated by the SMT solver, the interval is checked, whether it actually contains both boolean values and may thus be shrinked by evaluating the SMT expression. This improvement provides a performance benefit, especially for variant models, in which constant booleans are used to configure a variant. A similar enhancement is applied during the evaluation of divisions. First, the interval is evaluated if it contains zero and then the SMT solver is invoked to find a solution, yielding a division by zero.

Vice versa, optimizations from the SMT solver are feed back to intervals. First, if the SMT solver proves or disproves a boolean formula, the interval is adjusted and the according constant is removed. Second, if a divisor is proven to be non-zero, the zero is removed from the interval, before the operation is carried out, which reduces the number of potential division by zero warnings.

Since formulas grow along paths, we evaluate each boolean expression along the path to potentially decrease the size of the formula. In this way expressions like $x \wedge \neg x$ are reduced to zero, which is the signal value being passed to the next ports.

5   Evaluation

After having presented, how we combine abstract interpretation with interval sets and symbolic execution with SMT to perform value range analysis on block diagrams, we demonstrate the performance and discuss benefits and drawbacks of our approach. We compare results of our analysis with results of the Math-Works Simulink Design Verifier (SLDV)[4], which performs a value range analysis on Simulink models, too. We have applied our methods to several block diagrams to highlight the main aspects of our technique. Table 2 provides an overview of all models which have been evaluated. The second and third column in Table 2 lists blocks and lines, while the fourth column presents the number of virtual blocks[5], i.e. blocks performing no operation and serving only as visual aids. Structural properties of the systems are given in the last three columns. The fifth column lists the number of subsystems, including conditional and atomic ones, while column six denotes the hierarchy, i.e. the maximum number of nested subsystems. Finally, the last column determines, whether the system is a feedback systems and contains a loop.

Table 2. Model metrics

Model	Blocks	Lines	Virtual blocks	Subsystems	Hierarchy	Closed loop
ABS Brake	48	50	16	5	2	yes
Quarter Car	57	70	11	3	2	yes
Suspension	46	55	13	3	1	yes
DAS	970	915	562	189	13	yes
8 Bit Counter	190	213	126	20	4	no

The first three systems represent applications from the automotive domain and contain continuous blocks, which are not supported by the SLDV. Therefore, we have discretized the systems with MathWorks model discretizer, using Tustins method [10] (trapezoidal integration). Further adaptions, which are described below, were necessary for some models. The ABS Brake represents an anti-lock braking system and is taken from the Simulink examples[6]. In addition to the discretization, we replaced the stop simulation block with an *Out*-block yielding a feasible model for the SLDV. Given our current implementation, we had to exchange the user defined function block, computing the relative slip[7] by $1 - u_1/u_2$ with a subsystem, an addition and division block, respectively. The Quarter Car (we analyzed not the entire system) and Suspension systems, both

---

[4] See http://www.mathworks.com/products/sldesignverifier/.
[5] See http://mathworks.com/help/simulink/ug/nonvirtual-and-virtual-blocks.html.
[6] See http://de.mathworks.com/help/simulink/examples/modeling-an-anti-lock-braking-system.html.
[7] In case $u_2 = 0$, ε is used, which is considered in our verification.

model vehicle suspension in the automotive domain and are taken from the Simulink examples and Matlab Central[8]. To analyze both models, no further modification, except the discretization, was necessary. As a pure discrete system, the 8 Bit Counter, taken from Matlab Central and extended by an additional *Out*-block, is being evaluated. Due to the nature of the hardware related model, the entire system consists mainly of *Memory*- and *Truth Table*-blocks. The DAS model is an industrial example of an assistance system from the automotive domain.

Our evaluation platform is a computer with an Intel i5 2.67 GHz CPU, eight gigabytes memory, with a 64-bit Windows 7 operating system and Matlab 2015b. The logged analysis times of the SLDV exclude the duration of model compilation and translation to the internal intermediate representation. Thus, we exclude for our algorithm the time for starting Matlab, loading the model and translating it to our intermediate abstract block diagram representation. Additionally to time elapse for analysis, we compare the number and type of issued warnings.

Table 3. Analysis results

Model	Time (s)			Warnings		
	SMTR	SMTF	SLDV	SMTR	SMTF	SLDV
ABS Brake	4.838	81.777	102	30 (1)	30 (1)	4
Quarter Car	1.315	1.255	11	35 (0)	35 (0)	2
Suspension	28.483	30.388	12	83 (0)	83 (0)	1
DAS	37.658	1317.478	75	225 (5)	225 (5)	31
8 Bit Counter	44.273	32.165	44	97 (0)	97 (0)	12

In Table 3, an overview of the comparison is given. On the left part of the table, the time elapse is denoted, while the right part contains the number of warnings issued by each algorithm, including symbolic execution with reals (SMTR), floats (SMTF) and the Simulink Design Verifier (SLDV). Since the SLDV uses rational number approximations and no IEEE-754 floats, we extended the evaluation by adding the symbolic execution with reals, to highlight the computational cost for sound floating point abstractions. Hence, our solution issues warning types, which are not considered by the SLDV, such as potential NaN values or implicit rate transitions. Consequently, our algorithm issues more warnings on all chosen models. Therefore, we indicated the number of warnings, excluding warning types not being issued by the SLDV, in parenthesis.

As expected, because of the more complicated theory used for SMTF, the time elapse using SMTR is for most models lower. Moreover, SMTF scales worse

---

[8] See http://de.mathworks.com/matlabcentral/.

than SMTR to larger models. Comparing SMTR to SLDV, it can be noticed, that SLDV is faster analyzing the Suspension model. Regarding the issued warnings, SMTR and SMTF differ for no evaluated model, which we find to be plausible. This is due to the fact, that no model was constructed, using IEEE-754 specific blocks, such as isNaN or isInf. In addition, no model was chosen which exploits differences between SMTR and SMTF. The SMTR yields also NaN warnings, because IEEE-754 operations are also covered by the interval sets. However, differences between the number of warnings of our approach and the SLDV will further be discussed for the evaluated models.

The main difference concerns the *Result could be NaN warning* which is non-existent for SLDV. However, SLDV computes for many signals the same reachable values as SMTF/SMTR, which are often $(-\infty; \infty)$ due to overapproximations and thus could lead to a NaN result in case the sum of two signals with reachable values $(-\infty; \infty)$ is computed, as in many of the benchmark models. The further discussion will focus on warnings which are supported by both approaches. SLDV detects for the ABS Brake model, two *potential divisions by zero* (DbZ) and two potential *data type overflows* (DTO). Using SMTF/SMTR, we were able to avoid the detection of three false positives to only one potential DbZ warning. Regarding the Quarter Car model, SLDV issues two DbZ warnings. However, these result from constant values which were different from zero at the time of analysis and were thus not detected by SMTF/SMTR. The Suspension model causes SLDV to detect a false positive DTO warning. The SMTF/SMTR warnings, however, are limited to potential NaN and *implicit rate transition* warnings.

Comparing the warnings and computed reachable values for the DAS model, we detected that SLDV is in general less overapproximative regarding data stores (which are not yet supported by our tool) and triggered subsystems. However, SLDV issues 19 DbZ and 12 DTO warnings which are caused by lookup tables and divisions by constants or constant signals and data types as float64 which may not overflow. Besides warnings for unsupported features, NaN occurrences and implicit rate transitions, we were able to detect two paths in the model which do not contribute to any model result. Furthermore a violation of the specified design ranges has been detected, which might be a false positive warning.

For the 8 Bit Counter model, SLDV issues 12 overflow warnings. However, these relate to signals which are either of integer types or of boolean type as a result of a lookup. Inspecting the correspondent blocks and paths of the model, these warnings can be identified as false positives and are, furthermore, not detected using SMTR/SMTF.

6   Conclusion

This paper presented the combination of abstract interpretation with symbolic execution based on SMT with IEEE-754 floating point arithmetic for static value range analysis of block diagrams. The evaluation of the presented approach against an industrial state of the art tool showed, that the industrial tool scales better to large models regarding the time elapse for analysis. However, it is not able to detect IEEE-754 related modeling flaws, such as potential occurrences of NaN or correct handling of infinity values due to the used rational number approximation. Moreover, we were able to show that our presented approach is able to reduce the number of false positives regarding warnings for potential overflows and divisions by zero, compared to the industrial tool.

Future work will focus on extending the support of Simulink features, e.g. Stateflow which is only partly supported yet, and to reduce over approximations for special system classes.

References

1. Agrawal, A., Simon, G., Karsai, G.: Semantic translation of Simulink/Stateflow models to hybrid automata using graph transformations. Electron. Notes Theor. Comput. Sci. **109**, 43–56 (2004)
2. Alefeld, G., Mayer, G.: Interval analysis: theory and applications. J. Comput. Appl. Math. **121**(12), 421–464 (2000)
3. Bochot, T., Virelizier, P., Waeselynck, H., Wiels, V.: Model checking flight control systems: the airbus experience. In: ICSE Companion (2009), pp. 18–27 (2009)
4. Broy, M., Kirstan, S., Krcmar, H., Schätz, B., Zimmermann, J.: What is the benefit of a model-based design of embedded software systems in the car industry? In: Software Design and Development: Concepts, Methodologies, Tools, and Applications: Concepts, Methodologies, Tools, and Applications, p. 310 (2013)
5. Chapoutot, A., Martel, M.: Abstract simulation: a static analysis of simulink models. In: International Conference on Embedded Software and Systems, 2009. ICESS 2009, pp. 83–92, May 2009
6. Cousot, P., Cousot, R.: Abstract interpretation: a unified lattice model for static analysis of programs by construction or approximation of fixpoints. In: Proceedings of the 4th ACM SIGACT-SIGPLAN Symposium on Principles of Programming Languages, pp. 238–252 (1977)
7. de Moura, L., Bjørner, N.S.: Z3: an efficient SMT solver. In: Ramakrishnan, C.R., Rehof, J. (eds.) TACAS 2008. LNCS, vol. 4963, pp. 337–340. Springer, Heidelberg (2008)
8. Dernehl, C., Hansen, N., Kowalewski, S.: Static value range analysis for Matlab/Simulink-models. In: 13. Workshop Automotive Software, INFORMATIK 2015, pp. 1649–1660 (2015)
9. ISO: ISO 26262–6 - Road vehicles - functional safety - Part 6 product development software level. Technical report, Geneva, Switzerland (2011)
10. Korlinchak, C., Comanescu, M.: Discrete time integration of observers with continuous feedback based on Tustin's method with variable prewarping. In: 6th IET International Conference on Power Electronics, Machines and Drives (PEMD 2012), pp. 1–6. IET (2012)
11. Leino, K.R.M., Logozzo, F.: Using widenings to infer loop invariants inside an SMT solver, or: a theorem prover as abstract domain. In: Workshop on Invariant Generation, pp. 70–84 (2007)
12. Moore, R.E., Kearfott, R.B., Cloud, M.J.: Introduction to Interval Analysis. Society for Industrial and Applied Mathematics, Philadelphia (2009)

13. de Moura, L., Bjørner, N.: Satisfiability modulo theories: an appetizer. In: Oliveira, M.V.M., Woodcock, J. (eds.) SBMF 2009. LNCS, vol. 5902, pp. 23–36. Springer, Heidelberg (2009)

14. Reicherdt, R., Glesner, S.: Formal verification of discrete-time MATLAB/Simulink models using Boogie. In: Giannakopoulou, D., Salaün, G. (eds.) SEFM 2014. LNCS, vol. 8702, pp. 190–204. Springer, Heidelberg (2014)

15. Selic, B.: The pragmatics of model-driven development. IEEE Softw. **20**(5), 19–25 (2003)

16. Tripakis, S., Sofronis, C., Caspi, P., Curic, A.: Translating discrete-time Simulink to Lustre. ACM Trans. Embed. Comput. Syst. (TECS) **4**(4), 779–818 (2005)

Model Checking

Program Generation Using Simulated Annealing and Model Checking

Idress Husien$^{(\boxtimes)}$ and Sven Schewe

Department of Computer Science, University of Liverpool, Liverpool, UK
`idress.husien@liv.ac.uk`

Abstract. Program synthesis can be viewed as an exploration of the search space of candidate programs in pursuit of an implementation that satisfies a given property. Classic synthesis techniques facilitate exhaustive search, while genetic programming has recently proven the potential of generic search techniques. But is genetic programming the right search technique for the synthesis problem? In this paper we challenge this belief and argue in favor of simulated annealing, a different class of general search techniques. We show that, in hindsight, the success of genetic programming has drawn from what is arguably a hybrid between simulated annealing and genetic programming, and compare the fitness of classic genetic programming, the hybrid form, and pure simulated annealing. Our experimental evaluation suggests that pure simulated annealing offers better results for automated programming than techniques based on genetic programming.

1 Introduction

The development of correct code can be quite challenging, especially for concurrent systems. Classical software engineering methods, where the validation is based on testing, do not seem to provide the right way to approach this type of involved problems, as bugs easily elude predefined tests. Guaranteeing correctness for such programs is also not trivial. Manual proof methods for verifying the correctness of the code against a given formal specification were suggested in the late 60s. The next step for achieving more reliable software has been to offer an automatic verification procedure through model checking [1–3,6,15,18,26,27].

The holy grail of such techniques would be synthesis: the automated construction of programs that are correct by construction. Such synthesis techniques have long been held to be impossible for reactive systems due to the complexity of synthesis, which ranges from EXPTIME for CTL synthesis [5,25] to undecidable for distributed systems [13,30,33,34].

This line of thought has come under attack on many fronts. On the theoretical side, bounded [14] and succinct [11] synthesis techniques have levelled the playing field between the verification and synthesis of reactive systems by shifting the

This work was supported by the Ministry of Higher Education in Iraq through the University of Kirkuk and by the EPSRC through grant EP/M027287/1.

R. De Nicola and E. Kühn (Eds.): SEFM 2016, LNCS 9763, pp. 155–171, 2016.
DOI: 10.1007/978-3-319-41591-8_11

focus from the input complexity to the cost measured in the minimal explicit and symbolic solution, respectively. One could argue that this is the theoretical underpinning of successful approaches, including implementations of bounded synthesis [10,12] and methods based on genetic programming [20–23].

The success of genetic programming is also based on the observation that the neighborhood of good solutions are often 'not bad', and would often still display many sought after properties, such as satisfying a number of sub-specifications fully, and others partially. Such properties are translated to a high fitness of the candidate solution. Vice versa, the higher the fitness of a candidate, the more likely is it to find a full solution in its proximity. This observation is also at the heart of traditional engineering techniques: usually the elimination of a bug does not cause errors in other places. It is also the assumption used when applying program repair [19,36] techniques. The successive development into correct programs is also distantly related to counter-example-guided inductive synthesis [35] for inductive programs, where a genetic approach has also been discussed [7].

Our work is at the same time inspired by the success of genetic programming and driven by the doubt if genetic programming is the right generic search technique to use. The success of genetic programming for synthesis is thoroughly documented by a series of papers by Katz and Peled [21–23]. The doubts, on the other hand, are fueled by the general observation that genetic programming is often outperformed by simulated annealing [8,28,31].

On a conceptual level, the difference between simulated annealing and genetic programming techniques are rather minor. These difference are threefold. The first difference is in the number of candidates considered in each iteration. In genetic programming, these are many. In the Katz and Peled papers [21–23], for example, these are typically 150, 5 from the previous cycle and 145 mutated programmes—numbers we have copied for our own experiments with genetic programming. In simulated annealing, there is typically one new implementation in each iteration. The second difference is that genetic approaches may use crossovers, a proper mix of two candidate solutions, in addition to mutations, whereas simulated annealing only uses mutations[1]. The third difference is the way the selection takes place. The rules for selection is typically static for genetic programming, while the entropy falls over time in simulated annealing.

It is important to note that crossovers are not always used in genetic programming, and we are not aware of any genetic programming approach that has tried to exploit crossovers for synthesis. Personal communication with the authors of [21–23] showed that they did not believe that crossover would be useful in the context of synthesis. Simulated annealing has been reported [8,28,31] to outperform genetic programming when crossovers do not provide an advantage or are not used. Broadly speaking, this is because keeping only a single instance increases the update speed (where the factor is roughly the number

---

[1] The changes are usually not referred to as mutations, but the rules of obtaining them are the same. We use the term mutations for simulated annealing, too, in order to ease the comparison between simulated annealing and genetic programming.

of instances), whereas many instances reduce the search depth or increase the likelihood of success in a bounded search with a fixed number of iterations. Overall, the speed-up of the update tends to outweigh the increase in depth, or the reduction in the success rate, of a bounded search. This led us to the hypothesis that the same holds when these techniques are used in synthesis.

Finally, the paper series on genetic programming by Katz and Peled [21–23] has used a layered approach, where the weighing of the search function differs over time, starting with establishing the safety properties. The effect of this difference is comparable to the effect of cooling when a stable level of quality is reached. We took this as another hint that simulated annealing is the more appropriate technique when implementing synthesis based on general search with model checking as a fitness measure. In this work we suggest to use simulated annealing for program synthesis and compare it to similar approaches based on genetic programming. We use a formal verification technique, model checking, as a way of assessing its fitness in an inductive automatic programming system. We have implemented a synthesis tool, which uses multiple calls to the model checker NuSMV [3] to determine the fitness for a candidate program. The candidate programs exist in two forms. The main form is a simple imperative language. This form is subject to mutation, but it is translated to a secondary form, the modeling language of NuSMV, for evaluating its fitness. All choices of how exactly a program is represented and how exactly the fitness is evaluated are disputable. Generic search techniques are, however, usually rather robust against changes in such details. While there has been further research on how to measure partial satisfaction [17], we believe that the best choice for us is to keep to the choices made for promoting genetic programming [21–23], as this is the only choice that is completely free of suspicion of being selected for being more suitable for simulated annealing than for genetic programming. A second motivation for this selection is that it results in very simple specifications and, therefore, in fast evaluations of the fitness. Noting that synthesis entails on average hundreds of thousands to millions of calls to a model checker, only simple evaluations can be considered. We have implemented six different combinations of selection and update mechanism to test our hypothesis: besides simulated annealing, we have used genetic programming both without crossover (as discussed in [21–23]) and with crossover. The tests we have run confirmed that simulated annealing performs significantly better than genetic programming. As a side result, we found that the assumption of the authors of [21–23] that crossover does not accelerate genetic programming did not prove to be entirely correct, but the advantages we observed were minor.

2   The Approach in a Nutshell

In a nutshell, our synthesiser (cf. Fig. 1) consists of four main components: a modifier/seeder for programs (Program Generation), a compiler into a model checker format (Program Translation), a quantitative extension of a model checker, using NuSMV [3] as a back-end, and a selector that determines which program to keep (Simulated Annealing). The specification is provided in form of a list of sub-specifications, which is then automatically extended to additional weaker specifications that are used to obtain a quantitative measure for partial satisfaction. Broadly speaking, the extension takes partial satisfaction of a specification into account by giving different weights to different weaker versions of sub-specifications (cf. Sect. 4). The result can be manually modified, but the results reported in Sect. 6 refer to the automatically produced extension.

The internal representation of a program is a tree. The seeder/modifier produces an initial seed. (Alternatively, one could start with an initial program provided by the user.) The modifier/seeder also produces modifications of existing programs by changing sub-trees (cf. Sect. 4). The programs are then translated to the input language of a model checker (NuSMV in our case), which is then called several times to determine the level of satisfaction, which is the core of the fitness (cf. Sect. 4) of a program.

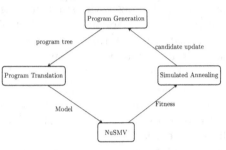

Fig. 1. Synthesis Tool

Broadly speaking, the number of candidate programs kept depends on the search technique used. We have implemented both genetic programming approaches and simulated annealing in order to obtain a clean point of comparison.

3   Background

Simulated Annealing. Simulated annealing [4,16] is a general local search technique that is able to escape from local optima, easy to implementation, and has good convergence properties.

When applied to an optimisation problem, the fitness function (objective) generates values for the quality of the solution constructed in each iteration. The fitness of this newly selected solution is then compared with the fitness of the solution from the previous round. Improved solutions are always accepted, while some of the other solutions are accepted in the hope of escaping local optima in search of global optima. The probability of accepting solutions with reduced fitness depends on a temperature parameter, which is typically falling monotonically with each iteration of the algorithm.

Simulated annealing starts with an initial candidate solution. In each iteration, a neighboring solution is generated by mutating the previous solution. Let, for the ith iteration, F_{i-1} be the fitness of the 'old' solution and F_i the fitness of its mutation constructed in the ith iteration. If the fitness is not decreased ($F_i \geq F_{i-1}$), then the mutated solution is kept. If the fitness is decreased ($F_i < F_{i-1}$), then the probability p that this mutated solution is kept is

$$p = e^{\frac{F_i - F_{i-1}}{T_i}},$$

where T_i is the temperature parameter for the ith step. The chance of changing to a mutation with smaller fitness is therefore reduced with an increasing gap in the fitness, but also with a falling temperature parameter. The temperature parameter is positive and usually non-increasing $(0 < T_i \leq T_{i-1})$. The development of the sequence T_i is referred to as the *cooling schedule* and inspired by cooling in the physical world [16].

Algorithm 1. Simulated Annealing algorithm

$i := 0$
loop local search with cooling
repeat
  $i := i + 1$
  derive a neighbor x' of x
  $\Delta F := F(x') - F(x)$
  if $\Delta F < 0$ **then**
    $x := x'$
  else
    derive random number $p[0, 1]$
    if $p < e^{\frac{\Delta F}{T(i)}}$ **then**
      $x := x'$
    end if
  end if
until the goal is reached or $i = i_{\mathsf{max}}$

The effect of *cooling* on the simulation of annealing is that the probability of following an unfavorable move is reduced. In practice, the temperature is often decreased in stages. During each stage the temperature is kept constant until a balanced solution is reached. The set of parameters that determines how the temperature is reduced (i.e., the initial temperature, the stopping criterion, the temperature decrements between successive stages, and· the number of transitions for each temperature value) is called the cooling schedule. We have used a simple cooling schedule, where the temperature is dropped by a constant in each iteration. The algorithm is described in Algorithm 1.

Genetic programming. Genetic programming [24] is a different general search technique that has been used for program synthesis in a similar setting [20–23]. In genetic programming, a population of λ candidate programs is first generated randomly. In each step, a small share of the population consisting of μ candidates (with $\mu \ll \lambda$) is maintained based on the fitness. Usually, a random function that makes it more likely for fitter candidate programs to be selected for spawning the next generation is applied. The selected candidates are then mated to retain a population of λ, and mutations are applied to a high share of the resulting programs (e.g., on all duplicates).

We have implemented genetic programming as a comparison point, using the values $\lambda = 150$ and $\mu = 5$ from [21]. We also use the $2,000$ iterations suggested there as a cut-off point, where the algorithm is re-started. In its pure form, it uses the sum of the partial satisfaction values of all sub-specifications as a foundation of the fitness function.

We have additionally implemented a hybrid form that changes the selection technique over time. This technique works in layers: it first establish the safety properties, and then the liveness properties. Specifications with better values for the safety properties are always given preference, while liveness properties are—for equal values for the safety properties—used to determine the fitness. I.e., they are merely tie-breakers.

This approach has been used in [21–23]. We refer to it as a *hybrid approach* as it introduces a property known from simulated annealing: in the beginning, the algorithm is applying changes more flexibly, while it becomes more rigid later.

We have implemented the genetic approaches with and without crossover, and used both evaluation techniques for simulated annealing, where we refer to using the classic fitness function as a *rigid* evaluation, and to the hybrid approach as *flexible* evaluation.

Model checking. Model checking [2,6] is a technique used to determine whether a program satisfies a number of specifications. A model checker takes two inputs. The first of them, the specification, is a description of the temporal behavior a correct system shall display, given in a temporal logic. The second input, the model, is a description of the dynamics of the system that the user wants to evaluate. This might be a computer program, a communications protocol, a state machine, a circuit diagram, etc.

A model checker uses a symbolic representation of the model to decide efficiently if the model satisfies the specification. Standard temporal logic used in model checking are linear-time temporal logic (LTL) [32] and computation tree logic (CTL) [5]. We focus on the latter.

Given a finite set Π of atomic propositions, the syntax of a CTL formula is defined as follows:

$$\phi ::= p \mid \neg\phi \mid \phi \vee \phi \mid A\psi \mid E\psi,$$
$$\psi ::= X\phi \mid \phi U \phi \mid G\phi,$$

where $p \in \Pi$. For each CTL formula ϕ we denote the length of ϕ by $|\phi|$.

Let $T = (V, E)$ be an infinite directed tree, with all edges pointing away from the root. (In model checking, this is the unraveling of the model.) Let $l : V \to 2^{\Pi}$ be a labeling function. The semantics of CTL is defined as follows. For each $v \in V$ we have:

- $v \models p$ if, and only if, $p \in l(v)$.
- $v \models \neg\phi$ if, and only if, $v \not\models \phi$.
- $v \models \phi \vee \psi$ if, and only if, $v \models \phi$ or $v \models \psi$.
- $v \models A\psi$ if, and only if, for all paths π starting at v, we have $\pi \models \psi$.
- $v \models E\psi$ if, and only if, there exists a path π starting at v with $\pi \models \psi$.

Let $\pi = v_1, v_2, \ldots$ be an infinite path in T. We have:

- $\pi \models X\phi$ if, and only if, $v_2 \models \phi$.
- $\pi \models \phi U \phi'$ if, and only if, there exists an $i \in \mathbb{N}$ such that $v_i \models \phi'$ and, for all j in the range $1 \le j < i$, we have $v_j \models \phi$.
- $\pi \models G\phi$ if, and only if, $v_i \models \phi$ for all $i \in \mathbb{N}$.

Note that the ϕ and ϕ' here are state formulas.

The pair (T, l), where T is a tree and l is a labeling function, is a *model* of ϕ if, and only if, $r \models \phi$, where $r \in V$ is the root of the tree. If (T, l) is a model of ϕ, then we write $T, l \models \phi$.

For the candidate programs in our paper, the tree is the tree of all runs / interleaving of the programs under asynchronous composition, and the labels are the program states.

4 Synthesis Tool Architecture

Our tool consists of four main parts: a generator and mutator of abstract programs (Program Generation); a translator from abstract programs to models (Program Translator); a model checker as a basis for determining the fitness, and the simulated annealing mechanism for selecting the candidate program to continue with (cf. Fig. 1).

We use NuSMV [3] as a model checker. The translator therefore translates the abstract programs into the model language of NuSMV. The other parts of the tool are written in C++. Figure 1 gives an overview on the main components of our tool.

When comparing simulated annealing to genetic programming, we merely replace the simulated annealing component by a similar component for the respective genetic programming variant and optionally add crossover to the available mutations.

The user provides specifications for the desired properties of a system in the form of a list of CTL specifications for the system dynamics that the program has to satisfy. The simulated annealing component then derives the intermediate specifications (full and partial compliance) that are used to determine the fitness of a candidate (cf. Sect. 4).

If the candidate program satisfied all required properties, then the synthesiser returns it as a correct program.

Otherwise, it will compare the fitness of the current candidate with the (stored) fitness value of the program it is derived from by mutation. (This is the currently stored candidate.) If the fitness is lower, then the tool will update the stored candidate with the probability $e^{\Delta F / T(i)}$ defined by the loss $\Delta F = F_i - F_{i-1}$ in fitness and the current temperature $T(i)$ taken from the cooling schedule. If the fitness is not lower, the tool will always replaces the stored candidate by the mutated one. When the end of the cooling schedule is reached, the tool aborts. The synthesis process is then re-started, either with a fresh cooling schedule (usually with a higher starting temperature or slower cooling) or with the same cooling schedule. We have implemented the latter. Additional information about the tool can be found at: http://cgi.csc.liv.ac.uk/~idresshu/index2.html.

Model checking as a fitness function. We use model checking to determine the fitness of a candidate program in the same way as it has been used for genetic programming [21–23]. Based on the model checking results, we derive a quantitative measure for the fitness (as a level of partial correctness) of a program. This can be the share of properties that are satisfied so far, or mechanically produced simpler properties. For example, if a property shall hold on all paths, it is better if it holds on some paths, and yet better if it holds almost surely.

Our implementation considers the specification as a list of sub-specifications and assigns full marks for each sub-specification, which is satisfied by the candidate program. For cases where the sub-specification is not satisfied, we distinguish between different levels of partial satisfaction.

We offer an automated translation of properties with up to two universal quantifiers that occur positively. 100 points are assigned when the sub-specification is satisfied, 80 points if the specification is satisfied when replacing one universal path quantifier by an existential path quantifier, and 10 points are assigned if the specification is satisfied after replacing both universal path quantifiers by existential ones. (Existential quantifiers that occur negatively are treated accordingly.) Examples of this automated translation are shown in Sect. 5.

The output of the model checker is used to evaluate the fitness of the current candidate. The main part of the fitness is the average of the values for all sub-specifications in the rigid evaluation and the average of all liveness specifications in the flexible evaluation. Following [21], we apply a penalty for long programs by deducing the number of inner nodes of a program from this average when assigning the fitness of a candidate program. The resulting fitness value will be used by simulated annealing to compare the current candidate with the previous one when using rigid evaluation, and to make a decision whether the changes will be preserved or discarded. When using flexible evaluation, this only happens if the value for the safety specification is equal; falling resp. rising values for safety specifications always result in discarding resp. selecting the update when using flexible evaluation.

Programs as trees. The main form of the programs is a tree, in which each *leaf node* represents a parameter or constant, while each *parent node* represents an operation like assignments, comparisons, or algorithm instruction like *if* or *while*. The candidate programs are built from the root down to the terminal nodes (cf. [21,24]). Figure 2 shows the tree representation of the program

while (turn==me)
other=0

on the left, and two mutations of these programs in the middle and on the right.

Mutations are changes in the program tree. Changes can be applied as follows:

1. Randomly select a node to be changed.

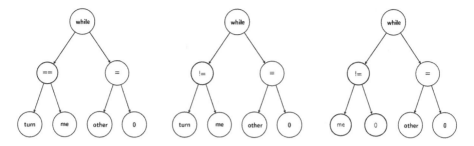

Fig. 2. Program tree (left) with two mutations (middle and right)

2. Apply one of the following changes:
   (a) Replace a boolean comparator by a different boolean comparator. E.g., the middle program from Fig. 2 can result from the left program when '==' is replaced by '!='.
   (b) Replace a leaf by a different parameter or constant from a user defined set.
   (c) Replace a sub-tree (which is no leaf) by a different sub-tree of size 3 with the same type. E.g., the right program from Fig. 2 can result from the left program when by replacing the left sub-tree.
   (d) Add a new internal node, using the node that was there as one sub-tree and creating further offspring of minimal size (which is ≤ 3) to make the resulting tree well typed.

Crossovers between two programs P1 and P2 randomly select nodes N1 of P1 and N2 of P2, and swap the sub-trees rooted in N1 and N2. This way, they produce a proper mix of the two programs.

Besides standard commands—'while', 'if', assignments, boolean connectives and comparators—there are also variable names and constants. They have to be provided by the user. The user also needs to specify, which variables are local and which are global. She can provide an initial tree with nodes that the modifier is not allowed to alter. Examples of this are provided in Sect. 5.

To evaluate the fitness of the produced program, it is first translated into the language of the model checker NuSMV [3]. We have used the translation method suggested by Clarke, Grumberg, and Peled [6]. In this translation, the program is converted into very simple statements (similar to assembly language). To simplify the translation, the program lines are first labeled, and this label is then uses as a pointer that represents the program counter *(PC)*. From this intermediate language, the NuSMV model is then built by creating *(case)* and *(next)* statements that use the *PC*. Figure 3 shows the translation of a mutual exclusion algorithm. At first, each line in the source algorithm labelled, then a variable pc (which is local for each MODULE) is added to represent the control state.

process me
while (true) **do**
  noncritical section
  while (turn==me) **do**
    skip
  end while
  critical section
  turn=other
end while
 	
'me' and 'other' are (different) variable valuations, in this example implemented as boolean variables. In other instances, they might be have a different (finite) datatype.
	MODULE p(turn)
	VAR
	pc: {11, 12, 14,15};
	ASSIGN
	init(pc) := 11;
	next(pc) :=
	case
	(pc=11) : {11, 12};
	(pc=12)&(turn=me) : 14;
	(pc=14) : 15;
	(pc=15) : 11;
	TRUE: pc;
	esac;
	next(turn):=
	case
	(pc=15): other;
	TRUE :turn;
	esac;

Fig. 3. Translation example – source(left) and target (right)

5   Case Studies

We have selected mutual exclusion [9] and leader election [23,29] as case studies, because these are the examples, for which genetic programming has been successfully attempted.

Mutual exclusion. In mutual exclusion, no two processes are allowed to be in the *critical section* at the same time. In addition, there are liveness properties that essentially require non-starvation.

For the mutual exclusion example, we consider programs that progress through four sections, a 'non-critical section', an 'entry section', a 'critical section', and an 'exit section'. The 'non-critical section' and 'critical section' parts are not targets of the synthesis process. In this example, we start with a small program tree that includes the non-critical section and the critical section as privileged commands that cannot be changed by the modifier. Neither can any of their ancestors in the program tree. The entry and exit sections, on the other hand, are standard parts of the tree that can be changed.

The modifier is also provided with the vocabulary it can use. Besides the standard commands and the privileged commands for the critical and non-critical sections, these are the variables 'me' and 'other' that identify the two processes involved and, depending on the benchmark, two or three global / shared boolean variables.

The mutual exclusion example uses one safety specification: only one process can be in the critical sections at a time. This is represented by the CTL formula

$$!EF(P0 \text{ in critical section } \& P1 \text{ in critical section}).$$

When using this sub-specification for determining the fitness, we assign

100 points when the sub-specification is satisfied, and
80 points when $!AF(P0$ in critical section & $P1$ in critical section) holds.

In addition, there is a non-starvation property that, whenever a process enters its entry section, it will eventually enter the critical section. For process, one this is

$$AG(P1 \text{ in entry section} \rightarrow AFP1 \text{ in critical section}).$$

When using this sub-specification for determining the fitness, we assign

100 points when the sub-specification is satisfied,
80 points when $EG(P1$ in entry section $\rightarrow AFP1$ in critical section) holds,
80 points when $AG(P1$ in entry section $\rightarrow EFP1$ in critical section) holds, and
10 points when $EG(P1$ in entry section $\rightarrow EFP1$ in critical section) holds.

Leader election. As a second case study, we consider synthesising a solution for the leader election problem [23, 29]. For that purpose, we use clockwise unidirectional ring networks with two different sizes, three or four nodes, respectively.

For leader election, we do not consider any privileged commands. Again, the modifier needs to be provided with vocabulary. Besides the standard commands, this includes

- *id:* a specific integer value for each node in the ring, which have the values $1, \ldots, i$ for rings of size i.
- *myval, other, leaderID:* local variables; leaderID is initialized to 0.
- *Send (myval):* a command that refers to sending the value of 'myval' to the next node in the ring. (It is placed in a variable the next process can read using the following command.)
- *Receive (other):* a command that reads the last value sent by the previous node.

The specification for leader election requires the safety specification that there is never more than one leader, and the liveness requirement that a leader will eventually be elected. For both requirement, we assign

100 points when the sub-specification is satisfied on all paths, and
80 points when the sub-specification is satisfied on some path.

6   Results

We have implemented the simulated annealing and genetic programming algorithms as described, using NuSMV [3] as a solver when deriving the fitness of candidate programs. For simulated annealing, we have set the initial temperature to 20,000. The cooling schedule decreases the temperature by 0.8

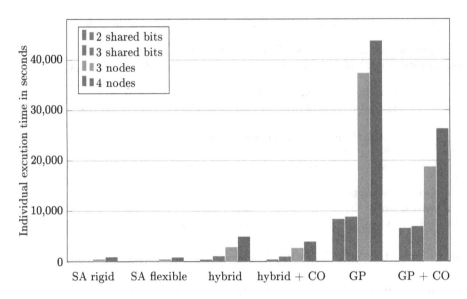

Fig. 4. Average time required for synthesising a correct program (Color figure online)

in each iteration. The schedule ends after 25, 000 iterations, when the temperature hits 0. In a failed execution, this leads to determining the fitness of 25, 001 candidate programs.

As described in Sect. 3, we have taken the values suggested in [21] for genetic programming: $\lambda = 150$ candidate programs are considered in each step, $\mu = 5$ are kept, and we abort after 2, 000 iterations. In a failed execution, this leads to determining the fitness of 290, 150 candidate programs.

For the mutual exclusion benchmark, we distinguish between programs that use two and three shared bits, respectively. For the leader election benchmark we use ring networks with three and four nodes, respectively. The results are shown in Figs. 4 and 5 and summarised in Table 1. The experiments have been conducted using a machine with an Intel core i7 3.40 GHz CPU and 16GB RAM. Figure 4 shows the average time needed for synthesising a correct program. The two factors that determine the average running time are the success rate and the running time for a full execution, successful or not. These values are shown in Fig. 5.

An individual execution of simulated annealing ends when a correct program is found or when the stopping temperature is reached after 25, 000 iterations. Similarly, the genetic programming approaches stop when they have found a solution or when the number or iterations has reached its maximum of 2, 000 iterations. Note that, while simulated annealing incurs more iterations before reaching its termination criterion, it needs to perform only a fraction of the model checking tasks in each iteration. While the number of iterations is slightly more than an order of magnitude higher, the number of programs, for which the

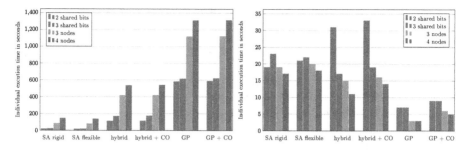

Fig. 5. Average running time of an individual execution (left) and success rate of individual executions (right) (Color figure online)

fitness needs to be calculated, is slightly more than an order of magnitude lower (25,001 vs. 290,150).

For the model checking community, success rates of around 20 % may sound very low, but this is the appropriate range for such techniques. Note that it is very simple to drive the success rate up: one can decrease the cooling speed for simulated annealing and increase the number of iterations for genetic programming, respectively. However, this also increases the running time for individual full executions. A very high success rate is therefore not the goal when devising these algorithms, but a low expected overall running time. A 20 % success rate is in a good region for achieving this goal. Table 1 shows the average running time for single executions in seconds, the success rate in %, and the resulting overall running time. The best values (shortest expected running time or highest success rate) for each comparison printed in bold. Both simulated annealing and the hybrid approach significantly outperform the pure genetic programming approach. The low success rate for pure genetic programming suggests that the number of iterations might be too small. However, as the individual execution time is already ways above the average time simulated annealing needs for constructing a correct program, we did not increase the number of iterations.

The advantage in the individual execution time between the classic and the hybrid version of genetic programming is in the range that is to be expected, as the number of calls to the model checker is reduced. It is interesting to note that simulated annealing, where the shift from rigid to flexible evaluation might be expected to have a similar effect, does not benefit to the same extent. It is also interesting to note that the execution time suggests that determining the fitness of programs produced by simulated annealing is slightly more expensive. This was to be expected, as the average program length grows over time. The penalty for longer programs reduces this effect, but cannot entirely remove it. (This potential disadvantage is the reason why an occasional re-start provides better results than prolonging the search.)

The advantage in running of simulated annealing compared to the hybrid approach reach from factor 4 to factor 10, and the comparison to pure genetic programming reach from factor 35 to factor 76. It is interesting to note that

Table 1. Search techniques comparison

	Search technique	Single execution	Success rate	Overall time
2 shared bits	SA rigid	20	19	105.26
	SA flexible	**18**	21	**85.71**
	Hybrid w/o crossover	113	31	364.51
	Hybrid with crossover	115	**33**	348.48
	GP w/o crossover	583	7	8,328.57
	GP with crossover	589	9	6,544.44
3 shared bits	SA rigid	23	**23**	100
	SA flexible	**20**	22	**90.9**
	Hybrid w/o crossover	171	17	1,005.88
	Hybrid with crossover	175	19	921.05
	GP w/o crossover	615	7	8,785.71
	GP with crossover	620	9	6,888.88
3 nodes	SA rigid	84	19	442.1
	SA flexible	**81**	**20**	**405**
	Hybrid w/o crossover	418	15	2,786.66
	Hybrid with crossover	421	16	2,631.25
	GP w/o crossover	1120	3	37,333.33
	GP with crossover	1123	6	18,716.66
4 nodes	SA rigid	145	17	852.94
	SA flexible	**138**	**18**	**766.66**
	Hybrid w/o crossover	536	11	4,872.72
	Hybrid with crossover	541	14	3,864.28
	GP w/o crossover	1311	3	43,700.00
	GP with crossover	1314	5	26,280.00

both the pure and the hybrid approach to genetic programming benefit from crossovers, but while the benefit for the pure approach is significant, almost halving the average time for synthesising a program in one case, the benefit for the superior hybrid approach is small.

7   Conclusion

We have implemented an automated programming technique based on simulated annealing and genetic programming, both in the pure form of [20] and the arguably hybrid form of [21,22]. The implementations from these papers were unavailable for comparison, but this is, in our view, a plus: the performance is naturally sensitive to the quality of the integration, the suitability of the model checker used, and hidden details, like how the seed is chosen or details of how the fitness is computed. The integrated comparison makes sure that all methods are on equal footage in these regards.

The results are very clear and in line with the expectation we had drawn from the literature [8,28,31]. When crossovers are not used, the main difference between the established genetic programming techniques and simulated annealing is the search strategy of using many and using a single instance, respectively. The data gathered confirms that an increase of the number of iterations can easily overcompensate the broader group of candidates kept in genetic programming. In our experiments, we have used an increase that fell short of creating the same expected running time for a single full execution (with or without success), and yet outperformed even the hybrid approach w.r.t. the success rate on three of our four benchmarks. We have also added variations of genetic programming that include crossover to validate the assumption that crossovers do not lead to an annihilation of the advantage, but it proved that the hybrid approach, and thus the stronger competitor, does not benefit much from using crossover. The double advantage of shorter running time and higher success rate led to an improvement of 1.5 to 2 orders of magnitude compared to pure genetic programming (with and without crossover), and between half an order and one order of magnitude when compared to the hybrid approach (with or without crossover).

It will be interesting to see if future work will show that these factors are essentially constant, or if they depend heavily on the circumstances.

References

1. Alur, R., Henzinger, T.A., Mang, F.Y.C., Qadeer, S., Rajamani, S.K., Tasiran, S.: MOCHA: modularity in model checking. In: Hu, A.L., Vardi, M.Y. (eds.) CAV 1998. LNCS, vol. 1427, pp. 521–525. Springer, Heidelberg (1998)
2. Burch, J.R., Clarke, E.M., McMillan, K.L., Dill, D.L., Hwang, L.J.: Symbolic model checking: 10^{20} states and beyond. Inf. Comput. **98**(2), 142–170 (1992)
3. Cimatti, A., Clarke, E., Giunchiglia, E., Giunchiglia, F., Pistore, M., Roveri, M., Sebastiani, R., Tacchella, A.: NuSMV 2: an opensource tool for symbolic model checking. In: Brinksma, E., Larsen, K.G. (eds.) CAV 2002. LNCS, vol. 2404, pp. 359–364. Springer, Heidelberg (2002)
4. Clark, J.A., Jacob, J.L.: Protocols are programs too: the meta-heuristic search for security protocols. Inf. Softw. Technol. **43**, 891–904 (2001)
5. Clarke, E.M., Emerson, E.A.: Design and synthesis of synchronization skeletons using branching time temporal logic. In: Kozen, D. (ed.) Logics of Programs. LNCS, vol. 131, pp. 52–71. Springer, Heidelberg (1982)
6. Clarke Jr., E.M., Grumberg, O., Peled, O.: Model Checking. MIT Press, Cambridge (1999)
7. David, C., Kroening, D., Lewis, M.: Using program synthesis for program analysis. In: Davis, M., Fehnker, A., McIver, A., Voronkov, A. (eds.) LPAR-20 2015. LNCS, vol. 9450, pp. 483–498. Springer, Heidelberg (2015). doi:10.1007/978-3-662-48899-7_34
8. Davis, L.: Genetic Algorithms and Simulated Annealing. Morgan Kaufmann Publishers Inc., San Francisco (1987)
9. Dijkstra, E.W.: Solution of a problem in concurrent programming control. Commun. ACM **8**, 569 (1965)

10. Ehlers, R.: Unbeast: symbolic bounded synthesis. In: Abdulla, P.A., Leino, K.R.M. (eds.) TACAS 2011. LNCS, vol. 6605, pp. 272–275. Springer, Heidelberg (2011)

11. Fearnley, J., Peled, D., Schewe, S.: Synthesis of succinct systems. J. Comput. Syst. Sci. **81**(7), 1171–1193 (2015)

12. Filiot, E., Jin, N., Raskin, J.-F.: An antichain algorithm for LTL realizability. In: Bouajjani, A., Maler, O. (eds.) CAV 2009. LNCS, vol. 5643, pp. 263–277. Springer, Heidelberg (2009)

13. Finkbeiner, B., Schewe, S.: Uniform distributed synthesis. In: LICS, pp. 321–330. IEEE Computer Society Press (2005)

14. Finkbeiner, B., Schewe, S.: Bounded synthesis. Int. J. Softw. Tools Technol. Transfer **15**(5–6), 519–539 (2013)

15. Hahn, E.M., Li, Y., Schewe, S., Turrini, A., Zhang, L.: ISCASMC: a web-based probabilistic model checker. In: Jones, C., Pihlajasaari, P., Sun, J. (eds.) FM 2014. LNCS, vol. 8442, pp. 312–317. Springer, Heidelberg (2014)

16. Henderson, D., Jacobson, S.H., Johnson, A.W.: The theory and practice of simulated annealing. In: Glover, F., Kochenberger, G.A. (eds.) Handbook of Metaheuristics, pp. 287–319. Springer, New York (2003)

17. Henzinger, T.A., Otop, J.: From model checking to model measuring. In: D'Argenio, P.R., Melgratti, H. (eds.) CONCUR 2013 – Concurrency Theory. LNCS, vol. 8052, pp. 273–287. Springer, Heidelberg (2013)

18. Holzmann, G.J.: The model checker SPIN. Softw. Eng. **23**(5), 279–295 (1997)

19. Jobstmann, B., Griesmayer, A., Bloem, R.: Program repair as a game. In: Etessami, K., Rajamani, S.K. (eds.) CAV 2005. LNCS, vol. 3576, pp. 226–238. Springer, Heidelberg (2005)

20. Johnson, C.G.: Genetic programming with fitness based on model checking. In: Ebner, M., O'Neill, M., Ekárt, A., Vanneschi, L., Esparcia-Alcázar, A.I. (eds.) EuroGP 2007. LNCS, vol. 4445, pp. 114–124. Springer, Heidelberg (2007)

21. Katz, G., Peled, D.A.: Model checking-based genetic programming with an application to mutual exclusion. In: Ramakrishnan, C.R., Rehof, J. (eds.) TACAS 2008. LNCS, vol. 4963, pp. 141–156. Springer, Heidelberg (2008)

22. Katz, G., Peled, D.: Model checking driven heuristic search for correct programs. In: Peled, D.A., Wooldridge, M.J. (eds.) MoChArt 2008. LNCS, vol. 5348, pp. 122–131. Springer, Heidelberg (2009)

23. Katz, G., Peled, D.: Synthesizing solutions to the leader election problem using model checking and genetic programming. In: Namjoshi, K., Zeller, A., Ziv, A. (eds.) HVC 2009. LNCS, vol. 6405, pp. 117–132. Springer, Heidelberg (2011)

24. Koza, J.R.: Genetic Programming: On the Programming of Computers by Means of Natural Selection. MIT Press, Cambridge (1992)

25. Kupferman, O., Vardi, M.Y.: Church's problem revisited. Bull. Symb. Logic **5**(2), 245–263 (1999)

26. Kupferman, O., Vardi, M.Y., Wolper, P.: An automata-theoretic approach to branching-time model checking. J. ACM **47**(2), 312–360 (2000)

27. Kwiatkowska, M., Norman, G., Parker, D.: PRISM 4.0: verification of probabilistic real-time systems. In: Gopalakrishnan, G., Qadeer, S. (eds.) CAV 2011. LNCS, vol. 6806, pp. 585–591. Springer, Heidelberg (2011)

28. Lahtinen, J., Myllymäki, P., Silander, T., Tirri, H.: Empirical comparison of stochastic algorithms. In: 2NWGA, pp. 45–60 (1996)

29. Lichtenstein, O., Pnueli, A.: Checking that finite state concurrent programs satisfy their linear specification. In: POPL, pp. 97–107. ACM (1985)

30. Madhusudan, P., Thiagarajan, P.S.: Distributed controller synthesis for local specifications. In: Orejas, F., Spirakis, P.G., van Leeuwen, J. (eds.) ICALP 2001. LNCS,
vol. 2076, pp. 396–407. Springer, Heidelberg (2001)
31. Mann, J., Smith, G.: A comparison of heuristics for telecommunications traffic
routing. In: Modern Heuristic Search Methods, pp. 235–254 (1996)
32. Pnueli, A.: The temporal logic of programs. In: FOCS, pp. 46–57. IEEE Computer
Society Press (1977)
33. Pnueli, A., Rosner, R.: Distributed reactive systems are hard to synthesize. In:
FOCS, pp. 746–757. IEEE Computer Society Press (1990)
34. Schewe, S., Finkbeiner, B.: Synthesis of asynchronous systems. In: Puebla, G. (ed.)
LOPSTR 2006. LNCS, vol. 4407, pp. 127–142. Springer, Heidelberg (2007)
35. Solar-Lezama, A.: Program sketching. Int. J. Softw. Tools Technol. Transf.
15(5–6), 475–495 (2013)
36. von Essen, C., Jobstmann, B.: Program repair without regret. In: Sharygina, N.,
Veith, H. (eds.) CAV 2013. LNCS, vol. 8044, pp. 896–911. Springer, Heidelberg
(2013)

LTL Parameter Synthesis of Parametric Timed Automata

Peter Bezděk[(✉)], Nikola Beneš, Jiří Barnat, and Ivana Černá

Faculty of Informatics, Masaryk University, Brno, Czech Republic
bezdek@mail.muni.cz, {xbenes3,barnat,cerna}@fi.muni.cz

Abstract. The parameter synthesis problem for parametric timed automata is undecidable in general even for very simple reachability properties. In this paper we introduce restrictions on parameter valuations under which the parameter synthesis problem is decidable for LTL properties. The investigated bounded integer parameter synthesis problem could be solved using an explicit enumeration of all possible parameter valuations. We propose an alternative symbolic zone-based method for this problem which results in a faster computation. Our technique extends the ideas of the automata-based approach to LTL model checking of timed automata. To justify the usefulness of our approach, we provide experimental evaluation and compare our method with explicit enumeration technique.

1 Introduction

Model checking [1] is a formal verification technique applied to check for logical correctness of discrete distributed systems. While it is often used to prove the unreachability of a bad state (such as an assertion violation in a piece of code), with a proper specification formalism, such as the *Linear Temporal Logic* (LTL), it can also check for many interesting liveness properties of systems, such as repeated guaranteed response, eventual stability, live-lock, etc.

Timed automata have been introduced in [2] and have emerged as a useful formalism for modelling time-critical systems as found in many embedded and cyber-physical systems. The formalism is built on top of the standard finite automata enriched with a set of real-time clocks and allowing the system actions to be guarded with respect to the clock valuations. In the general case, such a timed system exhibits infinite-state semantics (the clock domains are continuous). Nevertheless, when the guards are limited to comparing clock values with integers only, there exists a bisimilar finite state representation of the original infinite-state real-time system referred to as the region abstraction. A practically efficient abstraction of the infinite-state space came with the so called zones [3]. The zone-based abstraction is much coarser and the number of zones *reachable*

N. Beneš—The author has been supported by the Czech Science Foundation grant no. GA15-11089S.

R. De Nicola and E. Kühn (Eds.): SEFM 2016, LNCS 9763, pp. 172–187, 2016.
DOI: 10.1007/978-3-319-41591-8_12

from the initial state is significantly smaller. This in turns allows for an efficient implementation of verification tools for timed automata, see e.g. UPPAAL [4].

Very often the correctness of a time-critical system relates to a proper timing, i.e. it does not only depend on the logical result of the computation, but also on the time at which the results are produced. To that end the designers are not only in the need of tools to verify correctness once the system is fully designed, but also in the need of tools that would help them derive proper time parameters of individual system actions that would make the system as a whole satisfy the required specification. After all this problem of *parameter synthesis* is more urgent in practice than the verification as such.

Related Work. The problem of the existence of a parameter valuation for a reachability property of a parametric timed automaton in continuous time has been shown to be undecidable in [5,6] for a parametric timed automaton with as few as 3 clocks. This problem remains undecidable even for integer-valued parameters [7]. A solution for the parameter synthesis problem and reachability properties is presented in [8] where the authors provide a semi-decision algorithm which is not guaranteed to terminate in all cases. Authors also introduce a subclass of parametric timed automata, called L/U automata for which the emptiness problem is decidable. Decidability results for the class of L/U automata are further extended in [9]. In particular, the authors show that emptiness, finiteness and universalitity problems of the set of parameter valuations for which there is an infinite accepting run are decidable.

To obtain a decidable version of parameter synthesis problem for parametric timed automata we need to restrict parameter valuations to bounded integers. When modelling a real-time system, designers can usually provide practical bounds on time parameters of individual system actions. Therefore, introducing a parameter synthesis method with such a restriction is still reasonable. In [10] the authors show that the problem of existence of bounded integer parameter value such that a given property is satisfied is PSPACE-complete for a significant number of properties, which include Timed Computational Tree Logic. They give symbolic algorithms only for reachability and unavoidability properties.

Contribution. The main contribution of this paper is a symbolic method that solves the parameter synthesis problem for specifications given in the Linear Time Logic (LTL) and parametric timed automata with bounded integer parameters. To this end, we introduce a finite abstraction of parametric timed automata with bounded integer parameters and provide an algorithm working over this abstraction. To evaluate our technique we implemented both a symbolic approach and explicit enumeration technique in a proof-of-concept tool and compare the techniques on a case study. The finite abstraction does not provide a unique representation of states and therefore we design an efficient state storage mechanism that deals with this problem. The experiments demonstrate the strength of the symbolic approach which may be faster by an order of magnitude.

Outline. The rest of the paper is organised as follows. The problem definition is given in Sect. 2 that also introduces the basic notions. We then define the symbolic semantics of a parametric timed Büchi automaton and its finite abstraction in Sect. 3. Section 4 describes the parameter synthesis algorithm itself. Section 5 describes the implementation and used heuristics. Then, in Sect. 6 we experimentally evaluate the proposed algorithm and compare it with explicit enumeration. Finally, Sect. 7 concludes the paper.

2 Preliminaries and Problem Statement

In order to state our main problem formally, we need to describe the notion of a parametric timed automaton. We start by describing some basic notation.

Let P be a finite set of *parameters*. An *affine expression* is an expression of the form $z_0 + z_1 p_1 + \ldots + z_n p_n$, where $p_1, \ldots, p_n \in P$ and $z_0, \ldots, z_n \in \mathbb{Z}$. We use $E(P)$ to denote the set of all affine expressions over P. A *parameter valuation* is a function $v : P \to \mathbb{Z}$ which assigns an integer number to each parameter. Let $lb : P \to \mathbb{Z}$ be a lower bound function and $ub : P \to \mathbb{Z}$ be an upper bound function. For an affine expression e, we use $e[v]$ to denote the integer value obtained by replacing each p in e by $v(p)$. We use $max_{lb,ub}(e)$ to denote the maximal value obtained by replacing each p with a positive coefficient in e by $ub(p)$ and replacing each p with a negative coefficient in e by $lb(p)$. We say that the parameter valuation v respects lb and ub if for each $p \in P$ it holds that $lb(p) \leq v(p) \leq ub(p)$. We denote the set of all parameter valuations respecting lb and ub by $Val_{lb,ub}(P)$. In the following, we only consider parameter valuations from $Val_{lb,ub}(P)$.

Let X be a finite set of *clocks*. We assume the existence of a special *zero clock*, denoted by x_0, that has always the value 0. A *guard* is a finite conjunction of expressions of the form $x_i - x_j \sim e$ where $x_i, x_j \in X$, $e \in E(P)$ and $\sim \in \{\leq, <\}$. We use $G(X, P)$ to denote the set of all guards over a set of clocks X and a set of parameters P. A *simple guard* is a guard containing only expressions of the form $x_i - x_j \sim e$ where $x_i, x_j \in X$, $e \in E(P)$, $\sim \in \{\leq, <\}$, and $x_i = x_0$ or $x_j = x_0$. We also use $\overline{G}(X, P)$ to denote the set of all simple guards over a set of clocks X and a set of parameters P. A *clock valuation* is a function $\eta : X \to \mathbb{R}_{\geq 0}$ assigning non-negative real numbers to each clock such that $\eta(x_0) = 0$. We denote the set of all clock valuations by $Val(X)$. Let $g \in G(X, P)$ and v be a parameter valuation and η be a clock valuation. Then $g[v, \eta]$ denotes a boolean value obtained from g by replacing each parameter p with $v(p)$ and each clock x with $\eta(x)$. A pair (v, η) *satisfies* a guard g, denoted by $(v, \eta) \models g$, if $g[v, \eta]$ evaluates to true. The *semantics* of a guard g, denoted by $[\![g]\!]$, is a set of all valuation pairs (v, η) such that $(v, \eta) \models g$. For a given parameter valuation v we write $[\![g]\!]_v$ for the set of clock valuations $\{\eta \mid (v, \eta) \models g\}$.

We define two operations on clock valuations. Let η be a clock valuation, d a non-negative real number and $R \subseteq X$ a set of clocks. We use $\eta + d$ to denote the clock valuation that adds the delay d to each clock, i.e. $(\eta + d)(x) = \eta(x) + d$ for all $x \in X \setminus \{x_0\}$. We further use $\eta\langle R \rangle$ to denote the clock valuation that resets clocks from the set R, i.e. $\eta\langle R \rangle(x) = 0$ if $x \in R$, $\eta\langle R \rangle(x) = \eta(x)$ otherwise.

Definition 2.1 (PTA). *A parametric timed automaton (PTA) is a tuple $M = (L, l_0, X, P, \Delta, Inv)$ where*

- *L is a finite set of locations,*
- *$l_0 \in L$ is the initial location,*
- *X is a finite set of clocks,*
- *P is a finite set of parameters,*
- *$\Delta \subseteq L \times \overline{G}(X, P) \times 2^X \times L$ is a finite transition relation, and*
- *$Inv : L \to \overline{G}(X, P)$ is an invariant function.*

We use $q \xrightarrow{g,R}_\Delta q'$ to denote $(q, g, R, q') \in \Delta$. The semantics of a PTA is given as a labelled transition system. A *labelled transition system* (LTS) over a set of symbols Σ is a triple $(S, s_0, \to)$, where S is a set of states, $s_0 \in S$ is an initial state and $\to \subseteq S \times \Sigma \times S$ is a transition relation. We use $s \xrightarrow{a} s'$ to denote $(s, a, s') \in \to$.

Definition 2.2 (PTA semantics). *Let $M = (L, l_0, X, P, \Delta, Inv)$ be a PTA and v be a parameter valuation. The semantics of M under v, denoted by $[\![M]\!]_v$, is an LTS $(\mathbb{S}_M, s_0, \to)$ over the set of symbols $\{act\} \cup \mathbb{R}_{\geq 0}$, where*

- *$\mathbb{S}_M = L \times Val(X)$ is a set of all states,*
- *$s_0 = (l_0, \mathbf{0})$, where $\mathbf{0}$ is a clock valuation with $\mathbf{0}(x) = 0$ for all x, and*
- *the transition relation $\to$ is specified for all $(l, \eta), (l', \eta') \in \mathbb{S}_M$ as follows:*
  - *$(l, \eta) \xrightarrow{d} (l', \eta')$ if $l = l'$, $d \in \mathbb{R}_{\geq 0}$, $\eta' = \eta + d$, and $(v, \eta') \models Inv(l')$,*
  - *$(l, \eta) \xrightarrow{act} (l', \eta')$ if $\exists g, R : l \xrightarrow{g,R}_\Delta l'$, $(v, \eta) \models g$, $\eta' = \eta\langle R\rangle$, and $(v, \eta') \models Inv(l')$.*

The transitions of the first kind are called delay *transitions, the latter are called* action *transitions.*

We write $s_1 \xrightarrow{act}_d s_2$ if there exists $s' \in \mathbb{S}_M$ and $d \in \mathbb{R}^{\geq 0}$ such that $s_1 \xrightarrow{act} s' \xrightarrow{d} s_2$. A proper run π of $[\![M]\!]_v$ is an infinite alternating sequence of delay and action transitions that begins with a delay transition $\pi = (l_0, \eta_0) \xrightarrow{d_0} (l_0, \eta_0 + d_0) \xrightarrow{act} (l_1, \eta_1) \xrightarrow{d_1} \cdots$. A proper run is called Zeno if the sum of all its delays is finite.

Let M be a PTA, $\mathcal{L} : L \to 2^{Ap}$ be a labelling function that assigns a set of atomic propositions to each location of M, v be a parameter valuation, and φ be an LTL formula. We say that M under v with $\mathcal{L}$ satisfies φ, denoted by $(M, v, \mathcal{L}) \models \varphi$ if for all proper runs π of $[\![M]\!]_v$, π satisfies φ where atomic propositions are determined by $\mathcal{L}$.

Given a parametric timed automaton M, a labelling function $\mathcal{L}$, and an LTL property φ, the *parameter synthesis problem* is to compute the set of all parameter valuations v such that $(M, v, \mathcal{L}) \models \varphi$. Unfortunately, it is known that the parameter synthesis problem for a PTA is undecidable even for very simple (reachability) properties [5]. Instead of solving the general problem, we thus focus on a more constrained version which is still reasonable for practical purposes.

Problem Formulation. Given an LTL property φ, a parametric timed automaton $M = (L, l_0, X, P, \Delta, Inv)$, a labelling function $\mathcal{L}$, a lower bound function lb and an upper bound function ub, *the bounded integer parameter synthesis problem* is to compute the set of all parameter valuations v such that $(M, v, \mathcal{L}) \models \varphi$ and $lb(p) \le v(p) \le ub(p)$ for each $p \in P$.

This problem is trivially decidable using the standard zone-based abstraction and explicit enumeration of all parameter valuations. In order to avoid the necessity of the explicit enumeration of all parameter valuations we use a combination of the zone-based abstraction and a symbolic representation of parameter valuation sets. Our algorithmic framework which solves this problem consists of three steps.

As the first step, we apply the standard automata-based LTL model checking of timed automata [2] to parametric timed automata. We employ this approach in the following way. From a PTA M and an LTL formula φ we produce a product parametric timed Büchi automaton (PTBA) A. The accepting runs of the automaton A correspond to the runs of M violating the formula φ.

As the second step, we employ a symbolic semantics of a PTBA A with a suitable extrapolation. From the symbolic state space of a PTBA A we finally produce a Büchi automaton B in which each state is associated symbolic information about parameter valuations. This transformation is described in Sect. 3.

As the last step, we need to detect all parameter valuations for which there exists an accepting run in Büchi automaton B. To that end, we employ a new algorithm, which we call the Cumulative NDFS. The algorithm is described in detail in Sect. 4.

We now proceed with the definitions of a Büchi automaton, a parametric timed Büchi automaton and its semantics.

Definition 2.3 (BA). *A Büchi automaton (BA) is a tuple $B = (Q, q_0, \Sigma, \rightarrow, F)$, where Q is a finite set of states, $q_0 \in Q$ is an initial state, Σ is a finite set of symbols, $\rightarrow \subseteq Q \times \Sigma \times Q$ is a set of transitions, and $F \subseteq Q$ is a set of accepting states (acceptance condition). An ω-word $w = a_0 a_1 a_2 \ldots \in \Sigma^\omega$ is accepting if there is an infinite sequence of states $q_0 q_1 q_2 \ldots$ such that $q_i \xrightarrow{a_i} q_{i+1}$ for all $i \in \mathbb{N}$, and there exist infinitely many $i \in \mathbb{N}$ such that $q_i \in F$.*

Definition 2.4 (PTBA). *A parametric timed Büchi automaton (PTBA) is a pair $A = (M, F)$ where $M = (L, l_0, X, P, \Delta, Inv)$ is a PTA, and $F \subseteq L$ is a set of accepting locations.*

Zeno runs represent non-realistic behaviours and it is desirable to ignore them in analysis. Therefore, we are interested only in non-Zeno accepting runs of a PTBA. There is a syntactic transformation to the so-called strongly non-Zeno form [11] of a PTBA, which guarantees that each accepting run is non-Zeno. For the rest of the paper, we thus assume that there are no Zeno accepting runs in the PTBA.

Definition 2.5 (PTBA semantics). *Let $A = (M, F)$ be a PTBA and v be a parameter valuation. The semantics of A under v, denoted by $[\![A]\!]_v$, is defined as $[\![M]\!]_v = (\mathbb{S}_M, s_0, \rightarrow)$.*

We say a state $s = (l, \eta) \in \mathbb{S}_M$ is accepting if $l \in F$. A proper run $\pi = s_0 \xrightarrow{d_0} s_0' \xrightarrow{act} s_1 \xrightarrow{d_1} s_1' \xrightarrow{act} \ldots$ of $[\![A]\!]_v$ is accepting if there exists an infinite set of indices i such that s_i is accepting.

3 Symbolic Semantics

In this section we show the construction of a finite system which represents the semantics of a given PTBA. First, we describe a parametric extension of the zone abstraction. This extension is based on constrained parametric difference bound matrices, described in [8]. However, this abstraction itself does not guarantee finiteness in our setting. To solve this problem we further introduce a finite parametric extrapolation.

3.1 Constrained Parametric Difference Bound Matrix

A *constraint* is an inequality of the form $e \sim e'$ where $e, e' \in E$ and $\sim \in \{>, \geq, \leq, <\}$. We define $c[v]$ as the boolean value obtained by replacing each p in c by $v(p)$. A valuation v *satisfies* a constraint c, denoted $v \models c$, if $c[v]$ evaluates to true. The *semantics* of a constraint c, denoted $[\![c]\!]$, is the set of all valuations that satisfy c. A finite set of constraints C is called a *constraint set*. A valuation *satisfies* a constraint set C if it satisfies each $c \in C$. The *semantics* of a constraint set C is given by $[\![C]\!] = \bigcap_{c \in C} [\![c]\!]$. A constraint set C is *satisfiable* if $[\![C]\!] \neq \emptyset$. A constraint c *covers* a constraint set C, denoted $C \models c$, if $[\![C]\!] \subseteq [\![c]\!]$.

As in [8], we identify the relation symbol $\leq$ with the boolean value true and $<$ with the boolean value false. Then, we treat boolean connectives on relation symbols $\leq, <$ as operations with boolean values. For example, $(\leq \Longrightarrow <) = <$.

We now define the parametric difference bound matrix, the constrained parametric difference bound matrix, several operations on them, and the symbolic semantics of a PTBA.

Definition 3.1. *A* parametric difference bound matrix *(PDBM) over P and X is a set D which contains for all $0 \leq i, j \leq |X|$ a guard of the form $x_i - x_j \prec_{ij} e_{ij}$ where $x_i, x_j \in X$ and $e_{ij} \in E(P) \cup \{\infty\}$ and $i = j \implies e_{ii} = 0$. We denote by D_{ij} a guard of the form $x_i - x_j \prec_{ij} e_{ij}$ contained in D. Given a parameter valuation v, the semantics of D is given by $[\![D]\!]_v = [\![\bigwedge_{i,j} D_{ij}]\!]_v$. A PDBM D is satisfiable with respect to v if $[\![D]\!]_v$ is non-empty.*

Definition 3.2. *A* constrained parametric difference bound matrix *(CPDBM) is a pair (C, D), where C is a constraint set and D is a PDBM and for each $0 \leq i \leq |X|$ it holds that $C \models e_{0i} \geq 0$. The semantics of (C, D) is given by $[\![C, D]\!] = \{(v, \eta) \mid v \in [\![C]\!] \wedge \eta \in [\![D]\!]_v\}$. We call (C, D) satisfiable if $[\![C, D]\!]$ is non-empty. A CPDBM (C, D) is said to be in the canonical form if and only if for all i, j, k, $C \models e_{ij}(\prec_{ik} \wedge \prec_{kj})e_{ik} + e_{kj}$.*

Resetting a Clock. Suppose (C, D) is a CPDBM in the canonical form. The reset of the clock x_r in (C, D), denoted by $(C, D)\langle x_r \rangle$, is given as $(C, D\langle x_r \rangle)$ where:

$$D\langle x_r \rangle_{ij} = \begin{cases} D_{0j} & \text{if } i \neq j \text{ and } i = r, \\ D_{i0} & \text{if } i \neq j \text{ and } j = r, \\ D_{ij} & \text{else.} \end{cases}$$

We can again generalise this definition to a set of clocks:

$$(C, D)\langle x_{i_0}, x_{i_1}, \ldots, x_{i_k} \rangle \overset{def}{\Leftrightarrow} (C, D)\langle x_{i_0} \rangle \langle x_{i_1} \rangle \ldots \langle x_{i_k} \rangle.$$

Applying a Guard. Suppose g is a guard of the form $x_i - x_j \prec e$, (C, D) is a CPDBM in the canonical form and $D_{ij} = (e_{ij}, \prec_{ij})$. The application of the guard g on (C, D) generally results in a set of CPDBMs and is defined as follows:

$$(C, D)[g] = \begin{cases} \{(C, D[g])\} & \text{if } C \models \neg(e_{ij}(\prec_{ij} \implies \prec)e), \\ \{(C, D)\} & \text{if } C \models e_{ij}(\prec_{ij} \implies \prec)e, \\ \{(C \cup \{e_{ij}(\prec_{ij} \implies \prec)e\}, D), & \text{otherwise,} \\ (C \cup \{\neg e_{ij}(\prec_{ij} \implies \prec)e\}, D[g]), \} \end{cases}$$

where $D[g]$ is defined as follows:

$$D[g]_{kl} = \begin{cases} (e, \prec) & \text{if } k = i \text{ and } l = j, \\ D_{kl} & \text{else.} \end{cases}$$

We can generalise this definition to conjunctions of guards as follows:
$$D[g_{i_0} \wedge g_{i_1} \wedge \ldots \wedge g_{i_k}] \overset{def}{\Leftrightarrow} D[g_{i_0}][g_{i_1}] \ldots [g_{i_k}].$$

Time Successors. Suppose (C, D) is a CPDBM in the canonical form. The time successor of (C, D), denoted by $(C, D)^\uparrow$, represents a CPDBM with all upper bounds on clocks removed and is given as $(C, D^\uparrow)$ where:

$$D_{ij}^\uparrow = \begin{cases} (\infty, <) & \text{if } i \neq 0 \text{ and } j = 0, \\ D_{ij} & \text{else.} \end{cases}$$

The reset and time successor operations preserve the canonical form of a CPDBM. After the application of a guard the CPDBM may no longer be in the canonical form and thus a transformation to the canonical form needs to be performed. However, due to the presence of parameters the standard canonisation [12] process can be ambiguous. The canonisation procedure is therefore extended to cope with this ambiguity. As a consequence, the result of the canonisation is not a single CPDBM, but may generally be a set containing potentially more CPDBMs in the canonical form with mutually disjoint constraint sets.

To canonise the given CPDBM we need to derive the tightest constraint on each clock difference. Deriving the tightest constraint on a clock difference can be seen as finding the shortest path in the graph interpretation of the CPDBM. In [8] the authors implement the canonisation using a nondeterministic extension of the Floyd-Warshall algorithm where on each relaxation a split into two different CPDBMs can occur.

Canonisation. First, we define a relation $\longrightarrow_{FW}$ on constrained parametric bound matrices as follows, for all $0 \leq k, i, j \leq |X|$:

- $(k, i, j, C_1, D_1) \longrightarrow_{FW} (k, i, j+1, C_2, D_2)$
  if $(C_2, D_2) \in (C_1, D_1)[x_i - x_j(\prec_{ik} \wedge \prec_{kj})e_{ik} + e_{kj}]$
- $(k, i, |X|+1, C_1, D_1) \longrightarrow_{FW} (k, i+1, 0, C_1, D_1)$
- $(k, |X|+1, 0, C_1, D_1) \longrightarrow_{FW} (k+1, 0, 0, C_1, D_1)$

The relation $\longrightarrow_{FW}$ can be seen as a representation of the computation steps of the extended Floyd-Warshall algorithm.

Suppose now (C, D) is a CPDBM. The canonical set of (C, D), denoted as $(C, D)_c$, represents a set of CPDBMs with the tightest constraint on each clock difference in D and is defined as follows:

$$(C, D)_c = \{(C', D') \mid (0, 0, 0, C, D) \longrightarrow^*_{FW} (|X|+1, 0, 0, C', D')\}$$

Example 3.3. Let $x, y \in X$ and $p, q \in P$. For a CPDBM $(C, D) = (\emptyset, \{x \leq p, y \leq q, y \leq x, y \leq x\})$ we obtain by canonisation $(C, D)_c = \{((\{p \leq q\}, \{x \leq p, y \leq p, y \leq x, y \leq x\}), (\{q < p\}, \{x \leq q, y \leq q, y \leq x, y \leq x\})\}$.

Definition 3.4. (PTBA symbolic semantics). *Let* $A = ((L, l_0, X, P, \Delta, Inv), F)$ *be a PTBA. Let lb and ub be a lower bound function and an upper bound function on parameters. The* symbolic semantics *of* A *with respect to lb and ub is a transition system* $(\mathbb{S}_A, \mathbb{S}_{init}, \Longrightarrow)$, *denoted as* $[\![A]\!]_{lb,ub}$, *where*

- $\mathbb{S}_A = L \times \{[\![C, D]\!] \mid (C, D) \text{ is a CPDBM}\}$ *is the set of all symbolic states,*
- *the set of initial states* $\mathbb{S}_{init} = \{(l_0, [\![C, D]\!]) \mid (C, D) \in (\emptyset, E^\uparrow)[Inv(l_0)]\}$, *where*
  • E *is a PDBM with* $E_{i,j} = (0, \leq)$ *for each* i, j, *and*
  • *for each* $p \in P$, *the constraints* $p \geq lb(p)$ *and* $p \leq ub(p)$ *are in* C.
- *There is a transition* $(l, [\![C, D]\!]) \Longrightarrow (l', [\![C'_c, D'_c]\!])$ *if*
  • $l \xrightarrow{g,R}_\Delta l'$ *and*
  • $(C'', D'') \in (C, D)[g]$ *and*
  • $(C''_c, D''_c) \in (C'', D'')_c$ *and*
  • $(C', D') \in (C''_c, D''_c\langle R\rangle^\uparrow)[Inv(l')]$ *and*
  • $(C'_c, D'_c) \in (C', D')_c$.

We say that a state $S = (l, [\![C, D]\!]) \in \mathbb{S}_A$ *is accepting if* $l \in F$. *We say that* $\pi = S_0 \Longrightarrow S_1 \Longrightarrow \ldots$ *is a* run *of* $[\![A]\!]_{lb,ub}$ *if* $S_0 \in \mathbb{S}_{init}$ *and for each* i, $S_i \in \mathbb{S}_A$ *and* $S_{i-1} \Longrightarrow S_i$. *A run* respects *a parameter valuation* v *if for each state* $S_i = (l_i, [\![C_i, D_i]\!])$ *it holds that* $v \in [\![C_i]\!]$. *A run* π *is* accepting *if there exists an infinite set of indices* i *such that* S_i *is accepting. For the rest of the paper we fix lb, ub and use* $[\![A]\!]$ *to denote* $[\![A]\!]_{lb,ub}$.

3.2   Finite Abstraction

Similarly to the nonparametric case, the symbolic transition system $[\![A]\!]$ may be infinite. In order to obtain a finite transition system we need to apply a finite abstraction over $[\![A]\!]$. In the standard case of timed automata without parameters we use one of the extrapolation techniques [13,14]. In our parametric setup we define a new finite abstraction called the *pk-extrapolation* which is a parametric extension of the widely used *k-extrapolation* [13]. The k-extrapolation identifies states which are identical except for the clock values which exceeds the maximal constant from guards and invariants.

In our parametric setup, we need to define the maximal constant with which each clock within a PTBA is compared. We define $M(x)$ as the maximal value in $\{max_{lb,ub}(e) \mid e$ is compared with x in a guard or an invariant of the considered PTBA$\}$. The core idea of pk-extrapolation is the same as the idea of k-extrapolation. We substitute each bound on clock difference in the CPDBM whenever this bound exceeds the maximal constant. The precise description of this substitution process is given in the Definition 3.5. Contrary to the nonparametric case, due to the occurrence of parameters in the CPDBM bounds, the substitution process may be ambiguous. In these situations we restrict the parameter values in order to obtain an unambiguous situation. This solution is similar to the constraint set splitting that is done in the application of a guard and in the canonisation procedure. Therefore, the result of pk-extrapolation is a set of CPDBMs instead of a single CPDBM.

Definition 3.5. *Let A be a PTBA, $(l, [\![C, D]\!])$ be a symbolic state of $[\![A]\!]$ and $D_{ij} = x_i - x_j \prec_{ij} e_{ij}$ for each $0 \le i, j \le |X|$. We define the* pk-extrapolation α_{pk} *in the following way.* $\alpha_{pk}(l, [\![C, D]\!])$ *is the set of all $(l, [\![C', D']\!])$ such that for each i, j, $0 \le i, j \le |X|$ one of the following conditions holds:*

- $D'_{ij} = x_i - x_j \prec_{ij} e_{ij}$ *and the constraint* $(e_{ij} \le M(x_i)) \in C'$,
- $D'_{ij} = x_i - x_j < \infty$ *and the constraint* $(e_{ij} > M(x_i)) \in C'$,
- $D'_{ij} = x_i - x_j \prec_{ij} e_{ij}$ *and the constraint* $(e_{ij} \ge -M(x_j)) \in C'$,
- $D'_{ij} = x_i - x_j < -M(x_j)$ *and the constraint* $(e_{ij} < -M(x_j)) \in C'$.

Example 3.6. Consider $x, y \in X$, $p \in P$, $p \in [0, 7]$, $M(x) = M(y) = 10$, and the symbolic state $(l, [\![C, D]\!])$ where $C = \emptyset$ and $D = \{x \le y, y \le x, y \le 2p\}$. Now, $\alpha_{pk}(l, [\![C, D]\!])$ contains two symbolic states: $(l, [\![C_1, D_1]\!])$ and $(l, [\![C_2, D_2]\!])$ where $C_1 = \{2p \le 10\}$, $D_1 = \{x \le y, y \le x, y \le 2p\}$, $C_2 = \{2p > 10\}$, $D_2 = \{x \le y, y \le x, y < \infty\}$.

Theorem 3.7. *Let A be a PTBA. The pk-extrapolation is a finite abstraction that preserves all accepting runs of $[\![A]\!]_v$ for each parameter valuation v.*

Proof Idea. We can transform the proof of Theorem 1 of [15] as well as the corresponding lemmata and definitions into our parametric setup. Due to space constraints, we did not include the full technically detailed proof and we kindly refer the reader to [16].

4   Parameter Synthesis Algorithm

We recall that our main objective is to find all parameter valuations for which the parametric timed automaton satisfies its specification. In the previous sections we have described the standard automata-based method employed under a parametric setup which produces a Büchi automaton. For the rest of this section we use $s.[\![C]\!]$ to denote the set $[\![C]\!]$ where $s = (l, [\![C, D]\!])$ is a state of the input Büchi automaton. We say that a sequence of states $s_1 \Longrightarrow s_2 \Longrightarrow \ldots \Longrightarrow s_n \Longrightarrow s_1$ is a cycle under the parameter valuation v if each state s_i in the sequence satisfies $v \in s_i.[\![C]\!]$. A cycle is called accepting if there exists $0 \leq i \leq n$ such that s_i is accepting.

The standard automata-based LTL model checking checks the emptiness of the produced Büchi automaton. The emptiness check can be performed using the Nested Depth First Search (NDFS) algorithm [17]. The NDFS algorithm is a modification of the depth first search algorithm which allows a detection of an accepting cycle in the given Büchi automaton.

Contrary to the standard LTL model checking, it is not enough to check the emptiness of the produced Büchi automaton. Our objective is to check the emptiness of the produced Büchi automaton for each considered parameter valuation. To solve this objective, we introduce a new algorithm called the Cumulative NDFS algorithm which is an extension of the NDFS algorithm. The pseudocode of Cumulative NDFS is given in Algorithm 1. Our modification is based on the set *Found* which accumulates all detected parametric valuations such that an accepting cycle under these valuations was found. In contrast to the NDFS algorithm, whenever Cumulative NDFS detects an accepting cycle, parameter valuations are saved to the set *Found* and the computation continues with a search for another accepting cycle. Note the fact that whenever we reach a state s' with $s'.[\![C]\!] \subseteq Found$ we already have found an accepting cycle under all valuations from $s'.[\![C]\!]$ and there is no need to continue with the search from s'. Therefore, we are able to speed up the computation whenever we reach such a state.

The crucial property the algorithm is based on is that of monotonicity. The set of parameter valuations $s.[\![C]\!]$ can not grow along any run of the input automaton. Lemma 4.1 states this observation formally. The observation follows from the definition of successors in $[\![A]\!]^{\alpha}$ and the definition of operations on CPDBMs. The clear corollary of Lemma 4.1 is the fact that each state s on a cycle has the same set $s.[\![C]\!]$.

Lemma 4.1. *Let A be a PTBA, α be an abstraction and s be a state in $[\![A]\!]^{\alpha}$. For every state s' reachable from s it holds that $s'.[\![C]\!] \subseteq s.[\![C]\!]$.*

Theorem 4.2. *Let A be a PTBA and α an abstraction over $[\![A]\!]$. A parameter valuation v is contained in the output of the CumulativeNDFS($[\![A]\!]^{\alpha}$) if and only if there exists an accepting run respecting v in $[\![A]\!]^{\alpha}$.*

Due to space constraints, we did not include the full technically detailed proof and we kindly refer the reader to [16].

Algorithm *CumulativeNDFS(G)*

1 | *Found ← ∅; Stack ← ∅*
   | *Outer ← ∅; Inner ← ∅*
2 | *OuterDFS(s_{init})*
3 | **return** *Accepted ← Found*

Procedure *OuterDFS(s)*

4 | *Stack ← Stack ∪ {s}*
5 | *Outer ← Outer ∪ {s}*
6 | **foreach** *s′ such that s → s′* **do**
7 | | **if** *s′ ∉ Outer ∧ s′ ∉ Stack ∧ s′.[[C]] ⊈ Found* **then**
8 | | | *OuterDFS(s′)*
9 | **if** *s ∈ Accepting ∧ s.[[C]] ⊈ Found* **then**
10 | | *InnerDFS(s)*
11 | *Stack ← Stack \ {s}*

Procedure *InnerDFS(s)*

12 | *Inner ← Inner ∪ {s}*
13 | **foreach** *s′ such that s → s′* **do**
14 | | **if** *s′ ∈ Stack* **then**
15 | | | "Cycle detected"
16 | | | *Found ← Found ∪ s′.[[C]]*
17 | | | **return**
18 | | **if** *s′ ∉ Inner ∧ s′.[[C]] ⊈ Found* **then**
19 | | | *InnerDFS(s′)*

Algorithm 1. Cumulative NDFS

As the last step in the solution to our problem, we need to complement the set *Accepted*. Thus, the solution is the complement of the set *Accepted*, more precisely the set $Val_{lb,ub}(X, P) \setminus Accepted$. To conclude this section, we state that Theorem 4.2 together with Theorem 3.7 imply the correctness of our solution.

5 Implementation

We have implemented our approach in a proof-of-concept tool. We are able to process models given as networks of parametric timed automata. A network represents a product of several parametric timed automata where handshake synchronization of two components at a time is allowed. We also extend the parametric timed automata with data variables which enable the usage of guards on data values and transition effects on data values. Such model is considered standard in the field and is used as the modelling language in the tool UPPAAL.

Deadlocks. Cumulative NDFS algorithm returns all parameter valuations for which LTL property does not hold. However, state space can contain deadlock states which also need to be detected and reported. In the nonparametric setting a state is a deadlock state if there are no enabled outgoing transitions. In a parametric setting the deadlock status of a state depends on the parameter valuation. To decide for which parameter valuations a state $(l, [[C, D]])$ is a deadlock we need to consider all guards $g_1, \ldots, g_n$ of the outgoing transitions of l. The state $(l, [[C, D]])$ is a deadlock for all parameter valuations in $[[C, D]][\neg g_1 \wedge \ldots \wedge \neg g_n]$. Applying this detection to each reachable state, all parameter valuations leading to deadlock are detected during computation.

Procedure $InitializeStorage()$

1 | $Storage \leftarrow \emptyset; M_1 \leftarrow \emptyset; M_2 \leftarrow \emptyset$

Procedure $SetData(l, C, D, data)$

2 | **if** $M_2(C, D) \neq \emptyset$ **then**
3 | | $(C', D') \leftarrow M_2(C, D)$
4 | | $Storage(l, C', D') \leftarrow data$
5 | **else**
6 | | $IH \leftarrow integerHull(C, D)$
7 | | **foreach** (C', D') in $M_1(IH)$ **do**
8 | | | **if** $[\![C', D']\!] = [\![C, D]\!]$ **then**
9 | | | | $M_2(C, D) \leftarrow (C', D')$
10 | | | | $Storage(l, C', D') \leftarrow data$
11 | | $M_2(C, D) \leftarrow (C, D)$
12 | | $M_1(IH) \leftarrow M_1(IH) \cup \{(C, D)\}$
13 | | $Storage(l, C, D) \leftarrow data$

Procedure $GetData(l, C, D)$

14 | **if** $M_2(C, D) \neq \emptyset$ **then**
15 | | $(C', D') \leftarrow M_2(C, D)$
16 | | **return** $Storage(l, C', D')$
17 | **else**
18 | | $IH \leftarrow integerHull(C, D)$
19 | | **foreach** (C', D') in $M_1(IH)$ **do**
20 | | | **if** $[\![C', D']\!] = [\![C, D]\!]$ **then**
21 | | | | $M_2(C, D) \leftarrow (C', D')$
22 | | | | **return** $Storage(l, C', D')$
23 | | $M_2(C, D) \leftarrow (C, D)$
24 | | $M_1(IH) \leftarrow M_1(IH) \cup \{(C, D)\}$
25 | | $Storage(l, C, D) \leftarrow initialData$
26 | | **return** $initialData$

Algorithm 2. State space storage operations

State space storage. One of the performance critical parts of the implementation is the state space storage. We use the state space storage to look up and store information about presence of each state in the sets *Inner*, *Outer*, and *Stack*. We refer to this information as *data*. A straightforward implementation would simply store each state together with its data. Such a solution is only efficient when a unique representation of states is available. Without such a unique representation the storage operations have to perform expensive equivalence checks with each stored state in the worst case scenario. In [10] the authors introduce unique representation based on a computation of an integer hull. The integer hull of a given set is a convex hull of all integer elements of a given set.

The solution of [10] assumes the existence of an upper bound for each clock. We do not have such an upper-bound assumption and therefore this solution is not directly applicable in our technique. However, we use the integer hull as a heuristic approximation of a unique representation of a CPDBM instead. This way we obtain a practically efficient solution that deals with the non-existence of a unique representation of a state.

The solution is based on two mappings. The first mapping, denoted by M_1 maps a given integer hull to a list of CPDBM representations. Each such list contains the representations of semantically different CPDBMs with the same integer hull. Thanks to M_1 we can quickly distinguish states with different integer hulls. However, each storage operation still needs to perform the expensive computation of the integer hull. In order to reduce number of the integer hull computations, we introduce the second mapping, denoted by M_2. This second mapping serves as a cache which maps a given CPDBM to its unique representative in the storage. Once a CPDBM representative is resolved, it is saved in M_2.

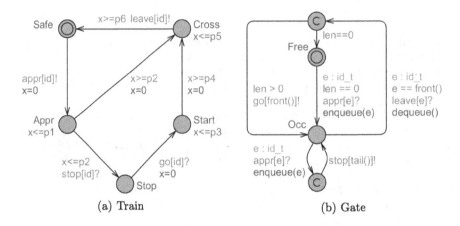

Fig. 1. Parametric TrainGate model

The pseudo code of state space storage operations is given in Algorithm 2. Note that the procedures *SetData* and *GetData* are analogous. In our prototype tool, the two mappings as well as the storage itself are implemented using hash tables. Checking whether two states are semantically equivalent is implemented using Parma Polyhedra Library [18]. The library is also used to check parametric constraint satisfaction in the CPDBM operations.

6   Experimental Evaluation

We have implemented the proposed technique for integer parameter synthesis in our proof-of-concept tool. Our goal is to compare our method with the explicit enumeration technique. To be able to compare performance of both techniques under similar conditions we also implemented the standard DBM-based LTL model checker for timed automata. Both tools use the same LTL to BA translation method [19] and analogous extrapolation techniques.

Our evaluation was performed on a parametric extension of the case study TrainGate [20] provided with the tool UPPAAL. In the TrainGate model we substitute all 6 integer bounds with separate parameters and consider two trains. This model is presented in Fig. 1. We checked two LTL properties. The first property *prop1* states that the two trains can not cross the bridge simultaneously $(G!(Train_1.cross$ and $Train_2.cross))$. The second property *prop2* states that whenever the first train is approaching the bridge it will cross the bridge eventually $(G\ Train_1.appr \implies F\ Train_1.cross)$. For all considered parameter valuations which do not lead to the deadlock, *prop1* and *prop2* are satisfied.

Experiments were performed on a PC with CPU i5-4690 and 16 GB RAM. We considered a timeout of 12 h for each task. We provide percentage of solved parameter valuations if the timeout was reached by explicit enumeration.

Table 1 shows the impact of the number of parameters used in the model. For models with a small number of parameters and small value ranges the explicit

Table 1. Impact of model parameter count

TrainGate model 2 trains	3 params	4 params	5 params	6 params
	$p_1 \in [20, 50]$	$p_1 \in [20, 50]$	$p_1 \in [20, 50]$	$p_1 \in [20, 50]$
	$p_2 \in [10, 50]$	$p_2 \in [10, 50]$	$p_2 \in [10, 50]$	$p_2 \in [10, 50]$
	$p_3 \in [15, 50]$	$p_3 \in [15, 50]$	$p_3 \in [15, 50]$	$p_3 \in [15, 50]$
	$p_4 = 7$	$p_4 \in [\ 7, 50]$	$p_4 \in [\ 7, 50]$	$p_4 \in [\ 7, 50]$
	$p_5 = 5$	$p_5 = 5$	$p_5 \in [\ 5, 50]$	$p_5 \in [\ 5, 50]$
	$p_6 = 3$	$p_6 = 3$	$p_6 = 3$	$p_6 \in [\ 3, 50]$
prop1 explicit enumeration	0:01:03	0:44:50	Timeout(51 %)	Timeout(2 %)
prop1 cumulative algorithm	0:08:16	0:54:39	3:20:25	7:58:42
prop2 explicit enumeration	0:01:21	0:58:17	Timeout(42 %)	Timeout(1 %)
prop2 cumulative algorithm	0:12:20	1:23:37	5:11:01	10:48:16

Table 2. Impact of parameter range size

TrainGate model	$p_1 \in [20, 50]$	$p_1 \in [20, 100]$	$p_1 \in [10, 100]$
2 trains	$p_2 \in [10, 50]$	$p_2 \in [10, 100]$	$p_2 \in [10, 100]$
4 parameters	$p_3 \in [15, 50]$	$p_3 \in [15, 100]$	$p_3 \in [10, 100]$
$p_5 = 5$ $p_6 = 3$	$p_4 \in [\ 7, 50]$	$p_4 \in [\ 7, 100]$	$p_4 \in [10, 100]$
prop1 explicit enumeration	0:44:50	Timeout(68 %)	Timeout(63 %)
prop1 cumulative algorithm	0:54:39	7:39:43	6:56:49
prop2 explicit enumeration	0:58:17	Timeout(56 %)	Timeout(53 %)
prop2 cumulative algorithm	1:23:37	10:25:28	8:59:11

enumeration can be more efficient. However, higher parameter count significantly favours the cumulative algorithm. Table 2 shows the impact of the parameter range size on the execution times. Note that for larger parameter ranges the cumulative algorithm is faster than explicit enumeration.

7   Conclusion and Future Work

We have presented an algorithmic framework for the bounded integer parameter synthesis for parametric timed automata with an LTL specification. The proposed framework allows the avoidance of the explicit enumeration of all possible parameter valuations.

Our symbolic technique is based on the zone abstraction and uses a parametric extension of difference bound matrices. To be able to employ the zone-based method successfully we have introduced a finite abstraction called the pk-extrapolation. To be able to synthesize all violating parameter valuations we have introduced the Cumulative NDFS algorithm which is an extension of the NDFS algorithm.

We have implemented the proposed technique in an experimental tool and our experiments confirm that this technique can be significantly faster than the explicit enumeration technique.

As for future work we plan to introduce different finite abstractions based on different extrapolations and compare their influence on the state space size. We also plan to introduce a parallel version of the cumulative algorithm. Other area that can be investigated is the employment of different linear specification logics, e.g. Clock-Aware LTL [21] which enables the use of clock-valuation constraints as atomic propositions.

References

1. Clarke, E., Grumberg, O., Peled, D.: Model Checking. MIT Press, Cambridge (1999)
2. Alur, R., Dill, D.L.: A theory of timed automata. Theoret. Comput. Sci. **126**(2), 183–235 (1994)
3. Daws, C., Tripakis, S.: Model checking of real-time reachability properties using abstractions. In: Steffen, B. (ed.) TACAS 1998. LNCS, vol. 1384, pp. 313–329. Springer, Heidelberg (1998)
4. Behrmann, G., David, A., Larsen, K.G., Hakansson, J., Petterson, P., Yi, W., Hendriks, M.: Uppaal 4.0. In: QEST, pp. 125–126. IEEE (2006)
5. Alur, R., Henzinger, T.A., Vardi, M.Y.: Parametric real-time reasoning. In: Proceedings of the Twenty-Fifth Annual ACM Symposium on Theory of Computing, pp. 592–601. ACM (1993)
6. Miller, J.S.: Decidability and complexity results for timed automata and semi-linear hybrid automata. In: Lynch, N.A., Krogh, B.H. (eds.) HSCC 2000. LNCS, vol. 1790, p. 296. Springer, Heidelberg (2000)
7. Beneš, N., Bezdĕk, P., Larsen, K.G., Srba, J.: Language emptiness of continuous-time parametric timed automata. In: Halldórsson, M.M., Iwama, K., Kobayashi, N., Speckmann, B. (eds.) ICALP 2015. LNCS, vol. 9135, pp. 69–81. Springer, Heidelberg (2015)
8. Hune, T., Romijn, J., Stoelinga, M., Vaandrager, F.: Linear parametric model checking of timed automata. J. Logic Algebraic Programm. **52**, 183–220 (2002)
9. Bozzelli, L., La Torre, S.: Decision problems for lower/upper bound parametric timed automata. Formal Methods Syst. Des. **35**(2), 121–151 (2009)
10. Jovanovic, A., Lime, D., Roux, O.H.: Integer parameter synthesis for real-time systems. IEEE Trans. Softw. Eng. **41**(5), 445–461 (2015)
11. Tripakis, S., Yovine, S., Bouajjani, A.: Checking timed büchi automata emptiness efficiently. Formal Methods Syst. Des. **26**(3), 267–292 (2005)
12. Dill, D.L.: Timing assumptions and verification of finite-state concurrent systems. In: Sifakis, J. (ed.) Automatic Verification Methods for Finite State Systems. LNCS, vol. 407, pp. 197–212. Springer, Heidelberg (1990)
13. Bouyer, P.: Forward analysis of updatable timed automata. Formal Methods Syst. Des. **24**(3), 281–320 (2004)
14. Behrmann, G., Bouyer, P., Larsen, K.G., Pelánek, R.: Lower and upper bounds in zone-based abstractions of timed automata. Int. J. Softw. Tools Technol. Transf. **8**(3), 204–215 (2006)

15. Li, G.: Checking timed Büchi automata emptiness using LU-abstractions. In: Ouaknine, J., Vaandrager, F.W. (eds.) FORMATS 2009. LNCS, vol. 5813, pp. 228–242. Springer, Heidelberg (2009)
16. Bezděk, P., Beneš, N., Barnat, J., Černá, I.: LTL parameter synthesis of parametric timed automata. CoRR abs/1409.3696 (2016)
17. Courcoubetis, C., Vardi, M., Wolper, P., Yannakakis, M.: Memory-efficient algorithms for the verification of temporal properties. In: Clarke, E.M., Kurshan, R.P. (eds.) CAV. LNCS, vol. 531, pp. 233–242. Springer, Heidelberg (1992)
18. Bagnara, R., Hill, P.M., Zaffanella, E.: The parma polyhedra library: toward a complete set of numerical abstractions for the analysis and verification of hardware and software systems. Sci. Comput. Programm. **72**(1–2), 3–21 (2008)
19. Gastin, P., Oddoux, D.: Fast LTL to Büchi automata translation. In: Berry, G., Comon, H., Finkel, A. (eds.) CAV 2001. LNCS, vol. 2102, p. 53. Springer, Heidelberg (2001)
20. Behrmann, G., David, A., Larsen, K.G.: A tutorial on UPPAAL. In: Bernardo, M., Corradini, F. (eds.) SFM-RT 2004. LNCS, vol. 3185, pp. 200–236. Springer, Heidelberg (2004)
21. Bezděk, P., Beneš, N., Havel, V., Barnat, J., Černá, I.: On clock-aware LTL properties of timed automata. In: Ciobanu, G., Méry, D. (eds.) ICTAC 2014. LNCS, vol. 8687, pp. 43–60. Springer, Heidelberg (2014)

Model Checking Simulation Rules
for Linearizability

Graeme Smith[(✉)]

School of Information Technology and Electrical Engineering,
The University of Queensland, Brisbane, Australia
smith@itee.uq.edu.au

Abstract. Linearizability is the standard notion of correctness for concurrent objects. A number of approaches have been developed for proving linearizability along with associated tool support. In this paper, we extend the tool support for an existing simulation-based method. We complement the current theorem-prover support with model checking to allow a means of quickly finding problems with an implementation before attempting a full verification. Our model checking approach is novel in that it is used to verify the simulation rules, rather than directly trying to check an object being accessed by a number of threads. As a consequence, verification can be done for an arbitrary number of accessing threads; something that is not possible with existing approaches based on model checking.

1 Introduction

Concurrent objects are objects which have been designed to allow simultaneous access by more than one thread. They include locks and data structures, and are common in modern software libraries such as `java.util.concurrent`. They may employ *coarse-grained locking*, where one thread locks the object forcing all others to wait, but for efficiency are more likely to employ *fine-grained locking*, where only parts of the object are locked, e.g., two adjacent nodes in a linked list, or *non-blocking algorithms*, where no locking is employed [11]. In the cases of fine-grained locking and non-blocking algorithms, lines of the object's code being executed by different threads are interleaved leading to subtle behaviour that is difficult to verify.

The main notion of correctness for concurrent objects is *linearizability* [12]. It compares an abstract specification of a concurrent object, where all operations are atomic, and a concrete specification (or implementation), where operations may overlap. It requires that each operation of the concrete specification *appears* to take place atomically at some point between its invocation and return – the operation's *linearization point* [12] – and that the resulting sequence of such points corresponds to a sequence of operations on the abstract specification. Effectively this means that overlapping concrete operations can occur in any order in the abstract sequence, but when one concrete operation returns before another is invoked that order must be preserved in the abstract sequence.

© Springer International Publishing Switzerland 2016
R. De Nicola and E. Kühn (Eds.): SEFM 2016, LNCS 9763, pp. 188–203, 2016.
DOI: 10.1007/978-3-319-41591-8_13

A number of approaches have been developed for proving linearizability along with associated tool support [1,4,7–9,18,24]. In particular, Derrick et al. [7,8,18] have developed a simulation-based method for proving linearizability supported by the interactive theorem prover KIV [17]. This approach has been proved sound and complete, the soundness and completeness proofs themselves being done in KIV.

Although not automatic, a strength of Derrick et al.'s approach is the fact that, being based on theorem proving, the size of the concurrent object's state space is not restricted, and verification can be done for an arbitrary number of accessing threads. This is not possible with existing approaches based on model checking where both the size of the data structure, and the number of threads needs to be restricted [2,14,22,25,26,28]. In each model checking approach, the size of stacks and queues is limited to between 2 and 5 items. In all approaches other than [28], the number of threads is limited to between 2 and 4 (depending on the complexity of the object). In [28], which uses partial-order reduction and symmetry reduction to increase the number of threads, that number is still limited to between 3 and 6 for the objects verified.

In this paper, we provide a model checking approach that, while similarly limited in terms of state space, allows an arbitrary number of threads. This is achieved by using the model checker to verify the simulation rules of Derrick et al.'s approach, rather than trying to directly check an object being accessed by a number of threads. The approach is intended to complement, rather than act as a replacement for, the use of KIV. In particular, it is intended to be used as a means of quickly finding problems with implementations before attempting a full verification in KIV.

We show how the approach is encoded in TLC [27], the model checker for TLA+ [13],[1] but other state-based model checkers, e.g. SAL [5], could be used. We do not try to optimise the model checking; this paper is a proof of concept and we leave the development of an efficient tool to future work.

The paper is structured as follows. In Sect. 2, we introduce the simulation rules of Derrick et al. and our running example, the Treiber stack [23]. In Sect. 3, we show how the simulation rules can be encoded in TLC when the abstract specification's operations are deterministic; as argued by Burkhardt et al. [2] this is nearly always the case. For completeness, we provide an alternative encoding to handle cases where the abstract specification has one or more nondeterministic operations in Sect. 4. We conclude with a discussion of future work in Sect. 5.

2   Simulation-Based Proof Method

The work of Derrick et al. [7,8,18] identifies different proof rules for use with 3 classes of linearizability proofs of increasing complexity. The first and simplest class of proofs are those where each operation's linearization point can be determined from the current state of the calling thread and object [7]. The next

---

[1] This choice was partly inspired by the use of TLA+ and TLC at Amazon [15,16].

class involves operations whose linearization points are determined by future states, possibly resulting from the operations of other threads [8]. The final class includes objects whose linearization points can only be determined by examining the whole global history [18].

In the first two cases, the proof rules reduce reasoning about an arbitrary number of processes to thread-local reasoning about one process and its environment which is abstracted to one other process. In the latter case, proving linearizability is reduced to finding a backward simulation relation between simple extensions of the abstract and concrete specifications of the concurrent object. This latter approach is complete in itself, but is generally more difficult to apply than the approaches for the first two cases. In all cases, proofs are *step-local* meaning reasoning is performed on one line of code at a time.

In this paper, we focus on the first class of proofs. Extending our work to the other classes is discussed in Sect. 5.

2.1 The Treiber Stack

To illustrate the proof method and our model checking approach in the rest of the paper, we introduce as a case study the Treiber stack [23]. The Treiber stack was the first proposed non-blocking implementation of a concurrent list-based stack. A typical implementation (taken from [7]) is given below, where Node is a class with two fields val:T and next:Node, and T_empty is the type T augmented with the additional value empty.

```
head : Node;    \\ global variable
n, ss, ssn : Node;  lv:T;   \\ thread-local variables

push(v : T) :                pop() : T_empty
1  n = new(Node);              repeat
2  n.val = v;              7      ss = head;
   repeat                  8      if ss = null
3     ss = head;           9          return empty;
4     n.next = ss;        10      ssn = ss.next;
5  until CAS(head, ss, n) 11      lv = ss.val;
6  return;                12  until CAS(head, ss, ssn);
                          13  return lv;
```

A thread doing a push operation assigns the value being pushed onto the stack to the val variable of a new node stored in local variable n. It then repeatedly tries to make n the head of the stack by setting a local variable ss to the global variable head, setting n's next variable to ss, and then assigning head to n provided it is still equal to ss (i.e., provided another thread has not in the meantime changed the value of head). CAS(a,b,c) is an atomic operation (supported by most microprocessors) which compares a and b and, if they are equal, sets a to c and returns true; otherwise it leaves a unchanged and returns false.

A thread doing a pop operation repeatedly sets ss to head, returning empty if ss is null, and otherwise setting ssn to ss's next variable and local variable lv to ss's val variable and, finally, assigning ssn to head and returning lv provided head is still equal to ss.

The Treiber stack is linearizable with respect to the following abstract specification of a stack (given in Z [21][2]). The linearization point of push is the final CAS which returns true. The linearization point of pop is either line 7 (when ss is assigned null), or the final CAS which returns true.

$$
\begin{array}{|l}
\hline [T] \\
\\
\underline{} AS \underline{} \\
\quad stack : seq\,T \\
\hline
\end{array}
\qquad
\begin{array}{|l}
\hline ASInit \underline{} \\
\quad AS \\
\hline
\quad stack = \langle\,\rangle \\
\hline
\end{array}
$$

$$
\begin{array}{|l}
\hline Push \underline{} \\
\quad \Delta AS \\
\quad v? : T \\
\hline
\quad stack' = \langle v?\rangle \frown stack \\
\hline
\end{array}
\qquad
\begin{array}{|l}
\hline Pop \underline{} \\
\quad \Delta AS \\
\quad v! : T \cup \{empty\} \\
\hline
\quad stack = \langle\,\rangle \Rightarrow \\
\qquad v! = empty \wedge stack' = stack \\
\quad stack \neq \langle\,\rangle \Rightarrow stack = \langle v!\rangle \frown stack' \\
\hline
\end{array}
$$

We use set union to add the special value *empty* to the type T in operation *Pop* although strictly this should be done using a free type definition in Z [21].

2.2 Simulation-Based Proof

To apply the approach of [7], we first need to derive a concrete Z specification from the implementation. This specification has one or two operations for each line of code. The state is described by two schemas representing the global and thread-local variables. For the Treiber stack, the global state GS includes a variable $head$ and the shared memory in which nodes are stored. Let Ref be the set of all references to nodes, and T be the type of values in a node.

---

[2] Following [7] we adopt the blocking semantics of Z in which operations are *guarded*, i.e., unable to occur when their predicate cannot be satisfied [6].

$$
\begin{array}{|l}
\hline
\quad GS\,\underline{\hspace{4cm}} \\
\hline
head : Ref \cup \{null\} \\
mem : Ref \nrightarrow (T \times (Ref \cup \{null\})) \\
\hline
\end{array}
\qquad
\begin{array}{|l}
\hline
\quad GSInit\,\underline{\hspace{3cm}} \\
GS \\
\hline
head = null \\
mem = \varnothing \\
\hline
\end{array}
$$

The local state LS includes the variables n, ss, ssn, lv and v (the input variable) appearing in the code, as well as a variable pc denoting the program counter. Let $PC == 0..13$ where 0 denotes that the thread is idle, i.e., not executing an operation.

$$
\begin{array}{|l}
\hline
\quad LS\,\underline{\hspace{3.5cm}} \\
\hline
n, ss, ssn : Ref \\
lv, v : T \\
pc : PC \\
\hline
\end{array}
\qquad
\begin{array}{|l}
\hline
\quad LSInit\,\underline{\hspace{3cm}} \\
LS \\
\hline
pc = 0 \\
\hline
\end{array}
$$

For each operation, there is an invocation operation which requires pc to be 0 and sets it to the first line of the operation.[3]

$$
\begin{array}{|l}
\hline
\quad Push0\,\underline{\hspace{3cm}} \\
\Xi GS \\
\Delta LS \\
v? : T \\
\hline
pc = 0 \wedge v' = v? \wedge pc' = 1 \\
\hline
\end{array}
\qquad
\begin{array}{|l}
\hline
\quad Pop0\,\underline{\hspace{3cm}} \\
\Xi GS \\
\Delta LS \\
\hline
pc = 0 \wedge pc' = 7 \\
\hline
\end{array}
$$

Then for each non-branching line of code there is a single operation. For example, for lines 2 and 3 we have

$$
\begin{array}{|l}
\hline
\quad Push2\,\underline{\hspace{3cm}} \\
\Delta GS \\
\Delta LS \\
\hline
pc = 2 \wedge pc' = 3 \\
mem'(n) = (v, second(mem(n))) \\
\hline
\end{array}
\qquad
\begin{array}{|l}
\hline
\quad Push3\,\underline{\hspace{3cm}} \\
\Xi GS \\
\Delta LS \\
\hline
pc = 3 \wedge pc' = 4 \\
ss' = head \\
\hline
\end{array}
$$

---

[3] Following [7], we assume all values of variables and values in the range of functions that are not explicitly changed by a Z operation, remain unchanged.

For each branching line of code there are 2 operations. For example, for line 5 we have

$$\frac{Push5t}{\begin{array}{l} \Delta GS \\ \Delta LS \end{array}}$$
$$pc = 5 \wedge head = ss \wedge pc' = 6$$
$$head' = n$$

$$\frac{Push5f}{\begin{array}{l} \Xi GS \\ \Delta LS \end{array}}$$
$$pc = 5 \wedge head \neq ss \wedge pc' = 3$$

Following the approach of [7], we then have two proof obligations for each operation of the concrete specification.

Step 1. Firstly, we need to show that the lines of code defining the concrete operations simulate the abstract operations. To do this, we identify one line of code as the *linearization step*. This line of code must simulate the abstract operation, all others simulating an abstract skip. For example, for the operation **push** we require that line 5 simulates the abstract operation when **head** equals **ss**, and all other lines simulate an abstract skip (see Fig. 1 for a possible execution of the operation).

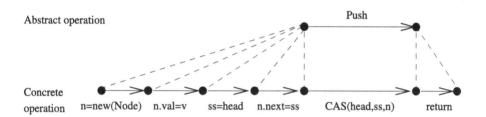

Fig. 1. Simulation of *Push*

To do this we need to define an abstraction relation relating the global concrete state space gs and abstract state space as. The abstraction relation ABS for the Treiber stack is defined recursively as follows.

$$ABS(as, gs) == ABS0(as.stack, gs.head, gs.mem)$$
$$ABS0(s, h, m) == (h = null \Rightarrow s = \langle \rangle) \wedge$$
$$(h \neq null \Rightarrow s \neq \langle \rangle \wedge h \in \text{dom } m \wedge first(m(h)) = head(s)$$
$$\wedge ABS0(tail(s), second(m(h)), m)$$

We also need to define an invariant to enable the simulation of each line of code to be proven independently. In our example, to prove that the line of code

`CAS(head,ss,ssn)` simulates the effect of the abstract operation when `head` equals `ss`, this invariant needs to ensure that when pc $= 5$ and $head = ss$ we have

$$n \in \text{dom } mem \wedge first(mem(n)) = v \wedge second(mem(n)) = ss \wedge$$
$$(\forall r : \text{dom } mem \bullet second(mem(r)) \neq n) \wedge ss \neq n$$

The second line of this predicate ensures that n is a new node not referenced by any other.

Such an invariant is stated in terms of the global concrete state space gs and the local concrete state space ls. Hence, the invariant $INV(gs, ls)$ must imply the following.

$$ls.pc = 5 \wedge gs.head = ls.ss \Rightarrow ls.n \in \text{dom } gs.mem \wedge$$
$$first(gs.mem(n)) = ls.v \wedge second(gs.mem(n)) = ls.ss) \wedge$$
$$(\forall r : \text{dom } gs.mem \bullet second(gs.mem(r)) \neq ls.n) \wedge ls.ss \neq ls.n$$

Each simulation is then proved by one of 5 rules depending on whether the line of code is an invocation (beginning an operation), return (ending an operation) or internal step (neither an invocation nor return), and whether it occurs before or after the linearization step. A function $status(gs, ls)$ is defined to identify the linearization step. Before invocation, $status(gs, ls)$ is $IDLE$. After invocation but before the linearization step it is equal to $IN(in)$, where $in : In$ is the input to the abstract operation, and after the linearization step it is equal to $OUT(out)$, where $out : Out$ is the output of the abstract operation. The types In and Out have a special value $\perp$ denoting no input or output, respectively. As well as identifying the linearization point, the $status$ function is used to store the input of the invocation step until it is needed at the linearization point, and to store the abstract output of the linearization step until it is need at the return step.

Let σ and σ' be status values, and λ be a list of parameters comprising gs, gs', ls and ls', and possibly in or out. For a step COP which is not a linearization step, the proof obligation is always of the following form.

$$\forall as : AS; \; gs, gs' : GS; \; ls, ls' : LS; \; in : In; \; out : Out \bullet$$
$$ABS(as, gs) \wedge INV(gs, ls) \wedge status(gs, ls) = \sigma \wedge COP(\lambda) \Rightarrow$$
$$status(gs', ls') = \sigma' \wedge ABS(as, gs') \wedge INV(gs', ls') \qquad (1)$$

For a linearization step such as the step $Push5t$ which simulates an abstract operation AOP, the proof obligation is of the following form.

$$\forall as : AS; \; gs, gs' : GS; \; ls, ls' : LS; \; in : In \bullet$$
$$ABS(as, gs) \wedge INV(gs, ls) \wedge status(gs, ls) = \sigma \wedge COP(\lambda) \Rightarrow$$
$$(\exists as' : AS; \; out : Out \bullet AOP(in, as, as', out) \wedge$$
$$status(gs', ls') = \sigma' \wedge ABS(as', gs') \wedge INV(gs', ls') \qquad (2)$$

Step 2. Secondly, we need to prove non-interference between threads. This amounts to showing that a thread p (with local state ls) cannot invalidate the invariant $INV(gs, lsq)$ or change the status $status(gs, lsq)$ which another thread q (with local state lsq) relies on. To do this we require a further invariant $D(ls, lsq)$ relating the local states of two threads. For the Treiber stack, this invariant includes a predicate that the local variable n of two threads cannot be the same reference. That is, D includes the conjunct $pcq \in 2..5 \wedge pc \in 2..5 \Rightarrow n \neq nq$.

The proof obligation then requires we prove

$$\forall \, as : AS; \; gs, gs' : GS; \; ls, ls', lsq : LS \, \bullet$$
$$ABS(as, gs) \wedge INV(gs, ls) \wedge INV(gs, lsq) \wedge D(ls, lsq) \wedge COP(\lambda)$$
$$\Rightarrow INV(gs', lsq) \wedge D(ls', lsq) \wedge status(gs', lsq) = status(gs, lsq) \quad (3)$$

Additionally, we have a proof obligation related to initialisation.

$$\forall \, gs : GSInit \, \bullet \, \exists \, as : ASInit \, \bullet \, ABS(as, gs) \wedge$$
$$(\forall \, ls : LSInit \, \bullet \, INV(gs, ls)) \wedge (\forall \, ls, lsq : LSInit \, \bullet \, D(ls, lsq)) \quad (4)$$

Each of these proof obligations is step-local, involving a single line of code, and involving the states of at most two threads. Together they have been shown to prove linearizability between the abstract and concrete specifications [7].

3   Encoding the Rules for Deterministic Specifications

To verify the Treiber stack, the theorem proving approach using KIV proposed in [7] requires 295 proof steps, 85 of which are interactive. If an error is found in either the implementation or the abstraction relation and invariants, all proof steps need to be redone once it is corrected. Our model checking approach can be applied to find such errors automatically before any proof steps are attempted. It uses the abstraction relation and invariants proposed for the proof steps in order to do this. KIV can then be applied to ensure no errors have been missed due to the limited state space used during the model checking.

In this section, we show how to encode each proof obligation as a separate model checking problem in TLC. We can alternatively encode a model checking problem that checks several, or even all, of the proof obligations at once. Separating the proof obligations, however, improves scalability; each model checking problem involves only one step of a single, generally deterministic operation.[4] Whether this separation needs to be done depends on the size of the state space of our abstract and concrete specifications.

A TLC model checking problem comprises a TLA+ module (encoding a specification in terms of variables, constants and definitions, including an initial-state and next-state definition), and a configuration file assigning finite values to constants, and listing the properties that need to be checked.

---

[4] An example of a nondeterministic operation is an invocation operation that takes an input. Such an operation is nondeterministic on the value of that input.

For each concrete step, we need to prove the proof obligations for the one or two operations derived from the line of code. Part of these obligations is that the *status* function is updated correctly. We assume we have already classified the type of each step, e.g., whether it is a linearization step or not. The remaining purpose of *status* is to store the input and output values until they are needed. To capture this we include *in* and *out* as variables, and introduce an invariant *STATUS* over them. For the Treiber stack, we have

$$STATUS \;\widehat{=}\; (pc \in 1..5 \Rightarrow in = v) \land (pc \in 8..9 \Rightarrow out = empty)$$
$$\land\; (pc = 13 \Rightarrow out = lv)$$

3.1 Non-linearization Steps

For each concrete step which is not a linearization step, we need to prove proof obligation (1) for each operation *COP* derived from the line of code. As an example, consider the operation *Push0*. We need to show that when this operation occurs from a state satisfying *ABS* ∧ *INV* ∧ *STATUS*, it results in a state satisfying these conditions. Hence, we build a model which, from such a state, can do a single *Push0* operation, and prove that *ABS*, *INV* and *STATUS* are invariants.[5]

The initial state space of such a model will be large, and hence we employ some simple strategies to reduce it. Firstly, we can ignore local variables that are not used in the push operation, i.e., the variables ssn and lv do not have to be included in the state. Similarly, since the operation has no output, the variable *out* can be left out of the state. Since these variables can occur in *INV* and *STATUS* we additionally remove all conjuncts of *INV* and *STATUS* that are not relevant immediately before or after the step, i.e., for *Push0* all conjuncts that are not relevant when $pc = 0$ or $pc = 1$. Also, to reduce the size of the initial state, we can equate all local variables and *in* to default values (since they have not yet been assigned values at this step of push).

For *Push0*, the state is defined in terms of variables *stack*, *head*, *mem*, *n*, *ss*, *v*, *pc* and *in*. We also have constants *Ref*, *T* and *null*, as well as 2 additional constants *N* and *undef*. *N* is the maximum size of the stack, and *undef* is required since, unlike Z, TLA+ does not support partial functions; we model a partial function with a total function f by letting $f[e] = undef$ when e is not in the domain of the partial function. The initial state is then

$Init \;\widehat{=}\; stack \in FiniteSeq(T, N)$
$\qquad \land\; mem \in [Ref \rightarrow ((T \times (Ref \cup \{null\})) \cup undef)]$
$\qquad \land\; head \in Ref \cup \{null\} \land ABS \land n = null \land ss = null \land v = 0$
$\qquad \land\; pc = 0 \land INV \land in = 0 \land STATUS$

---

[5] The output of the model checker run can be checked to ensure that this model does not have an empty set of initial states.

where *FiniteSeq* is defined in terms of the function *Seq* of TLA+ [13]. Since TLC evaluates predicates from left to right it is necessary that all variables appearing in the definitions *ABS*, *INV* and *STATUS* are typed in a conjunct appearing to the left of them. Furthermore, since these definitions constrain the set of states under consideration, it is more efficient to have them as early as possible in the predicate, i.e., immediately following the typing of their variables.

The next-state relation is then defined in terms of the single operation

$$Push0 \mathrel{\widehat{=}} pc = 0 \land pc' = 1 \land v' \in Ref \land in' = v'$$
$$\land\ UNCHANGED\langle stack, head, mem, n, ss\rangle$$

where *UNCHANGED* is a TLA+ operator for stating that particular variables are not changed by an operation.

The complete TLA+ module is shown below.[6]

──────────────── MODULE *Push0* ────────────────

EXTENDS *FiniteSequences*, *Naturals*
VARIABLES *stack*, *head*, *mem*, *n*, *ss*, *v*, *in*, *pc*
CONSTANTS *Ref*, *T*, *null*, *N*, *undef*

$ABS0[s \in FiniteSeq(T, N), h \in Ref \cup \{null\}] \mathrel{\widehat{=}}$
    $(h = null \Rightarrow Lens(s) = 0)$
    $\land\ (h \neq null \Rightarrow Len(s) \neq 0 \land mem[h] \neq undef \land mem[h][1] = Head(s)$
                  $\land\ ABS0[Tail(S), mem[h][2]])$
$ABS \mathrel{\widehat{=}} ABS0[stack, head]$
$INV \mathrel{\widehat{=}} ...$ as described in the text
$STATUS \mathrel{\widehat{=}} pc \in 1..5 \Rightarrow in = v$

$Init \mathrel{\widehat{=}} ...$ as given above
$Push0 \mathrel{\widehat{=}} ...$ as given above
$Spec \mathrel{\widehat{=}} Init \land \Box[Push0]_{\langle stack, head, mem, n, ss, v, in, pc\rangle}$

───

Modules for other non-linearization steps are constructed similarly. For example, the module for operation *Push2* has the same variables and constants. However, the initial state cannot assign *n* to *null* as it is assigned a value in the previous line of code. Therefore, we have $n \in Ref$, rather than $n = null$ in *Init*; the other conjuncts of *Init* being the same as before.

The next-state relation for *Push2* is

$$Push2 \mathrel{\widehat{=}} pc = 2 \land pc' = 3 \land mem' = [mem\ EXCEPT\ ![n] = \langle v, @[2]\rangle]$$
$$\land\ UNCHANGED\langle stack, head, n, ss, v, in\rangle$$

───────────

[6] The notation $Init \land \Box[Op]_{\langle v_1,...,v_n\rangle}$ describes the module's behaviours whose initial states satisfy *Init* and whose state transitions satisfy *Op*, and specifies that the environment of the module is unable to change the values of $v_1, \ldots, v_n$.

where the TLA+ notation $f' = [f \; EXCEPT \; ![n] = e]$ updates the function f so that $f'[n] = e$, where @ in e equals $f[n]$, e.g., $\langle v, @[2]\rangle = \langle v, mem[n][2]\rangle$ in *Push2* above.

3.2 Linearization Step

For each linearization step, we need to prove proof obligation (2). This proof obligation again requires that *ABS*, *INV* and *STATUS* hold after the concrete step. However, the values for *out* and the abstract states after the step are values reached by applying the abstract operation *AOP*. To simplify the encoding, we assume two properties of the abstract operation in this section. We return to more general abstract operations in Sect. 4.

The first property is that abstract operations are deterministic. The second is that they are *total*, i.e., have a true guard and so can be applied at any time. Both of these properties are true of our specification of the Treiber stack in Sect. 2.1.

Proof obligation (2) is of the form

$$\forall x, y, y' \bullet P(x, y, y') \Rightarrow (\exists x' \bullet Q(x, x') \wedge R(x', y'))$$

where $Q(x, x')$ is the abstract operation. If this operation is deterministic, we have $Q(x, x') \equiv q(x) \wedge x' = e$ for some expression e and predicate $q(x)$. If it is also total then $q(x) = true$ and we have $Q(x, x') \equiv x' = e$. Therefore, proof obligation (2) can be written as

$$\forall x, y, y' \bullet P(x, y, y') \Rightarrow (\exists x' \bullet x' = e \wedge R(x', y'))$$

Applying the one-point rule for existential quantification ($\exists x \bullet x = e \wedge P(x) \equiv P(e)$), to $\exists x' \bullet x' = e \wedge R(x', y')$ we get

$$\forall x, y, y' \bullet P(x, y, y') \Rightarrow R(e, y')$$

Then, applying the one-point rule for universal quantification ($P(e) \Rightarrow R(e) \equiv \forall x \bullet P(x) \wedge x = e \Rightarrow R(x)$), to $P(x, y, y') \Rightarrow R(e, y')$ we get

$$\forall x, x', y, y' \bullet P(x, y, y') \wedge x' = e \Rightarrow R(x', y')$$

which is

$$\forall x, x', y, y' \bullet P(x, y, y') \wedge Q(x, x') \Rightarrow R(x', y')$$

Hence, we can prove proof obligation (2) in the same way we prove proof obligation (1) after extending the next-state relation to produce the unique values for the abstract specification. For example, for *Push5t* we have

$$Push5t \; \widehat{=} \; pc = 5 \wedge head = ss \wedge pc' = 6 \wedge head' = n$$
$$\wedge \; stack' = \langle in \rangle \circ stack \wedge UNCHANGED\langle mem, n, ss, v, in \rangle$$

where $s \circ t$ concatenates sequences s and t. That is, *stack* is updated according to the abstract operation *Push* of Sect. 2.1.

3.3 Non-interference

For each concrete step, whether a linearization step or not, we need to prove proof obligation (3). This proof obligation requires that under an invariant D the actions of one thread p do not break the invariant INV of another thread q. Again, for scalability, we decide to encode the proof obligation for a single step of p and for a single state of q. For example, we will have one TLA+ module for the case when p executes $Push5t$ while q is at line 2.

To encode such a module we need to have local variables for both p and q and invariants $INVq$ and $STATUSq$ for q, as well as the new invariant D. The module is as follows.

─────────────────── MODULE $Push5tPush2$ ───────────────────

EXTENDS $FiniteSequences, Naturals$

VARIABLES $stack, head, mem, n, ss, v, in, pc, nq, ssq, vq, inq, pcq$

CONSTANTS $Ref, T, null, N, undef$

$ABS \; \hat{=} \; ...$ as before

$INV \; \hat{=} \; ...$ as before

$INVq \; \hat{=} \; ...$ like INV but in terms of nq, etc.

$D \; \hat{=} \; ...$ as described in the text

$STATUS \; \hat{=} \; ...$ as before

$STATUSq \; \hat{=} \; ...$ like STATUS but in terms of nq, etc.

$Init \; \hat{=} \; stack \in FiniteSeq(T, N)$
       $\wedge \; mem \in [Ref \rightarrow ((T \times (Ref \cup \{null\})) \cup undef)]$
       $\wedge \; head \in Ref \cup \{null\} \wedge ABS \wedge n \in Ref \wedge ss \in Ref \cup \{null\}$
       $\wedge \; v \in T \wedge pc = 5 \wedge INV \wedge in \in T \wedge STATUS \wedge nq \in Ref$
       $\wedge \; ssq = null \wedge vq \in T \wedge pcq = 2 \wedge INVq \wedge D \wedge inq \in T$
       $\wedge \; STATUSq$

$Push5t \; \hat{=} \; ...$ as given above except nq, etc. in the $UNCHANGED$ list

$Spec \; \hat{=} \; Init \wedge \square[Push5t]_{\langle stack,head,mem,n,ss,v,in,pc,nq,ssq,vq,inq,pcq \rangle}$

──

Given this module, we then prove $INVq$, D and $STATUSq$ are invariants to discharge proof obligation (3).

3.4 Initialisation

The final proof obligation (4) is proved by creating a module with 2 local states (as above). All variables, global and local, are initialised according to the abstract and concrete initialisation schemas, or in the case of local variables, given a default value (since they are not assigned a value initially when the threads are idle). Then we check that ABS, INV, $INVq$ and D are invariants under the empty next-state relation. That is, the required module is

─────────────────────── MODULE *Init* ───────────────────────

EXTENDS *FiniteSequences*, *Naturals*

VARIABLES *stack*, *head*, *mem*, *n*, *ss*, *ssn*, *v*, *lv*, *pc*, *nq*, *ssq*, *ssnq*, *vq*, *lvq*,
           pcq

CONSTANTS *Ref*, *T*, *null*, *N*, *undef*

$ABS \;\hat=\; ...$ as before

$INV \;\hat=\; ...$ as before

$INVq \;\hat=\; ...$ like INV but in terms of nq, etc.

$D \;\hat=\; ...$ as described in the text

$Init \;\hat=\; stack = \{\} \land mem \in [Ref \rightarrow \{undef\}] \land head = null$
$\qquad \land\ n = null \land ss = null \land ssn = null \land v = 0 \land lv = 0 \land pc = 0$
$\qquad \land\ nq = null \land ssq = null \land ssnq = null \land vq = 0 \land lvq = 0$
$\qquad \land\ pcq = 0$

$Stop \;\hat=\; FALSE$

$Spec \;\hat=\; Init \land \Box[Stop]_{\langle stack, head, mem, n, ss, ssn, v, lv, pc, nq, ssq, ssnq, vq, lvq, pcq \rangle}$

───

3.5 Discussion

To make our approach practical we need to address the fact that it requires many model checking jobs to be run. A batch program is required to handle these jobs and report any errors that are encountered. While developing our approach, we ran the jobs manually[7] and were able to successfully verify the Treiber stack, a test-and-test-and-set spinlock implementation taken from [10] and an implementation of the Linux reader-writer mechanism, seqlock, taken from [3].

Checking a single proof obligation for the Treiber stack with a maximum stack size of 4 takes around 16 s on an iMac with a 2.7 GHz Intel Core i5 processor and 4GB RAM. Since it is intended that the full verification of the stack is to be carried out using KIV, this stack size is sufficient for our purposes.

In general, however, checking larger state spaces has the potential to uncover more errors. One area of future work is to look at improving the efficiency of our approach. Although TLC is capable of running multiple threads, these are only employed after the initial states have been computed [27]. Hence, reducing the number of initial states by ignoring unused local variables, and setting local variables which have not been assigned a value to a default value is important. Since we can determine when to apply these state space reductions statically, this process can be automated. Using a different encoding where the initial state is built up over a number of state transitions would enable us to use TLC's option

─────────────

[7] To save time, we often ran multiple jobs at once, i.e., using one module, at the expense of a smaller state space.

to run a user-defined number of threads. Then efficiency could be improved by using more and better hardware. For example, Amazon run TLC on a cluster of 10 machines, each with eight cores plus hyperthreads and 23 GB of RAM [16].

Another area of future work is to investigate encoding the simulation rules in other model checkers such as SAL [5] to compare efficiency.

4   Encoding the Rules for Nondeterministic Specifications

Consider a bounded version of the Treiber stack whose specification abstracts from what happens when a push occurs and the stack is full. The state schema and operation *Push* are updated as follows.

$$
\begin{array}{|l}
\hline AS \\\hline
stack : seqT \\\hline
\#stack \leq Max \\\hline
\end{array}
\qquad
\begin{array}{|l}
\hline Push \\\hline
\Delta AS \\
v? : T \\\hline
\#stack < Max \Rightarrow \\
\quad stack = \langle v? \rangle \frown stack \\\hline
\end{array}
$$

We could implement *Push* to simply ignore the new value when the stack is full. Alternatively, we could implement it to delete the oldest value in the stack, in order to make place for the new value. Whether such implementations are sensible would depend on the envisaged application.

To prove any such implementation is linearizable with respect to *Push*, we cannot use the approach of Sect. 3.2 which relies on *Push* being deterministic. Instead we encode proof obligation (2) more directly. Instead of proving that *ABS* is an invariant for all concrete steps, we instead prove that for the linearization step of a nondeterministic operation that there exists an execution of the abstract operation which leads to *ABS* being true. That is, for the module corresponding to step *Push5t* we prove *ABS1* is an invariant, where

$$
\begin{aligned}
ABS1 \widehat{=}\ & (pc = 5 \Rightarrow ABS) \\
& \wedge\, (pc = 6 \Rightarrow (\exists\, s \in FiniteSeq(T, N) \bullet \\
& \qquad Len(stack) < Max \Rightarrow s = (\langle in \rangle \circ stack) \wedge ABS0[s, head]))
\end{aligned}
$$

and *Push5t* is encoded in the same way as a non-linearization step. The model checking time for this encoding is comparable to that of Sect. 4, taking around 16 s for a stack of maximum size 4.

A similar approach can be used for an abstract operation which is not total, ensuring the linearization step occurs only when the operation is enabled.

5   Conclusion

In this paper, we have provided model checking support for a simulation-based approach to proving linearizability [7]. The approach enables developers of concurrent objects to quickly check their designs for errors before attempting a full verification using a theorem prover. The approach is the only model checking approach we are aware of that allows checking linearizability for an arbitrary number of threads. Other approaches are typically limited to between 2 and 4 threads depending on the concurrent object.

At present, the approach can only be used with concurrent objects whose linearization points can be determined from the current state of the calling thread and object. As future work, we would like to extend this to other concurrent objects. As a first step, we will investigate encoding the additional simulation rules of [8], allowing objects whose linearization points are determined by future states. These simulation rules are only slightly more complicated than the ones we encoded in this paper. Following this, we will investigate handling the complete approach, for all possible concurrent objects, described in [18]. This approach requires that the implementation is a backward simulation of the specification. Earlier work on verifying backward simulations using model checking [19,20] will provide a starting point for this investigation.

Acknowledgements. Thanks to Kirsten Winter for her helpful comments. This work was supported by ARC Discovery Grant DP160102457.

References

1. Amit, D., Rinetzky, N., Reps, T., Sagiv, M., Yahav, E.: Comparison under abstraction for verifying linearizability. In: Damm, W., Hermanns, H. (eds.) CAV 2007. LNCS, vol. 4590, pp. 477–490. Springer, Heidelberg (2007)
2. Burckhardt, S., Dern, C., Musuvathi, M., Tan, R.: Line-up: a complete and automatic linearizability checker. In: PLDI 2010, pp. 330–340. ACM (2010)
3. Burckhardt, S., Gotsman, A., Musuvathi, M., Yang, H.: Concurrent library correctness on the TSO memory model. In: Seidl, H. (ed.) Programming Languages and Systems. LNCS, vol. 7211, pp. 87–107. Springer, Heidelberg (2012)
4. Calcagno, C., Parkinson, M., Vafeiadis, V.: Modular safety checking for fine-grained concurrency. In: Riis Nielson, H., Filé, G. (eds.) SAS 2007. LNCS, vol. 4634, pp. 233–248. Springer, Heidelberg (2007)
5. de Moura, L., Owre, S., Rueß, H., Rushby, J., Shankar, N., Sorea, M., Tiwari, A.: SAL 2. In: Alur, R., Peled, D.A. (eds.) CAV 2004. LNCS, vol. 3114, pp. 496–500. Springer, Heidelberg (2004)
6. Derrick, J., Boiten, E.: Refinement in Z and Object-Z: Foundations and Advanced Applications, 2nd edn. Springer, London (2014)
7. Derrick, J., Schellhorn, G., Wehrheim, H.: Mechanically verified proof obligations for linearizability. ACM Trans. Program. Lang. Syst. **33**(1), 4 (2011)
8. Derrick, J., Schellhorn, G., Wehrheim, H.: Verifying linearisability with potential linearisation points. In: Butler, M., Schulte, W. (eds.) FM 2011. LNCS, vol. 6664, pp. 323–337. Springer, Heidelberg (2011)

9. Doherty, S., Groves, L., Luchangco, V., Moir, M.: Formal verification of a practical lock-free queue algorithm. In: de Frutos-Escrig, D., Núñez, M. (eds.) FORTE 2004. LNCS, vol. 3235, pp. 97–114. Springer, Heidelberg (2004)
10. Gotsman, A., Musuvathi, M., Yang, H.: Show no weakness: sequentially consistent specifications of TSO libraries. In: Aguilera, M.K. (ed.) DISC 2012. LNCS, vol. 7611, pp. 31–45. Springer, Heidelberg (2012)
11. Herlihy, M., Shavit, N.: The Art of Multiprocessor Programming. Morgan Kaufmann, San Francisco (2008)
12. Herlihy, M., Wing, J.M.: Linearizability: a correctness condition for concurrent objects. ACM Trans. Program. Lang. Syst. $12(3)$, 463–492 (1990)
13. Lamport, L.: Specifying Systems: The TLA+ Language and Tools for Hardware and Software Engineers. Addison-Wesley Longman, Boston (2002)
14. Liu, Y., Chen, W., Liu, Y.A., Sun, J.: Model checking linearizability via refinement. In: Cavalcanti, A., Dams, D.R. (eds.) FM 2009. LNCS, vol. 5850, pp. 321–337. Springer, Heidelberg (2009)
15. Newcombe, C.: Why Amazon Chose TLA$^+$. In: Ait Ameur, Y., Schewe, K.-D. (eds.) ABZ 2014. LNCS, vol. 8477, pp. 25–39. Springer, Heidelberg (2014)
16. Newcombe, C., Rath, T., Zhang, F., Munteanu, B., Brooker, M., Deardeuff, M.: How Amazon Web Services uses formal methods. Commun. ACM $58(4)$, 66–73 (2015)
17. Reif, W., Schellhorn, G., Stenzel, K., Balser, M.: Structured specifications and interactive proofs with KIV. In: Automated Deduction, pp. 13–39. Kluwer (1998)
18. Schellhorn, G., Wehrheim, H., Derrick, J.: A sound and complete proof technique for linearizability of concurrent data structures. ACM Trans. Comput. Logic $15(4)$, 31:1–31:37 (2014)
19. Smith, G., Derrick, J.: Verifying data refinements using a model checker. Formal Aspects Comput. $18(3)$, 264–287 (2006)
20. Smith, G., Winter, K.: Model checking action system refinements. Formal Aspects Comput. $21(1–2)$, 155–186 (2009)
21. Spivey, J.M.: The Z Notation: A Reference Manual. Prentice Hall, London (1992)
22. Travkin, O., Mütze, A., Wehrheim, H.: SPIN as a linearizability checker under weak memory models. In: Bertacco, V., Legay, A. (eds.) HVC 2013. LNCS, vol. 8244, pp. 311–326. Springer, Heidelberg (2013)
23. Treiber, R.K.: Systems programming: Coping with parallelism. Technical report RJ 5118, IBM Almaden Res. Ctr. (1986)
24. Vafeiadis, V.: Modular fine-grained concurrency verification. Ph.D. thesis, University of Cambridge (2007)
25. Černý, P., Radhakrishna, A., Zufferey, D., Chaudhuri, S., Alur, R.: Model checking of linearizability of concurrent list implementations. In: Touili, T., Cook, B., Jackson, P. (eds.) CAV 2010. LNCS, vol. 6174, pp. 465–479. Springer, Heidelberg (2010)
26. Vechev, M., Yahav, E., Yorsh, G.: Experience with model checking linearizability. In: Păsăreanu, C.S. (ed.) SPIN 2009. LNCS, vol. 5578, pp. 261–278. Springer, Heidelberg (2009)
27. Yu, Y., Manolios, P., Lamport, L.: Model checking TLA+ specifications. In: Pierre, L., Kropf, T. (eds.) CHARME 1999. LNCS, vol. 1703, pp. 54–66. Springer, Heidelberg (1999)
28. Zhang, S.J.: Scalable automatic linearizability checking. In: ICSE 2011, pp. 1185–1187. ACM (2011)

LTL Model Checking under Fairness in PROB

Ivaylo Dobrikov$^{(\boxtimes)}$, Michael Leuschel, and Daniel Plagge

Institut für Informatik, Universität Düsseldorf,
Universitätsstr. 1, 40225 Düsseldorf, Germany
{dobrikov,leuschel,plagge}@cs.uni-duesseldorf.de

Abstract. Model checking of liveness properties often results in unrealistic, unfair infinite behaviors as counterexamples. Fairness is a notion where the search is constrained to infinite paths that do not ignore infinitely the execution of a set of enabled actions. In this work we present an implementation for efficient checking of LTL formulas under strong and weak fairness in PROB, available for model checking B, Event-B, Z, CSP and CSP∥B models. The fairness checking algorithm can cope with both weak and strong fairness conditions, where the respective fairness conditions can be joined by means of the logical operators for conjunction and disjunction, which makes setting up and checking fairness to a property more flexible. We evaluate the implementation on various CSP models and compare it to t he fairness implementation of the PAT tool.

1 Introduction and Motivation

Many system requirements can be readily specified in temporal logic such as the linear-time temporal logic (LTL). Subsequently, using an LTL model checker one can check automatically the property specified in LTL on the respective finite state model. There are two general approaches for developing an LTL model checker: the tableau approach [10] and the automata-theoretic approach [14].

The PROB LTL model checker, introduced in [11], follows the tableau approach from [10] and can check properties specified in LTL$^{[e]}$[11], an extended version of LTL providing also support for transition propositions. The algorithm presented in [11] can cope with deadlock states and partially explored state spaces. The LTL search algorithm of PROB is implemented in C using a callback mechanism for exploring the states and evaluating the atomic propositions in SICStus Prolog.

Adding fairness constraints to liveness properties is sometimes necessary in order to exclude unreasonable behaviors of the model and to direct the search for counterexamples on "fair" paths only. The fact that the PROB LTL model checker can deal with transition propositions using LTL$^{[e]}$ enables the user to easily express the fairness conditions as an LTL$^{[e]}$ formula [15]. That is, fairness constraints *fair* can be added as a premise to a liveness property f by means of implication. Then, one can check "*fair* $\Rightarrow$ f" in order to restrict the search for fault system behaviors on paths fair in regard to the imposed fairness constraints *fair*. However, setting fairness constraints to an LTL$^{[e]}$ formula via

© Springer International Publishing Switzerland 2016
R. De Nicola and E. Kühn (Eds.): SEFM 2016, LNCS 9763, pp. 204–211, 2016.
DOI: 10.1007/978-3-319-41591-8_14

re-formulating the formula causes an exponential growth of the search graph and on that account is considered to be in most cases a very inefficient approach.

In this work we briefly describe the implementation of the fairness algorithm in PROB's LTL model checker [11] and explain how one can flexibly impose fairness conditions. Additionally, we discuss the enhancements of the LTL model checking process in PROB and evaluate the fairness implementation by comparing PROB and PAT on various CSP specifications.

2   Preliminaries

Linear time properties that require some progress in the system are called *liveness* properties. Intuitively, liveness properties state that "something good" will happen in the future [8]. Liveness properties are violated by infinite computations comprising a bad cycle for the property.

The LTL model checker of PROB uses a tableau approach for checking whether an LTL$^{[e]}$ formula is satisfied or violated by a model. In general, the model checker algorithm searches for a strongly connected component (SCC) with certain properties, referred also as *self-fulfilling* SCC [10]. Such an SCC contains a (bad) cycle that represents a violation of the liveness property.

Fairness is used to rule out bad behaviors that may be considered as unrealistic by the developer of the formal model. There are different variants of fairness in terms of at which granularity level of the system are imposed: *action-based* [7], *state-based* fairness [4], *process* fairness [5], etc. In this work we concentrate on *action-based* fairness and more particularly, on *weak* and *strong* fairness, notions often used in verification of many applied systems [2,15].

An infinite computation is weakly fair with respect to an action a when: if a is continuously enabled from some point, then a is executed infinitely often. Further, an infinite computation is said to be strongly fair with respect to an action a when: if a is enabled infinitely many times, then it is executed infinitely often. In LTL$^{[e]}$ the fairness conditions can be imposed by means of the execution operator $[\cdot]$ and the derived LTL operators G (globally) and F (eventually). If, for example, a search for a counterexample for some LTL formula f should be constrained on infinite paths that are weakly fair with respect to some action a, then one can re-formulate f as follows:

$$(FG\ e(a) \Rightarrow GF\ [a]) \Rightarrow f.$$

Similarly, one can constrain the search to computations violating the property f which are strongly fair in regard to some event a by re-formulating f as follows:

$$(GF\ e(a) \Rightarrow GF[a]) \Rightarrow f.$$

In both formulae $e(a)$ is an atomic proposition stating that a is enabled at the currently processed state.

3   Fairness Algorithm and Implementation

Given a model M and an LTL$^{[e]}$ formula f, the PROB LTL model checker checks $M \vDash f$ by searching for self-fulfilling strongly connected components (SCCs) that can be reached from some initial state of M. In case that such a self-fulfilling SCC is found the model checker will return a counterexample for f. Otherwise, if no self-fulfilling SCC is discovered, we have proven that $M \vDash f$. The search for SCCs in the PROB LTL$^{[e]}$ model checker is based on the Tarjan's algorithm [13].

We extended the search algorithm of the LTL model checker [11] for supporting fairness checking separately, i.e. not adding the fairness constraints by encoding them as a premise to the original LTL$^{[e]}$ formula. In general, the idea of our fairness implementation is to check if each found self-fulfilling SCC C satisfies the imposed fairness conditions. If C is unfair with respect to the fairness constraints, then the model checker declines C as a possible counterexample for f and continues the search for fair self-fulfilling SCCs until a fair self-fulfilling SCC is found or all possible states are visited. Otherwise, if the discovered SCC C is fair, then the search finishes with generating a counterexample satisfying the imposed fairness constraints and violating the formula being checked. The process of model checking under fairness in PROB can be illustrated as in Fig. 1.

Since the fairness checks are performed on the discovered self-fulfilling SCCs, it was not necessary to modify the main search algorithm. Basically, we added a new procedure testing additionally the respective SCC in case the user has set some fairness constraints. We implemented support for action-based weak and strong fairness. The implementation allows setting fairness constraints on all possible actions of the system or on a subset thereof. Furthermore, both the weak and strong fairness assumptions can be imposed simultaneously for a

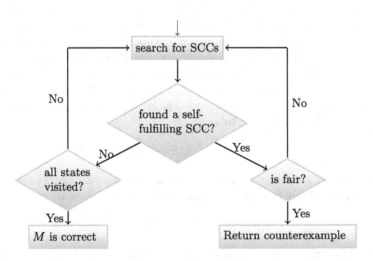

Fig. 1. LTL model checking under fairness

given formula. That is, a property that should be satisfied under certain weak and strong fairness conditions can be checked in one run of the model checker.

We extended the LTL$^{[e]}$ grammar with four new operators: sef and wef for imposing strong fairness and weak fairness in regard to all actions of the system, respectively, and sf($\cdot$) (strong fairness) and wf($\cdot$) (weak fairness) for setting fairness conditions on single actions of the system. Both operators sf($\cdot$) and wf($\cdot$) expect a transition proposition as an argument and can be used in combination with conjunction and disjunction in order to allow to impose more sophisticated fairness assumptions. The syntactic extensions enable the user to set the fairness constraints *fair* to a formula f in the well-known way: *fair* $\Rightarrow f$. Both the strong and weak fairness requirements, can be given simultaneously as a premise to the LTL$^{[e]}$ property by joining them with the conjunction operator. The fairness constraints are recognised on the syntactical level by the LTL$^{[e]}$ parser and are not included in the original property. The syntax for imposing fairness conditions in ProB can be outlined by the following grammar:

$$
\begin{array}{lll}
fair & ::= wfair \mid sfair & \mid wfair \wedge sfair \mid \textbf{wef} & \mid \textbf{sef} \\
wfair & ::= & \textbf{wf}(tp) \mid wfair \vee wfair \mid wfair \wedge wfair \mid (wfair) \\
sfair & ::= & \textbf{sf}(tp) \mid sfair \vee sfair \mid sfair \wedge sfair \mid (sfair)
\end{array}
$$

where tp is a transition proposition, and wef and sef are the tokens for setting weak and strong fairness conditions on all possible transitions, respectively.

To give an example of how one can set up fairness constraints to an LTL$^{[e]}$ formula in ProB consider a semaphored-based mutual exclusion algorithm for two processes.[1] Assume that each process is simplified to perform three types of actions: *req* (sending a request for entering the critical section), *enter* (entering the critical section), and *rel* (leaving the critical section). Further, consider the following property P: "*each process gets access to its critical section infinitely often*". To prove P on the model one needs to assume that all executions are weakly fair in regard to the *req* actions of both processes and that every execution is strongly fair in regard to the *enter* actions of both processes. Suppose that *req*. 1 and *req*. 2 denote the request actions of process 1 and process 2, respectively; and *enter*.1 and *enter*.2 the enter actions of process 1 and process 2, respectively. The corresponding fairness conditions can then be expressed by the grammar above as follows:

$$\big(\textbf{wf}(req.\,1) \wedge \textbf{wf}(req.\,2)\big) \wedge \big(\textbf{sf}(enter.1) \wedge \textbf{sf}(enter.2)\big)$$

Evaluation. First of all, encoding the fairness conditions by means of an LTL$^{[e]}$ formula and then adding it as a premise to the property is very inefficient since the state space of the search graph grows exponentially in the length of the formula [10]. For instance, if we encode the fairness conditions of the semaphored-based mutual exclusion model for two processes in LTL$^{[e]}$ and then check the re-formulated formula on the model, then the ProB LTL model checker would need to explore overall 1,048,576 atoms (the number of nodes in the search

---

[1] A detailed description of the algorithm could be viewed, for example, in [1] Chap. 2.

graph) to check P. On the other hand, checking P on the model using the fairness checking capabilities of PROB will need to explore only 44 atoms.

For the evaluation of the algorithm we have tested various CSP specifications where imposing fairness constraints is necessary to prove certain liveness properties. Further, we have evaluated model checking under fairness on PROB and PAT. PAT provides among others support for LTL model checking with fairness assumptions [12] for CSP#. A part of the results[2] of the evaluation is given in Table 1. It has been acquired by executing each test case 10 times with PROB 1.5.1 and PAT 3.5.1 on a Virtual Machine Version of Windows 7 (64 Bit) installed on a MacBook Pro Intel Core i5 Dual 2.90 GHz with 16 GB RAM.

All models in Table 1 are provided as examples with the PAT tool and have been translated into CSP-M and CSP ∥ B to be tested also within PROB. In all test cases the respective fairness constraints (Weak and Strong) were imposed on all transitions. The first sub-column of the State Space column reports the number of states of the model, whereas the second one the number of states of the product of the system with the respective automaton of the formula. In the Time column we have listed the time needed for checking the LTL[e] formula on the model. In the parentheses of the Time column we have also given the times needed for the exploration of the complete state space of the respective model.[3]

In all test cases in Table 1 the PAT tool has outperformed PROB. Observing the times just for the state space exploration (the times in parentheses), we can see that the discrepancy in the performance of both tools remains. On the other hand, comparing the overhead in PAT caused for checking the property on the model and for performing all fairness checks with this of PROB one can

Table 1. Part of the experimental Results (times in seconds)

Model & # Procs	LTL[e] formula	Fairness	Tool	State space		Time ($^+$)
				States	States×Aut	
Peterson* # Procs: 3	$GF[cs.0]$	Weak	PROB	514	2,113	1.415 (1.387)
			PAT	513	2,099	0.092 (0.052)
Peterson* # Procs: 4	$GF[cs.0]$	Weak	PROB	10,369	42,001	38.869 (37.035)
			PAT	10,368	53,122	1.504 (0.207)
DP # Procs: 6	$GF[eat.0]$	Strong	PROB	1,763	7,604	4.131 (3.898)
			PAT	1,762	4,273	0.333 (0.121)
DP # Procs: 8	$GF[eat.0]$	Strong	PROB	22,363	96,500	188.800 (149.220)
			PAT	22,362	240,620	24.098 (1.291)
Scheduler # Procs: 7	$G([enter.1] \Rightarrow F[leave.1])$	Strong	PROB	9,478	46,656	16.644 (11.976)
			PAT	7,290	61,238	4.785 (0.384)
Scheduler # Procs: 8	$G([enter.1] \Rightarrow F[leave.1])$	Strong	PROB	30,619	148,716	97.913 (87.074)
			PAT	24,057	227,450	18.233 (0.808)

(∗) In PROB the model is specified and verified using the CSP ∥ B methodology [9].
($^+$) The time needed for exploring the state space of the model.

---

[2] The models and the results of the experiments can be obtained from the following web page http://nightly.cobra.cs.uni-duesseldorf.de/fairness/.

[3] Generally, we have performed deadlock checking on the model for both tools in order to measure the times for state space exploration.

Table 2. Experimental results on MINT Linux (64 Bit) - (times in seconds)

Model	LTL[e] Formula	Fairness	Tool	States × Aut	Time
DP # Procs: 8	$GF[eat.0]$	Strong	PROB	96,500	362.452
			PAT (Mono)	240,620	380.755
Scheduler # Procs: 8	$G([enter.1] \Rightarrow F[leave.1])$	Strong	PROB	148,716	110.454
			PAT (Mono)	227,450	777.441

observe that the differences are very small. For instance, for **Scheduler8** PROB needed 87.074 s to explore the state space of the model and 97.913 to explore the state space of the specification and check the LTL[e] formula, i.e. PROB needed about ten seconds to check the property on the already explored state space and perform all necessary fairness checks. In the same time, the overhead for testing the LTL property under fairness in PAT is about 17 s. This suggests that the main reason for PROB being outperformed by PAT is due to the poor performance of PROB's CSP interpreter responsible for the state space exploration of CSP specifications.

To reproduce the results from Table 1 one needs to run the experiments on Windows as PAT is mainly developed for Windows. On other operating systems such as Linux one can run PAT with the mono platform. However, experiments have shown that PAT 3.5.1 with mono performs poorly on other systems such as Linux and in most cases will be outperformed by PROB as can be seen in Table 2. The PAT experments in Table 2 were performed with mono 3.2.8.

In Table 3 we have listed several experiments run with PROB to reveal the overhead caused by the fairness check. We have measured the time needed for checking and rejecting of all non-fair SCCs violating the checked property. Although the number of non-fair SCCs is considerably high, the fairness checking times in all cases are very small in comparison to the overall checking times.

Related Work. Besides the two notions of action-based fairness discussed in this paper, PAT [12] supports also verification under weak and strong process fairness. Furthermore, PAT provides also support for strong global fairness, fairness notion concerned with the infinite execution of both actions and states. One of the most prominent model checkers, SPIN [6], provides support for weak fairness.

Table 3. Fairness checking statistics in PROB (times in seconds)

Model & # Procs	LTL[e] Formula	# Atoms	# Rejected SCCs	Fairness Checking Time	Total Time
DP 7	$sef \Rightarrow GF[eat.0]$	27,093	291	0.824	29.188
DP 8	$sef \Rightarrow GF[eat.0]$	96,501	824	4.311	205.559
ME_Sem 10	$sef \Rightarrow GF[enter.1]$	26,628	2,305	0.664	36.044
ME_Sem 11	$sef \Rightarrow GF[enter.1]$	57,349	5,121	1.898	162.136

In [12], the performance of verification under weak fairness in SPIN is compared with that of PAT. In most of the test cases in [12], PAT performed better than SPIN. Another model checker that provides support for fairness is NuSMV [3], a symbolic model checker supporting two types of state-based fairness: justice and compassion. A justice constraint assumes that a given state formula is fulfilled infinitely often, whereas the compassion assumption requires that a formula must be true infinitely often if another state formula is true infinitely often.

Conclusion. We have presented a fairness implementation in PROB supporting verification under weak and strong action-based fairness for B, Event-B, Z, CSP, and CSP∥B. Fairness assumptions in PROB can be easily imposed on all actions of the checked model, or on a subset thereof; it is even possible to specify action parameters. It appears that for LTL model checking of large-scale CSP specifications PROB performs poorly compared to other model checkers for CSP. However, the main motivation of PROB's CSP support was to provide an FDR/CSP-M compliant interpreter which can be used for CSP∥B, and which has not been tuned for model checking. On the positive side, experiments have shown that the overhead caused by the fairness checking procedure is considerably small and it can be applied to a wide range of specification formalisms.

Acknowledgements. We would like to thank David Williams for the ideas, very useful feedback and support on this work.

References

1. Baier, C., Katoen, J.-P.: Principles of Model Checking. The MIT Press, Cambridge (2008)
2. Chouali, S., Julliand, J., Masson, P.-A., Bellegarde, F.: Pltl-partitioned model checking for reactive systems under fairness assumptions. ACM Trans. Embed. Comput. Syst. **4**(2), 267–301 (2005)
3. Cimatti, A., Clarke, E., Giunchiglia, F., Roveri, M.: Nusmv: a new symbolic model checker. Int. J. Softw. Tools Technol. Transf. **2**(4), 410–425 (2000)
4. Clarke, E.M., Grumberg, O., Peled, D.A.: Model Checking. MIT Press, Cambridge (1999)
5. Francez, N.: Fairness. Springer-Verlag New York Inc., New York (1986)
6. Holzmann, G.: Spin Model Checker: Primer and Reference Manual, 1st edn. Addison-Wesley Professional, Boston (2003)
7. Kwiatkowska, M.: Event fairness and non-interleaving concurrency. Formal Aspects Comput. **1**(1), 213–228 (1989)
8. Lamport, L.: Proving the correctness of multiprocess programs. IEEE Trans. Softw. Eng. **3**(2), 125–143 (1977)
9. Butler, M., Leuschel, M.: Combining CSP and B for specification and property verification. In: Fitzgerald, J.S., Hayes, I.J., Tarlecki, A. (eds.) FM 2005. LNCS, vol. 3582, pp. 221–236. Springer, Heidelberg (2005)
10. Lichtenstein, O., Pnueli, A.: Checking that finite state concurrent programs satisfy their linear specification. In: POPL 1985, pp. 97–107. ACM, New York (1985)

11. Plagge, D., Leuschel, M.: Seven at one stroke: LTL model checking for high-level specifications in B, Z, CSP, and more. STTT **12**(1), 9–21 (2010)
12. Sun, J., Liu, Y., Dong, J.S., Pang, J.: PAT: Towards flexible verification under fairness. In: Bouajjani, A., Maler, O. (eds.) CAV 2009. LNCS, vol. 5643, pp. 709–714. Springer, Heidelberg (2009)
13. Tarjan, R.: Depth first search and linear graph algorithms. SIAM J. Comput. **1**(2), 146–160 (1972)
14. Vardi, M.Y., Wolper, P.: An automata-theoretic approach to automatic program verification. In: Proceedings of 1st Symposium on Logic in Computer Science, pp. 332–344, Cambridge, June 1986
15. Williams, D.M., de Ruiter, J., Fokkink, W.: Model checking under fairness in ProB and its application to fair exchange protocols. In: Roychoudhury, A., D'Souza, M. (eds.) ICTAC 2012. LNCS, vol. 7521, pp. 168–182. Springer, Heidelberg (2012)

Verification

Counterexamples from Proof Failures in SPARK

David Hauzar[1,2,3], Claude Marché[1,2(✉)], and Yannick Moy[3]

[1] Inria, Université Paris-Saclay, 91893 Palaiseau, France
Claude.Marche@inria.fr
[2] LRI, CNRS & Univ. Paris-Sud, 91405 Orsay, France
[3] AdaCore, 75009 Paris, France

Abstract. A major issue in the activity of deductive program verification is the understanding of the reason why a proof fails. To help the user understand the problem and decide what needs to be fixed in the code or the specification, it is essential to provide means to investigate such a failure. We present our approach for the design and the implementation of *counterexample generation* within the SPARK 2014 environment, exhibiting values for the variables of the program where a given part of the specification fails to be validated. To produce a counterexample, we exploit the ability of SMT solvers to propose, when a proof of a formula is not found, a *counter-model*. Turning such a counter-model into a counterexample for the initial program is not trivial because of the many transformations leading from a given code and specification to a verification condition.

1 Introduction

Deductive program verification is an activity that aims at checking that a given program respects a given functional behavior. In this context, the expected behavior must be expressed formally by logical assertions, *i.e.* preconditions and postconditions, forming a *contract*. Deductive program verification typically proceeds by generating, from both the code and the formal specification, a set of logic formulas called *verification conditions* (VCs). If one proves that all generated VCs are tautologies, then the program is guaranteed to satisfy its specification. In recent program verification environments like Dafny [20], Open-JML [12] and Why3 [7], VCs are discharged using automated theorem provers, in particular those of the *Satisfiability Modulo Theories* (SMT) family such as Alt-Ergo [5], CVC4 [2] and Z3 [22]. These theorem provers are used as black-boxes that, given a VC, may produce three kinds of results:

1. The prover answers something meaning "yes, the VC is a tautology"
2. The prover answers anything else, meaning "I don't know", in order words the prover is not able to prove the VC for any reason
3. The prover runs for a too long time (seemingly infinitely) or runs out of memory

---

Work partly supported by the Joint Laboratory ProofInUse (ANR-13-LAB3-0007, http://www.spark-2014.org/proofinuse) of the French national research organization.

R. De Nicola and E. Kühn (Eds.): SEFM 2016, LNCS 9763, pp. 215–233, 2016.
DOI: 10.1007/978-3-319-41591-8_15

The case where the prover runs for too long time is handled in practice by setting a given time limit, so that the prover process is killed when exceeding this limit. The cases 2 and 3 are the same from the user's perspective: the VC is not proved. Note that we do not distinguish a case where the prover would answer "no it is not a tautology", because the VCs typically involve undecidable logic features (*e.g.* non-linear integer arithmetic, first-order quantification) so provers are in practice incomplete: there is no way for them to be sure that a given VC is not provable.

A major issue in the activity of deductive verification is thus understanding the reasons for a proof failure. There are various reasons why it may fail:

1. The property to prove is indeed invalid: the code is not correct with respect to the given specification.
2. The property is in fact valid, but is not proved, again for two possible reasons:
   - The prover is not able to obtain a proof (in the given time and memory limits): this is the incompleteness of the proof search;
   - The proof may need extra intermediate annotations, such as loop invariants, or more complete contracts of the subprograms

For the user to be able to fix the code or the specification of their program, it is essential to understand into which of the two above cases any undischarged VC falls. The solution we propose in this paper is to generate *counterexamples*, or more precisely *potential* counterexamples. Such a counterexample should give values for the variables of the program, demonstrating a particular case where a given annotation may not hold. To produce a counterexample, we exploit an additional feature of SMT solvers: the ability to propose, when a proof of a formula is not found, a *counter-model*, exhibiting an interpretation of the free variables where the formula cannot be proved true. Turning such a counter-model into a counterexample for the initial program is not a trivial task because of the many transformations that lead to a VC from a given code and specification. For this work, our goal was to design and implement counterexample generation within the SPARK 2014 [21] environment for the development of safety-critical Ada programs. In this context, the initial program with annotations is first translated into the intermediate language WhyML. The Why3 tool [7] processes WhyML to generate verification conditions using a weakest precondition calculus. These VCs are then passed to SMT solvers after several possible transformations: simplifications and encoding of features not natively supported by SMT-LIB. Then, to turn the counter-model into a counterexample, one has to relate the model produced by the SMT solver back to the original problem, taking into account the entire transformation chain.

In Sect. 2 we present the support for counterexamples in SPARK 2014, from a user's point of view, illustrated by simple examples. In Sect. 3 we go into the internals of the tools, and explain how we designed our approach to generate counterexamples. We discuss related work and future work in Sect. 4. More details can be found in a technical report [16].

2   Counterexamples in SPARK

Ada 2012 is the latest version of the Ada language [1], a general purpose language, traditionally used in embedded software development. This version adds new features for specifying the behavior of programs, such as subprogram contracts and type invariants. SPARK is a subset of Ada targeted at formal verification [21]. Its restrictions ensure that the behavior of a SPARK program is unambiguously defined. The SPARK language and toolset for static verification has been applied for many years in on-board aircraft systems, control systems, cryptographic systems, and rail systems [8]. SPARK also provides dedicated features that are not part of Ada 2012: essential constructs for deductive verification (*e.g.* loop invariants, ghost code) have been added. To formally prove a SPARK 2014 program, GNATprove uses WhyML as an intermediate language. The SPARK program is translated into an equivalent WhyML program which can then be verified using the Why3 tool.

```
saturation.adb
3  procedure Saturate (Val : in out Unsigned_16)
4     with
5        Post =>
6           (if Val'Old <= 255 then Val = Val'Old) and
7           (if Val'Old >  255 then Val = 255)
8  is
9  begin
10       Val := Val and 16#FF#;
11   end Saturate;
Saturate
```

```
Messages   Locations
▲  -  ▣   ⬚  ▤                              Q▾ filter
   Builder results (1 item)
   ▾  saturation.adb (1 item)
         6:7        medium: postcondition might fail
```

Fig. 1. A failed postcondition.

Figure 1 shows an example of a saturation procedure, ensuring that values stay in a given range. In this example, the procedure should ensure that the output value is less or equal to 255. More precisely, the postcondition requires that if the input value is in the range, it is unmodified, and set to 255 otherwise. Note the attribute 'Old that refers to the values that expressions had at procedure entry. The procedure is implemented using bit-wise AND with mask 0xFF. As the message at the bottom shows, GNATprove does not succeed in proving the postcondition.

The means for the user to investigate the possible reason of the failure are:

– Execute code and properties during tests, in a way that violations of the property will stop execution with an exception. This depends of course on the availability of tests that exercise the violation, but testing is a well-known software engineering discipline that engineers usually master, hence uncovering incorrect code and properties is comparatively easier than investigating other reasons for proof failure.

- A focused manual review of the code and assertions can efficiently diagnose many cases of missing annotations.
- The user can try to increase the proof power along different axes, in order to combine the results of different provers and allocate more resources (in particular time) for each proof attempt. In GNATprove, in addition to the lower level switches, there are predefined *proof levels* between 0 and 4 that the user can increase to augment the proof power: more time allocated, use more provers.

GNATprove also helps users by pinpointing the part of a larger assertion which is not proved, and the execution path along which the proof fails. During interactions, the IDE integration is of utmost importance to allow focusing the proof on a single subprogram or even a single line of code. Yet, testing and manual review may not identify all errors and missing annotations, and increasing the proof power may prove the property either. The burden is then on the user to verify the unproved property by other means: more tests, manual reviews, or using an interactive prover whose proof script is checked by GNATprove.

Adding Counterexamples in SPARK. We describe now the new facilities to generate counterexamples that is the purpose of this paper. There are multiple ways to integrate counterexamples in a development environment, depending on the expected degree of interactions with users. In SPARK, we have chosen to simplify the interactions to a minimum, so that users are directly presented with the most relevant information. GNATprove displays the values of relevant variables in the message displayed to the user for an unproved check. The message displayed by GNATprove on the example from Fig. 1 is:

```
medium: postcondition might fail (e.g. when Val'Old = 4096 and Val = 0)
```

This information alone might be sufficient to understand the problem. Otherwise, GNATprove has pre-computed for every unproved check a counterexample trace that can be displayed in the IDE. This trace consists of a sequence of program lines, annotated with values of relevant variables.

For example, Fig. 2 shows the trace computed by GNATprove and displayed in GNAT Programming Studio on the example seen before. A variable is selected as *relevant* in the summary message if it appears in the expression being checked. A variable on any given line is selected as *relevant* in the trace if it is assigned a new value on this line. As visible from Fig. 2, the counterexample trace is displayed inside special lines in the editor, that are not part of the code and cannot be edited manually (note the absence of a line number). These lines are prefixed with the token -- that introduces comments in Ada code to make it clear to users that they are not part of the code. The lines in the program

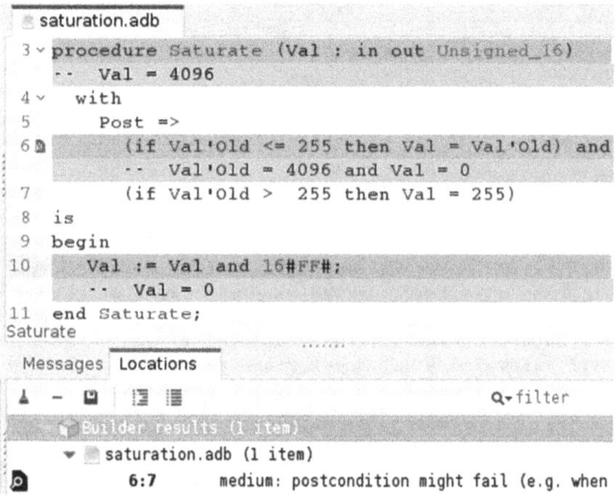

```
saturation.adb
 3 ⌄ procedure Saturate (Val : in out Unsigned_16)
    -- Val = 4096
 4 ⌄   with
 5       Post =>
 6 ▸          (if Val'Old <= 255 then Val = Val'Old) and
             -- Val'Old = 4096 and Val = 0
 7           (if Val'Old >  255 then Val = 255)
 8   is
 9   begin
10       Val := Val and 16#FF#;
         -- Val = 0
11   end Saturate;
Saturate
```

Messages Locations

🔺 — 💾   ▤ ▤   Q▾filter

Builder results (1 item)

▾ saturation.adb (1 item)
      6:7   medium: postcondition might fail (e.g. when

Fig. 2. Counterexample interleaved with code.

to which the trace applies (lines 3, 6 and 10) are emphasized in the editor. The counterexample shows that the implementation is indeed not correct with respect to the specification. Bitwise AND of 4096 and 0xFF is 0, while the specification requires that the returned value of Val be 255.

Counterexamples with Records and Arrays. Counterexamples can contain values of record types and array types. Their values are displayed in the usual Ada syntax as aggregates, as illustrated in Fig. 3. If the counterexample value of a field is not known, it is displayed as question mark. If there is more than one such field, then these fields are aggregated under the name others. On Fig. 3, type Saturable_Value defined at line 5–8 contains a field Value representing the actual value and a field Upper_Bound being an upper bound of the saturation range. The postcondition of the function Saturate is analogous to the postcondition of the procedure Saturate from Fig. 2. The field Value of the returned record must contain the value of the field Value of the input record if it is in the range, otherwise it must contain the upper bound of the range. The saturation is now implemented using function Unsigned_16'Max. The counterexample shows that if Val.Value is 16383 and Val.Upper_Bound is 49152, Saturate'Result.Val is 49152. Indeed, instead of the function Unsigned_16'Max, the function Unsigned_16'Min should be used.

Similarly for records, the content of arrays is shown in Ada syntax for array aggregates. For arrays with statically unknown ranges, the array range is also part of the counterexample, shown again in Ada syntax using the attributes 'First and 'Last. See the report [16] for a more detailed example.

```
saturation.adb
 5    type Saturable_Value is record
 6        Value : Unsigned_16;
 7        Upper_Bound : Unsigned_16;
 8    end record;
 9
10    function Saturate (Val : Saturable_Value) return Saturable_Value
      --  Val = (Value => 16383, Upper_Bound => 49152)
11      with SPARK_Mode,
12      Post =>
13        (if Val.Value <= Val.Upper_Bound then
            --  Saturate'Result = (Value => 49152, Upper_Bound => ?) and
            --  Val = (Value => 16383, Upper_Bound => 49152)
            Saturate'Result.Value = Val.Value) and
14        (if Val.Value > Val.Upper_Bound then
15
16            Saturate'Result.Value = Val.Upper_Bound)
17    is
18    begin
19        return Val'Update
          --  Saturate'Result = (Value => 49152, Upper_Bound => 49152)
20        (Value => Unsigned_16'Max (Val.Value, Val.Upper_Bound));
21    end Saturate;
```

Fig. 3. Counterexample with a record type.

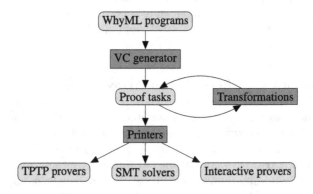

Fig. 4. Why3 architecture

3   Implementation of Counterexamples

3.1   Short Introduction to Why3

Why3 (http://why3.lri.fr) is an environment for deductive program verification, providing the language WhyML for specification and programming [14]. WhyML is used as an intermediate language for verification of SPARK programs as well as C and Java programs [13], and can also be used as a primary programming language (it can be compiled to Ocaml).

A schematic view of Why3's components is shown in Fig. 4. The specification component of WhyML [6], used to write program annotations and background theories, is an extension of first-order logic. It features ML-style polymorphic types (prenex polymorphism), algebraic datatypes (in particular records), abstract types, and functions and predicates specified axiomatically. Why3 comes with a rich standard library providing general-purpose theories useful for specifying programs [7]. This includes integer and real arithmetic, arrays, and bit-vectors. The specification part of the language serves as a common format for theorem proving problems, *proof tasks* in Why3's jargon. The programming part of WhyML is a dialect of ML with a number of restrictions to make verification easier [14]. WhyML function definitions are annotated with preconditions and postconditions both for normal and exceptional termination, and loops are also annotated with invariants. Why3 generates proof tasks from user lemmas and annotated programs (using a weakest precondition calculus), then dispatches them to multiple provers. We detail below a few features of Why3 that are of particular interest for the counterexamples feature.

Transformations. A Why3 transformation is any procedure taking a proof task as an argument and producing another proof task, or more generally a set of proof tasks. Transformations must be *sound* in the sense that validity of the resulting tasks must imply the validity of the input task. The converse is generally true but not always. A typical example is the *split* transformation: for a given proof task of the form $H_1, \ldots, H_k \vdash \forall \boldsymbol{x}.H \rightarrow (G_1 \wedge \cdots \wedge G_n)$, that is, if the goal ends with a conjunction, it produces the set of n tasks $H_1, \ldots, H_k \vdash \forall \boldsymbol{x}.H \rightarrow G_i$ for $1 \leq i \leq n$. As most of the provers do not support some of the language features, (*e.g.* pattern matching, polymorphic types, recursion), Why3 applies a series of encoding transformations to eliminate unsupported constructions before dispatching a proof task to provers. Other transformations can also be imposed by the user in order to simplify the proof search: inlining of definitions, simplification by computation, case analysis, application of inductive schemes, etc.

Labels. Why3 *labels* are arbitrary character strings, written between double quotes. They can be attached to any logic formula or term, and also to any declaration. Their interpretation is not fixed *a priori*; in some cases they are interpreted by specific transformations. For example, the *asymmetric conjunction* of Why3's logic is a connective written as &&. Internally, it is in fact the usual conjunction $\wedge$ with the label "asym_split" on the first argument. The split transformation interprets this label so that a goal of the form f1 && f2 is split into the goals f1 and f1 $\rightarrow$ f2. Transformations that do not interpret labels keep them attached to formulas and terms, if possible. For example, a transformation may rename a variable, in that case it should propagate labels from the original variable to the new one. Analogously, if a transformation rewrites a given sub-term into another, it should also propagate labels of the old term to the new one.

Locations. To help traceability of errors from its various front-ends, WhyML has a mechanism of source locations similar to the #line directive of C preprocessor. Instead of being line-oriented, it is character-precise: any term or declaration can be given an annotation of the form #*file* l b e# meaning that this term or declaration originates from the source file *file*, at line l, from first character b to last character e. Similarly as for labels, transformations should propagate locations.

The Weakest Precondition calculus. The VC generator, which implements a variant of the weakest precondition calculus (WP for short), takes any WhyML function and creates a proof task. If that proof task is a tautology then the input function satisfies its contract. This formula is typically quite large, as it collects all the necessary checks that need to hold for the function to be safe: postcondition, but also initialization and preservation of loop invariants if any, any kind of runtime checks, etc. To present the resulting formula to the user in a more friendly manner, a default application of the `split` transformation is applied, so as to obtain a set of VCs that corresponds to the various checks to perform on the original program. To make this more user-friendly, Why3's WP calculus is instrumented so that each of the sub-formulas that corresponds to a program check is annotated with a label of the form `"expl: text"`. The *text* is an explanation of the VC, and is interpreted by the graphical interface. Regarding the counterexample feature, an important aspect is that during the computation of the WP, for each program statement that updates a program variable as a side-effect, a fresh logical variable holding this new value is created. This is the case for assignment statements, but also occurs in case of function calls and in presence of loops.

Metas. Why3's *metas* provide a way to associate metadata to a proof task that, unlike labels, are not attached to any particular sub-term or declaration, but are declared globally to the task. A meta is characterized by a name and a set of parameters that can be nearly of any kind of object: a number, a boolean, a string, but also a reference to another declaration: a type, a function symbol, an hypothesis. As for labels, metas can be interpreted by transformations, but are usually kept unchanged. Unlike labels, the name of metas, and the type of their arguments, must be declared first.

3.2   Model Features of SMT-LIB

An SMT solver takes as input a set of formulas, and checks whether this set is satisfiable or not. To prove that a given proof task $H \vdash G$ is a tautology, we query the solver for the satisfiability of H and the negation of G: if the solver answers that this set is unsatisfiable, it means that proof task is valid. If the solver terminates with any other answer, the SMT solver may propose a potential model of H and $\neg G$ describing why $H \vdash G$ cannot be proved. To get such a model, we use features of SMT-LIB [3], and the solvers CVC4 and Z3. SMT-LIB defines commands `get-model` and `get-value` for getting models. The command `get-model` returns a set of interpretations for all user-declared function symbols in the input task. The command (`get-value` $t_1 \cdots t_n$) returns for each term t_i a value term that is equivalent to t_i in the potential model.

3.3   Counterexamples at Why3 Level

Our goal is to exploit the generation of models by SMT solvers to construct a potential counterexample to the input Why3 program. This means that we need to add counterexample generation to the Why3 architecture described in Fig. 4: some feedback from the bottom (prover results) to the top (input program) must be implemented. Because the VC generation and the Why3 transformations can rename variables and introduce fresh ones, re-interpreting the model returned by the solver into a counterexample of the input source is a non-trivial process.

A first choice we have to make is on whether using the `get-model` or the `get-value` command of SMT-LIB. The command `get-model` might seem easier to use at first because no argument needs to be given. However, from the large set of function symbols and their values returned by `get-model`, it would be a hard task to extract which part of it corresponds to the initial program, because we have no trace of the extra logical variables and renamings made by WP and transformations. That's why we decided to use the `get-value` command instead. We provide the variables or terms to query as arguments of this command by properly propagating traceability information along the WP and the Why3 transformations. This is done using Why3 labels and metas instrumenting the different processing steps as shown in Fig. 5. This has to be performed regarding different aspects that are detailed in the subsections below.

Marking variables to show in a counterexample. In a Why3 task, variables that should be shown in a counterexample are marked with the label `"model"`. When the task is printed into SMT-LIB format, SMT-LIB terms corresponding to these variables are collected and then passed as parameters of the `get_value` command. As an example, see the following Why3 task:

```
constant x "model" :int
goal G : x+x > 0
```

When printing the task into SMT-LIB syntax, the SMT-LIB term corresponding to the constant x will be collected and queried for counterexample value v. The counterexample will be displayed to the user in the form x = v and this equality will be associated to the location of the goal G. For a Why3 task that is generated from WhyML or SPARK program, we additionally need to annotate each variable with two things. First, with a location in the original source code and second with the name of the variable in the source language.

```
constant x "model" "model_trace:X" #file.adb 42 1 2#:int
goal G : x+x > 0
```

In such a case the counterexample will be displayed in the form X = v and associated with location in file `file.adb`, line 42 (in practice inside a comment as in Fig. 2).

Instrumenting WP calculus for counterexamples. The user expects that all successive values of a variable, marked with label `"model"`, appear in a counterexample. WP creates a fresh logical variable for every modification of a given variable. For variables marked with label `"model"`, counterexample labels are propagated

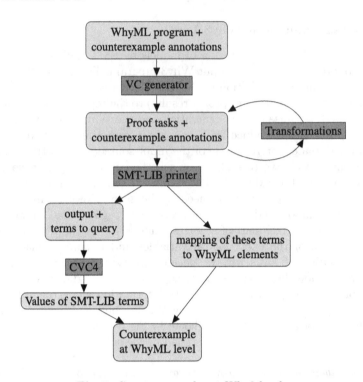

Fig. 5. Counterexamples at Why3 level.

to these fresh logical variables. Moreover, each of these fresh variables is given the location of the expression that triggers its creation. As an example, let us consider the following WhyML code implementing a simple loop:

```
let test_loop ( x "model" "model_trace:X" : ref int ): unit
  requires { !x > 0 }
= while !x > 0 do                          (* counterexample: X = 1 *)
    invariant { !x ≥ 0 }
    x := !x - 2                            (* counterexample: X = -1 *)
  done
```

The variable `x` is marked with labels `"model"` and `"model_trace"` as counterexample variable. The property preserving loop invariant is not proved, and a counterexample, shown in comments, is generated. The formula encoding this property is shown in Fig. 6. The vari-

```
forall x "model" "model_trace:X".
  (x ≥ 2) →
  (forall x1 "model" "model_trace:X@loop".
   x1 ≥ 0 →
   x1 > 0 →
     (forall x2 "model" "model_trace:X@call".
      (x2 = (x1 - 2)) → x2 ≥ 0)))
```

Fig. 6. Logical formula generated by WP.

able `x` quantified at the top of the formula stands for the input value of the variable `x` of the `test_loop` function. Then, WP creates another fresh variable x1 for the value of variable x at the beginning of some arbitrary loop iteration. Finally, WP creates a fresh variable x2 for the value of variable x after the assignment statement.

```
let test_post
    (x "model" "model_trace:X" : int)
    (y "model" "model_trace:Y" :
                        ref int): unit
        (* counterexample: X = 1 *)
    ensures { "model_vc" !y ≥ x }
        (* counterexample: Y = 0, X = 1 *)
= y := x - 1
        (* counterexample: Y = 0 *)
```

Fig. 7. Counterexample located at post-condition annotated with `"model_vc"`

As shown on Fig. 6, the `"model"` label on the variable xof `test_loop` is propagated to all those logical fresh variables corresponding to x. A similar propagation occurs with label `"model_trace"` with some additional information (after the `"@"` sign) to explain the origin of the fresh variable. Source code locations are not displayed here for readability.

Get values of variables from a given assertion. In practice, it is useful for the user to see values of counterexample variables at the location of the assertion that fails. As an example, see Fig. 2. Both initial and final value of variable Val are displayed on line 6, which is the location of the failed postcondition and this information is also a part of the message summarizing the unproved assertion in the "messages" panel.

```
type byte
function to_rep byte : int
predicate in_range (x : int) =
  -128 ≤ x ≤ 127
axiom range_axiom : forall x:byte.
  in_range (to_rep x)
meta "model_projection"
  function to_rep
constant a "model_projected"
            "model_trace:A" : byte

type r = {f : byte; g : bool}
function proj_f
  "model_trace:.F" (x:r) : byte =
    x.f
meta "model_projection"
  function proj_f
function proj_g
  "model_trace:.G" (x:r) : bool =
    x.g
meta "model_projection"
  function proj_g
constant b "model_projected"
          "model_trace:B" : r
```

Fig. 8. Projections of abstract types and records.

During WP, all modifications of variables relevant for counterexamples are marked, and their values are displayed at the respective locations that triggered the modifications. However, the user expects to see also, at the location of a failed check, the values of the variables involved in that check. One way to display these variables at the location of a failed check would be to retrieve the last point of modification of a variable and display this counterexample value at the location of a failed proof. However, this is quite complex to do when multiple program paths are encoded in a VC.

That is why we preferred to explicitly mark variables that appear at the location of a failed check. In WhyML programs, expressions that trigger generating a proof task are marked with label `"model_vc"`. These expressions can be asserts, preconditions, and postconditions. We implemented a dedicated Why3 transformation that uses this label to find the expression that triggers generating the current proof task. The transformation then marks all counterexample variables read in this expression as a part of the counterexample at locations of the expression.

The example of Fig. 7 shows a function with a postcondition marked with a label `"model_vc"`. This postcondition cannot be proved and a counterexample is generated. At the location of the postcondition, the values of the variable x at the function start and the variable y at exit are displayed.

Projections in models. For some types, SMT-LIB standard does not specify how values of these types should be displayed. Most notably, this is the case for abstract types. When an SMT solver is queried for values of such a type, it usually returns just an internal reference. To display values of these types in a counterexample, we decided to *project* them to values of types that can be displayed. To project values of a type T_1 to a type T_2, a meta `"model_projection"` must be declared taking as argument some function P_1 from T_1 to T_2. If some element E of type T_1 is labeled with `"model_projected"`, then instead of querying for a value for E, the solver is queried for a value of $P_1(E)$. Projections are applied transitively: if there is a projection function P_2 from T_2 to T_3, a value of $P_2(P_1(E))$ is queried. Moreover, if there are more than one projection for a projected type, all of them are applied. Projecting values is implemented as a Why3 transformation `intro_projections_cntexmp`.

Figure 8 defines an abstract type `byte` to represent integers from -128 to 127. Values of this type can be projected to integers using function `to_rep`. This function is marked as a projection using meta `"model_projection"`. The variable a of type `byte` is marked with the label `"model_projected"`. This means that a will be queried in counterexamples and will be projected from `byte` to `int` using `to_rep`.

Querying record values reuses projection mechanism to extract their fields. For each field, a projection function is defined, marked using meta `"model_projection"`, and annotated with a `"model_trace"` label specifying the name of the field. When the transformation `intro_projections_cntexmp` uses this function to project a record value to the record field, it adds the name of the field to the content of `"model_trace"` label of the record value. Remember that projections are applied transitively: if a field is of a type with a defined projection, it is further projected. Figure 8 shows an example of definition of record type r with fields f and g. Functions `proj_f` and `proj_g` project a value of type r to field f and g and they are annotated with `"model_trace"` labels capturing the names of the fields that will be displayed in a counterexample. The constant b is marked to be queried for a counterexample with `"model_projected"` label meaning that the value must be projected before being displayed and it is annotated with `"model_trace"` label that captures the name of the variable that will be displayed in a counterexample.

Arrays. SMT-LIB does not define how values of array types should be output in a counterexample. To get values of array types, we rely on the form in which values of array types are returned by the CVC4 solver: an array as a constant array and series of store operations defining relevant indices. Here are two examples of array values that CVC4 may return:

```
(store (store ((as const (Array Int Int)) 0) 1 2) 3 4)
((as const (Array Int (Array Int Int))) ((as const (Array Int Int)) 0))
```

The first array is a single-dimensional array with index 1 equal to 2, index 3 equal to 4, and other indices equal to 0. The second array is a two-dimensional array with all indices equal to 0. The values stored in the array may be of abstract or record types so we need to project them. The problem is that we cannot proceed as for records by introducing projections for each array index because there are infinitely many of them. To overcome this problem, for an array `orig_arr` that should be queried for a counterexample and has values of an abstract type `t_val`, a projection function `pf_val` from the abstract type `t_val` to concrete type `t_val_c` is defined. Then, new array `proj_arr` with values of the type `t_val_c` is defined together with an axiom stating that projections of values in the original array are equal to the values in the new array:

```
constant proj_arr: map int t_val_c
axiom proj_axiom : (forall i : int. proj_arr[i] = pf_val(orig_arr[i]))
```

Instead of querying the solver for the original array, the solver is queried for the new, projected array.

3.4   Building Counterexamples for SPARK

A SPARK program is translated by the tool `gnat2why` into a WhyML program with counterexample annotations. Why3 generates VCs and tries to prove each resulting proof task with selected provers. If all fail, the task is split into smaller tasks. When a task can be neither proved nor split, it is attempted to be proved in the counterexample mode described in Sect. 3.3. The generated counterexample is returned back to `gnat2why` and post-processed, before being displayed to the user.

Generating WhyML code. `gnat2why` marks all WhyML elements corresponding to declarations of SPARK variables or to declarations of arguments of SPARK functions to be part of a counterexample using `"model"` or `"model_projected"` labels, generates projection functions for abstract and record types generated by `gnat2why` and marks WhyML elements that trigger generating of a VC by `"model_vc"` labels. `gnat2why` also generates `"model_trace"` labels storing traceability information to corresponding elements in SPARK program. Instead of storing names, `"model_trace"` labels store unique identifiers from SPARK internal representation (AST). `gnat2why` generates Why3 location tags, which make it possible to explicitly specify source code locations of WhyML elements.

Post-processing counterexamples. The counterexample returned from Why3 to `gnat2why` is a map from locations in SPARK source code to lists of counterexample elements at these locations. A counterexample element consists of an identifier and a value. The identifier has the form $x.f_1 \ldots f_n$ $(n \geq 0)$ where x

(resp. f_i) is the internal AST identifier of a variable (resp. field). Counterexample elements are post-processed in the following way: identifiers are mapped back to names in the source code, elements in the same source code line corresponding to same record are grouped together as an aggregate (as in Fig. 3). Values are converted to SPARK syntax.

3.5 Experimental Evaluation

Our implementation of counterexample generation is publicly available in Why3 0.87 and SPARK 16.0. On the full SPARK regression test-suite consisting in 1472 tests, enabling counterexample generation only induce a small slowdown if any on all supported platforms.

Figure 9 presents the results on the section of the test-suite that was initially created for the Riposte tool [25], which was used in the previous versions of SPARK to generate counterexamples. Overall, in most of the cases, counterexamples were obtained and they were of a good quality. The main difficulty for counterexample generation was the use of non-linear arithmetic (tests `arithmetic`, `alpha_launch_examples`, and `victor_divmod_rules`) and the presence of arrays (tests `array_aggregates`, `arrays`, `simple_arrays`, `arrays_multidim`, `array_application`, and `complex_arrays`). In the case of arrays, this is likely caused by the additional projections and axioms that are generated for arrays when generating counterexamples, as described in Sect. 3.3.

Test	VCs	Unproved	Counterexamples		Good Counterexamples	
			Number	Percentage	Number	Percentage
basic	42	4	4	100%	4	100%
logic	46	11	11	100%	11	100%
enums	34	4	4	100%	4	100%
real_world	10	4	4	100%	4	100%
mixed	9	2	2	100%	2	100%
array_algorithms	44	2	2	100%	2	100%
records	115	19	18	95%	18	95%
alpha_launch_examples	17	8	6	75%	6	75%
array_aggregates	172	25	19	76%	19	76%
arrays	51	13	12	92%	8	62%
simple_arrays	109	50	50	100%	30	60%
usergroup_examples	15	4	2	50%	2	50%
victor_divmod_rules	58	9	4	44%	4	44%
arithmetic	126	24	10	42%	10	42%
arrays_multidim	20	13	10	77%	2	15%
array_applications	44	9	1	11%	1	11%
complex_arrays	39	10	10	100%	0	0%
All	**951**	**211**	**169**	**80%**	**127**	**60%**

Fig. 9. Results of counterexample generation on Riposte tests.

4   Conclusions and Perspectives

We added the generation of counterexamples to SPARK 2014, by exploiting the model generation feature of SMT solvers, and appropriately instrumenting the process of generating VCs from a SPARK program, through the intermediate WhyML program, weakest precondition calculus and logic transformations. Instead of complex post-processing of the complete model that would be returned by the SMT-LIB `get-model` command, we instrumented the processing steps so that only the adequate terms are queried with the `get-value` command, and then a simple mapping from the terms queried to the initial program variables can be applied to build the counterexample.

Recent user training sessions showed a clear appeal of counterexamples to users, which motivated our choice to enable them by default in SPARK (versions 16.0 and later). Based on our initial feedback with the use of counterexamples inside SPARK, counterexamples may be the most useful feature in SPARK for investigating unproved properties, after the possibility to execute contracts and assertions in tests.

Related Work. The model returned by a SAT or SMT solver on a satisfiable problem is exploited in several areas of program verification, a major case being the one of model checking, as for example in the Alloy analyzer [26] or the CBMC model checker for C programs [15]. In the case of deductive verification, generating counterexamples is not as common. The Riposte tool based on answer set programming [25] was used in the previous versions of SPARK to generate counterexamples, but only at the level of VCs without source traceability. There is also the case of the NitPick tool inside the Isabelle proof assistant [4].

In the more specific case of program verifiers using SMT solvers, the idea of instrumenting the generation of VCs originates from the old system ESC/Modula-3, that generates VCs for the Simplify solver, adding specific labels to determine the source location and the path of execution leading to the potential program error. The same mechanism was reused in ESC/Java [19]. The potential counterexample proposed by Simplify can be displayed to the user, but is very hard to understand because of the various encodings from the input program to the VC. Only recently a way to reinterpret the counterexample in terms of variables of the source code was designed in the OpenJML framework [12]. They use SMT-LIB command `get-value` to get counterexample values for all sub-expressions in the original program, supporting values of scalar types only, and also to get values of block predicates, which they use to determine the control-flow path of the failed assertion [11]. In SPARK, it is possible to generate VCs for individual control-flow paths and display control-flow path for such VCs if they cannot be proved. In OpenJML, SMT-LIB VCs are generated directly, without using intermediate representation. On one hand, this make it easier to maintain mapping between source-code variables and logical variables. On the other hand, using Why3 as intermediate language makes it possible to use the power of Why3 transformations to transform a proof task to forms well suited for different provers. Another deductive program verification framework that makes use of SMT counter-models is the Boogie Verifier Debugger [18]. Boogie is used as an intermediate language by Dafny [20] and VCC [10]. Boogie also has its own way of reinterpreting the counter-model, generated by its back-end prover Z3, in terms of the source code. Besides scalar values, Boogie makes it possible to display the content of dynamically allocated data structures such as objects. Unlike SPARK and OpenJML, Boogie encodes locations and source variable names in the generated VC, uses SMT-LIB command `get-model` to get whole SMT-LIB counterexample and then relies on reverse transformations to map the SMT-LIB counterexample into the source code.

Both OpenJML and Boogie present the counterexample in a user-friendly manner, in their respective graphical interfaces (Eclipse, Visual Studio). Their presentation is a bit different from our way of presenting the counterexample, where we give values of relevant variables inside comments at proper locations of the source code. We have no evidence that our approach is better than these other approaches in terms of quality of the generated counterexamples. We designed our approach so that it is the best fit for SPARK users.

Another recent approach for helping users in debugging their specification and code is to use some kind of symbolic execution, as is proposed by the Visual Studio dynamic debugger [23] and the Verifast verifier [17].

Future Work. During this work, we encountered a few issues that could be addressed by authors of SMT solvers.

First, SMT-LIB standard does not fix any rule for displaying model values. In particular, it is not standardized how values of array types and bit-vector types should be displayed. This need for standardization is already known and it is likely to appear in the near future. Related to this, we believe that the feature of projections that we introduced could be handled by the solvers themselves as part of the standard to display counterexamples. This would be particularly useful in the case of arrays: the solution we proposed, involving the introduction of another array and an axiom, makes the problem harder to prove because of the additional universal quantification.

A second issue concerns the validity of generated counterexamples. In principle, one should query SMT solvers for models only if the answer was 'sat'. However, on a VC generated by a program verification task, most of the time the answer is 'unknown' or the solver hits the time limit given. As expected, in this case the model is not guaranteed to be a true model. However, there are some cases where the model returned is *trivially wrong* because it is not even a model of the ground part of the goal. A suggestion for improvement is as follows: since the main source of incompleteness comes from the quantified hypotheses, there could be two different modes of operation, with two corresponding time limits. A first time limit, say a "soft" one, gives the time during which the solver is allowed to instantiate quantifiers as it wants. After this soft time limit is reached, a "hard" time limit should give the solver extra time to continue its search but in a specific mode where no new quantifier instantiation is performed. In this second mode, it is likely that the solver would terminate its search, and if a model is returned, it would be valid with respect to the ground part of the goal. If such modes were implemented in SMT solvers, it would be of major interest for counterexample generation.

Another technical issue is the ability to support model generation for all supported theories. This is not always the case, for example CVC4 does not produce models when non-linear arithmetic is selected. It is understandable since this logic is undecidable, there is no way to be sure that the model returned would be a true one. However, a similar degraded mode as described above could be implemented, for example in the degraded mode non-linear parts of the formulas could be ignored.

To double-check that a counterexample produced by our technique is a true one, one may consider turning it into a test case and run the program with the given values. This is unfortunately not an easy task because of the procedure calls: a procedure has a concrete semantics given by concrete execution and abstract semantics given by contracts. Since only the abstract semantics is visible to a solver, it may happen that a counterexample is true with respect to the abstract semantics, but false with respect to the concrete semantics and moreover it can happen that there is a different counterexample, not returned by the solver, true with respect to both semantics. Thus, properly combining counterexamples generated by failed proof attempts and run-time verification needs to investigated further. Recent work by Christakis et al. [9] and Petiot et al. [24] pursue such a direction.

Acknowledgements. We would like to thank David Cok, Clément Fumex, Rustan Leino, Andrei Paskevich, Florian Schanda, as well as the anonymous reviewers for their useful comments. We are pleased that a reviewer specifically agreed with us on "the suggested improvement to SMT solvers regarding hard and soft limits" and another confirmed that "the insights discussed as future work are very interesting".

References

1. Barnes, J.: Programming in Ada 2012. Cambridge University Press, Cambridge (2014)
2. Barrett, C., Conway, C.L., Deters, M., Hadarean, L., Jovanović, D., King, T., Reynolds, A., Tinelli, C.: CVC4. In: Gopalakrishnan, G., Qadeer, S. (eds.) CAV 2011. LNCS, vol. 6806, pp. 171–177. Springer, Heidelberg (2011)
3. Barrett, C., Stump, A., Tinelli, C.: The SMT-LIB standard: version 2.0. In: 8th International Workshop on Satisfiability Modulo Theories (2010)
4. Blanchette, J.C., Nipkow, T.: Nitpick: a counterexample generator for higher-order logic based on a relational model finder. In: Kaufmann, M., Paulson, L.C. (eds.) ITP 2010. LNCS, vol. 6172, pp. 131–146. Springer, Heidelberg (2010)
5. Bobot, F., Conchon, S., Contejean, E., Iguernelala, M., Lescuyer, S., Mebsout, A.: The Alt-Ergo automated theorem prover (2008). http://alt-ergo.lri.fr/
6. Bobot, F., Filliâtre, J.C., Marché, C., Paskevich, A.: Why3: Shepherd your herd of provers. In: International Workshop on Intermediate Verification Languages, Wrocław, Poland, pp. 53–64 (2011)

7. Bobot, F., Filliâtre, J.C., Marché, C., Paskevich, A.: Let's verify this with Why3. Int. J. Softw. Tools Technol. Transfer **17**(6), 709–727 (2015)
8. Chapman, R., Schanda, F.: Are we there yet? 20 years of industrial theorem proving with SPARK. In: Klein, G., Gamboa, R. (eds.) ITP 2014. LNCS, vol. 8558, pp. 17–26. Springer, Heidelberg (2014)
9. Christakis, M., Leino, K.R.M., Müller, P., Wüstholz, V.: Integrated environment for diagnosing verification errors. In: Chechik, M., Raskin, J.-F. (eds.) TACAS 2016. LNCS, vol. 9636, pp. 424–441. Springer, Heidelberg (2016). doi:10.1007/978-3-662-49674-9_25
10. Cohen, E., Dahlweid, M., Hillebrand, M., Leinenbach, D., Moskal, M., Santen, T., Schulte, W., Tobies, S.: VCC: a practical system for verifying concurrent C. In: Berghofer, S., Nipkow, T., Urban, C., Wenzel, M. (eds.) TPHOLs 2009. LNCS, vol. 5674, pp. 23–42. Springer, Heidelberg (2009)
11. Cok, D.R.: Improved usability and performance of SMT solvers for debugging specifications. Int. J. Softw. Tools Technol. Transf. **12**(6), 467–481 (2010)
12. Cok, D.R.: OpenJML: Software verification for Java 7 using JML, OpenJDK, and Eclipse. In: Formal Integrated Development Environments (2014). Elec. Proc. Theor. Comput. Sci. 149, 79–92 (2014)
13. Filliâtre, J.-C., Marché, C.: The Why/Krakatoa/Caduceus platform for deductive program verification. In: Damm, W., Hermanns, H. (eds.) CAV 2007. LNCS, vol. 4590, pp. 173–177. Springer, Heidelberg (2007)
14. Filliâtre, J.-C., Paskevich, A.: Why3 — where programs meet provers. In: Felleisen, M., Gardner, P. (eds.) ESOP 2013. LNCS, vol. 7792, pp. 125–128. Springer, Heidelberg (2013)
15. Groce, A., Kroning, D., Lerda, F.: Understanding counterexamples with explain. In: Alur, R., Peled, D.A. (eds.) CAV 2004. LNCS, vol. 3114, pp. 453–456. Springer, Heidelberg (2004)
16. Hauzar, D., Marché, C., Moy, Y.: Counterexamples from proof failures in the SPARK program verifier. Research Report 8854, Inria (2016). https://hal.inria.fr/hal-01271174
17. Jacobs, B., Smans, J., Philippaerts, P., Vogels, F., Penninckx, W., Piessens, F.: VeriFast: a powerful, sound, predictable, fast verifier for C and Java. In: Bobaru, M., Havelund, K., Holzmann, G.J., Joshi, R. (eds.) NFM 2011. LNCS, vol. 6617, pp. 41–55. Springer, Heidelberg (2011)
18. Le Goues, C., Leino, K.R.M., Moskal, M.: The boogie verification debugger (tool paper). In: Barthe, G., Pardo, A., Schneider, G. (eds.) SEFM 2011. LNCS, vol. 7041, pp. 407–414. Springer, Heidelberg (2011)
19. Leino, K.R.M., Millstein, T., Saxe, J.B.: Generating error traces from verification-condition counterexamples. Sci. Comput. Program. **55**(1–3), 209–226 (2005)
20. Leino, K.R.M., Wüstholz, V.: The Dafny integrated development environment. In: Formal Integrated Development Environments (2014). Elec. Proc. Theor. Comput. Sci. 149, 3–15 (2014)
21. McCormick, J.W., Chapin, P.C.: Building High Integrity Applications with SPARK. Cambridge University Press, Cambridge (2015)
22. de Moura, L., Bjørner, N.S.: Z3: an efficient SMT solver. In: Ramakrishnan, C.R., Rehof, J. (eds.) TACAS 2008. LNCS, vol. 4963, pp. 337–340. Springer, Heidelberg (2008)
23. Müller, P., Ruskiewicz, J.N.: Using debuggers to understand failed verification attempts. In: Butler, M., Schulte, W. (eds.) FM 2011. LNCS, vol. 6664, pp. 73–87. Springer, Heidelberg (2011)

24. Petiot, G., Kosmatov, N., Botella, B., Giorgetti, A., Julliand, J.: Your proof fails? testing helps to find the reason (2015). http://arxiv.org/abs/1508.01691
25. Schanda, F., Brain, M.: Using answer set programming in the development of verified software. In: Technical Communications of the 28th International Conference on Logic Programming. LIPIcs, vol. 17, pp. 72–85. Leibniz-Zentrum fuer Informatik (2012)
26. Torlak, E., Jackson, D.: Kodkod: a relational model finder. In: Grumberg, O., Huth, M. (eds.) TACAS 2007. LNCS, vol. 4424, pp. 632–647. Springer, Heidelberg (2007)

Proving Termination of Programs with Bitvector Arithmetic by Symbolic Execution

Jera Hensel, Jürgen Giesl$^{(\boxtimes)}$, Florian Frohn, and Thomas Ströder

LuFG Informatik 2, RWTH Aachen University, Aachen, Germany
{hensel,giesl,florian.frohn,stroeder}@informatik.rwth-aachen.de

Abstract. In earlier work, we developed an approach for automated termination analysis of C programs with explicit pointer arithmetic, which is based on symbolic execution. However, similar to many other termination techniques, this approach assumed the program variables to range over mathematical integers instead of bitvectors. This eases mathematical reasoning but is unsound in general. In this paper, we extend our approach in order to handle fixed-width bitvector integers. Thus, we present the first technique for termination analysis of C programs that covers both byte-accurate pointer arithmetic and bit-precise modeling of integers. We implemented our approach in the automated termination prover AProVE and evaluate its power by extensive experiments.

1 Introduction

In [14], we developed an approach for termination analysis of C with explicit pointer arithmetic, which we implemented in our tool AProVE [9]. AProVE won the termination category of the *International Competition on Software Verification (SV-COMP)*[1] at *TACAS* in 2015 and 2016. However, like the other termination tools at *SV-COMP*, our approach was restricted to mathematical integers.

In general, this is unsound: The function f below does not terminate if x has the maximum value of its type[2]. But we can falsely prove termination if we treat x and j as mathematical integers. For g, we could falsely conclude non-termination, although g always terminates due to the wrap-around for unsigned overflows.

```
void f(unsigned int x)  {          void g(unsigned int j) {
    unsigned int j = 0;                while (j > 0) j++; }
    while (j <= x) j++; }
```

Supported by the DFG grant GI 274/6-1.

[1] See http://sv-comp.sosy-lab.org/.

[2] In C, adding 1 to the maximal unsigned integer results in 0. In contrast, for signed integers, adding 1 to the maximal signed integer results in undefined behavior. However, most C implementations return the minimal signed integer as the result.

R. De Nicola and E. Kühn (Eds.): SEFM 2016, LNCS 9763, pp. 234–252, 2016.
DOI: 10.1007/978-3-319-41591-8_16

In this paper, we adapt our approach for termination of C from [14] to handle the bitvector semantics correctly. To avoid dealing with the intricacies of C, we analyze programs in the platform-independent intermediate representation of the LLVM compilation framework [12]. Our approach works in two steps: First, a *symbolic execution graph* is automatically constructed that represents an over-approximation of all possible program runs (Sects. 2 and 3). This graph can also be used to prove that the program does not result in undefined behavior (so in particular, it is memory safe). In a second step (Sect. 4), this graph is transformed into an *integer transition system (ITS)*, whose termination can be proved by existing techniques. In Sect. 5, we compare our approach with related work and evaluate our corresponding implementation in AProVE. Appendix A discusses details on the semantics of abstract states and Appendix B gives the proofs of the theorems.

To extend our approach to fixed-width integers, we express relations between bitvectors by corresponding relations between mathematical integers $\mathbb{Z}$. In this way, we can use standard SMT solving over $\mathbb{Z}$ for all steps needed to construct the symbolic execution graph. Moreover, this allows us to obtain ITSs over $\mathbb{Z}$ from these graphs, and to use standard approaches for generating ranking functions to prove termination of these ITSs. So our contribution is a general technique to adapt byte-accurate symbolic execution to the handling of bitvectors, which can also be used for many other program analyses besides proving termination.

Limitations. To simplify the presentation and to concentrate on the issues related to bitvectors, we restrict ourselves to a single LLVM function and to LLVM *types* of the form in (for n-bit integers), in* (for pointers to values of type in), in**, in***, etc. Moreover, we assume a 1 byte data alignment (i.e., values may be stored at any address) and only handle memory allocation by the LLVM instruction `alloca`. See [14] for an extension of our approach to programs with several LLVM functions, arbitrary alignment, and external functions like `malloc`. As discussed in [14], some LLVM concepts are not yet supported by our approach (e.g., `undef`, floating point values, vectors, `struct` types, and recursion). Another limitation is that our approach cannot directly *disprove* properties like memory safety or termination, as it is based on over-approximating all possible program runs.

2   LLVM States for Symbolic Execution

In this section, we define concrete and abstract LLVM states that represent sets of concrete states. These states will be needed for symbolic execution in Sect. 3. As an example, consider the function g from Sect. 1. In the corresponding[3] LLVM code in Fig. 1, the integer variable j has the type i32, as it is represented as a bitvector of length 32. The program is split into the *basic blocks* entry, cmp,

---

[3] This LLVM program corresponds to the code obtained from g with the Clang compiler [3]. To ease readability, we wrote variables without "%" in front (i.e., we wrote "j" instead of "%j" as in proper LLVM) and added line numbers.

body, and done. We will explain this LLVM code in detail when constructing the symbolic execution graph in Sect. 3.

In our abstract domain, an LLVM state consists of the current program position, the values of the local program variables, a knowledge base with information about these values, and two sets to describe allocations and the contents of memory. The *program position* is represented by a pair (b, k). Here, b is the name of the current basic block and k is the index of the

```
define i32 @g(i32 j) {
entry:  0:  ad = alloca i32
        1:  store i32 j, i32* ad
        2:  br label cmp
cmp:    0:  j1 = load i32* ad
        1:  j1pos = icmp ugt i32 j1, 0
        2:  br i1 j1pos, label body, label done
body:   0:  j2 = load i32* ad
        1:  inc = add i32 j2, 1
        2:  store i32 inc, i32* ad
        3:  br label cmp
done:   0:  ret void }
```

Fig. 1. LLVM code for the function g

next instruction. So if *Blks* is the set of all basic blocks, then the set of program positions is $Pos = Blks \times \mathbb{N}$. We represent an assignment to the *local program variables* $\mathcal{V}_\mathcal{P}$ (e.g., $\mathcal{V}_\mathcal{P} = \{j, ad, \ldots\}$) by an injective function $LV : \mathcal{V}_\mathcal{P} \to \mathcal{V}_{sym}$, where $\mathcal{V}_{sym}$ is an infinite set of symbolic variables with $\mathcal{V}_{sym} \cap \mathcal{V}_\mathcal{P} = \varnothing$. Let $\mathcal{V}_{sym}(LV) \subseteq \mathcal{V}_{sym}$ be the set of all symbolic variables v where $LV(x) = v$ for some $x \in \mathcal{V}_\mathcal{P}$.

The third component of states is the *knowledge base* $KB \subseteq QF\_IA(\mathcal{V}_{sym})$, a set of first-order quantifier-free integer arithmetic formulas. For concrete states, KB uniquely determines the values of symbolic variables, whereas for abstract states several values are possible. We identify *sets* of formulas $\{\varphi_1, \ldots, \varphi_n\}$ with their *conjunction* $\varphi_1 \wedge \ldots \wedge \varphi_n$ and require that KB is just a conjunction of equalities and inequalities in order to speed up SMT-based arithmetic reasoning.

The fourth component of a state is an *allocation list* AL. It contains expressions of the form $[\![v_1, v_2]\!]$ for $v_1, v_2 \in \mathcal{V}_{sym}$, which indicate that $v_1 \leq v_2$ and that all addresses between v_1 and v_2 have been allocated by an alloca instruction.

The fifth component PT is a set of "*points-to*" atoms $v_1 \hookrightarrow_{ty,i} v_2$ where $v_1, v_2 \in \mathcal{V}_{sym}$, ty is an LLVM type, and $i \in \{u, s\}$. This means that the value v_2 of type ty is stored at the address v_1, where $i \in \{u, s\}$ indicates whether v_2 represents this value as an *unsigned* or *signed* integer. As each memory cell stores one byte, $v_1 \hookrightarrow_{i32,i} v_2$ states that v_2 is stored in the four cells $v_1, \ldots, v_1 + 3$.

Finally, we use a special state ERR to be reached if we cannot prove absence of undefined behavior (e.g., if a non-allowed overflow or a violation of memory safety by accessing non-allocated memory might take place).

Definition 1 (States). LLVM states *have the form* (p, LV, KB, AL, PT) *where* $p \in Pos$, $LV : \mathcal{V}_\mathcal{P} \to \mathcal{V}_{sym}$, $KB \subseteq QF\_IA(\mathcal{V}_{sym})$, $AL \subseteq \{[\![v_1, v_2]\!] \mid v_1, v_2 \in \mathcal{V}_{sym}\}$, *and* $PT \subseteq \{(v_1 \hookrightarrow_{ty,i} v_2) \mid v_1, v_2 \in \mathcal{V}_{sym}, ty \text{ is an LLVM type}, i \in \{u, s\}\}$. *In addition, there is a state* ERR *for undefined behavior. For* $a = (p, LV, KB, AL, PT)$, *let* $\mathcal{V}_{sym}(a)$ *consist of* $\mathcal{V}_{sym}(LV)$ *and all symbolic variables in* KB, AL, *or* PT.

We often identify the mapping LV with the equations $\{x = LV(x) \mid x \in \mathcal{V}_{\mathcal{P}}\}$. As an example, consider the following abstract state for our function g:

$$(\ (\texttt{entry}, 2), \{j = v_j, \texttt{ad} = v_{\texttt{ad}}\}, \{v_{end} = v_{\texttt{ad}} + 3\}, \{\llbracket v_{\texttt{ad}}, v_{end} \rrbracket\}, \{v_{\texttt{ad}} \hookrightarrow_{\texttt{i32},u} v_j\}) \quad (1)$$

It represents states in the entry block immediately before executing the instruction in line 2. Here, $LV(j) = v_j$, the memory cells between $LV(\texttt{ad}) = v_{\texttt{ad}}$ and $v_{end} = v_{\texttt{ad}} + 3$ have been allocated, and v_j is stored in the 4 cells $v_{\texttt{ad}}, \ldots, v_{end}$.

In contrast to [14], we partition the program variables $\mathcal{V}_{\mathcal{P}}$ into two disjoint sets $\mathcal{U}_{\mathcal{P}}$ and $\mathcal{S}_{\mathcal{P}}$. If $x \in \mathcal{U}_{\mathcal{P}}$ (resp. $x \in \mathcal{S}_{\mathcal{P}}$), then $LV(x)$ is x's value as an unsigned (resp. signed) integer. This is advantageous when formulating rules to execute LLVM instructions like icmp ugt and sgt, since the LLVM types do not distinguish between unsigned and signed integers. Instead, some LLVM instructions consider their arguments as "unsigned" whereas others consider them as "signed".

To determine $\mathcal{U}_{\mathcal{P}}$ and $\mathcal{S}_{\mathcal{P}}$, we use the following heuristic which statically scans the program $\mathcal{P}$ for variables which are (mainly) used in unsigned resp. signed interpretation. We iteratively add a variable x to $\mathcal{U}_{\mathcal{P}}$ if

- x is an address (i.e., it has a type of the form ty∗),
- x occurs in an unsigned comparison instruction (e.g., icmp ugt for the integer comparison "unsigned greater than") or in another unsigned operation (e.g., udiv or urem for "unsigned division" or "remainder"),
- x occurs in a sign neutral comparison (icmp eq or ne) or in a phi or select instruction together with another variable $y \in \mathcal{U}_{\mathcal{P}}$, where y is not the condition,
- x occurs in an add, sub, mul, or shl instruction without nsw flag ("no signed wrap-up" means that overflow of signed integers yields undefined behavior),
- x occurs in a binary or conversion instruction with another $y \in \mathcal{U}_{\mathcal{P}}$,
- x is the result of icmp or the condition of a branch (br) or select instruction,
- x occurs in a lshr ("logical shift right") instruction,
- x occurs in a zext instruction (the "zero extension" adds zero bits in front),
- x is loaded from an address where a variable $y \in \mathcal{U}_{\mathcal{P}}$ is stored to, or
- x is stored to an address where a variable $y \in \mathcal{U}_{\mathcal{P}}$ is loaded from.

Afterwards, we iteratively remove x from $\mathcal{U}_{\mathcal{P}}$ again if

- x is one of the two arguments of a signed comparison (e.g., icmp sgt) or x occurs in another signed operation (e.g., sdiv or srem),
- x occurs in a comparison or in a phi or select instruction together with another variable $y \in \mathcal{V}_{\mathcal{P}} \setminus \mathcal{U}_{\mathcal{P}}$, where x is not the condition,
- x occurs in an instruction flagged by nsw,
- x occurs in a binary or conversion instruction with another $y \in \mathcal{V}_{\mathcal{P}} \setminus \mathcal{U}_{\mathcal{P}}$,
- x occurs in an ashr ("arithmetic shift right") instruction,
- x occurs in a sext instruction (the "sign extension" adds copies of the most significant bit in front),
- x is loaded from an address where a variable $y \in \mathcal{V}_{\mathcal{P}} \setminus \mathcal{U}_{\mathcal{P}}$ is stored to, or
- x is stored to an address where a variable $y \in \mathcal{V}_{\mathcal{P}} \setminus \mathcal{U}_{\mathcal{P}}$ is loaded from.

We then define $\mathcal{S}_\mathcal{P} = \mathcal{V}_\mathcal{P} \setminus \mathcal{U}_\mathcal{P}$. In this way, we make sure that in each instruction in $\mathcal{P}$, all occurring program variables of type $\mathtt{i}n$ with $n > 1$ are either from $\mathcal{U}_\mathcal{P}$ or from $\mathcal{S}_\mathcal{P}$. In our example, we obtain $\mathcal{U}_\mathcal{P} = \mathcal{V}_\mathcal{P} = \{\mathtt{j}, \mathtt{ad}, \ldots, \mathtt{inc}\}$ and $\mathcal{S}_\mathcal{P} = \varnothing$. Note that there is no guarantee that all variables in $\mathcal{U}_\mathcal{P}$ resp. $\mathcal{S}_\mathcal{P}$ are used as unsigned resp. signed integers in the original C program (e.g., if $\mathtt{y}, \mathtt{z} \in \mathcal{S}_\mathcal{P}$ and the C program contains "$\mathtt{unsigned\ int\ x\ =\ y\ +\ z;}$", then our heuristic would conclude $\mathtt{x} \in \mathcal{S}_\mathcal{P}$, since the resulting LLVM code has the instruction "$\mathtt{x\ =\ add}$ $\mathtt{i32\ y,\ z}$"). Our analysis remains correct if there are (un)signed variables that we do not recognize as being (un)signed (i.e., failure of the above heuristic for $\mathcal{U}_\mathcal{P}$ and $\mathcal{S}_\mathcal{P}$ only affects the performance, but not the soundness of our approach).

To construct symbolic execution graphs, for any state a we use a first-order formula $\langle a \rangle_{FO}$, which is a conjunction of equalities and inequalities containing KB and obvious consequences of AL and PT. Moreover, $\langle a \rangle_{FO}$ states that all integers belong to intervals corresponding to their types. Here, let $\mathsf{umax}_n = 2^n - 1$, $\mathsf{smin}_n = -2^{n-1}$, and $\mathsf{smax}_n = 2^{n-1} - 1$. Moreover, $size(\mathtt{ty})$ is the number of bits required for values of type $\mathtt{ty}$ (e.g., $size(\mathtt{i}n) = n$ and $size(\mathtt{ty}*) = 32$ (resp. 64) on 32-bit (resp. 64-bit) architectures). As usual, "$v \in [k, m]$" is a shorthand for "$k \le v \wedge v \le m$" and "$\models \varphi$" means that φ is a tautology.

Definition 2 (FO Formulas for States). $\langle a \rangle_{FO}$ is the smallest set with[4]

$$
\begin{aligned}
\langle a \rangle_{FO} = \; & KB \cup \{0 < v_1 \le v_2 \mid [\![v_1, v_2]\!] \in AL\} \cup \\
& \{v_2 = w_2 \mid (v_1 \hookrightarrow_{\mathtt{ty},i} v_2), (w_1 \hookrightarrow_{\mathtt{ty},i} w_2) \in PT \text{ and } \models \langle a \rangle_{FO} \Rightarrow v_1 = w_1\} \cup \\
& \{v_1 \ne w_1 \mid (v_1 \hookrightarrow_{\mathtt{ty},i} v_2), (w_1 \hookrightarrow_{\mathtt{ty},i} w_2) \in PT \text{ and } \models \langle a \rangle_{FO} \Rightarrow v_2 \ne w_2\} \cup \\
& \{0 < v_1 \wedge v_2 \in [0, \mathsf{umax}_{size(\mathtt{ty})}] \mid (v_1 \hookrightarrow_{\mathtt{ty},u} v_2) \in PT\} \cup \\
& \{0 < v_1 \wedge v_2 \in [\mathsf{smin}_{size(\mathtt{ty})}, \mathsf{smax}_{size(\mathtt{ty})}] \mid (v_1 \hookrightarrow_{\mathtt{ty},s} v_2) \in PT\} \cup \\
& \{LV(\mathtt{x}) \in [0, \mathsf{umax}_{size(\mathtt{ty})}] \mid \mathtt{x} \in \mathcal{U}_\mathcal{P}, \mathtt{x} \text{ has type } \mathtt{ty}\} \cup \\
& \{LV(\mathtt{x}) \in [\mathsf{smin}_{size(\mathtt{ty})}, \mathsf{smax}_{size(\mathtt{ty})}] \mid \mathtt{x} \in \mathcal{S}_\mathcal{P}, \mathtt{x} \text{ has type } \mathtt{ty}\}.
\end{aligned}
$$

Concrete states determine the values of variables and the contents of the memory *uniquely*. To enforce a uniform representation, in concrete states we only allow statements of the form $(w_1 \hookrightarrow_{\mathtt{ty},i} w_2)$ in PT where $\mathtt{ty} = \mathtt{i8}$ and $i = u$. In addition, concrete states (p, LV, KB, AL, PT) must be *well formed*, i.e., for every $(w_1 \hookrightarrow_{\mathtt{ty},i} w_2) \in PT$, there is an $[\![v_1, v_2]\!] \in AL$ such that $\models KB \Rightarrow v_1 \le w_1 \le v_2$. So PT only contains information about addresses that are known to be allocated.

Definition 3 (Concrete States). *An* LLVM *state c is* concrete *iff $c = ERR$ or $c = (p, LV, KB, AL, PT)$ is well formed, $\langle c \rangle_{FO}$ is satisfiable, and*

- *For all $v \in \mathcal{V}_{sym}(c)$ there exists an $n \in \mathbb{Z}$ such that $\models \langle c \rangle_{FO} \Rightarrow v = n$.*
- *For all $[\![v_1, v_2]\!] \in AL$ and for all integers n with $\models \langle c \rangle_{FO} \Rightarrow v_1 \le n \le v_2$, there exists $(w_1 \hookrightarrow_{\mathtt{i8},u} w_2) \in PT$ for some $w_1, w_2 \in \mathcal{V}_{sym}$ such that $\models \langle c \rangle_{FO} \Rightarrow w_1 = n$ and $\models \langle c \rangle_{FO} \Rightarrow w_2 = k$, for some $k \in [0, \mathsf{umax}_8]$.*
- *There is no $(w_1 \hookrightarrow_{\mathtt{ty},i} w_2) \in PT$ for $\mathtt{ty} \ne \mathtt{i8}$ or $i = s$.*

---

[4] Of course, $\langle a \rangle_{FO}$ can be extended by more formulas, e.g., on the connection between v_2 and v_2' if $(v_1 \hookrightarrow_{\mathtt{i}n,u} v_2), (v_1 \hookrightarrow_{\mathtt{i}m,u} v_2') \in PT$ for $n < m$. Then we can also handle programs which load an $\mathtt{i}n$ integer from an address where an $\mathtt{i}m$ integer was stored.

In [14], for every abstract state a, we also introduced a *separation logic* formula $\langle a \rangle_{SL}$ which extends $\langle a \rangle_{FO}$ by detailed information about the memory. (We recapitulate $\langle a \rangle_{SL}$ and the semantics of separation logic in Appendix A.) For this semantics, we use *interpretations* (as, mem). Here, $as : \mathcal{V}_\mathcal{P} \rightarrow \mathbb{Z}$ is an *assignment* of the program variables, where for $\mathbf{x} \in \mathcal{V}_\mathcal{P}$ of type $\mathtt{ty}$, we have $as(\mathbf{x}) \in [0, \mathsf{umax}_{size(\mathtt{ty})}]$ if $\mathbf{x} \in \mathcal{U}_\mathcal{P}$ and $as(\mathbf{x}) \in [\mathsf{smin}_{size(\mathtt{ty})}, \mathsf{smax}_{size(\mathtt{ty})}]$ if $\mathbf{x} \in \mathcal{S}_\mathcal{P}$. The partial function $mem : \mathbb{N}_{>0} \rightharpoonup \{0, \ldots, \mathsf{umax}_8\}$ with finite domain describes the memory contents at allocated addresses (as unsigned integers). We use "$\rightharpoonup$" for partial functions. For any abstract state a, we have $\models \langle a \rangle_{SL} \Rightarrow \langle a \rangle_{FO}$. So $\langle a \rangle_{FO}$ is a weakened version of $\langle a \rangle_{SL}$, used to construct symbolic execution graphs. This allows us to use standard first-order SMT solving for all reasoning in our approach.

Now we define which concrete states are represented by an abstract state a. We extract an interpretation (as^c, mem^c) from every concrete state $c \neq ERR$. Then a *represents* all concrete states c where (as^c, mem^c) is a model of some concrete instantiation of $\langle a \rangle_{SL}$. A *concrete instantiation* is a function $\sigma : \mathcal{V}_{sym} \rightarrow \mathbb{Z}$. So σ does not instantiate $\mathcal{V}_\mathcal{P}$. Instantiations are extended to formulas as usual.

Definition 4 (Representing Concrete by Abstract States). *Let* $c = (p, LV^c, KB^c, AL^c, PT^c)$ *be a concrete state. For every* $\mathbf{x} \in \mathcal{V}_\mathcal{P}$, *let* $as^c(\mathbf{x}) = n$ *for the number* $n \in \mathbb{Z}$ *with* $\models \langle c \rangle_{FO} \Rightarrow LV^c(\mathbf{x}) = n$. *For* $n \in \mathbb{N}_{>0}$, *the function* $mem^c(n)$ *is defined iff there exists a* $(w_1 \hookrightarrow_{i8,u} w_2) \in PT$ *such that* $\models \langle c \rangle_{FO} \Rightarrow w_1 = n$. *Let* $\models \langle c \rangle_{FO} \Rightarrow w_2 = k$, *where* $k \in [0, \mathsf{umax}_8]$. *Then* $mem^c(n) = k$.

We say that an abstract state $a = (p, LV^a, KB^a, AL^a, PT^a)$ *represents a concrete state* $c = (p, LV^c, KB^c, AL^c, PT^c)$ *iff* a *is well formed and* (as^c, mem^c) *is a model of* $\sigma(\langle a \rangle_{SL})$ *for some concrete instantiation* σ *of the symbolic variables. The only state that represents the error state* ERR *is* ERR *itself.*

So the abstract state (1) represents all concrete states $c = ((\mathtt{entry}, 2), LV, KB, AL, PT)$ where mem^c stores the 32-bit integer $as^c(\mathbf{j})$ at the address $as^c(\mathbf{ad})$.

3 From **LLVM** to Symbolic Execution Graphs

We now show how to automatically generate a *symbolic execution graph* that over-approximates all executions of a program. To this end, we define operations to convert any integer expression t into an unsigned resp. signed n-bit integer[5]:

$$\mathsf{uns}_n(t) = t \bmod 2^n \qquad\qquad \mathsf{sig}_n(t) = ((t + 2^{n-1}) \bmod 2^n) - 2^{n-1}$$

The correctness of uns_n is obvious and by Theorem 5, sig_n is correct as well.

Theorem 5 (Converting Integers to Signed n-Bit Integers). *Let* $n \in \mathbb{N}$ *with* $n \geq 1$. *Then* $\mathsf{sig}_n(t) \in [\mathsf{smin}_n, \mathsf{smax}_n]$ *and* $t \bmod 2^n = \mathsf{sig}_n(t) \bmod 2^n$.

---

[5] As usual, mod is defined as follows: For any $m \in \mathbb{Z}$ and $n \in \mathbb{N}_{>0}$, we have $t = m \bmod n$ iff $t \in [0, n-1]$ and there exists a $k \in \mathbb{Z}$ such that $t = k \cdot n + m$.

Moreover, we extend LV to apply it also to concrete integers. To this end, we use $LV_{u,n}, LV_{s,n} : \mathcal{V}_{\mathcal{P}} \uplus \mathbb{Z} \rightarrow \mathcal{V}_{sym} \uplus \mathbb{Z}$, where $LV_{u,n}(t)$ (resp. $LV_{s,n}(t)$) is t represented as an unsigned (resp. signed) integer with n bits, for any $t \in \mathcal{V}_{\mathcal{P}} \uplus \mathbb{Z}$:

$$LV_{u,n}(t) = \begin{cases} LV(t), & \text{if } t \in \mathcal{U}_{\mathcal{P}} \\ \mathrm{uns}_n(LV(t)), & \text{if } t \in \mathcal{S}_{\mathcal{P}} \\ \mathrm{uns}_n(t), & \text{if } t \in \mathbb{Z} \end{cases} \qquad LV_{s,n}(t) = \begin{cases} \mathrm{sign}_n(LV(t)), & \text{if } t \in \mathcal{U}_{\mathcal{P}} \\ LV(t), & \text{if } t \in \mathcal{S}_{\mathcal{P}} \\ \mathrm{sign}_n(t), & \text{if } t \in \mathbb{Z} \end{cases}$$

We developed symbolic execution rules for all LLVM instructions that are affected by the adaption to bitvectors. We handle overflows by appropriate case analyses (Sect. 3.1) or by introducing "modulo" relations (Sect. 3.2). Moreover, Sect. 3.3 presents rules for bitwise binary and conversion instructions. The remaining bitvector instructions of LLVM are handled in an analogous way (see [1] for details), and rules for other LLVM instructions can be found in [14].

3.1 Handling Bitvector Operations by Case Analysis

We start with the initial states that one wants to analyze for termination, e.g., with the abstract state A where j has an unknown value. In the symbolic execution graph for g in Fig. 2, we abbreviated parts by "..." and wrote $\hookrightarrow_{i32}$ and umax instead of $\hookrightarrow_{i32,u}$ and umax_{32}. To ease readability, we replaced some symbolic variables by their values (e.g., we wrote $\mathtt{j1pos} = 1$) and explicitly depicted formulas like $v_{\mathtt{j}} \in [0, \mathsf{umax}]$ that follow from $\langle A \rangle_{FO}$ since $\mathtt{j} \in \mathcal{U}_{\mathcal{P}}$ and $LV(\mathtt{j}) = v_{\mathtt{j}}$.

The function g allocates $[\![v_{\mathsf{ad}}, v_{end}]\!]$ and stores the value $v_{\mathtt{j}}$ of j at address ad. Next, we jump to the block cmp for the loop comparison. After loading the value $v_{\mathtt{j}}$ (stored at address ad) to the program variable j1, in State E we check whether j1's value in <u>un</u>signed interpretation is greater <u>than</u> 0 (icmp ugt).

The following rule evaluates such instructions symbolically. In our rules, "p: ins" states that ins is the instruction at position p. Let a always denote the abstract state *before* the execution step (i.e., above the horizontal line of the rule), where we write $\langle a \rangle$ instead of $\langle a \rangle_{FO}$. Moreover, $LV[\mathtt{x} := v]$ is the function where $(LV[\mathtt{x} := v])(\mathtt{x}) = v$ and $(LV[\mathtt{x} := v])(\mathtt{y}) = LV(\mathtt{y})$ for $\mathtt{y} \neq \mathtt{x}$. If $p = (\mathtt{b}, k)$, then $p^+ = (\mathtt{b}, k+1)$ is the position of the next instruction in the same block.

---

icmp ugt (p: "x = icmp ugt ty t_1, t_2" with $\mathtt{x} \in \mathcal{V}_{\mathcal{P}}$, $t_1, t_2 \in \mathcal{V}_{\mathcal{P}} \cup \mathbb{Z}$)

$$\frac{(p, \ LV, \ KB, \ AL, \ PT)}{(p^+, \ LV[\mathtt{x} := v], \ KB \cup \{\varphi\}, \ AL, \ PT)} \quad \text{if } v \in \mathcal{V}_{sym} \text{ is fresh and if}$$

either $\models \langle a \rangle \Rightarrow (LV_{u,size(\mathtt{ty})}(t_1) > LV_{u,size(\mathtt{ty})}(t_2))$ and φ is "$v = 1$"
or $\models \langle a \rangle \Rightarrow (LV_{u,size(\mathtt{ty})}(t_1) \leq LV_{u,size(\mathtt{ty})}(t_2))$ and φ is "$v = 0$"

However, in our example the value of $LV_{u,32}(\mathtt{j1}) = LV(\mathtt{j1}) = v_{\mathtt{j}}$ is unknown. Therefore, we first have to *refine* State E to States F and G such that the comparison can be decided. For this case analysis, we use the following rule.

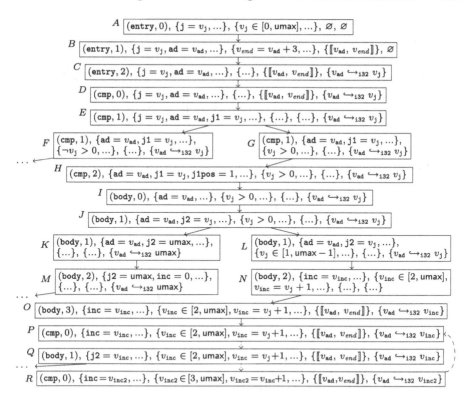

Fig. 2. Symbolic execution graph for the function g

---

icmp ugt refinement (p: "x = icmp ugt ty t_1, t_2" with x $\in \mathcal{V}_P$, $t_1, t_2 \in \mathcal{V}_P \cup \mathbb{Z}$)
$\dfrac{(p,\ LV,\ KB,\ AL,\ PT)}{(p, LV, KB \cup \{\varphi\}, AL, PT) \quad | \quad (p, LV, KB \cup \{\neg\varphi\}, AL, PT)}$ **if**
φ is "$LV_{u,size(\mathrm{ty})}(t_1) > LV_{u,size(\mathrm{ty})}(t_2)$" and we have both $\not\models \langle a \rangle \Rightarrow \varphi$ and $\not\models \langle a \rangle \Rightarrow \neg\varphi$

The rules for other comparisons are analogous. So the rules for the *signed* "greater than" comparison (**sgt**) are obtained by replacing $LV_{u,size(\mathrm{ty})}$ with $LV_{s,size(\mathrm{ty})}$.

If y is compared by **ugt** and y $\in \mathcal{U}_P$, then $LV(\mathrm{y})$ is y's value as an unsigned integer, which makes the comparison very simple. (Similarly, $LV(\mathrm{y})$ is signed if y is compared by **sgt**). In contrast, if LV represented the value of *all* program variables as signed integers, then for **icmp ugt** we would have to consider more cases, which results in a significantly larger graph (i.e., in a less efficient approach)[6].

---

[6] Then we would have to check first whether $LV_{s,size(\mathrm{ty})}(t_1) < 0$ and $LV_{s,size(\mathrm{ty})}(t_2) \geq 0$. In that case, "**icmp ugt ty** t_1, t_2" is *true*, since the most significant bits of t_1 and t_2 are 1 and 0, respectively. The other cases are $LV_{s,size(\mathrm{ty})}(t_1) \geq 0 \wedge LV_{s,size(\mathrm{ty})}(t_2) < 0$, and the two cases where $LV_{s,size(\mathrm{ty})}(t_1)$ and $LV_{s,size(\mathrm{ty})}(t_2)$ have the same sign and either $LV_{s,size(\mathrm{ty})}(t_1) > LV_{s,size(\mathrm{ty})}(t_2)$ or $LV_{s,size(\mathrm{ty})}(t_1) \leq LV_{s,size(\mathrm{ty})}(t_2)$.

In our example, if $\neg v_\mathsf{j} > 0$ (State F), we return from the function. If $v_\mathsf{j} > 0$ (State G), the conditional branch instruction leads us to the block that corresponds to the body of the while-loop. In the step from State I to J, again the value v_j stored at address v_ad is loaded to a program variable j2. The next instruction is an overflow-sensitive addition: If $v_\mathsf{j} < \mathsf{umax}_{32}$, then $v_\mathsf{j} + 1$ is assigned to inc. But if $v_\mathsf{j} = \mathsf{umax}_{32}$, then there is an overflow. If KB does not contain enough information to decide whether an overflow occurs, we perform a case analysis.

---

unsigned add refinement (p: "x = add in t_1, t_2" with $\mathsf{x} \in \mathcal{V}_\mathcal{P}$, $t_1, t_2 \in \mathcal{V}_\mathcal{P} \cup \mathbb{Z}$)

$$\frac{(p, \ LV, \ KB, \ AL, \ PT)}{(p, LV, KB \cup \{\varphi\}, AL, PT) \ \mid \ (p, LV, KB \cup \{\neg\varphi\}, AL, PT)} \quad \text{if } \mathsf{x} \in \mathcal{U}_\mathcal{P} \text{ and}$$

φ is "$LV_{u,n}(t_1) + LV_{u,n}(t_2) \leq \mathsf{umax}_n$", where $\not\models \langle a \rangle \Rightarrow \varphi$ and $\not\models \langle a \rangle \Rightarrow \neg\varphi$

Therefore, State J is refined to K and L. In K, j2 has the value umax_{32}, i.e., adding 1 results in an overflow. In State L, this overflow cannot happen.

The rule for "signed add refinement" is analogous, but here we have $\mathsf{x} \in \mathcal{S}_\mathcal{P}$ and we obtain three instead of two cases: "$LV_{s,n}(t_1) + LV_{s,n}(t_2) < \mathsf{smin}_n$", "$LV_{s,n}(t_1) + LV_{s,n}(t_2) \in [\mathsf{smin}_n, \mathsf{smax}_n]$", and "$LV_{s,n}(t_1) + LV_{s,n}(t_2) > \mathsf{smax}_n$".

Now we define rules for add. If no overflow can occur, then the result is the addition of the operators. Thus, State L evaluates to N, where $v_\mathsf{inc} = v_\mathsf{j} + 1$.

---

add without overflow (p: "x = add [nsw] in t_1, t_2" with $\mathsf{x} \in \mathcal{V}_\mathcal{P}$, $t_1, t_2 \in \mathcal{V}_\mathcal{P} \cup \mathbb{Z}$)

$$\frac{(p, \ LV, \ KB, \ AL, \ PT)}{(p^+, \ LV[\mathsf{x} := v], \ KB \cup \{\varphi\}, \ AL, \ PT)} \quad \text{if } v \in \mathcal{V}_{sym} \text{ is fresh and if}$$

either $\quad \mathsf{x} \in \mathcal{U}_\mathcal{P}, \models \langle a \rangle \Rightarrow (LV_{u,n}(t_1) + LV_{u,n}(t_2) \in [0, \mathsf{umax}_n])$,
and φ is "$v = LV_{u,n}(t_1) + LV_{u,n}(t_2)$"

or $\quad\ \ \mathsf{x} \in \mathcal{S}_\mathcal{P}, \models \langle a \rangle \Rightarrow (LV_{s,n}(t_1) + LV_{s,n}(t_2) \in [\mathsf{smin}_n, \mathsf{smax}_n])$,
and φ is "$v = LV_{s,n}(t_1) + LV_{s,n}(t_2)$"

If an overflow occurs, then due to the wrap-around, the unsigned result value is the sum of the operands minus the type size 2^n. For example, in the evaluation of State K to M, we add the relation $v_\mathsf{inc} = \mathsf{umax}_{32} + 1 - 2^{32} = 0$.

---

unsigned add with overflow (p: "x = add in t_1, t_2" with $\mathsf{x} \in \mathcal{V}_\mathcal{P}$, $t_1, t_2 \in \mathcal{V}_\mathcal{P} \cup \mathbb{Z}$)

$$\frac{(p, \ LV, \ KB, \ AL, \ PT)}{(p^+, \ LV[\mathsf{x} := v], \ KB \cup \{v = LV_{u,n}(t_1) + LV_{u,n}(t_2) - 2^n\}, \ AL, \ PT)} \quad \text{if}$$

$\mathsf{x} \in \mathcal{U}_\mathcal{P}$, $v \in \mathcal{V}_{sym}$ is fresh, and $\models \langle a \rangle \Rightarrow (LV_{u,n}(t_1) + LV_{u,n}(t_2) > \mathsf{umax}_n)$

When adding two signed integers in C, an overflow leads to undefined behavior. Thus, this is translated into an LLVM instruction with the flag nsw. However, when adding an unsigned and a signed integer in C, an overflow does not yield undefined behavior (i.e., the resulting LLVM instruction is not flagged with nsw). Our heuristic for $\mathcal{U}_\mathcal{P}$ and $\mathcal{S}_\mathcal{P}$ would consider this to be "signed" addition. Thus, we also need a rule for overflow of signed add without the flag nsw.

Moreover, most C implementations use a wrap-around semantics also for signed integers. Thus, they compile C to LLVM code where nsw is not used at all. Our approach is independent of the actual C compiler, as it analyzes termination of the resulting LLVM program instead and it can also handle signed overflows.

Thus, we use a similar rule for $x \in \mathcal{S}_\mathcal{P}$. If $\models \langle a \rangle \Rightarrow (LV_{s,n}(t_1) + LV_{s,n}(t_2) > \mathsf{smax}_n)$, then we add "$v = LV_{s,n}(t_1) + LV_{s,n}(t_2) - 2^n$" to the knowledge base KB. If $\models \langle a \rangle \Rightarrow (LV_{s,n}(t_1) + LV_{s,n}(t_2) < \mathsf{smin}_n)$, we add "$v = LV_{s,n}(t_1) + LV_{s,n}(t_2) + 2^n$". However, a potential signed overflow that is flagged with nsw leads to ERR.

---

signed add with nsw overflow (p: "x = add nsw in t_1, t_2", $x \in \mathcal{V}_\mathcal{P}$, $t_1, t_2 \in \mathcal{V}_\mathcal{P} \cup \mathbb{Z}$)

$$\frac{(p,\ LV,\ KB,\ AL,\ PT)}{ERR} \quad \text{if } x \in \mathcal{S}_\mathcal{P} \text{ and } \not\models \langle a \rangle \Rightarrow (LV_{s,n}(t_1) + LV_{s,n}(t_2) \in [\mathsf{smin}_n, \mathsf{smax}_n])$$

For M, the execution ends after some more steps. For N, after storing $v_{\mathtt{inc}}$ to $v_{\mathtt{ad}}$, we branch to block cmp again. State P is like D (but ad points to j in D whereas ad points to inc in P). Therefore, we continue the execution, where the steps from P to Q are similar to the steps from D to J. Here, dotted arrows abbreviate several steps. Q is again refined and in the case where no overflow occurs, we finally reach State R at the same program position as D and P.

To obtain *finite* symbolic execution graphs, we can *generalize* states whenever an evaluation visits a program position (b, k) multiple times. We say that a' is a *generalization* of a with the instantiation μ whenever the conditions (b) – (e) of the following rule from [14] are satisfied. Again, a is the state *before* the generalization step and a' is the state *resulting* from the generalization.

---

generalization with μ

$$\frac{(p,\ LV,\ KB,\ AL,\ PT)}{(p',\ LV',\ KB',\ AL',\ PT')} \quad \text{if}$$

(a) a has an incoming "evaluation edge" (not just refinement or generalization edges)
(b) $LV(x) = \mu(LV'(x))$ for all $x \in \mathcal{V}_\mathcal{P}$
(c) $\models \langle a \rangle \Rightarrow \mu(KB')$
(d) if $[\![v_1, v_2]\!] \in AL'$, then $[\![\mu(v_1), \mu(v_2)]\!] \in AL$
(e) for $i \in \{u, s\}$, if $(v_1 \hookrightarrow_{\mathsf{ty},i} v_2) \in PT'$, then $(\mu(v_1) \hookrightarrow_{\mathsf{ty},i} \mu(v_2)) \in PT$

Clearly, we have $\models \langle a \rangle_{SL} \Rightarrow \mu(\langle a' \rangle_{SL})$. Condition (a) is needed to avoid cycles of refinement and generalization steps, which do not correspond to any computation. See [14] for a heuristic to compute suitable generalizations automatically.

In our graph, P is a generalization of State R. If we use an instantiation μ with $\mu(v_j) = v_{\mathtt{inc}}$ and $\mu(v_{\mathtt{inc}}) = v_{\mathtt{inc2}}$, then all conditions of the rule are satisfied. So we can conclude the graph construction with a (dashed) *generalization edge* from R to P. A symbolic execution graph is *complete* if all its leaves correspond to ret instructions (so in particular, the graph does not contain ERR states). As shown in [14], any LLVM evaluation of concrete states can be simulated by our symbolic execution rules. So in particular, a program with a complete symbolic execution graph does not exhibit undefined behavior (thus, it is memory safe).

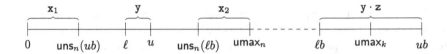

Fig. 3. Multiplication of unsigned integers

3.2 Handling Bitvector Operations by Modulo Relations

We now consider further LLVM instructions whose symbolic execution rules have to be adapted to bitvector arithmetic. A refinement with two cases was sufficient to express the result of unsigned addition (or subtraction): if $y + z$ exceeds $\mathsf{umax}_n = 2^n - 1$ for unsigned integers y and z, then the result of the addition is $(y + z) - 2^n \in [0, \mathsf{umax}_n]$, since $y + z$ can never exceed $2 \cdot \mathsf{umax}_n$. But for multiplication, if $y \cdot z$ exceeds umax_n, then $(y \cdot z) - 2^n$ is not necessarily in $[0, \mathsf{umax}_n]$. In contrast, one might have to subtract 2^n multiple times. Even worse, if one only knows that y and z are values from some interval, then for some values of $y \cdot z$ one may have to subtract 2^n more often than for others in order to obtain a result in $[0, \mathsf{umax}_n]$. So for multiplication, performing case analysis to handle overflows is not practical[7]. Thus, we use modulo relations instead, which hold regardless of whether an overflow occurs or not: for unsigned integers, if x is the result of multiplying y and z, then the relation "$x = y \cdot z \bmod 2^n$" (i.e., $x = \mathsf{uns}_n(y \cdot z)$) correctly models the overflow of bitvectors of size n. To use standard SMT solvers for "modulo", any expression "$t = m \bmod n$" can be transformed into "$t = k \cdot n + m$", where $0 \le t < m$ and k is an existentially quantified fresh variable.

In some cases, the result of a multiplication "$x = \mathtt{mul}\ \mathtt{in}\ t_1,\ t_2$" can be in disjoint intervals. For example, if $y \in [\ell, u]$ such that $\ell \cdot z \le \mathsf{umax}_k < u \cdot z$ for some k, then there can be two intervals (x_1, x_2 in Fig. 3) for $x = y \cdot z$, when x is regarded as an unsigned integer in $[0, \mathsf{umax}_n]$. Here, it is useful to extend KB by additional information on the intervals of the result. If $LV_{u,n}(t_1) \in [\ell_1, u_1]$ and $LV_{u,n}(t_2) \in [\ell_2, u_2]$ for numbers $\ell_1, \ell_2, u_1, u_2 \in \mathbb{N}$, then for $\ell b = \ell_1 \cdot \ell_2$ and $ub = u_1 \cdot u_2$, we have $LV_{u,n}(t_1) \cdot LV_{u,n}(t_2) \in [\ell b, ub]$. However, our goal is to infer information on the possible value of $\mathsf{uns}_n(LV_{u,n}(t_1) \cdot LV_{u,n}(t_2))$.

To this end, we compute the size of the interval $[\ell b, ub]$. If $ub - \ell b + 1 \ge 2^n$, then $[\ell b, ub]$ contains more numbers than those that can be represented with n bits and $LV(x)$ can be any n-bit integer. Otherwise, we check whether $\mathsf{uns}_n(\ell b) \le \mathsf{uns}_n(ub)$ holds. In this case, we add "$LV(x) \in [\mathsf{uns}_n(\ell b), \mathsf{uns}_n(ub)]$" to KB. Finally, if the size of $[\ell b, ub]$ is $< 2^n$ but $\mathsf{uns}_n(\ell b) > \mathsf{uns}_n(ub)$, then $LV(x) \in [0, \mathsf{uns}_n(ub)] \cup [\mathsf{uns}_n(\ell b), \mathsf{umax}_n]$, i.e., $LV(x)$ is not between the inner bounds $\mathsf{uns}_n(ub)$ and $\mathsf{uns}_n(\ell b)$, cf. Fig. 3. However, we cannot add "$LV(x) \le \mathsf{uns}_n(ub) \lor LV(x) \ge \mathsf{uns}_n(\ell b)$" to KB as it contains "$\lor$", but KB is a conjunction of (in)equalities.

---

[7] If $y, z \in [0, 2^n - 1]$, then $y \cdot z \in [0, 2^{2 \cdot n} - 2^{n+1} + 1]$. So there are $\mathcal{O}(2^n)$ many potential intervals of size 2^n for the result, i.e., we would have to consider $\mathcal{O}(2^n)$ many cases.

Hence, Theorem 6 shows how to express a condition of the form "$t \in [\min, u] \cup [\ell, \max]$" for $\min \leq u < \ell \leq \max$ by a single inequality. To this end, we subtract ℓ so that the second subinterval $[\ell, \max]$ (x_2 in Fig. 4) starts with 0. Then we apply "mod 2^n" (this results in moving the first subinterval x_1, cf. the dashed arrow in Fig. 4). Afterwards, we shift the whole interval back (by adding ℓ again).

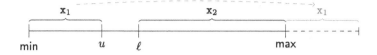

Fig. 4. Expressing unions of intervals

Theorem 6 (Expressing Unions of Intervals in a Single Inequality). *Let $n \in \mathbb{N}_{>0}$, $\min \in \mathbb{Z}$, $\max = \min + 2^n - 1$, $t \in [\min, \max]$, and $\min \leq u < \ell \leq \max$. Let* $\mathsf{inBounds}(t, \min, u, \ell, \max)$ *be the formula* "$((t - \ell) \bmod 2^n) + \ell \leq 2^n + u$". *Then we have* $t \in [\min, u] \cup [\ell, \max]$ *iff* $\mathsf{inBounds}(t, \min, u, \ell, \max)$ *holds.*

---

unsigned mul (p: "$\mathtt{x}$ = $\mathtt{mul}$ in t_1, t_2" with $\mathtt{x} \in \mathcal{V}_\mathcal{P}$, $t_1, t_2 \in \mathcal{V}_\mathcal{P} \cup \mathbb{Z}$)

$$\frac{(p, \ LV, \ KB, \ AL, \ PT)}{(p^+, \ LV[\mathtt{x} := v], \ KB \cup \{\varphi, \psi\}, \ AL, \ PT)} \quad \text{if } \mathtt{x} \in \mathcal{U}_\mathcal{P}, \ v \in \mathcal{V}_{sym} \text{ is fresh, and}$$

- If $\models \langle a \rangle \Rightarrow (LV_{u,n}(t_1) \cdot LV_{u,n}(t_2) \in [0, \mathsf{umax}_n])$, then φ is "$v = LV_{u,n}(t_1) \cdot LV_{u,n}(t_2)$".
  Otherwise, φ is "$v = \mathsf{uns}_n(LV_{u,n}(t_1) \cdot LV_{u,n}(t_2))$".
- $\ell_1, \ell_2, u_1, u_2 \in \mathbb{N}$ such that $\models \langle a \rangle \Rightarrow (LV_{u,n}(t_1) \in [\ell_1, u_1] \wedge LV_{u,n}(t_2) \in [\ell_2, u_2])$
- $\ell b = \ell_1 \cdot \ell_2$ and $ub = u_1 \cdot u_2$
- If $ub - \ell b + 1 \geq 2^n$, then ψ is *true*.
  Otherwise, if $\mathsf{uns}_n(\ell b) \leq \mathsf{uns}_n(ub)$, then ψ is "$v \in [\mathsf{uns}_n(\ell b), \mathsf{uns}_n(ub)]$".
  Otherwise, ψ is $\mathsf{inBounds}(v, 0, \mathsf{uns}_n(ub), \mathsf{uns}_n(\ell b), \mathsf{umax}_n)$.

We have an analogous rule for signed multiplication by using $\mathtt{x} \in \mathcal{S}_\mathcal{P}$ instead of $\mathcal{U}_\mathcal{P}$, $LV_{s,n}$ instead of $LV_{u,n}$, smin_n and smax_n instead of 0 and umax_n, sig_n instead of uns_n, $\mathbb{Z}$ instead of $\mathbb{N}$, and by defining ℓb (resp. ub) as the minimum (resp. maximum) of $\{x_1 \cdot x_2 \mid x_1 \in [\ell_1, u_1], x_2 \in [\ell_2, u_2]\}$. Moreover, for signed multiplication with the flag "$\mathtt{nsw}$", we reach *ERR* if $\not\models \langle a \rangle \Rightarrow (LV_{s,n}(t_1) \cdot LV_{s,n}(t_2) \in [\mathsf{smin}_n, \mathsf{smax}_n])$. We also use similar rules for division and remainder (where LLVM has separate instructions for unsigned and signed integers), cf. [1].

3.3 Handling Bitwise Operations

For bitwise binary LLVM operations like "and" (computing bitwise logical conjunction), we also infer knowledge about the range of the result. For instance, the conjunction of 3 ($0\,1\,1$) and 5 ($1\,0\,1$) is 1 ($0\,0\,1$). So if "$\mathtt{x}$ = $\mathtt{and}$ in t_1, t_2" and $\mathtt{x} \in \mathcal{U}_\mathcal{P}$, then $LV(\mathtt{x}) \leq LV_{u,n}(t_1)$ and $LV(\mathtt{x}) \leq LV_{u,n}(t_2)$, since a "1" on a position of the bitvector results in a larger number than a "0" on that position.

The same is true for signed integers, if both are positive or negative. So the conjunction of -1 ($11\ldots11$) and -2 ($11\ldots10$) is -2. The conjunction of a negative and a positive signed integer is at most as large as the positive integer.

---

signed and (p: "x = and in t_1, t_2" with $\mathbf{x} \in \mathcal{V}_\mathcal{P}$, $t_1, t_2 \in \mathcal{V}_\mathcal{P} \cup \mathbb{Z}$)

$$\frac{(p, \ LV, \ KB, \ AL, \ PT)}{(p^+, \ LV[\mathbf{x} := v], \ KB \cup \{\varphi\}, \ AL, \ PT)} \quad \text{if } \mathbf{x} \in \mathcal{S}_\mathcal{P}, \, v \in \mathcal{V}_{sym} \text{ is fresh, and}$$

- $\ell_1, \ell_2, u_1, u_2 \in \mathbb{Z}$ such that $\models \langle a \rangle \Rightarrow (LV_{s,n}(t_1) \in [\ell_1, u_1] \wedge LV_{s,n}(t_2) \in [\ell_2, u_2])$
- If $\langle a \rangle \Rightarrow (LV_{s,n}(t_1) = LV_{s,n}(t_2))$, then φ is "$v = LV_{s,n}(t_1)$".
  Otherwise, if $\ell_1 \geq 0 \wedge \ell_2 \geq 0$ or $u_1 < 0 \wedge u_2 < 0$, φ is "$v \leq LV_{s,n}(t_1) \wedge v \leq LV_{s,n}(t_2)$".
  Otherwise, if $\ell_1 \geq 0$ then φ is "$v \leq LV_{s,n}(t_1)$" and if $\ell_2 \geq 0$ then φ is "$v \leq LV_{s,n}(t_2)$".
  Otherwise, φ is "$v \leq \max(u_1, u_2)$".

In the corresponding rule for unsigned **and**, φ is "$v = LV_{u,n}(t_1)$" if $\langle a \rangle \Rightarrow (LV_{u,n}(t_1) = LV_{u,n}(t_2))$. Otherwise, φ is "$v \leq LV_{u,n}(t_1) \wedge v \leq LV_{u,n}(t_2)$".

Moreover, we adapt the rules for conversion instructions (e.g., extension and truncation). *Sign extension* (**sext**) copies the most significant bit to all extension bits, while for zero extension (**zext**) only zeros are used. So for 101, the sign extension is $1\ldots1101$ and the zero extension is $0\ldots0101$. The following rule for **sext** (resp. **zext**) considers its argument as a signed (resp. unsigned) integer. Then these instructions do not change the value of their operands.

---

extension (p: "x = sext/zext in t to im" with $\mathbf{x} \in \mathcal{V}_\mathcal{P}$, $t \in \mathcal{V}_\mathcal{P} \cup \mathbb{Z}$, $n < m$)

$$\frac{(p, \ LV, \ KB, \ AL, \ PT)}{(p^+, \ LV[\mathbf{x} := v], \ KB \cup \{\varphi\}, \ AL, \ PT)} \quad \text{if } v \in \mathcal{V}_{sym} \text{ is fresh and if}$$

either $\quad p$: "x = sext in t to im", $\mathbf{x} \in \mathcal{S}_\mathcal{P}$, and φ is "$v = LV_{s,n}(t)$"

or $\qquad\ p$: "x = zext in t to im", $\mathbf{x} \in \mathcal{U}_\mathcal{P}$, and φ is "$v = LV_{u,n}(t)$"

The instruction **trunc** truncates a value to the n least significant bits. Similar to the rules for multiplication, we again use the operations sig_n (resp. uns_n) and inBounds to express our knowledge about the result of the truncation.

---

signed trunc (p: "x = trunc im t to in" with $\mathbf{x} \in \mathcal{V}_\mathcal{P}$, $t \in \mathcal{V}_\mathcal{P} \cup \mathbb{Z}$, $n < m$)

$$\frac{(p, \ LV, \ KB, \ AL, \ PT)}{(p^+, \ LV[\mathbf{x} := v], \ KB \cup \{\varphi, \psi\}, \ AL, \ PT)} \quad \text{if } \mathbf{x} \in \mathcal{S}_\mathcal{P}, \, v \in \mathcal{V}_{sym} \text{ is fresh, and}$$

- If $\models \langle a \rangle \Rightarrow (LV_{s,m}(t) \in [\mathsf{smin}_n, \mathsf{smax}_n])$, then φ is "$v = LV_{s,m}(t)$".
  Otherwise, φ is "$v = \mathsf{sig}_n(LV_{s,m}(t))$".
- $\ell, u \in \mathbb{Z}$ such that $\models \langle a \rangle \Rightarrow (LV_{s,m}(t) \in [\ell, u])$
- If $u - \ell + 1 \geq 2^n$, then ψ is *true*.
  Otherwise, if $\mathsf{sig}_n(\ell) \leq \mathsf{sig}_n(u)$, then ψ is "$v \in [\mathsf{sig}_n(\ell), \mathsf{sig}_n(u)]$".
  Otherwise, ψ is $\mathsf{inBounds}(v, \mathsf{smin}_n, \mathsf{sig}_n(u), \mathsf{sig}_n(\ell), \mathsf{smax}_n)$.

In the rule for unsigned **trunc**, we have $\mathbf{x} \in \mathcal{U}_\mathcal{P}$ instead of $\mathcal{S}_\mathcal{P}$, $LV_{u,m}(t)$ instead of $LV_{s,m}(t)$, 0 and umax_n instead of smin_n and smax_n, and uns_n instead of sig_n.

4   From Symbolic Execution Graphs to Integer Systems

After the graph construction has been completed, we extract an *integer transition system* (ITS) from the cycles of the symbolic execution graph and then use existing tools to prove its termination.

ITSs can be represented as graphs whose nodes correspond to program locations and whose edges correspond to transitions. A transition is labeled with conditions that are required for its application. These conditions are quantifier-free formulas over a set of variables $\mathcal{V}$ and a corresponding set $\mathcal{V}' = \{x' \mid x \in \mathcal{V}\}$ which refers to the values of the variables *after* applying the transition.

The only cycle of the symbolic execution graph in Fig. 2 is the one from P to R and back. The resulting ITS is shown in Fig. 5. The values of the variables do not change in transitions that correspond to evaluation edges of the symbolic execution graph. For the generalization edge from R to P with the instantiation μ, the corresponding transition in the ITS gets the condition $v' = \mu(v)$ for all $v \in$

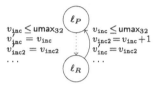

Fig. 5. ITS for function g

$\mathcal{V}_{sym}(P)$. So we obtain the condition $v'_{\text{inc}} = \mu(v_{\text{inc}})$, i.e., $v'_{\text{inc}} = v_{\text{inc2}} = v_{\text{inc}} + 1$. In contrast, v_{inc2}'s value can change arbitrarily here, since $v_{\text{inc2}} \notin \mathcal{V}_{sym}(P)$. Moreover, the transitions of the ITS contain conditions like $v_{\text{inc}} \leq \text{umax}_{32}$, which are also present in the states P – R. Standard tools can easily prove termination of this ITS. See [14] for details on extracting ITSs from symbolic execution graphs.

Recall that the bitvector arithmetic is covered by the rules to construct the symbolic execution graph, whereas the variables in the graph and in the resulting ITS range over $\mathbb{Z}$. Therefore, the following theorem from [14] still holds. It states that termination of the ITS implies termination of the analyzed LLVM program.

Theorem 7 (Termination). *Let $\mathcal{P}$ be an LLVM program with a complete symbolic execution graph $\mathcal{G}$ and let $\mathcal{I}_\mathcal{G}$ be the ITS resulting from $\mathcal{G}$. If $\mathcal{I}_\mathcal{G}$ terminates, then $\mathcal{P}$ also terminates for all concrete states represented by the states in $\mathcal{G}$.*

5   Related Work, Experiments, and Conclusion

We adapted our approach for proving memory safety and termination of C (resp. LLVM) programs to bitvectors. Since we represent bitvectors by relations on $\mathbb{Z}$, we can use standard SMT solving and standard termination analysis on $\mathbb{Z}$ for the symbolic execution and the termination proofs in our approach.

There are few other methods and tools for termination of bitvector programs (e.g., KITTeL [7,8], TAN [4,11], 2LS [2], Juggernaut [5], Ultimate [10][8])[9]. Compared to related work, our approach has the following characteristics:

---

[8] However, there is not yet any paper describing Ultimate's adaption to bitvectors.

[9] Outside of termination analysis, there exist several tools for overflow detection. However, we cannot easily apply such external tools in our approach, since we want to use the result of potential overflows to continue our symbolic execution and analysis.

(a) Handling Memory: KITTeL, TAN, 2LS, and Juggernaut either do not handle dynamic data structures, strings, and arrays, or they abstract their properties to arithmetic ones. Thus, they fail for programs whose termination depends on explicit pointer arithmetic. Note that without considering the memory, termination of bitvector programs is decidable in *PSPACE* [4]. In contrast, our approach is the first which combines the handling of bitvectors with the precise representation of low-level memory operations, by using symbolic execution.

(b) Representation with $\mathbb{Z}$*:* Similar to KITTeL and the first approach in [4], we represent bitvectors by relations on $\mathbb{Z}$. In contrast, 2LS, Juggernaut, and the second approach in [4] use vectors of Boolean variables instead and reduce the termination problem to second-order satisfiability. This would have drawbacks when constructing symbolic execution graphs, where large numbers of SMT queries have to be solved. Here, using $\mathbb{Z}$ instead of bitvectors often simplifies the graph structure and lets us benefit from the efficiency of SMT solving over $\mathbb{Z}$.

(c) Unsigned resp. Signed Representation: We use a heuristic to determine whether we represent information about the unsigned or the signed value of variables in the states for symbolic execution. In contrast, KITTeL resp. the first approach of [4] represent only the signed resp. the unsigned values. The drawback is that then one needs a larger case analysis for instructions like icmp ugt resp. sgt which differ for unsigned and signed integers. Thus, this affects efficiency.

(d) Case Analysis vs. "Modulo": When representing bitvectors by relations on $\mathbb{Z}$, the wrap-around for overflows can either be handled by case analysis or by "modulo" relations. We use a hybrid approach with case analysis for instructions like addition (to avoid "modulo" which is less efficient for SMT solving) and with "modulo" for operations like multiplication (where case analysis could lead to an exponential blow-up). KITTeL only uses case analysis. While [4] also applies "modulo", our approach infers more complex relations about the ranges of variables, even if these ranges are unions of disjoint intervals. For an efficient SMT reasoning during symbolic execution, we express such "disjunctive properties" by single inequalities, cf. the formula inBounds(t, min, u, ℓ, max).

We implemented our approach in AProVE [14] using the SMT solvers Yices [6] and Z3 [13] in the back-end. The previous version of AProVE won the *SV-COMP* 2015 and 2016 competitions for termination of C programs (where tools were restricted to mathematical integers). To evaluate the new version of AProVE with bitvectors, we performed experiments on 118 C programs. We took the 61 *Windows Driver Development Kit* examples used for the evaluation of [4] and [8], 61 of the 62 examples from the repository of Juggernaut where we excluded one example containing float, 7 of the 9 examples of [5] where we excluded two examples with float, 4 new examples where termination depends on overflows of multiplication, and 4 new examples combining pointer and bitvector arithmetic. From these 137 examples, we removed 19 examples which are known to be non-terminating. Since Ultimate does not support bitvector arithmetic for signed integers yet, the right half of the table in Fig. 6 consists of those examples where termination does not depend on signed integers. We ran all tools in a mode where signed overflows are allowed and result in a wrap-around behavior.

	T	**F**	**TO**	**RT**	**T**	**F**	**TO**	**RT**	**%**
AProVE	34	9	9	10.23	61	3	2	5.55	80.5
2LS	23	29	0	0.37	45	21	0	0.33	57.6
KITTeL	27	4	21	1.81	33	3	30	14.17	50.8
Juggernaut	10	19	23	34.12	22	26	18	6.22	27.1
Ultimate	–	–	–	–	11	54	1	12.77	16.7

Fig. 6. Experimental evaluation

Figure 6 shows the performance of the tools for a time limit of 300 s per example on an Intel Core i7-950 with 6 GB memory. We did not compare with TAN, since it was outperformed by its successor 2LS in [2]. "**T**" is the number of examples where termination was proved, "**F**" states how often the termination proof failed in ≤ 300 s, "**TO**" is the number of time-outs, "**RT**" is the average run time in seconds for the examples where the tool showed termination, and "**%**" is the percentage of examples where termination was proved.

So on our collection (which mainly consists of the examples from the evaluations of the other tools), AProVE is most powerful. To evaluate the benefit of representing both unsigned and signed values (cf. *(c)*), we also ran AProVE in a mode where all values are represented as signed integers (i.e., $\mathcal{S}_\mathcal{P} = \mathcal{V}_\mathcal{P}$). Here, we lost 11 termination proofs. To evaluate the use of case analysis vs. "modulo" (cf. *(d)*), we tested a version of AProVE where we used "modulo" also for operations like addition. Here, we failed on 13 more examples. For details on our experiments, to access our implementation via a web interface, and for symbolic execution rules for further LLVM instructions, we refer to [1]. In future work, we plan to extend our approach to recursion, to inductive data structures, and to a compositional treatment of LLVM functions (the main challenge is to combine these tasks with the handling of explicit pointer arithmetic).

Acknowledgments. We are grateful to M. Heizmann, D. Kroening, M. Lewis, and P. Schrammel for their help with the experiments.

A   Separation Logic Semantics of Abstract States

To formalize the semantics of an abstract state a, in [14] we introduced a separation logic formula $\langle a \rangle_{SL}$, which extends $\langle a \rangle_{FO}$ by information about the memory (i.e., about AL and PT). In $\langle a \rangle_{SL}$, we combine the elements of AL with the separating conjunction "$*$" to express that different allocated memory blocks are disjoint. As usual, $\varphi_1 * \varphi_2$ means that φ_1 and φ_2 hold for disjoint parts of the memory. In contrast, the elements of PT are combined by the ordinary conjunction "$\wedge$". So $(v_1 \hookrightarrow_{\mathsf{ty},i} v_2) \in PT$ does not imply that v_1 is different from other addresses in PT. Similarly, we also combine the two formulas resulting from AL and PT by "$\wedge$", as both express different properties of the same addresses.

Definition 8 (*SL* **Formulas for States**). *For $v_1, v_2 \in \mathcal{V}_{sym}$, let $\langle [\![v_1, v_2]\!] \rangle_{SL} = (\forall x. \exists y. \ (v_1 \leq x \leq v_2) \Rightarrow (x \hookrightarrow y))$. For any* LLVM *type* ty, *we define*

$$\langle v_1 \hookrightarrow_{\mathtt{ty},u} v_2 \rangle_{SL} = \langle v_1 \hookrightarrow_{size(\mathtt{ty})} v_2 \rangle_{SL}.$$

To handle the two's complement representation of signed integers, we define $\langle v_1 \hookrightarrow_{\mathtt{ty},s} v_2 \rangle_{SL} =$

$$\langle v_1 \hookrightarrow_{size(\mathtt{ty})} v_3 \rangle_{SL} \ \wedge \ (v_2 \geq 0 \Rightarrow v_3 = v_2) \ \wedge \ (v_2 < 0 \Rightarrow v_3 = v_2 + 2^{size(\mathtt{ty})}),$$

where $v_3 \in \mathcal{V}_{sym}$ is fresh. We assume a little-endian data layout (where least significant bytes are stored in the lowest address). Hence, we define $\langle v_1 \hookrightarrow_0 v_3 \rangle_{SL} = true$ and $\langle v_1 \hookrightarrow_{n+8} v_3 \rangle_{SL} = (v_1 \hookrightarrow (v_3 \bmod 2^8)) \wedge \langle (v_1 + 1) \hookrightarrow_n (v_3 \operatorname{div} 2^8) \rangle_{SL}$.

A state $a = (p, LV, KB, AL, PT)$ is represented in separation logic by

$$\langle a \rangle_{SL} = \langle a \rangle_{FO} \ \wedge \ (\text{\Large$*$}_{\varphi \in AL} \ \langle \varphi \rangle_{SL}) \ \wedge \ (\bigwedge_{\varphi \in PT} \ \langle \varphi \rangle_{SL}).$$

We use *interpretations* (as, mem) for the semantics of separation logic (Sect. 2).

Definition 9 (Semantics of Separation Logic). *Let $as : \mathcal{V}_{\mathcal{P}} \to \mathbb{Z}$ be an assignment, $mem : \mathbb{N}_{>0} \rightharpoonup \{0, \ldots, \mathsf{umax}_8\}$, and φ be a formula. Let $as(\varphi)$ result from replacing all local variables $\mathbf{x}$ in φ by the value $as(\mathbf{x})$. By construction, local variables $\mathbf{x}$ are never quantified in our formulas. Then we define $(as, mem) \models \varphi$ iff $mem \models as(\varphi)$.*

We now define $mem \models \psi$ for formulas ψ that may contain symbolic variables from $\mathcal{V}_{sym}$. As usual, all free variables $v_1, \ldots, v_n$ in ψ are implicitly universally quantified, i.e., $mem \models \psi$ iff $mem \models \forall v_1, \ldots, v_n. \psi$. The semantics of arithmetic operations and predicates as well as of first-order connectives and quantifiers are as usual. In particular, we define $mem \models \forall v. \psi$ iff $mem \models \sigma(\psi)$ holds for all instantiations σ where $\sigma(v) \in \mathbb{Z}$ and $\sigma(w) = w$ for all $w \in \mathcal{V}_{sym} \setminus \{v\}$.

We still have to define the semantics of $\hookrightarrow$ and $*$ for variable-free formulas. For $n_1, n_2 \in \mathbb{Z}$, let $mem \models n_1 \hookrightarrow n_2$ hold iff $mem(n_1) = n_2$[10]. The semantics of $*$ is defined as usual in separation logic: For two partial functions $mem_1, mem_2 : \mathbb{N}_{>0} \rightharpoonup \mathbb{Z}$, we write $mem_1 \perp mem_2$ to indicate that the domains of mem_1 and mem_2 are disjoint. If $mem_1 \perp mem_2$, then $mem_1 \uplus mem_2$ denotes the union of mem_1 and mem_2. Now $mem \models \varphi_1 * \varphi_2$ holds iff there exist $mem_1 \perp mem_2$ such that $mem = mem_1 \uplus mem_2$ where $mem_1 \models \varphi_1$ and $mem_2 \models \varphi_2$.

---

[10] We use "$\hookrightarrow$" instead of "$\mapsto$" in separation logic, since $mem \models n_1 \mapsto n_2$ would imply that $mem(n)$ is undefined for all $n \neq n_1$. This would be inconvenient in our formalization, since PT usually only contains information about a *part* of the allocated memory.

B   Proofs

Proof of Theorem 5. Since the result of "mod 2^n" is always in the interval $[0, 2^n - 1]$, we immediately obtain $\text{sig}_n(t) = ((t + 2^{n-1}) \bmod 2^n) - 2^{n-1} \in [0 - 2^{n-1}, 2^n - 1 - 2^{n-1}] = [-2^{n-1}, 2^{n-1} - 1] = [\text{smin}_n, \text{smax}_n]$. Moreover, we have

$$t \bmod 2^n$$
$$= (t + 2^{n-1} - 2^{n-1}) \bmod 2^n$$
$$= (((t + 2^{n-1}) \bmod 2^n) - 2^{n-1}) \bmod 2^n$$
$$= \text{sig}_n(t) \bmod 2^n.$$

$\square$

Proof of Theorem 6. We consider three cases.

Case 1: $t \in [\text{min}, u]$

Clearly, $u < \ell$ implies $u - \ell < 0$. Moreover, we also have $u - \ell \geq \text{min} - \text{max} = -2^n + 1$, which together implies

$$-2^n < u - \ell < 0. \tag{2}$$

Thus, we have:
$$
\begin{aligned}
t \leq u \quad &\Rightarrow & t - \ell &\leq u - \ell \\
&\Rightarrow & (t - \ell) \bmod 2^n &\leq u - \ell + 2^n & \text{by (2)} \\
&\Rightarrow & ((t - \ell) \bmod 2^n) + \ell &\leq u + 2^n \\
&\Rightarrow & \text{inBounds}(t, \text{min}, u, \ell, \text{max}) &\text{ holds}
\end{aligned}
$$

Case 2: $t \in [u + 1, \ell - 1]$

This entails $u + 1 \leq \ell - 1$, i.e., $u - \ell + 1 < 0$. Moreover, we also have $u - \ell + 1 \geq \text{min} - \text{max} + 1 = -2^n + 2$, which together implies

$$-2^n < u - \ell + 1 < 0. \tag{3}$$

We obtain:
$$
\begin{aligned}
t \geq u + 1 \quad &\Rightarrow & t - \ell &\geq u - \ell + 1 \\
&\Rightarrow & (t - \ell) \bmod 2^n &\geq u - \ell + 1 + 2^n & \text{by (3)} \\
&\Rightarrow & ((t - \ell) \bmod 2^n) + \ell &\geq u + 1 + 2^n \\
&\Rightarrow & \text{inBounds}(t, \text{min}, u, \ell, \text{max}) &\text{ does not hold}
\end{aligned}
$$

Case 3: $t \in [\ell, \text{max}]$

Note that $\text{max} - \ell \geq 0$ and moreover, $\text{max} - \ell < \text{max} - \text{min} = 2^n - 1$, i.e.,

$$0 \leq \text{max} - \ell < 2^n. \tag{4}$$

In addition, we have

$$\text{max} = \text{min} + 2^n - 1 \leq u + 2^n - 1. \tag{5}$$

Here, we obtain:
$$
\begin{aligned}
t \leq \text{max} \quad &\Rightarrow & t - \ell &\leq \text{max} - \ell \\
&\Rightarrow & (t - \ell) \bmod 2^n &\leq \text{max} - \ell & \text{by (4)} \\
&\Rightarrow & ((t - \ell) \bmod 2^n) + \ell &\leq \text{max} \\
&\Rightarrow & ((t - \ell) \bmod 2^n) + \ell &\leq u + 2^n & \text{by (5)} \\
&\Rightarrow & \text{inBounds}(t, \text{min}, u, \ell, \text{max}) &\text{ holds} & \square
\end{aligned}
$$

Proof of Theorem 7. The proof of Theorem 7 is identical to the proofs of
Theorems 10 and 13 in [14]. It relies on the fact that our symbolic execution
rules correspond to the actual execution of LLVM when they are applied to
concrete states (this also holds for the new bitvector rules of the current paper).
So if a concrete state c is represented in the symbolic execution graph, then
every LLVM evaluation of c corresponds to a path in the graph. The generation
of an ITS from the graph is done in such a way that termination of the ITS
implies that there is no such infinite path in the graph. As all integers in the
symbolic execution graphs and in the ITSs are still *mathematical* integers, the
construction of ITSs has not changed in the current paper, i.e., the corresponding
proof of [14] directly carries over to the present setting.

References

1. AProVE. http://aprove.informatik.rwth-aachen.de/eval/Bitvectors/
2. Chen, H.Y., David, C., Kroening, D., Schrammel, P., Wächter, B.: Synthesising interprocedural bit-precise termination proofs. In: Cohen, M.B., Grunske, L.,
   Whalen, M. (eds.) ASE 2015, pp. 53–64. IEEE (2015)
3. Clang compiler. http://clang.llvm.org
4. Cook, B., Kroening, D., Rümmer, P., Wintersteiger, C.: Ranking function synthesis
   for bit-vector relations. Formal Methods Syst. Des. **43**(1), 93–120 (2013)
5. David, C., Kroening, D., Lewis, M.: Unrestricted termination and non-termination
   arguments for bit-vector programs. In: Vitek, J. (ed.) ESOP 2015. LNCS, vol. 9032,
   pp. 183–204. Springer, Heidelberg (2015)
6. Dutertre, B., de Moura, L.M.: The Yices SMT solver (2006). Tool paper at http://
   yices.csl.sri.com/tool-paper.pdf
7. Falke, S., Kapur, D., Sinz, C.: Termination analysis of C programs using compiler
   intermediate languages. In: Schmidt-Schauß, M. (ed.) RTA 2011. LIPIcs, vol. 10,
   pp. 41–50 (2011)
8. Falke, S., Kapur, D., Sinz, C.: Termination analysis of imperative programs using
   bitvector arithmetic. In: Joshi, R., Müller, P., Podelski, A. (eds.) VSTTE 2012.
   LNCS, vol. 7152, pp. 261–277. Springer, Heidelberg (2012)
9. Giesl, J., et al.: Proving termination of programs automatically with AProVE. In:
   Demri, S., Kapur, D., Weidenbach, C. (eds.) IJCAR 2014. LNCS, vol. 8562, pp.
   184–191. Springer, Heidelberg (2014)
10. Heizmann, M., Hoenicke, J., Leike, J., Podelski, A.: Linear ranking for linear lasso
    programs. In: Van Hung, D., Ogawa, M. (eds.) ATVA 2013. LNCS, vol. 8172, pp.
    365–380. Springer, Heidelberg (2013)
11. Kroening, D., Sharygina, N., Tsitovich, A., Wintersteiger, C.M.: Termination
    analysis with compositional transition invariants. In: Touili, T., Cook, B., Jackson,
    P. (eds.) CAV 2010. LNCS, vol. 6174, pp. 89–103. Springer, Heidelberg (2010)
12. Lattner, C., Adve, V.S.: LLVM: a compilation framework for lifelong program
    analysis & transformation. In: CGO 2004, pp. 75–88. IEEE (2004)
13. de Moura, L., Bjørner, N.S.: Z3: an efficient SMT solver. In: Ramakrishnan, C.R.,
    Rehof, J. (eds.) TACAS 2008. LNCS, vol. 4963, pp. 337–340. Springer, Heidelberg
    (2008)
14. Ströder, T., Giesl, J., Brockschmidt, M., Frohn, F., Fuhs, C., Hensel, J., Schneider-
    Kamp, P.: Proving termination and memory safety for programs with pointer arith-
    metic. In: Demri, S., Kapur, D., Weidenbach, C. (eds.) IJCAR 2014. LNCS, vol.
    8562, pp. 208–223. Springer, Heidelberg (2014)

SMT-Based Automatic Proof
of ASM Model Refinement

Paolo Arcaini[1]([✉]), Angelo Gargantini[2], and Elvinia Riccobene[3]

[1] Charles University in Prague, Faculty of Mathematics and Physics,
Prague, Czech Republic
arcaini@d3s.mff.cuni.cz
[2] Dipartimento di Ingegneria, Università degli Studi di Bergamo, Bergamo, Italy
angelo.gargantini@unibg.it
[3] Dipartimento di Informatica, Università degli Studi di Milano, Milan, Italy
elvinia.riccobene@unimi.it

Abstract. Model refinement is a technique indispensable for modeling large and complex systems. Many formal specification methods share this concept which usually comes together with the definition of refinement correctness, i.e., the mathematical proof of a logical relation between an abstract model and its refined models.

Model refinement is one of the main concepts which the Abstract State Machine (ASM) formal method is built on. Proofs of correct model refinement are usually performed manually, which reduces the usability of the ASM model refinement approach. An automatic support to assist the developer in proving refinement correctness along the chain of refinement steps could be of extreme importance to improve, in practice, the adoption of ASMs.

In this paper, we present how the integration between the ASMs and Satisfiability Modulo Theories (SMT) can be used to automatically prove correctness of model refinement for the ASM method.

1 Introduction

Modeling is a fundamental activity of system life-cycle: models allow developers to reason about the systems under construction and represent central artifacts of their development. Building models of large and complex systems is, however, not an easy task since lots of requirements have to be taken into consideration.

To manage such a complexity, many specification methods share a modeling process based on *model refinement* [1]. It consists in developing models starting from a high-level description of the system and proceeding through a sequence of more detailed models each introducing, step-by-step, design decisions and implementation details. The concept of model refinement usually comes together with the definition of *refinement correctness*, i.e., the mathematical proof of a logical relation between an abstract model and its refined models.

This work was partially supported by the Grant Agency of the Czech Republic project 14-11384S.

R. De Nicola and E. Kühn (Eds.): SEFM 2016, LNCS 9763, pp. 253–269, 2016.
DOI: 10.1007/978-3-319-41591-8_17

Model refinement is a key concept for the *Abstract State Machine* (ASM) formal method. The ASM modeling process is based on the concept of a *ground model* representing a precise but concise high-level system specification, and on the *refinement principle* that allows to capture all details of the system design by a sequence of refined machines to the desired level of detail, possibly to the code level. In [12,14], Börger presents the ASM refinement, discusses its characteristics compared to other refinement approaches, and provides the definition of correctness proofs, namely the guaranty that a machine is a correct refinement of an abstract machine.

In developing ASM specifications of different case studies [3,4,6,8], we have modeled through refinement and we have observed that (a) the usual refinement schema a modeler uses is a (1:n) refinement in which one step of the abstract machine corresponds to n steps of the refined machine; (b) each refinement step introduces very small changes, either in terms of data and of control structure; (c) along the chain of models, the proofs of refinement correctness are similar and often tedious to repeat. Such observations reinforced in us the idea, felt for a long time, of having a tool assisting the modeler along the refinement steps and being able to provide automatic proof of the refinement correctness.

A mechanized approach to prove correctness of the ASM refinement already exists [22]. It requires the encoding of an ASM model into dynamic logic, a deep knowledge of the KIV theorem prover and an active role of the modeler in conducting the proofs. The tool is not integrated in any existing framework for ASM model development and manipulation [7,17], thus this verification activity appears separated with respect to other activities on models and does not permit reusing information. Our goal is, instead, to have a prover of correct model refinement fully integrated into a framework for editing, simulating, validating and verifying ASM models, so to improve the practical usability of the ASM method. We cannot expect practitioners to have deep skills in theorem provers or verification strategies, and we are aware of the necessity to compensate these lacks with suitable mechanized support which hides the mathematical complexity of the proof obligations that model refinement requires.

By exploiting the symbolic representation of ASMs into Satisfiability Modulo Theories (SMT), already presented in [5] as part of an SMT-based technique for runtime verification, we here present an automatic approach where the proof of ASM refinement is performed by means of satisfiability checking.

We introduce the definition of ASM stuttering refinement between two ASMs. It is a restricted form of the ASM model refinement defined in [12], but we have found it recurring in our modeling experience and shared with other formal approaches [2,20]. It has also the advantage of allowing the reduction of the ASM correct refinement problem to an SMT problem, since the proof strategy to guarantee stuttering refinement does not reason on possible corresponding subruns of the two machines, but on the concept of a state to be initial and to be in (transition) relation with another state. This SMT problem consists of two conditions (initial refinement and step refinement) that guarantee a machine to be a stuttering refinement of an abstract machine. An SMT solver is used to prove the validity of such properties.

The paper is organized as follows. Section 2 briefly introduces the ASMs and their use when modeling through refinement. A running case study is used for exemplification purposes. In Sect. 3 we give our notion of refinement and in Sect. 4 we provide a technique for proving it. Section 5 presents the SMT encoding of the model refinement correctness problem. Section 6 gives a preliminary evaluation of the approach. Section 7 presents work related to the verification of correct refinement for ASMs, and Sect. 8 concludes the paper.

2   Abstract State Machines

Abstract State Machines (ASMs) [14] are an extension of FSMs, where unstructured control states are replaced by states with arbitrary complex data. The method has a rigorous mathematical foundation; however, a practitioner can understand ASMs as pseudo-code or virtual machines working over abstract data structures. We here give the necessary background to understand our approach.

ASM *states* are algebraic structures, i.e., domains of objects with functions and predicates defined on them. An ASM *location*, defined as the pair (*function-name*, *list-of-parameter-values*), represents the abstract ASM concept of basic object containers. The couple (*location*, *value*) represents a machine memory unit. Therefore, ASM states can be viewed as abstract memories.

Location values are changed by firing *transition rules*. They express the modification of functions interpretation from one state to the next one. Note that the algebra signature is fixed and that functions are total (by interpreting undefined locations $f(x)$ with value *undef*). Location *updates* are given as assignments of the form $loc := v$, where loc is a location and v its new value. They are the basic units of rules construction. There is a limited but powerful set of *rule constructors* to express: guarded actions (**if-then**), simultaneous parallel actions (**par**), sequential actions (**seq**), nondeterminism (existential quantification **choose**), and unrestricted synchronous parallelism (universal quantification **forall**).

An ASM *computation* is, therefore, defined as a finite or infinite sequence $S_0, S_1, \ldots, S_n, \ldots$ of states of the machine, where S_0 is an initial state and each S_{n+1} is obtained from S_n by firing the unique *main rule* which in turn could fire other transitions rules. An ASM can have more than one *initial state*. It is possible to specify state *invariants*.

During a machine computation, not all the locations can be updated. Indeed, functions are classified as *static* (never change during any run of the machine) or *dynamic* (may change as a consequence of agent actions or *updates*). Dynamic functions are distinguished between *monitored* (only read by the machine and modified by the environment) and *controlled* (read and written by the machine). A further classification is between *basic* and *derived* functions, i.e., those coming with a specification or computation mechanism given in terms of other functions.

```
asm LGS_GM

signature:
  enum domain HandleStatus = { UP | DOWN }
  enum domain DoorStatus =
    {CLOSED | OPENING | OPEN | CLOSING}
  enum domain GearStatus =
    {RETRACTED|EXTENDING|EXTENDED|RETRACTING}
  dynamic monitored handle: HandleStatus
  dynamic controlled doors: DoorStatus
  dynamic controlled gears: GearStatus

definitions:
  rule r_closeDoor =
    switch doors
      case OPEN: doors := CLOSING
      case CLOSING: doors := CLOSED
      case OPENING: doors := CLOSING
    endswitch
```

```
rule r_retractionSequence =
  if gears != RETRACTED then
    switch doors
      case CLOSED: doors := OPENING
      case CLOSING: doors := OPENING
      case OPENING: doors := OPEN
      case OPEN:
        switch gears
          case EXTENDED:
            gears := RETRACTING
          case RETRACTING:
            gears := RETRACTED
          case EXTENDING:
            gears := RETRACTING
        endswitch
    endswitch
  else
    r_closeDoor[]
  endif
```

```
main rule r_Main =
  if handle = UP then
    r_retractionSequence[]
  else
    r_outgoingSequence[]
  endif

default init s0:
  function doors = CLOSED
  function gears = EXTENDED
```

Code 1. Landing Gear System – Abstract model

ASMs allow modeling any kind of computational paradigm, from a *single* agent executing parallel actions, to distributed *multiple* agents interacting in a synchronous or asynchronous way. Moreover, an ASM can be nondeterministic due to the presence of monitored functions (external nondeterminism) and of choose rules (internal nondeterminism).

A set of tools exists to support the ASM modeling process. Tools are part of the ASMETA (ASM mETAmodeling) framework[1] [7], and are strongly integrated in order to permit reusing information about models during different development phases. ASMETA provides basic functionalities for ASM models creation and manipulation (as editing, storage, interchange, access, etc.), and supports advanced model analysis techniques (as validation, verification, testing, model review, requirements analysis, runtime verification, etc.).

Example 1 (Landing Gear System case study). We here consider, as supporting case study, the Landing Gear System [11] (LGS), which is the airplane component responsible for the maneuvering of the landing gears and associated doors. The system can be in *nominal* mode or in *emergency* mode. In nominal mode, a landing sequence is: opening of the doors of the landing gear boxes, extension of the landing gears, and closing of the doors. The system also elaborates health parameters for all the equipments and, if necessary, switches to emergency mode.

Model LGS_GM (shown in Code 1) specifies the system behavior at a very abstract level: we only represent the statuses of the gears and of their doors and how they change in the retraction and outgoing sequences. Although there are three landing sets, we abstract and we model all of them as one. Functions **doors** and **gears** represent the status of the doors and of the gears, respectively. The state transitions are driven by the value of the monitored function **handle**. As long as **handle** is UP, the *retraction sequence* is executed; when **handle** is DOWN, the *outgoing sequence* is executed. Let us see how the retraction sequence works. We assume **handle** to be UP in each state. In the initial state, the **doors** are CLOSED and the **gears** are EXTENDED; then the **doors** start OPENING. When the **doors** become OPEN, the **gears** start RETRACTING. When the **gears** become

---

[1] http://asmeta.sourceforge.net/.

RETRACTED, the doors start CLOSING. The retraction sequence terminates with the doors CLOSED and the gears RETRACTED. The outgoing sequence behaves similarly. Note that a retraction (resp. an outgoing) sequence can be always interrupted by switching the value of the handle; in this case, an outgoing (resp. a retraction) sequence begins, starting from the status of the doors and the gears reached in the previous sequence.

2.1 ASM Modeling Through Refinement

Modeling by ASMs starts by developing an initial abstract model, called *ground model*, which is a precise and concise high-level system description and can be considered as reference model for the further steps of the design. Model LGS_GM shown in Code 1 is an example of ground model.

Modeling proceeds by *model refinement*, namely by a chain of step-wise refined models, starting from the ground model. At each refined level, further details are added to capture the major design decisions and provide descriptions of the complete software architecture and component design of the system. The end point of the chain is decided by the designer, and it should be a model detailed enough to be mapped into executable code or at least a model against which the code can be automatically tested for conformance checking.

Several examples [9,21,24] show the applicability of this approach which permits to keep the complexity of the system under control, and to bridge, in a seamless manner, the gap between specification and code.

In model refinement, a key point is to prove that a refined model is correct w.r.t. the abstract one. For ASMs, the original description of the refinement method and the definition of correct model refinement are due to Börger in [12]. That definition of refinement is very general and makes it difficult to prove refinement correctness in an automatic way or, at least, to find proof patterns.

3 Stuttering Refinement

We here define stuttering refinement between two ASMs, which is a restricted form of the ASM model refinement as in [12] (a comparison is given in Sect. 7). This notion of refinement allows us to provide an automatic approach to refinement proof, based on a logic representation of ASM signatures and transition rules. We consider deterministic and nondeterministic single-agent ASMs.

As stated in Sect. 2, a state S of an ASM M is a set of locations with value. We here denote by $val(l, S)$ the value of a location l at state S.

A model refinement first requires the definition of corresponding *locations of interest*, i.e., pairs of (possibly sets of) locations one wants to relate in corresponding abstract and refined states.

Definition 1 (Corresponding Locations of Interest). *Given two ASMs A and R, we denote by* corrLoc *the correspondence over the set of locations of interest of the refined machine R and their corresponding locations of the abstract machine A, i.e.,* corrLoc(l_R, l_A) *is true iff l_R is a location of interest in R and l_A is its unique corresponding location in A.*

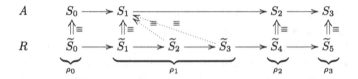

Fig. 1. Stuttering refinement – Relation between a refined run and an abstract run

On the base on the corresponding locations of interest, we define *conformant states* between the abstract and refined machines, namely states having equivalent values for the corresponding locations of interest. Obviously, a notion of equivalence ≡ of the data in the locations of interest is assumed available.

Definition 2 (Conformance). *Let S be a state of the abstract machine A (also called* abstract state*), $\widetilde{S}$ a state of the refined machine R (also called* refined state*). The two states are* conformant *iff corresponding locations of interest have equivalent values, i.e.,*

$$conf(\widetilde{S}, S) \quad \text{iff} \quad \forall l_R \forall l_A \, corrLoc(l_R, l_A) \rightarrow val(l_R, \widetilde{S}) \equiv val(l_A, S)$$

Typically, *corrLoc* is a one-to-one correspondence between the locations of interest of A and R and the designer uses the same function symbols to denote these corresponding locations. We here assume – as in [16] – linked locations to have the same names and equality as equivalence relation. More complicated conformance relations can be easily reduced to this simplified form by introducing convenient derived functions representing predicates over the abstract or refined states. Suppose to have a function fuelStatus in the abstract machine defined over the domain {NORMAL, RESERVE} and that this function is refined by the function fuelLevel defined over the interval [1,30]. The two specifications can be linked by introducing in the refined machine a derived function fuelStatus that specifies the desired conformance relation (e.g., fuelStatus = **if** fuelLevel > 10 **then** NORMAL **else** RESERVE **endif**).

Once the notions of corresponding locations of interest and of state conformance have been determined, one can define that R is a correct stuttering refinement of A as follows:

Definition 3 (Stuttering Refinement). *An ASM R is a correct stuttering refinement of an ASM A if and only if each R-run can be split in a sequence of subruns $\widetilde{\rho}_0, \widetilde{\rho}_1, \ldots$ and there is an A-run $S_0, S_1, \ldots$ such that for each $\widetilde{\rho}_i$ it holds $\forall \widetilde{S} \in \widetilde{\rho}_i: conf(\widetilde{S}, S_i)$.*

Note that infinite R-runs can be split in an infinite number of finite subruns, or in a finite number of subruns where only the last one is infinite. Figure 1 depicts a stuttering refined run and a corresponding abstract run.

```
asm LGS_SE                                   rule r_retractionSequence =
                                               if gears != RETRACTED then
signature:                                       switch doors
   ...                                             case CLOSED:
   dynamic monitored doorsOpen: Boolean               par
   dynamic monitored doorsClosed: Boolean                generalEV := true
   dynamic monitored gearsExtended: Boolean              openDoorsEV := true
   dynamic monitored gearsRetracted: Boolean             doors := OPENING
definitions:                                          endpar
   rule r_closeDoor =                              case OPENING:
      switch doors                                    if doorsOpen then
         case CLOSING:                                   par
            if doorsClosed then                             openDoorsEV := false
               par                                          doors := OPEN
                  generalEV := false                     endpar
                  closeDoorsEV := false                endif
                  doors := CLOSED                   ...
               endpar
            endif              invariant over doorsClosed, doorsOpen: not(doorsClosed and doorsOpen)
   ...                         invariant over gearsExtended, gearsRetracted: not(gearsExtended and gearsRetracted)
```

Code 2. Landing Gear System – Refined model

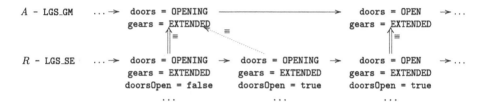

Fig. 2. LGS case study – Relation between a refined run and an abstract run

Example 2 (Refinement of the case study). We modeled the LGS by means of four refinement steps. The model LGS_GM in Code 1 is the ground ASM. In the refined model LGS_SE, we have added the modeling of the sensors that detect when the doors and the gears change their status. Code 2 shows the new elements introduced in the model. Four boolean monitored functions are used to indicate whether the gears are extended (**gearsExtended**) or retracted (**gearsRetracted**), and whether the doors are closed (**doorsClosed**) or open (**doorsOpen**). In this model, we have refined some rules by adding the reading of sensors. Some update rules have been guarded by conditional rules checking the value of the monitored functions; for example, we can see in Code 2 that if the **doors** are **CLOSING**, they become **CLOSED** only if the sensor **doorsClosed** is turned on (i.e., the guard of conditional rule is true). Note that LGS_SE is a stuttering refinement of LGS_GM because when the sensors do not detect any change, the state is still conformant to the previous abstract state (i.e., the doors and the gears have not changed their statuses). See Fig. 2 as an example of corresponding runs.

4   Proving Refinement

We here aim at automating the proof of stuttering refinement between two ASMs by reducing it to a satisfiability checking problem (to be solved by, e.g., an SMT solver). Therefore, we need to describe the concepts of ASM state and ASM transition by means of suitable predicates, and Definition 3 as a first order formula. The validity of such a formula should guarantee the stuttering machine refinement.

We introduce the following predicates capturing the concepts of initial state, next state, and conformant states.

– $init(S)$ iff S is an initial state;
– $step(S, S')$ iff the state S' can be obtained by applying the main rule at S;
– $conf(\widetilde{S}, S)$ iff states S and $\widetilde{S}$ are conformant (see Definition 2).

In the following, let us indicate by S a state of the abstract machine A and by S' the next state of S. Similarly, $\widetilde{S}$ and $\widetilde{S}'$ are two subsequent states of the refined machine R.

Theorem 1. *If the following properties hold*

$$\forall \widetilde{S}\colon (init(\widetilde{S}) \to \exists S\colon (init(S) \land conf(\widetilde{S}, S))) \tag{1}$$

$$\forall \widetilde{S} \forall \widetilde{S}' \forall S\colon \left[\begin{pmatrix} step(\widetilde{S}, \widetilde{S}') \\ \land \\ conf(\widetilde{S}, S) \end{pmatrix} \to \begin{pmatrix} \exists S'\colon (step(S, S') \land conf(\widetilde{S}', S')) \\ \lor \\ conf(\widetilde{S}', S) \end{pmatrix} \right] \tag{2}$$

then R is a stuttering refinement of A.

Proof. Definition 3 follows from properties (1) and (2) by induction on the length of a run of the refined machine R.

Let $\widetilde{\rho} = \widetilde{S}_0, \widetilde{S}_1, \ldots$, be a run of R. $\widetilde{\rho}$ can be splitted in subruns $\widetilde{\rho}_0, \widetilde{\rho}_1, \ldots$ such that all the states in each $\widetilde{\rho}_i$ have the same values of the linking variables, whereas states of two consecutive subruns $\widetilde{\rho}_i$ and $\widetilde{\rho}_{i+1}$ have different values for the linking variables.

We build a run $\rho = S_0, S_1, \ldots$ of A such that ρ and $\widetilde{\rho}$ satisfy Definition 3.

By property (1), it holds $conf(\widetilde{S}_0, S_0)$ by taking $\widetilde{S}_0$ as $\widetilde{S}$ and S_0 as one existing state S satisfying the implication in (1).

Let us suppose that Definition 3 holds till state $\widetilde{S}_j$ of $\widetilde{\rho}_k$ and that $\widetilde{S}_j$ conforms to the abstract state S_k of ρ. We now consider the next state $\widetilde{S}_{j+1}$ (i.e., $step(\widetilde{S}_j, \widetilde{S}_{j+1})$). By inductive hypothesis, it holds $conf(\widetilde{S}_j, S_k)$. By property (2), considering $\widetilde{S} = \widetilde{S}_j$, $\widetilde{S}' = \widetilde{S}_{j+1}$, $S = S_k$, one of the two conditions must hold: $\exists S'\colon (step(S_k, S') \land conf(\widetilde{S}_{j+1}, S'))$ or $conf(\widetilde{S}_{j+1}, S_k)$. In the first case, we take $S_{k+1} = S'$ and we start considering a new subrun $\widetilde{\rho}_{k+1}$ of refined states conformant to S_{k+1}, while in the second case $\widetilde{S}_{j+1}$ is still part of the subrun $\widetilde{\rho}_k$ whose states conform to S_k. In both cases the A-run satisfies the property of Definition 3.

In the sequel, we refer to property (1) as *initial refinement*, and to property (2) as *step refinement*.

```
asm M0
signature:
    controlled x: Integer
definitions:
    main rule r_Main = x := x + 1

default init s0:
    function x = 0
```

```
asm M1
signature:
    controlled x: Integer
definitions:
    main rule r_Main =
        if x > 0 then x := x + 1
        else x := 1
        endif

default init s0: function x = 0
```

Code 3. Abstract model   **Code 4.** Refined model of Code 3

Example 3 (Proof of LGS stuttering refinement). The model LGS_SE is a correct stuttering refinement of LGS_GM. The two models have the same initial state and then property (1) of Theorem 1 is guaranteed. Moreover, model LGS_SE step refines model LGS_GM (i.e., property (2) of Theorem 1 is guaranteed). Indeed, in each state, the refined machine can move to a state in which the doors status or the gears status are either changed (if the sensors detect the changing) or unchanged (if the sensors do not detect any change). Therefore, if a state $\widetilde{S}$ of the refined model LGS_SE is conformant with a state S of the abstract model LGS_GM, a step in the refined model can lead to a state $\widetilde{S}'$ that is either conformant with S (if the sensors do not detect any change) or with the next state S' of the abstract model (if the sensors detect the changing).

4.1 Using Invariants in Refinement Proof

The step refinement property in Theorem 1 is a sufficient but not a necessary condition for a correct (stuttering) refinement. A machine R could be a correct refinement of a machine A but it may not guarantee step refinement. Indeed, step refinement is also checked over states that are not reachable in R: if step refinement is violated only in unreachable states, then we falsely judge the refinement not correct.

Example 4. Let us consider the ASM model *M0* in Code 3 that simply increments function x, and the model *M1* in Code 4 that increments x if it is greater than 0, otherwise updates it to 1. Model *M1* does not step refine model *M0* (property (2) of Theorem 1), because, when x is negative, x is incremented in *M0* and updated to 1 in *M2*: therefore, by Theorem 1 we could not state that model *M1* is a correct stuttering refinement of model *M0*. However, *M1* is a correct stuttering refinement of *M0*; indeed, states in which x is negative are not reachable in both models.

Theorem 1 can be modified by strengthening the inductive hypothesis by introducing a state invariant I over the refined machine as follows:

Theorem 2. *If there exists an invariant I such that the following properties hold*

$$\forall \widetilde{S}\colon (init(\widetilde{S}) \to (I(\widetilde{S}) \wedge \exists S\colon (init(S) \wedge conf(\widetilde{S}, S)))) \qquad (3)$$

$$\forall \widetilde{S} \forall \widetilde{S}' \forall S\colon \left[\begin{pmatrix} I(\widetilde{S}) \wedge \\ step(\widetilde{S}, \widetilde{S}') \wedge \\ conf(\widetilde{S}, S) \end{pmatrix} \to I(\widetilde{S}') \wedge \begin{pmatrix} \exists S'\colon (step(S, S') \wedge conf(\widetilde{S}', S')) \\ \vee \\ conf(\widetilde{S}', S) \end{pmatrix} \right] \qquad (4)$$

then R is a stuttering refinement of A.

Proof. The invariant used in the formulas simply restricts the set of states of the refined machine over which we need to verify refinement correctness. For this reason, the proof of Theorem 1 is applicable also in this case.

Example 5. The refinement between model *M0* in Code 3 and *M1* in Code 4 is correctly proved correct using the invariant $I = x \geq 0$ in Formulas 3 and 4.

Although finding a suitable invariant I may be difficult, thanks to Theorem 2 designers can prove arbitrary complex stuttering refinements.

4.2   Towards an SMT Encoding

To be useful for our final goal, namely reducing the proof of initial and step refinement to an SMT problem, in Formulas (1) and (2) we need to symbolically represent the states and the transition relation.

Functions of any arity are supported by our technique (and by the tool implementation), provided that all the function domains are finite; note that infinite domains may introduce quantifications that are not evaluated (i.e., **unknown** result) by the SMT solver. In the following, in order not to over complicate the notation of our formulas, we only consider 0-ary functions.

Let $\bar{f}_A = [fa_1, \ldots, fa_n]$ be the ordered list of the functions of the abstract machine A and $\bar{f}'_A = [fa'_1, \ldots, fa'_n]$ a renamed copy of the functions in the next state. Similarly, we define ordered lists $\bar{f}_R = [fr_1, \ldots, fr_m]$ and $\bar{f}'_R = [fr'_1, \ldots, fr'_m]$ for the refined machine R. We order the functions of all the previous lists such that the first L functions are the locations of interest. When necessary, we split a list of functions $\bar{f}$ between the functions corresponding to locations of interest (those for which we are interested in checking the conformance relation) and those which are not related: $\bar{f} = \bar{f}^c + \bar{f}^{nc}$.

We can express the predicates *init*, *step*, *conf*, and I used in Theorem 2, in terms of the function lists of a machine.

- Given a machine M with functions $\bar{f}_M$, we introduce the predicates $init_M(\bar{f}_M)$ and $step_M(\bar{f}_M, \bar{f}'_M)$ formalizing the initial predicate and the step predicate of the machine.
- We can define the conformance relation between states of two related machines by using a relation between the lists of machine functions. Given two ordered

lists $\bar{p} = [p_1, \ldots, p_L, \ldots]$ and $\bar{q} = [q_1, \ldots, q_L, \ldots]$, both long at least L, we introduce

$$conf(\bar{p}, \bar{q}) \quad \equiv \quad \bigwedge_{i=1}^{L} p_i = q_i \quad \equiv \quad \bar{p}^c = \bar{q}^c \tag{5}$$

to represent conformance: if $conf(\bar{p}, \bar{q})$ is true, all the locations of interest have equal values in $\bar{p}$ and $\bar{q}$.
- The invariant I, if necessary, is provided by the user as a predicate over the functions $\bar{f}_R$.

In order to prove initial refinement (property (3) of Theorem 2), we check whether the following formula is valid:

$$\forall \bar{f}_R : (init_R(\bar{f}_R) \rightarrow (I(\bar{f}_R) \wedge \exists \bar{f}_A : (init_A(\bar{f}_A) \wedge conf(\bar{f}_R, \bar{f}_A)))) \tag{6}$$

In order to prove step refinement (property (4) of Theorem 2), we check whether the following formula is valid:

$$\forall \bar{f}_R \, \forall \bar{f}_R' \, \forall \bar{f}_A : \\ \left[\begin{pmatrix} I(\bar{f}_R) \wedge \\ step_R(\bar{f}_R, \bar{f}_R') \wedge \\ conf(\bar{f}_R, \bar{f}_A) \end{pmatrix} \rightarrow I(\bar{f}_R') \wedge \begin{pmatrix} \exists \bar{f}_A' : (step_A(\bar{f}_A, \bar{f}_A') \wedge conf(\bar{f}_R', \bar{f}_A')) \\ \vee \\ conf(\bar{f}_R', \bar{f}_A) \end{pmatrix} \right] \tag{7}$$

We can transform Formulas 6 and 7 in order to eliminate universal quantifiers (by Herbrandization) and reduce the number of variables (by exploiting the equality of variable values induced by the conformance), as follows:

$$init_R(\bar{f}_R) \rightarrow (I(\bar{f}_R) \wedge \exists \bar{f}_A^{nc} : init_A(\bar{f}_R^c + \bar{f}_A^{nc})) \tag{8}$$

$$\begin{pmatrix} I(\bar{f}_R) \wedge \\ step_R(\bar{f}_R, \bar{f}_R') \end{pmatrix} \rightarrow I(\bar{f}_R') \wedge \begin{pmatrix} \exists \bar{f}_A^{nc'} : step_A(\bar{f}_R^c + \bar{f}_A^{nc}, \bar{f}_R^{c'} + \bar{f}_A^{nc'}) \\ \vee \\ \bar{f}_R^{c'} = \bar{f}_R^c \end{pmatrix} \tag{9}$$

Formulas 8 and 9 no longer contain the variable lists $\bar{f}_A^c$ and $\bar{f}_A^{c'}$; so we can avoid the duplication for A of all the locations of interest in the current and next state.

5   Proving Refinement by SMT

In this section, we show how we can prove stuttering refinement in an automatic way by reducing it to a Satisfiability Modulo Theories (SMT) problem.

An SMT problem is a decision problem for logical formulas with respect to combinations of background theories expressed in classical first-order logic with equality. An SMT instance is a generalization of a boolean SAT instance in which various sets of variables are replaced by predicates from a variety of underlying theories. SMT solvers can be used, as in our case, as automatic theorem provers by checking unsatisfiability.

5.1   SMT-Based Refinement Proof

We need to represent the initial states and a generic step of the ASM machine in an SMT solver and prove initial and step refinement (i.e., Theorem 2 encoded as Formulas 8 and 9). In order to do this, we here extend the mapping from ASM to SMT already presented in [5] for different purposes.

Given a machine $M = \langle sig, funcDefs, funcInit, r\_main \rangle$, being sig the signature containing the functions $\bar{f}$, $funcInit = \{fi_1, \ldots, fi_p\}$ the sequence of function initializations and $funcDefs = \{fd_1, \ldots, fd_q\}$ the sequence of function definitions, we define the predicates $init_M$ and $step_M$, formalizing the initial state and the generic step of the machine (see Sect. 4), as follows:

$$init_M = (\textbf{and}\ T_d(fi_1)\ \ldots\ T_d(fi_p)) \qquad step_M = (\textbf{and}\ T_r(r\_main)\ T_d(fd_1)\ \ldots\ T_d(fd_q))$$

where T_d and T_r are functions that map, respectively, ASM function definitions and transition rules to SMT formulas. Note that $T_r(r\_main)$ fully captures the semantics of ASM transition rules: it specifies that a location must be updated under some given conditions, and must be kept unchanged otherwise. ASMs semantics prescribes that non-updated locations are kept unchanged; in SMT this must be specified explicitly. We refer to [5] for details on the mapping.

We now show how we verify the validity of Formulas 8 and 9 using two SMT instances. Let $\{Da_1, \ldots, Da_n\}$ be the codomains of the functions $\bar{f}_A$ of the abstract machine A and $\{Dr_1, \ldots, Dr_m\}$ those of the functions $\bar{f}_R$ of the refined machine R. We identify with inv the mapping of the proof invariant, i.e., $inv = T_t(I)$, being T_t the map function from ASM terms to SMT.

For Formula 8, we build the following SMT instance:

(**declare−fun** fr_1 () Dr_1) ... (**declare−fun** fr_m () Dr_m)
(**define−fun** $init_R$ () Bool $init_R(\bar{f}_R)$)
(**define−fun** inv_R () Bool $inv(\bar{f}_R)$)
(**define−fun** $existsInit_A$ () Bool
$\qquad\qquad$ (**exists** ((fa_{L+1} Da_{L+1}) ... (fa_n Da_n)) $init_A(\bar{f}_R^c + \bar{f}_A^{nc})$)))
(**assert** (**not** (=> $init_R$ (**and** inv_R $existsInit_A$))))

where the antecedent of the implication is represented through the SMT function $init_R$, and the consequent by the conjunction of functions inv_R and $existsInit_A$.

For Formula 9, we build the following instance[2]:

(**declare−fun** fr_1 () Dr_1) ... (**declare−fun** fr_m () Dr_m)
(**declare−fun** fr'_1 () Dr_1) ... (**declare−fun** fr'_m () Dr_m)
(**declare−fun** fa_{L+1} () Da_{L+1}) ... (**declare−fun** fa_n () Da_n)
(**define−fun** $step_R$ () Bool $step_R(\bar{f}_R, \bar{f}'_R)$)
(**define−fun** inv_R () Bool $inv(\bar{f}_R)$)
(**define−fun** inv'_R () Bool $inv(\bar{f}'_R)$)
(**define−fun** $existsStep_A$ () Bool
$\qquad\qquad$ (**exists** ((fa'_{L+1} Da_{L+1}) ... (fa'_n Da_n)) $step_A(\bar{f}_R^c + \bar{f}_A^{nc}, \bar{f}_R^{c'} + \bar{f}_A^{nc'})$)))

---

[2] Note that in concrete instances we also do not declare constants for monitored and derived functions belonging to $\bar{f}_R^{nc'}$ and $\bar{f}_A^{nc'}$, as they do not appear in the asserted formulas.

(**define−fun** stutteringState () Bool (and (= fr$'_1$ fr$_1$) ... (= fr$'_L$ fr$_L$)))
(**assert** (not (=> (and inv$_R$ step$_R$) (and inv$'_R$ (or existsStep$_A$ stutteringState)))))

where the conjunction of the antecedent of the implication is represented by functions inv$_R$ and step$_R$. The consequent is represented by functions inv$'_R$, existsStep$_A$ and stutteringState; the latter one models the equality of vectors in the stuttering state (i.e., $\bar{f}_R^{c'} = \bar{f}_R^{c}$ in Formula 9) as a conjunction of equalities.

As usual in SMT solvers, in order to prove validity of a formula, we check that its negation is unsatisfiable. Therefore, if both previous two instances are proved to be unsatisfiable, the refinement is proved correct. However, since the step refinement condition is sufficient but not necessary, when Formula 9 is proved not valid (i.e., the corresponding SMT instance is satisfiable), we cannot state that the refinement is not correct.

Note that, when the refinement is not proved correct, the SMT solver provides us a model (over functions $\bar{f}_R$, $\bar{f}'_R$, and $\bar{f}_a^{nc}$) that acts as a *witness* of the refinement incorrectness: by examining the witness, we can understand whether it is really the case that the refinement is not correct, or it is a false negative result and so we have to strengthen the invariant. For example, proving refinement between Codes 3 and 4 (without any invariant) returns as witness (= x0 -1) (= x1 1). The witness tells us that step refinement does not hold from the state in which x is -1; however, since x cannot be negative, the result is a false negative and we can strengthen the proof by adding the invariant $x \geq 0$.

Example 6. Codes 5 and 6 show the SMT instances built for proving initial and step refinement between the ASMs shown in Codes 1 and 2 for the LGS. In this case, there is no need to specify any invariant.

```
(define−fun doors0 () DoorStatus) (define−fun gears0 () GearStatus)
(define−fun doorsOpen0 () Bool) (define−fun doorsClosed0 () Bool) ...
(define−fun generalElectroValve0 () Bool) ...
(define−fun init_LGS_SE () Bool (and (= doors0 CLOSED) (= gears0 EXTENDED)
                     (not generalElectroValve0) (not extendGearsElectroValve0) ...))
(define−fun existsInit_LGS_GM () Bool (and (= doors0 CLOSED) (= gears0 EXTENDED)))
(assert (not (=> init_LGS_SE existsInit_LGS_GM )))
(check−sat)
```

Code 5. LGS case study – Initial refinement proof (from Code 1 to Code 2)

```
(define−fun doors0 () DoorStatus) (define−fun gears0 () GearStatus)
(define−fun doorsOpen0 () Bool) (define−fun doorsClosed0 () Bool) ...
(define−fun generalElectroValve0 () Bool) ...
(define−fun doors1 () DoorStatus) (define−fun gears1 () GearStatus)
(define−fun doorsOpen1 () Bool) (define−fun doorsClosed1 () Bool) ...
(define−fun generalElectroValve1 () Bool) ...
(define step_LGS_SE () Bool (and (if (= handle0 UP) ...)))
(define existsStep_LGS_GM () Bool (exists (handle HandleStatus)
                     (and (if (= handle UP) (if (/= gears0 RETRACTED) ...))))
(define−fun stutteringState () Bool (and (= gears0 gears1) (= doors0 doors1)))
(assert (not (=> step_LGS_SE (or existsStep_LGS_GM stutteringState))))
(check−sat)
```

Code 6. LGS case study – Step refinement proof (from Code 1 to Code 2)

6 Evaluation

Based on the translation presented in previous sections, we have developed a tool[3] that, given two ASMs, builds the SMT instances and calls the SMT solver Yices in order to prove refinement correctness. The refinement prover is *integrated* in the ASMETA toolset.

The effectiveness of our approach has been tested on different case studies. Some are taken from the literature [13] and are examples of ASM model refinement whose correctness was manually proved. Others are specification case studies developed by ourselves in different contexts: Cloud-based applications [8], a Landing Gear System [6], and the validation of medical software [3,4]. In almost all the cases, the refinement has been proved in less than 10 secs on a Linux machine, Intel(R) Core(TM) i7, 4 GB RAM. However, for one refinement step in [4], we were not able to complete the proof in less than 5 min, the fixed timeout after which we stop the proof. The limiting factor for scalability is the number of monitored functions that are existentially quantified in Formula 9; the refined model whose refinement correctness we were not able to prove has 32 boolean monitored functions. As future work, we plan to assess the approach scalability and apply techniques to reduce the time and memory consumption of the tool (e.g., using cone of influence reduction techniques).

7 Related Work

Formal methods whose computational model is a transition system, e.g., B [2], Z [15], I/O automata [18,19], support the concept of model refinement. The ASM refinement can be compared to that of all the other formalisms and this has already been extensively done in [12]. For this reason, we here relate our work only with Börger's original notion of ASM refinement and its definition of correct model refinement.

Börger's refinement definition [12] is based on checking correspondence between run segments of abstract and refined machines, in a way that the starting and ending states (those of interest) of such corresponding subruns are conformant. The definition allows (m, n)-refinements, namely a run segment of length n in the refined machine simulates as a run segment of length m in the abstract machine. Moreover, it permits that some abstract/refined states don't have corresponding refined/abstract states. We keep the concepts of locations of interests and state conformance given in terms of data equivalence relation between locations of interest. Stuttering refinement is a particular case of Börger's definition, i.e., $(1, n)$-refinement with the constraint of total conformance relation on the states of the refined machine. In our opinion, the restriction of Börger's schema of refinement we propose here is not particularly disadvantageous. Firstly, $(1, n)$-refinement is a kind of refinement that is already considered in literature (with the name of *action refinement* [10]). Secondly, this restricted schema applies to

---

[3] The tool and experimental results can be found at http://asmeta.sourceforge.net/download/asmrefprover.html.

all the ASM specifications we have considered to evaluate the effectiveness of our approach (see Sect. 6). Furthermore, when modeling, it is often useful to guarantee that invariants holding in the abstract level, still hold in the refined one (this was the case for the Landing Gear System specification [6]). The classical refinement [12] preserves the invariants only weakly, since intermediate refined states are not required to conform to some abstract state, while stuttering refinement preserves all the invariants (as also the approach in [23]): if a property is true in every abstract state, it will be true also in every refined state (modulo the *conf* relation). The need to guarantee preservation of those state invariants inspired our definition.

Another framework supporting ASM refinement is that proposed by Schellhorn [22], which is based on the use of the KIV theorem prover. With respect to that framework, ours has several differences. Our *definition of conformity* is much simpler than that used by the KIV tool, because we simply assume that a refined state conforms to its abstract one if they have equal values of functions having the same name (which are the functions of interest). If the user wants to define an ad hoc conformance relation, (s)he must add a derived function representing a predicate over the abstract or refined states (see Sect. 3). In order to *prove refinement*, a relation between the runs must be proved in [22], while we require to prove only a relation between the initial states and between two consecutive states. Using runs permits completeness but requires the use of temporal logics, while our proof is much simpler. Our approach is analogous to induction-based bounded model checking, in which the *next* relation suffices in proving the validity of temporal invariants. KIV supports interactive verification, while we aim to a *completely automatic* technique. Also for this reason, we have chosen an SMT solver. In case the proof fails, we are able to show a counterexample in which the refinement is not preserved. As shown before, there are some cases in which our technique produces spurious counterexamples and it is unable to prove the refinement. These spurious counterexamples can be eliminated by invariant strengthening.

8   Conclusions

We have presented an approach for proving the refinement correctness of Abstract State Machines. The approach considers a particular type of refinement (i.e., stuttering refinement) that frequently occurs in concrete case studies. The proposed approach exploits the symbolic representation of an ASM model in an SMT solver, and reduces the proof of refinement correctness to a satisfiability problem that is automatically solved by the SMT solver. The technique has been implemented in a tool integrated in the ASMETA framework. Although the limits in terms of completeness (some refinements could be very hard to prove) and expressive power (some refinements may be not stuttering), the tool has the advantages of usability, integration in an existing framework, and automation in proving refinement correctness. This relieves the modeler of the necessity to drive a mathematical proof manually or in an interactive way (as requested in [22,23]), which requires certain verification skills. Furthermore, in case a model is not proved a correct stuttering refinement of another model, our framework provides counterexamples useful to reason about incorrect modeling of the refined machine.

In this work, we have considered deterministic and nondeterministic single-agent ASMs. As future work, we plan to prove refinement of multi-agent ASMs. Moreover, we want to study techniques for automatic invariant generation.

References

1. Abadi, M., Lamport, L.: The existence of refinement mappings. Theor. Comput. Sci. **82**(2), 253–284 (1991)
2. Abrial, J.-R., Hallerstede, S.: Refinement, decomposition, and instantiation of discrete models: Application to Event-B. Fundam. Inform. **77**(1), 1–28 (2007)
3. Arcaini, P., Bonfanti, S., Gargantini, A., Mashkoor, A., Riccobene, E.: Formal validation and verification of a medical software critical component. In: Proceedings of MEMOCODE 2015, pp. 80–89. IEEE (2015)
4. Mashkoor, A.: The hemodialysis machine case study. In: Butler, M., Schewe, K.-D., Mashkoor, A., Biro, M. (eds.) ABZ 2016. LNCS, vol. 9675, pp. 329–343. Springer, Heidelberg (2016). doi:10.1007/978-3-319-33600-8_29
5. Arcaini, P., Gargantini, A., Riccobene, E.: Using SMT for dealing with nondeterminism in ASM-based runtime verification. In: ECEASST, vol. 70 (2014)
6. Arcaini, P., Gargantini, A., Riccobene, E.: Rigorous development process of a safety-critical system: from ASM models to Java code. Int. J. Softw. Tools Technol. Transf. 1–23 (2015)
7. Arcaini, P., Gargantini, A., Riccobene, E., Scandurra, P.: A model-driven process for engineering a toolset for a formal method. Softw. Pract. Experience **41**, 155–166 (2011)
8. Arcaini, P., Holom, R.-M., Riccobene, E.: ASM-based formal design of an adaptivity component for a cloud system. Formal Aspects Comput. 1–29 (2016)
9. Beierle, C., Börger, E., Durdanović, I., Glässer, U., Riccobene, E.: Refining abstract machine specifications of the steam boiler control to well documented executable code. In: Abrial, J.-R., Börger, E., Langmaack, H. (eds.) Dagstuhl Seminar 1995. LNCS, vol. 1165, pp. 52–78. Springer, Heidelberg (1996)
10. Boiten, E.A.: Introducing extra operations in refinement. Formal Aspects Comput. **26**(2), 305–317 (2012)
11. Boniol, F., Wiels, V.: The landing gear system case study. In: Boniol, F., Wiels, V., Ait Ameur, Y., Schewe, K.-D. (eds.) ABZ 2014. CCIS, vol. 433, pp. 1–18. Springer, Heidelberg (2014)
12. Börger, E.: The ASM refinement method. Formal Aspects Comput. **15**(2), 237–257 (2003)
13. Börger, E.: The Abstract State Machines method for high-level system design and analysis. In: Formal Methods: State of the Art and New Directions, pp. 79–116. Springer, London (2010)
14. Börger, E., Stärk, R.: Abstract State Machines: A Method for High-Level System Design and Analysis. Springer, Heidelberg (2003)
15. Derrick, J., Boiten, E.: Refinement in Z and object-Z: Foundations and Advanced Applications. Springer, London (2001)

16. Ernst, G., Pfähler, J., Schellhorn, G., Reif, W.: Modular refinement for submachines of ASMs. In: Ait Ameur, Y., Schewe, K.-D. (eds.) ABZ 2014. LNCS, vol. 8477, pp. 188–203. Springer, Heidelberg (2014)

17. Farahbod, R., Glässer, U.: The CoreASM modeling framework. Softw. Pract. Experience **41**(2), 167–178 (2011)

18. Lynch, N.A., Tuttle, M.R.: An introduction to input/output automata. CWI Q. **2**, 219–246 (1989)

19. Lynch, N.A., Vaandrager, F.W.: Forward and backward simulations: Part I. untimed systems. Inf. Comput. **121**(2), 214–233 (1995)

20. Meseguer, J., Palomino, M., Martí-Oliet, N.: Algebraic simulations. J. Logic Algebraic Program. **79**(2), 103–143 (2010)

21. Riccobene, E., Schmid, J.: Capturing requirements by abstract state machines: The light control case study. J. UCS **6**(7), 597–620 (2000)

22. Schellhorn, G.: Verification of ASM refinements using generalized forward simulation. J. UCS **7**(11), 952–979 (2001)

23. Schellhorn, G.: ASM refinement preserving invariants. J. UCS **14**(12), 1929–1948 (2008)

24. Stärk, R., Schmid, J., Börger, E.: Java and the Java Virtual Machine, vol. 24. Springer, Heidelberg (2001)

Coq Implementation of OO Verification Framework VeriJ

Ke Zhang$^{(\boxtimes)}$ and Zongyan Qiu

LMAM and Department of Informatics, School of Mathematics,
Peking University, Beijing, China
zksms@pku.edu.cn, qzy@math.pku.edu.cn

Abstract. We implement an OO specification and verification framework VeriJ in the proof assistant Coq. This framework covers the main OO features like encapsulation, inheritance and polymorphism. It can modularly specify and verify programs, while only one specification per method is necessary. In this paper, we introduce the framework VeriJ, our tool in Coq, and an example to illustrate how to specify/verify the program in a modular and abstract way.

1 Introduction

The main features of Object Orientation (OO), such as inheritance and polymorphism, bring challenges to formal verification, as discussed in [1]. To address the challenges, we need a specification/verification framework to: verify OO program modularly; achieve information hiding in the specification; and handle the complicated problems brought by inheritance.

The OO specification and verification framework VeriJ [2] is able to solve the problems above. VeriJ uses behavioral subtyping [3] to address inheritance and polymorphism, and uses specification predicates to support modular verification of OO programs, and improve information hiding.

We implement the framework VeriJ in the proof assistant Coq [4], giving some functions and lemmas for users to define and specify the programs. Thus, we can formally prove that a program satisfies its specification.

The paper is organized as follows: Sect. 2 introduces the main idea and design of VeriJ; Sect. 3 introduces our Coq implementation, and shows an example as an illustration; Sect. 4 discusses the related work and concludes.

2 The VeriJ Framework

Now we briefly introduce VeriJ, which consists of a simple OO language which supports the main OO features; a general OO memory model; a revised separation logic for describing states and transitions of OO programs; and a verification

---

K. Zhang—Supported by the NSFC under grant No. 61272160, No. 61202069 and No. 61532019.

R. De Nicola and E. Kühn (Eds.): SEFM 2016, LNCS 9763, pp. 270–276, 2016.
DOI: 10.1007/978-3-319-41591-8_18

framework which give facilities to support modular specification and verification. More details about VeriJ can be found in [2,5].

The programming language in VeriJ is a sequential subset of Java. It is relatively simple to facilitate theoretical study, and large enough for covering important OO issues such as dynamic binding, object sharing, aliasing, casting, etc. The syntax is shown below, here x is a variable, y a local variable, z a parameter, C a class name, I an interface name, π a method specification, a and m field and method names respectively. Assertion $p(\textbf{this}, \bar{r})$ is the specification predicate, we will explain it below.

$$v ::= \textbf{this} \mid x \qquad e ::= \textbf{true} \mid \textbf{false} \mid \textbf{null} \mid v \mid numeric\_exps$$
$$b ::= \textbf{true} \mid \textbf{false} \mid e = e \mid e < e \mid \neg b \mid b \vee b \mid b \wedge b$$
$$c ::= \textbf{skip} \mid x := e \mid x := b \mid v.a := e \mid x := v.a \mid x := (C)v \mid x := v.m(\bar{e})$$
$$\mid \ x := \textbf{new}\ C(\bar{e}) \mid \textbf{return}\ e \mid c;c \mid \textbf{if}\ b\ c\ \textbf{else}\ c \mid \textbf{while}\ b\ c$$
$$T ::= \textbf{Bool} \mid \textbf{Int} \mid \textbf{Object} \mid C \mid I \qquad P ::= \ \textbf{def}\ p(\textbf{this}, \bar{r})$$
$$M ::= T\ m(\overline{T_1}) \qquad L ::= \ \textbf{interface}\ I[: \bar{I}]\ \{\overline{P;\ M\ [\pi];}\}$$
$$K ::= \textbf{class}\ C : C\ [\triangleright \bar{I}]\ \{\overline{T\ a;}\ \overline{P : \psi;}\ \overline{C(\overline{T_1})\ [\pi]\ \{\overline{T_2\ y;}\ c\}}\ \overline{M\ [\pi]\ \{\overline{T_2\ y;}\ c\}}\ \}$$
$$G ::= (K \mid L) \mid (K \mid L)\ G$$

VeriJ takes a pure reference memory model. A runtime state $s = (\sigma, O) \in$ State consists of a stack and a heap:

$$\text{Stack} \ \hat{=}\ \text{Name} \rightarrow \text{Ref} \qquad \text{Heap} \ \hat{=}\ \text{Ref} \rightarrow \text{Name} \rightarrow \text{Ref}$$
$$\text{State} \ \hat{=}\ \text{Stack} \times \text{Heap}.$$

A stack $\sigma \in$ Stack maps variables and constants to references, and a heap maps references to field-reference pairs.

The assertion language is similar to that of Separation Logic [6] with some revisions to fit the needs of OO verification.

$$\rho ::= \textbf{true} \mid \textbf{false} \mid r_1 = r_2 \mid r : T \mid r <: T \mid v = r$$
$$\eta ::= \textbf{emp} \mid r_1.a \mapsto r_2 \mid \textsf{obj}(r, T)$$
$$\psi ::= \rho \mid \eta \mid p(\bar{r}) \mid \neg \psi \mid \psi \vee \psi \mid \psi * \psi \mid \psi -\!\!* \psi \mid \exists r \cdot \psi$$

- Here r denotes a reference; ρ denotes assertions independent of heaps; $r_1 = r_2$ holds iff r_1 and r_2 are identical; and $v = r$ denotes v holds the reference r. $r : T$ and $r <: T$ denote that r refers to an object of type T, or of some subtype of T respectively.
- η denotes the assertions involving heaps. Empty and singleton assertions are similar to those in Separation Logic. The singleton $r_1.a \mapsto r_2$ means the heap only contains the field $r_1.a$, whose value is r_2. $\textsf{obj}(r, T)$ indicates the heap contains exactly an object of type T, and r refers to this object.
- Connectors $*$ and $-\!\!*$ comes from Separation Logic. $\psi_1 * \psi_2$ indicates the heap can be split into two parts, where ψ_1 and ψ_2 holds respectively.

In a class C, we can declare specification predicates in the form of $p(\textbf{this}, \bar{r})$: ψ. Here $\textbf{this}$ and $\bar{r}$ are the parameters, and ψ is the definition of predicate p. ψ is only visible in C or subclasses of C. Out of the scope, p can be used only as an atomic assertion. Predicates can also be defined recursively.

The subclass inherits all the predicates defined in its superclass, and can override them. Using the specification predicates, we are able to reason about OO programs at an abstract level, without exposing the implementation details. It also allows us to define abstract specifications for interfaces.

The verification rules of VeriJ can be found in [2,5], and we will not introduce them in this paper, due to the space limit.

3   Coq Implementation of VeriJ

In this section, we introduce our implementation of VeriJ in Coq. Then we use a simple example to show how to use our tool to verify OO program. Our coq code can be found at https://github.com/fm-pku/VeriJ-tool.

3.1   Modules

We implement VeriJ as the following Coq modules: Util (Utilities), Heap, Stack, Expr (Expression), Lang (Language), Env (Static environment), State, Asn (Assertion Language), Sem (Operation semantics), Spec (Specification). Each module has an interface for the users, showing which functions and lemmas are provided in this module.

Heap and Stack define the memory model; Expr, Lang and Sem define the programming language and its semantics; Env stores useful information such as the class hierarchy and method declarations. When verifying real programs, users do not need to be concerned about these modules too much. The most important modules are as follows:

- State. It contains the information about the static environment Env and the runtime state (Heap and Stack). When declaring the program, we need to call the functions like build_class and build_method in this module.
- Asn. It defines the assertion language of VeriJ and its semantics. The assertion can be evaluated with respect to any given heap, stack and type environment. Besides, this module also provides several lemmas about first order logic and separation logic.
- Spec. It defines the specification of the programs. All the verification rules of VeriJ are defined as lemmas in this module. When verifying a program against its specification, the generated proof obligations are: all methods in all classes satisfy their specifications; and each subclass is a behavioral subtype of its superclass (and the interfaces that it implements). For inherited methods, we can prove a specification refinement relation (rule [H-INH] in [2]) instead of re-verifying the method body.

3.2   Example

Code in Fig. 1 is modified from the example in [7], which is a typical example in OO verification. *Cell* declares a specification predicate *cell* for describing its

class *Cell* : **Object** {
  Int *x*;
  def *cell*(**this**, *v*) : **this**.*x* ↦ *v*;
  void *set*(**Int** *v*)
  ⟨*cell*(**this**, -)⟩⟨*cell*(**this**, *v*)⟩
  { **this**.*x* := *v*; }
  Int *get*() ⟨*cell*(**this**, *v*)⟩
  ⟨*cell*(**this**, *v*) ∧ res = *v*⟩
  { **Int** *c*; *c* := **this**.*x*; **return** *c*; }
}

interface *Undoable* {
  def *cell*(**this**, *v*);
  def *bak*(**this**, *v*);

  void *set*(**Int** *v*) ⟨*cell*(**this**, *b*)⟩
  ⟨*cell*(**this**, *v*) ∧ *bak*(**this**, *b*)⟩
  Int *get*() ⟨*cell*(**this**, *v*)⟩
  ⟨*cell*(**this**, *v*) ∧ res = *v*⟩;
  void *undo*() ⟨*bak*(**this**, *b*)⟩⟨*cell*(**this**, *b*)⟩;
}

class *ReCell* : *Cell* ▷ *Undoable* {
  Int *y*;
  def *cell*(**this**, *v*) : **this**.*x* ↦ *v* * **this**.*y* ↦ -;
  def *bak*(**this**, *v*) : **this**.*x* ↦ - * **this**.*y* ↦ *v*;
  void *set*(**Int** *v*) { **Int** *c*;
    c := **this**.*x*; **this**.*y* := *c*; **this**.*x* := *v*; }
  void *undo*() { **Int** *c*;
    c := **this**.*y*; **this**.*x* := *c*; }
}

Fig. 1. Interface *Undoable* and Classes *Cell*, *ReCell*

behavior, and *ReCell* overrides predicate *cell* by adding a field *y*. Here ⟨·⟩⟨·⟩ stands for pre and post-conditions of methods, and res denotes the return value.

To verify this example in Coq, we need to define the program and its specification at first. For example, *ReCell* is defined by the following Coq code:

```
Module ReCell.
 Definition fields := RType.update_field_type "y" Int.
 Definition cell : pred := .\(fun this => .\(fun v =>
    =| (fun r' => this'"x" |-> v * this'"y" |-> r'))).
 Definition bak : pred := .\(fun this => .\(fun v =>
    =| (fun r' => this'"x" |-> r' * this'"y" |-> v))).
 Definition set_cmd := Lang.fread "c" "this" "x";
                       Lang.fwrite "this" "y" (^"c");
                       Lang.fwrite "this" "x" (^"v").
 Definition undo_cmd := Lang.fread "c" "this" "y";
                       Lang.fwrite "this" "x" (^"c").
 Definition declare (s : state) : state :=
    State.build_method "ReCell" "undo" ...
    (State.build_method "ReCell" "set" ...
    (State.build_class "ReCell" ("Cell"::"Undoable"::nil) fields s)).
End ReCell.
```

The function `declare` maps a state into a new state, in which the static environment is updated, adding the information about class *ReCell* and its methods. The method *get* and all the method specifications are inherited, thus do not need to be declared in module ReCell. Here the predicate `cell` means:

$$\lambda this \cdot \lambda v \cdot \exists r' \cdot this.x \mapsto v * this.y \mapsto r'.$$

Modules `Cell` and `Undoable` are defined similarly. Therefore, the state

```
Definition program :=
   ReCell.declare (Undoable.declare (Cell.declare init_state))).
```

contains all the information about the program of this example.

Then we can verify this program in Coq by proving:

```
Lemma verify_cell: program + preds |= spec.
```

It denotes that for the given program and predicate environment, the specification of the program holds, i.e. (1) each method satisfies its specification; (2) *ReCell* is a behavioral subtype of both *Cell* and *Undoable*. We successfully verify this example in Coq. Besides, we verify a more complicated example about two different implementations of *Queue*, which can be found in our Coq project.

4   Related Work and Conclusion

In recent years, researchers have proposed many OO verification tools, such as jStar [8] and VeriFast [9]. However, these tools do not generate formal proof of the program correctness. To solve this problem, some works [10,11] use proof assistants—such as Coq, Isabelle—to verify programs, since they can generate machine-checkable proofs.

Bengtson *et al.* [11,12] present a verification tool Charge! for verifying Java-like programs using higher-order separation logic. Charge! is also implemented in Coq, and its goal is analogous to ours, but the logic it uses and the way it models the OO programs are quite different from VeriJ. As shown in Sect. 3.2, VeriJ supports both class inheritance and interface-based inheritance. However, Charge! does not support class inheritance. Therefore, VeriJ allows code re-use, and can avoid re-verifying the inherited methods. Furthermore, it is more structured to declare programs using VeriJsince VeriJ defines a static environment which Charge! lacks. For example, in VeriJ the proof obligations for behavioral subtyping are automatically generated, but in Charge! those proof obligations need to be manually declared in the sub-interfaces.

Parkinson and Bierman [13,14] propose a framework based on separation logic and abstract predicate family, and they use a pair of static and dynamic specifications to specify each method. Based on this, Distefano and Parkinson develop a semi-automatic program verifier jStar [8] for Java programs. Compared to their work, the specification predicate in VeriJ is similar with the abstract predicate family, but VeriJ introduces visibility, inheritance and over-riding rules for specification predicates. Thus the specification predicates provide better encapsulation for implementation details, meanwhile, each method only need one specification in VeriJ.

In conclusion, we implement the OO specification and verification framework VeriJ in Coq. It uses behavioral subtyping to solve the problems brought by inheritance and polymorphism, and uses specification predicates to ensure a modular reasoning system. VeriJ is able to specify and verify programs of a subset of Java, including dynamic/static binding, interfaces, implementation of multiple interfaces, etc. Inherited fields/methods/specifications do not need to be re-declared or re-verified.

We have developed a set of Coq functions, as a tool, which allows user to define and specify the programs in Coq. All the verification rules of VeriJ are defined as lemmas in Coq, users can use them to prove the specifications of programs. We provide two examples *Cell* and *Queue*, together with their correctness proof in the Coq project.

As the future work, we are going to:

- Prove more examples using our tool, to get more experience for improving the tool. In addition, we plan to develop a more user-friendly syntax in Coq for the users to describe programs with specification in VeriJ.
- Define the weakest pre-condition semantics of VeriJ in Coq, and also define more Coq tactics, to make the tool more automatic. With these facilities, the tool may automatically derive the specification of intermediate states, instead of asking for manual declarations.
- Define more specific tactics to improve the speed of verification. Although some Coq built-in tactics work well in the verification, they are relatively slow. Some specific tactics for VeriJ would be helpful.
- Apply more static checks to the real programs. Now we only prove the partial correctness of programs (i.e. if a program successfully terminates, then it satisfies the specification). Based on the static environment, we can further check the well-typedness, termination, etc.

References

1. Leavens, G.T., Leino, K.R.M., Müller, P.: Specification and verification challenges for sequential object-oriented programs. Formal Aspects Comput. **19**(2), 159–189 (2007)
2. Liu, Y., Hong, A., Qiu, Z.: Inheritance and modularity in specification and verification of OO programs. In: TASE 2011, pp. 19–26. IEEE Computer Society (2011)
3. Liskov, B., Wing, J.M.: A behavioral notion of subtyping. ACM Trans. Program. Lang. Syst. **16**(6), 1811–1841 (1994)
4. The Coq Development Team: The Coq Proof Assistant Reference Manual (Version 8.4) (2012)
5. Qiu, Z., Hong, A., Liu, Y.: Modular verification of OO programs with interfaces. In: Aoki, T., Taguchi, K. (eds.) ICFEM 2012. LNCS, vol. 7635, pp. 151–166. Springer, Heidelberg (2012)
6. Reynolds, J.C.: Separation logic: a logic for shared mutable data structures. In: Proceedings 17th Annual IEEE Symposium on Logic in Computer Science 2002, pp. 55–74. IEEE (2002)
7. Abadi, M., Cardelli, L.: A Theory of Objects. Springer, Heidelberg (1996)
8. Distefano, D., Parkinson, M.J.: jStar: towards practical verification for Java. ACM SIGPLAN Notices, vol. 43, No. 10, pp. 213–226 (2008)
9. Jacobs, B., Smans, J., Philippaerts, P., Vogels, F., Penninckx, W., Piessens, F.: VeriFast: a powerful, sound, predictable, fast verifier for C and Java. In: Bobaru, M., Havelund, K., Holzmann, G.J., Joshi, R. (eds.) NFM 2011. LNCS, vol. 6617, pp. 41–55. Springer, Heidelberg (2011)

10. McCreight, A.: Practical tactics for separation logic. In: Berghofer, S., Nipkow, T., Urban, C., Wenzel, M. (eds.) TPHOLs 2009. LNCS, vol. 5674, pp. 343–358. Springer, Heidelberg (2009)

11. Bengtson, J., Jensen, J.B., Birkedal, L.: Charge!. In: Beringer, L., Felty, A. (eds.) ITP 2012. LNCS, vol. 7406, pp. 315–331. Springer, Heidelberg (2012)

12. Bengtson, J., Jensen, J.B., Sieczkowski, F., Birkedal, L.: Verifying object-oriented programs with higher-order separation logic in Coq. In: van Eekelen, M., Geuvers, H., Schmaltz, J., Wiedijk, F. (eds.) ITP 2011. LNCS, vol. 6898, pp. 22–38. Springer, Heidelberg (2011)

13. Parkinson, M.J., Bierman, G.M.: Separation logic, abstraction and inheritance. In: POPL 2008, pp. 75–86. ACM (2008)

14. Parkinson, M., Bierman, G.: Separation logic for object-oriented programming. In: Clarke, D., Noble, J., Wrigstad, T. (eds.) Aliasing in Object-Oriented Programming. LNCS, vol. 7850, pp. 366–406. Springer, Heidelberg (2013)

Towards a Proof Framework for Information Systems with Weak Consistency

Peter Zeller$^{(\boxtimes)}$ and Arnd Poetzsch-Heffter

University of Kaiserslautern, Kaiserslautern, Germany
{p_zeller,poetzsch}@cs.uni-kl.de

Abstract. Weakly consistent data stores are more scalable and can provide a higher availability than classical, strongly consistent data stores. However, it is much harder to reason about and to implement applications, when the underlying infrastructure provides only few guarantees. In this paper, we report on work in progress on a proof framework, which can be used to formally reason about the correctness of such applications. The framework supports the verification of functional properties, which go beyond the guarantees given by the data store and can cover relations between multiple interactions with clients and invariants between several objects. Additionally, we modeled and support modern database features, like causal consistency, snapshot-transactions, and conflict-free replicated data types (CRDTs). The framework and the proofs are developed within the interactive theorem prover Isabelle/HOL.

1 Introduction

Today, many information systems are built without a strongly consistent data store. There is a variety of reasons for this trend: For services which are offered world-wide, the concept of Geo-Replication allows for low latency in all regions, by replicating data at servers, which are geographically close to the users. However, Geo-Replication does not work well with the concepts of strong consistency. In particular, distributed transactions are incompatible with low latency and high availability [6]. Mobile applications have problems comparable to Geo-Replicated systems. Since the network connection is sometimes slow or unavailable, it is not feasible to use strong consistency to synchronize data between mobile devices and cloud services.

Programming applications using weak consistency is inherently complex. Most importantly, convergence must be ensured, meaning that all replicas represent the same abstract state when they have observed the same set of operations, without losing writes. To help programmers handle this problem, conflict-free replicated data types (CRDTs) [14] have been developed. A CRDT is a reusable data type, which embodies a certain strategy to handle concurrent updates. Examples are counters, sets, and maps. When an application is written using CRDTs, the convergence property comes for free and thus the development effort is reduced.

© Springer International Publishing Switzerland 2016
R. De Nicola and E. Kühn (Eds.): SEFM 2016, LNCS 9763, pp. 277–283, 2016.
DOI: 10.1007/978-3-319-41591-8_19

However, convergence is not the only desirable property of an application. It is also important that concurrent updates are handled in a way that makes sense for the application (see Sect. 2). These correctness properties are often overlooked by developers. One reason for this is that there is no systematic method to reason about the correctness of an implementation. While there are multiple program logics for working with sequential and concurrent programs, there are no frameworks yet, which support reasoning about eventual consistency and CRDTs on a higher level. Thus, it is not feasible to use existing frameworks to reason about nontrivial correctness properties of these kinds of applications.

To make the verification practical, our work aims to considerably reduce the required proof work. We are developing a proof framework in Isabelle/HOL [13], which captures commonalities of applications, which are built on top of weakly consistent data stores with replicated data types. With the common verification tasks lifted to the framework level, the verification of a concrete application can be done on a higher level and focus on the application specific properties and invariants. We discuss our approach to verification in Sect. 3.

2   Developing Applications with Weak Consistency

To show the need to reason about causal consistency and the choice of data types, we consider a small application to manage user accounts. This application provides the following API to clients:

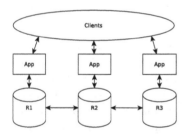

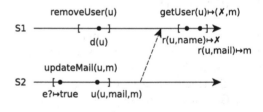

Fig. 1. System architecture   **Fig. 2.** Problematic execution

The function `registerUser(name, email)` creates a new user account with the given data and returns the unique identifier of the newly created user. To update the mail address of a user with a given identifier, there is a function `updateMail(id, newMail)`. To remove a user from the system, `removeUser(id)` can be called. The data of a user can be retrieved via `getUser(id)`, which returns a record with the name and the mail address of a given user, or `not_found` when the user does not exist.

We assume an architecture similar to the one shown in Fig. 1 on which we want to implement our application. At the bottom there are several (full) replicas of the database, which asynchronously synchronize their states. At the top

```
def registerUser(name, mail) {          def removeUser(id) {
  result = newId()                        users[id].delete()
  atomic {                              }
    users[result]['id'].write(result)
    users[result]['name'].write(name)  def getUser(id) {
    users[result]['mail'].write(mail)    atomic {
  }                                        val exists = users[id].exists()
  return result                            if (exists) {
}                                            val name = users[id]['name'].read()
                                             val mail = users[id]['mail'].read()
def updateMail(id, newMail) {                result = {'name': name, 'mail': mail}
  atomic {                                 } else {
    val exists = users[id].exists()          result = not_found
    if exists {                            }
      users[id]['mail'].write(newMail)   }
    }                                    return result
  }                                    }
}
```

Fig. 3. Pseudocode implementation of example application to manage user accounts.

there is a set of clients, for which we do not have any additional assumptions. In particular clients might be stateful and communicate with each other. The application layer itself is stateless, all data is assumed to be stored in the database or by clients.

In this scenario, an application consists of a set of methods, which can be called by clients. The application can then interact with the database by querying the data and by issuing updates to the database. Queries and updates can be enclosed in a transaction, which works on a causally consistent snapshot and guarantees atomicity of the enclosed operations, but transactions do not provide serializability. In particular, it is possible to read from stale states and there can be concurrent updates on the same object. The data store is parametrized by a data type specification, which defines how concurrent updates are merged. Often, the top-level data type is a map which results in a key-value data store. Furthermore we assume, that the database provides session guarantees as in [4].

Implementation: Figure 3 shows a pseudocode implementation of the user management example. The variable `users` refers to a map data type in the database and maps user identifiers to another map containing the user data. The inner map contains entries for id, name, and mail which all are last-writer-wins registers [14]. The registers provide `write` and `read` methods. The maps allow to look up a key (squared brackets syntax) and they allow to `delete` entries and to check whether an entry `exists`. We use an add-wins map, which means that a delete-operation will win over concurrent update operations.

One difficulty in implementing this example on a weakly consistent data store is to make `removeUser` work correctly. As an example we consider the following property, which links the invocation of the `removeUser`-method with the expected effect and therefore is more than just an integrity constraint: "A user that is removed should eventually be removed on all replicas, and not reappear because of other operations being called afterwards or concurrently".

When using CRDTs, eventual consistency and high availability come for free. However, a developer still has to reason about the behavior of the application. For example, consider the scenario in Fig. 2. In this scenario, an update operation on user u is first executed in session 2. Concurrently, user u is removed in session 1. Later, the update from session 2 is received in session 1 and the CRDT handles the concurrent updates by letting the update-operation win over the remove-operation of the user. Thus the getUser-operation in session 1 will return a user-record, although the user has been removed. Even worse, the user record would be inconsistent, since the name was removed, but the mail exists because of the write-operation from the concurrent update.

Choosing a last-writer-wins semantics for the map would lead to similar problems, as the previously explained add-wins semantics. With a remove-wins semantics for the map, the application would work as intended, as we demonstrate in the next section. But there are more pitfalls, into which a developer can run. Even with the remove-wins semantics at the database level, if the update method would not check, whether the user is deleted and just did a blind update, then a user could reappear after being removed. A user could also reappear, if the users identifier was not generated in a way which guarantees uniqueness.

The chosen example of object-deletion often comes up in practice. Riak, a distributed key-value store, uses tombstones for deletion, which means that remove operations win over concurrent updates. However, in the default settings tombstones are purged after $3\,\mathrm{s}$[1], which can lead to objects which reappear after they have been deleted.

3   Specification and Verification

Having seen some possible pitfalls of the example, the question arises, how we can assure ourself, that the given implementation is indeed correct, when a remove-wins map is used. We want to describe application properties from the clients perspective. The clients can only observe the procedure calls sent to the system and the responses of the system, which we model as a trace of request and response-events. However, it is hard to specify the system just in terms of this trace, because of the inherent nondeterminism of the system. The response depends on the internal delivery of messages at the database level.

Specification: To handle the problem of nondeterminism, we adapt a technique used for specifying replicated data types [5,15], where the outcome of operations is expressed using the happens-before relation on update-operations in the history of operations. We lift the happens before relation from the database level to the level of client-calls, by defining that a call c_1 happens before a call c_2 (we write $c_1 \prec c_2$), when all database calls in c_1 happen before every database call in c_2. Using the happens before relation and the set of all client-calls, we can specify invariants about the communication history between the application and

---

[1] See "Configuring Object Deletion" at http://docs.basho.com/riak/latest/ops/advanced/deletion/. The behavior in Cassandra is similar.

its clients. For example, we can formalize the property from Sect. 2, which states that a removed user should not reappear:

$$\forall c_1, c_2 \in clientCalls. \ \forall u. \ args(c_1) = removeUser(u) \wedge c_1 \prec c_2$$
$$\wedge \ args(c_2) = getUser(u) \quad \longrightarrow \quad res(c_2) = \texttt{not\_found}$$

Verification: For verification we have to express additional invariants about the internals of the application. In particular, we have to relate the client-calls with the corresponding database operations and we have to reason about the internal, local steps done by the application. We explain how our framework supports the verification of the different kind of invariants using a proof sketch for the example property.

Property 1: When *removeUser(id)* has been called, then there must be a corresponding database operation *users[id].delete()*. To support properties like this, our framework provides a mapping function, which maps each database operation to the corresponding client-call. This function can be used in invariants and is automatically updated by the framework in each step.

Property 2: There are no map update operations on a removed user, which happen causally after the remove (except for other removes).

The operations in the *registerUser* procedure cannot come afterwards, because *newUID* never returns an identifier known to clients. Therefore *removeUser(id)* must happen at a point in time after *registerUser* and no happens-before relation can exist which points into the past.

The operations in *updateMail* cannot happen after a remove, because the procedure checks whether the user exists before doing any updates. Because the code is packed in an atomic unit, the check and the map updates see the same set of operations. So if the update operations were executed after a remove, the existence check would have returned false.

The maintenance of property 2 has to be shown for the code of each method. Our framework supports this by annotating the code with assertions, similar to work by Ashcroft [1]. Some proof obligations can already be handled automatically using general properties proven in the framework. In particular, the framework restricts local assertions so that it is not necessary to consider the effect of local steps on other, concurrent procedure invocations. We believe that we can further reduce the effort by automatically generating verification conditions from the code and a few invariants.

Property 3: When *getUser* is called after a *remove*, we get that there is a database operation for deleting the user by property 1. By property 2 we know that no database operation on the same user happened after the remove. There can be concurrent updates, but since we used a remove-wins semantics for the map, we always get the required result, that the user does not exist.

For the reasoning about CRDT semantics, out framework supports high-level specifications of CRDTs, as used in work on verification of CRDTs [3,5,7,15]. Users can write custom CRDT specifications for their applications or reuse and compose the existing specifications of some commonly used CRDTs.

4   Related Work

Gotsman and others have worked on modeling and verifying replicated data types [4,5,7]. This work is mostly focused on pen and paper proofs and therefore requires too much effort for realistic applications. Still, the work on Composite Replicated Data Types [7] is the work most similar to ours, since it also uses transactions to build bigger applications from simpler data types.

CISE [8] is a framework which concentrates on the combination of weak consistency with strong consistency and pessimistic concurrency control. The work presents proof rules for this scenario and a tool based on an approximation of these rules, which can automatically check whether enough locks are used to ensure the maintenance of data integrity constraints. However, the tool mostly concentrates on locks and cannot handle more complicated interactions with replicated data types and properties which go beyond integrity constraints and is therefore not applicable to our userbase example.

Chapar [12] is a proof framework for causally consistent databases, which was developed using Coq. The work also includes a simple model checker for applications, which can explore different schedules consistent with causal consistency, but cannot be used to prove the correctness of complex applications. Also the work only considers simple key-value stores without support for replicated data types.

Finally there is a lot of work on general purpose tools like TLA+ [11] or Alloy [9]. While these tools can be applied to check the applications we are interested in, they require to model the complete system, including the database and the data types. Hence the models can be quite big, and the automated checkers become infeasible.

5   Conclusion and Future Work

We aim to reduce the amount of manual work required for performing proofs in the future by capturing more general properties in proof rules and by using more automation. In particular we believe that it will be possible to handle atomic blocks as one single step and to generate verification conditions with more automation, which would significantly reduce the manual effort. The formalization in Isabelle/HOL allows us to improve on this incrementally, since manual proofs are always available, when no automation has been developed yet.

The primitive proof rule we use currently, already helps with informal reasoning about program correctness. We hope that developing more specialized proof rules will also lead to more insights for informal reasoning and thus help developers in writing correct applications.

Acknowledgement. This research is supported in part by European FP7 project 609 551 SyncFree https://syncfree.lip6.fr/ (2013–2016).

References

1. Ashcroft, E.A.: Proving assertions about parallel programs. J. Comput. Syst. Sci. **10**(1), 110–135 (1975)
2. Bodik, R., Majumdar, R. (eds.): Proceedings of the 43rd Annual ACM SIGPLAN-SIGACT Symposium on Principles of Programming Languages, POPL 2016, St. Petersburg, FL, USA, 20–22 January 2016. ACM (2016)
3. Bouajjani, A., Enea, C., Hamza, J.: Verifying eventual consistency of optimistic replication systems. In: Jagannathan and Sewell [10], pp. 285–296
4. Burckhardt, S., Gotsman, A., Yang, H.: Understanding eventual consistency. Technical report MSR-TR-2013-39, this document is work in progress. Feel free to cite, but note that we will update the contents without warning (the first page contains a timestamp), and that we are likely going to publish the content in some future venue, at which point we will update this paragraph, March 2013
5. Burckhardt, S., Gotsman, A., Yang, H., Zawirski, M.: Replicated data types: specification, verification, optimality. In: Jagannathan and Sewell [10], pp. 271–284
6. Gilbert, S., Lynch, N.A.: Brewer's conjecture and the feasibility of consistent, available, partition-tolerant web services. SIGACT News **33**(2), 51–59 (2002)
7. Gotsman, A., Yang, H.: Composite replicated data types. In: Vitek, J. (ed.) ESOP 2015. LNCS, vol. 9032, pp. 585–609. Springer, Heidelberg (2015)
8. Gotsman, A., Yang, H., Ferreira, C., Najafzadeh, M., Shapiro, M.: 'Cause I'm strong enough: reasoning about consistency choices in distributed systems. In: Bodik and Majumdar [2], pp. 371–384
9. Jackson, D.: Software Abstractions - Logic, Language, and Analysis. MIT Press, Cambridge (2006)
10. Jagannathan, S., Sewell, P. (eds.) The 41st Annual ACM SIGPLAN-SIGACT Symposium on Principles of Programming Languages, POPL 2014, San Diego, CA, USA, 20–21 January 2014. ACM (2014)
11. Lamport, L.: Specifying Systems, The TLA+ Language and Tools for Hardware and Software Engineers. Addison-Wesley, Reading (2002)
12. Lesani, M., Bell, C.J., Chlipala, A.: Chapar: certified causally consistent distributed key-value stores. In: Bodik and Majumdar [2], pp. 357–370
13. Nipkow, T., Paulson, L.C., Wenzel, M. (eds.): Isabelle/HOL. LNCS, vol. 2283. Springer, Heidelberg (2002)
14. Shapiro, M., Preguiça, N., Baquero, C., Zawirski, M.: A comprehensive study of convergent and commutative replicated data types. Rapport de recherche RR-7506, INRIA, January 2011
15. Zeller, P., Bieniusa, A., Poetzsch-Heffter, A.: Formal specification and verification of CRDTs. In: Ábrahám, E., Palamidessi, C. (eds.) FORTE 2014. LNCS, vol. 8461, pp. 33–48. Springer, Heidelberg (2014)

Interaction and Adaptation

A Cognitive Framework
Based on Rewriting Logic
for the Analysis of Interactive Systems

Antonio Cerone[(✉)]

IMT School for Advanced Studies, Lucca, Italy
antonio.cerone@imtlucca.it
http://sysma.imtlucca.it/people/antonio-cerone/

Abstract. Interactive systems may appear to work correctly and safely when analysed in isolation from the human environment in which they are supposed to work. In fact, the same cognitive skills that enable humans to perform complex tasks may also become the source of critical errors in the interaction with systems and devices designed as supports for such tasks. It is thus essential to verify the desired properties of an interactive system using a model that not only includes a user-centered description of the task, but also incorporates a representation of human cognitive processes within the task execution.

In this paper we consider automatic and deliberate cognitive processes in combination with the use of the Short Term Memory (STM), and provide a formal notation to model the set of basic tasks that a human component (user or operator) has to carry out to accomplish a goal by interacting with an interface. The semantics of the notation is given in terms of a cognitive framework that makes use of rules driven by the basic tasks to rewrite both the system state and the STM until all necessary tasks have been completed. Potential human errors are then detected using model checking. Our notation, which is implemented using the MAUDE rewrite system, and our formal verification methodology are finally illustrated by two case studies: a user of an Automatic Teller Machine (ATM) and an operator of an Air Traffic Control (ATC) system.

Keywords: Formal modelling and verification · Rewriting logic · Interactive systems · Model checking · MAUDE

1 Introduction

Interactive systems are characterised by a cooperative work between a *human component* and the *interface* of a system, which can be a computer system, a device, a control system, a transportation system, etc. The purpose of the cooperation is the accomplishment of a goal, which may be a specific objective to achieve, such as purchasing a product from a vending machine, or a correct state of the system to be preserved. In the former situation the human component

© Springer International Publishing Switzerland 2016
R. De Nicola and E. Kühn (Eds.): SEFM 2016, LNCS 9763, pp. 287–303, 2016.
DOI: 10.1007/978-3-319-41591-8_20

is the *user* of the system underlying the interface, in the latter the *operator*, through the interface, of a plant control (e.g. a nuclear plant) or a control service (e.g. traffic control).

The systematic analysis of human errors in interactive systems has its roots in Human Reliability Assessment (HRA) techniques [12], which mostly emerged in the 1980's. However, these first attempts in the safety assessment of interactive systems were typically based on *ad hoc* techniques [13], with no efforts to incorporate a representation of human cognitive processes within the model of the interaction. Although Mach already stated at the beginning of last century that "knowledge and error flow from the same mental sources, only success can tell the one from the other" [15], we had to wait until the 1990's to clearly understand that "correct performance and systematic errors are two sides of the same coin" [21]. At that time the increasing use of formal methods yielded more objective analysis techniques [9] that resulted, on the one hand, in the notion of *cognitively plausible user behaviour*, based on formal assumptions to bound the way users act driven by cognitive processes [1] and, on the other hand, in the formal description of expected effective operator behaviour [20] and the formal analysis of errors performed by the operator as reported by accident analysis [11]. Thus, research in the formal analysis of interactive systems branched into two separate directions: the analysis of cognitive errors of users involved in everyday-life [2] and work-related [18,22] interactive tasks, and the analysis of skilled operators behaviour in traditionally critical domains, such as transportation, chemical and nuclear plants, health and defence [3,4,7,17,23]. The different interaction contexts of a user, who applies attention very selectively and acts mainly under automatic control [2,19], and an operator, who deals with high cognitive load and whose attentional mechanisms risk to be overloaded due to coping with Stimulus Rich Reactive Interfaces (SRRIs) [23], have led to the development of distinct approaches, keeping separate these two research directions. However, users have sometimes to deal with decision points or unexpected situations, which require a "reactivation" of their attentional mechanisms, and operators must sometime resort to automatisms to reduce attentional and cognitive loads.

In this paper, we try to unify these two research directions by providing a general framework to reconcile automatic control with attentional and cognitive loads. Section 2 adopts the information processing approach in explaining human behaviour and defines a framework, together with a formal notation, to describe the cognitive processes underlying human behaviour and the way they exploit human memory. Section 3 provides the semantics of our notation in terms of a rewriting system model (Sect. 3.1) and briefly presents its implementation and use (Sect. 3.2). Section 4 illustrates the generality of our cognitive framework on two case studies: a user of an Automatic Teller Machine (ATM), and an operator of an Air Traffic Control (ATC) system. Both case studies had been previously modelled [2–4] using the CSP (Communicating Sequential Processes) process algebra [10]. While in such previous work two distinct *ad hoc* frameworks had been developed to model a user [2] and an operator [3,4], in this paper we unify the two contexts within the same formal framework, which is based on rewriting logic [16] and is implemented within the MAUDE rewrite system [5].

2   Modelling Cognitive Processes

Following the *information processing* approach normally used in cognitive psychology, we model human cognitive processes as processing activities that make use of input-output channels, to interact with the external environment, and three main kinds of memory, to store information: *sensory memory*, where information perceived through the senses persists for a very short time; *short-term memory (STM)*, which has a limited capacity and where the information that is needed for processing activities is temporary stored with rapid access and rapid decay; *long-term memory (LTM)*, which has a virtually unlimited capacity and where information is organised in structured ways, with slow access but little or no decay [8].

2.1   Input as Perceptions and Output as Actions

Input and output occur in humans through senses. In our work we give a general representation of input channels in term of *perceptions*, with little or no details about the specific senses involved in the perception, but with a strong emphasis on the semantics of the perception in terms of its potential cognitive effects. For instance, if the user of a vending machine perceives that the requested product has been delivered, the emphasis is on the fact that the user will be induced to collect the product and not on whether the user has seen or rather heard the product coming out of the machine.

We represent output channels in term of *actions*. Actions are performed in response to perceptions. We are interested in the urgency to react created by the perception: for example, if we are withdrawing cash, we need to collect the delivered cash before the machine takes it back. Analogously, if an operator perceives an anomalous system behaviour, in general we are not interested in whether such perception occurs through sight, hearing, or even by touching a hot component or through a burning smell; instead, we are interested in the action that the operator has to carry out to solve the problem and in the urgency of such an action.

2.2   Attention and Processing Control

Perceptions are briefly stored in the sensory memory and only relevant perceptions are transfered to the STM using *attention*, a selective processing activity that aims to focus on one aspect of the environment while ignoring others. Inspired by Norman and Shallice [19], we consider two levels of cognitive control:

automatic control fast processing activity that does not require attention to occur and is carried out outside awareness with no conscious effort;

deliberate control processing activity triggered and focussed by attention and carried out under the intentional control of the individual, who is aware and conscious of the required effort.

For example, automatic control is essential in driving a car and, in such a context, it develops throughout a learning process based on deliberate control: during the learning process the driver has to make a conscious effort to use gear, indicators, etc. in the right way (deliberate control) and would not be able to do this while talking or listening to the radio. Once automaticity in driving is acquired, the driver is aware of the high-level tasks that are carried out, such as driving to office, turning to the right and waiting at a traffic light, but is not aware of low-level details such as changing gear, using the indicator and the colour of the light, amber or red, while stopping at a traffic light (automatic control).

2.3   Tasks and Short-Term Memory (STM)

The purpose of an interaction between a human and an interface is to allow the human to accomplish a goal. In Sect. 2.2 we have referred to high-level and low-level tasks. The goal is associated with the top-level task. For both users and operators the top-level task can be decomposed in a hierarchy of tasks until reaching basic tasks, which cannot be further decomposed. A difference between the user and operator cases is that the user's goal is normally associated with the basic task that accomplishes it, whereas there is no such basic task in the operator case.

We model a basic task as a quadruple

$$info_i \uparrow perc_h \Longrightarrow act_h \downarrow info_j$$

where perception $perc_h$ triggers the retrieval of information $info_i$ from the STM, the execution of action act_h and the storage of information $info_j$ in the STM.

Information is kept promptly available, while it is needed to perform the current top-level task, by storing it in the STM. Several kinds of information may be stored in the STM: the goal of the interaction (which we identify with the top-level task), a partial result of a calculation, a piece of information retrieved from the LTM, a perception transferred from the sensory memory through the attention mechanism, a reference to a future action to be performed, the current state of the ongoing reasoning process or plan currently carried out. For the purpose of our work we consider only three kinds of information that can be stored in the STM:

task goal represented as the action that leads to the direct achievement of the goal (user), or as the action that contributes to preserve the correct system state or a placeholder if such an action cannot be identified (operator);
action reference which refers to a future action to be performed;
cognitive state that is the state of the plan developed by the user/operator.

A task goal is formally modelled as

$$goal(act, type)$$

where *act* is the action that either leads to the direct achievement of the goal, if *type* = *achieve*, or contributes to preserve the correct system state, if *type* = *preserve* (in this case the action may be left unspecified).

We formally denote by *none* when an entity (information, perception, action) of a task or the action of a task goal is absent or left unspecified (*none* is a placeholder in the latter case). When *none* is used as information it denotes the absence of action reference.

We model the two levels of control considered in Sect. 2.2 as three categories of basic tasks:

automatic task triggered by a perception, or an information in the STM;
cognitive task triggered by a cognitive state;
decision task triggered by a task goal in the STM.

An automatic tasks must include an action, but may not include a perception or may not use the STM (thus it may have one or both information fields empty). A cognitive task must always have the two information fields to contain the current cognitive state to retrieve from STM and the next cognitive state to store in the STM, but it has neither perception nor action. A decision task must include a perception and store in the STM a reference to an action that is related to the task goal contained in the retrieval information field, with the perception triggering the retrieval of the task goal; for instance, if the first part of the driving route to our workplace is in common with the driving route to our favourite supermarket and our goal is driving to work, the perception of approaching the branching point will trigger the storage of a reference to the action related to the goal (i.e. taking the road to drive to work) in the STM.

Automatic tasks are performed under automatic control, whereas cognitive and decision tasks are performed under deliberate control. Normally, a user works mainly under automatic control [19], with most of the performed tasks being automatic tasks, whereas an operator works mainly under deliberate control [21], with most of the performed tasks being cognitive tasks.

2.4   Interface

In our context a user perception refers to a stimulus produced by an action of the interface with which the human is interacting. Hence we identify an interface state created by an interface action with the perception such an action produces in humans. For example, the interface state created by the action of giving change, performed by the interface of a vending machine, is identified with the perception (sound of falling coins or sight of the coins) produced. Thus, in our notation, interface state and corresponding human perception are denoted by the same formal entity (which, assuming the user's perspective, we call "perception").

In Sect. 2.1 we anticipated that perceptions may induce different degrees of urgency in reacting. Since we identify a perception with the interface state caused by the interface action that produced that perception, the urgency of a perception can be modelled by associating a timeout with such an interface state (hence with the perception itself). For example the urgency of the user of a cash machine in collecting the delivered cash is associated with the machine timeout for taking back the cash. In order to use perceptions as interface states, possibly with timeouts, to define interface transitions, we decorate a perception *perc* as follows.

perc!0 state that produces a perception inducing no urgency in reacting and is not associated with a timeout;

perc!1 state that produces a perception inducing urgency and is associated with a timeout that is not expired;

perc!2 state that produces a perception inducing urgency and is associated with a timeout that has already expired.

By interpreting perceptions in terms of the interface states that caused them, we model an interface transition as a triple

$$perc_h!m \xrightarrow{act_h} perc_k!n$$

where interface state $perc_h$, with possible timeout characterised by m, triggers the execution of action act_h with a transition of the interface to state $perc_k$, whose possible timeout is characterised by n. An action $act \neq none$ is, therefore, performed through a cooperation between human and interface and thus belongs to both a task and an interface transition and represents the basic form of interaction. An action $act = none$ is denoted by an unlabelled arrow. The initial state of the interface is normally an idling state (the interface is available for an interaction), thus it is not associated with a timeout (*perc*!0). In our formal representation we keep track of the action act that produced the state *perc* by defining an interface state as a pair $act \gg perc!m$. The initial state becomes then $none \gg perc!0$. We will exploit this redundant notation in Sect. 3.1.

2.5   Closure and Post-completion Error

An important phenomenon that occurs in automatic behaviour is *closure* [8]. When the goal of a task has been achieved there is a tendency to flush out the STM to be ready to start a new task. This may cause the removal from the STM of some important subtasks that are still not completed and result in some form of failure of the main task, called *post-completion error*. Undesired closure most commonly occurs when the main goal of the task is achieved before completing some subsidiary tasks, due to the task sequentialisation forced by the interface. A classical example is provided by an ATM that delivers cash before returning the card. Since the user's main goal is to get cash, once the cash is collected, the STM is flushed out and the user may terminate the task, thus forgetting the card in the ATM. That is why modern ATMs return the card before delivering cash. Closure has been formally modelled in previous works using Higher Order Logic (HOL) [6] and the CSP process algebras [2].

2.6   Long-Term Memory (LTM) and Supevisory Attentional System

LTM is used for long-term storage of "factual information, experiential knowledge, procedural rules of behaviour — in fact, everything that we know" [8]. Information may be transferred from the STM to the LTM through *rehearsal*, the well-known recycling mechanism functionally equivalent to the idea of repeating things to yourself.

In our cognitive framework, we do not consider transfer of information from STM to LTM. In fact, we assume that the LTM already contains procedural rules of behaviour, such as the basic tasks (automatic, cognitive and decision tasks) introduced in Sect. 2.3. Moreover, during automatic control, experiential knowledge already stored in the LTM may be used to solve situations in which automatic tasks result inappropriate. Norman and Shallice [19] propose the existence of a *Supervisory Attentional System* (SAS), sometimes also called *Supervisory Activating System*, which becomes active whenever none of the automatic tasks are appropriate. The activation of the SAS is triggered by perceptions that are assessed as danger, novelty, requiring decision or the source of strong feelings such as temptation and anger.

We formalise such an assessment as a function $assess(act, perc)$, where $perc$ is the perception that triggered the SAS activation and act is the last interaction before that perception. The function returns one of the following values: *danger*, *decision*, *novelty*, *anger* and *auto*. For example, if we start overtaking a car (act) and we hear honking from behind ($perc$) the assessment will be $assess(act, perc) = danger$. Normally the automatic response to a danger is to abandon the ongoing task without accomplishing the goal, in our example the overtaking task/goal. Responses to novelties (*novelty*) and feelings (e.g. *anger*) vary from individual to individual and cannot be captured by our framework. Response to requiring decision (*decision*) are driven by a specific basic task of the model. Value *auto* denotes that the SAS is not activated.

Therefore, the assessment function is a way of formalising experiential knowledge that has been stored in the LTM, in our example the experience that honking is a warning of danger.

3   Rewriting System Model and Analysis

3.1   Rewrite Rules

Let Π be a set of perceptions, Σ be a set of actions, Γ be a set of action references and Δ a set of cognitive states, with $\Gamma \cap \Delta = \emptyset$. We model our cognitive framework on Π, Σ, Γ and Δ as a rewrite system consisting of four sets of objects

$\mathcal{T}$ a set of basic tasks;
$\mathcal{I}$ a set of interface transitions;
$\mathcal{C}$ a singleton containing the current interface state and its causal action;
$\mathcal{M}$ the set of entities in the STM;

and a set $\mathcal{R}$ of rewriting rules

$$\mathcal{T} \, \mathcal{I} \, \mathcal{C} \, \mathcal{M} \overset{\text{rewrite}}{\Longrightarrow} \mathcal{T} \, \mathcal{I} \, \mathcal{C}' \mathcal{M}'$$

that are defined as follows:

interacting: if $info_i \uparrow perc_h \Longrightarrow act_h \downarrow info_j \in \mathcal{T}$, with $act_h \neq none$

and $\mathcal{C} = \{act \gg perc_h!m\}$ and $perc_h!m \overset{act_h}{\longrightarrow} perc_k!n \in \mathcal{I}$, with $m < 2$,
and $info_i \in \mathcal{M}$ and there exists a goal in $\mathcal{M}$
then $\mathcal{C}' = \{act_h \gg perc_k!n\}$
and $\mathcal{M}' = \mathcal{M} - \{info_i\} \cup \{info_j\}$

closure: if $info_i \uparrow perc_h \Longrightarrow act_h \downarrow info_j \in \mathcal{T}$, with $act_h \neq none$

and $\mathcal{C} = \{act \gg perc_h!m\}$ and $perc_h!m \overset{act_h}{\longrightarrow} perc_k!n \in \mathcal{I}$ and $m < 2$
and $goal(act_h, achieve), info_i \in \mathcal{M}$
then $\mathcal{C}' = \{act_h \gg perc_k!n\}$
and $\mathcal{M}' = \{info_j\}$

danger: if $info_i \uparrow perc_h \Longrightarrow act_h \downarrow info_j \in \mathcal{T}$, with $act_h \neq none$

and $\mathcal{C} = \{act \gg perc_h!m\}$ and $perc_h!m \overset{act_h}{\longrightarrow} perc_k!n \in \mathcal{I}$ and $m < 2$
and $info_i \in \mathcal{M}$
and $assess(act, perc_h) = danger$
then $\mathcal{C}' = \{act_h \gg perc_k!expired(n)\}$ where

$$expired(n) = \begin{cases} 2 & \text{if } n = 1 \\ n & \text{otherwise} \end{cases}$$

and $\mathcal{M}' = \{info_j\}$

timeout: if $\mathcal{C} = \{act \gg perc_h!m\}$ and $perc_h!m \longrightarrow perc_k!n \in \mathcal{I}$ and $m > 1$
then $\mathcal{C}' = \{none \gg perc_k!n\}$
and $\mathcal{M}' = \mathcal{M}$

cognitive: if $info_i \uparrow perc_h \Longrightarrow none \downarrow info_j \in \mathcal{T}$
and $info_i \in \mathcal{M} \cap \Delta$ and $info_j \in \Delta$
then $\mathcal{C}' = \mathcal{C}$
and $\mathcal{M}' = \mathcal{M} - \{info_{\rangle}\} \cup \{info_{|}\}$

decision: if $info_i \uparrow perc_h \Longrightarrow none \downarrow info_j \in \mathcal{T}$
and $info_i \in \mathcal{M}$ is a goal
and $assess(none, perc_h) = decision$
then $\mathcal{C}' = \mathcal{C}$
and $\mathcal{M}' = \mathcal{M} \cup \{info_{|}\}$

Automatic tasks enable the application of rules **interacting, closure** and **danger**, which involve an interaction between user and interface ($act_h \neq none$). Cognitive and decision tasks enable the application of rules **cognitive** and **decision**, respectively, which operate on the STM only, without involving any interaction with the interface ($act_h = none$) and with no change to the interface state ($\mathcal{C}' = \mathcal{C}$). Rule **timeout** refers to an autonomous action of the interface, with no involvement of the human component (there is no basic task involved).

The **interacting** rule is applied if there is a perception $perc_h$ in the current state $\mathcal{C}$ and/or information $info_i$ in the STM $\mathcal{M}$ that are associated in a task of $\mathcal{T}$ with the execution of action act_h, there is a goal in the STM $\mathcal{M}$ and there is no expired timeout ($m < 2$) associated with the interface state $perc_h!m$ that has generated perception $perc_h$. The next state $\mathcal{C}'$ of the interface is $perc_k!n$, which results by executing action act_h, and the next STM $\mathcal{M}'$ is obtained by removing information $info_i$ and storing information $info_j$.

The **closure** rule is very similar to the interacting rule, but now the goal in the STM $\mathcal{M}$ must be of type *achievement* ($goal(act_h, achieve)$) and the execution of action act_h results in emptying the STM before storing information $info_j$.

The **danger** rule is applied if the current perception $perc_h$ that follows the execution of action act is assessed as a danger ($assess(act, perc_h) = danger$). The user performs action act_h. Moreover, since, as we have seen in Sect. 2.6, the user's normal response to a danger is to abandon the task, if there is a timeout associated with the current state ($perc_k!1$), then the next state is $perc_k!2$, which is the current state now associated with an expired timeout (since $expired(1) = 2$), otherwise it is $perc_k!n$ (since $expired(n) = n$ for $n \neq 1$). The next STM $\mathcal{M}'$ is obtained by removing all information and storing information $info_j$, as it happens for the closure. The need for this rule to assess a perception with respect to the action that has caused it explains why, in Sect. 2.4, we have kept track, in the formal notation of an interface state, of the action that produced that state.

The **timeout** rule is triggered by the expiration of the timeout ($m > 1$) and leads through the autonomous action act_h to the new interface state $perc_k!n$.

The **cognitive** rule refers to a cognitive process of the human, with cognitive state $info_i$ retrieved from and cognitive state stored in the STM.

Finally, the **decision** rule differs from the cognitive rule because the retrieved information is a goal, which is then stored again in the STM, and because of the presence of the assessment as a precondition. It models the SAS-induced switch from automatic control to deliberate control due to a required decision.

3.2   Implementation and Analysis with MAUDE

The MAUDE implementation, which can be downloaded at

http://sysma.imtlucca.it/cognitive-framework-sefm-2016/,

consists of the following generic modules

entities which defines the basic sorts that model perceptions, actions, and information that can be stored in the STM;

cognitive architecture which defines the structures of tasks, STM, LTM, and interfaces (including the current interface state) and the MAUDE rewrite rules that work on such structures;

and the following modules that are specific to the case study under analysis

tasks which defines the basic tasks and the goals of the case study;
interfaces which includes the different interfaces to be analysed;
LTM information such as the assessment function introduced in Sect. 2.6.

Simulation is performed by running the rewrite commands available in MAUDE.

Model-checking analysis requires the use of the **model-checker** predefined
MAUDE module and the definition of two further modules that are specific to
the case study:

preds which defines predicates on perceptions, actions and STM information;
check which includes properties to be verified and runs the model checker.

We define the truth value of predicates on an entity e as follows:

$$\mathcal{P}_x(e) = \begin{cases} true & \text{if } x = cogn \text{ and } e \in \mathcal{M} \\ & \text{or } x = act \text{ and there exist } p, m \text{ such that } e \gg p!m \in \mathcal{C} \\ & \text{or } x = perc \text{ and there exist } a, m \text{ such that } a \gg e!m \in \mathcal{C} \\ false & \text{otherwise} \end{cases}$$

The **preds** module implements predicates $\mathcal{P}_{cogn}(e)$, $\mathcal{P}_{act}(e)$ and $\mathcal{P}_{perc}(e)$.

4   Case Studies

In this section our cognitive framework is illustrated through two case studies by
effectively using it in two distinct ways: to formally verify properties of interfaces
in the context of human usage and compare different interface designs (Sect. 4.1);
and to analyse the operator's behaviour by formally checking whether a given
decomposition of the operator's task failure is sound and complete (Sect. 4.2).
These two case studies were presented in our previous work [2,3] using two
independent *ad hoc* approaches, both based on the CSP process algebra.

4.1   Automatic Teller Machine (ATM) User

Let be $\Pi = \{cardR, pinR, cashO, cardO\}$, $\Sigma = \{cardI, pinI, cashC, cardC\}$,
$\Gamma = \{cardB\}$ and $\Delta = \emptyset$. A simple ATM task, in which the user has only the
goal to withdraw cash, is modelled by the following four basic tasks:

$none \uparrow cardR \Longrightarrow cardI \downarrow cardB$
  When the interface is perceived ready $(cardR)$, the user inserts the card
  $(cardI)$ and remembers (in the STM) that the card has to be taken back
  $(cardB)$ at a later stage;
$none \uparrow pinR \Longrightarrow pinI \downarrow none$
  When the interface is perceived to request a pin $(pinR)$, the user inputs the
  pin $(pinI)$;
$none \uparrow cashO \Longrightarrow cashC \downarrow none$
  When perceiving that the cash has been delivered $(cashO)$, the user collects
  the cash $(cashC)$;

$cardB \uparrow cardO \Longrightarrow cardC \downarrow none$

When perceiving that the card has been returned ($cardO$), the user collects the card ($cardC$) and no longer needs to remember to collect it ($cardB$);

The goal ("to withdraw cash") is identified with the act of collecting cash (action $cashC$) and is formally modelled as $goal(cashC, achieve)$.

We model an old interface that sequentially requests a card, requests a pin, delivers the cash and returns the card, and a new interface that returns the card before delivering the cash. The two interface models are as follows.

Old ATM: transitions	New ATM: transitions
1. $cardR!0 \xrightarrow{cardI} pinR!1$	1. $cardR!0 \xrightarrow{cardI} pinR!1$
2. $pinR!1 \xrightarrow{pinI} cashO!1$	2. $pinR!1 \xrightarrow{pinI} cardO!1$
3. $cashO!1 \xrightarrow{cashC} cardO!1$	3. $cardO!1 \xrightarrow{cardC} cashO!1$
4. $cardO!1 \xrightarrow{cardC} cardR!0$	4. $cashO!1 \xrightarrow{cashC} cardR!0$
5. $pinR!2 \longrightarrow cardO!1$	5. $pinR!2 \longrightarrow cardO!1$
6. $cashO!2 \longrightarrow cardO!1$	6. $cashO!2 \longrightarrow cardR!0$
7. $cardO!2 \longrightarrow cardR!0$	7. $cardO!2 \longrightarrow cardR!0$

For both interfaces the initial state is $none \gg cardR!0$.

In both interfaces, transitions 1–4 model the normal sequences of interactions for the specific design (old or new). The last three transitions model interface autonomous actions. In both interfaces, if the timeout expires after requesting a pin, then the card is returned (transitions 5). If the timeout expires after delivering the cash (transitions 6), then in the old ATM the card is returned, whereas in the new ATM the control goes back to the initial state, so inhibiting a cash collection action and, as a result, implicitly modelling that the cash is taken back by the ATM. Finally, in both interfaces, if the timeout expires after returning the card, then the control goes back to the initial state, so inhibiting a card collection action and, as a result, implicitly modelling that the card is confiscated (transitions 7).

We model the user experience for the two ATM designs as follows.

Old ATM: user experience	New ATM: user experience
1. $assess(cardI, pinR) = auto$	1. $assess(cardI, pinR) = auto$
2. $assess(pinI, cashO) = auto$	2. $assess(pinI, cardO) = auto$
3. $assess(cashC, cardO) = auto$	3. $assess(cardC, cashO) = auto$
4. $assess(cardC, cardR) = auto$	4. $assess(cashC, cardR) = auto$
5. $assess(pinI, cardO) = danger$	5. $assess(cardC, cardR) = anger$
6. $assess(pinI, cardR) = anger$	6. $assess(act, perc) = novelty,$
7. $assess(act, perc) = novelty,$	otherwise
otherwise	

In both experiences the value of the assessment is $auto$ when the sequence of action and perception is the same as in the experienced interface (assessments 1–4, corresponding to the tasks 1–4 above). A user who has experience with the old ATM design could interpret: the perception that the card is returned after having input the pin as if the pin were incorrect and there were a danger for the card to be confiscated at one of the next attempts (5. $assess(pinI, cardO) = danger$); the perception that the ATM goes back to the initial card request without returning the card after having input the pin as if the card were confiscated (6. $assess(pinI, cardR) = anger$); and any other sequence of action and perception as a novelty. A user who has experience with the new ATM design could interpret: the perception that the ATM goes back to the initial card request after returning the card without delivering cash as a sign that cash cannot be withdrawn, e.g. because the ATM is out of cash (5. $assess(cardC, cardR) = anger$); and any other sequence of action and perception as a novelty.

We want to verify, for each interface design, whether there are cognitive errors that may prevent the user from collecting the card and from collecting the cash. The properties that the user is always able to collect a returned card (property AlwaysCardBack) and is always able to collect the delivered cash (property AlwaysCashGot) are specified as follows:

$$\text{AlwaysCardBack} = \Box(\mathcal{P}_{perc}(cardO) \rightarrow (\neg\mathcal{P}_{perc}(cardR) \; \mathcal{U} \; \mathcal{P}_{act}(cardC)))$$
$$\text{AlwaysCashGot} = \Box(\mathcal{P}_{perc}(cashO) \rightarrow (\neg\mathcal{P}_{perc}(cardR) \; \mathcal{U} \; \mathcal{P}_{act}(cashC)))$$

The model checking analysis shows that AlwaysCardBack is true with the new ATM and not with the old ATM, independently of the user experience, while AlwaysCashGot is false only with the new ATM and a user experienced with the old ATM. Property AlwaysCardBack detects possible post-completion errors in using the old design of the ATM and shows that such errors cannot occur in the new design of the ATM. Property AlwaysCashGot detects the possibility of missing the collection of delivered cash. Although the new design of the ATM works in an ideal world where all ATMs are designed according to the new criterion, there are countries, in the developing world, where ATMs are still designed according to the old criterion. Thus we can imagine that a user from one of such countries, while visiting a country where all ATMs are designed according to the new criterion, is likely to assess the early return of the card as a danger and is prone to abandon the interaction forgetting to collect the cash (falsifying AlwaysCashGot).

4.2   Air Traffic Control (ATC) Operator

The goal of an ATC task is to avoid that the distance between aircraft goes below a minimum prescribed distance. If this happens, we say that the aircraft violate separation. The ATC operator has to monitor the local air traffic situation and execute communication actions to urge aircraft to change speed, altitude and/or direction in order to avoid separation violation. Aircraft whose trajectories are leading to separation violation are called "in conflict".

We consider a purely cognitive task, which models the cognitive processes of the operator after having perceived the state of the system, independently of whether such a perception is correct or erroneous. Thus basic tasks will have no perceptions. Let be $\Pi = \emptyset$ $\Sigma = \{act\}$, $\Gamma = \emptyset$ and $\Delta =$

$\{scan, part, con, non\ decide, reclassify, intend\}$. Following the Operator Choice Model (OCM), defined by Lindsay and Connelly [14], we decompose the ATC task into a number of basic tasks that the operator has to perform:

$scan \uparrow none \Longrightarrow none \downarrow part$
   The operator scans the interface ($scan$) until finding a part where there are aircraft that may violate separation ($part$).
$part \uparrow none \Longrightarrow none \downarrow con$
   In the part of the interface under analysis ($part$) the operator identifies aircraft that are in conflict (con).
$part \uparrow none \Longrightarrow none \downarrow non$
   In the part of the interface under analysis ($part$) the operator does not identify aircraft that are in conflict (non).
$con \uparrow none \Longrightarrow none \downarrow scan$
   If the conflict (con) does not require urgent action, the operator goes back to scan the interface ($scan$), looking for more urgent conflicts.
$non \uparrow none \Longrightarrow none \downarrow scan$
   If no conflict has been identified (non) in the part under analysis, the operator goes back to scan the interface ($scan$).
$con \uparrow none \Longrightarrow none \downarrow decide$
   The operator develops a plan ($decide$) to solve the conflict under investigation (con).
$con \uparrow none \Longrightarrow none \downarrow reclassify$
   The operator reclassifies ($reclassify$) a conflict (con) under investigation as a non conflict.
$reclassify \uparrow none \Longrightarrow none \downarrow scan$
   After reclassifying ($reclassify$), the operator goes back to scan the interface ($scan$).
$decide \uparrow none \Longrightarrow none \downarrow scan$
   After developing a plan to solve a conflict ($decide$), the operator goes back to scan the interface ($scan$), looking for other conflicts.
$decide \uparrow none \Longrightarrow none \downarrow intend$
   After developing a plan to solve a conflict ($decide$), the operator intends to carry out a specific action to solve the conflict ($intend$).
$intend \uparrow none \Longrightarrow act \downarrow scan$
   The operator implements the intention ($intend$) by performing an action (act) and then goes back to scan the interface ($scan$).

The goal ("to prevent separation violation") is expressed simply as the preservation of the state by performing actions (act models a generic action) and is formally modelled as $goal(act, preserve)$. Note that only the last basic task is an automatic task; all other tasks are cognitive tasks. Once the intention is established, the cognitive process terminates and the execution of the action is a purely automatic activity triggered by the intention.

   In this case study we focus on the cognitive aspects of the ATC operator rather than on the specific aspects of the interface that may induce the operator's errors. Many cognitive errors may occur in the execution of the tasks above independently of the characteristics of the interface that presents the air traffic situation to the operator. Our aim is the analysis of a set of task failures that have been identified by psychologists through the observation of operators while using an ATC simulator [3,4,14], in order to find out if such a set is a sound and complete decomposition of the top-level ATC task failure, that is the occurrence of separation violation. As in our previous work [3,4], we use temporal logic to formalise the task failures and model checking to verify the soundness and completeness of the decomposition. However, in that previous work, the OCM and a "toy environment" consisting of three aircrafts were formalised using the CSP process algebra, and the results could not be generalised to any environment. Here, instead, we use our cognitive framework to formalise the OCM as a list of basic tasks, as shown above, and we model the environment as the following trivial interface consisting of just one transition, which is independent of the number of aircrafts involved and the number of conflicts between them.

1. $none!0 \xrightarrow{act} none!0$

The initial state is obviously $none \gg none!0$. In this case study there is no information on previous experience. Hence, there is no need to introduce an assessment function.

We can characterise a separation violation as an operator who persistently misses the intention to carry out a specific action to solve the conflict [3,4]. Hence the top-level task failure is formalised as $\Box\neg\mathcal{P}_{cogn}(intend)$. We distinguish between intention (intend) and action (act) to be able to model an unintended action that does not match the intention [21]. Although this is not part of our analysis, such a mismatch would be relevant in the analysis of errors induced by a specific interface design, which could be carried out on this case study by introducing alternative interface designs and using our formal cognitive framework as in the ATM case study.

The formalisation of the ATC task failure decomposition suggested by Lindsay and Connelly [14] is

$$\mathcal{D} = \{\text{FailureOfScanning, PerMisClass, PerMisPrior, DeferAction}\}$$

where

FailureOfScanning $= \Box\neg\mathcal{P}_{cogn}(part)$
PerMisClass $= \Diamond\mathcal{P}_{cogn}(part) \land \Box(\mathcal{P}_{cogn}(part) \lor \mathcal{P}_{cogn}(con) \rightarrow \bigcirc\mathcal{P}_{cogn}(non))$
PerMisPrior $= \Diamond\mathcal{P}_{cogn}(con) \land \Box(\mathcal{P}_{cogn}(con) \rightarrow \bigcirc\mathcal{P}_{cogn}(scan))$
DeferAction $= \Diamond\mathcal{P}_{cogn}(decide)) \land \Box(\mathcal{P}_{cogn}(decide) \rightarrow \bigcirc\mathcal{P}_{cogn}(scan))$

Failure of scanning (FailureOfScanning) occurs when the operator fails to monitor a specific part of the interface, thus missing possible conflicts. *Persistent mis-classification* (PerMisClass) occurs when the operator persistently classifies as a non conflict what is actually a conflict. *Persistent mis-prioritisation* (PerMisPrior) occurs when the operator persistently gives a low priority to a conflict, thus missing to solve it. *Defer action for too long* (DeferAction) occurs when the operator persistently delays to implement an already developed plan to solve a conflict. Note that the "eventually" part in the last three formulae guarantees that the task failures are not overlapping.

The soundness of the decomposition is expressed by model-checking formula

$$\bigwedge_{F \in \mathcal{D}} (F \rightarrow \Box \neg \mathcal{P}_{cogn}(intend))$$

The completeness of the decomposition is expressed by model-checking formula

$$(\Box \neg \mathcal{P}_{cogn}(intend)) \rightarrow \bigvee_{F \in \mathcal{D}} F$$

Model checking analysis using MAUDE shows that decomposition $\mathcal{D}$ is sound but not complete. However, if we redefine PersMisClass as

$$\text{PersMisClass'} = \Diamond \mathcal{P}_{cogn}(part)) \wedge \Box(\mathcal{P}_{cogn}(part) \rightarrow \bigcirc \mathcal{P}_{cogn}(non))$$

and we define

$$\text{ConDecPro} = \Diamond \mathcal{P}_{cogn}(reclassify) \wedge$$
$$\Box(\mathcal{P}_{cogn}(con) \rightarrow \bigcirc(\mathcal{P}_{cogn}(scan) \vee \mathcal{P}_{cogn}(reclassify))$$

then model checking analysis using MAUDE shows that decomposition

$$\mathcal{D}' = \{\text{FailureOfScanning, PerMisClass', PerMisPrior, ConDecPro, DeferAction}\}$$

is sound and complete.

Contrary decision process (ConDecPro) new task failure occurs when a conflict is persistently reclassified as a non conflict. Details on the psychological interpretation of all task failures can be found in our previous work [3].

5   Conclusion

We have presented a cognitive framework for the formal analysis of the interaction between humans and interfaces both in the case of a user, who acts mainly under automatic control using selective attention, and in the case of an operator, who deals with high cognitive and attentional load. The ATC case study presented in Sect. 4.2 illustrates how cognitive processes carried out under deliberate control result in automatic activities performed under automatic control.

This is a major generalisation with respect to our two previous CSP works. In fact, in one work [2] the user model captured automatic control with attentional mechanisms limited to automatic responses to unexpected events but not sensitive to decisional clues that trigger responses carried out under deliberate control (decisions); in the other work [3,4] the operator model expressed deliberate control with no capability to formalise perceptions, which are instead fundamental in the SRRIs used in plant and traffic control, and was *ad hoc* for an ATC task in a fixed "toy environment".

References

1. Butterworth, R., Blandford, A.E., Duke, D.: Demonstrating the cognitive plausability of interactive systems. Formal Aspects Comput. **12**, 237–259 (2000)
2. Cerone, A.: Closure and attention activation in human automatic behaviour: a framework for the formal analysis of interactive systems. In Proceedings of FMIS 2011. Electronic Communications of the EASST, vol. 45 (2011)
3. Cerone, A., Connelly, S., Lindsay, P.: Formal analysis of human operator behavioural patterns in interactive surveillance systems. Softw. Syst. Model. **7**(3), 273–286 (2008)
4. Cerone, A., Lindsay, P., Connelly, S.: Formal analysis of human-computer interaction using model-checking. In: Proceedings of SEFM 2005, pp. 352–361. IEEE (2005)
5. Clavel, M., Durán, F., Eker, S., Lincoln, P., Martí-Oliet, N., Meseguer, J., Talcott, C.: The maude 2.0 system. In: Nieuwenhuis, R. (ed.) RTA 2003. LNCS, vol. 2706, pp. 76–87. Springer, Heidelberg (2003)
6. Curzon, P., Blandford, A.: Formally justifying user-centred design rules: a case study on post-completion errors. In: Boiten, E.A., Derrick, J., Smith, G.P. (eds.) IFM 2004. LNCS, vol. 2999, pp. 461–480. Springer, Heidelberg (2004)
7. De Oliveira, R.A.: Formal specification and verification of interactive systems with plasticity : applications to nuclear-plant supervision. Ph.D. thesis, University of Grenoble (2015)
8. Dix, A., Finlay, J., Abowd, G., Beale, R.: Human-Computer Interaction. Pearson Education, Englewood Cliffs (1998)
9. Dix, A.J.: Formal Methods for Interactive Systems. Academic Press, Cambridge (1991)
10. Hoare, C.: Communicating Sequential Processes. International Series in Computer Science. Prentice Hall, Upper Saddle River (1985)
11. Johnson, C.: Reasoning about human error and system failure for accident analysis. In: Howard, S., Hammond, J., Lindgaard, G. (eds.) INTERACT 1997. IFIP, pp. 331–338. Chapman and Hall, London (1997)
12. Kirwan, B.: Human reliability assessment (chap. 28). In: Evaluation of Human Work. Taylor and Francis, London (1990)
13. Leveson, N.G.: Safeware: System Safety and Computers. Addison-Wesley, Boston (1995)
14. Lindsay, P., Connelly, S.: Modelling erroneous operator behaviours for an air-traffic control task. In: Proceedings of AUIC 2002. Conferences in Research and Practice in Information Technology, vol. 7, pp. 43–54. Australian Computer Society (2002)
15. Mach, C.: Knowledge and Error. Reidel (1905). English Translation (1976)
16. Martí-Oliet, N., Meseguer, J.: Rewriting logic: roadmap and bibliography. Theoret. Comput. Sci. **285**(2), 121–154 (2002)
17. Martinie, C., Palanque, P., Fahssi, R., Blanquart, J.P., Fayollas, C., Seguin, C.: Task model-based systematic analysis of both system failures and human errors. IEEE Trans. Human-Mach. Syst. **46**(2), 243–254 (2016)
18. Masci, P., Rukšėnas, R., Oladimeji, P., Cauchi, A., Gimblett, A., Li, Y., Curzon, P., Thimbleby, H.: The benefits of formalising design guidelines: a case study on the predictability of drug infusion pumps. Innovations Syst. Softw. Eng. **11**(2), 73–93 (2015)
19. Norman, D.A., Shallice, T.: Attention to action: willed and automatic control of behaviour. In: Consciousness and Self-Regulation. Advances in Research and Theory, vol. 4. Plenum Press (1986)

20. Palanque, P., Bastide, R., Paterno, F.: Formal specification as a tool for objective assessment of safety-critical interactive systems. In: Howard, S., Hammond, J., Lindgaard, G. (eds.) INTERACT 1997. IFIP, pp. 323–330. Chapman and Hall, London (1997)

21. Reason, J.: Human Error. Cambridge University Press, Cambridge (1990)

22. Rukšėnas, R., Curzon, P., Blandford, A.E., Back, J.: Combining human error verification and timing analysis: a case study on an infusion pump. Formal Aspects Comput. **26**, 1033–1076 (2014)

23. Su, L., Bowman, H., Barnard, P., Wyble, B.: Process algebraic model of attentional capture and human electrophysiology in interactive systems. Formal Aspects Comput. **21**(6), 513–539 (2009)

Incentive Stackelberg Mean-Payoff Games

Anshul Gupta[1]([⊠]), Sven Schewe[1], Ashutosh Trivedi[2],
Maram Sai Krishna Deepak[2], and Bharath Kumar Padarthi[2]

[1] University of Liverpool, Liverpool, UK
Anshul.Gupta@liverpool.ac.uk
[2] Indian Institute of Technology Bombay, Mumbai, India

Abstract. We introduce and study incentive equilibria for multi-player mean-payoff games. Incentive equilibria generalise well-studied solution concepts such as Nash equilibria and leader equilibria. Recall that a strategy profile is a Nash equilibrium if no player can improve his payoff by changing his strategy unilaterally. In the setting of incentive and leader equilibria, there is a distinguished player—called the leader—who can assign strategies to all other players, referred to as her followers. A strategy profile is a leader strategy profile if no player, except for the leader, can improve his payoff by changing his strategy unilaterally, and a leader equilibrium is a leader strategy profile with a maximal return for the leader. In the proposed case of incentive equilibria, the leader can additionally influence the behaviour of her followers by transferring parts of her payoff to her followers. The ability to incentivise her followers provides the leader with more freedom in selecting strategy profiles, and we show that this can indeed improve the leader's payoff in such games. The key fundamental result of the paper is the existence of incentive equilibria in mean-payoff games. We further show that the decision problem related to constructing incentive equilibria is NP-complete. On a positive note, we show that, when the number of players is fixed, the complexity of the problem falls in the same class as two-player mean-payoff games. We present an implementation of the proposed algorithms, and discuss experimental results that demonstrate the feasibility of the analysis.

1 Introduction

The classical mean-payoff games [7,30] are two-player zero-sum games that are played on weighted finite graphs, where two players—Max and Min—take turn to move a token along the edges of the graph to jointly construct an infinite play. The objectives of the players Max and Min are to respectively maximise and minimise the limit average reward associated with the play. Mean-payoff games enjoy a special status in verification, since μ-calculus model checking and parity games can be reduced in polynomial-time to solving mean-payoff games. Mean-payoff objectives can also be considered as quantitative extensions [13,15] of classical Büchi

This work was supported by the EPSRC through grant EP/M027287/1 (Energy Efficient Control), by DARPA under agreement number FA8750-15-2-0096 and by the US National Science Foundation (NSF) under grant numbers CPS-1446900.

R. De Nicola and E. Kühn (Eds.): SEFM 2016, LNCS 9763, pp. 304–320, 2016.
DOI: 10.1007/978-3-319-41591-8_21

objectives, where we are interested in the limit-average share of occurrences of accepting states rather than merely in whether or not infinitely many accepting states occur. For a broader discussion on quantitative verification, in general, and the transition from the classical qualitative to the modern quantitative interpretation of deterministic Büchi automata, we refer the reader to Henzinger's survey on quantiative reactive modelling and verification [15].

We focus on multi-player extension of mean-payoff games where a finite number of players control various vertices and move a token along the edges to collectively produce an infinite run. There is a player-specific reward function that, for every edge of the graph, gives an immediate reward to each player. The payoff to a player associated with a play is the limit average of the rewards in the individual moves. The most natural question related to the multi-player game setting is to find an optimal 'stable' *strategy profile* (a set of strategies, one for each player). Broadly speaking, a strategy profile is stable, if no player has an incentive to deviate from it. Nash equilibria [19] and leader equilibria [13,29] (also known as *Stackelberg equilibria*) are the most common notions of stable strategy profiles for multi-player games.

A strategy profile is called a Nash equilibrium if no player can improve his payoff by unilaterally changing his strategy. In a setting where we have a distinguished player (called the leader) who is able to suggest a strategy profile to other players (called followers), a strategy profile is stable if no follower can improve his payoff by unilaterally deviating from the profile. A leader equilibrium is a stable strategy profile that maximises the reward for the leader.

In this paper, we introduce and study a novel notion of stable strategy profiles for multi-player mean-payoff games that we call incentive Stackelberg equilibria (or incentive equilibria for short). In this setting, the leader has more powerful strategies, where she not only puts forward strategies that describe how the players move, but also gives non-negative incentives to the followers for compliance. These incentives are then added to the overall rewards the respective follower would receive in each move of the play, and deduced from the overall reward of the leader. Like for leader equilibria, a strategy profile is stable if no *follower* has an incentive to deviate. An *incentive equilibrium* is a stable strategy profile with maximal reward for the leader.

Using incentive equilibria has various natural justifications. The techniques we discussed here can be applied where distributed development of a system is considered. That is, when several rational components interact among themselves along with a rational controller and they try to optimise their individual objectives and specifications. Our techniques can be applied to maximise utility of a central controller while also complying with individual component specifications. Transferring utilities is also quite natural where the payoffs on the edges directly translate to the gains incurred by individual components. These techniques can also be used to maximise social optima where rational controller follow the objective of maximising joint utility. We now discuss two simple examples that exemplify the role that incentives can play to achieve good stable solutions of multi-player mean-payoff games.

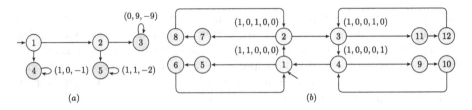

Fig. 1. (a) Incentive equilibrium beats leader equilibrium and Nash equilibrium and (b) incentive equilibrium gives much better system utilisation.

Example 1. Consider the multi-player mean-payoff game shown in Fig. 1(a). Here we have three players: Player 1, Player 2 (the leader), and Player 3. The vertex labelled 1 is controlled by Player 1, while the vertex labelled 2 is controlled by Player 2. All other vertices are controlled by Player 3. We further annotate the rewards of various players on the edges of the graph by giving a triple, where the reward of the players 1, 2, and 3 are shown in that order. We omit the labels when the rewards of all players are 0. An incentive equilibrium would be given by (a strategy profile leading to) the play $\langle 1, 2, 3^\omega \rangle$, where the leader pays an incentive of 1 to Player 1 for each step and 0 to Player 3. By doing this, she secures a payoff of 8 for herself. The reward for the players 1 and 3 in this incentive equilibrium are each 1 and -9, respectively. A leader equilibrium would result in the play $\langle 1, 2, 5^\omega \rangle$ with rewards of 1 for Player 1 and the leader and -2 for Player 3: when the leader cannot pay any incentive to Player 1, then the move from Vertex 2 to Vertex 3 will not be part of a stable strategy. The only Nash equilibrium in this game would result in the play $\langle 1, 4^\omega \rangle$ with the rewards of 1 for Player 1, 0 for the leader, and -1 for Player 3. This example shows how leader benefits from her additional choices in leader and incentive equilibria. □

Example 2. Consider the multi-player mean-payoff game shown in the Fig. 1(b) with five players—Player 0 (or: leader) and Player 1 to 4 (followers). For $i \in \{1, 2, 3, 4\}$, Player i controls the vertex labelled i in the game and gets a reward of 1 whenever token is at vertex i. (To keep the rewards on the edges, one could encode this by giving this reward whenever vertex i is entered.) Player 0 gets a reward of 1 in all of these vertices. The payoff of all other players is 0 in all other cases. Notice that the only play defined by Nash or leader equilibria in this example is $\langle (1, 5, 6)^\omega \rangle$, which provides a payoff of $\frac{1}{3}$ to Player 0 and Player 1, and a payoff of 0 to all other players. For incentive equilibria, however, the leader can give an incentive of $\frac{1}{12}$ to all followers when they follow the play $\langle (1, 2, 3, 4)^\omega \rangle$. It is easy to see that such a strategy profile is incentive stable. The leader will then receive a payoff of $\frac{2}{3}$, i.e., her payoff from the cycle, 1, minus the incentives given to the other players, $4 \cdot \frac{1}{12}$. All other players receive a payoff of $\frac{1}{3}$, consisting of the payoff from the cycle, $\frac{1}{4}$, plus the incentive they receive from the leader, $\frac{1}{12}$. Notice that this payoff is not only better from the leader's point-of-view, the other players are also better off in this equilibrium. □

In both examples, we saw that the incentive equilibria are strictly better than Nash and leader equilibria. It is not a coincidence—note that leader reward from any Nash equilibrium cannot be greater than her reward from any leader equilibrium, as in the case of leader strategy profiles, leader can select from a wider range of strategy profiles. Thus, if compared to a Nash equilibrium, a leader equilibrium can only be superior w.r.t. the leader reward. Similarly, a leader equilibrium cannot beat an incentive equilibrium, as here also, leader can select from a wider range of strategy profiles ('leader stable' strategy profiles can be viewed as an 'incentive stable' strategy profiles with 0 incentives). It again implies that leader reward from any leader equilibrium cannot be greater than her reward from any incentive equilibrium.

Related Work. Ummels and Wojtczak [27,28] considered Nash equilibria for mean-payoff games and showed that the decision problem of finding a Nash equilibria is NP-complete for pure (not allowing randomisation) strategy profiles, while the problem is undecidable for arbitrary randomised strategies. Gupta and Schewe [13] have extended these results to leader equilibria. The undecidability result of [28] for Nash equilibria in arbitrary randomised strategies can be easily extended to leader equilibria. For this reason, we focus on non-randomised strategies throughout this paper. Leader equilibria were introduced by von Stackelberg [29] and were further studied in [11]. The strategy profiles we study here are inspired from [12] and are studied in detail for infinite games in [13]. Incentive equilibria have recently been introduced for bi-matrix games [14], but have, to the best of our knowledge, not been used in infinite games. Two-player mean-payoff games were first studied in [9] and were shown to be positionally determined. They can be solved in pseudo-polynomial time [6,30], smoothed polynomial time [3], PPAD [10] and randomised subexponential [2] time. Their decision problem is also known to be in UP∩co-UP [16,30].

Contributions. The key contribution of the paper is the concept of incentive equilibria to system analysis in general and to multi-player mean-payoff games in particular. We show that the complexity of finding incentive equilibria is same as that for finding leader equilibria [13] for multi-player mean-payoff games: it is NP-complete in general, but, for a fixed number of players, it is in the same complexity class as solving two-player mean-payoff games (2MPGs). In other words, solving two-player mean-payoff games is the most expensive step involved. We have implemented an efficient version of the optimal strategy improvement algorithm from [24] as a backbone, and equipped it with a logarithmic search to expand it from the qualitative evaluation (finding mean partitions) of mean-payoff games to their quantitative evaluation. We construct incentive equilibria by implementing a constraint system that gives necessary and sufficient conditions for a strategy profile to be (1) stable and (2) provide optimal leader return among them. The evaluation of the constraint system involves evaluating a bounded number of calls to the linear programming solver. The contribution of the paper is therefore two-fold—first to conceptualise incentive equilibria in multi-player mean-payoff games (Sects. 2 and 3), and second to present a tool

(Sect. 4) deriving optimal return for the leader by evaluating a number of multi-player games.

2   Incentive Equilibrium

We introduce the concept of incentive equilibria for multi-player mean-payoff games. These games are played among multiple players on a multi-weighted finite directed graph arena where a distinguished player, called the leader, is able to put forward a strategy profile. She will follow the strategy she assigned for herself, while all other players, called her followers, will comply with the strategy she suggested, unless they benefit from unilateral deviation. The leader is further allowed to incentivise the behaviour of her followers by sharing her payoff with them, in order to make compliance with the strategy she has put forward sufficiently attractive. This, in turn, may improve the leader's payoff. Before we define incentive equilibria, let us recall a few key definitions.

Definition 1 (Multi-player Mean-Payoff Games). *A multi-player mean-payoff game (MMPG) arena $\mathcal{G}$ is a tuple $(P, V, (V_p)_{p \in P}, v_0, E, (r_p)_{p \in P})$ where*

- *P is a finite set of players with a distinguished leader player $l \in P$,*
- *V is a finite set of vertices with a distinguished initial vertex $v_0 \in V$,*
- *$(V_p)_{p \in P}$ is a partition of V characterising vertices controlled by players,*
- *$E \subseteq V \times V$ is a set of edges such that for all $v \in V$ there is $v' \in V$ with $(v, v') \in E$, and*
- *$(r_p)_{p \in P}$ is a family of reward functions $r_p : E \to \mathbb{Q}$, that for each player $p \in P$, assigns reward for player p associated with that edge.*

A finite play $\pi = \langle v_0, v_1, \ldots, v_n \rangle$ of the game $\mathcal{G}$ is a sequence of vertices such that v_0 is the initial vertex, and for every $0 \leq i < n$, we have, $(v_i, v_{i+1}) \in E$. An infinite play is defined in an analogous manner. A multi-player mean-payoff game is played on a game arena $\mathcal{G}$ among several players by moving a token along the edges of the arena. The game begins by placing a token on the initial vertex. Each time the token is on the vertex controlled by a player $p \in P$, the player p chooses an outgoing edge and moves the token along this edge. The game continues in this fashion forever, and the players thus construct an infinite play of the game. The (raw) payoff $r_p(\pi)$ of a player $p \in P$ associated with a play $\pi = \langle v_0, v_1, \ldots \rangle$ is the limit average reward of the path, given as $r_p(\pi) \stackrel{\text{def}}{=} \liminf_{n \to \infty} \frac{1}{n} \sum_{i=0}^{n-1} r_p((v_i, v_{i+1}))$. We refer to this value as the raw payoff of the player p to distinguish it from the payoff for the player that also includes the incentive given to the player by the leader.

A strategy of a player is a recipe for the player to choose the successor vertex. It is given as a function $\sigma_p : V^* V_p \to V$ such that $\sigma_p(\pi)$ is defined for a finite play $\langle v_0, \ldots, v_n \rangle$ when $v_n \in V_p$ and it is such that $(v_n, \sigma_p(\pi)) \in E$. A family of strategies $\overline{\sigma} = (\sigma_p)_{p \in P}$ is called a strategy profile. Given a strategy profile $\overline{\sigma}$, we write $\overline{\sigma}(p)$ for the strategy of player $p \in P$ in $\overline{\sigma}$. A strategy profile $\overline{\sigma}$ defines a unique play $\pi_{\overline{\sigma}}$, and therefore a raw payoff $r_p(\overline{\sigma}) = r_p(\pi_{\overline{\sigma}})$ for each player p.

We write $\Sigma_p^{\mathcal{G}}$ for the set of strategy of player $p \in P$ and $\Pi^{\mathcal{G}}$ for the set of strategy profiles in a game arena $\mathcal{G}$. When the game arena is clear from the context, we omit it from the superscript.

For a strategy profile $\overline{\sigma}$, a player $p \in P$, and a strategy σ' of p, we write $\overline{\sigma}_{p,\sigma'}$ for the strategy profile $\overline{\sigma}'$ such that $\overline{\sigma}'(p) = \sigma'$ and $\overline{\sigma}'(p') = \overline{\sigma}(p')$ for all $p' \in P \setminus \{p\}$. We can now define Nash and leader (aka Stackelberg) equilibria.

Definition 2 (Nash Equilibria and Leader Equilibria). *A strategy profile* $\overline{\sigma}$ *is a Nash equilibrium if no player would gain from unilateral deviation, i.e., for all* $p \in P$ *we have* $r_p(\overline{\sigma}) \geq r_p(\overline{\sigma}_{p,\sigma'})$ *for all* $\sigma' \in \Sigma_p$. *A strategy profile* $\overline{\sigma}$ *is a leader strategy profile if no player, except for the leader, would gain from unilateral deviation, i.e., for all* $p \in P \setminus \{l\}$ *we have* $r_p(\overline{\sigma}) \geq r_p(\overline{\sigma}_{p,\sigma'})$ *for all* $\sigma' \in \Sigma_p$. *A leader equilibrium is a maximal leader strategy profile.*

We next define an *incentive strategy profile* as a strategy profile which satisfies the stability requirements of the leader equilibria and allows the leader to give incentives to the followers. We refer to an optimal strategy profile in this class that provides maximal reward to the leader as an *incentive equilibrium*.

An incentive to a player p is a function $\iota_p : V^* V_p \rightarrow \mathbb{R}_{\geq 0}$ from the set of histories to incentives. Incentives can be extended to infinite play $\pi = \langle v_0, v_1, \ldots \rangle$ in the usual mean-payoff fashion: $\iota_p(\pi) \stackrel{\text{def}}{=} \liminf_{n \to \infty} \frac{1}{n} \sum_{i=0}^{n-1} \iota_p(v_0 \ldots v_{n-1})$. The overall payoff $\rho_p(\pi)$ to a follower in run π is the raw payoff plus all incentives, $\rho_p(\pi) \stackrel{\text{def}}{=} r_p(\pi) + \iota_p(\pi)$, while the overall payoff of the leader $\rho_l(\pi)$ is her raw payoff after deducting all incentives, $\rho_l(\pi) \stackrel{\text{def}}{=} r_l(\pi) - \sum_{p \in P \setminus \{l\}} \iota_p(\pi)$.

We extend the notion of a strategy profile in the presence of incentives as a pair $(\overline{\sigma}, \overline{\iota})$, where $\overline{\sigma}$ is a strategy profile assigned by the leader, in which the leader pays an incentive given by the incentive profile $\overline{\iota} = (\iota_p)_{p \in P \setminus \{l\}}$. We write $\overline{\iota}_p$ for the incentive for player $p \in P \setminus \{l\}$. We write $\overline{\iota}_p(\overline{\sigma})$ for the incentive to player p for the unique run $\pi_{\overline{\sigma}}$ under incentive profile $\overline{\iota}$. In any incentive strategy profile $(\overline{\sigma}, \overline{\iota})$, no player but the leader may benefit from deviation. An optimal strategy profile among this class would form an *incentive equilibrium*.

Definition 3 (Incentive Equilibria). *A strategy profile* $(\overline{\sigma}, \overline{\iota})$ *is an incentive strategy profile, if no follower can improve his overall payoff from a unilateral deviation, i.e., for all players* $p \in P \setminus \{l\}$ *we have that* $r_p(\overline{\sigma}) + \overline{\iota}_p(\overline{\sigma}) \geq r_p(\overline{\sigma}_{p,\sigma'}) + \overline{\iota}_p(\overline{\sigma}_{p,\sigma'})$ *for all* $\sigma' \in \Sigma_p$. *An incentive strategy profile* $(\overline{\sigma}, \overline{\iota})$ *is an incentive equilibrium if the leader's total payoff for this profile is maximal among all incentive strategy profiles, i.e., for all* $(\overline{\sigma}', \overline{\iota}')$ *we have that* $r_l(\overline{\sigma}) - \sum_{p \in P \setminus \{l\}} \overline{\iota}_p(\overline{\sigma}) \geq r_l(\overline{\sigma}') - \sum_{p \in P \setminus \{l\}} \overline{\iota}'_p(\overline{\sigma}')$.

An incentive strategy profile is a *leader strategy profile* if all incentives are 0, and a *Nash strategy profile* if, in addition, $\overline{\sigma}$ is also a Nash equilibrium. We write SP, ISP, LSP, and Nash SP for the set of strategy profiles, incentive strategy profiles, leader strategy profiles, and Nash strategy profiles respectively. It is clear that Nash SP $\subseteq$ LSP $\subseteq$ ISP $\subseteq$ SP. This observation, together with Example 1(a) yield the following result.

Theorem 1 (IE ≥ LE ≥ NE). *Incentive equilibria do not provide smaller return than leader equilibria, and leader equilibria do not provide smaller return than Nash equilibria. Moreover, there are games for which the leader reward from three equilibria are different.*

3   Existence, Construction, and Complexity

This section is dedicated to the existence, construction, and complexity of incentive equilibria. Similar results were developed by Gupta and Schewe [13] for leader equilibria for multi-player mean-payoff games. If we are only interested in complexity classes, the results in the following section can be obtained by a simple reduction to leader equilibria [13] using a gadget (Fig. 2) that replaces each state by intuitively circling through the followers and allowing the leader to transfer a large part h (for *high* incentive) of her utility to each of the followers[1]. Following this approach leads, however, to an increase in the size of the linear programs, simply because we would incur a blow-up of the game by a factor of $2|P|$. To avoid this unnecessary blowup, we adapt the proofs from [13] that result in a more efficient algorithm.

 Proof Sketch. We first introduce a canonical class of incentive strategy profiles—the *perfectly-incentivised strategy profiles* (PSPs)—that corresponds to

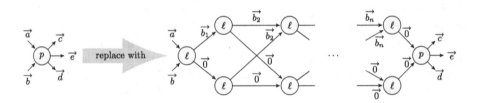

Fig. 2. Gadget reducing incentive equilibrium to leader equilibrium. Here we assume that ℓ is the leader player and $1, \ldots, n$ are n followers. Here we label a state by ℓ if it is controlled by leader, and by p if it is controlled by a player p. Every state p of the original game arena is replaced by $2n + 2$ states in the gadget in the manner shown above. Here reward vector b_i corresponds to reward $-h$ for the leader, reward $+h$ to follower i, and reward 0 to all other followers.

---

[1] When translating a strategy in the presence of incentives (σ, ι), the translation can be done by simulating the runs. The translation of the strategy profile σ is straight forward; it determines the choices at the respective last states from the gadgets. The translation of the incentives refer to the choices within the gadgets. They can be obtained by letting the leader make the decision to transfer h to follower p if, and only if, the sum of the incentives this follower p has collected in the game on the original MMPG is at least h higher than the sum of the utilities the leader has so far transferred to p in the gadgets. If passing through a gadget is counted as one step, all lim inf values agree on the original and its simulation. The back translation is even more direct: it suffices to wait till the end of each gadget, and then assign incentives accordingly.

the Stackelberg version of the classic subgame perfection. Keep in mind that not all perfectly-incentivised strategy profiles (PSPs) are valid incentive strategy profiles (ISPs). On the other hand, we show that every ISP has a corresponding PSP (which is also an ISP) with the same leader reward. Thanks to this result, in order to construct incentive equilibrium it suffices to consider PSPs that are also ISPs.

Further, we show that, for PSPs that are ISPs, it suffices to find a maximum in a *well behaved* class of strategy profiles: strategy profiles where every edge has a limit share of the run—by showing that the supremum of general strategies cannot be higher than the supremum of these well behaved ones. We then show how to construct well behaved PSPs that are ISPs based on a family of constraint systems that depend on the occurring and recurring vertices on the play. At the same time, we show that no general ISP that defines a play with this set of occurring and recurrent vertices can have a higher value. The set of occurring and recurrent vertices can be guessed and the respective constraint system can be build and solved in polynomial time, which also provides inclusion of the related decision problem in NP.

3.1 Perfectly-Incentivised Strategy Profiles

We define a canonical form of an incentive equilibrium with this play that we call *perfectly-incentivised strategy profiles* (PSP). In a PSP, a deviator (a deviating follower) is punished, and the leader incentivises all other followers to collude against the deviator. While the larger set of strategies and plays that define them (when compared to Nash and leader equilibria) lead to a better value, this incentive scheme leads to a higher stability: the games are subgame perfect relative to the leader. A strategy profile $(\overline{\sigma}, \overline{\iota})$ is a subgame perfect incentive strategy profile, if every reachable subgame is also an incentive strategy profile. This term adjusts the classic notion of subgame perfect equilibria to our setting. In a subgame perfect Nash equilibrium, it is required that the subgame started on each history also forms a Nash equilibrium. Note that the leader is allowed to benefit from deviation in our setting.

The means to obtain subgame perfection after deviation is to make all players harm the most recent deviator. Thus, we essentially resort to a two-player game. For a multi-player mean-payoff game $\mathcal{G}$, we define, for each follower p, the two-player mean-payoff game (2MPG) $\mathcal{G}_p$ where p keeps his reward function, while all other players have the same antagonistic reward $-r_p$. Two-player mean-payoff games are memoryless determined, such that every vertex v has a value, which we denote by $r_p(v)$. This value clearly defines a minimal payoff of a follower: when he passes by a vertex in a play, then he cannot expect an outcome below $r_p(v)$, as he would otherwise deviate.

PSP strategy profiles are in the tradition of reward and punish strategy profiles [13]. In any 'reward and punish' strategy profile, the leader facilitates the power of all remaining followers to punish a deviator. If a player p chooses to deviate from the strategy profile at history h, the game would turn into a two-player game, where all the other followers and the leader forsake their own interests, and jointly try to 'punish' p. That is, player p may still try to maximise his reward and his objective remains exactly the same, but the rewards of the rest of the players have changed to negative of the reward of player p. As they form a coalition with the joint objective to harm p, this is an ordinary two-player mean-payoff game that starts at the vertex $\mathsf{last}(h)$.

For a strategy profile $\overline{\sigma}$ and a history h, we call h a deviating history, if it is not a prefix of $\pi_{\overline{\sigma}}$. We denote by $\mathsf{dev}(h, \overline{\sigma})$ the last player p, who has deviated from his or her strategy $\overline{\sigma}_p$ on a deviating history h. A perfectly-incentivised strategy profile is defined as a strategy profile (PSP) $(\overline{\sigma}, \overline{\iota})$ with the following properties. For all prefixes h and h' of $\pi_{\overline{\sigma}}$ and for all followers p, it holds that $\overline{\iota}_p(h) = \overline{\iota}_p(h')$. We also refer to this value by $\overline{\iota}_p$. For deviator histories h', the incentive $\overline{\iota}_p(h')$ is 0 except for the following cases. On every deviating history h with deviating player $p = \mathsf{dev}(h, \overline{\sigma})$, the player p' who owns the vertex $v = \mathsf{last}(h)$ follows the strategy from the 2MPG $\mathcal{G}_p$. If, under this strategy, player p' selects the successor v' at a vertex v in the 2MPG $\mathcal{G}_p$ (and thus $\overline{\sigma}_{p'}(h) = v'$), p' is a follower, and $p' \neq p$, then player p' receives an incentive, such that $r_{p'}(v, v') + \overline{\iota}_{p'}(h \cdot v') = r_{\max} + 1$.

Note that, technically, the leader punishes herself in this definition. This is only to keep definitions simple; she is allowed to have an incentive to deviate, and the subgame perfection does not impose a criterion upon her. Note also that a PSP is not necessarily an incentive strategy profile, as it does not guarantee anything about $\pi_{\overline{\sigma}}$. The following theorem states the importance of PSPs in constructing incentive equilibrium.

Theorem 2. *Let $(\overline{\sigma}, \overline{\iota})$ be an ISP that defines a play $\pi_{\overline{\sigma}}$. Then we can define a PSP $(\overline{\sigma}, \overline{\iota})$, that is also an ISP, with the same reward, and defines the same play.*

The proof of this theorem follows from Lemmas 1 and 2.

Lemma 1. *Let $(\overline{\sigma}', \overline{\iota}')$ be a strategy profile that defines a play $\pi_{\overline{\sigma}'}$, which contains precisely the reachable vertices Q. Let $(\overline{\sigma}', \overline{\iota}')$ satisfy that, $\forall$ followers $p \in P \setminus \{l\}$ and all vertices $v \in Q \cap V_p$ owned by p we have that $\overline{\iota}_p(\overline{\sigma}') + r_p(\overline{\sigma}') \geq r_p(v)$. Then we can define a PSP $(\overline{\sigma}, \overline{\iota})$ with the same reward, which defines the same play.*

Proof. We note that a PSP $(\overline{\sigma}, \overline{\iota})$ is fully defined by the play $\pi_{\overline{\sigma}}$ and the $\overline{\iota}$ restricted to the prefixes of $\pi_{\overline{\sigma}}$. We now define the PSP $(\overline{\sigma}, \overline{\iota})$ with the following property: $\pi_{\overline{\sigma}} = \pi_{\overline{\sigma}'}$, that is the play of the PSP equals the play defined by the ISP we started with. For all followers p and all prefixes h of $\pi_{\overline{\sigma}}$, we have $\overline{\iota}_p(h) = \overline{\iota}'_p(\overline{\sigma})$. It is obvious that $(\overline{\sigma}', \overline{\iota}')$ and $(\overline{\sigma}, \overline{\iota})$ yield the same reward for all followers and the same reward for the leader. We now assume for contradiction that the resulting PSP is not an incentive strategy profile. If this is the case, then a follower p must benefit from deviation at some history h. Let us start with the case that h is a deviator history. In this case, the reward for p upon not deviating is $r_{\max} + 1$, while it is the outcome of some game upon deviation, which is clearly bounded by $r_{\max}$.

We now turn to the case that h is not a deviator history, and therefore a prefix of $\pi_{\overline{\sigma}}$. Let p be the owner of $v = \mathsf{last}(h)$. If p is the leader, we have nothing to show. If p is a follower and does not have an incentive to deviate in $(\overline{\sigma}, \overline{\iota})$, we have nothing to show. If p is a follower and has an incentive to deviate in $(\overline{\sigma}, \overline{\iota})$, we note that his payoff after deviation would be bounded from above by $r_p(v)$. Thus, he does not have an incentive to deviate (contradiction).   □

Lemma 2. *Let $(\overline{\sigma}, \overline{\iota})$ be an ISP that defines a play $\pi_{\overline{\sigma}}$, which contains precisely the vertices Q. Then, for all followers $p \in P \setminus \{l\}$ and all vertices $v \in Q \cap V_p$ owned by p, we have that $\overline{\iota}_p(\overline{\sigma}') + r_p(\overline{\sigma}') \geq r_p(v)$.*

Proof. Assume that this is not the case for a follower p and a vertex $v \in Q$ owned by p. Then p would benefit upon deviating when visiting v.   □

3.2   Existence and Construction of Incentive Equilibria

We say that a strategy profile $\overline{\sigma}$ is *well-behaved* if in the resulting play $\pi_{\overline{\sigma}}$, the frequency (ratio) of occurrence of every edge of the game arena occurs has a limit, i.e., each edge here occurs with a limit probability (the limes inferior and superior of the share of its occurrence on $\pi_{\overline{\sigma}}$ are equal). Such notion of well-behaved strategy profiles were also defined in [13] for the case of leader equilibria. We first construct optimal ISPs among well behaved PSPs, and then show that no ISP give a better payoff for leader.

Let $\overline{\sigma}$ is a well-behaved perfectly-incentivised strategy profile and let Q be the set of vertices visited in $\pi_{\overline{\sigma}}$ and $S \subseteq Q$ be the set of vertices that are visited infinitely often (note that S is strongly connected). Let $p_{(s,t)}$ be the limit ratio (frequency) of occurrence of an edge $(s, t) \in E \cap S \times S$ in $\pi_{\overline{\sigma}}$ and let p_v be the limit ratio of each vertex $v \in S$.

Thanks to the proof of Lemma 1, the following constraint system (linear program) characterises the necessary and sufficient conditions for the well-behaved perfectly-incentivised strategy profile $\overline{\sigma}$ to be an ISP.

1. $p_v = 0$ if $v \in V \setminus S$ and $p_v \geq 0$ if $v \in S$.
2. $p_e = 0$ if $e \in E \setminus S \times S$ and $p_e \geq 0$ if $e \in E \cap S \times S$
3. $\sum_{v \in V} p_v = 1$
4. $p_s = \sum_{(s,t) \in E} p_{(s,t)}$ for all $s \in S$ and $p_t = \sum_{(s,t) \in E} p_{(s,t)}$ for all $t \in S$
5. $\overline{\iota}_p + \sum_{e \in E} p_e r_p(e) \geq \max_{v \in Q}(r_p(v))$ where $r_p(v)$ is the value at vertex v in the 2MPG $\mathcal{G}_p$ characterising minimum payoff expected by player p.

The constraints presented above are quite self-explanatory. Constraints 1 and 2 state that the limit ratio of occurrence of a vertex and edge is positive only when it is visited infinitely often. Constraint 3 expresses that the sum of ratio of occurrence of vertices is equal to 1, while constraint 4 expresses the fact the limit ratio of a vertex should be equal to limit ratios of all incoming edges, and equal to limit ratio of all outgoing edges from that vertex. The last constraint stems from the proof of Lemma 1 combined with the observation that reward $r_p(\overline{\sigma})$ of a player p in $\overline{\sigma}$ is simply $\sum_{e \in E} p_e r_p(e)$, that is, it is the weighted sum of the raw rewards of the individual edges. Before we define the objective function, we state a simple corollary from the proof of Lemma 1.

Corollary 1. *Every well behaved PSP that is an ISP satisfies these constraints, and every well behaved strategy profile $(\overline{\sigma}, \overline{\iota})$, whose play $\pi_{\overline{\sigma}}$ satisfies these constraints, defines a PSP, which is then an ISP.*

Note that the resulting PSP is an ISP even if $(\overline{\sigma}, \overline{\iota})$ is not. This is because the satisfaction of the constraints are enough for the final contradiction in the proof of Lemma 1.

Construction of Incentive Equilibria. The objective of the leader is obviously to maximise $r_l(\overline{\sigma}) - \sum_{p \in P \smallsetminus \{l\}} \overline{\iota}_p = \sum_{e \in E} p_e r_l(e) - \sum_{p \in P \smallsetminus \{l\}} \overline{\iota}_p$. Once we have this linear programming problem, it is simple to determine a solution in polynomial time [17,18]. We first observe that it is standard to construct a play defining a PSP from a solution. A key observation is that, if the linear program detailed above for sets Q of reachable vertices and S of vertices visited infinitely often has a solution, then there is a well behaved reward and punish strategy profile that meets this solution.

Theorem 3. *Non-well behaved PSPs that are also ISPs cannot provide better rewards for the leader than those from well behaved PSPs that are also ISPs.*

Proof. Corollary 1 shows that there exists a well defined constraint system obeyed by all well behaved PSPs that are also ISPs with a set Q of reachable vertices and a set S of recurrent vertices. Let us assume for contradiction that there is a reward and punish strategy profile $(\overline{\sigma}, \overline{\iota})$ that defines a play $\pi_{\overline{\sigma}}$ with the same sets Q and S of reachable and recurrent vertices, respectively, that provides a strictly better reward $r_l(\overline{\sigma}) - \sum_{p \in P \smallsetminus \{l\}} \overline{\iota}_p$, which exceeds the maximal reward obtained by the leader in well behaved PSPs that are also ISPs by some $\varepsilon > 0$.

We now construct a well behaved PSPs that are also ISPs and that also provides a better return. First, we take a $\overline{\iota}'$ with $\overline{\iota}_p = \overline{\iota}'_p$ for all followers p. This allows us to focus on the raw rewards only. Let k be some position in $\pi_{\overline{\sigma}}$ such that, for all $i \geq k$, only positions in the infinity set S of $\pi_{\overline{\sigma}}$ occur. Let π be the tail $v_k v_{k+1} v_{k+2} \ldots$ of $\pi_{\overline{\sigma}}$ that starts in position k. Obviously $r_p(\pi) = r_p(\overline{\sigma})$ holds for all players $p \in P$. We observe that, for all $\delta > 0$, there is an $l \in \mathbb{N}$ such that, for all $m \geq l$, $\frac{1}{m} \sum_{i=0}^{m-1} r_p((v_i, v_{i+1})) > r_p(\pi) - \delta$ holds for all $p \in P$, as otherwise the limes inferior property would be violated. We now fix, for all $a \in \mathbb{N}$, a sequence $\pi_a = v_k v_{k+1} v_{k+2} \ldots v_{k+m_a}$, such that $v_{k+m_a+1} = v_k$ and $\frac{1}{m} \sum_{i=0}^{m_a-1} r_p((v_i, v_{i+1})) > r_p(\pi) - \frac{1}{a}$ holds for all $p \in P$. Let $\pi_0 = v_0 v_1 \ldots v_{k-1}$. We now select $\pi' = \pi_0 \pi_1^{b_1} \pi_2^{b_2} \pi_3^{b_3} \ldots$, where the b_i are natural numbers big enough to guarantee that $\frac{b_i \cdot |\pi_i|}{|\pi_{i+1}| + |\pi_0| + \sum_{j=1}^{i} b_j \cdot |\pi_j|} \geq 1 - \frac{1}{i}$ holds. Letting b_i grow this fast ensures that the payoff, which is at least $r_p(\pi) - \frac{1}{i}$ for all players $p \in P$, dominates till the end of the first iteration[2] of $|\pi_{i+1}|$. The resulting play belongs to a well behaved (as the limit exists) strategy profile, and can thus be obtained

---

[2] Including the first iteration of π_{i+1} is a technical necessity, as a complete iteration of π_{i+i} provides better guarantees, but without the inclusion of this guarantee, the π_j's might grow too fast, preventing the existence of a limes.

by a well behaved PSP by Corollary 1. It thus provides a solution to the linear program from above, which contradicts our assumption. □

Consequently, it suffices to guess the optimal sets Q of vertices that occur and S of vertices that occur infinitely often to obtain a constraint system that describes an incentive equilibrium, which is well behaved and a PSP—and therefore subgame perfect.

Corollary 2. *The decision problems 'is there a (subgame perfect) incentive equilibrium with leader reward $\geq r$' is in NP, and the answer to these two questions is the same.*

Note that, if we have a fixed number of players, the number of possible constraint systems is polynomial. Like in [13], there are only polynomially many (for n vertices and k followers $O(n^k)$ many) second parts (the constraints on the follower rewards) of the constraint systems. For them, it suffices to consider the most liberal sets Q (which is unique) and S (the SCCs in the game restricted to Q, at most n). For a fixed number of players, finding incentive equilibria is therefore in the same class as solving 2MPGs. We adapt the NP hardness proof for leader equilibrium in mean-payoff games from [13] by reducing the 3SAT satisfiability formula over n atomic propositions with m conjuncts to solve a MMPG with $2n+1$ players and $5m+4n+2$ vertices with payoffs 0 and 1 only.

Theorem 4. *The problem of deciding whether an incentive equilibrium σ with reward $r_l(\sigma) \geq 1 - 1/n$ of the leader exists in games with rewards in $\{0,1\}$, is NP-complete.*

4 Experimental Results

We have implemented a tool [1] in C++ to evaluate the performance of the proposed algorithms for multi-player mean-payoff games (MMPG) for a small number of players. We implemented an algorithm from [24] to find mean values at the vertices. We then infer and solve a number of constraint systems. We describe our main algorithm here.

4.1 Algorithm Specific Details

We first evaluate MMPGs using reduction to solving underlying 2MPGs. We then infer and solve a number of linear programming problems to find a solution. For few number of players, the number of different solutions to these games is usually small, and, consequently, the number of linear programming problems to solve is small, too. In order to find the individual mean partition, we use an algorithm from [24], that finds 0-mean partitions, and expand it quantitatively to find the value of 2MPGs. We recall that for 2MPG both players have optimal memoryless strategies. Under such strategies, the game will follow a 'lasso path' from every starting vertex: a finite (and possibly empty) path, followed by a cycle, which is repeated infinitely many times. The value of a game position is defined by the average of the edge weights on this cycle.

In our context, the edge weights are either 0 or 1. The values of the vertices are therefore fractions $\frac{a}{l}$ with $0 \leq a \leq l \leq n$, where l is the length of the cycle, and a is the number of 'accepting' events in the DBA that refers to the objective of the respective player, i.e., the edges with value 1, occurring on this cycle.

An α-mean partition of a 2MPG is the subset of vertices, for which the return is $\geq \alpha$. Conceptually, to find the $\frac{a}{l}$-mean partition, one would simply subtract $\frac{a}{l}$ from the weight of every edge and look for the 0-mean partition. However, to stay with integers, it is better to use integer values on the edges, e.g., by replacing the 0s by $-a$, and the 1s by $l - a$. For games with n vertices, there are only $O(n^2)$ values for the fraction $\frac{a}{l}$ to consider, as optimal memoryless strategies always lead to lasso paths and only the cycle at the end of the lasso determines the values for a and l, where $0 < a < l \leq n$.

We start by narrowing down the set of values by classifying the mean partition in a logarithmic search. After determining the $\frac{1}{2}$ mean partition, we know which values are < 0.5 and ≥ 0.5, respectively. The two parts of the game can then be analysed further, determining the $\frac{1}{4}$ and $\frac{3}{4}$ mean partition, respectively. After s such partitionings, all values in a partition of the game are either known to be in an $[k \cdot 2^{-s}, (k+1) \cdot 2^{-s}[$ interval for some $k < 2^s - 1$, or in the interval $[1 - 2^{-s}, 1]$. We stop to bisect when the size p of a partition is at most 2^s. In this case, the respective interval has $f \leq p$ fractions with a denominator $\leq p$. We determine them, store them in a balanced tree, and use it to determine the correct value of all vertices of the partition in $\lceil \log_2 f \rceil$ steps.

The number of different values of nodes in a 2MPG is usually small, and certainly it would be much smaller than the number of vertices in the game. Consequently, the number of constraint systems is also small for a small number of players. We use this algorithm to evaluate a number of randomly created three player mean-payoff games, where the player take turns. We consider three players – player 1, player 2 and a leader and two different evaluations on the same game graph. We first see how each player fares when they try to maximise their return against a coalition of all other players, including the leader. In the first evaluation, leader forms a coalition with player 1 (minimiser) against player 2 (maximiser) on the payoffs defined for player 2. We find the different possible mean values at the nodes in this evaluation, using the algorithm from above. In the second evaluation, leader forms a coalition with player 2 (minimiser) against player 1 (maximiser) on the payoffs defined for player 1. We also note the different possible mean values at the nodes in this evaluation, using again the algorithm from above. The resultant two-player games provide the constraints for the linear programming problems that we presented in Sect. 3.2. These different values form the different thresholds that we have to consider. We now consider all possible combinations of these different threshold values for the followers and determine the vertices that comply with them.

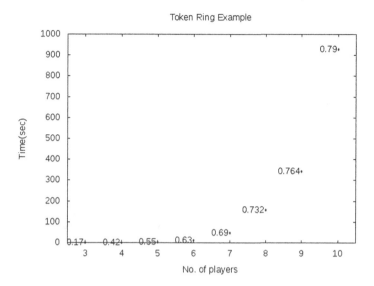

Fig. 3. The figure shows results for a generalisation of example 2 for multiple players with n nodes in the inner cycle and $n-1$ in outer cycles where n is number of players.

4.2 Experimental Results

Experiments indicate that our implementation of the algorithm can solve examples of size 100 nodes and 10 players within 30 min. The algorithm is, of course, much faster for the games with two or three players. Figures 3 and 4 show the experimental results for the following two problem classes.

- Recall the example from Fig. 1(b). We generalise this example for token ring graph parameterised by 2 variables, n and d. It has 'n' nodes on the inner cycle, each of which correspond to 'n' different players and each of these 'n' nodes is also present on another cycle of length 'd'. The weights are set such that, all players except the leader get '1/n' if they chose the inner ring and get '1/d' if they chose their respective outer ring. The leader reward is '1' in the inner ring and '1/d' in all the other rings. The data supports the pen-and-paper analysis that incentives are useful iff $n > d > n(n-1)/(2n-1)$ holds. Figure 3 shows the leader reward for this example and the running time of our tool to compute it.
- Fig. 4 (left plot) shows the difference between incentive equilibrium and leader equilibrium for randomly generated 3 player MMPGs, while the right plot shows similar results on random graphs, where the number of players range from 3 to 10.

The evaluation results confirm that the leader reward increases significantly in incentive equilibria when compared to leader equilibria.

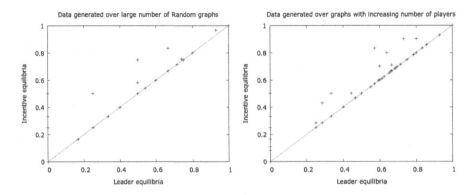

Fig. 4. The left figure shows the results for randomly generated MMPGs with 3 players, while the right one is for randomly generated MMPGs with 3 to 10 players.

5 Discussion

The main contribution of this paper is the introduction of incentive equilibria in multi-player mean-payoff games and the implementation of our techniques in a tool. We study how a rational leader might improve over her outcome by paying small incentives to her followers. At first, it may not seem to be a rational move of the leader, but close insight would show how a leader might improve her reward in this way. The incentive equilibria are seen as an extension to leader equilibria, where a rational leader, by giving an incentive to every other player in the game, can derive an optimal strategy profile. We believe that these techniques are helpful for the leader when maximising the return for a single player and would also be instrumental in defining stable rules and optimising various outcomes. The evaluation results from Sect. 4 show that the results are significantly better for the leader in an incentive equilibrium as compared to her return in a leader equilibrium.

References

1. MMPGSOLVER. http://www.cse.iitb.ac.in/~trivedi/mmpgsolver/
2. Björklund, H., Vorobyov, S.: A combinatorial strongly subexponential strategy improvement algorithm for mean-payoff games. Discrete Appl. Math. **155**(2), 210–229 (2007)
3. Boros, E., Elbassioni, K., Fouz, M., Gurvich, V., Makino, K., Manthey, B.: Stochastic mean payoff games: smoothed analysis and approximation schemes. In: Aceto, L., Henzinger, M., Sgall, J. (eds.) ICALP 2011, Part I. LNCS, vol. 6755, pp. 147–158. Springer, Heidelberg (2011)
4. Brihaye, T., Bruyère, V., De Pril, J.: Equilibria in quantitative reachability games. In: Ablayev, F., Mayr, E.W. (eds.) CSR 2010. LNCS, vol. 6072, pp. 72–83. Springer, Heidelberg (2010)

5. Brihaye, T., De Pril, J., Schewe, S.: Multiplayer cost games with simple Nash equilibria. In: Artemov, S., Nerode, A. (eds.) LFCS 2013. LNCS, vol. 7734, pp. 59–73. Springer, Heidelberg (2013)

6. Brim, L., Chaloupka, J., Doyen, L., Gentilini, R., Raskin, J.-F.: Faster algorithms for mean-payoff games. Formal Methods Syst. Des. **38**(2), 97–118 (2011)

7. Chatterjee, K., Henzinger, T.A., Jurdzinski, M.: Mean-payoff parity games. In: Proceedings of LICS 2005, pp. 178–187 (2005)

8. Chatterjee, K., Henzinger, T.A., Jurdzinski, M.: Games with secure equilibria. Theor. Comput. Sci. 67–82 (2006)

9. Ehrenfeucht, A., Mycielski, J.: Positional strategies for mean payoff games. Int. J. Game Theory **8**(2), 109–113 (1979)

10. Etessami, K., Yannakakis, M.: On the complexity of Nash equilibria and other fixed points. SIAM J. Comput. **39**(6), 2531–2597 (2010)

11. Friedman, J.W.: Oligopoly and the Theory of Games. Advanced Textbooks in Economics. North-Holland Pub. Co. (1977)

12. Friedman, J.W.: A Non-cooperative equilibrium for supergames. Rev. Econ. Stud. 1–12 (1971)

13. Gupta, A., Schewe, S.: Quantitative verification in rational environments. In: Proceedings of TIME, pp. 123–131 (2014)

14. Gupta, A., Schewe, S.: It pays to pay in bi-matrix Ggmes - a rational explanation for bribery. In: Proceedings of AAMAS, pp. 1361–1369 (2015)

15. Henzinger, T.A.: Quantitative reactive modeling and verification. Comput. Sci. R&D **28**(4), 331–344 (2013)

16. Jurdziński, M.: Deciding the winner in parity games is in UP ∩ co-UP. Inf. Process. Lett. **68**(3), 119–124 (1998)

17. Karmarkar, N.: A new polynomial-time algorithm for linear programming. In: Proceedings of STOC, pp. 302–311 (1984)

18. Khachian, L.G.: A polynomial algorithm in linear programming. Dokl. Akad. Nauk SSSR **244**, 1093–1096 (1979)

19. Nash, J.F.: Equilibrium points in n-person games. Proc. Natl. Acad. Sci. **36**(1), 48–49 (1950)

20. Osborne, M.J., Rubinstein, A.: A course in game theory. The MIT Press, Cambridge (1994). Electronic edition

21. Puterman, M.L.: Markov Decision Processes: Discrete Stochastic Dynamic Programming. Wiley, Hoboken (1994)

22. Pnueli, A., Rosner, R.: On the synthesis of a reactive module. In: Proceedings of POPL, pp. 179–190 (1989)

23. Ramadge, P.J.G., Wonham, W.M.: The control of discrete event systems. Proc. IEEE **77**(2), 81–98 (1989)

24. Schewe, S.: An optimal strategy improvement algorithm for solving parity and payoff games. In: Kaminski, M., Martini, S. (eds.) CSL 2008. LNCS, vol. 5213, pp. 369–384. Springer, Heidelberg (2008)

25. Schewe, S.: From parity and payoff games to linear programming. In: Královič, R., Niwiński, D. (eds.) MFCS 2009. LNCS, vol. 5734, pp. 675–686. Springer, Heidelberg (2009)

26. Ummels, M.: Rational behaviour and strategy construction in infinite multiplayer games. In: Arun-Kumar, S., Garg, N. (eds.) FSTTCS 2006. LNCS, vol. 4337, pp. 212–223. Springer, Heidelberg (2006)

27. Ummels, M.: The complexity of Nash equilibria in infinite multiplayer games. In: Amadio, R.M. (ed.) FOSSACS 2008. LNCS, vol. 4962, pp. 20–34. Springer, Heidelberg (2008)

28. Ummels, M., Wojtczak, D.: The complexity of Nash equilibria in limit-average games. In: Katoen, J.-P., König, B. (eds.) CONCUR 2011. LNCS, vol. 6901, pp. 482–496. Springer, Heidelberg (2011)

29. von Stackelberg, H.: Marktform und Gleichgewicht. Springer, Vienna (1934)

30. Zwick, U., Paterson, M.S.: The complexity of mean-payoff games on graphs. Theor. Comput. Sci. **158**(1–2), 343–359 (1996)

Stability-Based Adaptation of Asynchronously Communicating Software

Carlos Canal[1](✉) and Gwen Salaün[2]

[1] University of Málaga, Málaga, Spain
canal@lcc.uma.es
[2] University of Grenoble Alpes, Inria, LIG, CNRS, Grenoble, France

Abstract. Software Adaptation aims at composing incompatible black-box components or services (peers) whose individual functionality is as required for the new system. Adaptation techniques aim at automatically generating new components called adapters. An adapter works as an orchestrator and makes the involved peers work correctly together by receiving all messages exchanged in the system and by correcting mismatch between them. A challenging issue in this area is to consider that peers are described with (possibly cyclic) behavioural models and interact asynchronously, that is, exchanging messages via message buffers. The synthesis of adapters in this context is difficult because the composition of peers may result in infinite systems. In this paper, we propose new adaptation techniques, which rely on a property of communicating systems called stability. Stability aims at verifying whether a communicating system exhibits the same observational behaviour from a certain buffer bound on. We also provide adapter generation techniques using process algebra encodings and enumerative analysis techniques.

1 Introduction

New software is constructed in many cases by reusing and composing existing software elements, hereafter called *peers*. These peers correspond to a large variety of software, such as software components, Web servers, databases, Graphical User Interfaces, Software-as-a-Service in the cloud, or Web services. The composition of such heterogeneous software pieces is possible because peers are equipped with public interfaces, which exhibit their provided/required services as well as any other composition requirements that must be respected to ensure the correct execution of the system. A problem in this context is that some peer may be relevant *wrt.* a new composition-to-be from a functional point of view, but does not exactly match with the partner peers from an interface point of view. Mismatch takes different forms such as disparate operation names or unspecified message receptions, and it prevents the direct assembly of the peers.

Software Adaptation [7,26] is a non-intrusive solution for composing black-box software peers that present interface mismatch, leading to deadlock or other undesirable behaviour when they are combined. Adaptation techniques aim at automatically generating new components called *adapters*, and usually rely on

© Springer International Publishing Switzerland 2016
R. De Nicola and E. Kühn (Eds.): SEFM 2016, LNCS 9763, pp. 321–336, 2016.
DOI: 10.1007/978-3-319-41591-8_22

an *adaptation contract*, which is an abstract description of how mismatch can be worked out. The adapter acts as an orchestrator and makes the involved peers work correctly together by receiving all messages and by compensating for mismatch. Many solutions have been proposed since the seminal work by Yellin and Strom [26], but most of them assume that peers interact using synchronous communication, that is, synchronization via rendez-vous.

One of the main open challenges in the adaptation area is to assume that peers interact using asynchronous communication, which is a valid assumption given that nowadays many systems rely on this communication model (cloud computing, Web, grid computing, GALS, multi-core architectures, IoT, etc.). Asynchronous communication highly complicates the adapter generation process, because the corresponding systems are not necessarily bounded and may result into infinite systems. It is known that in this context, the verification problem is undecidable for communicating finite state machines [4]. An option is to arbitrary bound the sources of infiniteness (buffers, cycles, number of participants, etc.), but we want to avoid imposing this kind of constraints, since it would unnecessarily restrict the behaviour of the whole system.

We assume that peers are modelled using behavioural descriptions and interact asynchronously via (possibly unbounded) FIFO buffers. In a previous work [9], we presented a preliminary proposal for asynchronous adaptation in which a sufficient condition, called *synchronizability*, was required. However, many asynchronous systems are not synchronizable. Hence, in order to widen the number of systems to be adapted, in this paper we propose new synthesis techniques, which rely on an encoding into the LNT process algebra [10] on the one hand, and on a property of *stability* [1] on the other hand. Using stability is an improvement over synchronizability, as many systems in practice are not synchronizable yet stable. A set of peers is stable if from some buffer bound k, the k-bounded asynchronous composition is equivalent to the $k + 1$-bounded asynchronous composition, considering only the ordering of output messages and ignoring that of input messages. If this k exists, it is proved [1] that the observable behaviour remains the same for any larger buffer bound. This property can be verified using equivalence checking techniques on finite systems, although the set of peers interacting asynchronously can result in infinite systems. Based on this result, one can check on the system a property, concerning output messages, for the smallest bound satisfying stability and claim that this property is also satisfied for any larger bound. We use stability here for verifying whether an adapter generated for a certain bound k can be used with any larger bound, or even with unbounded buffers.

As far as the adapter synthesis techniques are concerned, we encode all inputs (peers, contract, buffers) into the LNT process algebra and use the CADP verification toolbox [13] for generating the corresponding adapter model. The stability property is also checked automatically using the CADP equivalence checker. Since the adaptation contract is manually written, the designer can take advantage of the LNT encoding to verify using CADP that the final adapter works correctly, that is, respects certain properties of interest. We have validated our approach on several case studies, one of them presented in detail throughout this paper.

The rest of this paper is organized as follows. Section 2 introduces the behavioural model for peers and the notation for specifying adaptation contracts. Section 3 overviews the encoding into LNT. In Sect. 4, we present the stability property and how we use it in our context. Section 5 shows how we generate the adapter model from the LNT encoding and using CADP verification techniques. In this section, we also present our whole adaptation method for asynchronous environments. Finally, Sect. 6 surveys related work, and Sect. 7 concludes this paper.

2 Models

In this section, we first introduce the interface model through which peers are accessed and used. Then, we define adaptation contracts, and present the motivating example that will be used throughout the paper.

2.1 Interface LTS

We assume that peers are described using a behavioural *interface* in the form of a Labelled Transition System (LTS).

Definition 1 (LTS). *A* Labelled Transition System *is a tuple* (S, s^0, Σ, T) *where: S is a set of states, $s^0 \in S$ is the initial state, $\Sigma = \Sigma^! \cup \Sigma^?$ is a finite alphabet partitioned into a set $\Sigma^!$ ($\Sigma^?$, resp.) of send (receive, resp.) message events, and $T \subseteq S \times \Sigma \times S$ is the transition function.*

The alphabet of the LTS is built on the set of operations used by the peer in its interaction with the world. This means that for each operation p provided by the peer, there is a message event $p? \in \Sigma^?$ in the alphabet of the LTS describing the behaviour of the peer, and for each operation r required from its environment, there is a message event $r! \in \Sigma^!$. When two peers present events with the same name and complementary directions $(a!, a?)$ they can be matched for inter-peer communication through message-passing.

Note that as usually done in the literature [11,16,23], our interfaces abstract from operation arguments, types of return values, and exceptions. Nevertheless, they can be easily extended to explicitly represent operation arguments and their associated data types, by using Symbolic Transition Systems (STSs) [18] instead of LTSs. However, this renders the definitions and results presented in this work much longer and cumbersome, without adding anything substantial to the technical aspects of our proposal. Hence, it is omitted in this paper.

It is worth observing that other formalisms, such as process algebra, could be used alternatively to LTS [8]. However, for this paper we have preferred to use LTS as the input notation of our proposal, since they provide a compact representation, graphical, and easy to understand for all developers.

2.2   Adaptation Contracts and Adapter LTS

Typical mismatch situations between peers appear when event names do not correspond, the order of events is not respected, or an event in one peer has no counterpart or matches several events in another one. All these cases of behavioural mismatch can be worked out by specifying an adaptation contract [8]. Adaptation contracts consist of rules that express correspondences between operations of the peers, like bindings between ports or connectors in architectural descriptions. Adaptation rules are given as vectors, as defined below:

Definition 2 (Vector). *An* adaptation vector *(or* vector *for short) for a set of peers* $\{\mathcal{P}_1, \ldots, \mathcal{P}_n\}$ *with* $\mathcal{P}_i = (S_i, s_i^0, \Sigma_i, T_i)$, *is a tuple* $\langle e_1, \ldots, e_n \rangle$ *with* $e_i \in \Sigma_i \cup \{\epsilon\}$, ϵ *meaning that a peer does not participate in the vector.*

In order to unambiguously identify them, we prefix event names with the name of the peer, *e.g.*, $\mathcal{P}_i : p?$, or $\mathcal{P}_j : r!$, and in that case ϵ can be omitted. For instance, the vector $\langle p_1 : a!, \ p_3 : b?, \ p_4 : c? \rangle$ represents an adaptation rule indicating that the output event $a!$ from peer p_1 should match both input events $b?$ and $c?$ in p_3 and p_4, respectively, while peer $p2$ does not participate in this interaction.

In some complex adaptation scenarios, adaptation rules must be taken contextually (*i.e.*, vectors cannot be applied at any time, but only in certain situations). For this purpose, we may use regular expressions (regex) on vectors [9], indicating a pattern for applying them that will constrain the adaptation process, enforcing additional properties on the adapter. This endows adaptation contracts with extended expressivity, though in this work we do not show their use, in order to avoid additional complexity in the presentation of our proposal.

Definition 3 (Adaptation Contract). *An* adaptation contract V *for a set of peers* $\{\mathcal{P}_1, \ldots, \mathcal{P}_n\}$ *is a set of adaptation vectors for those peers.*

Writing the adaptation contract is the only step of our approach which is not handled automatically. This step is crucial because an inadequate contract would induce the generation of an adapter that will not make the composition of peers to behave correctly. However, the adaptation methodology that we propose is iterative, which helps in writing the contract contract. Furthermore, in [5,6], we presented a tool-supported approach for assisting and making easier the specification of the adaptation contract. For more details on adaptation contracts and the kinds of mismatch that can be resolved with them, we refer to [8].

Given a set of peers represented by their LTS interfaces and an adaptation contract, our goal is to generate an adapter, which will play the role of *man-in-the-middle*, solving the mismatch presented by the peers. The adapter is also represented by an LTS consisting of messages to be consumed from its buffer and messages to be sent to the other peers. The adapter also keeps track of the messages received by its own local buffer. This information is important to enforce the adapter to execute the correct behaviour, avoiding engaging in a branch that may lead to an erroneous execution of the whole system.

Definition 4 (Adapter LTS). *An adapter LTS is a tuple* (S, s^0, Σ, T) *where:* S *is a set of states,* $s^0 \in S$ *is the initial state,* $\Sigma = \Sigma^! \cup \Sigma^? \cup \Sigma^B$ *is a finite alphabet partitioned into a set* $\Sigma^!$ $(\Sigma^?,$ *resp.) of send (receive, resp.) messages and a set of messages received by its buffer* Σ^B, *and* $T \subseteq S \times \Sigma \times S$ *is the transition function.*

In the following we will show how this adapter LTS can be automatically generated from the LTS interfaces of the peers and the adaptation contract.

2.3   Running Example

In order to illustrate the main features of our proposal, the following motivating example will be used throughout this paper. Consider a simple Client/Server system, in which clients are identified to the server by their username and password, and submit requests for a certain service. Upon receiving the result of the request, the client issues an acknowledging message, and then quits. The interface LTS representing the behaviour of clients is shown in Fig. 1, top, where the black dot indicates the initial state.

On the other side, the server follows a similar behaviour, as shown in Fig. 1, left bottom. The main differences, which are used in the example in order to show how to perform adaptation, are: *(i)* connections are expected by the server with a single *login?* message (instead of two separate *usr!* and *pwd!* messages issued by the client); *(ii)* after login, the server is ready to receive several consecutive requests or a logout message, while the client only sends one request before quitting; and *(iii)* messages for disconnection are also named differently in the client and the server. Finally the server interacts with a third peer, a database log (Fig. 1, right bottom), which stores all the requests fulfilled by the server.

The example above has been chosen deliberately simple in order to avoid it taking too much space in this paper. However, it shows the different kinds of adaptation that our proposal addresses: differences in message names (*e.g., quit!* and *logout?*), differences in the granularity or the order of messages (*e.g., user!,*

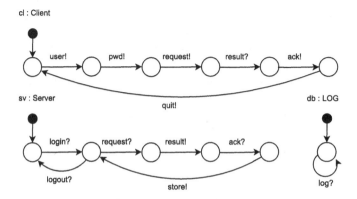

Fig. 1. Interface LTSs of the peers.

pwd! and *login?*), and differences in decision-taking roles and other higher level behavioural aspects (*e.g.,* the client decides to quit after a request, while the server allows new requests). How to address all these differences or mismatch between the interfaces of the peers is specified with an adaptation contract. Assuming that *sv* refers to a server, *cl* to its client and *db* to the database log, these three peers can be adapted by means of the following contract, which shows how message names are interconnected between the different peers involved in this system:

$$\{ \ \langle cl{:}user!, \ sv{:}login? \rangle,$$
$$\langle cl{:}pwd! \rangle,$$
$$\langle cl{:}quit!, \ sv{:}logout? \rangle,$$
$$\langle cl{:}request!, \ sv{:}request? \rangle,$$
$$\langle cl{:}result?, \ sv{:}result! \rangle,$$
$$\langle cl{:}ack!, \ sv{:}ack? \rangle,$$
$$\langle sv{:}store!, \ db{:}log? \rangle \ \}$$

3   Process Algebra Encoding

Our asynchronous adapter generation techniques rely on an encoding into LNT [10] that we overview in this section. LNT is a formal specification language which combines traits of process calculi, functional and imperative languages. We chose LNT for two main reasons. First, it is expressive enough for encoding all inputs (LTSs, contract, buffers, architecture) of our problem. Second, it is equipped with a rich verification toolbox (CADP) that we use for checking the existence of an adapter and, if this is the case, for generating an adapter LTS and for analyzing properties of interest on it.

Interface LTSs. An LNT process is generated for each state in the interface LTS of a peer. The alphabet of the process contains the set of messages appearing in the transitions of the LTS. The behaviour of the process encodes all the transitions of the LTS going out from the corresponding state. If there is no such transition, the body of the process is the null statement. If there is a single transition, the body of the process corresponds to the message labelling this transition, followed by a call to the process encoding the target state of the transition. If there is more than one transition, we use the select operator, which encodes a nondeterministic choice between the different transitions going out of that state. Name clashes are avoided by prefixing each message with the name of the corresponding peer. We encode emitted messages (received messages, resp.) with a _EM (_REC, resp.) suffix. These suffixes are necessary because LNT symbols ! and ? are used for data transfer only.

Adaptation Contract. The vectors are encoded into an LNT process called *contract*. The process alphabet is composed of all received and emitted messages between the adapter-to-be and the involved participant peers, that is, all messages appearing in the vectors. Each vector is encoded as a sequence of actions starting with the emissions and followed by the receptions. Notice that in the LNT process representing the adaptation contract, message directions are reversed with respect to the peers because the adapter will receive the output messages and emit the input messages expected by the recipient peers.

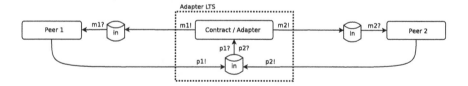

Fig. 2. Architecture and exchanged messages.

Asynchronous Assembling. Now, we need to encode how all participants (peer interfaces and adaptation contract) are composed together using asynchronous communication. The architecture of the whole assembly is shown in Fig. 2. The contract represents an abstract description of the future adapter, and all messages must go through this adapter, which acts as a centralized orchestrator. Each participant is equipped with an input FIFO buffer. A buffer in LNT is first encoded using an LNT list and LNT functions are used to describe classic operations on these buffers (*e.g.*, adding and retrieving messages). Then, for the behavioural part, a buffer is encoded using a process with a buffer data type as parameter. This process can receive messages from the other participants, and it synchronizes with its own participant when the latter wants to read a message. More precisely, when a participant reads a message, it reads the oldest message in its buffer. When a participant sends a message to another participant, it sends the message to the input buffer of that participant. In the next sections, we will show how buffer bounds are determined for generating the adapter LTS while avoiding the manipulation of infinite state spaces.

We also generate a process encoding each couple (*participant*, *buffer*) that corresponds to a parallel composition (par) of the participant with its buffer. The synchronization set contains messages consumed by the participant from its buffer. Finally, the whole system (main process in LNT) consists of the parallel composition of all these couples. It is worth noting that since the involved peers communicate via the adapter, they evolve independently from one another and are therefore composed using the par operator without synchronizations. In contrast, the couple (*contract*, *buffer*) must synchronize with all couples (*peer*, *buffer*) on all emissions from/to the peers, and this is made explicit in the corresponding synchronization set of this parallel composition.

4   Stability of Adapted Systems

In this section, we characterize the stability property for adapted systems, where peers communicate with the adapter asynchronously via FIFO buffers. Hence, each peer $\mathcal{P}_i$ is equipped with an input message buffer Q_i, and the adapter $\mathcal{A}$

with an input buffer Q. A peer can either send a message $m \in \Sigma^!$ to the tail of the adapter buffer Q at any state where this send message is available, or either read a message $m \in \Sigma^?$ from its buffer Q_i if the message is available at the buffer head. We recall that we focus on output events, since reading from the buffer is private non-observable information, which is encoded as an internal transition in the asynchronous system.

Definition 5 (Adapted Asynchronous Composition). *Given a set of peers* $\{\mathcal{P}_1, \ldots, \mathcal{P}_n\}$ *with* $\mathcal{P}_i = (S_i, s_i^0, \Sigma_i, T_i)$, Q_i *being its associated input buffer, and an adapter* $\mathcal{A} = (S, s^0, \Sigma, T)$ *with input buffer* Q, *their asynchronous composition is the labelled transition system* $LTS_{aa} = (S_{aa}, s_{aa}^0, \Sigma_{aa}, T_{aa})$ *where:*

- $S_{aa} \subseteq S_1 \times Q_1 \times \ldots \times S_n \times Q_n \times S \times Q$ *where* $\forall i \in \{1, \ldots, n\}$, $Q_i \subseteq (\Sigma_i^?)*$ *and* $Q \subseteq (\Sigma^?)*$
- $s_{aa}^0 \in S_{aa}$ *such that* $s_{aa}^0 = (s_1^0, \epsilon, \ldots, s_n^0, \epsilon, s^0, \epsilon)$ *(where* ϵ *denotes an empty buffer)*
- $\Sigma_{aa} = \cup_i \Sigma_i \cup \Sigma$
- $T_{aa} \subseteq S_{aa} \times \Sigma_{aa} \times S_{aa}$, *and for* $s = (s_1, Q_1, \ldots, s_n, Q_n, s_a, Q) \in S_{aa}$ *and* $s' = (s_1', Q_1', \ldots, s_n', Q_n', s_a', Q') \in S_{aa}$ *we have that*

(p2a!) $s \xrightarrow{m!} s' \in T_{aa}$ *if* $\exists i \in \{1, \ldots, n\} : m \in \Sigma_i^! \cap \Sigma^?$, *(i)* $s_i \xrightarrow{m!} s_i' \in T_i$, *(ii)* $Q' = Qm$, *(iii)* $s_a' = s_a$, *(iv)* $\forall k \in \{1, \ldots, n\} : Q_k' = Q_k$, *and (v)* $\forall k \in \{1, \ldots, n\} : k \neq i \Rightarrow s_k' = s_k$

(p2a?) $s \xrightarrow{\tau} s' \in T_{aa}$ *if* $m \in \Sigma^?$, *(i)* $s_a \xrightarrow{m?} s_a' \in T$, *(ii)* $mQ' = Q$, *(iii)* $\forall k \in \{1, \ldots, n\} : Q_k' = Q_k$, *and (iv)* $\forall k \in \{1, \ldots, n\} : s_k' = s_k$

(a2p!) $s \xrightarrow{m!} s' \in T_{aa}$ *if* $\exists j \in \{1, \ldots, n\} : m \in \Sigma^! \cap \Sigma_j^?$, *(i)* $s_a \xrightarrow{m!} s_a' \in T$, *(ii)* $Q_j' = Q_j m$, *(iii)* $Q' = Q$, *(iv)* $\forall k \in \{1, \ldots, n\} : k \neq j \Rightarrow Q_k' = Q_k$, *and (v)* $\forall k \in \{1, \ldots, n\} : s_k' = s_k$

(a2p?) $s \xrightarrow{\tau} s' \in T_{aa}$ *if* $\exists i \in \{1, \ldots, n\} : m \in \Sigma_i^?$, *(i)* $s_i \xrightarrow{m?} s_i' \in T_i$, *(ii)* $mQ_i' = Q_i$, *(iii)* $\forall k \in \{1, \ldots, n\} : k \neq i \Rightarrow Q_k' = Q_k$, *(iv)* $\forall k \in \{1, \ldots, n\} : k \neq i \Rightarrow s_k' = s_k$, *(v)* $Q' = Q$, *and (vi)* $s_a' = s_a$

We denote by LTS_{aa} an unbounded adapted asynchronous composition, while we use LTS_{aa}^k for referring to the k-*bounded* adapted asynchronous composition, where each message buffer is bounded to size k. The definition of LTS_{aa}^k can be obtained from Definition 5 by allowing send transitions only if the message buffer of the receiving peer has less than k messages in it. Otherwise, the sender is blocked, *i.e.*, we assume reliable communication without message losses.

The stability property applies here by considering the adapter as a peer whose peculiarity is to interact with all the other participants.

Definition 6 (Stability). *A set of peers* $\{\mathcal{P}_1, \ldots, \mathcal{P}_n\}$ *and an adapter* $\mathcal{A}$ *are stable if* $\exists k$ *such that* $LTS_{aa}^k \equiv_{br} LTS_{aa}^q$ $(\forall q > k)$.

A sufficient condition for ensuring stability was presented in [1]: if there exists a bound k such that the k-bounded and the $(k + 1)$-bounded asynchronous systems are branching equivalent, *i.e.*, $LTS_{aa}^k \equiv_{br} LTS_{aa}^{k+1}$, then the system remains stable, meaning that the observable behaviour is always the same for any bound greater than k. The smallest k satisfying the stability property can be found using heuristics and a search algorithm. However, stability is undecidable. Therefore an arbitrary max bound is used during these computations and the algorithm stops when the current value goes beyong that arbitrary value. In that case, stability checking is inconclusive.

5   Adapter Generation and Methodology

In the previous section we have defined stability for adapted asynchronous systems. If a system is stable for a certain bound k, we are able to generate an adapter model that communicates asynchronously with the peers, where all the participants use buffers of size k. The adapter will play the role that until now had taken the adaptation contract. This adapter is obtained from our LNT encoding by keeping only the behaviour we expect from the adapter point of view, that is, we need to preserve send and receive messages for the adaptation contract. To do so, we hide message exchanges corresponding to consumptions of the peers from their buffers and we rename emissions from peers to the adaptation contract (Σ^B) in order to distinguish these messages from the adapter regular behaviour $(\Sigma^!$ and $\Sigma^?)$. In order to keep only the behaviour corresponding to the most permissive adapter, we use CADP compilers, which explore all the possible executions of the generated LNT specification. We also make use of minimization techniques available in CADP for eliminating all internal actions, removing duplicated paths, and determinizing the final LTS. The whole adapter generation process is achieved automatically.

Figure 2 shows an example of architecture with the contract/adapter and two peers. Each participant is equipped with one input buffer. The dashed box shows the messages we keep in order to generate the adapter LTS where $m_i! \in \Sigma^!$, $p_i? \in \Sigma^?$, and $p_i! \in \Sigma^B$, $i \in \{1, 2\}$.

Note that stability is checked on the whole LNT encoding. We show below that this property is preserved when we extract the adapter LTS from this encoding for using it with the peer LTSs, all interacting via FIFO buffers.

Theorem 1 (Stability Preservation). *Given a set of peers $\{\mathcal{P}_1, ..., \mathcal{P}_n\}$ and an adaptation contract V, if the corresponding asynchronous LNT encoding is stable for a certain k, then the system where all peers interact through the generated adapter LTS A via k-bounded FIFO buffers is also stable for this k.*

Proof. Let $S_1^k = ((\mathcal{P}_1|Q_1)|...|(\mathcal{P}_n|Q_n))|(V|Q)$ be the encoding into LNT of the peers $\{\mathcal{P}_1, ..., \mathcal{P}_n\}$, of the contract V, and of FIFO buffers Q_i for peers and Q for the contract/adapter-to-be. The alphabet $\Sigma_V = \Sigma_V^! \cup \Sigma_v^?$ of V coincides with the alphabet $\Sigma = \Sigma_A^! \cup \Sigma_A^? \cup \Sigma_A^B$ of the adapter LTS A, that is, $\Sigma_V^! = \Sigma_A^!$ and $\Sigma_V^? = \Sigma_A^?$, but for actions Σ_A^B. However, actions in Σ_A^B are not synchronized with the system, they are internally used in the adapter LTS for keeping track of the content of its buffer Q only.

Once the adapter is generated, the current behaviour of the whole system is as follows: $S_2^k = ((\mathcal{P}_1|Q_1)|\ldots|(\mathcal{P}_n|Q_n))|(A|Q)$. Actually, the adapter LTS A is obtained by extraction from S_1^k, by keeping the behaviour of V constrained by the peers' behaviours as explained beforehand in this section, which is exactly the behaviour of A. Thus, $(C|V) \equiv_{br} (C|A)$, where C stands for the context, *i.e.*, the rest of the system. Hence, $S_1^k \equiv_{br} S_2^k$ and this proves the theorem. ∎

Figure 3 gives an overview of our approach for generating an adapter LTS in asynchronous environments. First of all, we assume that the peers are incompatible and thus cannot be reused and composed directly without using adaptation techniques for compensating mismatch. This can be checked using existing compatibility techniques as those presented, *e.g.*, in [21]. If an adapter is required, the user needs to provide an adaptation contract. The next step consists in encoding all these inputs (peer LTSs and adaptation contract) into LNT as presented in Sect. 3.

Then, we check stability directly on the LNT encoding, trying to find a k from which the k-bounded adapted asynchronous composition and the $k + 1$-bounded adapted asynchronous composition are equivalent. If this is the case, it means that the system is stable and its observable behaviour will remain the same whatever bound is chosen for buffers from that bound k. In that case, we can generate the adapter for that k, and it can be used in practice for whatever bound equal or greater than it. If the system is not stable, the sole solution is to fix an arbitrary bound before generating the adapter model, to generate the adapter LTS for that bound, and to use it further with that bound only.

Finally, since the adaptation contract is written manually, some mistake may appear at this level ending up with a faulty adapter. However, we can take advantage of the LNT encoding in order to formally analyse the system. This can be achieved by verifying the global LTS obtained direclty from the encoding and corresponding to the execution of the whole application (peers and adapter), or by verifying the adapter LTS obtained after synthesis from the LNT encoding as explained at the beginning of this section. In both cases, one can use the verification techniques and tools available in the CADP toolbox, and in particular, the Evaluator model checker, which accepts as input an LTS and an MCL formula [19], and returns a diagnostic (Boolean value + a counterexample if the property is false). If some property is not satisfied, we can go back to the contract writing, make corrections on it, and start again from this step the overall synthesis.

Coming back to our Client/Server example, we start from the LTSs of the peers, as presented in Sect. 2.3. As already explained there, the client, the server, and the database log show several sources of mismatch, the most obvious being that they communicate using different message names, but also that messages do not correspond one-to-one between the server and the client (during the login phase), and that the server admits several requests after connection, while the client does not. Hence, adaptation is required, and the adaptation contract presented in Sect. 2.3 is the first step of the adaptation process.

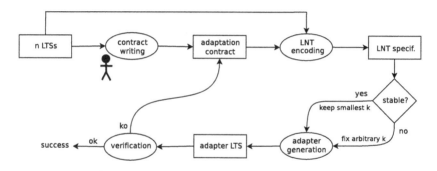

Fig. 3. Overview of our approach.

Then, we can check whether the system is synchronizable. If that were the case, we would be under the conditions defined in [9], which require the asynchronous system to be behaviourally equivalent to its synchronous version. This is not the case of our adapted Client/Server system, in which the client is able to issue several output messages (*user!*, *pwd!*, *request!*) in a row in the asynchronous version of the system, whereas this is not possible in the synchronous system because the adapter, after the reception of the two first messages (*user?*, *pwd?*), cannot receive the third one (*request?*) until it sends the *login!* message to the server. Hence, the results in [9] do not apply to our example, whereas the approach presented in this paper works as we will show in the rest of this section.

First of all, we need to check whether the system is stable. In order to analyse stability, both the interface LTSs of the peers and the adaptation contract are automatically encoded into LNT, as described in Sect. 3, and we check the LNT resulting system as defined in Sect. 4. We use the CADP toolbox for checking this property, which finds out that the asynchronous adapted system is stable for $k = 4$. Intuitively, this means than from buffers of that size, the observable collective behaviour of all peers remain the same, and hence, we can generate an asynchronous adapter using buffers bounded to that size. For this particular example, the asynchronous adapter presents 1,630 states and 4,278 transitions, though its generation takes only a few seconds. These figures show that, despite we have committed to a very simple system, asynchronous adaptation could not be possibly performed without automated techniques, as those presented in this paper. The asynchronous adapter, generated and visualized with CADP, is shown in Fig. 4, after the removal of internal transitions and identical paths, and abstracting for messages in Σ_B in order to make it fit in one page. We remind that event names in the adapter are reversed with respect to those of the peers and the adaptation contract, as explained in Sect. 3.

Once we have obtained the adapter, we can check the system (adapter alone or composition of the adapter with the peers) for properties of interest, like for instance deadlock freedom. Not fulfilling these properties would mean that the adaptation contract is ill-written, and from the counterexample provided we

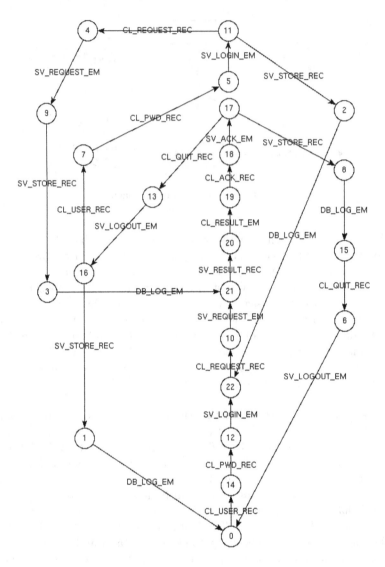

Fig. 4. Asynchronous adapter for the running example.

could adjust the contract, until the system behaves as expected. In our case, the adapted system is deadlock free, and we can also check for additional user-defined properties, which are expected to be enforced by the adapter. For instance, that every *request!* of the client will be followed by the delivery of the *result!* message, or that every *login?* message received by the server is followed by a corresponding *logout?* message. All these properties can be automatically analysed using the CADP model checker. When all properties of interest are satisfied, and this is the case with our example, we can conclude that our adaptation problem is solved.

6 Related Work

First of all, adaptation differs from automatic software composition approaches, particularly studied in the Web services area, *e.g.*, [3,17], where services involved into a new composition are assumed to perfectly match altogether with respect to certain compatibility property [12].

The major part of the contributions on the software adaptation area assume that peers interact synchronously, while our proposal addresses asynchronous communication. Van der Aalst *et al.* [25] propose a solution to behavioural adaptation based on open nets, a variant of Petri nets. A behavioural controller (a transition system and BPEL) is synthesised for the product net of the services and a set of message transformation rules. In [20], the authors provide a method for identification of the split/merge class of interface mismatch and a semi-automated, behaviour-aware approach for interface-level mismatch that results in identifying parameters of mapping functions that resolve that mismatch. In [8,18], the authors proposed automated techniques for generating an adapter model from a set of service.behavioural interfaces and an adaptation contract. Some BPEL code is automatically generated from the adapter model, which may finally be deployed.

Inverardi and Tivoli [15] formalise a method for the automated synthesis of modular connectors. A modular connector is structured as a composition of independent mediators, each of them corresponding to the solution of a recurring behavioural mismatch. Bennaceur *et al.* [2] propose a technique for automated synthesis of mediators using a quotient operator, that is based on behavioural models of the components and an ontological model of the data domain. The obtained mediator is the most general component that ensures deadlock-freedom and the absence of communication mismatch.

There are only a few attempts to generate adapters considering asynchronous communication. Padovani [22] presents a theory based on behavioural contracts to generate orchestrators between two services related by a subtyping (namely, sub-contract) relation. This is used to generate an adapter between a client of some service S and a service replacing S. An interesting feature of this approach is its expressiveness as far as behavioural descriptions are concerned, with support for asynchronous orchestrators and infinite behaviour. The author resorts to the theory of regular trees and imposes two requirements on the orchestrator, namely regularity and contractivity. However, this work does not support name mismatch nor data-related adaptation. Seguel *et al.* [24] present automatic techniques for constructing a minimal adapter for two business protocols possibly involving parallelism and loops. The approach works by assigning to loops a fixed number of iterations, whereas we do not impose any restriction, and peers may loop infinitely.

Gierds and colleagues [14] present an approach for specifying behavioural adapters based on domain-specific transformation rules that reflect the elementary operations that adapters can perform. The authors also present a novel way to synthesise complex adapters that adhere to these rules by consistently separating data and control, and by using existing controller synthesis algorithms.

Asynchronous adaptation is supported in this work, but buffers/places must be arbitrarily bounded for ensuring computability of the adapter.

In [9], we presented a solution to the software adaptation problem by using the synchronizability property and adapter generation techniques for synchronous communication. The adapter synthesis in this approach relies on an iterative process, which works properly in asynchronous environments. The main limitation of our previous work is that the synchronizability property is quite restrictive and requires asynchronous systems to behave *de facto* as synchronous. Stability is a much looser condition, allowing to address a wider class of asynchronous systems.

7   Conclusion

Software adaptation is an approach for simplifying the reuse of existing peers when building a new software by composition of these entities. Adaptation is particularly relevant when the peers to be composed fulfill the functional requirements of the system but they are not compatible from an interface point of view. In that case, we can rely on such techniques for synthesising an adapter, which acts as an orchestrator and intervenes on the messages exchanged for correcting mismatch among peer interfaces. Most solutions existing for this problem assume peers interact synchronously via rendez-vous communication.

In this paper, we consider they exchange messages asynchronously via FIFO buffers. We also focus on a behavioural description model for peers, involving non-determinism and cycles. We propose new synthesis techniques for asynchronous communication semantics, which are based on an encoding into LNT, a modern process algebra. As far as adapter generation is concerned, we use the CADP toolbox for compiling the generated process algebraic specification to an LTS, and for minimizing the obtained result using classic reduction techniques. Beyond synthesis techniques, we also provide two kinds of verification. The first one relies on the stability property and aims at ensuring that the generated adapter will work from a certain size chosen for buffers. The second one is to use model checking techniques in order to verify that the adapter respect certain properties of interest. Our approach has been applied to several examples for validation purposes.

Our main perspective is to find some sufficient conditions on the LTS models or on the adaptation contract specification that could help ensuring the stability property preservation. Such conditions would avoid to check this property and ensure by construction that the generated adapter would work in unconstrained asynchronous environments.

References

1. Akroun, L., Salaün, G., Ye, L.: Automated analysis of asynchronously communicating systems. In: Bošnacki, D., Wijs, A. (eds.) SPIN 2016. LNCS, vol. 9641, pp. 1–18. Springer, Heidelberg (2016). doi:10.1007/978-3-319-32582-8_1

2. Bennaceur, A., Chilton, C., Isberner, M., Jonsson, B.: Automated mediator synthesis: combining behavioural and ontological reasoning. In: Hierons, R.M., Merayo, M.G., Bravetti, M. (eds.) SEFM 2013. LNCS, vol. 8137, pp. 274–288. Springer, Heidelberg (2013)

3. Bertoli, P., Pistore, M., Traverso, P.: Automated composition of web services via planning in asynchronous domains. Artif. Intell. **174**(3–4), 316–361 (2010)

4. Brand, D., Zafiropulo, P.: On communicating finite-state machines. J. ACM **30**(2), 323–342 (1983)

5. Cámara, J., Martín, J.A., Salaün, G., Cubo, J., Ouederni, M., Canal, C., Pimentel, E.: ITACA: an integrated toolbox for the automatic composition and adaptation of web services. In: Proceedings of ICSE 2009, pp. 627–630. IEEE (2009)

6. Cámara, J., Salaün, G., Canal, C., Ouederni, M.: Interactive specification and verification of behavioral adaptation contracts. Inf. Softw. Technol. **54**(7), 701–723 (2012)

7. Canal, C., Murillo, J.M., Poizat, P.: Software adaptation. L'Objet **12**(1), 9–31 (2006)

8. Canal, C., Poizat, P., Salaün, G.: Model-based adaptation of behavioural mismatching components. IEEE Trans. Softw. Eng. **34**(4), 546–563 (2008)

9. Canal, C., Salaün, G.: Model-based adaptation of software communicating via FIFO buffers. In: Egyed, A., Schaefer, I. (eds.) FASE 2015. LNCS, vol. 9033, pp. 252–266. Springer, Heidelberg (2015)

10. Champelovier, D., Clerc, X., Garavel, H., Guerte, Y., Powazny, V., Lang, F., Serwe, W., Smeding, G.: Reference Manual of the LOTOS NT to LOTOS Translator (Version 5.4). INRIA/VASY, 149 p. (2011)

11. de Alfaro, L., Henzinger, T.A.: Interface automata. In: Proceedings of ESEC/FSE 2001, pp. 109–120. ACM Press (2001)

12. Durán, F., Ouederni, M., Salaün, G.: A generic framework for N-protocol compatibility checking. Sci. Comput. Program. **77**(7–8), 870–886 (2012)

13. Garavel, H., Lang, F., Mateescu, R., Serwe, W.: CADP 2010: a toolbox for the construction and analysis of distributed processes. In: Abdulla, P.A., Leino, K.R.M. (eds.) TACAS 2011. LNCS, vol. 6605, pp. 372–387. Springer, Heidelberg (2011)

14. Gierds, C., Mooij, A.J., Wolf, K.: Reducing adapter synthesis to controller synthesis. IEEE Trans. Serv. Comput. **5**(1), 72–85 (2012)

15. Inverardi, P., Tivoli, M.: Automatic synthesis of modular connectors via composition of protocol mediation patterns. In: Proceedings of ICSE 2013, pp. 3–12. IEEE/ACM (2013)

16. Magee, J., Kramer, J., Giannakopoulou, D.: Behaviour analysis of software architectures, pp. 35–49. Kluwer Academic Publishers (1999)

17. Marconi, A., Pistore, M.: Synthesis and composition of web services. In: Bernardo, M., Padovani, L., Zavattaro, G. (eds.) SFM 2009. LNCS, vol. 5569, pp. 89–157. Springer, Heidelberg (2009)

18. Mateescu, R., Poizat, P., Salaün, G.: Adaptation of service protocols using process algebra and on-the-fly reduction techniques. IEEE Trans. Softw. Eng. **38**(4), 755–777 (2012)

19. Mateescu, R., Thivolle, D.: A model checking language for concurrent value-passing systems. In: Cuellar, J., Sere, K. (eds.) FM 2008. LNCS, vol. 5014, pp. 148–164. Springer, Heidelberg (2008)

20. Motahari Nezhad, H.R., Xu, G.Y., Benatallah, B.: Protocol-aware matching of web service interfaces for adapter development. In: Proceedings of WWW 2010, pp. 731–740. ACM (2010)

21. Ouederni, M., Salaün, G., Bultan, T.: Compatibility checking for asynchronously communicating software. In: Fiadeiro, J.L., Liu, Z., Xue, J. (eds.) FACS 2013. LNCS, vol. 8348, pp. 310–328. Springer, Heidelberg (2014)

22. Padovani, L.: Contract-based discovery and adaptation of web services. In: Bernardo, M., Padovani, L., Zavattaro, G. (eds.) SFM 2009. LNCS, vol. 5569, pp. 213–260. Springer, Heidelberg (2009)

23. Plasil, F., Visnovsky, S.: Behavior protocols for software components. IEEE Trans. Softw. Eng. **28**(11), 1056–1076 (2002)

24. Seguel, R., Eshuis, R., Grefen, P.W.P.J.: Generating minimal protocol adaptors for loosely coupled services. In: Proceedings of ICWS 2010, pp. 417–424. IEEE Computer Society (2010)

25. van der Aalst, W.M.P., Mooij, A.J., Stahl, C., Wolf, K.: Service interaction: patterns, formalization, and analysis. In: Bernardo, M., Padovani, L., Zavattaro, G. (eds.) SFM 2009. LNCS, vol. 5569, pp. 42–88. Springer, Heidelberg (2009)

26. Yellin, D.M., Strom, R.E.: Protocol specifications and components adaptors. ACM Trans. Program. Lang. Syst. **19**(2), 292–333 (1997)

Compliance Checking in the Open Payments Ecosystem

Shaun Azzopardi[1]([✉]), Christian Colombo[1], Gordon J. Pace[1], and Brian Vella[2]

[1] University of Malta, Msida, Malta
shaun.azzopardi@um.edu.mt
[2] Ixaris Ltd., San Ġwann, Malta

Abstract. Given the strict legal frameworks which regulate the movements and management of funds, building financial applications typically proves to be prohibitively expensive for small companies. Not only is it the case that understanding legal requirements and building a framework of compliance checks to ensure that such legislation is adhered to is a complex process, but also, service providers such as banks require certification and reporting before they are willing to take on the risks associated with the adoption of applications from small application developers. In this paper, we propose a solution which provides a centralised Open Payments Ecosystem which supports compliance checking and allows for the matching of financial applications with service providers and programme managers, automatically providing risk analysis and reporting. The solution proposed combines static and dynamic verification in a real-life use case, which can shed new insights on the use of formal methods on large complex systems. We also report on the software engineering challenges encountered when analysing formal requirements arising from the needs of compliance to applicable legislation.

1 Introduction

Businesses often find themselves needing diverse ways of affecting or enabling payments in various contexts. As an example, consider a business providing a payment service to a travel agency to purchase flights, hotel bookings, etc. Having several such purchases from a single corporate card, particularly if that same card is also used for other purchases, would make reconciliation non-straightforward at best. On the other hand, providing one shot cards for use by the travel agency, which are cards that can be used once and disabled after the first purchase, makes reconciliation easier as only one purchase will be associated with any given card. However, for a business to set up such a payment programme, it is quite complex (implement cards processes for provisioning, reconciliation, dispute management, as well as creating a compliant application) and the costs may be prohibitive. In addition, negotiating with a bank or payment

The Open Payments Ecosystem has received funding from the European Union's Horizon 2020 research and innovation programme under grant number 666363.

© Springer International Publishing Switzerland 2016
R. De Nicola and E. Kühn (Eds.): SEFM 2016, LNCS 9763, pp. 337–343, 2016.
DOI: 10.1007/978-3-319-41591-8_23

service provider in order to use their services to perform the actual financial movements and the resulting investment required to guarantee compliance to national legislation can be daunting. Even understanding the legal requirements is a major task, let alone the building of the necessary infrastructure to ensure compliance and to perform the risk analysis required by law and the banks providing the services.

In this paper, we present a proposed architecture which addresses these issues, and we outline the research challenges ahead in deploying such an architecture. It is of particular interest to the formal methods community in that it is a real-life challenge with a solution built around the possibilities opened by formal verification and analysis techniques. The solution is also a showcase of how formal methods are applicable to the challenging area of financial application compliance, ranging from risk monitoring and capabilities analysis to regulatory compliance.

Open Payments Ecosystem (OPE) aims at building an infrastructure to address this need by providing an execution environment for financial transactions. In order to support developers, OPE makes a *development environment* available with the necessary APIs for application development and service provider integration. The OPE itself does not hold funds (which legally, can only be held by a regulated institution). Therefore, payment applications are submitted to the OPE by developers together with a corresponding model. Programme managers, in turn, perform an automated *compliance check* on the model and, if successful, pair the adopted application with an integrated service provider. Since service providers are regulated institutions, this arrangement enables the application to be executed on the OPE platform. In this manner, the OPE brings together a number of players[1] including: (i) *service providers* (typically banks) which affect the underlying financial transactions; (ii) *developers* who create the payment applications; (iii) *corporate customers* (the travel agent in our example) who in turn provide the payment applications to their customers; and (iv) *programme managers* who take responsibility of putting end to end financial services (programmes) together — combining applications to service providers — and provide them to corporate customers.

---

[1] In the rest of the paper, we will use the following terms:

Application: The artefact defining how instruments are issued and funds are moved.
Programme: An application deployed by a programme manager using a specific service provider(s).
Programme manager: An institution (not necessarily regulated) managing a number of programmes. Programme managers have contractual liability for the managed programmes.
Service Provider: A regulated institution providing some type of financial service to programme managers. Service providers have financial and regulatory liability for the services offered, some of which can be contractually transferred to programme managers while some would need to be evaluated against risk.

2   Compliance Engine

The compliance subsystem at the core of OPE (shown in Fig. 1) has multiple roles: (i) it is used to support programme managers when matchmaking an application and a service provider; (ii) it ensures that a programme does not violate national legislation and regulations based on the location where it is planned to be deployed; and (iii) provides runtime monitoring on the running programme to continually check whether the monitored constraints are violated.

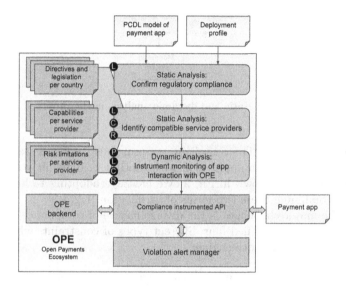

Fig. 1. The OPE compliance engine

Since the OPE architecture envisages that the payment application is executed outside the platform (typically on the end user's device or a web server), only accessing the OPE platform through API calls, it is possible that the application submitted for validation and matched with an appropriate service provider is compromised or tampered with. Furthermore, providing compliance algorithms which support different programming languages and technologies which developers may adopt is not scalable in the long run. The solution to be adopted is that of having the developer submit a suitable model of the application behaviour, sufficiently detailed to enable verification and matching with the service providers. The *Payment Application Modelling Language* (PAML) is a domain-specific language being developed specifically to enable the description of a model of a payments application — its components and attributes, and constraints amongst them. This is used for the verification phase which will be performed when a developer submits an application, but in order to ensure that the application is, in fact, a faithful implementation of the PAML model submitted, the application's interaction with the OPE will be monitored

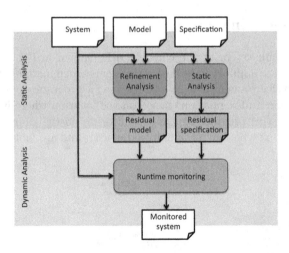

Fig. 2. The combination of static and dynamic analysis in the proposed architecture

at runtime to verify this. The compliance system thus combines static verification upon submission of an application with runtime or dynamic verification in a single framework as shown in Fig. 2. We envisage adopting techniques from recent work combining these two forms of verification [1, 2, 4, 8].

One of the major challenges is the diverse nature of compliance it attempts to address. We have identified four different types of constraints which need to be verified by the compliance engine:

Legal: In order to ensure interest from service providers, it is necessary that applications making use of payment accounts held by them, do not perform anything that is not allowed by regulations. For this reason, the compliance engine will require, in an encoded form, the definition and applicability of directives and legislation for different countries in which programmes may be deployed. For instance, UK e-money regulations require that funds on financial instruments must be redeemable at par value. This would require the compliance engine to (i) identify whether UK e-money legislation applies (confirm that the programme is regulated under UK law and that it deals with e-money), and if so; (ii) ensure that the application allows for redemption i.e. money remaining on a payment instrument (e.g. a card) after being closed can be withdrawn. However, checking that the amount of redemption is actually correct is not straightforward to check statically since the amount will depend on various runtime variables, thus splitting this compliance check into a static and a runtime verification component. The formalisation of the nuances of legislation is far from being straightforward, although we are considering techniques such as those developed in [3] to support this transformation, or validate it.

Capabilities: Service providers may have different capabilities e.g. in terms of what types of cards they can issue or amount of money they are able to handle, which means that when matching an application with potential service providers, the analysis must also cater for capabilities. These correspond more closely with traditional software engineering requirements, and we envisage that we can adopt existing techniques e.g. type systems, to enable their verification.

Risks: Service providers may also have guidelines in terms of risks they are willing to take. For instance, they may want a payment application not to issue more than a certain number of cards per person, or not to process more than a particular amount of money. As in the case of capabilities, this corresponds closely to business logic rules from financial transaction applications e.g. [6]. However, unlike regular properties, violation of which would require action to be taken, in this case, monitoring the properties as they approach thresholds, and giving the service providers the facility to act as they deem appropriate when these guidelines are not adhered to, is a more appropriate approach. For this reason, the compliance engine will be split into two tiers, one layer which computes these statistics (using an approach similar to [5]), and another layer processes them, generating alerts, notifications and actions automatically.

PAML compliance: Finally already discussed, some of the compliance checking will happen statically against the PAML model of an application. To ensure that this compliance holds for the application, the engine will also need to monitor the applications' behaviour to ensure that is faithful to the model describing it.

Figure 1 shows the architecture of this compliance engine, illustrating also at which stage the previous constraints are tackled (where L corresponds to legal constraints, C to capabilities, R to risks, and P to PAML compliance).

3   Formalising Regulatory Compliance

One of the major challenges of setting up the compliance engine is that of capturing what needs to be checked to ensure adherence to applicable regulations. To start with, the regulation come in the form of a number of regulatory texts, each consisting of a number of pages full of legal jargon. Secondly, regulations typically allow grey areas which leave room for interpretation. Furthermore, the lawyers who are familiar with the regulations are not technical people. In this context, we chose to apply an iterative process typical in software engineering practices [7] to ensure that the communication process between lawyers and developers does not leave room for misunderstandings. The steps we adopted were as follows:

Annotating regulations. As a first step, lawyers provided the technical team with the regulatory texts annotated with comments and explanations. The comments mainly consisted of their opinion on whether the regulation falls within the scope of the compliance engine. The explanations were aimed at clarifying jargon or providing an interpretation when the regulations left was room for one.

Shortlisting of applicable regulations. The technical team went through the annotated regulations, and for each regulation decided whether or not it falls within the scope of the compliance engine and in what way: which rules could be checked statically, which could be checked at runtime, etc. Once this list was compiled, it was discussed with the lawyers, having the technical team explaining the reasoning behind the adopted classification.

Summarising the shortlisted regulations. Each shorlisted regulation was summarised in a few words by the technical team, trying as far as possible to avoid ambiguity. These summaries were once more communicated to the lawyers and any disagreements on the choice of words were discussed.

Formalising the regulations. For each concisely described regulation approved by the lawyers, the technical team formulated the corresponding mathematics from which it is now straightforward to turn into code which automatically checks compliance. Once more, any questions which arose during formalisation process were discussed with the lawyers.

Following this iterative process, involving regular discussions based on evolving documentation, proved to be effective, leaving both the lawyers and technical team feeling confident the interpretation of the legal texts and the semantics of the formal specifications coincided.

4   Conclusions

Work on the OPE is still ongoing. We are currently completing the analysis of applicable legislation and incorporating these regulations within the compliance engine. Parts of this compliance process can be resolved statically, while other parts can only be verified dynamically at runtime. What we are currently looking into is how the two analysis approaches can be combined together in order to (i) enable the static checks to classify financial applications and match them with appropriate programme managers and service providers; (ii) ensure that none of the parts of the regulations which cannot be verified statically are violated at runtime through the use of runtime verification. Given the real-time nature and volume of transactions, it is crucial that runtime checks are reduced to a minimum, which can only be achieved by trying to verify as many of the properties as possible statically.

Compared to the current state of the art where banks have to manage risks by approving programs manually and requesting reports at particular intervals, the OPE will be offloading significant overheads off the risk takers, namely the banks, making the setting up and management of payment applications significantly more feasible. It is still be assessed to what degree the pre-deployment static analysis of the compliance process can alleviate the runtime overheads.

References

1. Ahrendt, W., Chimento, J.M., Pace, G.J., Schneider, G.: A specification language for static and runtime verification of data and control properties. In: Bjørner, N., de Boer, F. (eds.) FM 2015. LNCS, vol. 9109, pp. 108–125. Springer, Heidelberg (2015)
2. Ahrendt, W., Pace, G.J., Schneider, G.: A unified approach for static and runtime verification: framework and applications. In: Steffen, B., Margaria, T. (eds.) ISoLA 2012, Part I. LNCS, vol. 7609, pp. 312–326. Springer, Heidelberg (2012)
3. Azzopardi, S., Gatt, A., Pace, G.J.: Formally analysing natural language contracts. In: Computer Science Annual Workshop (2015)
4. Bodden, E., Lam, P., Hendren, L.: Clara: a framework for partially evaluating finite-state runtime monitors ahead of time. In: Barringer, H., et al. (eds.) RV 2010. LNCS, vol. 6418, pp. 183–197. Springer, Heidelberg (2010)
5. Colombo, C., Gauci, A., Pace, G.J.: LarvaStat: monitoring of statistical properties. In: Barringer, H., et al. (eds.) RV 2010. LNCS, vol. 6418, pp. 480–484. Springer, Heidelberg (2010)
6. Colombo, C., Pace, G.J., Abela, P.: Safer asynchronous runtime monitoring using compensations. Formal Methods Syst. Des. **41**(3), 269–294 (2012)
7. Larman, C., Basili, V.R.: Iterative and incremental developments. a brief history. Computer **36**(6), 47–56 (2003)
8. Wonisch, D., Schremmer, A., Wehrheim, H.: Zero overhead runtime monitoring. In: Hierons, R.M., Merayo, M.G., Bravetti, M. (eds.) SEFM 2013. LNCS, vol. 8137, pp. 244–258. Springer, Heidelberg (2013)

Development Methods

CoCoSpec: A Mode-Aware Contract Language for Reactive Systems

Adrien Champion[1(✉)], Arie Gurfinkel[2], Temesghen Kahsai[3], and Cesare Tinelli[1]

[1] The University of Iowa, Iowa City, USA
adrien.champion@email.com
[2] SEI/Carnegie Mellon University, Pittsburgh, USA
[3] NASA Ames/Carnegie Mellon University, Pittsburgh, USA

Abstract. Contract-based software development has long been a leading methodology for the construction of component-based reactive systems, embedded systems in particular. Contracts are an effective way to establish boundaries between components and can be used efficiently to verify global properties by using compositional reasoning techniques. A contract specifies the assumptions a component makes on its context and the guarantees it provides. Requirements in the specification of a component are often case-based, with each case describing what the component should do depending on a specific situation (or mode) the component is in. We introduce CoCoSpec, a mode-aware assume-guarantee-based contract language for embedded systems built as an extension of the Lustre language. CoCoSpec lets users specify mode behavior directly, instead of encoding it as conditional guarantees, thus preventing a loss of mode-specific information. Mode-aware model checkers supporting CoCoSpec can increase the effectiveness of the compositional analysis techniques found in assume-guarantee frameworks and improve scalability. Such tools can also produce much better feedback during the verification process, as well as valuable qualitative information on the contract itself. We presents the CoCoSpec language and illustrate the benefits of mode-aware model-checking on a case study involving a flight-critical avionics system. The evaluation uses Kind 2, a collaborative, parallel, SMT-based model checker extended to fully support CoCoSpec.

1 Introduction

The process of developing safety-critical embedded software (as used, for instance, in transportation, in aerospace and in medical devices) is becoming increasingly

---

This material is based upon work funded and supported by NASA under Grant # NNX14AI09G, and by the Department of Defense under Contract # FA8721-05-C-0003 with Carnegie Mellon University for the operation of the Software Engineering Institute, a federally funded research and development center. This material has been approved for public release and unlimited distribution. DM-0002921.

R. De Nicola and E. Kühn (Eds.): SEFM 2016, LNCS 9763, pp. 347–366, 2016.
DOI: 10.1007/978-3-319-41591-8_24

more challenging. The high number of functionalities now implemented at the software level, the inter-dependencies of software tasks, and the need to integrate different existing subsystems all lead to highly complex software-intensive cyber-physical systems. To manage this complexity embedded software is designed and implemented as the composition of several reactive components, each performing a specific, relatively simple functionality. A leading methodology to develop component-based software is *contract-based design*. In this paradigm, each component is associated with a contract specifying its input-output behavior in terms of *guarantees* provided by the component when its environment satisfies certain given *assumptions*. When contracts are specified formally for individual components, they can facilitate a number of development activities such as compositional reasoning during static analysis, stepwise refinement, systematic component reuse, and component-level and integration-level test case generation.

Embedded system components often exhibit complex discrete internal behavior akin to state transitions in finite-state machines. At any one time, the component is in some of a number of different *modes* as a consequence of past events, and its response to the current inputs differs depending on the mode(s) it is in. For instance, in a flight guidance system, modes govern the choice of a specific control algorithm: an *approach* mode enables a controller that attempts to land the airplane, whereas a *climb* mode enables a controller that attempts to take the aircraft to a suitably safe altitude. The behavior of a multi-component system emerges from complex interactions between the modes of these components.

Despite the prevalence of modes in embedded system design, common contract formalisms for such systems are not *mode-aware*, as they only allow one to express general assumptions and guarantees. As a consequence, mode-based behavior, which is ubiquitous in specification documents, ends up being encoded in conditional guarantees of the form "*situation* ⇒ *behavior*". Correspondingly, assume-guarantee-based tools are *mode-agnostic*, they cannot easily distinguish between mode-specific requirements and general guarantees such as "the output shall always be positive" although the two kinds of requirement describe very different expectations. We see mode-awareness as a natural and important evolution of assume-guarantee contracts and compositional reasoning based on them. We argue that by distinguishing between modes and guarantees in contract-based design we avoid losing fine-grained information that can be used to further improve the scalability and the user feedback of automated analyses.

Contributions. This paper focuses on a large class of embedded systems, (finite- and infinite-state) discrete synchronous reactive systems. For these systems, we introduce CoCoSpec, a mode-aware specification language for Contract-based Compositional verification of *safety properties* that extends the assume-guarantee paradigm, and describe the sort of advantages that mode-aware tools can provide. We focus on features of the language that help with *(i)* detecting shortcomings in the (modes of the) specification of a system independently of its implementation, *(ii)* improving fault localization, *(iii)* comparing the user's understanding of the contract/system pair with its actual behavior, and *(iv)* improving the scalability of the verification process.

For concreteness, we have developed and implemented CoCoSpec as an extension of the synchronous dataflow language Lustre [12], and so we will describe it as such here. We stress, however, that its theory and applications are generic with respect to the whole class of specification languages for discrete synchronous reactive systems.

We briefly introduce the Lustre language and the assume-guarantee paradigm in Sect. 2. The syntax and semantics of CoCoSpec are described in Sect. 3, along with a running example extracted from a medium-size case study we did to showcase CoCoSpec's main features. We present our case-study in more details in Sect. 5 and report on the benefits of mode-awareness to write and debug contracts, raise the trust in their accuracy, and improve the scalability of automatic contract verification.

Related Work. The notion of a *contract* has a long history in software engineering and traces its root to rely-guaranteed approaches introduced by Hoare, Dijkstra and others [10,14,17]. It is adopted in earnest in the *design by contract* methodology [16,25], which has been applied in different areas of software development and verification. Newer programming languages such as Dafny [22] incorporate formal contracts and compile-time contract checking as native features. Formal contracts have also been integrated into popular programming languages, via the addition of *ad hoc* specification languages, e.g., ACSL [20] for C/C++, JML [21] for Java, or SPARK [2] for Ada. ACSL in particular has a notion of *behavior* in function contracts which is similar to that of mode in CoCoSpec. One major difference is that predicates in an ASCL contract refer only to individual states (such as the pre- and the post-state of a function call), while in CoCoSpec, which is meant for reactive systems, they can use temporal operators.

A suitable notion of contract for reactive software, where components continuously process incoming data and produce output based on the input data and internal state information, is provided by the assume-guarantee paradigm for compositional verification [3]. A large number of contract formalisms have been proposed for reactive systems; for instance, Cimatti and Tonetta [7] develop a trace-based contract framework and adapt it to the properties specification language Othello [6]. Cofer *et al.* [8] follow a contract-based approach to perform compositional verification geared towards architectural models. Our approach differs from the techniques and languages above in the emphasis CoCoSpec puts on the mode-based behavior of the analyzed embedded system. In this sense, it is more in the spirit of Parnas tables [26], but for reactive systems.

2   Background

Lustre. CoCoSpec was conceived as a contract extension to languages, such as Lustre [12], for modeling systems composed of *synchronous reactive* components. Such languages are based on the theory of synchronous time in which all components maintain a permanent interaction with their environment (e.g., a larger component, or the physical environment in case of top level components) and are triggered by an abstract universal clock. Lustre is a stream-based executable modeling language for finite- and infinite-state reactive systems. Every system in Lustre takes as input one or more infinite streams of values of the same type, and produces one or more infinite streams as output. Lustre systems are assumed to run on a universal base clock that represents the smallest time span the system is able to distinguish. Individual components can, however, be defined to run on coarser-grained clocks. For simplicity, we ignore this feature here and pretend that all components run on the same clock. In that case, each stream of type τ can be understood mathematically as a function from $\mathbb{N}$ to τ.

System components are expressed in Lustre as *nodes* with an externally visible set of inputs and outputs. Variables are used to represent input, output and locally defined streams. Basic value types include *real* numbers, *integer* numbers, and *Booleans*. Operationally, a node has a cyclic behavior: at each clock tick t it reads the value of each input stream at position or *time* t, and instantaneously computes and returns the value of each output stream at time t. Lustre nodes can be made stateful by having them refer to stream values from (a fixed number of) previous instants.

Typically, the body of a Lustre node consists in a set of stream equations of the form $x = s$, where x is a variable denoting an output or a locally defined stream and s is a stream algebra over input, output, and local variables. Most stream operators are point-wise liftings of the usual operators over stream values. For example, if x and y are two integer streams, the expression $x + y$ is the stream denoting the function $\lambda t.x(t) + y(t)$; an integer constant c, denotes the constant function $\lambda t.c$. Two important additional operators are a unary right-shift operator **pre**, used to specify state computations, and a binary initialization operator **->**, used to specify initial state values. At time $t = 0$, the value $(\text{pre } x)(t)$ is undefined; for each time $t > 0$, it is $x(t-1)$. In contrast, the value $(x \text{ -> } y)(t)$ equals $x(t)$ for $t = 0$ and $y(t)$ for $t > 0$. Syntactic restrictions guarantee that all streams in a node are inductively well defined.

Since a node is itself a mapping from input to (one or more) output streams, once defined, it can be used like any other stream operator in the right-hand side of equations in the body of other nodes, by applying it to streams of the proper type.

Example 1. As an example, here is how a stopwatch could be modeled in Lustre.

```
node previous ( x : int ) returns ( y : int )
let
  y = 0 -> pre x ;
tel

node stopwatch ( toggle, reset : bool ) returns ( count : int );
var running : bool;
let
  running = (false -> pre running) <> toggle ;
  count = if reset then 0
          else if running then previous(count) + 1
          else previous(count) ;
tel
```

Auxiliary node `previous` defines an initializing delay operator for integer streams that takes a stream with values $x_0, x_1, x_2, \ldots$ and returns the stream $0, x_0, x_1, x_2, \ldots$ Node `stopwatch` models a stopwatch with two buttons, modeled respectively by the Boolean input variables `toggle` and `reset`, one to start/stop the stopwatch and the other to reset its time to zero. The locally defined auxiliary stream `running` keeps track of when the clock is running. Its value is `true` initially iff `toggle` is not equal to (`<>`) `false` at that time; it is `true` later iff its previous value is different from the current value of `toggle`. Stream `count` counts the number of instants the clock has been running since the beginning or the last reset, if any. Initially, it is 0 unless `reset` is `false` and `toggle` is `true`, in which case it is 1. Afterwards, it is reset to 0 every time `reset` is `true`, is incremented by 1 while the clock is running, and is kept at its previous value when the clock is stopped. The definition of `count` contains two applications of node `previous`, to `count` itself. Note that despite the apparent circularity of this definition, `count` is well defined because of the delay in `previous`.   □

Lustre has a formally specified semantics, which interprets nodes as a variant of extended-state Mealy machines [13] and node application as parallel composition. Discrete embedded systems developed in popular modeling languages such as Simulink or SCADE can be faithfully translated into Lustre (e.g., [9]). A large class of safety properties of Lustre models can be internalized as (Boolean) observer streams or observer nodes [11] and verified efficiently by SMT-based model checkers [18].

Assume-Guarantee Paradigm.   Assume-guarantee contracts [24] in component-based reactive systems provide a mechanism for capturing the information needed to specify and reason about component-level properties. An *assume-guarantee contract* for a component K is a pair of *past linear temporal logic* (pLTL) [19] predicates $\langle A, G \rangle$ where the *assumption* A ranges over the inputs of K, and the *guarantee* G ranges over its inputs and outputs.

pLTL is a rich logic that uniformly supports the formulation of *bounded liveness* and *safety* properties, the kind of properties we focus on in this work. In terms of standard LTL, the semantics of an assume-guarantee contract $\langle A, G \rangle$ is the formula $\mathbf{G}\, A \Rightarrow \mathbf{G}\, G$ where $\mathbf{G}$ is the *globally* operator. From a verification point of view, however, proving that a component K satisfies that formula amounts to proving that the pLTL formula $\mathbf{H}\, A \Rightarrow G$ is invariant for K where $\mathbf{H}$ is the *historically* modality of pLTL [23].[1]

Compositional reasoning is achieved by proving that each component satisfies its own contract *as well as* the guarantees of any component it provides input to. More precisely, for the latter proof obligation, if a component K_1 is composed in parallel with a component K_2 and provides inputs to K_2, one must also prove that those inputs always satisfy the assumptions of K_2. The proof that K_1 satisfies its contract can then assume that any output provided by K_2 satisfies

---

[1] Intuitively, $\mathbf{H}\, P$ states that P has been true in all states of an execution up to the current state.

the guarantees in K_2's contract. In Lustre terms, one must prove that every application $n(s_1, \ldots, s_n)$ of a node n inside another node m is *safe* in the sense that the actual parameters $s_1, \ldots, s_n$ satisfy at all times the assumptions of n on its inputs. To prove that m satisfies its own contract one can assume that the result of the application $n(s_1, \ldots, s_n)$ satisfies the guarantees in n's contract.

3   The CoCoSpec Language

CoCoSpec extends Lustre by adding constructs to specify contracts for individual nodes, either as special Lustre comments added directly inside the node declaration, or as external, stand-alone contract declarations. The latter are similar in shape to nodes but are introduced with the `contract` instead of the `node` keyword. A node can *import* an external contract using a special Lustre comment of the form

```
| (*@contract import <name>(<input params>) returns (<output params>); *)
```

For specification convenience, the body of a stand-alone contract can contain equalities defining local streams, using the `var` (`const`) keyword for (constant) streams. Besides local streams, a contract contains *assume* and *guarantee statements*, and *mode declarations*. Modes are named and consist of *require* and *ensure statements*. They have the form shown on Fig. 1. Statements can be any well-typed Lustre expressions of type `bool`. In particular, expressions can contain applications to previously defined Lustre nodes. This is convenient, for instance but not exclusively, if one wants to use pLTL operators since those can be defined as Lustre nodes.

Example 2. A possible contract, and associated import, for the `stopwatch` component from Example 1 could be the following:

```
contract stopwatchSpec ( tgl, rst : bool ) returns ( c : int ) ;
let
  var on: bool = tgl -> (pre on and not tgl) or (not pre on and tgl) ;
  assume not (rst and tgl) ; guarantee c >= 0 ;
  mode resetting ( require rst ; ensure c = 0 ; ) ;
  mode running ( require not rst ; require on ; ensure c = (1 -> pre c + 1) ; ) ;
  mode stopped ( require not rst ; require not on ; ensure c = (0 -> pre c) ; ) ;
tel


node stopwatch ( toggle, reset : bool ) returns ( time : int ) ;
(*@contract import stopwatchSpec(toggle, reset ) returns (time) ; *)
let ... tel
```

Note that `pre` binds more strongly than all other operators; `=>` is Boolean implication.

The contract has the same interface as the node. It uses an auxiliary Boolean variable `on` capturing the exact conditions under which the stopwatch should be on: initially when the start/stop button `tgl` is pressed (i.e., true); later when it was previously on and the start/stop button is not being pressed, or it was previously off and the start/stop button is being pressed. The contract contains a global assumption that the reset button `rst` and the start/stop button are never pressed at the same time, and a global guarantee that the time counter c is always non-negative. It also specifies three modes for the stopwatch. The component is in resetting mode if the reset button is pressed. When that button is not pressed, it is in running mode if the conditions captured by on hold, and is in stopped mode otherwise. The ensure statements of the three modes specify how c, the counter, should behave. It *(i)* is reset to 0 in resetting mode, *(ii)* is incremented by 1 in running mode, and *(iii)* maintains its previous value in stopped mode. To import the contract, node stopwatch instantiates the contract's formal (input an output) parameters with any expression of the same type. □

In our experience, the ability of a node to import a stand-alone contract provides great flexibility. It makes writing specifications and implementations more independent, and facilitates the reuse of contracts between components. In general, a node can import more than one contract and have also local assumptions, guarantees and modes. The contract of a node is the union of all the local and imported assumptions, guarantees and modes.

Expressions in contracts can refer to a mode directly by using its name as if it were a Boolean variable. This is just a shorthand for the conjunction of all the require statements in the mode. COCOSPEC avoids potential dependency cycles between modes due to this feature by prohibiting forward and self references. Each stand-alone contract defines a namespace, with :: as the namespace projection operator. As a consequence, modes can be referred to both inside and outside the contract they belong to. For example, in the stopwatch contract the require statement not on of mode stopped can be replaced, equivalently, by not ::running. In contrast, the require and ensure statements of running cannot contain a (forward) reference to mode stopped. The expression ::stopwatchSpec::running can be used in the contract of stopwatch to refer to the running mode of the imported stopwatchSpec contract, as in

```
node stopwatch ( toggle, reset : bool) returns ( time : int ) ;
(*@contract import stopwatchSpec(toggle, reset) returns (time) ;
   guarantee true -> (
     (pre ::stopwatchSpec::running and tgl) => ::stopwatchSpec::stopped
   ) ; *)
```

Finally, neither assume nor require statements can contain references to current values of an output stream—although they may refer to previous values of those streams via the pre operator. This is a natural restriction because it does not make sense in practice to impose *pre*conditions on the current output values.

3.1   Formal Semantics and Methodology

A COCOSPEC *contract* for a Lustre node N is a triple $\langle A, G, M \rangle$ where A is a set of *assumptions*, G is a set of *guarantees*, and M is a set of *modes*. A *mode* is a pair (R, E) where R is a set of *requires* and E is a set of *ensures*. Assumptions, guarantees, requires and ensures are all stream formulas, i.e., Boolean expressions over streams. A mode (R, E) in the contract of N is *active* at time t in in an execution of N if $\bigwedge R$ is true at that time.

Formally, we define a COCOSPEC contract $C = \langle A, G, M = \{(R_i, E_i)\}\rangle$ for some node N as the assume-guarantee contract $C' = \langle A, G'\rangle$, with $G' = G \cup \{R_i \Rightarrow E_i\}$.[2] Node N *satisfies* C if its corresponding extended-state machine satisfies contract C' in the standard sense, that is, if it satisfies $\mathbf{G}\,A \Rightarrow \mathbf{G}\,G'$.

We require for a contract $C = \langle A, G, M = \{(R_i, E_i)\}\rangle$ to be such that the formula

$$\mathbf{G}\,(A \wedge G \wedge \{R_i \Rightarrow E_i\}) \;\Rightarrow\; \mathbf{G}\,(\bigvee\{R_i\}) \tag{1}$$

is logically valid in LTL. Note that this is a (meta)requirement on the contract itself, not on its associated node(s). Intuitively, it states that in the scenario where the contract's assumptions and guarantees both hold, at least one of the requires holds at all times. COCOSPEC modes are meant to formalize requirements coming from specification documents that describe a transient behavior. If property (1) holds, then any node satisfying contract C, and used in a context where C's assumptions are always met, has at all times at least one active mode. This ensures that the contract covers all possible cases whenever its assumptions hold.

In practice, the first step when verifying a COCOSPEC contract is to check the defensive property (1). If it does not hold, a situation unspecified by the contract is reachable, hence the contract is incomplete and must be fixed. If one desires, temporarily perhaps, to have an underspecified contract on purpose, one can add a mode with an empty set of ensures and a set of requires that captures the missing cases. The point is that the underspecification of mode behavior should be formalized explicitly and not be a consequence of a missing set of requirements.

If the defensive property of a contract C of a node N holds, the next step is to verify, using assume-guarantee reasoning, that N respects C. We abstract each application of another node inside N by that node's contract, replacing the contract's formal parameters with the actual parameters in the application. We then prove that N respects C whenever its subnodes respect their own contract. We also prove that N contains only safe applications of other nodes. Overall, the analysis of a system is successful if we can prove that *(i)* none of the contracts used allow unspecified behavior, *(ii)* all nodes respect their contract, and *(iii)* all node applications are safe.

Note that a traditional assume-guarantee contracts $\langle A, G\rangle$ is expressible in COCOSPEC, as the contract $\langle A, G, \emptyset\rangle$. Property (1) is then trivially valid, and the analysis reduces to verifying $\langle A, G\rangle$. COCOSPEC is thus an extension of assume-guarantee contracts that natively supports, via the use of modes, requirements for transient behavior. We discuss the benefits that modes bring to mode-aware analyses in Sect. 5.

---

[2] We will identify sets of formulas, such as R_i and E_i, with the conjunction of their elements.

```
mode <id> (
  require <expr> ;
  ...
  require <expr> ;
  ensure <expr> ;
  ...
  ensure <expr> ;
) ;
```

```
node m1 (
  -- Control request flags.
  altRequest, fpaRequest : bool ;
  -- Deactivation flag.
  deactivate : bool ;
  -- Current and target altitude.
  altitude, targetAlt : real )
returns ( altEngaged, fpaEngaged: bool ) ;
```

```
node switch( on, off: bool )
returns ( out : bool ) ;
let
  out =
    not off and
    (on -> on or pre out) ;
tel
```

Fig. 1. Mode syntax.   **Fig. 2.** Activates one of the controllers.   **Fig. 3.** switch helper node.

3.2 Using CoCoSpec: An Example

We now describe an example of system specification in CoCoSpec that allows us to illustrate concretely the main features of the language. The example is derived from an extensive case study where we took a realistic Lustre model of an avionics system developed by NASA [4,15], and wrote CoCoSpec contracts based on a natural language requirement specification. We discuss the study in detail in Sect. 5. For the purposes of this subsection, it is not crucial to explain the whole model and its expected overall functionality except to say that the system has a component m1 that governs the engagement of two sub-controllers. Figure 2 shows the signature of the corresponding Lustre node[3]. This component decides whether two controllers, an *altitude controller* (alt) and a *flight path angle (FPA) controller* (fpa), should be engaged or not based on their respective request flags (altRequest and fpaRequest), a deactivation flag (deactivate), the current altitude (altitude), and the target altitude (targetAlt).[4]

Let *smallGap* be a predicate that holds iff the distance between the current and the target altitude is smaller than a certain value, say 200 ft. The requirements relevant to the m1 component, namely Guide 170, 180, and 210 in [15], state that when *smallGap* holds then the altitude controller has priority over the FPA controller: when requested to, the latter can engage provided that there is no request for the altitude controller to engage. When *smallGap* is false the FPA controller has priority instead (Guide 170 and 180). The request protocol is the following. An engagement request for a controller becomes active as soon as the corresponding input flag becomes true, and remains active until the deactivate flag becomes true. A generic auxiliary node modeling this protocol for an arbitrary pair of activation and deactivation flags is shown in Fig. 3.

The specification for the m1 component does not have any explicit assumptions. In the traditional assume-guarantee setting (e.g., in [1]) one would then be inclined to write a contract for m1 with the following guarantee:

---

[3] The node, called MODE_LOGIC_AltAndFPAMode in the original model, was slightly altered and its specification simplified for readability and simplicity.

[4] What the altitude and the FPA controllers actually do is not important at this point.

```
(     smallGap and altRequested                              => altEngaged) and
(     smallGap and fpaRequested and not altRequested => fpaEngaged) and
(not smallGap and fpaRequested                               => fpaEngaged) and
(not smallGap and altRequested and not fpaRequested => altEngaged)
```

where `altRequested = switch(altRequest, deactivate)` and `fpaRequested` is
defined similarly. A contract with a single, complex guarantee, leads to loss
of information in practice, for both human readers and static analysis tools
such as model checkers. In contrast, COCOSPEC allows one to provide the same
information but in a disaggregated form, explicitly accounting for the various
cases through the use of modes. With a mode-based specification, assumptions
only state general conditions on legal uses of the component—for instance,
that the altitude values are always positive. Similarly, guarantees specify mode-
independent behavior—in this case, that the altitude and FPA controllers never
engage at the same time.

```
contract ml ( altRequest, fpaRequest, deactivate : bool ; altitude, targetAlt : real )
returns ( altEngaged, fpaEngaged : bool ) ;
let
  var altRequested = switch(altRequest, deactivate) ;
  var fpaRequested = switch(fpaRequest, deactivate) ;
  var smallGap = abs(altitude - targetAlt) < 200.0 ;
  assume altitude >= 0.0 ;
  guarantee targetAlt >= 0.0 ;
  guarantee not altEngaged or not fpaEngaged ;
  mode guide210Alt ( require smallGap ; require altRequested; ensure altEngaged ; ) ;
  mode guide210FPA ( require smallGap ; require fpaRequested ; require not altRequested;
                     ensure fpaEngaged; ) ;
  mode guide180 ( require not smallGap ; require fpaRequested; ensure fpaEngaged; ) ;
  mode guide170 ( require not smallGap ; require altRequested ; require not fpaRequested;
                  ensure altEngaged ; ) ;
tel
```

Debugging the Specification Early on. We argue that, in addition to
enabling compositional reasoning, COCOSPEC contracts also lead to more
accurate analyses compared to traditional assume-guarantee by facilitating
blame assignment. A mode-aware tool knows which modes are active at each
step of a counterexample execution. Hence it can provide better feedback since
modes are in effect user-provided abstractions of concrete states. Designers can
reason about them to fix the system or its specification, instead of looking at
concrete values, which may be less readable and informative.

In our running example, attempting to prove `ml` correct does not go very far:
the defensive check fails right away and produces a counterexample triggering
unspecified behavior. The problem is resolved by noting that the English specification means to say that `fpaRequested` and `altRequested` should be true *only*
in the cases discussed above. Hence, this issue is easily addressed by adding the
following two modes:

```
mode noAlt ( require not altRequested ; ensure not altEngaged ; ) ;
mode noFPA ( require not fpaRequested ; ensure not fpaEngaged ; ) ;
```

Now, because this example is quite simple, an experienced reader may have
noticed the incompleteness in the specification already when we first introduced
it. As we argue in Sect. 5, however, mode-based blame assignment is a very

valuable feature on realistic systems with a large number of modes and complex require predicates.

Evaluating the Specification. We discuss next two approaches for checking that the semantics of a CoCoSpec contract corresponds to a user's understanding of it.

Unreachable Properties Over the Specification as Modes. Going back to the ml node, one could argue that mode guide170 should not be reachable from mode guide210FPA in one step (i.e., from time t to time $t+1$). That this is the case is not necessarily obvious because of the memorization capabilities provided by the switch component from Fig. 3.[5] Since the property is expected to hold, verifying it would raise trust in the contract. Moreover, if the specification or the system later evolved to the point of not satisfying that property anymore, it would be useful for a new analysis to reveal that. This can be achieved by formulating the property explicitly as a CoCoSpec mode:

```
mode no170From210FPA ( require false -> pre ::guide210FPA ; ensure not ::guide170 ; ) ;
```

Exploration of Reachable Modes. When the defensive property (1) holds, modes provide effectively a small, user-defined abstraction of a component's reachable state set, with each abstract state represented by a set of active modes. One can then use explicit-state model checking techniques to analyze the possible executions of a component at the level of mode transitions. For instance, one can unroll the abstract transition relation to some depth to verify the presence of expected mode transition sequences or see if unexpected ones occur. Figure 4 shows (up to depth 1 only, for space constraints) the graph of reachable modes for the ml system, starting from each possible initial mode combination. Even by simple visual inspection, one can obtain a better high-level validation of one's understanding of the contract against the actual behavior of the model. For instance, is it expected that guide170 is active only when noFpa is, or that the mode combination {noFpa, noAlt} can be reached from any initial mode combination?

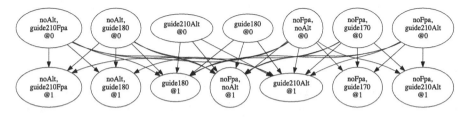

Fig. 4. Reachable combinations of modes in one transition from the initial state for ml.

---

[5] It is true in this instance because in the switch mode, off has priority over on.

4   Implementation

We added full support for CoCoSpec to Kind 2 [5], an open-source, multi-engine, SMT-based model checker for safety properties of Lustre programs, built as a successor of the PKind model checker [18].[6] Its basic version takes as input a Lustre file annotated with multiple properties to be proven invariant, and outputs for each property either a confirmation or a counterexample trace, a sequence of inputs that falsifies the property. Kind 2 is able to read Lustre models annotated with CoCoSpec contracts and verify them using compositional reasoning. We implemented all the features discussed in the previous section, including the exploration of the reachable modes of the input system to generate the corresponding graph.

Given a Lustre system S annotated with CoCoSpec contracts, Kind 2 can be run in *compositional mode* on S. In that case it will analyze the top node of S by abstracting its subnodes by their contracts, as discussed above. This is not enough to prove S correct though, since the correctness of the subsystems represented by the subnodes is not checked. Kind's *modular mode* addresses this shortcoming: in modular mode, Kind 2 will analyze each subsystem of the hierarchy, bottom-up, reusing previous results as it goes. When run in compositional and modular mode together, Kind 2 will analyze each subsystem compositionally, after proving the defensive check on its contract. If all systems of the hierarchy are proved correct, then the system as a whole is deemed safe.

Kind 2 also has a *refinement* mechanism. Say a node M contains an application of a node N, and the compositional analysis of M produces a counterexample. The counterexample might be spurious, as N was abstracted by its contract which might be too weak to verify M. In this case, if N was proved correct previously under some abstraction $\mathcal{A}$ of the node applications in its own body, then Kind 2 will launch a new analysis where the application of N in M is (in effect) replaced by the body of N under the abstraction $\mathcal{A}$. The failure of the compositional analysis signals that there is something wrong with the system and/or its specification. The refinement mechanism aims at giving more information about the problem. For instance, if M can be proved correct after refining the application of N as described above then probably the contract of N should be strengthened until the compositional analysis succeeds without having to use refinement.

5   Evaluation

As a case study to evaluate the usefulness and effectiveness of CoCoSpec, we chose a model derived from NASA Langley's Transport Class Model (TCM) [15], a control system for a mid-size ($\sim$250 K lb), twin-engine, commercial transport-class aircraft. While the TCM is not intended as a high-fidelity simulation of any particular transport aircraft, it was designed to be representative of the types of nonlinear behaviors of this class of aircraft. We specified in CoCoSpec some of the safety requirements for the TMC recently elicited by Brat *et al.* [4] from

---

[6] Kind 2 is available at http://kind.cs.uiowa.edu/.

Federal Aviation Regulations and other documents. We will refer to those as *FAR requirements*. In this section, we discuss our specification of the FAR requirements and how CoCoSpec aided their automated compositional verification.[7]

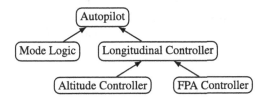

Fig. 5. Autopilot subsystem of the TCM.

The TCM includes submodels for the avionics (with transport delay), actuators, engines, landing gear, nonlinear aerodynamics, sensors (including noise), aircraft parameters, equations of motion, and gravity. It is primarily written in Simulink, consisting of approximately 5,700 Simulink blocks. The system also includes several thousand lines of C/C++ code in libraries, primarily used for the simulation of the aircraft engines and the nonlinear aerodynamics models. Here, we focus on the guidance and control submodels and their properties within the context of the TCM. These models are written entirely in Simulink and so can be faithfully converted automatically to a (multi-node) Lustre model. We will call *Autopilot* the subsystem of the TCM that combines these subcomponents.

The subsystem is depicted in Fig. 5. Each node in the graph corresponds to a component of the Autopilot system, and to a node in the Lustre model. The system actually has more nodes than this graph, which only shows the main components that are specified by a contract. While using the same name, we will distinguish between a component (for instance, the Autopilot node of the graph) and its corresponding subsystem, obtained as the composition of that component with all of its subcomponents. Of particular interest to us is the *Longitudinal Controller* subsystem, which combines two mutually exclusive subcontrollers, the *Altitude Controller* and the *FPA Controller*, to produce an elevation command for the aircraft. When engaged, the first subcontroller produces an elevation command aimed at reaching the target altitude it is given as input. The other subcontroller produces instead an elevation command aimed at reaching a target flight path angle (FPA). In practice, the two subcontrollers are not independent since the FPA Controller uses the output of the Altitude Controller to produce its output, regardless of which controller is engaged. The Longitudinal Controller and all its subcomponents are mostly numerical and include nonlinear arithmetic expressions.

---

[7] Full data on the case study, including models, contracts, reachability graphs, and instructions on how to reproduce our experimental results using the CoCoSpec version of Kind 2 are available at https://github.com/kind2-mc/cocospec_tcm_experiments.

Another subsystem of Autopilot, called *Mode Logic*, is in charge of deciding which of the subcontrollers, if any, should be active at any time. The decision is based on a number of parameters, including the aircraft's speed, altitude, and pitch, and the commands from the cockpit. A simplified version of the Mode Logic component is modeled by the ml Lustre node described in Sect. 3, and so we will not discuss it further here. Instead, we present the benefits of mode-awareness in the specification and verification of the Longitudinal Controller and of the Autopilot overall.

5.1 Benefits of CoCoSpec

Since we are not experts in flight control systems, we do not have a full understanding of the TCM or the details that the rather high-level FAR requirements leave unspecified. So, for our case study, we started from the FAR requirements and the TCM models (in Simulink and in their Lustre translation), and wrote naïve contracts for the Lustre components, which KIND 2 would then promptly disprove. In general, the concrete counterexample traces returned by KIND 2 were too detailed and specific for us to see what was wrong. However, thanks to the mode information, KIND 2 could point us relatively precisely to relevant parts of a trace. Additionally, knowing what modes were active at any point in the trace provided a nice abstraction that would allow us to reframe the problem in more general terms and help us find ways to revise the contract.

Probably the most useful feature was the exploration of reachable modes yielding the reachability graphs introduced in Sect. 3. Even when KIND 2 proved the correctness of the modes we wrote, the mode reachability graph it generated would often reveal significant gaps in our understanding of the system's behavior. Sometimes only *idle* modes would be reachable, because of problems in our require statements; some other times the graph would contain mode transitions we expected not to be possible; or, even worse, it would contain deadlocked states. We cannot overstate the usefulness of this feature in the case study: it quickly became impossible for us to trust a contract without examining the mode reachability graph first.

We discussed in Sect. 3.2 how easy it is to express in CoCoSpec mode properties by using a mode's identifier to refer to the conjunction of its require statements. For instance, properties like "mode m_2 cannot immediately follow mode m_1" and "modes m_3 and m_4 cannot be active at the same time" can be encoded respectively as:

```
guarantee true -> pre :: m₁ => not :: m₂ ;
guarantee not (:: m₃ and :: m₄) ;
```

Based on the reachability graphs and our understanding of the specification and the various subsystems, we ended up writing several properties like the above, to assess the quality of our contract. While reachability graphs provide a graphical mode-based exploration of the system and its specification up to some depth, expressing and checking properties over the specification itself considerably raises the trust in both the specification and the verification process. The fact that we do not duplicate mode requirements, but instead rely on a mode-aware tool to refer directly to mode identifiers, guarantees that these properties are synchronized with the current definition of each mode.

5.2   Verifying the Longitudinal Controller

KIND 2, like other model checkers for infinite-state systems, eventually relies on issuing queries to an SMT solver to reason about the system under analysis. Lustre models are converted internally into transition systems with an initial state condition and a two-state transition relation. These transition systems are then expressed as first-order formulas in one of the theories supported by the back-end SMT solver(s). Given the state of the art in SMT, without any compositional mechanism, an analysis of the Longitudinal Controller is currently impossible. The reason is that the system features nonlinear arithmetic constraints (with multiplications and divisions) which are very challenging for today's SMT solvers. On a system the size of this one, all solvers we tried give up as soon as we unroll the transition relation once, and return *unknown*.

The first step towards verifying any contract in the Autopilot system was thus for us to abstract the nonlinear expressions in it. To do so, we manually replaced nonlinear applications of the * and / Lustre operators with applications of Lustre nodes, written by us, meant to abstract those operators. For instance, an expression of the form $s * t$ with s and t of type `real` would be abstracted by `times`(s, t) where `time` is the node

```
node times( x, y : real ) returns ( z : real )
let
  z = x * y ;
tel
```

The abstracting nodes were provided with a contract specifying salient algebraic, and linear, properties of the abstracted operators, such as the existence of neutral and absorbing elements, sign, and proportionality. Because we isolated the nonlinear expressions, we were able to get the SMT solvers to prove these contracts. This allowed us to use just the contracts, which are on purpose weaker than the full implementation of the multiplication and division nodes, in the analysis of components using those nodes. As a nice side effect, by adding in the contract for the division node `divid` the assumption that the denominator argument is nonzero, we also got the analysis to check that no division by zero can happen in the system.

Armed with this sort of abstraction, we wrote contracts for the Longitudinal Controllers and its two subcontroller based on Guide 120 and 130 of the FAR requirements. A major challenge was that the output of the Altitude controller feeds also into the FPA controller, even when the former is disengaged. We thus had to write a contract for the Altitude Controller to specify its behavior even when it is not engaged. Now, the output in question is the result r of a nonlinear division of two values n and d, and is supposed to be within certain bounds. Our generic abstraction of division did not have a strong enough contract to guarantee that. However, the way the system is defined, when the Altitude Controller is disengaged both n and d are themselves bounded. So, we designed a custom abstraction for division, `divid_bounded_num`, which takes as input constant upper and lower bounds on the denominator and has a contract that extend our generic one for division with modes specifying that the result is within in an interval:[8]

```
contract divid_bounded_num( num, den: real ; const lbound, ubound: real )
returns ( res: real ) ;
let
   ...
   assume dem <> 0.0 and lbound <> 0.0 and u_bound <> 0.0 ;
   assume lbound <= den and den <= ubound ;
   ...
   mode num_pos_lbound_pos (
      require 0.0 <= num ; require 0.0 < lbound ;
      ensure  num/ubound <= res and res <= num/lbound ;
   ) ;
tel
```

There are six modes like `num_pos_lbound_pos` in the full contract, depending on the sign of the numerator and how the denominator compares to zero. Using this version of division we were able to prove that the output of the Altitude Controller is indeed within the expected bounds when the controller is disengaged.

Compositional Analysis. Due to the nonlinearities discussed above, KIND 2 is unable to perform a monolithic analysis of the Longitudinal Controller subsystem, that is, one that looks at the subsystem as a whole, ignoring that it is the composition of several components. Hence, we evaluated the compositional approach by comparing a *linearized-monolithic* analysis, where only the nonlinear expressions are abstracted, with a compositional one, where the two Altitude and the FPA subcontrollers are abstracted.

Both analysis were successful, but with no appreciable difference: they both terminate in a matter of seconds. This is not surprising because the implementation of those subcontrollers is not a lot more complex than their contract. In contrast, we did see a significant difference between the linearized monolithic analysis and the compositional one when we analyze the Autopilot system, as we explain next.

5.3 Verifying Autopilot

To verify the full Autopilot we wrote contracts also for its Mode Logic subsystem. The pertinent FAR requirements for that subsystem are Guide 170, 180, and 210, which specify how and when the altitude and the FPA controllers supposed to engage. We will not go over the contracts of Mode Logic here but describe instead our experience in verifying its composition with the Longitudinal Controller in the Autopilot system.

Before that, it is worth noting that during the verification of the Mode Logic component we found a bug in the Lustre model. The bug occurs when the input signals respectively enabling the Altitude and the FPA controller go from true

---

[8] Full contracts for times, divid, and divid_bounded_num are available on the case study website.

to false at the same time.[9] In that case, the output flag for the controller that has been given priority by Mode Logic will become true, as expected, but then alternate between true and false at every step afterwards. Since fixing the model was beyond our level of expertise, we side-stepped the problem for this case study by adding a `require` clause stating that the two input signals never fall together.

```
contract logic_alt_fpa(...) returns (...) ;
let
  mode alt_170 (...) ; mode alt_210 (...) ;
  mode fpa_180 (...) ; mode fpa_210 (...) ;
tel
```

```
contract mode_logic (...) returns (...) ;
let
  import logic_alt_fpa (...) returns (...) ;
tel
```

```
contract logic_longitudinal (
  head_engage, alt_engage, fpa_engage: bool ; alt, alt_target, hdot,
  fpa, fpa_target, pitch, speed, gskts, cas, elev, ail: real ;
) returns (
  head_engaged, alt_engaged, fpa_engaged: bool ; out_alt, out_pitch, out_elev: real ;
) ;
let
  import mode_logic (
    head_engage, alt_engage, fpa_engage, elev <> 0.0 or ail <> 0.0, alt, alt_target
  ) returns ( head_engaged, alt_engaged, fpa_engaged ) ;
  import longitudinal (
    ::mode_logic::logic_alt_fpa::alt_170 or ::mode_logic::logic_alt_fpa::alt_210,
    ::mode_logic::logic_alt_fpa::fpa_180 or ::mode_logic::logic_alt_fpa::fpa_210,
    alt, alt_target, hdot, fpa, fpa_target, pitch, speed, gskts, cas, elev
  ) returns ( out_alt, out_pitch, out_elev ) ;
tel
```

Fig. 6. A sketch of the contract for the Autopilot node.

Contracts for high-level components like Autopilot can be expressed in terms of the contracts for their subcomponents. Overall we found that lifting subcomponent contracts to their calling component is relatively straightforward thanks to the contract import feature discussed in Sect. 3. This feature is often flexible enough to let one write parametric contracts that can be adapted, by instantiation, to nodes with similar behavior. In the case of the Autopilot node, its contract can be created by importing and suitably connecting the contracts of its Mode Logic and Longitudinal Controller subcomponents, as illustrated in Fig. 6. Note that the two first parameters of the `longitudinal` import refer to the modes of the `mode_logic` contract to communicate whether the Altitude or the FPA controller is active. Reusing the contracts of the two subsystems through imports to write the contract for the Autopilot component reduces the duplication of specs across the overall system. This improves user-friendliness, maintainability and, hence, trust in the correctness of the specs.

There is still, however, room for errors in the contracts themselves. Mode information helps fix those errors that cause the contract to be falsifiable. Once a contract is proved, the exploration of reachable modes is again an invaluable

---

[9] This is possible in principle if these signals come from distinct physical on/off buttons, as opposed to a switch, that are released at the same time.

tool to make sure all the modes can actually be activated, and that the system and the contract behave as expected, at least up to the explored depth of the reachability graph.

Compositional Versus Linearized-Monolithic. The Autopilot system is rather complex. Recall that the Mode Logic component decides which controller is engaged based on information arbitrarily far in the past because of the request mechanism. Its outputs control the mutually-exclusive activation of the two subsystems of the Longitudinal Controller. Moreover, these subsystems are not independent as the FPA Controller takes as input the output of the Altitude Controller.

A monolithic analysis of this system in KIND 2 is again impossible because of the nonlinear expressions in the Longitudinal Controller subsystem, as discussed in Sect. 5.2. We therefore compared a linearized-monolithic analysis of Autopilot with a compositional one. The former could discharge some of the proof obligations generated for the Autopilot contract, but was overall inconclusive after running for one hour on an i7 (2014) CPU running Mac OS X. The compositional analysis, on the other hand, was able to prove the entire contract of the Autopilot node and all the proof obligations for the calls to its subcomponents in about 80 s.

We also had KIND 2 run a *full* analysis on Autopilot. As explained in Sect. 4, KIND 2 does that automatically by going through the hierarchy of nodes in a Lustre model bottom-up, and running a compositional analysis on each of them, where immediate subcomponents with contracts are abstracted by their contract. This guarantees that every node with a contract is correct, in the sense that it respects its contract as well as all the assumptions, if any, of the nodes it calls. The overhead of checking the correctness of *all* the subcomponents of Autopilot is minimal. The total runtime for this analysis, *including the nonlinear abstractions*, was under 100 s.

6 Conclusion

We described COCOSPEC, a mode aware assume-guarantee-based contract language for the specification of synchronous reactive systems. The starting point of COCOSPEC was the need to have a contract language able to accurately capture the behaviors of embedded systems. COCOSPEC is currently designed as an extension of the synchronous dataflow language Lustre. We have described COCOSPEC's main benefits, including *(i)* bringing the specification language closer to the specification documents, *(ii)* enabling defensive semantics checking of the specification for oversights, *(iii)* allowing more effective and more scalable compositional analyses, and *(iv)* providing better feedback for fault localization. In addition to these direct benefits come features such as the exploration of reachable modes or the formulation of properties about the specification (by referring to mode requirements). This allows a mode-aware tool supporting COCOSPEC to provide several means to raise trust in the specification.

We added full support for CoCoSpec to the Lustre model-checker Kind 2. We demonstrated the usefulness of compositional reasoning in the context of CoCoSpec by applying it successfully to the TCM, a flight-critical system case study which, due to its realistic functionality, size, and complexity, is not amenable to monolithic analyses.

Future Work. Kind 2 is also able to generate a concrete trace of inputs for each path in the tree of reachable modes. We conjecture that, by exploring the reachable modes of a contract, it is possible to generate specification-based test cases which are of better quality than those produced by syntactic test generation techniques. This is particularly relevant for outsourced components, which are often provided by subcontractors in executable form only. For such components, test cases are the only means to verify contract compliance. We plan to evaluate our conjecture experimentally in future work.

References

1. Backes, J., Cofer, D., Miller, S., Whalen, M.W.: Requirements analysis of a quad-redundant flight control system. In: Havelund, K., Holzmann, G., Joshi, R. (eds.) NFM 2015. LNCS, vol. 9058, pp. 82–96. Springer, Heidelberg (2015)
2. Barnes, J.G.P.: High Integrity Software - The SPARK Approach to Safety and Security. Addison-Wesley, Boston (2003)
3. Gheorghiu Bobaru, M., Păsăreanu, C.S., Giannakopoulou, D.: Automated assume-guarantee reasoning by abstraction refinement. In: Gupta, A., Malik, S. (eds.) CAV 2008. LNCS, vol. 5123, pp. 135–148. Springer, Heidelberg (2008)
4. Brat, G., Bushnell, D., Davies, M., Giannakopoulou, D., Howar, F., Kahsai, T.: Verifying the safety of a flight-critical system. In: Bjørner, N., de Boer, F. (eds.) FM 2015. LNCS, vol. 9109, pp. 308–324. Springer, Heidelberg (2015)
5. Champion, A., Mebsout, A., Sticksel, C., Tinelli, C.: The Kind 2 model checker. In: Chaudhuri, S., Farzan, A. (eds.) CAV 2016. LNCS, vol. 9780. Springer International Publishing, Switzerland (2016, to appear)
6. Cimatti, A., Roveri, M., Susi, A., Tonetta, S.: Validation of requirements for hybrid systems: a formal approach. ACM Trans. Softw. Eng. Methodol. **21**(4), 22 (2012)
7. Cimatti, A., Tonetta, S.: A property-based proof system for contract-based design. In: Cortellessa, V., Muccini, H., Demirörs, O. (eds.) 38th Euromicro Conference on Software Engineering and Advanced Applications, SEAA 2012. IEEE Computer Society (2012)
8. Cofer, D., Gacek, A., Miller, S., Whalen, M.W., LaValley, B., Sha, L.: Compositional verification of architectural models. In: Goodloe, A.E., Person, S. (eds.) NFM 2012. LNCS, vol. 7226, pp. 126–140. Springer, Heidelberg (2012)
9. Dieumegard, A., Garoche, P., Kahsai, T., Taillar, A., Thirioux, X.: Compilation of synchronous observers as code contracts. In: Wainwright, R.L., Corchado, J.M., Bechini, A., Hong, J. (eds.) Proceedings of the 30th Annual ACM Symposium on Applied Computing, 2015. ACM (2015)
10. Dijkstra, E.W.: A Discipline of Programming. Prentice-Hall, Englewood Cliffs (1976)

11. Halbwachs, N., Fernandez, J.C., Bouajjanni, A.: An executable temporal logic to express safety properties and its connection with the language lustre. In: Sixth International Symposium on Lucid and Intensional Programming, ISLIP 1993 (1993)

12. Halbwachs, N., Lagnier, F., Ratel, C.: Programming and verifying real-time systems by means of the synchronous data-flow language LUSTRE. IEEE Trans. Software Eng. **18**(9), 785–793 (1992)

13. Halbwachs, N., Lagnier, F., Raymond, P.: Synchronous observers and the verification of reactive systems. In: Nivat, M., Rattray, C., Rus, T., Scollo, G. (eds.) Algebraic Methodology and Software Technology (AMAST). Workshops in Computing, pp. 83–96. Springer, London (1993)

14. Hoare, C.A.R.: An axiomatic basis for computer programming. Commun. ACM **12**(10), 576–580 (1969)

15. Hueschen, R.M.: Development of the Transport Class Model (TCM) aircraft simulation from a sub-scale Generic Transport Model (GTM) simulation. Technical report, NASA, Langley Research Center (2011)

16. Jézéquel, J., Meyer, B.: Design by contract: the lessons of Ariane. IEEE Comput. **30**(1), 129–130 (1997)

17. Jones, C.: Development methods for computer programs including a notion of interference. Ph.D. thesis, Oxford University (1981)

18. Kahsai, T., Tinelli, C.: PKind: A parallel k-induction based model checker. In: Barnat, J., Heljanko, K. (eds.) Proceedings 10th International Workshop on Parallel and Distributed Methods in VerifiCation, PDMC 2011. EPTCS, vol. 72 (2011)

19. Kamp, J.: Tense logic and the theory of order. Ph.D. Thesis, UCLA (1968)

20. Kirchner, F., Kosmatov, N., Prevosto, V., Signoles, J., Yakobowski, B.: Frama-C: a software analysis perspective. Form. Asp. Comput. **27**(3), 573–609 (2015)

21. Leavens, G.T., Baker, A.L., Ruby, C.: JML: a notation for detailed design. In: Kilov, H., Rumpe, B., Simmonds, I. (eds.) Behavioral Specifications of Businesses and Systems. The Springer International Series in Engineering and Computer Science, vol. 523, pp. 175–188. Springer, New York (1999)

22. Leino, K.R.M.: Dafny: an automatic program verifier for functional correctness. In: Clarke, E.M., Voronkov, A. (eds.) LPAR-16 2010. LNCS, vol. 6355, pp. 348–370. Springer, Heidelberg (2010)

23. Manna, Z., Pnueli, A.: Temporal Verification of Reactive Systems. Springer, New York (1995)

24. McMillan, K.L.: Circular compositional reasoning about liveness. In: Pierre, L., Kropf, T. (eds.) CHARME 1999. LNCS, vol. 1703, pp. 342–346. Springer, Heidelberg (1999)

25. Meyer, B.: Applying "design by contract". IEEE Comput. **25**(10), 40–51 (1992)

26. Parnas, D.L.: Inspection of safety-critical software using program-function tables. In: Duncan, K.A., Krueger, K.H. (eds.) Linkage and Developing Countries, Information Processing, 1994, IFIP Transactions, vol. A-53. North-Holland (1994)

Modularizing Crosscutting Concerns in Component-Based Systems

Antoine El-Hokayem[1], Yliès Falcone[1(✉)], and Mohamad Jaber[2]

[1] Univ. Grenoble Alpes, Inria, LIG, Grenoble, France
{antoine.el-hokayem,ylies.falcone}@imag.fr
[2] American University of Beirut, Beirut, Lebanon
mj54@aub.edu.lb

Abstract. We define a method to modularize crosscutting concerns in the Behavior Interaction Priority (BIP) component-based framework. Our method is inspired from the Aspect Oriented Programming (AOP) paradigm which was initially conceived to support the separation of concerns during the development of monolithic systems. BIP has a formal operational semantics and makes a clear separation between architecture and behavior to allow for compositional and incremental design and analysis of systems. We thus distinguish local from global aspects. Local aspects model concerns at the component level and are used to refine the behavior of components. Global aspects model concerns at the architecture level, and hence refine communications (synchronization and data transfer) between components. We formalize global aspects as well as their integration into a BIP system through rigorous transformation primitives and overview local aspects. We present AOP-BIP, a tool for Aspect-Oriented Programming of BIP systems, and demonstrate its use to modularize logging, security, and fault-tolerance in a network protocol.

1 Introduction

A component-based approach [2] consists in building complex systems by composing components (building blocks). This confers numerous advantages (e.g., productivity, incremental construction, compositionality) that allow to deal with complexity in the construction phase. Component-based design is based on the separation between coordination and computation. The isolation of coordination mechanisms allows a global treatment and analysis on coordination constraints between components even if local computations on components are not visible (i.e., components are "black boxes").

A typical system consists of its main logic along with tangled code that implements multiple other functionalities. Such functionalities are often seen as secondary to the system. For example, logging is not particularly related to the main logic of most systems, yet it is often scattered throughout multiple locations in the code. Logging and the main code are separate domains and represent different *concerns*. A concern is defined in [5] as a *"domain used as a decomposition criterion for a system or another domain with that concern"*. Domains include logging, persistence and system policies like security. Concerns are often found in different parts

© Springer International Publishing Switzerland 2016
R. De Nicola and E. Kühn (Eds.): SEFM 2016, LNCS 9763, pp. 367–385, 2016.
DOI: 10.1007/978-3-319-41591-8_25

of a system, or in some cases multiple concerns overlap one region. These are called *crosscutting concerns*. AOP aims at modularizing crosscutting concerns by identifying a clear role for each of them in the system, implementing each concern in a separate module, and loosely coupling each module to only a limited number of other modules. At a glance, AOP defines mechanisms to determine the locations of the concerns in the system execution by introducing the concept of joinpoints and pointcuts. Then, it determines what to do at these locations by introducing advices. Finally, it provides a mechanism to coordinate all advices happening at a location by introducing a process called weaving.

Motivations and Challenges. In CBSs, crosscutting concerns arise at the levels of components [9, 19] (building blocks) and architectures (communications). Integrating crosscutting concerns in CBSs improves the progressiveness of building complex systems. More importantly, it allows users to reason about crosscutting concerns in separation, and favors correct-by-construction design.

Defining an AOP paradigm for CBSs poses multiple challenges. Firstly, the notion of program execution, while clear in a sequential program, needs to be redefined for CBSs. Indeed, the execution of a sequential program can be seen as a sequence of instructions, whereas the semantics of a CBS is generally more complex and relies on a notion of architecture imposing several constraints on their execution. Secondly, we aim to ensure that the locations where concerns arise in CBSs are represented homogeneously. This facilitates the verification and instrumentation of the system when incorporating crosscutting concerns (both at the syntactic and semantic levels). Finally, at any location, it is necessary to identify the possible modifications of a CBS that preserve semantics and coordination constraints.

Approach. We use the Behavior Interaction Priority (BIP) component-based framework [2, 20] with formal operational semantics. Coordination between components is achieved by using multiparty interactions and dynamic priorities for scheduling interactions. BIP consists of three layers: (1) Behavior which is handled by atomic components; (2) Interaction that describes the collaboration between the atomic components; (3) Priority chooses which interaction to execute out of many. BIP can be used to formally specify CBSs and generate efficient code that implements a CBS description.

We augment the BIP framework with the aspect-oriented paradigm. We begin by presenting the concepts of the BIP framework in Sect. 2. In general, concerns are expressed by determining their locations in the system, and their behavior at the given locations. Based on the formalization of concerns, we determine the *rules* that govern the integration of these concerns in a BIP system. Therefore, given an initial BIP system, and a description of concerns, we transform it so as to include the desired concerns. We distinguish and define two types of aspects: *Global* and *Local*. In Sect. 3, we give a full definition of global aspects and we briefly, for the lack of space, discuss local aspects and the composition of aspects. A full description of (1) local aspects, (2) aspect containers (which serve as a construct for composing aspects), (3) a high-level language for writing local and global aspects; and (4) the full example can all be found in [10]. Section 4 describes the AOP-BIP tool and its evaluation on network protocol case study. We present related work in Sect. 5 and future work in Sect. 6.

2   Behavior Interaction Priority

Behavior Interaction Priority (BIP) [2,20] allows to define systems as sets of atomic components with prioritized interactions. We present components, interactions, priorities, and their composition. An atomic component is the basic computation unit. It is defined by its interface (i.e., a set of ports) and behavior defined as a Labeled Transition System (LTS) extended with data. Transitions are labeled with update functions, guards, and ports. Ports define communication and synchronization points for components. A port can be associated with some variables (of the component), to exchange data with other components. Ports are said to be exported by the component as they define its interface.

Definition 1 (Update function). *An update function over a set of variables* X *is a sequence of assignments* $\langle x_1 := f^1(X_1), \ldots, x_n := f^n(X_n) \rangle$, *where* $\forall i \in [1, n] : x_i \in X \wedge X_i \subseteq X$.

Definition 2 (Port). *A port* $\langle p, x_p \rangle$ *is defined by an identifier* p *and a set of attached local variables* x_p *(denoted by* $p.vars$*).*

Definition 3 (Atomic component). *An atomic component is a tuple* $\langle P, L, T, X \rangle$, *where:*

- *X is a set of variables.*
- *L is a set of control locations.*
- *P is the set of ports such that* $\forall p \in P : p.vars \subseteq X$.
- *$T = L \times P \times \mathbb{B}[X] \times Exp[X] \times L$ is the set of transitions, where* $\mathbb{B}[X]$ *(resp.* $Exp[X]$*) is the set of boolean predicates (resp. update functions) over* X.

In a transition $\tau = \langle \ell, p_\tau, g_\tau f_\tau, \ell' \rangle \in T$, (1) ℓ is the source location; (2) ℓ' is the destination location; (3) p_τ is a port exported by the component; (4) g_τ is the guard (a boolean predicate), a boolean function over X; (5) f_τ is an update function over X. For a component $B = \langle P, L, T, X \rangle$ we denote P, L, T, X, by $B.locs$, $B.ports$, $B.trans$, $B.vars$, respectively. Additionally, we denote by $\mathcal{B}$ the set of all atomic components. Furthermore, for a transition $\tau = \langle \ell, p, g, f, \ell' \rangle$, we denote ℓ, p, g, f, ℓ' by $\tau.src$, $\tau.port$, $\tau.guard$, $\tau.func$, $\tau.dest$, respectively.

The semantics of an atomic component B is defined as an LTS. A state of the LTS consists of a location and valuation v of the variables of B. A transition is labeled with port along with valuation of its variables v_p, which is possibly received from other components. A transition $\langle l, p[X_p], g_\tau, f_\tau, l' \rangle$ is possible iff B has a transition $\tau = \langle \ell, p[X_p], g_\tau, f_\tau, \ell' \rangle \in T$ such that: (1) the guard before receiving the new valuation v_p of the port variables holds, i.e., $g_\tau(v) = true$; (2) the application of the computation function $f_\tau(v_p/v)$ yields v'.

Definition 4 (Semantics of an atomic component). *The semantics of an atomic component B is the LTS $S_B = \langle B.locs \times \boldsymbol{X}, B.ports \times \boldsymbol{X}, \rightarrow \rangle$, where:*
$\rightarrow = \{\langle\langle l, v \rangle, p(v_p), \langle l', v' \rangle\rangle \mid \exists \tau = \langle l, p[X_p], g_\tau, f_\tau, l' \rangle \in T.trans : g_\tau(v) \wedge v' = f_\tau(v_p/v)\};$ *and, $\boldsymbol{X}$ denotes the set of possible valuations of the variables in X.*

Furthermore, we say that a port p is enabled in a state $\langle \ell, v \rangle$, if there exists at least one transition τ from ℓ labeled by p and its guard $g_\tau(v)$ holds.

Interactions serve as the glue that coordinates (i.e., synchronization and data transfer) the components through their ports. An interaction consists of one or more ports of different atomic components, a guard on the variables of its ports, an update function that realizes data transfer between the ports.

Definition 5 (Interaction). *An interaction a is a tuple $\langle P_a, F_a, G_a \rangle$ s.t.:*

- *$P_a \subseteq \bigcup_{B \in \mathcal{B}}(B.ports)$ is a nonempty set of ports not containing more than one port per atomic component, i.e., $\forall B \in \mathcal{B} : |B.ports \cap P_a| \leq 1$.*
- *F_a is an update function over $\bigcup_{p_i \in P_a}(p_i.vars)$ executed with the interaction.*
- *G_a is a boolean expression, the guard of the interaction.*

For an interaction a, we denote P_a, G_a, F_a, as $a.ports$, $a.guard$, $a.func$ respectively.

We fix $\mathcal{B} = \{B_1, \ldots, B_n\}$ as the set of atomic components where the semantics of B_i is $S_{Bi} = \langle Q_{Bi}, P_{Bi}, \rightarrow \rangle$, $i \in [1, n]$, and γ as the set of interactions. A composite component is defined by composing atomic components using glue consisting of interactions and priorities.

Definition 6 (Semantics of composite component). *The semantics of the composite component built with $\mathcal{B}$ and γ (noted $\gamma(\mathcal{B})$) is the LTS $\langle Q, \gamma, \rightarrow \rangle$ where $Q = Q_{B_1} \times Q_{B_2} \times \ldots \times Q_{B_n}$, and $\rightarrow$ is the least set of transitions satisfying*

$$\frac{a = (\{p_i\}_{i \in I}, G_a, F_a) \in \gamma \qquad G_a(\{v_{pi}\}_{i \in I}) \qquad \forall i \in I, q_i \xrightarrow{p_i(v_i)}_i q_i' \wedge v_i = F_a^i(\{v_{pi}\}_{i \in I}) \qquad \forall i \notin I, q_i = q_i'}{\langle q_1, \ldots, q_n \rangle \xrightarrow{a} \langle q_1', \ldots, q_n' \rangle}$$

where v_{pi} is the valuation of the variables attached to port p_i and F_a^i is the partial update function derived from F_a restricted to the variables of p_i.

An interaction a is enabled iff its guard G_a holds and all of its ports are enabled. An enabled interaction is selected from the complete list of interactions, based on the current states of the atomic components. The BIP engine selects one of the enabled interactions and executes its update function F_a, which may modify its port variables. Then, the involved atomic components execute their corresponding transitions given the new valuations v_i received by the selected ports. In the following, we consider a composite component $\mathcal{C} = \gamma(\mathcal{B})$ with behavior $\langle Q, \gamma, \rightarrow \rangle$.

Multiple interactions can be enabled in a configuration. Priorities are used to filter the enabled interactions and reduce non-determinism.

Definition 7 (Priority). *A priority model π over $\mathcal{C}$ is a strict partial order on the set of interactions γ. We abbreviate $\langle a, a' \rangle \in \pi$ by $a \prec_\pi a'$. Adding π to $\mathcal{C}$ results in a new composite component $\mathcal{C}' = \pi(\mathcal{C})$ which semantics is the LTS $\langle Q, \gamma, \rightarrow_\pi \rangle$ where $\rightarrow_\pi$ is the least set of transitions satisfying the following rule:*

$$\frac{q \xrightarrow{a} q' \qquad \neg(\exists a' \in \gamma, \exists q'' \in Q : a \prec_\pi a' \wedge q \xrightarrow{a'} q'')}{q \xrightarrow{a}_\pi q'}$$

Whenever according to π an interaction $a \in \gamma$ is selected, there does not exist an enabled interaction in γ which has higher priority than a.

A composite component obtained by the composition of a set of atomic components can be composed with other components (composite or atomic) in a hierarchical and incremental fashion using the same operational semantics. For the scope of this paper, we flatten a hierarchical composite component to obtain a non-hierarchical one (i.e., consisting only of atomic components and simple interactions) using the method presented in [4]. The non-hierarchical composite component is subsequently referred to as the BIP model. A BIP system is constructed by composing atomic components using interactions and priorities (to form the BIP model), with an initial state (initial locations and variable initialization of atomic components).

Definition 8 (BIP system). *A BIP system is a tuple $\langle \mathcal{C}, q_0 \rangle$, where $q_0 = \langle Init, v \rangle$ is the initial state with $Init \in B_1.locs \times \ldots \times B_n.locs$ being the tuple of initial locations of atomic components, and $v \in \mathbf{X}^{Init}$ is the tuple formed by the initial valuations of all variables in atomic components $X^{Init} \subseteq \bigcup_{B \in \mathcal{B}} (B.vars)$.*

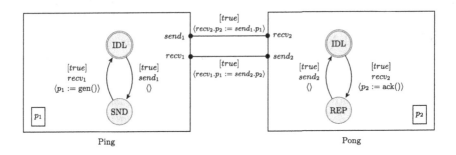

Fig. 1. Two communicating agents

Example 1 (BIP System). Figure 1 depicts a BIP system composed of two atomic components: `Ping` and `Pong`. The `Ping` component has one variable p_1 initialized to a random number and two locations IDL and SND, and two ports $send_1$ and $recv_1$. We associate the variable p_1 with both $send_1$ and $recv_1$. Initially, the `Ping` and `Pong` components are at the IDL locations. From location IDL, in component `Ping`, port send1 is enabled, since the guard of the transition from

IDL to SND holds. Similarly the transition from IDL to REP in Pong is possible, and $recv_2$ is enabled. The interaction that has both ports $send_1$ and $recv_2$ enabled, and its guard holding, is now enabled. Since no other interaction is enabled, it executes. Its update function executes the data transfer using the ports $send_1$ and $recv_2$ and their associated variables p_1 and p_2. Then, the update function of each transition executes (generating the acknowledgment packet in Pong). Ping will move to location SND and Pong to REP. Similarly, on the next step, the acknowledgement is sent back to Ping and it generates a new number. The two interactions ensure synchronization between the two components.

3   Modularizing Crosscutting Concerns in BIP

We address the concerns arising in the global view, namely the view where atomic components are black boxes and only the interactions are accessible.

3.1   Preliminaries

For the rest of the paper, we fix an arbitrary BIP-system $\langle C, q_0 \rangle$ where $C = \pi(\gamma(\mathcal{B}))$ with semantics $S = \langle Q, \gamma, \rightarrow \rangle$.

   We abstract the execution of a BIP system as a trace. Then, we define operations for inspecting data access and control flow.

Definition 9 (BIP trace). *A BIP trace* $\rho = (q_0 \cdot a_0 \cdot q_1 \cdot a_1 \cdots q_{i-1} \cdot a_{i-1} \cdot q_i)$ *is an alternating sequence of states of S and interactions in* γ; *and* $q_k \xrightarrow{a_k} q_{k+1} \in \rightarrow$, *for* $k \in [0, i-1]$.

A global event defines an interaction execution moving the system from a state to another state. From a trace, one can extract a sequence of global events.

Definition 10 (Global events). *The sequence of global events* E_ρ *extracted from the trace* $\rho = (q_0 \cdot a_0 \cdot q_1 \cdots a_{i-1} \cdot q_{i-1} \cdot a_{i-1} \cdot q_i)$ *is* $(E_0 \cdot E_1 \cdots E_{i-1})$ *where* $E_k = \langle q_k, a_k, q_{k+1} \rangle$, *for* $k \in [0, i-1]$.

Definition 11 (readvar and writevar). *Given a set of variables X and an update function* $f = \langle x_1 := f^1(X_1), \ldots, x_n := f^n(X_n) \rangle$ *as per Definition 1:*

- readvar$(f) = X_1 \cup X_2 \cup \ldots \cup X_n$ *denotes the read variables;*
- writevar$(f) = \{x_1, x_2, \ldots, x_n\}$ *denotes the modified variables.*

3.2   Global Joinpoints

In the global view, we focus on the atomic components used in a composite component. These components only export their ports, on which interactions are defined. Generally, each atomic component computes its enabled ports. Given the enabled ports and the guards of the interactions, the composite component executes one interaction which has: (1) all its ports enabled, (2) its guard holds, (3) there does not exist another interaction with higher priority which is also enabled. At the interaction level, the following operations exist: interaction enablement[1] and interaction execution.

Whenever an interaction executes, three kinds of global joinpoints can be identified: (1) Synchronization between different atomic components; (2) One or more atomic components sending data; (3) One or more atomic components receiving data. In the case of the global view, a joinpoint is simply any event appearing in the execution (in the sense of Definition 10). For the rest of the section, we consider $\mathcal{E}$ to be the set of all reachable events in $\langle \mathcal{C}, q_0 \rangle$ with $\rightarrow$.

Definition 12 (Global joinpoint). *A global joinpoint is a global event $E \in \mathcal{E}$.*

3.3 Global Pointcuts

Since we only consider the interaction execution joinpoint, we consider criteria for matching interactions and relate them to global joinpoints. To select a set of interactions, we use constraints over their associated ports (and their variables) and the involved data transfer. For this, a global pointcut expression has three parts: the ports themselves, a set of read variables, and a set of write variables. Note that the port variables should be involved in the computation function of the interaction. In Sect. 3.4, we use the read and written variables to define the context information passed to the advice.

Definition 13 (Global pointcut). *A global pointcut is a 3-tuple $\langle p, v_r, v_w \rangle$ that satisfies the following constraints:*

- $p \subseteq \bigcup_{B \in \mathcal{B}} (B.ports)$ *is a set of ports.*
- $v_r \subseteq \bigcup_{p_i \in p} (p_i.vars)$ *is the set of* read *variables.*
- $v_w \subseteq \bigcup_{p_i \in p} (p_i.vars)$ *is the set of* modified *variables.*

Definition 14 (Matching a global joinpoint with a global pointcut). *A global event $\langle q, a, q' \rangle$ is a joinpoint selected by a global pointcut $\langle p, v_r, v_w \rangle$ iff $\langle q, a, q' \rangle \models \langle p, v_r, v_w \rangle$, where:*

$$\langle q, a, q' \rangle \models \langle p, v_r, v_w \rangle \quad \textit{iff} \quad p \subseteq a.ports \wedge v_r \subseteq readvar(a.func) \wedge v_w \subseteq writevar(a.func).$$

A global event $\langle q, a, q' \rangle$ matches a global pointcut $\langle p, v_r, v_w \rangle$ if the interaction a involves all the ports in p, and its update function reads from the variables in v_r and writes to the variables in v_w.

A global pointcut captures interaction execution. For this purpose, we capture the interactions on the syntax of BIP models. Matching a global pointcut consists in selecting a subset of the interactions of a composite component.

Proposition 1. $(\langle q, a, q' \rangle \models gpc)$ *iff* $a \in match_g(\mathcal{C}, gpc)$, *where:* $match_g$ $(\mathcal{C}, \langle p, v_r, v_w \rangle) = \{a' \in \gamma \mid p \subseteq a'.ports \wedge v_r \subseteq readvar(a'.func) \wedge v_w \subseteq writevar(a'.func)\}$

---

[1] In this paper, we only consider *interaction execution* because of the complexity of matching *interaction enablement* which requires to include the BIP engine as part of the BIP model. To consider interaction enablement, it is better to interface with the BIP engine, meaning re-implement the BIP runtime.

The proposition ensures that an event is a joinpoint (i.e., $\langle q, a, q' \rangle \vDash gpc$)) iff its interaction a is syntactically selected (i.e., $a \in \mathrm{match_g}(\mathcal{C}, gpc)$).

Example 2 (Interactions matched by a pointcut). Figure 2a shows the interactions obtained by matching four pointcuts:

1. $\langle \{pa_1, pb_1\}, \emptyset, \emptyset \rangle$ matches all interactions including $\{pa_1, pb_1\}$ in their ports, that is, it only matches a_0 as it is the only interaction involving both ports.
2. $\langle \{pb_2\}, \emptyset, \emptyset \rangle$ matches all interactions including $\{pb_2\}$ in their ports, that is, it matches interactions a_1 and a_3, since they both involve pb_2.
3. $\langle \{pb_2\}, \{x_b\}, \emptyset \rangle$ matches interactions including $\{pb_2\}$ and which computation reads variable x_b associated with pb_2. The pointcut only matches a_1.
4. $\langle \{pd_1\}, \{x_d\}, \{x_d\} \rangle$ matches interactions that include $\{pd_1\}$ and which computation read and write the variable x_d associated with pd_1 (to receive data). The pointcut only matches a_1.

3.4   Global Advice and Global Aspect

A global advice defines the possible actions allowed on a global joinpoint $\langle q, a, q' \rangle$. These actions are restricted to two update functions f_b and f_a respectively before and after the interaction function $a.func$. Moreover, a global advice can only modify the ports that it matches, as interactions could include other ports. The non-matching ports and their variables are hidden from the advice as per application of Demeter's law [18]. Given a global pointcut $pc = \langle \{p_1, \ldots, p_n\}, v_r, v_w \rangle$, an advice is restricted to the ports $\{p_1, \ldots, p_n\}$ and their variables, and a set of extra variables V called the inter-type variables.

Definition 15 (Global advice). *Given a set of ports $p \subseteq \bigcup_{B \in \mathcal{B}} B.ports$ and a set of inter-type variables V, $X_{\mathrm{adv}} = V \cup \bigcup_{p_i \in p}(p_i.vars)$ is the set of advice variables. A global advice is a pair of functions $\langle f_b, f_a \rangle$ such that:*

- $(\mathrm{readvar}(f_b) \cup \mathrm{writevar}(f_b)) \subseteq X_{\mathrm{adv}}$, *and*
- $(\mathrm{readvar}(f_a) \cup \mathrm{writevar}(f_a)) \subseteq X_{\mathrm{adv}}$.

The global advice bound to p and V is noted $gadv(p, V)$.

The functions f_b and f_a are referred to as the before and after advice functions, respectively. The variables that they read and write (captured with readvar and writevar, respectively) should be variables of the advice.

We bind an advice to a pointcut expression with a global aspect. The advice should then apply to every joinpoint that the pointcut matches.

Definition 16 (Global aspect). *A global aspect is a tuple $\langle \mathcal{C}, V, gpc, \rangle$ $\langle gadv(p, V) \rangle$ such that:*

- $\mathcal{C}$ *is a composite component (as per Definition 8);*
- V *is the set of variables associated with the aspect;*
- $gpc = \langle p, v_r, v_w \rangle$ *is the global pointcut (as per Definition 13);*
- $gadv(p, V)$ *is the global advice (as per Definition 15).*

A global aspect therefore acts as a constraint between the pointcut and the advice. It ensures that the ports referred to the pointcut are the same for the advice, and that the advice has access to the variables of all ports in p and V.

Example 3 (Global Advice and Global Aspect). The global aspect:

$$\langle \mathcal{C}, \{v_0\}, \langle \{pd_1\}, \{x_d\}, \{x_d\}\rangle, \langle v_0 := x_d, x_d := v_0\rangle\rangle$$

defines the inter-type variable v_0. It also defines the pointcut to match the inter-actions that include port pd_1 and which update function reads and writes to x_d. The advice's before and after update functions are respectively $\langle v_0 := x_d\rangle$ and $\langle x_d := v_0\rangle$; saving the value of x_d in v_0 before the update function executes and then setting it back afterwards. The pointcut matches a_1 as shown in Fig. 2a and specifies that a_1 should execute the following sequence of instructions: $\langle (v_0 := x_d), (x_d := x_d + x_b), (x_d := v_0)\rangle$. An advice function in this case can only access $\{v_0\} \cup pd_1.vars$. The advice functions have no access to x_b, as it is not related to the port pd_1 but pb_2. This aspect disallows all interactions that read and write to x_d to modify its value.

3.5 Global Weaving

Using the binding of an advice to a pointcut, the weaving procedure instruments the BIP model. The procedure ensures that whenever a joinpoint matched by a pointcut occurs, the BIP system executes the advice. Recall that interactions are stateless (i.e., they have no variables of their own), but they rely on data transfer from ports. Variables can only be defined in atomic components. Therefore, the weaving procedure must create an extra atomic component (so called inter-type component) that contains the variables of the aspect along with necessary ports and interactions. The weaving operation is only concerned with syntactically modifying the system representation. For this, we separate the two notions of matching to find the locations to modify from the instrumentation itself. We therefore define first the transformation procedure and then its application with matching.

The transformation procedure uses the following parameters:

- A BIP composite component $\mathcal{C}$;
- A set of interactions $\mathcal{I}$ resulting from syntactically matching a pointcut;
- A set of extra variables (i.e., the inter-type variables);
- The two functions f_b and f_a of the advice.

Accordingly, we create a new BIP composite component where the update function of each $a \in \mathcal{I}$ is preceded by f_b and followed by f_a. In the following, we describe the weaving of a global aspect which requires weaving of the inter-type component and weaving of the advice.

Generating an Inter-type Component. We first define the inter-type component.

Definition 17 (Inter-type component). *The inter-type component asso- ciated to the set of inter-type variables V is defined as $B_V = \langle \{p_V\}, \{\ell_0\}, \{\langle \ell_0, p_V, true, \langle\rangle, \ell_0\rangle\}, V \rangle$ where $p_V = \langle pv, V \rangle$.*

B_V contains V as its variables, one port $p_V = \langle pv, V \rangle$ with all the variables attached to it, and one control location with a transition labeled with p_V and guarded with the expression *true*. This ensures that the port will not stop any other interaction from executing once connected to it. The inter-type component is added to the set of atomic components $\mathcal{B}$ of the BIP system.

Example 4 (Adding an inter-type component to a system). Figure 2b depicts $\mathcal{C}' = \pi(\gamma(\mathcal{B} \cup \{B_V\}))$ where $V = \{v_0, v_1\}$ and $\mathcal{C} = \pi(\gamma(\mathcal{B}))$. A new atomic component B_V is created. B_V has two local variables v_0 and v_1 and has its port p_V always enabled. The variables in V are attached to p_V.

Weaving the Advice. Once the inter-type component is added to the system, the advice is woven by connecting the existing interactions to it.

Definition 18 (Global weave). *Given a composite component $\mathcal{C} = \pi(\gamma(\mathcal{B}))$, a set of interactions $\mathcal{I}$, an inter-type V, and a global advice $adv = \langle f_b, f_a \rangle$, the global weave is defined as $\mathcal{C}' = weave_g(\mathcal{C}, \mathcal{I}, V, adv)$ where $\mathcal{C}' = \pi(\gamma'(\mathcal{B}'))$ is the new composite component; with:*

- $\mathcal{B}' = \mathcal{B} \cup \{B_V\}$ *is the new set of atomic components;*
- $B_V = \langle \{p_V\}, \{\ell_0\}, \{\langle \ell_0, p_V, true, \langle,\rangle \ell_0\rangle\}, V \rangle$ *is the inter-type component iden- tified by V (as per Definition 17);*
- γ' *is defined as* $\{m(a) \mid a \in \gamma\}$ *with:*

$$m(a) : \gamma \to \gamma' = \begin{cases} \langle a.ports \cup \{p_V\}, f_b \cdot a.func \cdot f_a, a.guard \rangle & if\, a \in \mathcal{I}, \\ a & otherwise. \end{cases}$$

The inter-type component B_V is added to $\mathcal{B}$. The interactions that require instru- mentation (i.e., $a \in (\gamma \cap \mathcal{I})$) are extended with the port p_V so as to have access to the inter-type variables and their computation function is prepended with f_b and f_a. The interactions not matched (i.e., $a \in (\gamma \setminus \mathcal{I})$) are unmodified and copied. Priorities (π) are not modified, thereby preserving the priorities on the interactions.

Example 5. Figure 2b displays the weave on the set of interactions $\{a_1\}$ with the set of inter-type variables $V = \{v_0, v_1\}$ of the advice $\langle f_b, f_a \rangle$. A new atomic component is created B_V that has two local variables v_0 and v_1 and has its port p_V always enabled. The variables in V are attached to p_V.

- The interaction a_1 is connected to p_V so as to allow access to V on which f_b and f_a can operate.
- The computation f_b is prepended to $a_1.func$ so as to execute before and f_a is appended to $a_1.func$ so as to execute after.

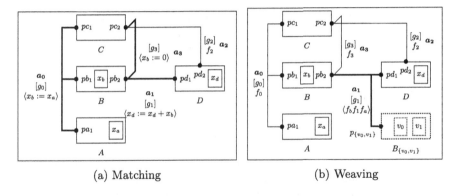

(a) Matching   (b) Weaving

Fig. 2. Matching and weaving a global aspect

– Since p_V is always enabled, the interaction a_1 will be enabled when pb_2 and pd_1 are both enabled and g_1 holds. The extension to p_V does not affect enablement.
– Once a_1 is executed if f_b or f_a write onto $p_V.vars$, they will then be received in B_V and changed accordingly.

We now define the operation that takes a global aspect, matches its pointcut expression, and weaves the result into the model.

Definition 19 (Weaving of a single global aspect). *Weaving a global aspect* $GA = \langle \mathcal{C}, V, gpc, \langle f_b, f_a \rangle \rangle$ *into a composite component* $\mathcal{C}$ *is noted* $\mathcal{C} \lhd_g GA$ *and yields a new composite component* $\mathcal{C}' = \text{weave}_g(\mathcal{C}, \text{match}_g(\mathcal{C}, gpc), V, \langle f_b, f_a \rangle)$.

Correctness of Weaving. We consider $\mathcal{E}'$ (resp. $\mathcal{E}$), to be the set of reachable events in the resulting (resp. original) BIP system $\langle \mathcal{C}', q_0' \rangle$ (resp. $\langle \mathcal{C}, q_0 \rangle$) where $\mathcal{C}' = \mathcal{C} \lhd_g \langle \mathcal{C}, V, gpc, \langle f_b, f_a \rangle \rangle$. We begin by defining function $\text{rem}_g : \mathcal{E}' \to \mathcal{E} \cup \{\epsilon\}$. Function rem_g removes the global advice from an event in $\mathcal{E}'$ and constructs a similar event in $\mathcal{E}$ or the empty event ϵ if it does not match the advice.

$$\text{rem}_g(\langle q_s, a, q_e \rangle) = \begin{cases} \langle q_s', a', q_e' \rangle & if \; \exists f : a.func = f_b \cdot f \cdot f_a \\ \epsilon & otherwise \end{cases}$$

with:

– $a' = \langle a.ports \setminus \{p_V\}, f, a.guard \rangle$ where $a.func = f$ s.t. $\exists f : f_b \cdot f \cdot f_a$.
– q_s' and q_e' exclude the valuations of V from q_s and q_e, respectively.

The following proposition expresses the correct application of the advice on the joinpoints selected by a pointcut expression.

Proposition 2 (Weaving correctness). $\forall \langle q, a, q' \rangle \in \mathcal{E}' : \exists f : a.func = \langle f_b \cdot f \cdot f_a \rangle$ *iff* $(e' \neq \epsilon \wedge e' \models gpc)$ *s.t.* $e' = \text{rem}_g(\langle q, a, q' \rangle)$

We say that an interaction's update function satisfies an advice application if its update function ($a.func$) starts with f_b and ends with f_a (i.e., the advice's before and after update functions). This proposition states that any event's interaction satisfies an advice application iff we can construct an event e' without the advice f_b and f_a ($e' = \text{rem}_g(\langle q, a, q' \rangle)$) which matches gpc ($e' \models gpc$) in the original system. Since an advice can add extra behavior like reading and writing to variables, it can cause the event to match more joinpoints, therefore it is removed before matching with gpc.

3.6   Overview of Local Aspects

Due to lack of space, we only give an overview of local aspects. In this view, we focus on atomic components seen as white boxes and seek to refine their behavior. An atomic component's state is studied to locate possible points where cross-cutting concerns apply. Since in this view we see components as whiteboxes, we have knowledge of the full BIP system and can extract a local execution trace for a given atomic component. An atomic component has control locations, variables, and transitions labeled with ports, guards and computation functions. At this level, concerns need to be managed at the following points: port execution/enablement, guard evaluation, access and modification of state's variables (i.e., location and local variables).

The local advice defines the possible actions to be injected at a local joinpoint. Similarly to a global advice (Definition 15), a local advice executes two functions before and after the local joinpoint. The functions of a local advice may only modify the variables of the atomic component and an extra set of inter-type variables V, specific to the local aspect. Furthermore, in order to increase the expressiveness of the local advice, a local advice may change the location of the atomic component depending on a specific guard.

3.7   Weaving Multiple Aspects

When weaving multiple aspects, specific problems and extra considerations arise. Whenever a new concern is added to the joinpoint, it is possible to interfere with the existing concern at the joinpoint. This behavior is called *interference*. We manage multiple aspects by grouping them in modules (called containers). Local containers (resp. global containers) apply to local (resp. global) aspects. Containers define an order on the aspects they encapsulate so that the weaving order is deterministic. Moreover, containers ensure that aspects share the same inter-type variables. In the case of local containers, local aspects are further required to operate on the same atomic component encouraging encapsulation, since aspects that operate on different atomic components do not interfere and cannot share inter-type variables. Weaving multiple aspects is fully described in [10].

4   Implementation

4.1   AOP-BIP: Aspect-Oriented Programming for BIP Systems

AOP-BIP is a proof-of-concept, aspect-oriented extension to BIP. AOP-BIP language supports both global and local aspects. Moreover, AOP-BIP's command line front-end takes as input: (1) a .bip file that represents a BIP system written in the BIP language [23]; and (2) a list of .abip files that describe the aspects. AOP-BIP produces an output BIP model where the aspects are woven.

4.2   Example

A network protocol is used to illustrate the handling of crosscutting concerns in BIP and is shown in Fig. 3. The Network composite component consists of a Server, Client and a Channel. The double circles denote the start locations for each component. The Server waits for the *clear-to-send* signal on its cts port

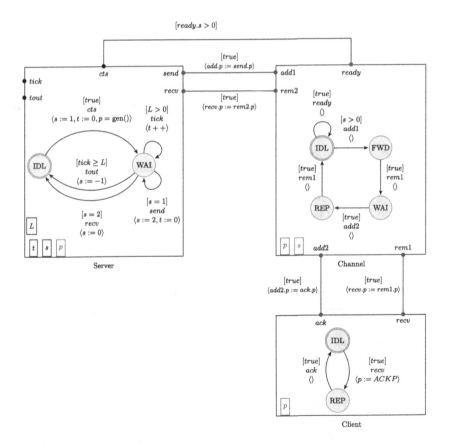

Fig. 3. The Network composite component

```
Aspect AddHash (server)   {
  portExecute(cts)
  do {} {p = wrap(p);}
}
Aspect VerifyHash (channel) {
  data int clear = 0
  portExecute(add1)
  do {} {clear = check(p); p = unwrap(p);}
     {(IDL, clear == 0)}
}
Aspect Carol { // Man-in-the-middle
  ports(a:server.send b:channel.add1)
  readPortVars(a.r)
  do {} {b.r = pfake(a.r);}
}
```

```
[Server.cts] Clear to Send
[Server.send ] -> 886|6 (Time: 0)
[Channel.add1] <- 386|6
[Channel.rem1] -> 386
[Client.recv ] <- ACK
[Client.ack  ] -> ACK
[Channel.add2] <- ACK
[Channel.rem2] -> ACK
[Server.recv ] <- ACK (Time: 3)

[Server.cts  ] Clear to Send
[Server.send ] -> 763|3 (Time: 0)
[Channel.add1] <- 736|3
[Server.tout ] Timeout
```

Fig. 4. Authentication aspects and trace

indicating that a channel is available. It then generates a packet and sends it to the channel. The channel forwards the packet to the client which acknowledges it. The channel will then send the acknowledgement back to the server.

Crosscutting Concerns. The network protocol is augmented by refining its specification. The correctness of our transformation ensures that the crosscutting concerns are rigorously handled. First, logging is introduced by capturing port executions locally in all components. Second, security is added in the form of authentication. A signature (hash) is added to the packet and checked. To accomplish the above we introduce two local aspects. The various aspects along with the output are displayed in Fig. 4. The first intercepts the Server's cts port execution and adds the signature once the server is ready to send, by modifying the packet stored in the local variable *p*. The second intercepts the Channel's add1 port execution, this port executes when a packet from the Server is sent. The advice verifies the signature (using check(p)) and stores the result (logical 0 or 1) in an inter-type variable clear. The advice also adds a reset location to IDL if the verification failed (clear == 0), preventing the Channel from forwarding the packet to the Client. The Carol aspect is added to modify the packet in transit to display a failed authentication. The global pointcut expression matches: (1) ports server.send and channel.add1, and (2) variable server.send.r. The advice in the Carol aspect changes the value of channel.add1.r after the execution of any interaction that matches the pointcut. Normally the system will execute the packet transfer by reading a.r and modifying b.r. The advice function instead will override b.r by generating a fake packet from a.r using pfake(a.r). The output displays a successful and an unsuccessful attempt. The packet is represented by a number and the signature is the last digit in the number. We first notice that the first aspect added |6 to the packet 886 and the second aspect removed it when the channel forwarded it (Channel1.rem1). Carol replaces the first packet 886 with 386, which both have the same signature (6). The verification succeeds in this case unlike in the second try, when 763 is replaced by 736 since the signature of 736 is 6 but not 3. Third, congestion avoidance is added by computing the round-trip time of the message and then waiting before sending further messages. Fourth, basic fault tolerance is introduced in the form of a failsafe mechanism. The system deadlocks and then terminates safely, after the server fails to receive a certain number of acknowledgments.

Coverage of Concerns. The coverage of the concerns is shown in Table 1. Column Transitions reports the number transitions that have been modified including the number of added transitions for reset locations. Column Interactions reports the number of modified interactions. Column OT (resp. OI) reports the number of transitions (resp. interactions) that overlap with other concerns. Interfering concerns are reported in column OC. Concerns are indicated by label (1–4). We illustrate concerns that target multiple areas in the system. Without using our tool, implementing these concerns would require to edit a significant part of the system. For instance, in the case of logging, the code must be inserted in 10 transitions, of which half overlap with other concerns.

Table 1. Crosscutting concerns in `Network`

#	Concern	Transitions	Interactions	OT	OI	OC
1	Logging	10	0	5	0	2,3
2	Authentication	2	1	2	1	1,3.4
3	Congestion	5	0	4	0	1,2
4	Fault Tolerance	0	3	0	1	2
`Network`		12	5			

5   Related Work

AOP for CBS. Pessemier et al. [21] present a framework to deal with crosscutting concerns in CBSs. It is a symmetric approach that presents aspects as components containing the advice and additional interfaces, and are therefore integrated homogeneously within the system. Joinpoints are a combination of interfaces of different components. Thus, components are seen as black boxes. The approach has several advantages. First it explicitly models dependencies between aspects and components, and allows for their composition at an architectural level. Second, it allows the aspects to be manipulated and reconfigured at runtime. Third, it clearly defines the relationships (1) between aspects and other aspects, and (2) between aspects and the components they modify. This approach however does not consider the semantics of interactions. It targets arbitrary interface signatures, so the implementation itself must explicitly address the synchronization amongst the different components and data transfer.

Similarly, other works such as [9,19] have been done to integrate AOP into CBSs as well. These approaches are however asymmetric and subsumed by [21].

Duclos' approach [9] defines two languages to integrate aspects. Lieberherr's approach [19] defines aspects as part of the modules they apply to, and compares the expressiveness of the approach with both AspectJ and HyperJ [22].

SAFRAN [6] differs from the above approaches by using AOP in the Fractal component model to define adaptation policies.

Formalization of Aspects. None of the above approaches relies on formal models. Work to formalize aspects in programs has been undertaken by [16]. The approach specifies different categories of aspects and how they affect various classes of properties (safety, liveness). The work has been extended by Djoko et al. [8] by expanding the categories and defining languages of aspects. The languages of aspects ensure by construction that aspects written with them fit a specific category. Additional tools for verification and analysis of aspects and their interferences have been developed and are presented in [17]. Larissa [1] is a language for handling crosscutting concerns in reactive systems modeled as the composition of Mealy automata. The matching is done by assigning monitor programs that look for a specific execution trace. Joinpoints are then associated with the input history. Advices consist of two types: `toInit` and `recovery`. The `toInit` advice places the program back in its original state. The `recovery` advice consists of restoring the program to the last recovery state it was in. A recovery state is determined by a monitor: the recovery program. The recovery states are associated with specific execution traces and are matched similarity to joinpoints. Compared to our approach, Larissa supports joinpoints based on the input history. It can also be seen as symmetric since aspects are introduced in the synchronous language used. However, the underlying model is conceived for reactive systems, and not CBSs, it does not have a clear distinction between communication and components, and thus does not distinguish between aspects related to components and communications. The communication model is based on simple input/output matching. Moreover, advices are not expressive and only consider reset/restore the state of the system. Formalizing aspects in the BRIC component model has been undertaken by [7]. BRIC formalizes component behavior and their interactions using the Communicating Sequential Processes (CSP) language. Unlike our approach, it is symmetric, aspects, pointcuts and advices are described in CSP, and woven using CSP operators. Additionally, it targets interactions and not the components themselves. It regards components as black boxes. Verification on the resulting woven system is possible in both approaches. However, BIP has a strong expressive synchronization primitive [3] which is more expressive than CSP [14]. This allows more concerns to be formalized.

6   Future Work

Future work comprises five directions. The first consists in capturing more joinpoints and extending the possible behavior of advices. Possible new joinpoints include variable in interaction guard, specific values of variables. Advices can be extended to modify guards on matching transitions and interactions.

The second consists in applying CBS methods to define advices and aspect composition. This helps integrate AOP in BIP symmetrically, where aspects are implemented as components and interactions within the existing system. This would allow to enable or disable aspects in the system, and specify more complex advices (i.e., advices as components instead of update functions and extra transitions). The third consists in elaborating new ways to compose aspects by finding new criteria to order them. Aspects can be re-ordered in a container based on their pointcut expressions, by grouping those which affect the same transitions or interactions, and whether or not they modify the existing variables (read/write aspects). Additionally, the language could be extended to allow the explicit definition of precedence rules. The fourth consists in implementing model-to-model transformations using Domain Specific Languages inspired by ATL [15] targeting the BIP model and comparing their expressiveness with our approach. The fifth is to integrate existing crosscutting concerns (such as monitoring [11]) with `AOP-BIP`, and in particular existing work such as [12,13].

Acknowledgement. The work reported in this article is in the context of the COST Action ARVI IC1402, supported by COST (European Cooperation in Science and Technology). Moreover, the authors acknowledge the support of the University Research Board (URB) at American University of Beirut.

A   Proofs

We first prove that the global joinpoints can be selected syntactically (Proposition 1), and then prove the correctness of advice application (Proposition 2).

Proof (Proof of Proposition 1). We consider a global event $\langle q, a, q' \rangle \in \mathcal{E}$ and a global pointcut expression $\langle p, v_r, v_w \rangle$. The proof follows from the definition of $\text{match}_g(\mathcal{C}, gpc)$ which selects all interactions matching the criteria that should be matched by $(E_i = \langle q, a, q' \rangle \vDash gpc)$.

$$(\langle q, a, q' \rangle \vDash \langle p, v_r, v_w \rangle) \text{ iff } p \subseteq a.ports$$
$$\wedge\, v_r \subseteq \text{readvar}(a.func)$$
$$\wedge\, v_w \subseteq \text{writevar}(a.func) \qquad \text{(Definition 14)}$$
$$\text{iff } a \in \text{match}_g(\gamma, gpc) \qquad \text{(Def. of match}_g)$$

Proof (Proof of Proposition 2). We assume that f_b and f_a can be uniquely determined and are not empty. It is possible to add an assignment statement at the start and end of each f_b and f_a which has no effect and is not present in the original system and acts as a marker (example: $x = x + NUM - NUM$, with NUM being a unique number not found in any other assignment). We consider an event $\langle q_s, a, q_e \rangle \in \mathcal{E}'$, and $\text{rem}_g(\langle q_s, a, q_e \rangle) = \langle q'_s, a', q'_e \rangle$ the constructed event without the advice.

$$\exists f : a.func = \langle f_b \cdot f \cdot f_a \rangle \text{ iff } \exists a' \in \gamma : m(a') = a \wedge a' \in \mathcal{I}) \quad (\text{Definition 18, m()})$$
$$\text{iff } a' \in \text{match}_g(\mathcal{C}, gpc) \quad (\text{Definition 19})$$
$$\text{iff } (\langle q'_s, a', q'_e \rangle \models gpc) \quad (\text{Proposition 1})$$
$$\text{iff } \text{rem}_g(\langle q_s, a, q_e \rangle) \models gpc)$$

An event interaction's update function $a.func$ starts with f_b and ends with f_a, according to the definition of m() in Definition 18 iff it is the result of weaving the advice on it from an interaction a' ($\exists a' \in \gamma : m(a') = a \wedge a' \in \mathcal{I}$). The interaction a' is in $\mathcal{I}$ iff it was selected by the local pointcut expression ($a' \in \text{match}_g(\mathcal{C}, gpc)$). According to Proposition 1, any event with interaction $a' \in \text{match}_g(\mathcal{C}, gpc)$ is a joinpoint, specifically $\langle q'_s, a', q'_e \rangle = \text{rem}_g(\langle q_s, a, q_e \rangle)$.

References

1. Altisen, K., Maraninchi, F., Stauch, D.: Aspect-oriented programming for reactive systems: larissa, a proposal in the synchronous framework. Sci. Comput. Program. **63**(3), 297–320 (2006)
2. Basu, A., Bensalem, S., Bozga, M., Combaz, J., Jaber, M., Nguyen, T.H., Sifakis, J.: Rigorous component-based system design using the BIP framework. IEEE Softw. **28**(3), 41–48 (2011)
3. Bliudze, S., Sifakis, J.: A notion of glue expressiveness for component-based systems. In: Proceedings of the 19th International Conference on Concurrency Theory, pp. 508–522 (2008)
4. Bozga, M., Jaber, M., Sifakis, J.: Source-to-source architecture transformation for performance optimization in BIP. IEEE Trans. Ind. Inform. **6**(4), 708–718 (2010)
5. Czarnecki, K., Eisenecker, U.W., Steyaert, P.: Beyond objects: generative programming. In: The 23rd International Conference on Software Engineering, pp. 5–14 (1997)
6. David, P.-C., Ledoux, T.: An aspect-oriented approach for developing self-adaptive fractal components. In: Löwe, W., Südholt, M. (eds.) SC 2006. LNCS, vol. 4089, pp. 82–97. Springer, Heidelberg (2006)
7. Dihego, J., Sampaio, A.: Aspect-oriented development of trustworthy component-based systems. In: Leucker, M., et al. (eds.) ICTAC 2015. LNCS, vol. 9399, pp. 425–444. Springer, Heidelberg (2015). doi:10.1007/978-3-319-25150-9_25
8. Djoko, S.D., Douence, R., Fradet, P.: Aspects preserving properties. Sci. Comput. Program. **77**(3), 393–422 (2012)
9. Duclos, F., Estublier, J., Morat, P.: Describing and using non functional aspects in component based applications. In: AOSD, pp. 65–75 (2002)
10. El-Hokayem, A., Falcone, Y., Jaber, M.: http://ujf-aub.bitbucket.org/aop-bip/
11. Falcone, Y., Havelund, K., Reger, G.: A tutorial on runtime verification. In: Engineering Dependable Software Systems, vol. 34, pp. 141–175. IOS Press (2013)
12. Falcone, Y., Jaber, M., Nguyen, T., Bozga, M., Bensalem, S.: Runtime verification of component-based systems in the BIP framework with formally-proved sound and complete instrumentation. Softw. Syst. Model. **14**(1), 173–199 (2015)
13. Falcone, Y., Jaber, M.: Fully automated runtime enforcement of component-based systems with formal and sound recovery. Int. J. Softw. Tools. Technol. Transf. 1–25, (2016). doi:10.1007/s10009-016-0413-6. ISSN:1433-2787

14. Hoare, C.A.R.: Communicating Sequential Processes. Prentice-Hall, Englewood Cliffs (1985)
15. Jouault, F., Allilaire, F., Bézivin, J., Kurtev, I.: ATL: a model transformation tool. Sci. Comput. Program. **72**(1–2), 31–39 (2008)
16. Katz, S.: Aspect categories and classes of temporal properties. In: Rashid, A., Akşit, M. (eds.) Transactions on Aspect-Oriented Software Development I. LNCS, vol. 3880, pp. 106–134. Springer, Heidelberg (2006)
17. Katz, S., Faitelson, D.: The common aspect proof environment. STTT **14**(1), 41–52 (2012)
18. Lieberherr, K.J., Holland, I.M.: Formulations and benefits of the law of demeter. SIGPLAN Not. **24**(3), 67–78 (1989)
19. Lieberherr, K.J., Lorenz, D.H., Ovlinger, J.: Aspectual collaborations: combining modules and aspects. Comput. J. **46**(5), 542–565 (2003)
20. Noureddine, M., Jaber, M., Bliudze, S., Zaraket, F.A.: Reduction and abstraction techniques for BIP. In: Lanese, I., Madelaine, E. (eds.) FACS 2014. LNCS, vol. 8997, pp. 288–305. Springer, Heidelberg (2015)
21. Pessemier, N., Seinturier, L., Duchien, L., Coupaye, T.: A component-based and aspect-oriented model for software evolution. IJCAT **31**(1/2), 94–105 (2008)
22. Tarr, P., Ossher, H.: Hyper/J: multi-dimensional separation of concerns for Java. In: Proceedings of the 23rd International Conference on Software Engineering, pp. 729–730 (2001)
23. Verimag: BIP Tools. http://www-verimag.imag.fr/BIP-Tools,93.html

Tightening a Contract Refinement

Alessandro Cimatti, Ramiro Demasi$^{(\boxtimes)}$, and Stefano Tonetta

Fondazione Bruno Kessler, Trento, Italy
{cimatti,demasi,tonettas}@fbk.eu

Abstract. Contract-based design is an emerging paradigm for correct-by-construction hierarchical systems: components are associated with assumptions and guarantees expressed as formal properties; the architecture is analyzed by verifying that each contract of composite components is correctly refined by the contracts of its subcomponents.

The approach is very efficient, because the overall correctness proof is decomposed into proofs local to each component. However, part of the complexity is delegated to the designer, who has the burden of specifying the contracts. Typical problems include understanding which contracts are necessary, and how they can be simplified without breaking the correctness of the refinement.

In this paper, we tackle these problems by proposing a new technique to understand and simplify a contract refinement. The technique, called tightening, is based on parameter synthesis. The idea is to generate a set of parametric proof obligations, where each parameter evaluation corresponds to a variant of the original contract refinement, and to search for tighter variants of the contracts that still ensure the correctness of the refinement. We cast this approach in the OCRA framework, where contracts are expressed with LTL formulas, and we evaluate its performance and effectiveness on a number of benchmarks.

1 Introduction

Embedded systems are growing in number and technical complexity. They are becoming more and more sophisticated towards open, interconnected and networked systems. Such complexity requires a rigorous analysis especially for those functions that have safety-critical requirements. Formal architectural models provide an important means to guarantee the correct refinement of system requirements along the design development and decomposition of the system.

Contract-based design, first conceived for software specification by Meyer in [20] and nowadays also applied to embedded systems (cfr. e.g., [2–4,12,14–16,22]), is an emerging paradigm for correct-by-construction systems which structures components properties into contracts. A contract specifies the properties assumed to be satisfied by the component environment (assumptions), and the properties guaranteed by the component in response (guarantees). The architecture is analyzed by verifying that each contract of composite components is correctly refined by the contracts of its subcomponents.

R. De Nicola and E. Kühn (Eds.): SEFM 2016, LNCS 9763, pp. 386–402, 2016.
DOI: 10.1007/978-3-319-41591-8_26

In the contract framework proposed in [12,13], assumptions and guarantees are specified as temporal formulas. Checking the correctness of contracts refinement is supported by generating a set of necessary and sufficient conditions. These proof obligations are temporal formulas obtained from assumptions and guarantees, which are valid if and only if the refinement is correct. The approach is implemented in the OCRA tool [8] and is parametrized by a linear-time temporal logic, either propositional LTL [21], or LTL with SMT predicates [11], or HRELTL [10,11], a variant of LTL where formulas represent sets of hybrid traces, mixing discrete- and continuous-time steps, and therefore amenable to model properties of hybrid systems. The approach has been used in several contexts and domains. A significant case study is presented in [5], where different variants of an industrial-size architectural model of a wheel braking system are analyzed, following the example outlined in the avionic AIR6110 standard.

The approach is very efficient, because the overall correctness proof is decomposed into proofs local to each component. However, part of the complexity is delegated to the designer, who has the burden of specifying the contracts. Typical problems include understanding which contracts are necessary, and how they can be simplified without breaking the correctness of the refinement.

In this paper, we tackle these problems by proposing a new technique to understand and simplify a contract refinement. The technique, called tightening, is based on parameter synthesis. The idea is to generate a set of parametric proof obligations, where each parameter evaluation corresponds to a variant of the original contract refinement, and to search for tighter variants of the contracts that still ensures the correctness of the refinement. We cast this approach in the OCRA framework and we evaluate its performance and effectiveness on a number of benchmarks, including the industrial-size architectures described in [5].

Related Work. We are not aware of similar works in the context of contract-based design. The problem of contract tightening is related to vacuity checking [18] and unsatisfiability core extraction [9]. The probably most related work is the notion of unsatisfiability core for LTL proposed in [23]. However, the design problem, the formal problem, and the technical solution are very different. First, differently from the above-mentioned problems, we are not weakening/strengthening the occurrence of a subformula, but we need to weaken/strengthen all occurrences of an assumption/guarantee inside the proof obligations in the same way. Second, we do not have just one property to simplify, but every assumption/guarantee that is simplified occurs in different proof obligations; this corresponds to different unsatisfiability or model checking problems to consider at the same time. Third, we reduce the problem to a parameter synthesis problem and we ensure the monotonicity of parameters to ensure scalable results.

Also the work described in [17] addresses the problem of simplifying a contract refinement, but with a different purpose and solution: the approach relies on a library of contracts and refinement relations considered as additional inputs to the refinement check problem, and simplifies the contract refinement based on such library. The main objective of the authors is to improve the performance of the refinement check based on the library, while we search a tighter version of the contracts that still ensure the correctness of the refinement.

Outline. The remainder of the paper is structured as follows. In Sect. 2 we introduce some notions used throughout the paper. In Sect. 3, we introduce the problem of tightening a contract refinement. We present in Sect. 4 the main algorithm for solving such problem. We describe the experimental evaluation performed in Sect. 5. Finally, we discuss some conclusions and directions for further work.

2 Background

2.1 Transition Systems

Given a finite set V of variables with a (potentially infinite) domain D, we denote with $\Sigma(V)$ the set of assignments to V, i.e. mapping from V to D. A *transition system* (TS) S is a tuple $S = \langle V, I, T \rangle$, where V is a set of (state) variables, $I \subseteq \Sigma(V)$ is the set of initial states, and $T \subseteq \Sigma(V) \times \Sigma(V)$ is the set of transitions. A state $s \in \Sigma(V)$ of S is an assignment to the variables V. A trace σ of S is an infinite sequence of states $\sigma = s_0, s_1, \cdots$ such that $s_0 \in I$ and for all $i \geq 0$, $\langle s_i, s_{i+1} \rangle \in T$. Given two transition systems $S_1 = \langle V_1, I_1, T_1 \rangle$ and $S_2 = \langle V_2, I_2, T_2 \rangle$, we define the synchronous product $S_1 \times S_2$ as $\langle V_1 \cup V_2, I_1 \wedge I_2, T_1 \wedge T_2 \rangle$. Since the product is commutative and associative, it can be generalized to a set of transitions systems.

2.2 LTL

Given a set of variables V, we assume to be given a set $Expr(V)$ of Boolean expressions over V as in [19]. In particular, in this paper we consider standard arithmetic predicates $(<, \leq, >, \geq, \ldots)$ and functions $(+, -, \ldots)$ over integer and real variables, although the proposed methods can be applied to more general settings.

We define the set of LTL formulas over the variables V with the following grammar rule:

$$\phi := p \mid \phi \wedge \phi \mid \phi \vee \phi \mid \neg \phi \mid X\phi \mid \phi U \phi \mid \phi R \phi$$

where p ranges in $Expr(V)$. We use the following standard abbreviations: $\top := p \vee \neg p$, $\bot := \neg \top$, $\phi \rightarrow \psi := (\neg \phi) \vee \psi$, $F\phi := \top U \phi$, $G\phi := \neg F \neg \phi$.

Traces over V are infinite sequences of assignments to V. Given a trace $\sigma = s_0, s_1, \ldots$, we denote with $\sigma[i]$ the $i+1$-th state s_i and with σ^i the suffix trace starting from $s[i]$.

Given a trace σ and an LTL formula ϕ over V, we define $\sigma \models \phi$ as follows:

- $\sigma \models p$ iff p evaluates to true given the assignment $\sigma[0]$
- $\sigma \models \neg \phi$ iff $\sigma \not\models \phi$
- $\sigma \models X\phi$ iff $\sigma^1 \models \phi$

- $\sigma \models \phi U \psi$ iff there exists $i \geq 0$ s.t. $\sigma^i \models \psi$ and for all j, $0 \leq j < i$, $\sigma^j \models \phi$
- $\sigma \models \phi R \psi$ iff for all $i \geq 0$ $\sigma^i \models \psi$ or there exists j, $0 \leq j < i$, s.t. $\sigma^j \models \phi$

The satisfiability problem is the problem of checking if for a given LTL formula ϕ there exists a trace σ such that $\sigma \models \phi$.

Given a TS $S = \langle V, I, T \rangle$ and an LTL formula ϕ over $V' \subseteq V$, $M \models \phi$ if for all traces σ of M, $\sigma \models \phi$. The satisfiability problem of an LTL formula over V can be reduced to model checking by considering the universal model as transition system: i.e., ϕ is satisfiable iff $\langle V, \Sigma(V), \Sigma(V) \times \Sigma(V) \rangle \not\models \neg\phi$.

Note that we are considering in general infinite-state transition systems for which these problems are undecidable. Our methods are based on SMT-based algorithms as those implemented in nuXmv [7].

2.3   Parameter Synthesis

The goal of parameter synthesis is to find the maximal set of values for some parameters, so that a given property is satisfied. Let S be a transition system and let U be a set of parameter, we define the parametric transition system $P = (V, U, I_U, T_U)$, where I and T are now defined on both the state variables and parameters. We define the parameters as frozen, i.e., we set their value in the initial state and preserve it during the execution of the system. Given a valuation for the parameters ($\gamma \in \Sigma(U)$), and a formula ψ we write $\gamma(\psi) = \psi[u \in U/\gamma(u)]$, to indicate that each parameter has been substituted with its value. Given a parametric transition system P and a valuation for the parameters γ, we can compute the *induced* transition system, by replacing the parameters with their valuation: $P_\gamma = (V, \gamma(I_U), \gamma(T_U))$. Given an LTL property ϕ expressed over the state variables and parameters, the parameter region ρ is the maximal set of assignments to the parameters, such that the property is satisfied by every trace of the induced system, formally: $\rho = \{\gamma \mid P_\gamma \models \gamma(\phi)\}$.

In this paper, we consider Boolean parameters and, with abuse of notation, we identify a parameter evaluation γ with the set $\{p \mid p \in U, \gamma(p) = \top\}$. The parameter region is monotonic iff whenever $\gamma \subseteq \gamma'$, if $\gamma \in \rho$ then $\gamma' \in \rho$. The monotonicity of the parameter region is typically exploited by parameter synthesis algorithms that enumerate the parameter evaluations γ such that $P_\gamma \not\models \gamma(\phi)$. In fact, one can proceed with γ of increasing cardinality and as soon as $P_\gamma \models \gamma(\phi)$ all γ' with $\gamma \subseteq \gamma'$ can be included in ρ.

2.4   Contract Refinement

In order to simplify the presentation, in this paper, we define a contract refinement independently from the component interfaces. In practice, in the tool support we consider, contracts are specified in terms of component input/output ports and the refinement has to take into account the connections among ports in component decomposition.

A contract C over the variables V is a pair $\langle A, G \rangle$ of LTL formulas over V_S representing respectively an *assumption* and a *guarantee*.

We also denote A by $\mathcal{A}(C)$, G by $\mathcal{G}(C)$, and the assertion $\neg A \vee G$ by $nf(C)$.

Let $C = \langle A, G \rangle$ be a contract over V. Let I and E be TS over V. We say that I is a correct implementation of C iff $I \models A \rightarrow G$. We say that E is a correct environment of C iff $E \models A$. We denote by $\mathcal{I}(C)$ and $\mathcal{E}(C)$, respectively, the set of correct implementations and the set of correct environments of C.

Given two contracts C and C' over V, we say that C refines C' (denoted by $C \preceq C'$) iff $\mathcal{I}(C') \subseteq \mathcal{I}(C)$ and $\mathcal{E}(C) \subseteq \mathcal{E}(C')$.

In a system architecture, each contract is associated to a component. If a component is decomposed into subcomponents, the associated contracts are implemented by the composition of the subcomponents' implementations. Similarly, the environment of the contract of a subcomponent is given by the composition of the environment of the composite component and the implementations of the other subcomponents. In order to prove that such decomposition is correct, we generalize the refinement notion to a set of contracts.

Given a contract C and a set of contracts $Sub = \{C_1, \ldots, C_n\}$, we say that Sub is a refinement of C, written $Sub \preceq C$, iff the following conditions hold:

1. The correct implementations of the sub-contracts form a correct implementation of C:

$$\{S_1 \times \ldots \times S_n \mid S_1 \in \mathcal{I}(C_1), \ldots, S_n \in \mathcal{I}(C_n)\} \subseteq \mathcal{I}(C)$$

2. For every $C_i \in Sub$, the correct implementation of the other sub-contracts and a correct environment of C form a correct environment of C_i:

$$\{E \times S_1 \times \ldots \times S_{j \neq i} \times \ldots \times S_n \mid E \in \mathcal{E}(C), \text{ for all } j, 1 \leq j \leq n, j \neq i, S_j \in \mathcal{I}(C_j)\} \subseteq \mathcal{E}(C_i)$$

In [12,13], we proved that the refinement is correct if and only if the following proof obligations are valid temporal formulas:

$$nf(C_1) \wedge \ldots \wedge nf(C_n) \rightarrow nf(C)$$

$$A \wedge \bigwedge_{1 \leq j \leq n, j \neq i} nf(C_j) \rightarrow A_i \text{ (for every } i, 1 \leq i \leq n)$$

3 The Problem of Tightening a Refinement

3.1 Motivation

Contract-Based Design. The contract-based design flow is depicted in Fig. 1, using the example of a Wheel Braking System (WBS), which takes care of translating the brake signals of the braking pedals into physical brake of the wheel. The brake pedal position is electrically fed to the braking computer, which in turn produces corresponding control signals to the brakes. This computer is named the Braking System Control Unit (BSCU). The BSCU is implemented with two redundant sub-systems, called subBSCU. Therefore, the BSCU takes as input two redundant `Pedal_Pos` brake positions and outputs a pressure on the `Brake_Line`.

The design starts with the view of the system as a whole black box with ports to interact with its environment. Then, it is decomposed into BSCU and Hydraulic components. The BSCU is in turn decomposed into two redundant subBSCU and a switch. The decomposition also defines how the ports of the component being decomposed are mapped down into the decomposition. For example, the "left" ports of the WBS are mapped onto the "left" ports of the BSCU.

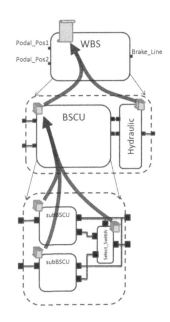

Fig. 1. Contract-based design flow.

Each component in the hierarchy is associated with a set of *contracts*, depicted in green, specifying the acceptable behaviors for the component and its environment. Contracts are refined, following the decomposition of components. For example, the contracts of the WBS are refined by some contracts of the BSCU and the Hydraulic subcomponents. The framework guarantees that, under specific conditions (corresponding to correct contract refinement), if the contracts of the subcomponents hold, then the contract of the parent component also holds.

Need for Tightening. The typical design of a system follows a top-down approach starting from the system requirements and iteratively deriving the requirements of subcomponents. The process is however quite expensive, especially if the requirements are formalized into formal properties. It may happen therefore to specify contracts on the subcomponents that are more demanding than necessary or that contain unwanted redundancies. It may happen also that the designer specifies a very strong assumption on the system to make the refinement correct and she/he wants to relax such assumption while keeping the design correct. In general, given a correct contract refinement, we would like to understand if the guarantees of subcomponents or assumption on the composite component can be weakened. We call this problem *top-down tightening* of a contract refinement.

In some cases, the guarantees of subcomponents or the assumption of the system are fixed. For example, the designer used the contract specification of an existing component. After having verified the contract refinement, the designer would like to understand if, using this subcomponents' specification, the system properties can be strengthened. Similarly, a given subcomponent specification can entail stronger assumptions on other subcomponents, which would allow the designer to choose alternative design solutions. We call *bottom-up tightening* of a contract refinement to this problem of strengthening the guarantees of a composite component and the assumptions of the subcomponents.

3.2 Formal Definition

Tightening. We now define formally the problem of tightening a contract refinement as follows. Given a contract C, and a set of contracts $C_1, \ldots, C_n$ such that $\{C_1, \ldots C_n\} \preceq C$, a *tightening* of this contract refinement is given by a set of contracts $C', C'_1, \ldots, C'_n$ such that:

- $\{C'_1, \ldots C'_n\} \preceq C'$
- $C' \preceq C$ and, for every i, $1 \le i \le n$, $C_i \preceq C'_i$.

A *top-down tightening* is a tightening as defined above such that $\mathcal{G}(C) = \mathcal{G}(C')$ and, for all i, $1 \le i \le n$, $\mathcal{A}(C_i) = \mathcal{A}(C'_i)$. We can easily prove that, equivalently, a top-down tightening is given by a set of contracts $C', C'_1, \ldots, C'_n$ such that:

- $\{C'_1, \ldots C'_n\} \preceq C'$
- $\mathcal{A}(C) \models \mathcal{A}(C')$ and, for every i, $1 \le i \le n$, $\mathcal{G}(C_i) \models \mathcal{G}(C'_i)$.

A *bottom-up tightening* is a tightening as defined above such that $\mathcal{A}(C) = \mathcal{A}(C')$ and, for all i, $1 \le i \le n$, $\mathcal{G}(C_i) = \mathcal{G}(C'_i)$. We can easily prove that, equivalently, a bottom-up tightening is given by a set of contracts $C', C'_1, \ldots, C'_n$ such that:

- $\{C'_1, \ldots C'_n\} \preceq C'$
- $\mathcal{G}(C') \models \mathcal{G}(C)$ and, for every i, $1 \le i \le n$, $\mathcal{A}(C'_i) \models \mathcal{A}(C_i)$.

4 The Algorithm

4.1 Overview

In this section, we present the main algorithm for tightening a contract refinement for the two variants of the problem we defined (*top-down* and *bottom-up*). The procedure first injects a set P of parameters in the contract specification to create a search space of weakened or strengthened assumptions and guarantees. Second, it creates the related proof obligations that are now parametrized by P and we want to find for which configurations of the parameters the contract refinement holds. This is a multiple parameter synthesis problem, because we have to search for the assignment to P such that all proof obligations are valid. Thus, as third step, we convert the problem to a single standard parameter synthesis problem and we call an off-the-shelf algorithm to solve it. In the first step, we make sure that the injection creates a monotonic parameter region by construction, which can be exploited by the synthesis algorithm.

These steps are formalized as follows, while the pseudo-code is shown in Algorithm 1. Suppose we want to obtain a top-down tightening of $Sub \preceq C$.

1. We transform C and Sub into a parametrized version C_P and Sub_P such that for every evaluation γ of P, if $\gamma(Sub_P) \preceq \gamma(C_P)$, then $\langle \gamma(C_P), \gamma(Sub_P) \rangle$ is a top-down tightening of $\langle C, Sub \rangle$.
2. We generate the proof obligations $PO(V, P)$ of $\gamma(Sub_P) \preceq \gamma(C_P)$.
3. We generate a single proof obligation ϕ that is equivalent to $PO(V, P)$ in the sense that $\{\gamma \in \Sigma(P) \text{ s.t. } \models \gamma(\phi) \text{ for every } \phi \in PO(V, P)\} = \{\gamma \in \Sigma(P) \text{ s.t. } \models \gamma(\phi_{PO})\}$.

Algorithm 1. Tightening a Contract Refinement

Input: a contract C, a set of contracts $Sub = \{C_1, \ldots, C_n\}$ such that $Sub \preceq C$, and
     $T =$ bottom-up or top-down
Output: $Sub' = \{C_1', \ldots C_n'\} \preceq C'$ and $C' \preceq C$ and, for every i, $1 \leq i \leq n$, $C_i \preceq C_i'$.
 1: {Calling top-down or bottom-up alg. on Sub and C}
 2: **if** $T =$ top-down **then**
 3:     $\langle \langle Sub_P, C_P \rangle, P \rangle = Top\_down\_tightening(Sub, C)$
 4: **else** {$T =$ bottom-up}
 5:     $\langle \langle Sub_P, C_P \rangle, P \rangle = Bottom\_up\_tightening(Sub, C)$
 6: **end if**
 7: {Construction of the Proof Obligations}
 8: $POs = ConstructPOs(Sub_P, C_P)$
 9: {Encodes all POs into a single PO}
10: $PO = BuildSinglePO(POs)$
11: {Calling Parameter Synthesis Algorithm}
12: $param\_region = ComputeParamRegion(PO, P)$
13: {Generate output}
14: $GenerateTightenedContractRef(PO, param\_region)$

4.2 Generation of the Parametric Problem

In this section, we describe how we introduce parameters in the contracts and generate a monotonic parameter synthesis problem. The high-level transformation is described in Algorithms 2 and 3 where assumptions and guarantees are weakened or strengthened depending on whether we are targeting a top-down or a bottom-up tightening of the contract refinement.

If the target is the top-down tightening of $Sub \preceq C$, the Algorithm 2 weakens every guarantee of the subcontracts in Sub and the assumption of the C. If the target is the bottom-up tightening, the Algorithm 3 strengthens the guarantee of C and every assumption of Sub.

The *Weaken* and *Strengthen* functions are described respectively in Algorithms 4 and 5. They take as input a formula and they return a parametric formula and a set of injected parameters. The definition assumes that every new parameter p is a fresh symbol. The number of parameters is linear in the size of the formula.

Parameters are injected so that every parameter evaluation yields a respectively weaker or stronger formula.

Algorithm 2. Top-down tightening $(Top\_down\_tightening(Sub, C))$

Input: a contract C and a set of contracts $Sub = \{C_1, \ldots, C_n\}$
Output: $\langle\langle Sub', C'\rangle, P\rangle$
 1: $Sub' = \emptyset$
 2: $P = \emptyset$ {Set of parameters}
 3: **for all** $C_i \in Sub$ **do**
 4:     $\langle \mathcal{G}(C_i'), P'\rangle = Weaken(\mathcal{G}(C_i))$
 5:     $Sub' = Sub' \cup \{\langle \mathcal{A}(C_i), \mathcal{G}(C_i')\rangle\}$
 6:     $P = P \cup P'$
 7: **end for**
 8: $\langle \mathcal{A}(C'), P'\rangle = Weaken(\mathcal{A}(C))$
 9: $C' = \langle \mathcal{A}(C'), \mathcal{G}(C)\rangle$
10: $P = P \cup P'$
11: **return** $\langle\langle Sub', C'\rangle, P\rangle$

Algorithm 3. Bottom-up tightening $(Bottom\_up\_tightening(Sub, C))$

Input: a contract C and a set of contracts $Sub = \{C_1, \ldots, C_n\}$
Output: $\langle\langle Sub', C'\rangle, P\rangle$
 1: $Sub' = \emptyset$
 2: $P = \emptyset$ {Set of parameters}
 3: **for all** $C_i \in Sub$ **do**
 4:     $\langle \mathcal{A}(C_i'), P'\rangle = Strengthen(\mathcal{A}(C_i))$
 5:     $Sub' = Sub' \cup \{\langle \mathcal{A}(C_i'), \mathcal{G}(C_i)\rangle\}$
 6:     $P = P \cup P'$
 7: **end for**
 8: $\langle \mathcal{G}(C'), P'\rangle = Strengthen(\mathcal{G}(C))$
 9: $C' = \langle \mathcal{A}(C), \mathcal{G}(C')\rangle$
10: $P = P \cup P'$
11: **return** $\langle\langle Sub', C'\rangle, P\rangle$

We remark that we do not aim to obtain the weakest or strongest version of a formula. In our approach, the definition of *Weaken* and *Strengthen* functions is pattern-based where new patterns can be investigated to complement or improve the current ones.

Theorem 1. *For any parameter evaluation* γ, $\phi \;\rightarrow\; \gamma(Weaken(\phi))$ *and* $\gamma(Strengthen(\phi)) \rightarrow \phi$.

Proof. We prove the theorem by induction on the structure of the formula. If $Weaken(\phi) = \langle \phi^W, P\rangle$, we denote with ϕ' the instantiation of ϕ^W with some evaluation γ. Similarly, if $Strengthen(\phi) = \langle \phi^S, P\rangle$, we denote with ϕ'' the instantiation of ϕ^S with some evaluation γ.

The result of *Weaken* and *Strengthen* is outlined in Tables 1 and 2. It is routine to check line by line that $\phi \rightarrow \phi'$ and $\phi'' \rightarrow \phi$, based on the inductive hypothesis that $\phi_1 \rightarrow \phi_1'$, $\phi_2 \rightarrow \phi_2'$, $\phi_1'' \rightarrow \phi_1$.   □

Algorithm 4. $Weaken(\phi)$

Input: a formula ϕ
Output: $\langle \phi^W, P \rangle$
1: **if** $\phi = a > b$ (similar for $\phi = a < b$) **then**
2:     $\phi^W = p_1 \rightarrow (a > b) \wedge p_2 \rightarrow (a \geq b)$
3:     **return** $\langle \phi^W, \{p_1, p_2\} \rangle$
4: **else if** $\phi = \phi_1 \wedge \phi_2$ **then**
5:     $\langle \phi_1^W, P_1 \rangle = Weaken(\phi_1)$, $\langle \phi_2^W, P_2 \rangle = Weaken(\phi_2)$
6:     $\phi^W = p_1 \rightarrow \phi_1^W \wedge p_2 \rightarrow \phi_2^W$
7:     **return** $\langle \phi^W, P_1 \cup P_2 \cup \{p_1, p_2\} \rangle$
8: **else if** $\phi = \phi_1 \vee \phi_2$ **then**
9:     $\langle \phi_1^W, P_1 \rangle = Weaken(\phi_1)$, $\langle \phi_2^W, P_2 \rangle = Weaken(\phi_2)$
10:     $\phi^W = \phi_1^W \vee \phi_2^W$
11:     **return** $\langle \phi^W, P_1 \cup P_2 \rangle$
12: **else if** $\phi = \phi_1 \mathcal{R} \phi_2$ **then**
13:     $\langle \phi_1^W, P_1 \rangle = Weaken(\phi_1)$, $\langle \phi_2^W, P_2 \rangle = Weaken(\phi_2)$
14:     $\phi^W = p_1 \rightarrow (\phi_1^W \wedge \phi_2^W) \wedge p_2 \rightarrow (\phi_1^W \mathcal{R} \phi_2^W)$
15:     **return** $\langle \phi^W, P_1 \cup P_2 \cup \{p_1, p_2\} \rangle$
16: **else if** $\phi = \phi_1 \mathcal{U} \phi_2$ **then**
17:     $\langle \phi_1^W, P_1 \rangle = Weaken(\phi_1)$, $\langle \phi_2^W, P_2 \rangle = Weaken(\phi_2)$
18:     $\phi^W = \phi_1^W \mathcal{U} \phi_2^W$
19:     **return** $\langle \phi^W, P_1 \cup P_2 \rangle$
20: **else if** $\phi = \neg \phi_1$ **then**
21:     $\langle \phi_1^S, P_1 \rangle = Strengthen(\phi_1)$
22:     **return** $\langle \neg \phi_1^S, P_1 \rangle$
23: **else**
24:     **return** $\langle p \rightarrow \phi, \{p\} \rangle$
25: **end if**

It follows immediately that Algorithms 2 and 3 yield a correct top-down/bottom-up tightening, as stated in the following corollary.

Corollary 1. *Let C be a contract and Sub a set of contracts. Let $\langle \langle Sub', C' \rangle, P \rangle$ be the result of $Top\_down\_tightening(Sub, C)$ or $Bottom\_up\_tightening(Sub, C)$. Then, for any evaluation γ of the parameters P, if $\gamma(Sub') \preceq \gamma(C')$ then $\langle \gamma(Sub'), \gamma(C') \rangle$ is a top-down or bottom-up tightening of $\langle Sub, C \rangle$, respectively.*

Moreover, the parameter injection is designed so that the semantics of the parametric formulas is monotonic with respect to the parameter evaluations.

Theorem 2. *If $\gamma \subseteq \gamma'$, $\gamma'(Weaken(\phi)) \rightarrow \gamma(Weaken(\phi))$ and $\gamma(Strengthen(\phi)) \rightarrow \gamma'(Strengthen(\phi))$.*

Proof. Looking again at Tables 1 and 2, one can check the monotonicity case by case. In fact, for each type of formula, the lines reporting the result of *Weaken* and *Strengthen* are sorted according to the strength of the parameter evaluation (third column). More precisely, if γ is below γ', then either they are incomparable or $\gamma \subset \gamma'$. Therefore it is routine to prove that, in the second case,

Table 1. Simplification table for $Weaken(\phi)$, where ϕ'_i denotes the instantiation of ϕ_i^W with some evaluation γ.

Formula ϕ	$Weaken(\phi) = \langle \phi^W, P \rangle$	Evaluation γ	$\gamma(Weaken(\phi))$
$a < b$	$p_1 \to (a < b) \wedge p_2 \to (a \le b)$	$\{p_1, p_2\}$	$a \le b$
		$\{p_1\}$	$a < b$
		$\{p_2\}$	$a \le b$
		$\emptyset$	$\top$
$\phi_1 \wedge \phi_2$	$p_1 \to \phi_1^W \wedge p_2 \to \phi_2^W$	$\{p_1, p_2\}$	$\phi'_1 \wedge \phi'_2$
		$\{p_1\}$	ϕ'_1
		$\{p_2\}$	ϕ'_2
		$\emptyset$	$\top$
$\phi_1 \vee \phi_2$	$\phi_1^W \vee \phi_2^W$	NA	$\phi'_1 \vee \phi'_2$
$\phi_1 \,\mathcal{R}\, \phi_2$	$p_1 \to (\phi_1^W \wedge \phi_2^W) \wedge p_2 \to (\phi_1^W \,\mathcal{R}\, \phi_2^W)$	$\{p_1, p_2\}$	$\phi'_1 \wedge \phi'_2$
		$\{p_2\}$	$\phi'_1 \,\mathcal{R}\, \phi'_2$
		$\{p_1\}$	$\phi'_1 \wedge \phi'_2$
		$\emptyset$	$\top$
$\phi_1 \,\mathcal{U}\, \phi_2$	$\phi_1^W \,\mathcal{U}\, \phi_2^W$	NA	$\phi'_1 \,\mathcal{U}\, \phi'_2$
$\neg \phi_1$	$\neg \phi_1^S$	NA	$\neg \phi'_1$

Table 2. Simplification table for $Strengthen(\phi)$, where ϕ''_i denotes the instantiation of ϕ_i^S with some evaluation γ.

Formula ϕ	$Strengthen(\phi) = \langle \phi^S, P \rangle$	Evaluation γ	$\gamma(Strengthen(\phi))$
$a \le b$	$\neg p_1 \to (a < b) \wedge \neg p_2 \to (a = b) \wedge$ $(p_1 \wedge p_2) \to (a \le b)$	$\{p_1, p_2\}$	$a \le b$
		$\{p_2\}$	$a < b$
		$\{p_1\}$	$a = b$
		$\emptyset$	$\bot$
$\phi_1 \vee \phi_2$	$\neg p_1 \to \phi_1^S \wedge \neg p_2 \to \phi_2^S \wedge$ $(p_1 \wedge p_2) \to (\phi_1^S \vee \phi_2^S)$	$\{p_1, p_2\}$	$\phi''_1 \vee \phi''_2$
		$\{p_2\}$	ϕ''_1
		$\{p_1\}$	ϕ''_2
		$\emptyset$	$\phi''_1 \wedge \phi''_2$
$\phi_1 \wedge \phi_2$	$\phi_1^S \wedge \phi_2^S$	NA	$\phi''_1 \wedge \phi''_2$
$\phi_1 \,\mathcal{U}\, \phi_2$	$\neg p \to \phi_2^S \wedge p \to \phi_1^S \,\mathcal{U}\, \phi_2^S$	$\{p\}$	$\phi''_1 \,\mathcal{U}\, \phi''_2$
		$\emptyset$	ϕ''_2
$\phi_1 \,\mathcal{R}\, \phi_2$	$\phi_1^S \,\mathcal{R}\, \phi_2^S$	NA	$\phi''_1 \,\mathcal{R}\, \phi''_2$
$\neg \phi_1$	$\neg \phi_1^W$	NA	$\neg \phi''_1$

$\gamma'(Weaken(\phi)) \to \gamma(Weaken(\phi))$ and $\gamma(Strengthen(\phi)) \to \gamma'(Strengthen(\phi))$ (fourth column). $\qquad\square$

Note that parameters are introduced per contract, so they are shared by difference occurrences of the assumption/guarantee in the proof obligations. It is immediate to show that, thanks to the structured way in which formulas are either strengthened or weakened according to the target top-down/bottom-up tightening, the resulting synthesis problem is monotonic, as stated in the following corollary.

Corollary 2. *Let C be a contract and Sub a set of contracts. Let $\langle\langle Sub', C'\rangle, P\rangle$ the result of $Top\_down\_tightening(Sub, C)$ or $Bottom\_up\_tightening(Sub, C)$. Then, for any evaluation γ, γ' of the parameters P such that $\gamma \subseteq \gamma'$, if $\gamma(Sub') \preceq \gamma(C')$ then $\gamma'(Sub') \preceq \gamma'(C')$.*

Algorithm 5. *Strengthen(ϕ)*

Input: a formula ϕ
Output: $\langle \phi^S, P \rangle$
1: **if** $\phi = a \leq b$ (similar for $a \geq b$) **then**
2:     $\phi^S = \neg p_1 \rightarrow (a < b) \wedge \neg p_2 \rightarrow (a = b) \wedge (p_1 \wedge p_2) \rightarrow (a \leq b)$
3:     **return** $\langle \phi^S, \{p_1, p_2\} \rangle$
4: **else if** $\phi = \phi_1 \vee \phi_2$ **then**
5:     $(\phi_1^S, P_1) = Strengthen(\phi_1), (\phi_2^S, P_2) = Strengthen(\phi_2)$
6:     $\phi^S = \neg p_1 \rightarrow \phi_1^S \wedge \neg p_2 \rightarrow \phi_2^S \wedge (p_1 \wedge p_2) \rightarrow (\phi_1^S \vee \phi_2^S)$
7:     **return** $\langle \phi^S, P_1 \cup P_2 \cup \{p_1, p_2\} \rangle$
8: **else if** $\phi = \phi_1 \wedge \phi_2$ **then**
9:     $(\phi_1^S, P_1) = Strengthen(\phi_1), (\phi_2^S, P_2) = Strengthen(\phi_2)$
10:     $\phi^S = \phi_1^S \wedge \phi_2^S$
11:     **return** $\langle \phi^S, P_1 \cup P_2 \rangle$
12: **else if** $\phi = \phi_1 \, \mathcal{U} \, \phi_2$ **then**
13:     $(\phi_1^S, P_1) = Strengthen(\phi_1), (\phi_2^S, P_2) = Strengthen(\phi_2)$
14:     $\phi^S = \neg p \rightarrow \phi_2^S \wedge p \rightarrow \phi_1^S \, \mathcal{U} \, \phi_2^S$
15:     **return** $\langle \phi^S, P_1 \cup P_2 \cup \{p\} \rangle$
16: **else if** $\phi = \phi_1 \, \mathcal{R} \, \phi_2$ **then**
17:     $(\phi_1^S, P_1) = Strengthen(\phi_1), (\phi_2^S, P_2) = Strengthen(\phi_2)$
18:     $\phi^S = \phi_1^S \, \mathcal{R} \, \phi_2^S$
19:     **return** $\langle \phi^S, P_1 \cup P_2 \rangle$
20: **else if** $\phi = \neg \phi_1$ **then**
21:     $(\phi_1^W, P_1) = Weaken(\phi_1)$
22:     **return** $\langle \neg \phi_1^W, P_1 \rangle$
23: **else**
24:     **return** $\langle \neg p \rightarrow \phi, \{p\} \rangle$
25: **end if**

4.3   Multiple Validity Parameter Synthesis Problem

The approach to solve the tightening problem proposed in Sect. 4.1 introduces the problem of finding the parameter evaluations γ such that each formula $\phi(P, V) \in PO$ instantiated with γ is valid. Each validity problem can be reduced to a model checking problem but the parameter evaluation is shared by the different verification problems. This is different from the standard parameter synthesis problem where only one verification problem is considered. We called this problem a multiple validity parameter synthesis problem (not to be confused with multiple objective parameter synthesis problem).

We propose to reduce the multiple validity to one validity problem by renaming the variables in V and taking the conjunction of the proof obligations. Namely, if $PO = \{\phi_1, \ldots, \phi_n\}$ we create the formula $\phi_{PO}(P, V_1, \ldots, V_n) = \bigwedge_{1 \leq j \leq n} \phi_j[V_j/V]$, where V_j contains one copy v_j for each variable $v \in V$ and $\phi_j[V_j/V]$ is the formulas obtained by substituting every variable $v \in V$ with v_j (while the parameters P remain unchanged).

Theorem 3. *For all parameter evaluation γ, $\gamma(\phi_{PO})$ is valid iff, for all formulas $\phi \in PO$, $\gamma(\phi)$ is valid.*

Proof. $\Rightarrow$) Suppose for some $\phi_j \in PO$, $\gamma(\phi_j)$ is not valid. Let σ be a trace over V satisfying $\neg\gamma(\phi_j)$. Let us define the trace σ_j such that, for every $i \geq 0$, for all $v \in V$, $\sigma_j[i](v_j) = \sigma[j](v)$. Let us extend σ_j to a trace σ'_j over $V_1 \cup \ldots V_n$ assigning variables not in V_j in an arbitrary way. Then σ'_j satisfies $\neg\gamma(\phi_{PO})$.

$\Leftarrow$) Suppose ϕ_{PO} is not valid. Let σ be a trace over $V_1 \cup \ldots \cup V_n$ satisfying $\neg\gamma(\phi_{PO})$. Then, there exists j, $1 \leq j \leq n$, such that $\sigma \models \neg\gamma(\phi_j[V_j/V])$. Let us define the trace σ_j such that, for every $i \geq 0$, for all $v \in V$, $\sigma_j[i](v) = \sigma[j](v_j)$. Then σ'_j satisfies $\neg\gamma(\phi_j)$. $\qquad\square$

5   Experimental Evaluation

5.1   Details of the Implementation

We have implemented the algorithms described in the previous section on top of OCRA [8], a tool for architectural design based on contract-based design. In more details, we implemented a new command in OCRA that takes as input an OCRA specification, a contract's name, a component's name, and a desired variant of tightening (top-down or bottom-up) and produces as output an OCRA specification containing the tightened version of the given contract and its subcontracts. Regarding the parameter synthesis algorithm, we have used as backend an implementation reported in [6]. Since the synthesis is quite expensive for large number of parameters, we arbitrarily limit the injection to 350 parameters. This allows to get a tightening also in cases in which the definitions would produce many more parameters making the synthesis blow up.

We also implemented self checks to validate the results: first, we automatically check that each tightened contract refinement is correct; second, we automatically check for each tightened specification that the original formula entails the weaken formula (top-down tightening) and the strengthened formula entails the original formula (bottom-up tightening), see Theorem 1.

5.2   Description of Benchmarks

We have taken several benchmarks from several case studies developed manually using the OCRA language. Some examples are: several versions of the Wheel Brake System described in Sect. 3, a Lift System, a system with Redundant Sensors, and Airbag system [1]. Particularly, an interesting case study is taken from [5], where the authors presented a complete formal analysis of the AIR6110, a document describing the informal design of a Wheel Brake System, covering all the phases of the process, and modeled the case study by means of a combination of formal methods including contract-based design using OCRA, model checking and safety analysis.

5.3   Experimental Results

We carried out an experimental evaluation for 875 contract refinements taking into account the simplification obtained on each tightened contract refinement with respect to the length of the formulas on the original contracts involved[1]. The results of applying top-down (red crosses) and bottom-up (grey circles) tightening are shown in Fig. 2. From the results, we can clearly see a significant simplification for top-down tightening. As for bottom-up tightening, we did not get important simplification, but we observed that the main reason is that the size of formulas of the contracts involved are much smaller compared to the ones involved on the top-down tightening.

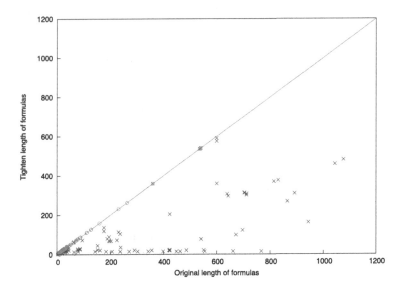

Fig. 2. Analysis of length of formulas for top-down and bottom-up. (Color figure online)

---

[1] We consider the standard definition of the length of a formula (number of symbols), apart from the length of $\top$ which is set to 0.

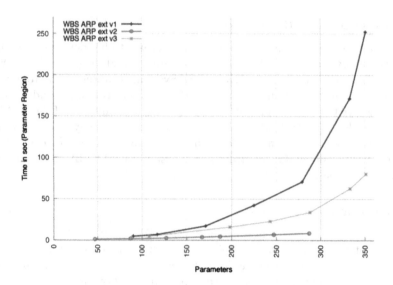

Fig. 3. Parameter scalability.

In Fig. 3 it is shown how our approach scales with respect to the number of parameters used for tightening a contract refinement and the time for computing the parameter region for three extended versions of the WBS example. All benchmarks have been performed with a time limit of 5 min for checking the contract refinement before and after tightening, the computation of the parameter region, and the check of the entailments properties. For the 875 contract refinements, 68 could not be completed within the timeout. We have run our experiments on a Linux machine with 8 CPU of 3.40 GHz Intel Xeon, with a memory of 15 GB.

The benchmarks and executables for reproducing the results are available at https://es-static.fbk.eu/people/demasi/SEFM2016/experiments.html.

6   Conclusions and Future Work

Motivated by validation problems of contract-based design, we defined the problem of tightening a contract refinement. We provided a solution based on the synthesis of parameters of temporal satisfiability problems. We evaluated the approach on a number of benchmarks and showed that the solution is effective and scalable. For future work, we will extend the approach to consider also the tightening of metric operators and the preservation of realizability.

References

1. Arts, T., Dorigatti, M., Tonetta, S.: Making implicit safety requirements explicit. In: Bondavalli, A., Di Giandomenico, F. (eds.) SAFECOMP 2014. LNCS, vol. 8666, pp. 81–92. Springer, Heidelberg (2014)

2. Bauer, S.S., David, A., Hennicker, R., Guldstrand Larsen, K., Legay, A., Nyman, U., Wąsowski, A.: Moving from specifications to contracts in component-based design. In: de Lara, J., Zisman, A. (eds.) Fundamental Approaches to Software Engineering. LNCS, vol. 7212, pp. 43–58. Springer, Heidelberg (2012)
3. Benveniste, A., Caillaud, B., Ferrari, A., Mangeruca, L., Passerone, R., Sofronis, C.: Multiple viewpoint contract-based specification and design. In: de Boer, F.S., Bonsangue, M.M., Graf, S., de Roever, W.-P. (eds.) FMCO 2007. LNCS, vol. 5382, pp. 200–225. Springer, Heidelberg (2008)
4. Benveniste, A., Caillaud, B., Nickovic, D., Passerone, R., Raclet, J.-B., Reinkemeier, P., Sangiovanni-Vincentelli, A., Damm, W., Henzinger, T., Larsen, K.G.: Contracts for system design. Technical report RR-8147, INRIA, November 2012
5. Bozzano, M., Cimatti, A., Fernandes Pires, A., Jones, D., Kimberly, G., Petri, T., Robinson, R., Tonetta, S.: Formal design and safety analysis of AIR6110 wheel brake system. In: Kroening, D., Păsăreanu, C.S. (eds.) CAV 2015. LNCS, vol. 9206, pp. 518–535. Springer, Heidelberg (2015)
6. Bozzano, M., Cimatti, A., Griggio, A., Mattarei, C.: Efficient anytime techniques for model-based safety analysis. In: Kroening, D., Păsăreanu, C.S. (eds.) CAV 2015. LNCS, vol. 9206, pp. 603–621. Springer, Heidelberg (2015)
7. Cavada, R., Cimatti, A., Dorigatti, M., Griggio, A., Mariotti, A., Micheli, A., Mover, S., Roveri, M., Tonetta, S.: The NUXMV symbolic model checker. In: Biere, A., Bloem, R. (eds.) CAV 2014. LNCS, vol. 8559, pp. 334–342. Springer, Heidelberg (2014)
8. Cimatti, A., Dorigatti, M., Tonetta, S.: OCRA: a tool for checking the refinement of temporal contracts. In: ASE, pp. 702–705 (2013)
9. Cimatti, A., Roveri, M., Schuppan, V., Tonetta, S.: Boolean abstraction for temporal logic satisfiability. In: Damm, W., Hermanns, H. (eds.) CAV 2007. LNCS, vol. 4590, pp. 532–546. Springer, Heidelberg (2007)
10. Cimatti, A., Roveri, M., Tonetta, S.: Requirements validation for hybrid systems. In: Bouajjani, A., Maler, O. (eds.) CAV 2009. LNCS, vol. 5643, pp. 188–203. Springer, Heidelberg (2009)
11. Cimatti, A., Roveri, M., Tonetta, S.: HRELTL: a temporal logic for hybrid systems. Inf. Comput. **245**, 54–71 (2015)
12. Cimatti, A., Tonetta, S.: A property-based proof system for contract-based design. In: SEAA (2012)
13. Cimatti, A., Tonetta, S.: Contracts-refinement proof system for component-based embedded systems. Sci. Comput. Program. **97**, 333–348 (2015)
14. Cofer, D., Gacek, A., Miller, S., Whalen, M.W., LaValley, B., Sha, L.: Compositional verification of architectural models. In: Goodloe, A.E., Person, S. (eds.) NFM 2012. LNCS, vol. 7226, pp. 126–140. Springer, Heidelberg (2012)
15. Damm, W., Hungar, H., Josko, B., Peikenkamp, T., Stierand, I.: Using contract-based component specifications for virtual integration testing and architecture design. In: DATE, pp. 1023–1028 (2011)
16. Graf, S., Passerone, R., Quinton, S.: Contract-based reasoning for component systems with complex interactions. In: TIMOBD 2011 (2011)
17. Iannopollo, A., Nuzzo, P., Tripakis, S., Sangiovanni-Vincentelli, A.L.: Library-based scalable refinement checking for contract-based design. In: DATE, pp. 1–6 (2014)
18. Kupferman, O., Vardi, M.Y.: Vacuity detection in temporal model checking. STTT **4**(2), 224–233 (2003)

19. Manna, Z., Pnueli, A.: The Temporal Logic of Reactive and Concurrent Systems. Springer, New York (1992)
20. Meyer, B.: Applying design by contract. Computer **25**(10), 40–51 (1992)
21. Pnueli, A.: The temporal logic of programs. In: FOCS, pp. 46–57 (1977)
22. Quinton, S., Graf, S.: Contract-based verification of hierarchical systems of components. In: SEFM, pp. 377–381 (2008)
23. Schuppan, V.: Towards a notion of unsatisfiable and unrealizable cores for LTL. Sci. Comput. Program. **77**(7–8), 908–939 (2012)

BMotionWeb: A Tool for Rapid Creation of Formal Prototypes

Lukas Ladenberger$^{(\boxtimes)}$ and Michael Leuschel

Institut für Informatik, Universität Düsseldorf, Düsseldorf, Germany
{ladenberger,leuschel}@cs.uni-dusseldorf.de

Abstract. The application of formal methods to the development of reliable interactive systems usually involves a multidisciplinary team with different roles and expertises (e.g. formal engineers, user interface designers and domain experts). While formal engineers provide the necessary expertise in formal methods, other roles may not be well versed in formal methods, such as user interface engineers or domain experts; consequently barriers may arise while working in a multidisciplinary team. For instance, communication problems and challenges in the rigorous use of formal method tools. Tools like BMotion Studio may reduce these barriers by creating visualizations of formal specifications, however, lacks features needed for the analysis of interactive systems. In this paper, we present a novel graphical environment that continues the ideas of BMotion Studio called *BMotionWeb* to provide support for the rapid creation of *formal prototypes*. A formal prototype links a mockup of a graphical user interface or device to an animated formal specification with the aim of providing lightweight formal validation of interactive systems. In order to demonstrate the application of BMotionWeb, we provide two case studies: a formal prototype of a simple phonebook software and a cruise control device.

Keywords: Formal methods · Animation · Visualization · Rapid prototyping · Validation · Mockup · Interactive user interface

1 Introduction

Formal methods are often applied in the field of safety-critical systems. They allow the specification and analysis of systems based on mathematical techniques with the main goal to ensure *reliability* and *robustness* of the system. The application of formal methods for the development of safety-critical systems usually involves a multidisciplinary team with different roles and expertise (e.g. formal engineers, domain experts and end users). Nowadays, however, safety-critical systems, such as, medical devices, airplane cockpits, or railway- and nuclear plant control systems, typically include interactive user interfaces (UI). Thus, the development of safety-critical systems also requires to properly account for user's cognition and to ensure the *usability* of the system. This task is typically performed by UI engineers. However, UI engineers, domain experts and end

© Springer International Publishing Switzerland 2016
R. De Nicola and E. Kühn (Eds.): SEFM 2016, LNCS 9763, pp. 403–417, 2016.
DOI: 10.1007/978-3-319-41591-8_27

users are rarely trained in formal methods. Consequently barriers could arise while working in a multidisciplinary team which can compromise the success of the project. For example, it can be challenging to find a common language for discussing potential system and design issues. The use of a formal specification as a basis for discussion requires significant knowledge about the mathematical notation of the respective formal method which non-formal method experts typically not have. Moreover, formal method tools may become inaccessible to non-formal method experts. On the other hand, formal engineers typically have no experience in common UI engineering techniques. As a consequence, there is a great demand for tools that can significantly reduce these barriers applying formal methods for developing interactive systems.

One tool that faces these barriers is BMotion Studio [9], a graphical environment for creating visualizations of formal specifications. While BMotion Studio provides a very convenient and fast approach to create simple visualizations of formal specifications, it makes it difficult to use and apply it when validating *interactive* systems. A reason for this is the limited reuse of existing components (e.g. interactive graphical elements and advanced UI techniques) and the lack of validation features needed for the analysis of UIs, such as logging of user interactions and deployment of visualizations.

In this paper we present a novel graphical environment called *BMotionWeb* that builds on the ideas of BMotion Studio to provide support for the light-weight validation of interactive systems by combining techniques known from the formal- and UI-engineering discipline: *animation* [8] and *mockup*. Animation allows the user to inspect the behavior of a formal specification by "executing it". Mockup is a common technique in the field of UI design to describe a model of a device or software UI. Combining an animation tool and a mockup, the formal specification becomes a "tool" in a real sense: it serves as a *formal prototype* that binds the intended functionality of the system to an interactive UI or device. BMotionWeb contributes new features for the rapid creation and lightweight validation of formal prototypes: (1) a visual editor that allows UI engineers to create mockups of a system UI or device; (2) the necessary technique to link a mockup with an animated formal specification; (3) and UI validation features such as logging of user interactions, visualizing the behavior of UI elements and deployment of formal prototypes. Throughout the paper, we demonstrate the application of BMotionWeb based on two case studies: a formal prototype of a simple phonebook software and a cruise control system.

The paper is organised as follows: Sect. 2 describes the architecture of BMotionWeb. In Sect. 3 we describe our approach for creating formal prototypes using BMotionWeb based on two case-studies. In Sect. 4 we demonstrate the application of a formal prototype for the lightweight validation of interactive systems. Finally, we compare our work with related work in Sect. 5 and conclude in Sect. 6. For more information and resources we refer the reader to our project website: http://stups.hhu.de/ProB/FormalPrototyping. The website contains the case-studies (specifications and formal prototypes) and interactive online-versions of the formal prototypes.

2   BMotionWeb

BMotionWeb builds on the ideas of BMotion Studio [9] to provide support for
the rapid creation of formal prototypes. BMotion Studio is a graphical environment for creating domain specific visualizations of formal specifications. It is
based on Eclipse and GEF (Graphical Editing Framework) [19] and comes as
a separate plug-in for Rodin [2] with support for the Event-B specification language [1]. BMotionWeb is a complete rewrite based on web technologies. Figure 1
gives an overview of the architecture of BMotionWeb. The overall architecture is
subdivided into a client front-end and a server back-end, where WebSockets [6]
are used to realise the communication between client and server. The client and
server can be run in a standalone application based on electron[1], a framework
for building cross-platform desktop applications using JavaScript or as separate
processes (either on the same machine or on different machines).

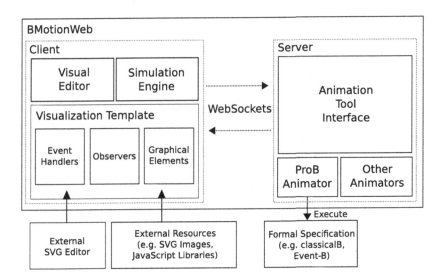

Fig. 1. Architecture overview of BMotionWeb for ProB

In the following subsections we describe the components of the client and
server in more detail.

2.1   Server Back-End

The server is entirely written in Java and provides an *animation tool interface*
capable of integrating external animation tools with BMotionWeb. Currently,
BMotionWeb integrates the ProB animator [11] that supports among others classical B [20] and Event-B [1]. The aim of the animation tool interface is to provide

---

[1] http://electron.atom.io/.

communication between the client front-end and the respective animation tool via WebSockets. For instance, to obtain information about the animated formal specification (e.g. values of state variables or results of evaluating formulas) and to trigger transitions (e.g. executing operations in classical B or events in Event-B).

2.2   Client Front-End

The client front-end consists of a *visual editor* and a *simulation engine* and is entirely written in JavaScript. The aim of the visual editor is to facilitate the creation and editing of *visualization templates*, whereas the simulation engine is responsible for executing visualization templates.

Visualization Template. At the heart of a formal prototype one finds a *visualization template*. A visualization template uses web-technologies to describe the mockup and its bindings to the animated formal specification of a formal prototype. In particular, it is composed of *graphical elements, observers* and *event handlers*:

- A *graphical element* is based on SVG (Scalable Vector Graphics) [22] and HTML [23], two markup languages which provide widgets like shapes, images, labels, tables and lists.
- An *observer* observes a specific part of the animated formal specification during the simulation. BMotionWeb provides various observers. For instance, a *formula observer* that binds a formula (e.g. an expression or a variable) to a graphical element and allows the tool to compute a visualization for any given state of the animated formal specification by changing the properties of the graphical element (e.g. the colour or position) according to the evaluation of the formula in the respective state.
- Finally, an *event handler* wires an interactive action to a graphical element. As an example, BMotionWeb provides an *execute event handler* that binds a classical B operation or an Event-B event to a graphical element and executes the operation or event respectively when the user clicks on the graphical element.

BMotionWeb also provides a JavaScript API for scripting observers and event handlers. Indeed, the use of web-technologies and especially the possibility to reuse existing resources like SVG images and external JavaScript libraries enables users to create formal prototypes for a wider range of systems.

Visual Editor. Figure 2 shows a snapshot of the visual editor. The editor consists of a palette for creating graphical elements, like shapes, labels, images and input fields and a view for managing the properties, observers and event handlers of graphical elements. Graphical elements can be added to a canvas which provides features known from modern graphical editors like drag and drop, undo/redo, copy/paste and zooming.

Simulation Engine. The simulation engine allows users to interact with the formal prototype and to explore its behavior. For this purpose, it renders a visualization template and manages the communication between the mockup and the animated formal specification. In particular, it sends requests from an observer (e.g. evaluating a formula) to the animation tool via the animation tool interface on the server side and forwards the returned results of the animation tool back to the observer. In addition, it triggers state changes in the animated formal specification based on user actions like clicking on an graphical element that wires an execute event handler.

Apart from the formal prototype view, several additional views for analysing a formal prototype have been made available from the ProB animator. For instance, a view that shows the values of variables and constants for the current and previous state of the animated formal specification and a view that lists all enabled and disabled transitions based on the current state of the animated formal specification.

3   Creating Formal Prototypes

In the following two subsections we give more details about the features of BMotionWeb based on two case studies: a classical B specification of a phonebook software (Sect. 3.1) and an Event-B specification of a cruise control device (Sect. 3.2). Both case studies are supported by code examples in which observers and event handlers are described using the BMotionWeb JavaScript API.

3.1   Formal Prototype of a Phonebook Software

In this section we demonstrate our approach based on a classical B specification of a phonebook software. The phonebook allows users to manage persons and telephone numbers and provides the following functionalities: adding and deleting persons with an associated number, searching for numbers and activating or deactivating persons. Moreover, the user can lock the phonebook which results in deactivating the phonebook, i.e. the user can not add new entries. The aim of this case-study is to exemplify the creation of software UI mockups, as well as to demonstrate how the connection between a software UI mockup and an animated formal specification can be established with BMotionWeb.

Mockup Software User Interfaces. Figure 2 shows a snapshot of the visual editor of BMotionWeb while creating the mockup of the input form of the phonebook software. As can be seen in Fig. 2, the mockup of the input form is composed of different graphical elements like input fields, buttons, a checkbox, shapes and labels. The UI engineer can change the properties of the selected graphical element by means of the properties view located on the right side of the editor. For instance, in Fig. 2, the phonenumber input field is selected. Thus, related properties like a property for defining the placeholder or the ID of the input field are made available to the UI engineer. Further, the input field element

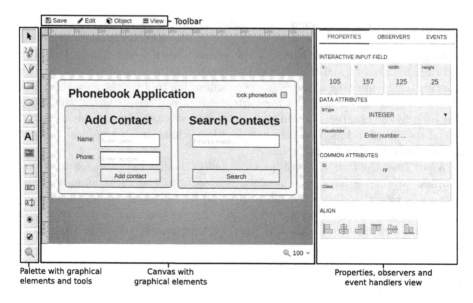

Fig. 2. UI mockup of the phonebook software in visual editor of BMotionWeb

provides a property that defines a classical B set like *INTEGER* or *NAT* or a custom set which comes from the animated formal specification. Defining a set causes a validation of the entered input, i.e. the input field checks whether the entered input is an element of the set or not.

```
1  bms.executeEvent({
2    selector:"#btAdd",
3    name:"add",
4    predicate: function(ui) {
5      var name = ui.find("#name");
6      var nr = ui.find("#nr");
7      return"name="+ name.val() +
8            "& nr="+ nr.val();
9  }});
```

```
1  add(name, nr) =
2    PRE
3      name ∈ STRING ∧
4      name ∉ dom(db) ∧
5      nr ∈ NATURAL ∧
6      lock = FALSE
7    THEN
8      db := db ∪ {name ↦ nr}
9    END;
```

Listing 1. Execute event handler for "Add contact" button (JavaScript)

Listing 2. Phonebook *add* Operation (classical B)

The values of the interactive graphical elements (e.g. the entered input of an input field or the value of a checked checkbox) can be used for defining event handlers. For instance, the "Add contact" button shown in Fig. 3 is wired to the event handler defined in Listing 1. Lines 1 and 2 state that we register a new *execute event handler* on the graphical element that matches the selector

"#btAdd" (The prefix "#" is used to match a graphical element by its ID.[2]), i.e. the graphical element that represents the "Add contact" button. Line 3 states that the event handler should execute the *add* operation of the classical B specification of the phonebook software (see Listing 2). In lines 4 to 9 we define a JavaScript function that returns a predicate determining the parameters of the *add* operation. The returned predicate (lines 7 to 8) is composed of the values of the name and number input fields (line 5 and 6). Figure 3 shows a snapshot of the formal prototype of the phonebook software where the user hovers the "Add contact" button. We have defined the event handler for the "Search" button in a similar fashion.

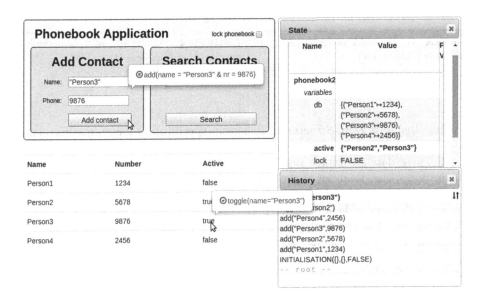

Fig. 3. Formal prototype of phonebook software

Listing 3 shows the *formula observer* for observing the *lock* variable of the phonebook specification (see Listing 4). Line 1 and 2 state that we register a new formula observer on the name and number input fields (#name and #nr) and on the "Add contact" button (#btAdd). Line 3 states that the observer should observe the variable *lock* during the simulation. In lines 4 to 6 we define a trigger function that is called whenever a state change has occurred. The reference to the matched graphical element (e) and the state values of the observed formulas (v) are passed as arguments to the trigger function. In line 6 we define the trigger action: the observer sets the *disabled* property of the graphical elements to the value of the lock variable (v[0]). Since we have set the *translate* property of the

---

[2] BMotionWeb makes use of the jQuery selector syntax to link event handlers and observers to graphical elements. For more information about the jQuery selector API we refer the reader to http://api.jquery.com/category/selectors/.

formula observer to *true* (see line 4) the value is automatically translated into a JavaScript object.

```
1  bms.observe("formula", {
2    selector:"#name,#nr,#btAdd",
3    formulas: ["lock"],
4    translate: true,
5    trigger: function(e, v) {
6      e.prop("disabled", v[0]);
7    }
8  });
```

Listing 3. Formula observer for lock variable (JavaScript)

```
1  VARIABLES db, active, lock
2  INVARIANT
3      lock : BOOL &
4      db : STRING +-> NATURAL &
5      active : POW(STRING)
6  INITIALISATION
7      db := {} || active := {} ||
8      lock := FALSE
```

Listing 4. Variables of phonebook specification (classical B)

Mockup Dynamic Data-Structures. In formal specification languages like classical B, the software is often modeled with data-structures like sets and relations. These data-structures typically contain a *dynamic* number of elements. For instance, the database of the phonebook is modeled as a relation between persons and numbers, where the size of the database increases or decreases, whenever the user adds or deletes a phonebook entry. In this section, we demonstrate the use of an external JavaScript library to connect HTML elements like tables and lists with dynamic data-structures like sets or relations.

In order to establish a connection between HTML elements and an animated formal specification we make use of the JavaScript MVC (Model View Controller) framework AngularJS [7].[3] AngularJS provides *controllers* and *directives*. A controller defines the data and behavior of HTML templates, whereas a directive can attach a specified behavior to an existing HTML element. As an example, consider the controller *pCtrl* in Listing 5. In lines 4 to 10 we register a new *formula observer* which observers the two state variables *db* and *active* (see Listing 4). The values of the variables are assigned to the *scope* of the controller and updated whenever a state change occurred in the animated formal specification (line 8 and 9). Moreover, in lines 12 to 14 we assign a helper function *isActive* to the scope that takes a person as its parameter and returns true whenever the person is in the *active* set. Otherwise it returns false.

A scope can be made available to an HTML template using the *ngController* directive as demonstrated in line 1 in Listing 6. Once the scope has been attached to the template, the values of the two variables *db* and *active* can be used within the template. For instance, in line 7 we assign a *ngRepeat* directive which creates a table row (lines 7 to 15) once per element from the *db* relation. Each row gets

---

[3] We choose AngularJS because BMotionWeb is also based on AngularJS, however, we could also use other JavaScript MVC libraries as well.

its own scope, where the current element (*el*) of the *db* relation is set to the row's scope. Thus, we can access the name ({{*el[0]*}}), the number ({{*el[1]*}}) and the status of each element ({{*isActive(el[0]*}})) and show them in the respective columns of the row (lines 8 to 14). In addition, we assign to each status column an *executeEvent* directive which creates a new execute event handler with *toggle* as the operation's name and *name=*"{{*el[0]*}}" as the operation's predicate. The lower left side of Fig. 3 demonstrates the HTML table during the simulation of the phonebook formal prototype.

```
1  angular.module('phone', [])
2  .controller('pCtrl', function() {
3
4    bms.observe("formula", {
5      formulas: ["db","active],
6      translate: true,
7      trigger: function(v) {
8        $scope.db = v[0];
9        $scope.act = v[1];
10     }});
11
12   $scope.isActive = function(n) {
13     return $scope.act.indexOf(n) > -1;
14   }
15
16 });
```

```
1  <table ng-controller="pCtrl">
2    <tr>
3      <th>Name</th>
4      <th>Number</th>
5      <th>Active</th>
6    </tr>
7    <tr ng-repeat="el in db">
8      <td>{{el[0]}}</td>
9      <td>{{el[1]}}</td>
10     <td execute-event
11       name="toggle"
12       predicate='name="{{el[0]}}"'>
13       {{isActive(el[0])}}
14     </td>
15   </tr>
16 </table>
```

Listing 5. Controller for database view (JavaScript)

Listing 6. Template for database view (HTML)

3.2 Formal Prototype of a Cruise Control Device

A common way to develop mockups is to create graphical sketches using the classical paper-and-pencil approach. In this section we demonstrate the application of BMotionWeb for reusing such graphical sketches for the creation of formal prototypes. For this purpose, we use an Event-B specification of a cruise control system (CCS) and a graphical sketch of a car cockpit including an exemplar of a device (see Fig. 4) as a case-study. A CCS is an automotive system implemented in software which automatically controls the speed of a car. The CCS device provides buttons to switch the CCS system on/off, to set the current speed of the car as the target speed of the CCS system and to increase and decrease the target speed. In addition, the speedometer provides information about the state of the CCS system and about the target speed in dependence on the current car speed.

Using the visual editor of BMotionWeb, UI engineers can select a picture (e.g. a graphical sketch or a photograph) of a device or a UI as a starting point

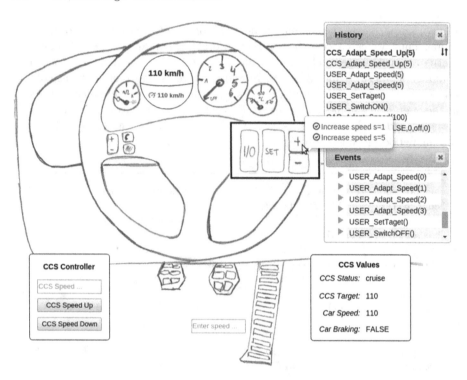

Fig. 4. Formal prototype of cruise control device

for creating a formal prototype. Once a picture is selected it can be extended with additional graphical elements. For this purpose, BMotionWeb contributes an *interactive area* graphical element which can be placed over the picture. An interactive area allows UI engineers to bind an execute event handler or a value of a variable to a specific area of a picture. As an example, Fig. 4 shows a snapshot of the formal prototype of the CCS device based on a graphical sketch, where the user hovers the "+" button on the graphical sketch. An interactive area overlays the button and binds an execute event handler (see Listing 7) that wires the event *USER_Adapt_Speed* (see Listing 8), one with with the predicate $s=1$ and one with the predicate $s=2$. In addition, the speedometer of the graphical sketch binds the two variables *car_speed* (the current speed of the car) and *ccs_target* (the target speed of the CCS system).

4   Validating Formal Prototypes

The use of a formal prototype for validation can take place at different stages of the development process. On the one hand, a formal prototype can be created of existing specifications (e.g. when the system is already implemented) as demonstrated in Sect. 3. On the other hand, a formal prototype can be maintained and used for validation at earlier stages of the development process, e.g. as a

```
1  bms.executeEvent({
2    selector:"#btSpeedUp",
3    events: [{ name: "USER_Adapt_Speed",
4              predicate: "s=1" },
5            { name: "USER_Adapt_Speed",
6              predicate: "s=5" }],
7    label: function(evt) {
8      return "Increase speed" +
9              evt.predicate";
10  }});
```

```
1  event USER_Adapt_Speed
2    any
3      s
4    where
5      @g1 ccs_status = cruise
6      @g2 s ∈ ℤ
7      @g3 ccs_target + s ≥ 0
8    then
9      @a1 ccs_target := ccs_target+s
10  end
```

Listing 7. Execute event handler "increase target speed" (JavaScript)

Listing 8. CCS "increase target speed" event (Event-B)

by-product of the developed formal specification. In the following we describe different application examples of a formal prototype to support the validation process of interactive systems.

Formal Prototype as a Base for Communication. A common understanding of the system in a multidisciplinary team is crucial for the success of the project. Indeed, it is important for the formal engineer to get feedback from the UI engineer for further development of the formal specification. On the other hand, the UI engineer needs to check whether his expectations are met in the formal specification. However, rarely all persons involved in a project are versed in formal methods. The application of a formal prototype can overcome this challenge: it allows UI engineers to validate the behavior of the system and the system's UI or device by interacting with a realistic prototype rather than by examining a substantial amount of mathematical formulas. Moreover, a formal prototype can be used to demonstrate features of the system's UI or device and to discuss validation results (e.g. system and design issues).

Deployment of Formal Prototypes. Running the client and server components of BMotionWeb as web-server processes allows the deployment of formal prototypes online. This can be in particularly useful for accessing a formal prototype from other devices, such as tablets and mobile phones and for sharing a formal prototype with other stakeholders (e.g. during an online project meeting). For example, a UI engineer could demonstrate a specific scenario of the system's UI or device by interacting with the formal prototype. All updates made on the formal prototype are automatically reflected to other stakeholders that have also opened the same formal prototype.

Logging and Visualizing User Interactions. BMotionWeb contributes new features for logging and visualizing user interactions. Figure 5 demonstrates the *user interactions log* view that lists the so far executed transitions of a simulation, where each transition shows the id of the graphical element that triggered the

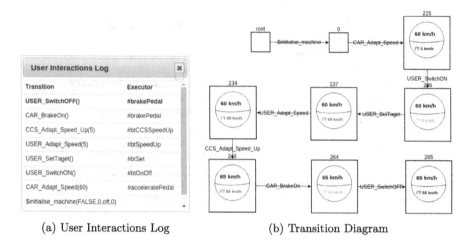

| (a) User Interactions Log | (b) Transition Diagram |

Fig. 5. User interactions log and transition diagram of a CCS device scenario

transition. The user can toggle between the states of a simulation by clicking on an entry of the list.

Based on the user interactions log, a *transition diagram* visualizing the behavior of graphical elements for a specific scenario can be generated. In order to generate a transition diagram, we apply the following approach: (1) the user selects the graphical elements for the transition diagram from the formal prototype; (2) we determine the observers of the selected graphical elements and derive their formulas (which can be simple variables or expressions) that are required to draw the state of the selected graphical elements; (3) for each state of the user interactions log we compute the representation of the selected graphical elements according to the value of the formulas in the respective state. As an example, Fig. 5(b) illustrates the behavior of the graphical element that represents the speedometer of the CCS device. Each rectangle represents a state, whereas a directed edge between two rectangles represents a transition labelled with the associated transition name.

Other Validation Features. BMotionWeb integrates other features that may support the validation of formal prototypes. For instance, a *projection diagram* can be generated for individual graphical elements following the approach presented in [10]. The objective of a projection diagram is to support human analysis of the system by highlighting relevant aspects of it, while hiding information that is not relevant from the diagram based on the state space of the animated formal specification.

Several additional views for analysing a formal prototype are made available from the ProB animator, e.g. a model-checking view with the goal to automatically check properties of the system like deadlock freeness and invariant preservation.

5 Related Work

Brama [21], AnimB [13] and the ProB based tool presented in [3] allow developers creating UIs of Event-B specifications using graphical elements provided by Flash[4] (e.g. labels and images, as well as interactive graphical elements like input fields and radio buttons). In Brama and AnimB the mapping between an animated formal specification and a UI is realised with the built-in programming language *ActionScript*, whereas the ProB based tool requires the developer to write Java as the gluing code. Although the use of Flash seems to be a promising tool for creating rich interactive prototypes, it involves some disadvantages for the developer: Since Flash is a self-contained tool the developer requires skills for using it. Furthermore, the developer requires additional programming skills for writing the gluing code that maps a state to the UI (e.g. ActionScript for Brama and AnimB and Java for [3]).

Other tools which provide comparable concepts to that of BMotionWeb are: JeB [24], an animator that provides an HTML5 canvas allowing the creation of UIs for Event-B specifications and WebASM [25], a web-based tool that brings the CoreASM [5] animator into the web and allows developing UIs for ASM [4] specifications. Similar to the previously mentioned Flash based tools, JeB and WebASM requires programmings skills to map a state to the UI. Moreover, the Flash- and web-based tools lack features for the validation of UIs (e.g. logging of user interactions).

PVSio-web [17] is a web environment including the animation engine PVSio [14] and a visual editor for creating interactive prototypes for the PVS formalism [18]. The visual editor of PVSio-web allows users to choose an image that represents the layout of the UI and to place interactive areas over it (e.g. areas to execute events and to display variable values). In contrast to PVSio-web, BMotionWeb allows users to compose a UI prototype of different graphical elements (e.g. images, labels and shapes). Moreover, in BMotionWeb variable values can also be mapped to the different attributes of the graphical elements using the observer concept of BMotionWeb.

The authors in [16] present three alternatives to extend the animation capabilities of VDMPad [15]. Especially the "Lively Walk-Through" approach can be compared to our work. It combines VDM animation with a UI to provide lightweight validation features for VDM specifications. For this, the approach introduces its own language called "LiveTalk" to wire interactive actions (e.g. executing an VDM operation) to UI widgets. In contrast to the "Lively Walk-Through" approach, in BMotionWeb at best no additional languages are required to create interactive actions (e.g. executing classicalB operations or Event-B events). Another difference between BMotionWeb and "Lively Walk-Through" is that the latter lacks of linking state variables to the UI.

6 Conclusion

In this paper we have presented BMotionWeb, a novel graphical environment for the *rapid* creation of *formal prototypes*. A formal prototype combines a mockup

---

[4] http://www.adobe.com/devnet/flash.html.

of a UI or device with the intended functionality of an animated formal specification. Thus, we eliminate (at least to a large degree) the need to implement and maintain the functional part of a prototype, e.g. using additional programming languages. BMotionWeb provides a visual editor that facilitates the creation of formal prototypes and different features for the lightweight validation of interactive systems, such as logging of user interactions, visualizing the behavior of graphical elements and deployment of formal prototypes. Since a formal prototype is based on web-technologies, external web-resources like third party JavaScript libraries and SVG images can be used to create formal prototypes for a wider range of interactive systems. We have demonstrated the application of BMotionWeb based on two case studies: a formal prototype of a classical B specification of a simple phonebook software and an Event-B specification of a cruise controller. The case studies (specifications and formal prototypes) and interactive online-versions of the formal prototypes have been made available at our project website.[5]

BMotionWeb can be used at any stage of the development process to support the validation of interactive systems. In summary, we believe that BMotion-Web can be useful for the following purposes: (i) to get a common understanding of the system between formal method and non-formal method experts; (ii) to demonstrate features of the system's UI or device; (iii) to discuss validation results (e.g. system and design issues).

Future Work. In future, we plan to apply BMotionWeb to create formal prototypes of other case studies, especially case studies coming from industrial projects. In this context, our aim is to integrate other animation tools with BMotionWeb to address a wider range of interactive systems. First experiments towards supporting the CoreASM animator [5] have already been made. We also plan to develop more features for the lightweight validation of interactive systems, such as A/B testing to compare two variants of a system UI or device. Finally, we plan to consider other techniques and tools to support the validation process, like the ProB constraint solver [12], e.g. to intelligently disable/enable graphical elements.

References

1. Abrial, J.-R.: Modeling in Event-B: System and Software Engineering. Cambridge University Press, Cambridge (2010)
2. Abrial, J.-R., Butler, M., Hallerstede, S., Hoang, T.S., Mehta, F., Voisin, L.: Rodin: an open toolset for modelling and reasoning in Event-B. Softw. Tools Technol. Transfer **12**(6), 447–466 (2010)
3. Bendisposto, J., Leuschel, M.: A generic flash-based animation engine for ProB. In: Julliand, J., Kouchnarenko, O. (eds.) B 2007. LNCS, vol. 4355, pp. 266–269. Springer, Heidelberg (2006)
4. Börger, E., Stärk, R.: Abstract State Machines: A Method for High-level System Design and Analysis. Springer Science & Business Media, New York (2012)

---

[5] http://www.stups.hhu.de/ProB/FormalPrototyping.

5. Farahbod, R., Gervasi, V., Glässer, U.: CoreASM: an extensible ASM execution engine. Fundamenta Informaticae **77**(1–2), 71–103 (2007)
6. Fette, I., Melnikov, A.: The websocket protocol (2011)
7. Green, B., Seshadri, S.: AngularJS. O'Reilly Media Inc., California (2013)
8. Hazel, D., Strooper, P., Traynor, O.: Requirements engineering and verification using specification animation. In: Automated Software Engineering, p. 302 (1998)
9. Ladenberger, L., Bendisposto, J., Leuschel, M.: Visualising Event-B models with B-motion studio. In: Alpuente, M., Cook, B., Joubert, C. (eds.) FMICS 2009. LNCS, vol. 5825, pp. 202–204. Springer, Heidelberg (2009)
10. Ladenberger, L., Leuschel, M.: Mastering the visualization of larger state spaces with projection diagrams. In: Butler, M., Conchon, S., Zaïdi, F. (eds.) Formal Methods and Software Engineering. LNCS, vol. 9407, pp. 153–169. Springer, Switzerland (2015)
11. Leuschel, M., Butler, M.: ProB: an automated analysis toolset for the B method. Softw. Tools Technol. Transfer (STTT) **10**(2), 185–203 (2008)
12. Leuschel, M., Bendisposto, J., Dobrikov, I., Krings, S., Plagge, D.: From animation to data validation: the ProB constraint solver 10 years on. In: Boulanger, J.-L. (ed.) Formal Methods Applied to Complex Systems: Implementation of the B Method, Chap. 14, pp. 427–446. Wiley ISTE, Hoboken (2014)
13. Mtayer, C.: AnimB Homepage. http://www.animb.org/. Accessed 12 Jan 2015
14. Munoz, C.A.: Pvsio reference manual. National Institute of Aerospace (NIA), Formal Methods Group, 100 (2005)
15. Oda, T., Araki, K.: Overview of VDMPad: an interactive tool for formal specification with vdm. In: Proceedings of International Conference on Advanced Software Engineering and Information Systems (ICASEIS) (2013)
16. Oda, T., Yamamoto, Y., Nakakoji, K., Araki, K., Larsen, P.G.: VDM animation for a wider range of stakeholders. Grace Technical reports, p. 18 (2015)
17. Oladimeji, P., Masci, P., Curzon, P., Thimbleby, H.: PVSio-web: a tool for rapid prototyping device user interfaces in PVS. In: FMIS2013 (2013)
18. Owre, S., Rushby, J.M., Shankar, N.: PVS: a prototype verification system. In: Kapur, D. (ed.) Automated Deduction–CADE-11. LNCS (LNAI), vol. 607, pp. 748–752. Springer, Heidelberg (1992)
19. Rubel, D., Wren, J., Clayberg, E.: The Eclipse Graphical Editing Framework (GEF). Addison-Wesley Professional, Boston (2011)
20. Schneider, S.: The B-Method: An Introduction. Palgrave Oxford, Oxford (2001)
21. Servat, T.: BRAMA: a new graphic animation tool for B models. In: Julliand, J., Kouchnarenko, O. (eds.) B 2007. LNCS, vol. 4355, pp. 274–276. Springer, Heidelberg (2006)
22. W3C SVG Working Group. Scalable Vector Graphics (SVG) 1.1 (2nd edn.), August 2011. http://www.w3.org/TR/SVG11/
23. W3C SVG Working Group. HTML5, A vocabulary and associated APIs for HTML and XHTML, October 2014. http://www.w3.org/TR/html5/
24. Yang, F.: A Simulation Framework for the Validation of Event-B Specifications. Ph.D. thesis, Université de Lorraine (2013)
25. Zenzaro, S., Gervasi, V., Soldani, J.: WebASM: an abstract state machine execution environment for the web. In: Ait Ameur, Y., Schewe, K.-D. (eds.) ABZ 2014. LNCS, vol. 8477, pp. 216–221. Springer, Heidelberg (2014)

Author Index

Printed in the United States
By Bookmasters